The Many Faces of Herod the Great

The Many Faces of Herod the Great

Adam Kolman Marshak

WILLIAM B. EERDMANS PUBLISHING COMPANY
GRAND RAPIDS, MICHIGAN / CAMBRIDGE, U.K.

© 2015 Adam Kolman Marshak
All rights reserved

Published 2015 by
Wm. B. Eerdmans Publishing Co.
2140 Oak Industrial Drive N.E., Grand Rapids, Michigan 49505 /
P.O. Box 163, Cambridge CB3 9PU U.K.

Library of Congress Cataloging-in-Publication Data

Marshak, Adam Kolman, 1979- author.
The many faces of Herod the Great / Adam Kolman Marshak.
pages   cm
Includes bibliographical references.
ISBN 978-0-8028-6605-9 (pbk.: alk. paper)
1. Herod I, King of Judea, 73 B.C.-4 B.C.
2. Jews — Kings and rulers — Biography.
3. Jews — History — 168 B.C.-135 A.D.
I. Title.

DS122.3.M37   2015
933′.05092 — dc23
[B]
2014027610

www.eerdmans.com

*To my wife Melissa,
the most reluctant (but insightful)
Herodian scholar in the world.*

Contents

List of Maps and Illustrations — xi

Foreword, by John J. Collins — xiii

Acknowledgments — xvi

Abbreviations — xviii

Introduction — xxii

SECTION I: CULTURAL AND INTELLECTUAL MILIEU

1. **Rome and Its Client Kings** — 3
   Rome and the Good Client King — 4
   The Advantages of Client Kingship — 20

2. **Hellenistic Monarchy in the Graeco-Roman World** — 25
   The King as a Virtuous Ruler — 27
   The King as Lawgiver — 29
   Possessing Majesty and Accumulating Wealth and Power — 30
   The King as Protector and Defender of His Subjects — 34
   Behaving Piously toward the Gods — 38
   Conclusion — 42

CONTENTS

3. **Judaean History from the Maccabees to Herod** — 43
   From Rebels to Rulers: The Rise of the Hasmoneans — 48
   The Hasmonean Dynasty — 54
   Hasmonean Political Ideology — 58

SECTION II: FROM HASMONEAN TO ANTONIAN

4. **Herod's Rise to Power (47-42 BCE)** — 75
   Herod in Galilee — 75
   Trial for Murder — 78
   Herod and Cassius — 82
   Herod and Antigonus — 89
   Conclusion — 90

5. **Herod and Antony (42-30 BCE)** — 92
   Negotiating the World of the Second Triumvirate — 92
   Herod and Rome: Becoming King — 98
   Resourceful King, Useful Ally — 104

6. **Herod the New Hasmonean** — 110
   Marriage, Family, and Hasmonean Blood — 111
   Herod's Architecture and the Hasmoneans — 116
   Herod's Coins and the Hasmonean Family — 126
   Conclusion: Herod the Hasmonean — 134

SECTION III: CLIENT KING IN AN AUGUSTAN WORLD

7. **Herod the Augustan Client King** — 139
   Military and Financial Support for Rome and Its Leaders — 141
   Honoring Rome's New Masters — 147
   Public Inscriptions to Honor Augustus and Herod Himself — 154
   Herod's Dated Coins: Donative and Advertisement — 156
   Herod's Undated Coins and Rome — 165
   Conclusion — 172

Contents

8. **Bringing Judaea into the Roman Sphere: Herod and Romanization** — 174
   - *A Roman Education* — 174
   - *Importation of Roman Luxury Goods* — 177
   - *Romanization of the Army* — 181
   - *Constructing Roman Buildings* — 191
   - *Using Roman Building Technology and Decoration* — 217
   - *Conclusion: Herod, Client King and Cultural Transmitter* — 227

9. **Herod the Hellenistic King in an Augustan World** — 230
   - *Herod and Euergetism* — 231
   - *Urban Construction and the Hellenistic Herod: Building in the Royal Tradition* — 250
   - *Hellenistic Kingship and Virtues in Herodian Judaea* — 264
   - *Herod and Hellenistic Piety* — 271
   - *Conclusion: Herod the Hellenistic King* — 275

10. **Herod, Melekh HaYehudim** — 278
    - *Herod, David, and Solomon* — 279
    - *Herod and Jewish Piety* — 284
    - *Patronage and Inclusion of the Diaspora* — 301
    - *Conclusion: Herod, Melekh HaYehudim* — 309

11. **Herod and the Temple** — 312
    - *Rebuilding the Temple in Jerusalem* — 312
    - *The Physical Layout of the Temple* — 316
    - *The Temple as Culmination of Herodian Political Ideology* — 325

    Conclusion: The Political Self-Presentation of Herod the Great — 335
    - *Herod the Courtier* — 335
    - *Herod's Early Reign as King of Judaea* — 336
    - *Herod's Later Reign as King of Judaea* — 337

Appendix A: A Recent Critique of My Chronology for the Dated Coins — 342

The Argument — 342

Response to Ariel and Fontanille's Critiques of Samaria/Sebaste as the Minting Site — 344

Appendix B: Did Herod Mint Silver Coinage? — 350

Bibliography — 355

Primary Sources — 355

Secondary Sources — 358

Index of Modern Authors — 389

Index of Ancient Writings — 395

Maps and Illustrations

MAPS

The Kingdom of Herod the Great	xxx
The Roman world (ca. 44-4 BCE)	2
The Near East under the Diadochs	24
The Near East under the Ptolemies and Seleucids	44
Hasmonean Judaea (ca. 166-40 BCE)	55
Herod's domestic building program (40-4 BCE)	263

ILLUSTRATIONS

Family Tree of the Antipatrid (Herodian) Dynasty	xxxi
Family Tree of the Hasmonean Dynasty	49
Bronze Prutah of John Hyrcanus I	68
Silver Tetradrachma of Cleopatra Thea	69
Bronze Prutah of Alexander Jannaeus	70
Comparison of Hasmonean and Herodian Palaces	121
Inscription-Anchor Coins of Herod the Great	128
Bronze Anchor-Double Cornucopia Prutah of Herod the Great	131
Gold Oktadrachma of Arsinoe II	132
The Dated Series of Herod the Great	159
Bronze Diadem-Table Series of Herod the Great	166

ILLUSTRATIONS

Bronze Anchor-Galley Lepton of Herod the Great	171
Isometric View of Herod's First and Third Palaces at Jericho	195
Isometric View of Herod's Palace Complex at Masada	198
Reconstructed Plan, Elevation, and Isometric View of the Northern Palace at Masada	199
Isometric View and Plan of the Jericho Hippostadium	202
Isometric Drawing and Plan of the *Augusteum* at Sebaste	210
Plan of Caesarea and the Sebastos Harbor	218
Reconstruction of Herod's Tomb Complex at Herodion	262
Bronze Single Cornucopia-Eagle Lepton of Herod the Great	288
Partly Reconstructed Plan of Herodian Jerusalem	304
Reconstructed Plan of Herod's Temple Mount	317
Reconstructed Elevations of the South Side of the Temple Mount Including the Huldah Gates	321
The Tyrian Shekel	351

Foreword

Few historical figures have worse reputations than Herod the Great. This is due in part to his cameo in the Gospel of Matthew, chapter 2. When he hears that a child has been born king of the Jews he becomes alarmed and asks the wise men to bring him word when they find him. When he realizes that they have not done so, he kills all the male children around Bethlehem who are aged two years or less. The story is fictional — Matthew 2 is a string of stories told to show how various prophecies were fulfilled in Jesus. But the brutality was in character for Herod, who was ruthless in killing anyone who might be a claimant to the throne. Those he had put to death included his wife Mariamme, who was of the Hasmonean line; her grandfather Hyrcanus II, who had been High Priest; his brother-in-law Jonathan, whom he had appointed high priest at the age of seventeen; his sons by Mariamme, Alexander and Aristobulus; and finally Antipater, whose mother he had divorced to marry Mariamme. The Roman emperor Augustus once quipped that it was better to be Herod's pig than his son. Yet he reigned for thirty-seven years. The Jewish historian Josephus wrote that "in his life as a whole he was blessed, if ever a man was, by fortune; a commoner, he mounted to a throne, retained it for all those years, and bequeathed it to his own children. In his family life, on the contrary, no man was more unfortunate."

Herod is called "the Great" because his reign in Jerusalem was the most splendid since the legendary days of Solomon. He was famous for his buildings, most notably for rebuilding the temple in Jerusalem, but also for building cities like Caesarea and fortresses like Herodium and Masada. He made bequests to cities throughout the eastern Mediterranean, and he even endowed the Olympic games. True, there was a famine in Judaea during his reign, but he was credited for his attempt to alleviate it from his personal resources. It is a matter of dispute whether his splendor was burdensome to his subjects, or they benefited from the employment his various projects provided.

Adam Kolman Marshak sets aside the familiar moralizing judgments on Herod to ask how he was so successful as a monarch despite a dubious lineage and claim to legitimacy. Marshak distinguishes three stages in Herod's career. In the first he was a courtier (47-40 BCE), then a young king (40-30), and finally (30-4) a mature sovereign. In the first stage, Herod succeeded because he fulfilled the expectations of his Roman and Judaean superiors, especially Marc Antony. He satisfied both constituencies by suppressing banditry, keeping the peace, and supporting the ethnarch, Hyrcanus II. In 40 BCE, however, his brother Phasael was captured by the Parthians and committed suicide, while Hyrcanus was mutilated to disqualify him from office. Herod now presented himself as the heir to the Hasmonean line and simultaneously as staunchly pro-Roman. He was installed as king of Judaea by the Romans, but he still needed to establish his legitimacy. He did this largely by ingratiating himself to Antony, giving him military and financial assistance and conferring honors on him. When Antony was defeated at Actium, however, Herod lost no time in proclaiming his allegiance to Augustus, using the same techniques he had used with Antony.

In the final phase of his career, Herod could portray himself at once as a glorious Hellenistic king and as the heir to David and Solomon. He constructed a vast monument to David, while his Temple project marked him as the new Solomon. Herod's Temple was more than twice the size of the original. He cultivated the good will of the Jewish Diaspora by defending its interests, while simultaneously displaying beneficence to Hellenistic cities. In this part of his career he no longer needed to worry about his legitimacy, but he wanted to build his reputation or, as modern politicians say, his "legacy."

Marshak sums up the achievement of Herod as follows: "what remained constant throughout Herod's reign was his astute ability to assess his political needs and present a public image that achieved his goals." He insists that oppression and repression were not the primary foundations of Herod's success, though he admittedly used both. Rather, he was politically adroit, with a profound grasp of self-presentation and propaganda. Very few political leaders have navigated their course so successfully in turbulent times.

Foreword

Does this mean that Herod should be forgiven for his undoubted savagery? No. As Walter Benjamin remarked, every great monument of civilization is simultaneously a monument of barbarity. The Pyramids were not built by beneficence, but they remain an impressive human accomplishment. Herod's character is beyond redemption, but this should not keep us from appreciating his very real achievements.

Marshak's book is a fine contribution not only to the history of Judaea but also to the study of Roman client kingship, and indeed to ancient politics, which have lost none of their relevance in the modern world.

JOHN J. COLLINS
Holmes Professor of Old Testament,
Yale Divinity School

Acknowledgments

My first research encounter with Herod the Great occurred at Stanford University during the winter quarter of 1998-99, when my professor, Susan Treggiari, assigned us a research paper for her Roman Republic class. I had to get special permission from her to do a paper on Herod because he technically post-dated the period we were studying. When she asked why I wanted to study Herod, my response was, "Oh, he seems kind of interesting, and there seem to be some good sources available." Little did I know that a semester paper would turn into a senior honors thesis, a dissertation, a plethora of articles, and now, finally, a full-length monograph. It has been a long, sometimes bumpy, but always fascinating road to this point, and there are so many people for whose help I am eternally grateful.

Thank you to Wm. B. Eerdmans for agreeing to publish my book. Thank you to Michael Thomson for your initial interest in my study and for all of your support and guidance along the way. Thank you to John W. Simpson Jr. for providing such helpful editorial feedback and for shepherding the book to completion so proficiently. Thank you to Victoria Fanning, and everyone else at Eerdmans who helped make this book a reality.

Thank you to Susan Treggiari for allowing me to go beyond our class's timeline and begin my so far fifteen-year obsession with Herod. Thank you for your guidance during my senior honors thesis, the success of which persuaded me to pursue graduate work. Thank you for circling every split infinitive in the first chapter of that thesis. Although a humbling experience at the time, the lesson it taught me on careful editing is one I hold dearly and impart to my students today. Thank you to Diana E. E. Kleiner, and John F. Matthews for your support and guidance while serving on my dissertation committee. Thanks especially to John J. Collins

Acknowledgments

for providing me with so much insight and support during the research and writing stages of the dissertation. Thank you for introducing me to Eerdmans and for writing the foreword to this book. Photographs of coins are, except where stated otherwise, used by permission of Jean-Philippe Fontanille (www.fontanillecoins.com). Plans and drawings of Herodian sites are used by courtesy of the Ehud Netzer estate and Roi Parat.

Thank you to all of my colleagues at Gann Academy in Waltham, Massachusetts, who have listened to me talk incessantly about Herod and Roman history for the past seven years. Thank you especially to the history department and my officemates (past and present), who have given me such a supportive, friendly, entertaining, and intellectually vibrant home. Thank you to my students, who have given me a mostly attentive forum to indulge my love of Rome and early Christianity while teaching them some claim, evidence, and analysis. My classrooms have kept me so inspired throughout these years, and that inspiration has helped me to finish this project. A special thank you to Michael Levine, who read through a number of my chapters and helped fix my minute (but significant) grammatical errors.

Lastly, thank you to my family (by blood and by marriage), who have been so loving and supportive throughout my life and have always humored me when I dragged them from archaeological site to archaeological site, some of which were no more than a few scattered column drums. Thank you to my parents and sister, who have given me such a loving and supportive safety net throughout my life and were my first companions as I began to explore the world of history, both ancient and modern. Thank you to my daughter Yaira. Your "editing help" has made me smile if not actually assisted me in finishing. Most importantly, thank you, thank you, thank you to my incredible, invaluable, indispensable wife Melissa, the most reluctant (but insightfully brilliant) Herodian scholar of them all.

ADAM KOLMAN MARSHAK

Abbreviations

AA	*Archäologischer Anzeiger*
ADAJ	*Annual of the Department of Antiquities of Jordan*
Ages.	Plutarch, *Agesilaus;* Xenophon, *Agesilaus*
AJ	Josephus, *Jewish Antiquities*
AJA	*American Journal of Archaeology*
AJP	*American Journal of Philology*
Ann.	Tacitus, *Annales*
ANRW	*Aufstieg und Niedergang der Römischen Welt*
ANSMN	*American Numismatic Society Notes*
Ant.	Plutarch, *Antony*
Ant. Rom.	Dionysius of Halicarnassus, *Roman Antiquities*
Att.	Cicero, *Epistulae ad Atticum*
Aug.	Suetonius, *Divus Augustus*
b.	Babylonian Talmud
BAIAS	*Bulletin of the Anglo-Israel Exploration Society*
B. Alex.	Caesar, *De Bello Alexandrino*
BAR	*Biblical Archaeology Review*
BASOR	*Bulletin of the American Schools of Oriental Research*
B. Civ.	Appian, *Civil Wars;* Caesar, *Civil War*
B. Gall.	Caesar, *Gallic War*
BiblArch	*Biblical Archaeologist*
BICS	*Bulletin of the Institute of Classical Studies*
BJ	Josephus, *Jewish War*
Brut.	Plutarch, *Brutus*
CAH	*Cambridge Ancient History*
Cat. Min.	Plutarch, *Cato the Younger*

Abbreviations

Chron.	Julius Africanus, *Chronographiae*
CIG	*Corpus inscriptionum graecarum*
CIJ	*Corpus inscriptionum judaicarum*
CIL	*Corpus inscriptionum latinarum*
CIRB	*Corpus Inscriptionum Regni Bosporani*
CJ	*Classical Journal*
Clem.	Seneca, *De clementia*
CP	*Classical Philology*
CQ	*Classical Quarterly*
Crass.	Plutarch, *Crassus*
Cyro.	Xenophon, *Cyropaedia*
DBSuppl	*Dictionnaire de la Bible: Supplément*
Demet.	Plutarch, *Demetrius*
Div. in Caec.	Cicero, *Divinatio in Caecilium*
Epit.	M. Junianus Justinus, *Epitoma Historiarum Philippecarum Pompei Trogi*
Evag.	Isocrates, *Evagorus*
Fam.	Cicero, *Epistulae ad Familiares*
FGrH	F. Jacoby, ed., *Die Fragmente der Griechischen Historiker*. Leiden: Brill, 1954-64.
Geog.	Strabo, *Geography*
GJ	*The Geographical Journal*
GRBS	*Greek, Roman, and Byzantine Studies*
Hist.	Tacitus, *Historiae*
HN	Pliny, *Natural History*
HTR	*Harvard Theological Review*
I. Alex. Ptol.	Étienne Bernand, *Inscriptions grecques d'Alexandrie ptolemaïque*. Cairo: Institut Français d'archéologie orientale, 2001.
Id.	Theocritus, *Idylls*
IEJ	*Israel Exploration Journal*
IGR	*Inscriptiones Graecae ad Res Romanas Pertinentes*
In Flacc.	Philo, *In Flaccum*
INJ	*Israel Numismatic Journal*
Ira	Seneca, *De ira*
JBL	*Journal of Biblical Literature*
JEA	*Journal of Egyptian Archaeology*
JHS	*Journal of Hellenic Studies*
JJS	*Journal of Jewish Studies*

ABBREVIATIONS

JNES	*Journal of Near Eastern Studies*
JQR	*Jewish Quarterly Review*
JRA	*Journal of Roman Archaeology*
JRS	*Journal of Religious Studies*
JSJ	*Journal for the Study of Judaism*
JSQ	*Jewish Studies Quarterly*
JThS	*Journal of Theological Studies*
Jug.	Sallust, *Bellum jugarthinum*
LCL	Loeb Classical Library
Leg.	Philo, *Allegorical Interpretation;* Plato, *Laws*
Legat.	Philo, *Legatio ad Gaium*
m.	Mishnah
MedAnt	*Mediterraneo Antico*
MemAmAc	*Memoirs of the American Academy in Rome*
MHR	*Mediterranean Historical Review*
Min.	Plato, *Minos*
Mith.	Appian, *Mithridatic Wars* (*Roman History* 12)
MRR	T. Robert S. Broughton, *The Magistrates of the Roman Republic.* Vol. 2. New York: American Philological Association, 1952.
NC	*Numismatic Chronicle*
NEAEHL	*The New Encyclopedia of Archaeological Excavations in the Holy Land,* ed. Ephraim Stern. Jerusalem: Israel Exploration Society, 1993.
Nic.	Isocrates, *Ad Nicoclem*
OCD	*Oxford Classical Dictionary,* ed. S. Hornblower and A. Spawforth. 3rd ed. Oxford: Oxford University Press, 1996.
OGIS	W. Dittenberger, ed., *Orientis graeci inscriptiones selectae.* Leipzig, 1903-05.
Or.	Dio Chrysostom, *Orationes*
PCPS	*Proceedings of the Cambridge Philological Society*
P. Ent.	Guéraud, Octave, ed. *Enteuxeis, requêtes et plaintes adressées au roi d'Égypte au IIIe siècle avant J. C.* 2 vols. Cairo: Institut Français d'archéologie orientale, 1931-32.
PEQ	*Palestine Exploration Quarterly*
Per.	Livy, *Periochae*
Pol.	Aristotle, *Politics*
P. Oxy.	*Oxyrhynchus Papyri*

Abbreviations

PssSol	*Psalms of Solomon*
Pun.	Appian, *Punic Wars* (*Roman History* 8)
Q. Fr.	Cicero, *Epistulae ad Quintum fratrem*
Q. C.	Quintus Curtius Rufus, *Historiarum Alexandri Magni Macedonis*
RB	*Revue Biblique*
Res Gest. Divi Aug.	*Res Gestae Divi Augusti*
Rh. Al.	Anaximenes, *Rhetorica ad Alexandrum*
RIN	*Rivista Italiana di numismatica e scienze affini*
SAN	*Society for Ancient Numismatics*
SEG	*Supplementum Epigraphicum Graecum*
SIG	W. Dittenberger, ed., *Sylloge Inscriptionum Graecarum*, 3rd ed. Leipzig: Herzel, 1915-24.
Sull.	Cicero, *Pro Sulla*
Syr.	Appian, *Syrian Wars*
TAPA	*Transactions of the American Philological Association*
TJC	Ya'akov Meshorer, *A Treasury of Jewish Coins: From the Persian Period to Bar Kokhba*. Nyack: Amphora, 2001.
YCS	*Yale Classical Studies*
ZAW	*Zeitschrift für die alttestamentliche Wissenschaft*
ZDPV	*Zeitschrift des Deutschen Palästina-Vereins*
ZPE	*Zeitschrift für Papyrologie und Epigraphik*

Introduction

An old and bloodthirsty tyrant hears from a group of magi of the birth of the Messiah, the new king of the Jews. He vengefully sends his soldiers to Bethlehem with orders to kill all the baby boys in the city and therefore preserve the tyrant's throne. For most of the Western World, this is Herod the Great, an icon of cruelty and evil, the epitome of a tyrant.

But is this really all of him, and is this all we can know about him? Because of his status within Christian communities as the archetype of evil, Herod has until recently been seen as one of history's *untouchables,* that group of individuals whose behavior and regimes defy objective analysis. And yet, one only needs to examine the mixed public reaction today to such autocrats as Bashar al-Assad, Augusto Pinochet, and Josef Stalin to understand that even the most oppressive regimes have their supporters, and even the most violent and ruthless of leaders have those who not only approve of their rule but glorify it.

So how can we truly *know* this controversial figure? Is it even possible? Is it even desirable? We should not attempt to whitewash his reign or explain away the cruelties of his regime. However, if we want to push aside the curtain of negative opinion and clear the mists of collective memory, we must put aside moral judgment and objectively assess the political processes that existed within Judaea during the end of the first century BCE. We must shed our preconception of *the Herod of the New Testament* in order to analyze effectively *the Herod of history.* This individual, far from being the culmination of all that is evil, was an astute and adept political player who skillfully manipulated the system to enhance his own position and power. He rewarded his friends, eliminated his enemies, and secured his hold on the throne with such skill and acumen that he became one

Introduction

of the most important and influential client kings in the Roman imperial system. His actions, while perhaps ruthless and at times cruel, were not much different from those of other rulers of the time who used political murder and execution to advance their agendas and secure their control. We must remember that the murder of wives and sons was a common, if unfortunate, practice among ancient kings, and even the most beloved and praised rulers engaged in such actions. Augustus Caesar himself, who was seen by many of the ancient sources as an exemplar of just rule, participated wholeheartedly in the proscriptions that led to the deaths of hundreds of Roman senators and *equites*. He also banished his daughter and granddaughter and exiled his grandson.[1]

Herod was a ruthless and cruel monarch, who executed his enemies and even turned on his friends. And yet, he was also the king who brought Judaea to its greatest economic and political prosperity. He was a magnificent and creative builder, the genius behind such imaginative and awe-inspiring structures as Masada and the Temple Mount. With any complex historical figure such as this, who rose to great heights of power and authority despite a dubious background and questionable legitimacy, numerous questions arise: How did such a man become king of Judaea? How did he survive and thrive in the turbulent period at the end of the Roman Republic when hundreds of other elites rose to dizzying heights of power only to end up defeated and dead? In essence, how did he succeed? Why was he able to reign in relative stability for over thirty years and pass on his kingdom to his chosen successors? Through a new analytical approach to politics, namely a focus on his self-presentation, we can begin to answer these questions. How Herod presented himself to his various audiences was a fundamental part of his ability to rule effectively and successfully. He thrived because he persuaded enough of those individuals with political agency that he was indeed a good king.

Ruling at the crossroads of three cultures (Roman, Hellenistic eastern, and Judaean), Herod incorporated aspects of each of these three worlds into his political self-presentation. In order to legitimate and solidify his rule, he integrated himself fully into the system of client kingship that thrived in the early reign of Augustus. He also utilized visual motifs to highlight his

---

1. Herod's life and reign as king of Judaea spanned several important periods in Roman history, none perhaps as important as the transformation of Gaius Octavius, first into Gaius Julius Caesar Octavianus (Octavian), and then into Augustus Caesar. For our purposes, I will refer to this man as Octavian when discussing his life prior to his renaming on January 16, 27 BCE, and as Augustus when discussing the period of time after this date.

INTRODUCTION

special relationship to Rome and its leaders. Furthermore, he drew on the cultural expectations of his Hellenized courtly elite and his royal neighbors in order to appear as the ideal Hellenistic king. Finally, he engaged with the Jewish past and attempted to portray himself first as a rightful successor to the previous dynasty, the Hasmoneans, and then as a glorious Jewish king in the vein of David and Solomon. He simultaneously became the good Roman ally, a Hellenistic monarch, and a Jewish king, consciously inserted himself into his political milieu, and strongly laid claim to legitimate succession, while keeping his three major audiences, Greek, Jewish, and Roman, in mind. The result of this conscious depiction was that Herod was able to persuade enough people with political agency that he was an effective king. Oppression and repression certainly had their role and function within the Herodian regime. However, they alone cannot account for his ability to minimize or quash dissent, nor can they explain why he was so popular with his Roman patrons, his royal neighbors, and the myriad of cities dotting the eastern Mediterranean, with whom he had rather friendly relationships. Some other factor besides oppression had to exist, and I believe that this factor was his ability to tap into the cultural mindset of his audiences and fulfill their expectations of him and his position.

Political self-presentation was thus a fundamental part of this success. It enabled him to surmount his dubious background, overcome the popularity of his predecessors, the Hasmoneans, survive the succession of civil wars that plagued the Roman world, and become arguably the most powerful king in the history of Judaea. It is therefore essential that we understand exactly how this presentation functioned within Herod's reign and how he used the multiple media available to him to achieve his goals.[2]

What is political self-presentation? How did and does it function? How can we discern it? All of these are essential questions that we must clarify before we can obtain a clear understanding of why Herod was so successful as a king. In short, it is the way in which a political actor or agent depicts himself in the public arena. It encompasses every aspect of his public persona, from the advertisement of political decisions to the publishing of

---

2. A possible counterargument to the approach I am taking is that Herod was merely the best of a group of bad options. We must, however, reject this argument. Rome, and in particular Marc Antony and Augustus, had many opportunities to remove Herod from power. It is noteworthy that not only did they not depose him, but they also promoted him from general to tetrarch and from tetrarch to king. Augustus also expanded Herod's territory, power, and influence on multiple occasions. It would seem undeniable then that Antony and Augustus perceived Herod as a useful ally and a competent ruler.

Introduction

his official portrait. Moreover, it need not reflect reality from an objective point of view. An individual can certainly present himself in a particular way even if others dispute the authenticity of this depiction.

In the ancient world, where the sources are often few and the distance from the present is great, it is often difficult to discern accurately a historical individual's self-presentation. A main facet of this difficulty is the highly stylized nature of the historical sources. In our case, our main source (Josephus's narratives) provides descriptions of Herod's actions, physical appearance, and character. However, these descriptions are also highly stylized presentations from an author (and sources) steeped in Graeco-Roman culture and rhetorically trained. Because of this background and rhetorical training, Josephus was well-versed in precisely the same cultural expectations that Herod was trying to fulfill. For example, for Josephus as for Herod, good kings were just men. If Josephus wished to describe a good king, he would depict him exercising justice. Consequently, what appears in the pages of Josephus's texts is a hybrid character, who is derived from both the authentic and historical person and the rhetorical-literary construction. Given these limitations, we would do best to focus on those aspects of Herod's character that have multiple points of reference. That is to say, we should focus our attention on Herodian actions that we can document using multiple sources.

And yet, historians can periodically peer through the haze of time and history and, using the available sources, sketch out a vivid image of an individual's public image. How does this individual see himself operating in the political realm? What image does he have of himself as a political figure? What type of ruler or statesman is he? Most importantly, how does he present himself to others? What images and ideas does he draw on to articulate his conception of himself? By answering these and related questions, we as historians can reveal how the individual depicted himself in the public sphere and how this display was fundamental to his creation of political power and support.

Additionally, it is sometimes possible to get beyond a discussion of presentation to one of identity. There may indeed be some correlation between how Herod presented himself in public and how he actually perceived himself. As the famous sociologist Erving Goffman has persuasively argued, human beings often do not perceive themselves as being self-contradictory in regard to their personal identity.[3] In other words,

---

3. Erving Goffman, *The Presentation of Self in Everyday Life* (Woodstock: Overlook, 1973).

INTRODUCTION

Herod might not have seen himself as being disingenuous. Since we cannot know for sure what he thought of himself, this study focuses instead on the public image he exhibited. Within the public realm, this identity was true, regardless of whether it was consistent with the private Herod.

Herod's public persona was quite real and tangible. Nevertheless, it was a constructed persona, created and shaped by several people whose names have been lost to history. It is impossible to know exactly how much personal control Herod the man exerted over his government.[4] The sources credit him with all of his actions, but in the same way that we do not assume kings and emperors personally wrote or dictated every letter signed by them, we cannot assume that he made every decision attributed to him by the authors Josephus and Nicolaus of Damascus or by the epigraphic sources. An established group of courtiers, advisors, and administrators probably carried out many of the political decisions enacted by the palace, and there may well have been a certain amount of departmental autonomy. And yet, Herod was the figurehead for this regime, so there is a level of truth in attributing these decisions to him or at least to his public persona, for that is what the overwhelming majority of his subjects would have encountered. Furthermore, it is entirely possible, and perhaps even probable given the evidence, that Herod the individual did participate in the management of his kingdom. Subordinates may indeed have exercised some autonomy, but it would have been wise for them to know whether their king would approve of their actions before committing them, since he could easily punish and even execute those who displeased him.[5] Because of the relative dearth of evidence as well as the interests of the sources we have, it is almost impossible to know the exact role that each courtier played in the decision-making of the Herodian regime or who was in charge of what. Given this inability to see the precise roles of specific ancient individuals, we must look at the regime as a whole rather than as a sum of its parts.

---

4. Ehud Netzer devotes a great deal of space to his theory that Herod was personally involved in the design and construction of his buildings. This hypothesis is certainly possible, but unverifiable. See Ehud Netzer, *The Architecture of Herod, the Great Builder* (Tübingen: Mohr, 2006), 295-301.

5. Autocracies are often extremely linear power systems in which the ruler sets an overall tone and environment and his subordinates act according to what they think he will approve of or with which he will be pleased. Adolf Hitler did not personally order every single anti-Jewish action, but he certainly set a tone and created an environment in which Nazi officials knew what was expected of them. See Ian Kershaw, *The Nazi Dictatorship: Problems and Perspectives of Interpretation* (London: Arnold, 1985).

Introduction

Moreover, at some level this distinction between what Herod *the actual man* decided, personally implemented, and achieved and what Herod *the public figure* received credit for is irrelevant to a discussion of how political self-presentation enabled the creation of legitimacy and maintenance of power. The average Judaean rarely, if ever, came into contact with the king. Even within the court, there may have been graduated levels of personal contact. Thus, an analysis of the regime as a whole is actually more accurate in the sense that most contemporary individuals looking at the regime would also not have been able to discern the discrete actions of individual advisors. Instead, the average Judaean would have credited the decisions to Herod himself as the figurehead. For the sake of clarity and ease of discussion, therefore, when I refer to *Herod,* I am referring to his public persona. In other words, I mean the regime for which the individual Herod, son of Antipater, was the figurehead and leader. Nevertheless, we must always keep in mind that this public persona was a construct of several individuals whose contributions and perhaps even identities have unfortunately been lost to modernity.

A final issue we must contend with is what it meant to be successful in the ancient world. To determine this, I have focused on the following main criteria: (1) a long reign, (2) a relatively peaceful and stable reign culminating in death from natural causes, and (3) the ability of a king to pass on his realm to his heirs. I have chosen these three because they are reasonable and rational indicators of success. While an early death might be simply a matter of chance and thus not always an indication of failure, having a long and stable reign necessitated a large degree of success. If a ruler could not govern properly, it was likely, considering the many pretenders to thrones, that his reign would be short.

The second criterion is also predicated on reason. Since the usual goal and duty of any ruler is to protect his citizenry and territory, a general absence of war and instability would mean that he had accomplished this task. I am not claiming that any instability is an immediate sign of failure. Even legendary kings such as David or Solomon were confronted by rebellions. However, the ability to control these periodic uprisings and keep the country's territorial integrity intact was the mark of a good ruler.

The final criterion, passing on the kingdom to a chosen heir, was a difficult task in the ancient world. Clearly, if one achieved a high level of peace and stability, it would not be too difficult for the designated heir to take the throne. Further, there was a belief in the ancient world that the skills of government could be passed from parent to child. Thus if the parent were successful, his son would have a good chance of receiving the necessary support to inherit his father's throne and kingdom.

It seems clear to me that Herod achieved all three of these criteria. Although there were minor revolts and riots, no major revolution occurred, and he rarely experienced defeat in the wars he fought. He also ruled for a considerable length of time. The Roman Senate made him king of Judaea in 40 BCE, and, while it took three years for him actually to secure his throne, he still managed to rule for thirty-three years afterward. Few Roman emperors lasted as long. Finally, he was able to pass his kingdom on to his children. Although the kingdom was split into three areas and lost certain cities such as Gaza, Herod himself determined this division.[6] The only major change Augustus made to the will was to grant the title *ethnarch* rather than king to Archelaus, with the opportunity for him to receive the title of king in the future if he deserved it (he did not).

Given our focus on political success, we should not be interested in making value judgments about whether Herod was a morally good king. Success in the ancient world did not require moral goodness or virtue; what it did require was strong leadership and political acumen. By consciously avoiding value judgments about his moral worth as a king and person, we will avoid the two major mistakes of past studies of Herod and his reign: (1) an unrealistic emphasis on his wickedness that does not take into account either the complexity of the Roman world, especially Judaea, and the reality that his behavior was not particularly unique, and (2) an overemphasis on force and repression as the sole factor in his success.

Herod the Great was not the most beloved of monarchs, but he was also not a completely immoral, sociopathic monster whose evil was and is so apparent that it defies rational historical analysis. We, as students of history, must advance beyond simplistic and biblically influenced interpretations of first-century BCE Judaea and treat Herod and his contemporaries as we would any other historical figures. By encompassing and engaging with all of the available evidence, both literary and material culture, I will suggest an alternative explanation for his success as king of Judaea and a possible method by which the political success or failure of other client

---

6. For Josephus's assessment of Herod's reign, see *AJ* 17.191-92. For the belief that a child could inherit political acumen from his parent, see Philo, *Leg.* 10.54-56. For Josephus's comment on Herod's general lack of military failure, see *BJ* 1.430.

Introduction

kings and even emperors can be examined. As such it allows us to move beyond simplistic explanations for political achievement and to begin to understand better the complex system in which kings such as Herod lived and thrived.

We begin with a simple question: How and why did Herod succeed as king of Judaea? As we shall see, it was his political self-presentation, his ability to depict himself as a worthy and effective king, that was fundamental to success. It is to this story of political dexterity, ruthlessness, and manipulation that we now turn.

The Kingdom of Herod the Great

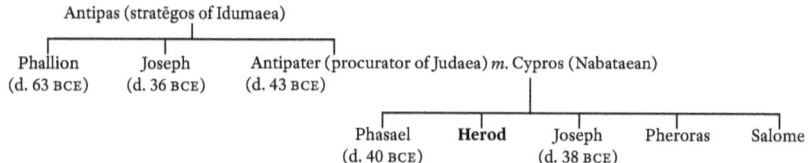

Family Tree of the Antipatrid (Herodian) Dynasty

SECTION I

Cultural and Intellectual Milieu

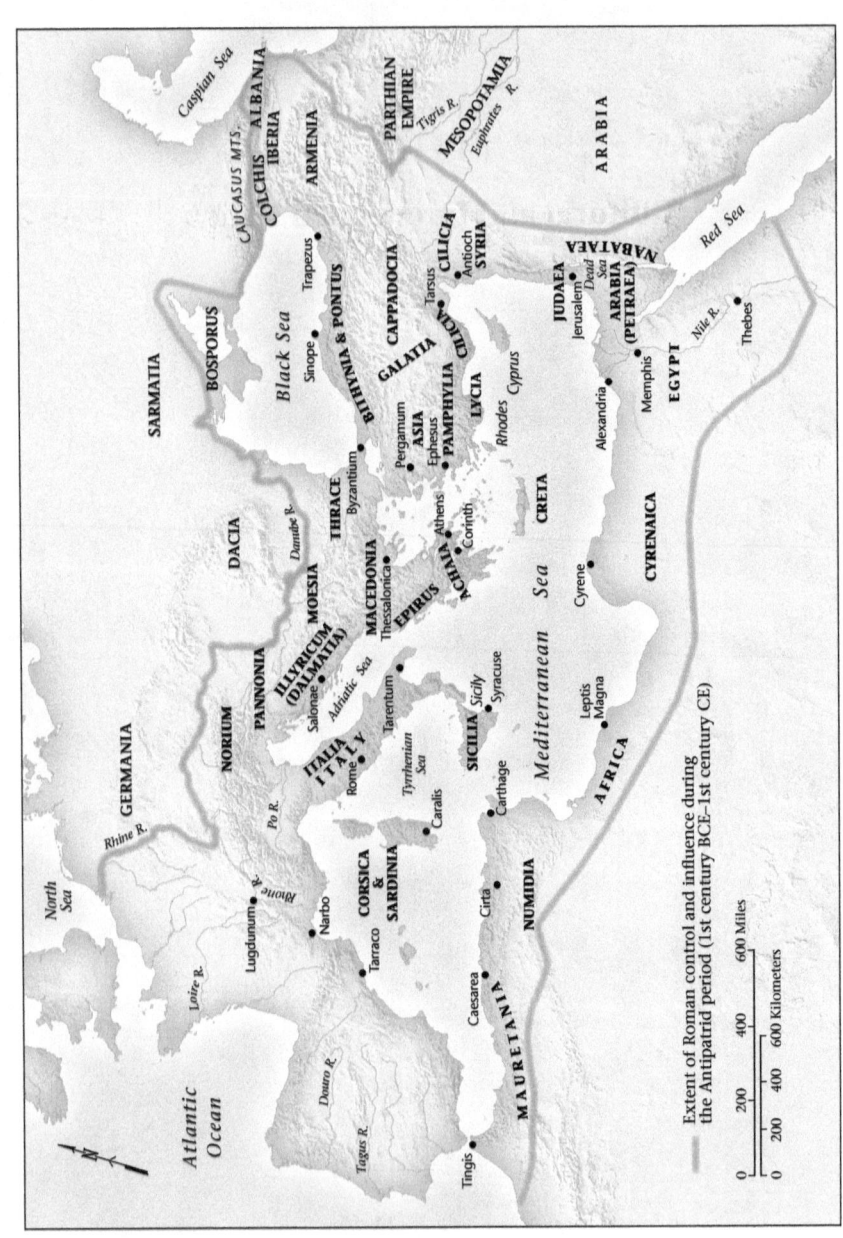

The Roman world (ca. 44-4 BCE)

CHAPTER 1

Rome and Its Client Kings

Before we can delve into the reign of Herod himself, it is essential that we clearly describe and delineate the politico-cultural milieu in which Herod operated. What did it mean to be a *good* king in the ancient world? What was expected of kings and princes? How was effectiveness determined? Who was interested in making such a judgment and, perhaps more importantly, who could? What follows is a brief discussion of the various expectations that Herod's political elite would have had for him as their king and ruler.[1] For the sake of simplicity and clarity, I will divide these qualities and characteristics into three categories corresponding to Herod's three dominant cultural identities: (1) criteria for good Roman client kingship, (2) criteria for good Hellenistic monarchy, and (3) criteria for good Jewish kingship.

Despite this tripartite division, we must remember that cultures and their values never exist in a vacuum and that, in as fluid a world as the ancient Mediterranean, there were considerable convergences and similarities among these three. Thus, although I have placed specific criteria in specific cultures, we should not imagine that they did not appear in the others. Many of the qualities desirable in a client king were also trademarks of a good Hellenistic monarch. Further, as Judaea was fully immersed in the Hellenistic world, it should not be surprising that Jews too shared many values and ideals with their non-Jewish neighbors. Nevertheless, it is our job as historians to categorize and differentiate, however artificial and over-

---

1. For a more detailed discussion of Roman client kingship, Hellenistic monarchy, and Jewish kingship, see Adam Kolman Marshak, "Herod the Great and the Power of Image: Political Self-Presentation in the Herodian Dynasty" (Ph.D. diss., Yale University, 2008), 36-71.

simplified our categories might be. To that end, I have attempted to place the characteristics and qualities in the chapter that seems to suit them best.

As we will see, many of the aspects of Hellenistic kingship presented in the next chapter do not entirely correspond to those that appear in this chapter. The main reason for this lack of symmetry is that client kingship was an institution in which the king was subordinate to a higher-status patron. One of the basic assumptions of Hellenistic political theory, however, was that the king was not subordinate to anyone. As such, issues of morality and philosophy played much larger roles than in the institution of client kingship. Client kings still were expected to behave justly and virtuously, but the relationship between patron and client king was more important and thus more readily visible.

One final note: we must not think that these criteria served as a concrete checklist of effective leadership. There was no umpire keeping score and making notes. Instead, these criteria, which permeated elite culture and its literature, acted as accepted and almost unconscious points of evaluation. Moreover, many were standard moral-philosophical and rhetorical values in the ancient world and sometimes extended beyond kings and rulers to all good men (namely aristocrats) and even philosophers. In order to persuade those with political agency (i.e., those who were in a position to affect who held the throne of Judaea) Herod did not need to satisfy all these criteria. However, if he had not fulfilled enough expectations, his reign would have been much shorter.

The haphazard survivability of ancient sources has resulted in relatively incomplete pictures of ancient rulers, even for those for whom there is an abundance of material (e.g., Augustus). Herod is no exception. The purpose of the following chapters is to paint a vivid but general picture of the cultural milieu in which Herod lived and thrived. Because of the nature of the sources and their particular interests, some aspects will be clearer and more vivid than others. Therefore, one should pay more attention to the picture as a whole and less to the individual details within.

Rome and the Good Client King

When the Roman Republic began to expand, it encountered a series of monarchies, and it was largely at the expense of these monarchies that Rome built its empire. However, Rome's relationship with these kingdoms was not simply one of conqueror and conquered. Instead of relying on outright conquest and annexation (indeed, the Romans were often loath to annex a territory formally), Rome often relied on alliances between itself and these semi-independent monarchies. These relationships were founded on diplomacy and "friendship" *(amicitia)* married to political dependence. In other words, Rome ruled indirectly through its allies, who, while maintaining large degrees of autonomy, were still ultimately accountable to Rome and the Senate.

Scholars have referred to these semi-independent monarchs as *client kings,* and have carefully analyzed exactly how this system functioned.[2] For our purposes, it is necessary only to lay out a general picture of the duties and obligations incumbent on a client king operating within the Roman sphere and of those required of the Romans vis-à-vis the client king. These expectations were an unconscious influence on any interactions Herod had with his Roman patrons. He would have known that he ought to behave in certain ways, and the Romans would have expected such behavior. If a king failed to fulfill these obligations, especially if such failure was a recurring problem, he could potentially lose Rome's friendship and support. Such a loss could result in the removal of the client king from power.

On the other hand, if Rome and its leaders neglected these obligations, they could easily find themselves losing the support of the client kings. If an individual Roman failed in his patronal duties, he might find client kings switching their political support from him to a rival aristocrat. If Rome as a state failed to uphold its obligations, the kings could, and in certain circumstances did, transfer their allegiance from Rome to other powers. In the first century BCE, Rome's main rival was Parthia. Rome could not afford to lose its allies to Parthia, and thus it took its commitments and obligations seriously.

I have isolated four major characteristics of good client kings: (1) a good client king was pro-Roman and provided peace and stability to Rome as a state; (2) he supported his individual aristocratic patrons politically and economically; (3) he lavished gifts, praise, and honors on his Roman

---

2. The two seminal works on Roman client kingship are Ernst Badian, *Foreign Clientelae* (Oxford: Clarendon, 1958), and David Braund, *Rome and the Friendly King: The Character of the Client Kingship* (New York: St. Martin's, 1984). For a discussion of the language and ideology of imperial patronage, see Richard Saller, *Personal Patronage under the Early Empire* (Cambridge: Cambridge University Press, 2002), 7-40. In my dissertation, I offer an updated examination of client kingship which, although deeply indebted to Braund and Badian, still covers new ground and offers new analysis of this important political relationship. For my analysis of client kingship, see Marshak, "Herod the Great and the Power of Image," 36-71.

allies and patrons. In the Republic the monarchs could choose any of the leading citizens as patrons, although men such as Sulla, Pompey, and Julius Caesar were preeminent. Finally, (4) client kings provided impetus and encouragement for the process of Romanization by which the country, its inhabitants, and certainly the ruling family slowly assimilated.

Providing a Friendly Ally to Rome

Recognition and Succession

Although perhaps the most obvious duty incumbent on client kings, loyally serving Rome's interests as a friendly ally was at the core of this political relationship. Such loyalty began with official Roman recognition and, in particular, the Roman custom of *appellatio*. In order for a king to obtain Roman recognition officially, the Senate had to recognize him as a *rex sociusque et amicus* ("allied and friendly king"). During the imperial period, the power and prominence of the Senate was transferred to the emperor. This recognition of the client king became so important that these monarchs often amended their titulature to include some reference to their Roman sanction. Examples include *philorhomaios* ("Friend of Rome"), *philokaisar* ("Friend of Caesar"), *philosebastos* ("Friend of Augustus"), and *philoklaudios* ("Friend of Claudius").[3]

Just as rulers needed Roman approval to become client kings, so too they needed Roman recognition of their succession plans. Indeed, when Herod died, his son Archelaus was very careful not to assume formally the title of king granted by his father. Instead, he insisted on waiting for Augustus's official approval.[4] There was a very practical motive for controlling

---

3. The first recorded use of the term *philorhomaios* in a king's titulature was in that of Ariobarzanes I of Cappadocia. For the election of Ariobarzanes as king, see Appian, *Mith.* 10; Justinus, *Epit.* 38.2. For Ariobarzanes' use of the term and a discussion of his kingship, see R. D. Sullivan, "The Dynasty of Cappadocia," in *ANRW* 2.7.2 (Berlin: de Gruyter, 1980), 1127-36. For the use of the term *philorhomaios* by his grandson Ariobarzanes III, see Cicero, *Fam.* 15.2. For Sauromates I's use of the terms *philokaisar* and *philorhomaios,* see *SEG* 27.445. For Herod of Chalcis's (41-48 CE) placement of the title *philoklaudios* on two of his coin types, see *TJC,* 263, 354 (coins 362-63). Also see Emil Schürer, *The History of the Jewish People in the Age of Jesus Christ (175 BC–AD 135),* ed., trans., and rev. Geza Vermes and Fergus Millar (Edinburgh: Clark, 1973-87), 1:571-72.

4. For Archelaus's refusal to assume his father's royal title, see *BJ* 2.2; *AJ* 17.202. It is important to note that men such as Archelaus, his brother Antipas, and his half-brother

succession. If a deceased king's heirs were not sufficiently pro-Roman or were too weak to run the country effectively, Rome likely would be forced to intervene to secure its own interests. Thus, in the interest of stability and peace, the emperors actively controlled the succession of client kings.[5]

Visiting Rome

As important as abrogating the right to control succession, kings felt a strong obligation to visit Rome at least a few times during their reigns. This pilgrimage was often in their own interest, since personal contact with the political center could facilitate closer relations and result in tangible benefits for a king and his family. For example, Rome's victory over Perseus at Pydna in 168 BCE resulted in a flood of embassies from eastern monarchs. Attalus of Pergamum, later Attalus II (220–138 BCE), was the leader of one of those embassies. When he arrived in Rome, he used the opportunity to press his claims to Aenus and Maroneia in Thrace as well as to request Roman support against the Galatians. When King Prusias II of Bithynia (ca. 182–149 BCE) visited Rome, he also congratulated the Senate on Rome's victory at Pydna.[6] Masinissa of Numidia (ca. 240-148 BCE), who happened to have sent his son to Rome on another issue, commanded him to congratulate the Senate for their victory and to obtain permission for Masinissa himself to visit Rome in person so that he could sacrifice on

---

Philip were explicitly not kings (Archelaus was an ethnarch, and Antipas and Philip were tetrarchs). Nevertheless, although they lacked the royal title, their role and function within the Roman system was similar to that of other kings. Thus, their experiences and Rome's expectation of them as rulers are still relevant to our discussion.

5. By giving Herod the right to choose his own successors, Augustus was bestowing a tremendous honor on the Judaean king. See *BJ* 1.454; *AJ* 16.192; cf. *AJ* 15.343; 16.92. *BJ* 1.454 seems to set Augustus's grant to Herod of the right to make his own will in the context of Herod's reconciliation with his son Alexander ca. 12 BCE. *AJ* 15.343 places the grant in 20 BCE, at the time that Augustus annexed Auranitis, Batanaea, and Trachonitis to Herod's kingdom. Braund argues that *BJ* 1.454 is correct in its chronology and that the episode in *AJ* 15.343 is anachronistic. He contends that the scene in *BJ* 1.454 (a hearing before Augustus arising out of a succession intrigue) would be a more appropriate context for Augustus's grant. See Braund, *Rome and the Friendly King*, 160 n. 54.

6. For Attalus's visit, see Polybius 30.1-3; Livy 45.19-20.1-3. For Prusias's visit, see Polybius 30.18; Livy 45.44.4-21. As will be discussed below, Prusias also used this visit to introduce his son and heir to the Senate, to reestablish ties with friends and patrons, and to press his own claims.

the Capitol. Masinissa's extreme age (he was already in his seventies) and fears that his absence might lead to instability, especially if he should die during his journey, persuaded the Senate to refuse his petition.[7] Masinissa's request, however, indicates the importance he placed on frequent personal contact with Rome and the Senate.

While all these examples are from the republican period, embassies to Rome to solicit support or reassert allegiance were also common during the empire. These visits were even more important when a new emperor came to the throne, as changes in Rome might lead to setbacks or large gains for client kings. For example, on the accession of Galba (one of the emperors of 69 CE), Herod Agrippa II set off for Rome to congratulate the new emperor and to learn what Galba wished done with regard to the Jewish revolt that was still raging in Judaea. While en route, Agrippa learned that Galba had fallen from power and that Otho had replaced him. Nevertheless, he continued his mission. Although the individual possessing the imperial office had changed, Agrippa's position vis-à-vis the emperor had not.[8]

Renewing ties with the imperial center was extremely important because a king's standing and status could quickly change, especially with the accession of a new emperor. For instance, Herod Antipas, who had enjoyed the privilege of being among Tiberius's closest friends, experienced a sharp change of fortune on the accession of Gaius in 37 CE. Indeed, he fell victim to the accusations of his nephew, Herod Agrippa I. As a result, Gaius forced him into exile, gave his territory to Agrippa, and appointed Agrippa king of Judaea.[9]

The Client King's Role in Defense

Once Rome acknowledged a client king as legitimate, he needed to play the role of the good ally by contributing to the defense of the Roman confederation. One way in which kings participated in this common defense was by eliminating or suppressing banditry and piracy. Additionally, those who ruled along the frontiers were also expected to create stable buffer states between Rome and its enemies. In the West, these buffer states protected

---

7. Livy 45.13-14.

8. For Agrippa's journey, see *BJ* 4.498-500. Initially, Agrippa was accompanying Vespasian's son Titus. However, when Titus learned that Galba was dead, he decided to return to Judaea and rejoin his father. Cf. Tacitus, *Hist.* 2.1-2, 81.

9. *BJ* 2.181-83; *AJ* 18.245-56.

Rome against barbarian tribes. However, it was the eastern front that especially concerned the Romans because Rome's only real rival, Parthia, bordered that frontier. Rome calculated that stable kingdoms with significant military strength could act as a deterrent to this hostile empire. Roman governors, in particular, depended on royal soldiers when constructing their defenses against possible Parthian incursions, although they often supplemented these light infantry and cavalry forces with Roman legions. Using royal armies for defense was less expensive than supplying Roman garrisons. Such forces did not often require Roman subsidies, which never amounted to an extraordinary amount of money. Thus, both alone and in concert with the legions, royal forces provided an essential military deterrent.[10]

Client kingdoms also acted as supply depots for incursions made by the Roman army. Furthermore, because they were located on the borders, many client kings were also able to provide valuable information to Roman officials about enemy troop movements. While governor of Cilicia (51-50 BCE), Cicero received warnings that the Parthians had crossed the Euphrates from Antiochus I of Commagene, Tarcondimotus I, ruler of part of Mount Amanus and later king of upper Cilicia, and Iamblichus I of Emesa. These client kings provided Cicero and the Roman state with valuable reconnaissance, which gave them an early warning and enabled them to respond expeditiously. Acting as advance warning for Rome was often in the best interests of these client kings. Not only would such reports strongly encourage Roman response and thus bolster the client king's own security, but simply by acting as an informant, a client king could dramatically improve his standing with the Roman state, especially in relation to other kings who did not provide such information.[11]

---

10. When Cicero became governor of Cilicia in 51/50 BCE, he explicitly stated in his letters that he would rely on the local troops of Deiotarus of Galatia in case of an invasion. See Cicero, *Att.* 6.1.14. For the combination of Roman legions with client kings' forces, see Livy 22.37. Cf. Tacitus, *Ann.* 12.15. For Rome's subsidizing of royal forces, see Braund, *Rome and the Friendly King*, 183.

11. As an example of a client kingdom acting as a supply depot, during the Third Macedonian War, Masinissa of Numidia sent a large supply of grain to the Roman soldiers. Rome did not wish to have this importation seen as a gift, so the Senate refused to accept the grain without paying for it (Livy 45.13-14). Marcus Licinius Crassus also relied on supplies from client states when preparing his failed Parthian campaign of 54-53 BCE (*AJ* 14.105-9). Although his plundering of the Temple in Jerusalem prior to this campaign is an example of Roman-allied relations gone awry, it does illustrate the fact that Roman officials believed the client kingdoms were places to accumulate money or supplies. For Cicero's use of local kings as advance warning for a Parthian invasion, see Cicero, *Fam.* 15.1-2. Cicero did not initially believe the reports coming from Antiochus I of Commagene because he doubted

Client kings also acted as guides for Roman forces. During Marcus Licinius Crassus's ill-fated Parthian campaign of 53 BCE, Abgar II of Osrhoene provided guides to the Roman commander. Although Dio accuses Abgar of betraying Crassus, the episode illustrates the Roman expectation that local chieftains and rulers would serve as guides for Roman armies. While good service as a guide could bring great reward, it also had its inherent risks. If things went wrong, as they did for Crassus, the client king could end up facing severe consequences and even a charge of treason.[12] Charges of treason or disloyalty did not just occur because of failed military expeditions. Precisely because these client kings were located on the borders between Rome and its enemies, their loyalty was often suspect and their actions sometimes resulted in their imprisonment on a charge of treason. Disloyalty need not have been blatant for a client king to fall under suspicion. Herod Antipas, who could hardly have been considered disloyal, suffered deposition and exile because his nephew Herod Agrippa persuaded the new emperor, Gaius Caligula, that Antipas was conspiring with Artabanus, king of Parthia. Ironically, Agrippa himself later fell under suspicion of treason during the reign of Claudius. The Syrian governor Gaius Vibius Marsus accused Agrippa of plotting both by restoring the walls of Jerusalem and by inviting neighboring monarchs to visit him at Tiberias.[13]

Nevertheless, even with a significant level of distrust, the buffer state system worked well for both sides. Not only did a client king provide a shield for Rome, but Rome also provided defense for the kings. The mere

---

Antiochus's loyalty. Instead, Cicero simply waited for confirmation from other more reliable sources. Cf. Caesar, *B. Gall.* 8.26 for Caesar's reception of information from Gallic client kings. For the benefits of aiding Roman generals, see *B. Gall.* 6.12; cf. 2.12; 5.53; 6.4; 8.6.

12. For Agbar's betrayal of Crassus, see Dio 40.20-24; Plutarch, *Crass.* 21-22. Julius Caesar also encountered treachery from guides who were supposedly loyal. For example, a Gaul named Ambiorix led Caesar's troops into a trap that resulted in a massacre (*B. Gall.* 5.27-37). Cf. Plutarch, *Ant.* 37, 39, 50.

13. See *AJ* 18.250 for Gaius's deposition and the exile of Herod Antipas. For Agrippa's alleged conspiracy, see *AJ* 19.327, 338-52. Charges of treason were also leveled against Antiochus IV of Commagene and his son Epiphanes. See *BJ* 7.219-29. The case of Eumenes II, who was a consistent Roman ally during the second century BCE, illustrates well how even the closest of allies could become suspect. Rome accused Eumenes of conspiring with Perseus of Macedon during the Third Macedonian War. Eumenes seems to have done nothing more than attempt to mediate peace between Perseus and Rome, although Polybius claims that he requested financial remuneration from Perseus in return for such services. See Polybius 29.5-9; 30.1-3; 19.6-17, 30. Some senators even urged Attalus to claim the Pergamene throne (30.1.7-10). For a discussion of this affair see Badian, *Foreign Clientelae*, 102-5.

possibility of Roman intervention was often a powerful enough deterrent to prevent invasion or revolt. If, in spite of this, revolts still occurred, Rome offered a refuge to which a king could flee. When Ptolemy VIII Euergetes II (also known as Ptolemy Physcon) ousted Ptolemy VI Philometor, Philometor promptly fled to Rome and soon returned with Roman support to help claim his throne.[14] Augustus in his *Res Gestae* gave a prominent position to this idea of foreign kings fleeing to Rome for assistance. The list of royal suppliants whom the *Res Gestae* states Augustus received included royalty from nations such as Parthia, Media, Adiabene, and even Britain. Therefore, if forced to flee their territories, client kings could have confidence in their eventual restoration by means of Roman legionary force.[15]

Providing a Political Ally for Individual Romans

We have seen how client kings had duties and obligations to Rome and how Rome had reciprocal duties to its client kings. However, as Fergus Millar argues, politics in the Roman world was conducted on a personal level. Kings had interactions both with the Senate as a body (or the emperor as a person) and with specific senators as individuals. These relationships with individual senators were certainly more important during the republican period. However, even when the Roman government was centralized in the hands of the emperor, senators continued to play large and influential roles in the management of the government, especially as provincial governors and proconsuls. Thus, even during the imperial period, the cultivation of relationships with senators and other powerful elites was still a necessity for any ambitious and politically astute client king.

Throughout the Republic and even into the imperial period, powerful Romans made personal connections with foreign rulers. Many of these relationships went back to the earliest times and were tied into the system of *hospitium* ("hospitality"). *Hospitium* was originally formally established between two parties, and a token of such a relationship was the *tessera hospitalis* ("token of hospitality").[16] A Roman aristocrat granting a *beneficium* ("benefit") to a foreigner in exchange for political honor and loyalty

---

14. See Diodorus 31.18 for Ptolemy VI Philometor's flight to Rome.
15. For Augustus's offer of refuge to royal exiles, see *Res Gest. Divi Aug.* 32.1.
16. The earliest known examples of a Roman *tessera hospitalis* come from the second century BCE. See *CIL* 1².23, 828, 1764.

was the foundation of these personal connections between Romans and non-Romans. Leading Romans would have *hospites* ("guests") all over the Mediterranean, and, especially as Roman power and influence increased, prominent non-Romans would take pride in their *hospitium* with important Romans. The balance of power between the Roman and his *hospes* also became increasingly unequal.

In addition to his obligations to the *Populus Romanus* (Roman people) as a state, the good client king also had obligations to his individual Roman patrons. This support would include public gestures of friendship and support. Moreover, client kings also were often called on to provide real political and economic assistance. This assistance could benefit the client king, since the appreciative Roman would likely reward the client king's services. When Herod Agrippa came to Rome ca. 36 CE, he used his connections with Tiberius and his sister-in-law Antonia to become the tutor of Tiberius's grandson Gemellus. Instead of paying attention to Gemellus, however, Agrippa spent his time with the future emperor Gaius Caligula. On Gaius's accession in 37, and probably in exchange for his services, Gaius appointed Agrippa king of his uncle Philip's territory. Further, in the aftermath of Gaius's assassination, Agrippa was instrumental in advising Claudius to claim the throne. In return, Claudius made Agrippa king of Judaea.[17]

Economic assistance could take the form of either money or supplies that the Roman patron required. For example, Gaius Flaminius had governed Sicily as praetor in 227 BCE. In 195, the Sicilians sent cheap corn to Rome to honor his memory and to enhance the political standing of his son Gaius, who was then serving as curule aedile. Additionally, it is no surprise that African beasts made their first appearance in Rome in large numbers in 169 BCE, in the aedileship of Publius Cornelius Scipio Nasica and Publius Lentulus. Scipio, who had strong family connections in Africa, no doubt requested such beasts from his clients there.

Finally, client kings were expected to provide safe haven for their patrons in times of trouble. Such havens were especially important at the end of the republican period, when a series of civil wars caused numerous prominent Romans to seek refuge overseas. Although Gaius Marius was the preeminent man in Roman politics at the end of the second century BCE, by 88 BCE he was forced to flee Rome. He first fled to Campania, but

---

17. For Agrippa's friendship with Gaius Caligula and his subsequent appointment by Gaius, see *BJ* 2.178-81; *AJ* 17.160-237. For Agrippa's role in Claudius's ascension, see *BJ* 2.204-17; *AJ* 19.236-47, 263-77. Cf. Dio 60.8.2.

he received little support there. Eventually he made his way to Africa, which was the site of one of his greatest victories and thus had a large concentration of his clients. Sullan supporters also made use of their overseas connections when they too were forced into exile. Marcus Licinius Crassus fled to Further Spain and Quintus Metellus Pius took refuge in Africa. Crassus had served in Further Spain under his father, the consul of 97 BCE. Metellus Pius could count on both the memory of his father's name and the connections he had personally made there while serving on his father's staff during the Jugurthine Wars (112-105 BCE). Thus, even in times of civil war, client kings actively assisted individual patrons, even if that patron had run afoul of the official Roman government.

Duties of the Individual Patron

What did the client king receive from the Roman aristocrat in exchange for all his services? Essentially, a Roman patron would facilitate diplomatic relations between Rome and his royal clients. Such facilitation often meant that he would introduce the king to the Senate and entertain his envoys while they were in the city. Indeed, it was often difficult for a less important king to get a hearing in the Senate without the efforts of his patrons. Patrons would also use their influence to obtain favorable settlements for their clients as well as look after their interests in the Senate. A patron might also be called on to settle an internal dispute or act as an arbitrator.[18]

Finally, and perhaps most importantly, a patron was expected to protect his client kings and cities from extortion and oppression. The towns of Sicily experienced such extortion and oppression at the hands of Gaius Verres while he was governor there. These towns requested the assistance of Cicero in their suit against Verres, because of their familiarity with him while he was quaestor there. In his speech, Cicero says that he had promised the Sicilians "that if any time should arrive when they wanted anything of me, I would not be wanting to their service."[19]

Client kings often had a number of potential patrons in Rome, and

---

18. For example, Publius Sulla in the case of Pompeii (Cicero, *Sull.* 60-62), Scipio Aemilianus in the case of the Macedonians (Polybius 35.4.110-11), and the dispute between Masinissa and Carthage (Appian, *Pun.* 72). For Roman patrons securing their client kings' introduction to the Senate see Livy 34.59.4; Plutarch, *Ti. Gracchus* 14; Dio 39.14.3; Strabo, *Geog.* 17.11.

19. Cicero, *Div. In Caec.* 2-6.

in times of trouble, it was not always clear which patron the client king would choose to support. It was therefore vital for patrons to fulfill their duties and obligations to their royal clients if they wanted to be able to rely on royal support. Thus, although the client kings had several duties and obligations toward individual Romans as well as to the Roman state, they did receive significant benefits and services in return.

Gifts and Honors

The third major characteristic of a good client king was that he lavished praise, gifts, and honors on his patrons whether they were prominent Romans, as in the Republic, or the imperial family, as in the empire. Kings often found it necessary to bribe both the Senate and leading citizens during the Republic and members of the imperial family during the empire. Freedmen as well as freeborn relatives of the emperor were often recipients of large gifts from kings. There are numerous accounts of foreign kings giving *gifts* to leading Romans in the Republic in order to secure their support for various pieces of legislation. The career of Jugurtha of Numidia (ca. 160-104 BCE) is a catalog of bribes and corruption among the highest officials in Rome. Additionally, Cicero wrote to his friend Atticus that when Ariarathes X of Cappadocia came to Rome (45 BCE) he hoped to achieve recognition by bribing Caesar.[20]

Additionally, client kings were also expected to entertain their patrons when they came to visit. This aspect of the relationship was so important that kings would try to outdo each other with ever-increasing entertainment and festivities. Hosting a Roman patron could enhance one's status or severely hurt it. This phenomenon was even more acute during the imperial period because there were fewer possible patrons. In reality, the imperial family held most of the power, and thus the members of the imperial household were the most worthwhile patrons to cultivate, although other non-imperial patrons did exist. As we will see later, Herod was an extremely successful host, and the visits by both Augustus and Agrippa only increased Herod's status in the Augustan regime.

Monetary rewards and hospitality were not the only ways to enhance the

---

20. Cicero, *Att.* 13.2a.2. A third example is that of Ptolemy XII Auletes, who had to bribe numerous Romans to restore his throne and ended up getting into a cycle of debt that led to subsequent ousters. When he died in 51 BCE, Caesar claimed that the Ptolemies owed him 17.5 million denarii.

patron-client relationship. Especially during the imperial period, kings often named their children after the emperor. The family of Herod Agrippa exemplifies this trend. First, his parents, Aristobulus and Berenice, named him, in all likelihood, after Herod the Great's friend and patron Marcus Agrippa. Later, Herod Agrippa named his son Agrippa, and afterward this name became a dynastic one along with Herod. Like his parents, Agrippa named a few of his children after two of his personal patrons' (Tiberius's and Gaius Caesar's) families. He had one son, whom he named Drusus after Tiberius's son, with whom Agrippa had been friends before Drusus's death in 23 CE. Agrippa also had a daughter, whom he named Drusilla after Gaius's beloved sister. According to Josephus, Drusilla (the Jewish princess) was six when her father died, which means that she was born in 38 CE, the same year that Gaius's sister Drusilla died. It seems, therefore, that Agrippa named his daughter in honor of the recently deceased favorite sister of his imperial patron.

Kings also often founded cities and named them after the emperor or prominent members of his family. Indeed, numerous *urbes Caesareae* (cities of Caesar) sprang up all over the Roman East. Although Herod's Caesarea Maritima is the best-documented example, there was also a Caesarea in his son Herod Philip's territory, Caesarea-Panion. Archelaus I of Cappadocia, Juba II of Mauretania, and Polemo I of Pontus and Bosporus all founded cities called Caesarea in honor of Augustus. Further, Archelaus I and Queen Pythodorida Philometor of Pontus also renamed cities Sebaste, which is the Greek equivalent of Augustus. The founding or renaming of cities in honor of the emperor continued after Augustus's death. Antiochus IV of Commagene founded a new city in Cetis called Germanicopolis in honor of Gaius as well as a city at Ninica called Claudiopolis for Claudius. Antiochus also built a new city in Lacanatis called Neronias. Finally, Agrippa II changed the named of Caesarea-Panion to Neronias.

Members of the imperial family could have also expected to receive naming honors. For instance, Herod Philip, tetrarch of Batanaea, Trachonitis, and Auranitis (4 BCE–ca. 33 CE), built up a village on the Sea of Galilee and renamed it Julias after either Augustus's daughter Julia or the Julian clan. Polemo I renamed Phanagoreia Agrippeia in honor of Augustus's friend and son-in-law Marcus Agrippa. As a close friend and colleague of Augustus, Marcus Agrippa had a considerable amount of power and influence. Further, he had helped Polemo to the throne, and the king probably felt a large amount of gratitude to the Roman.

Imperial names and even images also appeared on client kings' coins. A number of coins from the reign of Herod Philip illustrate this type. For example, Philip minted six major coin types during the reign of Augustus. Of those six, five have the portrait of Augustus on the obverse and one has the jugate heads of an emperor and Livia on it. On all these coins, the Greek translation of Augustus *(Sebastos)* appears around the coin edge. After the accession of Tiberius, Philip began minting coins with Tiberius's portrait on the obverse. Of the eleven main coin types unequivocally minted after 14 CE, eight have a portrait of Tiberius on the obverse, one has a bust of Livia, and one has a laureled head of Augustus. Unlike his brothers Antipas and Archelaus, Philip was free to use coin portraits on his coins because his territory was inhabited mostly by non-Jews. His brothers, on the other hand, ruled heavily Jewish areas, in which the inhabitants would have objected strongly to figural images on their coins. Accordingly, the brothers did not mint coins depicting portrait heads.[21]

The imperial cult was another medium through which kings could demonstrate their loyalty and appreciation, and its spread throughout the ancient world created a new forum for religious expression of loyalty by client kings. There is no hard evidence of kings participating in the regional cult of any Roman during the republican period, but as soon as the imperial cult became an established entity provincial kings began playing active roles. The rulers of the Bosporus, from Cotys I (46-63 CE) until the third century CE, regularly describe themselves as high priests of the Augusti.[22] The clearest example of eastern kings participating in the imperial cult, however, comes from Suetonius, who wrote that all the kings of the East jointly decided to complete the still-unfinished temple of Olympian Zeus at Athens and dedicate it to the *Genius Augusti*.[23] Participation in the

---

21. For Herod Philip's Tiberian era coins depicting the imperial family, see Meshorer, *TJC,* 87-89 (coins 101-4, 106, 109-11, plate 51). The remaining major coin type (Meshorer, *TJC,* coin 108, plate 51) depicts Philip on the obverse. For Antipas's and Archelaus's coins, see Meshorer, *TJC,* 78-85 (coins 67-94, plates 47-49).

22. *CIRB* 41, dated to 58/59 CE, is the earliest example. Cf. *CIRB* 69, 70. Antonia Tryphaena, the widow of Cotys VIII of Thrace, actively observed the cult of Gaius's sister Drusilla, whom Gaius had posthumously consecrated as the new Aphrodite. Antonia Tryphaena's sons, Rhoemetacles III of Thrace and Polemo II of Pontus, also joined their mother in observing the rites of this imperial cult. See *IGR* 4.145; cf. 144.

23. For the completion of the temple of Olympian Zeus at Athens, see Suetonius, *Aug.* 60. Cf. Livy 41.20 for the glory of this project. Pisistratus began work on the temple to Olympian Zeus, and Antiochus IV Epiphanes added to it. Hadrian finally completed the temple. Suetonius may have been exaggerating when he stated that all the kings of the Roman world were involved in the project. However, it is certainly true that many kings were active in building *urbes Caesareae,* and thus it is likely that a large number did participate in the construction of the temple.

imperial cult served a dual purpose. On the one hand, it was a powerful religious ceremonial expression of loyalty, but, on the other hand, it also vividly linked the king with the imperial family.

A final way that kings could show their allegiance and gratitude was through their royal wills. Before the principate, there were a few examples of monarchs leaving their entire kingdoms to Rome. King Ptolemy VIII Euergetes II Physcon provides the earliest. In 155 BCE he had his will carved on a large stele in Cyrene. There he bequeathed his kingdom to Rome in the event that he had no sons and heirs. As it happened, by the time Physcon died in 116 BCE, he did have sons and heirs. But by making Rome his heir and publishing his will he had publicly reaffirmed his friendship and alliance with Rome. This will protected Physcon while he was alive by publicly calling on Roman support for his rule and wishes and by reminding his internal audiences who his friends were. Attalus III Philometor of Pergamum's will, however, is the most famous example. Attalus, who died in 134 BCE, seems to have been a rather weak king, and he was more interested in studying botany and sculpture than ruling. Like Physcon's, Attalus's reign was marked by severe instability. There seem to have been a series of court executions, and the king isolated himself from his court and refused to govern. Further, the pretender Aristonicus raised a revolt and even succeeded in seizing the throne for short period. When Attalus died childless, he bequeathed his kingdom to Rome. After much politicking involving the tribune of the Plebs Tiberius Gracchus, Rome finally accepted the bequest, and Pergamum became the first territory successfully ceded to the Senate and People of Rome.

During the principate, the emperor, and in some cases his family usurped the position of the *Populus Romanus* (Roman people) as the potential heir(s) to royal estates. During the imperial period, many kings left legacies not only to the emperors but also to their wives, freedmen, or very close friends. Family members of the kings also included in their wills members of the imperial household with whom they had developed close relationships. Herod's sister Salome left Jamnia and its territory, along with Phasaelis and Archelais, to Livia, who was Augustus's wife and Salome's friend. Kings who wanted to pass on their kingdoms to their children left legacies to the imperial family, as did upper-class Romans who wanted their children to inherit the bulk of their estates. These legacies smoothed the transition from father to son and ensured continuation of the patron-client relationship. They also publicly advertised the honor and esteem with which the dead king held Rome and its ruler.

Cultural Transmission

Finally, a good client king also acted as an instigator and advocate of cultural and social transmission and integration. Often cultural transmission had to occur in the client king's own family before it could truly spread to the population. In order to facilitate such cultural integration, client kings, especially during the imperial period, often sent their children to Rome to be educated. The first documented case of such a visit occurred at the outbreak of the Third Macedonian War. According to Livy, Ariarathes IV of Cappadocia sent his son, Ariarathes V, to Rome to be educated and to "become familiar with Roman manners and men."[24]

As I have noted above, the Battle of Pydna ended the Third Macedonian War and ensured Roman domination of Greece and the eastern Mediterranean. It also marked a significant increase in the number and frequency of embassies from eastern kings. In three cases we know of, the kings brought their sons and heirs with them. In 167 BCE, King Prusias II of Bithynia brought his son, the future king Nicomedes II, to Rome with him. While in the city, Prusias visited a number of his friends and introduced his son to them. When Prusias and his son were received in the Senate, the king congratulated the Senate on the victory at Pydna and formally recommended his son. Similarly, in 153-152 BCE, Attalus III, while still a young boy, was formally introduced to the Senate and made several important contacts with friends of the Attalid family. Simultaneously, the young Demetrius II of Syria was also in Rome, presumably for the same purpose.[25] These cases seem to be the only three documented during the Republican period. It was more common for future kings to make short visits, although documentation for these trips is also rare. Furthermore, these short visits often achieved much of what was desired — formal contact with the Senate and personal interaction with leading Romans.

With the rise of Augustus and the *pax romana,* however, these visits become better documented and prolonged stays. Moreover, client kings increasingly saw it as vital to send both their heirs and their other sons. This rapid rise in the quantity, duration, and regularity of these visits by client princes seems to argue against the importance of Pydna and

---

24. Livy 42.19.
25. For the three embassies, see Livy 45.44.4-21; Polybius 33.18. In 30.18, Polybius offers a less than flattering interpretation of Prusias's actions.

against a view that princely educational visits to Rome were a custom that developed during the republican period. They certainly existed (it is also likely that more cases occurred than have been documented), but they seem not to have become customary until the Augustan period, when kings such as Herod sent all their male descendants to Rome to be educated.

Besides sending sons as educational tourists, kings also sent their sons to Rome as hostages. But these hostages' treatment often varied little from that of princes sent to be educated. The Roman government gave these hostages a large amount of freedom and respect. Further, these hostages did not suffer any loss of status or power. In particular, they usually had a good chance of eventually becoming kings in their own right. Although Juba II walked in Caesar's triumph in 47 BCE as a conquered prince, he received an education in Rome and in the army and finally, in 25 BCE, received the throne of Mauretania.

The education that these royal princes and hostages received was not simply academic. While in Rome these young men, who were future kings themselves, would make important connections with prominent Romans, men who might facilitate the future kings' rise to their thrones.[26] During the principate this process involved being introduced to the emperor and his family. Indeed, if a prince were lucky, he might even become part of the retinue of one of the members of the imperial family. Herod Agrippa I became friends with Tiberius's son Drusus and was the schoolmate of the future emperor Claudius. Later in life, Tiberius made Agrippa the tutor of Drusus's son Tiberius Gemellus, and on his own Agrippa cultivated the friendship of Gaius Caligula.

Another aspect of a prince's education was schooling in war. Princes sometimes had a chance to serve with the Roman army, and while in the service, they learned about Roman military techniques and strategy. This education served them well when they returned home and eventually began to reign themselves. According to Sallust, Micipsa sent Jugurtha to serve under Scipio Aemilianus at Numantia. While with Scipio, Jugurtha learned Latin, earned a good reputation, became friends with Aemilianus, and met many other important Romans who would help him in the future.

26. An example of a non-royal who was in Rome for similar reasons is Charops of Epirus, who came to Rome in the 170s BCE specifically to learn to speak and write Latin. His visit, like Ariarathes', was probably both educational and social, since it is highly likely that he also used his time in Rome to make connections with prominent Romans. His visit is mentioned in Polybius 27.15; cf. 32.5-6.

Antiochus IV Epiphanes, who spent time in Rome as a hostage, apparently paraded troops equipped in the Roman fashion at Daphne.[27]

Once in Rome, these royal princes would often meet each other, and these meetings and acquaintances likely facilitated future interactions and further bound the empire together. The practice of sending sons to Rome for education became a self-perpetuating cycle because a son sent to Rome would often become king and send his own sons. This exchange provided an intimate connection between Rome and its client kings and a greater chance for cultural and social integration and assimilation.[28]

It was only natural that the culturally integrated client prince would go back to his court and bring his newly acquired ideas and customs with him. In addition, he would also bring back new technologies and methods of building. The prince would then serve as a link between his native land, with its customs, and Rome. Royals were not the only ones who participated in this cultural exchange, but they were in a privileged position well suited to furthering the process of Romanization.

The Advantages of Client Kingship

In return for all their efforts, what benefits did client kings receive from their Roman patrons? First and most important, they received the support, both political and military, of the dominant power in the Mediterranean. As we have seen, Roman approval and Roman armies essentially installed

---

27. For Jugurtha's service under Scipio Aemilianus, see Sallust, *Jug.* 7; 9.3; 101.6. For Juba II's service in the army under Julius Caesar, see Dio 51.15.6. For Antiochus IV's use of Roman military gear, see Polybius 30.25, especially 25.3. For the Treaty of Apamea, by which Antiochus IV was sent to Rome as a hostage, see Polybius 21.40-44; Livy 38.38. Polybius 26.1a-1.14 describes Antiochus acting in a Roman way as a sign of his madness. As Braund rightly observes (*Friendly King*, 15), these behaviors are more likely signs of Romanization than of madness. Important Romans might also reciprocate this educational experience and send their children to live with a client king. Cicero sent his son and nephew to stay with Deiotarus in Galatia (*Att.* 17.3; 18.4). In the same vein, Cato the Younger sent his son to live in the Cappadocian royal court (Plutarch, *Cat. Min.* 73).

28. John Creighton, "Augustan Client Policy and Britain and the West," in *Herod and Augustus: Papers Presented at the IJS Conference, 21st-23rd June 2005*, ed. D. M. Jacobson and N. Kokkinos (Leiden: Brill, 2009), 361-81. Cf. John Creighton, "Links between the Classical Imagery in Post-Caesarean Belgica and the Rest of the Roman World," in *Die Kelten und Rom. Neue Numismatische Forschungen, Studien zu Fundmünzen der Antike*, ed. J. Metzler and D. Wigg-Wolf (Berlin: Mann, 2005), 87-108.

many client kings, such as Ptolemy XII Auletes, Polemo I of Pontus, and, of course, Herod. Furthermore, these monarchs maintained their positions, despite possible opposition, largely because of Roman support. Besides legitimacy from within, the might of Rome also dissuaded most external threats. When Antiochus IV Epiphanes invaded Egypt in 168 BCE, Rome intervened on behalf of the Ptolemies. In a famous historical incident, the Roman envoy, Gaius Popilius Laenas handed Antiochus the *senatus consultum*, ordered him to withdraw and then drew a circle around Antiochus and informed him that he could not leave the circle until he had answered the Senate's letter.[29] As we can see, simply having access to the Roman legions was often an effective deterrent to severe internal and external instability.

Second, client kings often received a share in the Roman imperial system through grants of citizenship. Once received, citizenship gave client kings a larger stake in the fortunes of Rome and her empire. This honor was not trivial. Romans during the late Republic and the principate were careful only to bestow citizenship on provincials who had performed great services to Rome. We should, therefore, evaluate Julius Caesar's grant of citizenship to Antipater, Herod's father, within this context. To repay Antipater for his support and heroism in battle, Caesar granted him and his children citizenship in 47 BCE. Because Herod and his family had a stake in the Roman Empire, they sought to further integrate themselves and their country into the Roman world. The grant of citizenship was, therefore, a major impetus to the Romanization of Palestine under the Herodians.[30]

Third, just as kings gave gifts to Rome, so too might they expect gifts in return. These might take the form of land grants, regular subsidies, or ad hoc presents. At some level, especially during the imperial period, a king, especially one with little natural claim to legitimacy, could consider his kingdom a gift from the Roman people. Periodically Rome also gave tracts of land to append to loyal monarchs' kingdoms. For example, as a reward for loyal service the emperor Claudius enlarged Herod Agrippa's territory so that it equaled the kingdom of his grandfather, Herod the Great.[31]

The practice of giving subsidies to client kings was somewhat ambig-

---

29. Polybius 28.18-23, 29.2, 27. Cf. *AJ* 12.242-46; 1 Macc 1:16-20.

30. *BJ* 1.194; *AJ* 14.137. For a similar grant of citizenship see the honors bestowed on Seleucus of Rhosus as collected in Victor Ehrenberg and A. H. M. Jones, *Documents Illustrating the Reigns of Augustus and Tiberius* (Oxford: Clarendon, 1955), 123 (301). Cf. Fergus Millar, "Triumvirate and Principate," *JRS* 63 (1973): 50-67, especially 58.

31. *BJ* 2.214-17; *AJ* 19.274-77. Cf. Dio 60.8.2. Cf. King Polemo I of Pontus, who received the kingdom of the Bosporus from Marcus Agrippa in 16 BCE (Dio 54.24.4-8).

uous. Subsidies could be sympathetically interpreted as essential aspects of diplomacy and foreign affairs, or they could be critically interpreted as bribes. It was even possible for Roman magistrates, such as the procurator Decianus Catus (60-61 CE), to view subsidies as loans to be repaid by the client kings. Ad hoc gifts seem to have been popular especially at the time of the Senate's *appellatio* of a king.[32] Nevertheless, there is evidence for Roman gifts at other times. In 203 BCE, Scipio Africanus gave his good friend Masinissa a golden crown, a curule chair, an ivory scepter, a tunic embroidered with palms, and a purple-bordered toga.[33] This custom continued during the imperial period, albeit modified slightly. In 24 CE, an unnamed senator revived ancient custom and presented an ivory scepter and an embroidered robe to Ptolemy of Mauretania.[34]

32. Livy 27.4 (King Syphax of the Masaesyli in 210 BCE), Cicero, *Q. Fr.* 2.10.2 (Antiochus I of Commagene in 59 BCE), Caesar, *B. Gall.* 1.43.4 (Ariovistus of the Suebi in 59 BCE).

33. For the gifts to Masinissa, see Livy 30.15, 17. These gifts may be not random but connected to the regalia of the old kings of Rome. Dionysius of Halicarnassus explicitly connects the royal gift giving and the Roman kings' regalia in his account of the first conferral of gifts by Rome: Lars Porsenna, having made a peace treaty with Rome, received "a throne of ivory, a scepter, a crown of gold, and a triumphal robe, which had been the insignia of the kings (of Rome)" (5.35.1; cf. 3.61). These items would thus be appropriate presents for the ritual of *appellatio*. However, this story must be accepted with reservation since, apart from Dionysius, no other source ever mentions the connection between Rome's regal past and the ritual of royal gift giving during the Republic or the empire. The fact that Dionysius has a particular antiquarian interest makes such silence even more suspicious. It is more likely that the gifts were evocative of kingship, in particular ancient Roman kingship, and, perhaps more importantly, of curule magistracy in both its military and civil aspects. For an analysis of this royal gift giving, see Braund, *Rome and the Friendly King*, 27-29.

34. For the gifts to Ptolemy of Mauretania, see Tacitus, *Ann.* 4.26.4. During the principate, from Gaius (37-41 CE) onward, kings received gifts explicitly connected to the curule office. These gifts were the *ornamenta praetoria* (accessories of a praetor) and *ornamenta consularia* (accessories of a consul). Herod Agrippa I is the first king known to have received either of these honors (the *ornamenta praetoria* from Gaius: Philo, *In Flacc.* 40). Cf. Schürer, *History of the Jewish People*, 1:314 n. 106. Under Claudius, he received the *ornamenta consularia*. At the same time, Agrippa's brother Herod of Chalcis received the *ornamenta praetoria* (Dio 60.8.2-3). The last king known to have received the honor is Agrippa II, who received the *ornamenta praetoria* from Vespasian in 75 (Dio 66.15.3-4). Since it seems that kings such as Agrippa I could proceed from receiving the *ornamenta praetoria* to receiving the *ornamenta consularia*, it is possible that the conferral of *ornamenta* might have constituted a form of ranking among the client kings of the principate. However, as Braund rightly observes (*Rome and the Friendly King*, 29), it is difficult to see the difference between the positions of kings such as Agrippa I, who received the *ornamenta consularia*, and kings such as Agrippa II, who only received the *ornamenta praetoria*. More important than a mark of rank within the principate, the *ornamenta* were likely evocative of the client kings' place in the imperial system as quasi-magistrates.

Fourth, client kings obtained access to Roman culture, in particular the benefits of Roman technology and engineering. As will be discussed later, the physical evidence for Herod's program of Romanization is extensive. He brought Roman buildings to Judaea and built using Roman-style construction techniques. He may even have imported Roman engineers to build his most massive projects, such as Caesarea and Sebaste. If Roman engineers were not used on the Temple, it is highly probable that they at least instructed Jewish masons and priests in certain techniques. All of these building projects were public edifices that exemplified both lifestyle and culture. Further, many of these structures, such as amphitheaters and baths, were places where people met and socialized. Although use of many of these buildings was limited to the elite, client kings' public works programs were a top-down version of acculturation in which the process started with royal supporters and slowly worked down to the less educated and less cosmopolitan general populace.

Finally, client kings maintained a great degree of local autonomy within the Roman sphere of influence. Given the distance between Rome and Judaea and the time it took for information to travel from the center outward, client kings often experienced great latitude in their decision-making. Consultation with Rome did occur, especially regarding important matters. However, Rome rarely usurped the authority and sovereignty of a king in areas that did not relate directly to Rome or Roman interests, and thus kings usually operated as autonomous rulers within a generally harmonious confederation of client states.

Our discussion of all the duties incumbent upon a client king and all the benefits that the Romans reaped from this relationship demonstrates that this patron-client relationship was reciprocal and mutually beneficial. In the next chapter, we will be examining the milieu of Hellenistic kingship. Although Herod was a client king in the Roman sphere of influence, he was also living in the Hellenistic East, a region that had its own well-established norms and cultural expectations of kingship. Without a proper understanding of these expectations of the good Hellenistic king, it would be impossible to understand Herod's kingship and his presentation to his Greek and Greek-influenced audiences.

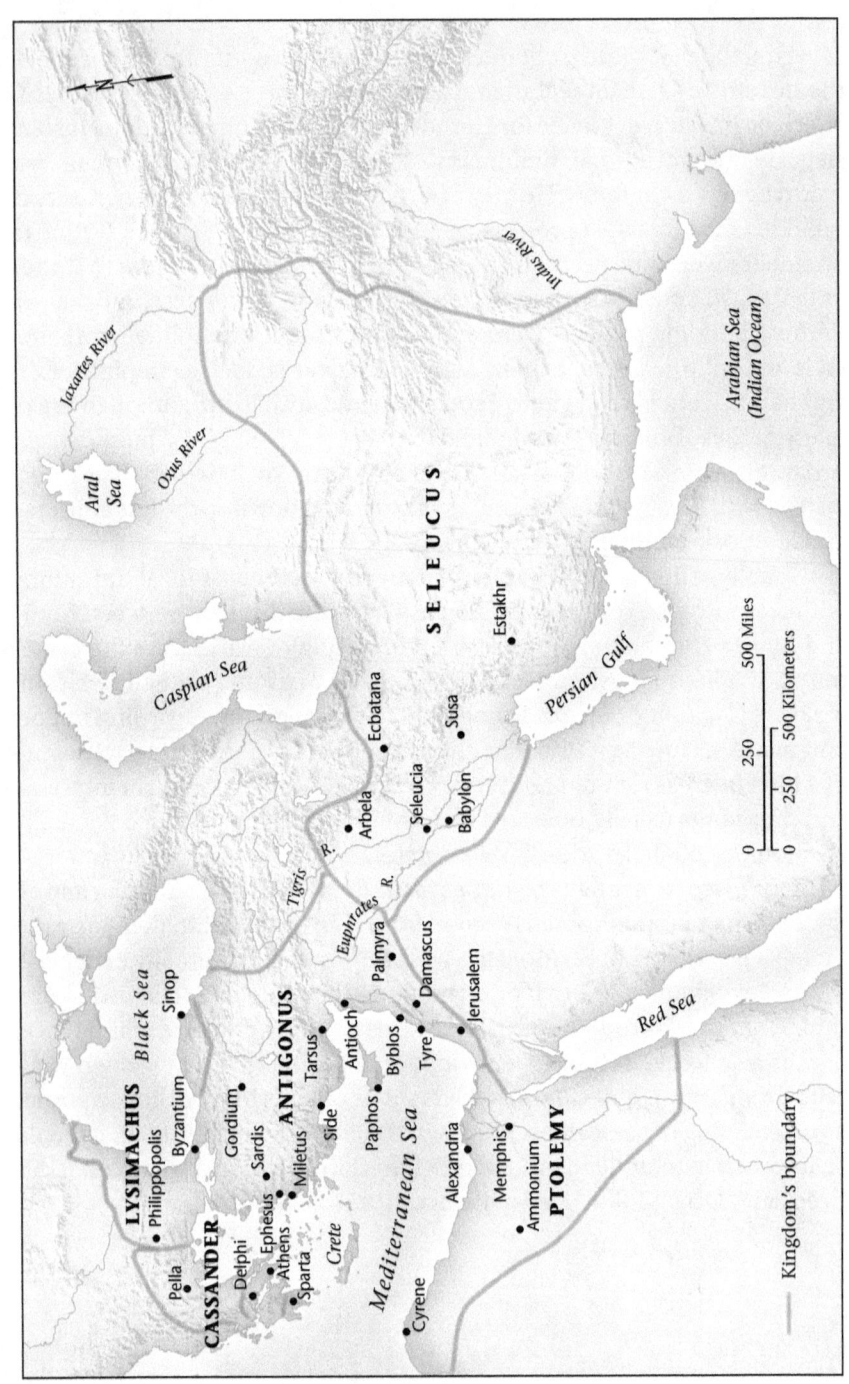

The Near East under the Diadochs

CHAPTER 2

Hellenistic Monarchy in the Graeco-Roman World

Although Rome and its system of client kingship cast a large shadow over first-century BCE Judaea, it is important to remember that Romanization was only beginning; the far more influential and pervasive cultural influence was Hellenism. Like most members of the Jewish elite of his time, Herod was thoroughly immersed in the Hellenistic world. He spoke Greek, read Greek, and acted Greek. Because of this cultural immersion, Hellenistic notions of good leadership would have been extremely important to Herod and would have provided him with a model familiar to those within his court.

The question thus becomes: What were these standard moral-philosophical and rhetorical values? Can we identify and describe the general philosophical milieu in which Herod, as a Hellenized monarch living in the Hellenistic East, would have resided? Fortunately, there was an increased philosophical interest in the role and duties of monarchs and aristocrats during the Hellenistic and Roman periods. This interest led to an explosion of treatises and speeches about the *good king*. Individual authors may have disagreed on minor points or specific facets of royal obligation. However, in general, there existed significant consensus on how the good king or ruler should behave toward his subjects, his neighbors, and his enemies. Within this nexus of conduct, we can locate general standards of royal behavior. From this massive literature, we can pare down the material and identify several general criteria of good kingship that appear repeatedly.[1]

1. F. W. Walbank provides a thorough introduction to Hellenistic monarchical theory. See F. W. Walbank, "Monarchies and Monarchic Ideals," in F. W. Walbank, A. E. Astin,

Nevertheless, all these texts would have little political importance if contemporary kings did not digest and follow their ideas. Although we cannot be sure that a particular monarch read a particular political theorist, the surviving archaeological, literary, and numismatic evidence strongly suggests that many kings were conscious of these criteria of good kingship and sought to fulfill them. It is therefore reasonable to assume that any reasonably educated and trained king who ascended the throne would have a basic understanding of what it meant to be a good king in the Hellenistic/Roman world even if he did not take these treatises as verbatim political guides. This inference is important to our study of Herod because he too would have been aware of the expectations of his Hellenized subjects, and he would have made all efforts to satisfy those expectations. Further, we know from Nicolaus of Damascus that Nicolaus himself tutored Herod in philosophy and history, among other subjects.[2] Although Nicolaus does not tell us exactly what Herod read, we can assume that Nicolaus gave the king a good Greek education. Such an education would no doubt have included some, if not all of the authors cited in this section. Even with limited specific information, we know that Herod would have been familiar with the ideas that appear throughout these works.[3]

M. W. Frederiksen, and R. M Ogilvie, eds., *CAH*² (Cambridge: Cambridge University Press, 2008), 7:63-100. However, his article is over twenty-five years old, and new discussions and issues have arisen in the field. Further, Walbank concentrates on Hellenistic political theory and does not make much of an effort to connect it with later Roman political and monarchical theory. Finally, his article does not focus on cultural expectations of kings. All of this requires us to engage in a review of the sources with a particular emphasis on the expected duties and obligations of kings and a cross-chronological and cross-geographical perspective. See also Richard A. Billows, *Antigonos the One-Eyed and the Creation of the Hellenistic State* (Berkeley: University of California Press, 1990), 155-60, 242-50; Helen Lund, *Lysimachus: A Study in Early Hellenistic Kingship* (London: Routledge, 1992), 153-83. For a brief overview of ideal Hellenistic kingship, especially as it regards Herod's kingdom, see Samuel Rocca, *Herod's Judaea: A Mediterranean State in the Classical World* (Tübingen: Mohr, 2008), 36-39.

2. *FGrH* 90 fragment 135. Ben Zion Wacholder, in his monograph on Nicolaus, offers a hypothetical list of Greek authors in Herod's library based on citations by Nicolaus and connections with the Herodian court. He lists forty-four authors, of whom only nineteen are well attested. While some of his inclusions are problematic, Wacholder's list does provide a possible snapshot of some of the authors Herod likely would have read. See Ben Zion Wacholder, *Nicolaus of Damascus* (Berkeley: University of California Press, 1962), 81-86.

3. This section examines the theoretical duties and obligations of Hellenistic kings as evidenced by the writings of several political theorists from Plato to Dio Chrysostom. Although men such as Dio (ca. 40–ca. 120 CE) and Lucius Annaeus Seneca (ca. 3 BCE–65 CE)

A final important note: the actual historicity of the events recounted in many of these philosophical texts such as the *Cyropaedia* and the biographies of Agesilaus, king of Sparta (ca. 440-360 BCE), is less important than the images evoked within the narratives. These images and the lessons offered within the treatises reflect general attitudes and beliefs about the institution of kingship. Such revelations enable us to better understand what people in antiquity expected of their leaders. Additionally, texts that we now believe to be more myth than fact were not read as such in the ancient world. Thus, mythical heroes such as Herakles were just as real to the ancient reader as Cyrus or Agesilaus and just as capable of teaching lessons to contemporary monarchs.

The King as a Virtuous Ruler

Among the entire corpus of Hellenistic philosophical treatises, one ideal that appears most frequently is the notion of the virtuous king. All good men were expected to be virtuous. However, because the king was the most powerful man in the kingdom, his moral status had to be unambiguously good in order for the state itself to be moral. For Isocrates, just as the king exceeds all in rank, so too must he surpass all in virtue. Aristo-

---

did not live in the Hellenistic period, the political ideas and ideals of the Hellenistic period carried over into the Roman republican and imperial periods. Thus, I believe it is perfectly reasonable to cite these men as evidence for a larger and extremely stable consensus about the duties and obligations of the good king that crossed geographical and chronological boundaries. Further, although there seems to have been quite a bit of interest in philosophical discussions of kingship during the Hellenistic and early imperial periods, many of these texts have not survived or have survived only in small fragments or as brief mentions in other literary sources. For example, a treatise on kingship by Theophrastus exists only as a citation in Dionysius of Halicarnassus (*Ant. Rom.* 5.73) and as fragments on a papyrus (*P. Oxy.* 1611.38-46). In a letter to Atticus (*Att.* 12.40), Cicero mentions an *Ad Alexandrum* of Theopompus but tells us nothing of its contents. A Stoic treatise, written by Persaeus of Citium, who was a disciple of Zeno and a member of the court of Antigonus II Gonatus, appears only by name in Diogenes Laertius (7.36). Given this dearth of available sources, I am relying on those that have survived, namely the writings of Isocrates, Plato, Xenophon, Aristotle, and Philodemus. Because of their general consensus on several issues relating to ideal kingship, I believe these texts represent well the original corpus of kingship treatises. See Walbank, "Monarchies," 77, where he argues that the surviving texts written by Hellenistic authors can provide us some idea of the general philosophical discussions and justifications of monarchy during that period. Cf. Erwin R. Goodenough, "The Political Philosophy of Hellenistic Kingship," *YCS* 1 (1928): 55-102.

tle concurs, remarking that in the ideal *politeia* (city-state), the king was chosen as king precisely because he possessed more virtue than everyone else.[4] We see this notion of the king as preeminent in virtue also in the *Peri Basileias* (On Kingship) of the neo-Pythagorean Diotogenes, who wrote that the king "must excel the rest in virtue and on that account be judged worthy to rule." Historical kings received praise for their virtue. For instance, an inscription dedicated to Attalus III praises him "because of his virtue" *(aretēs heneken)*.[5]

Among the virtues expected of kings were wisdom and justice. The importance of wisdom to Philodemus (ca. 110-35 BCE) is clear when one observes that the two kings he mentions more than any others were Odysseus and Nestor. Both were famous for their wisdom and counsel. For the author of the *Rhetorica ad Alexandrum,* wisdom was the foundation of good kingship. Wisdom enabled reason, and the good king used reason to rule well and to achieve justice, happiness, and well-being for himself and the state.[6] In his now fragmentary treatise *On Kingship,* Theophrastus asserted that the true king ruled by the scepter of justice rather than by the sword of tyranny. Diotogenes echoes this belief, declaring the king to be the prime source of justice in the realm and thus responsible for actively creating justice. This emphasis on the importance of the king displaying

---

4. Isocrates, *Nic.* 11-12. *Ad Nicoclem* is part of Isocrates' trilogy of *Cyprian Orations.* In this letter, which was likely written shortly after Nicocles ascended the throne of Salamis in 374 BCE, Isocrates addresses the new king and advises him on how to be a good ruler. Although this letter is specifically addressed to Nicocles, the ideas presented in it appear in other treatises of Isocrates and reflect his larger view of kingship. As we will see, Isocrates shares many ideas about the role of the good king with other Graeco-Roman philosophers. For an introduction to Isocrates and his political treatises, see Michael Gagarin, David Mirhady, Terry L. Papillon, Yun Lee Too, eds., *Isocrates,* 2 vols. (Austin: University of Texas Press, 2000-2004), 3-11 (3-13 in vol. 2). For Aristotle's view, see *Pol.* 5.10; cf. 1284a, 1288a.

5. Stobaeus, *Anthology* 4.7.62. Whether the fragments are Hellenistic or Roman (I am inclined to believe Louis Delatte, who dates them to the first to second century CE) is somewhat irrelevant to our interests. The ideas expressed in these treatises retain many of the ideas and notions found in earlier treatises that we can date more concretely. They thus can be used in our discussion of the duties and obligations of the good king. For the inscription praising Attalus III, see *OGIS* 332.

6. Pseudo-Aristotle, *Rhetorica ad Alexandrum* 1420a.24-25. Cf. David E. Hahm, "Kings and Constitutions: Hellenistic Theories," in *The Cambridge History of Greek and Roman Political Thought,* ed. Christopher Rowe and Malcolm Schofield (Cambridge: Cambridge University Press, 2000), 460. Although the *Rhetorica* was originally attributed to Aristotle because its ideas are similar to his, few scholars today believe that he wrote it. See Goodenough, "Political Philosophy," 91-92.

virtue, especially wisdom and justice, occurred because many philosophers, such as Isocrates, believed that the monarch could serve as a role model for others. When the king was wise and just, so too were his citizens.

The King as Lawgiver

Benevolence, wisdom, and justice were all necessary virtues because they also enabled the king to promulgate effective and moral laws, one of his central duties. According to Philodemus, the good king sustained just decisions. Isocrates urges Nicocles to effect fair and just law within his kingdom. He even encouraged him to copy the laws of other states if they were beneficial and moral.

Hellenistic philosophers believed that the good king was able to write just law because of his status as the animate or *living* law of the realm. Although later philosophers would expand on this idea and adapt increasingly popular notions of monotheism onto it, earlier writers such as Aristotle and Xenophon possessed a similar understanding of the relationship between the king and the law. Aristotle wrote in the *Politics* that if a king surpasses all others in virtue, then it is as if he is a law himself, and it is just for him to rule absolutely. Xenophon called the king "law with eyes for men" (*Cyropaedia* 8.1.22). Pseudo-Archytas and Diotogenes divided law into two types: animate and inanimate law. Animate law *(nomos empsychos)* was the king, and inanimate law was the legal code. Since the king was a form of living law, only he was capable of making just laws. Further, the true king, as animate law, was better than the average man. In the *Laws*, Plato argued that if a man existed who had a truly royal character and possessed "divine passion for self-control and justice," then the city should place itself under his control and obey any laws that he wrote.

Just laws could be instituted only where the king was able to judge impartially without passion or anger. Since all law and justice sprang from or was preeminently located in the mind of the king, it was absolutely vital that passion and desire never distract him. Only then could he make just law and decisions. Isocrates counseled Nicocles to render legal decisions with no sign of favoritism or inconsistency, both because it was just to do so and because it was practically beneficial, since then everyone in the kingdom would know the law of the land. Once these decisions were made, good kings were expected to be firm and punish those who disobeyed with firmness but clemency. Philodemus writes, "because of a decision he may appear gentle; because of his gentleness he may be loved, and because of his firmness, whenever necessary, he may not be despised" (*On Rhetoric* cols. 24-25). Mercy also had practical advantages. In his letter to Philip II of Macedon, Isocrates urged a policy of kindness rather than severity toward the Greeks because such a policy would lead to a greater reputation and greater loyalty. By acting compassionate and humane, Philip could gain greater honor for himself and secure the Greeks' loyalty more tightly than if he were a harsh and oppressive ruler.[7]

Possessing Majesty and Accumulating Wealth and Power

Virtue was undeniably important, but so was appearing virtuous. In particular, Hellenistic philosophers expected their ideal kings to be regal and majestic in appearance and to possess the wealth and power appropriate to their station. Since the king was the center of the state, he had to appear awe-inspiring. According to Aristotle, one of the causes of the destruction of a monarchy was contempt. When a king's subjects despised him and did not hold him in awe, they were less likely to tolerate his rule and more likely to revolt against it. It was therefore important for a king to impress and astonish his subjects. In other words, he had to look like and act like a king. Diotogenes recognized the importance of physical beauty when he wrote, "He [the king] will succeed in this [ruling] if first he make an impression of majesty by his appearance."[8] An important part of looking regal

---

7. Plato, *Leg.* 4.711E-712A. In the *Republic* (499B-C), Plato argues that the best constitution was the one that gave power to the philosopher-king. However, in the *Politics* (294A) he changes his opinion and asserts that a wisely conducted monarchy was superior to a constitution based on the rule of law. Cf. Hahm, "Kings and Constitutions," 459. This idea of the king as a higher being will be explained in greater detail later. For the benefits of impartial judgment, see Isocrates, *Nic.* 18.

8. Stobaeus, *Anthology* 4.7.62. Both the pose and physical appearance of royal statues and portraits were designed to emphasize the energetic and virile nature of the kings, who appeared either in armor or nude with or without a *chlamys*. Statues of kings in civilian dress have not been found. Royal sculptors frequently borrowed stances and schemes from athletic statuary. However, these royal statues exaggerated and intensified the athletic, muscular style, using it as a metaphor of power. Kings usually appeared as men of about twenty to thirty, even when the king's real age far exceeded that range. For example, a bronze statue of Seleucus I Nicator in the Museo Nazionale in Naples depicts him as a strong and dynamic individual of mature but youthful age even though he was likely in his sixties to seventies when the statue was commissioned. For a discussion of Hellenistic royal statuary,

was to be athletic, and it is not surprising that one of the more frequent royal pastimes was hunting. Philosophers such as Dio Chrysostom recommended this sport because it trained body and mind, making the king stronger, fitter, and better able to withstand heat, cold, hunger, and thirst.

Simple fitness was not enough. Many people in antiquity believed that external beauty was a sign of internal moral worth. Thus, one would want a handsome king because he would also be a moral ruler. Isocrates describes Evagoras as being handsome and physically attractive from a very young age. When he became an adult, he maintained his looks and added other kingly virtues to them. Dio Chrysostom used the myth of Herakles and Hermes to highlight the importance of physical beauty for the king. In the myth, Lady Royalty is radiant, elegant, and full of dignity. In order for a king truly to be regal, he had to imitate this physical beauty in some way. One of the ways a king could augment his physical appearance or highlight his comeliness was by dressing well. Unlike many Hellenistic philosophers, Philodemus saw no moral worth in physical beauty. However, he did realize that it could have the practical value of inspiring fear in one's enemies and loyalty in one's friends and subjects. Beauty made kings appear superhuman, and such an appearance instilled fear and reverence in subjects.

Political philosophers recognized, however, that sometimes kings were not physically attractive or imposing enough to awe their subjects. In those cases and even with men who were handsome, artificial means, for example dress and clothing, might be used to enhance the monarch's

---

see R. R. R. Smith, "Kings and Philosophers," in *Images and Ideologies: Self-Definition in the Hellenistic World,* ed. Anthony Bulloch, Erich S. Gruen, A. A. Long, and Andrew Stewart (Berkeley: University of California Press, 1993), 202-11. For the statue of Seleucus I depicting the old king as a mature and vibrant man see Smith, figure 5c. For other statues of Hellenistic kings see figures 5b (Demetrius Poliorcetes), 5d, and 6a-b (Attalus I). Cf. Jim Roy, "The Masculinity of the Hellenistic King," in *When Men Were Men: Masculinity, Power and Identity in Classical Antiquity,* ed. Lin Foxhall and John Salmon (London: Routledge, 1998), 111-26 for a discussion of the masculinity of the Hellenistic kings in their self-presentation. The Diadochs (the successors of Alexander the Great) and later Hellenistic kings also used coins to advertise their martial strength and physical prowess. As in their statuary, kings appeared on their coins with strong necks, solid round chins, wrinkles around the corners of their eyes, suggesting maturity and wisdom, severe expressions on their faces, and a curly hairstyle reminiscent of Alexander's *anastolē* but shorter on the sides and in the back. These depictions, which were influenced by and alluded to portraits of Herakles and Alexander, emphasized the energetic and powerful nature of these new kings. For examples see Robert Fleischer, "Hellenistic Royal Iconography on Coins," in *Aspects of Hellenistic Kingship,* ed. Per Bilde, et al. (Oakville: Aarhus University Press, 1996), 30-31, 33 (figures 8 and 9).

appearance. By dressing sumptuously and lavishly, a king displayed his majesty and distinguished himself from his subjects. The famous entry of Cleopatra into the city of Tarsus in 41 BCE is an excellent example of how a monarch used costume and visual effects to awe and entrance others. Antony had summoned Cleopatra to Tarsus to answer charges that she had aided the assassins of Julius Caesar. Bedecking herself in costly jewelry and other accoutrements and dressing up as Venus, Cleopatra sailed into the city in a luxuriously decorated boat with silver oars to the tunes of flutes, pipes, and lutes. She was accompanied by boys dressed as Cupids and girls dressed as Nereïds and Graces. Such costumes greatly impressed both Antony and the crowd assembled at the port. Antony not only acquitted Cleopatra of all charges, but this visit also marked the beginning of their love affair and alliance.

In addition to looking regal, a king also had to act dignified and graceful at all times. The way he behaved was a direct indication of his personal worth as an individual. Dio Chrysostom argued that no wicked or licentious person could ever become a king in the proper sense, since he could not even rule himself. A king who behaved regally and majestically would naturally have a large amount of personal charisma. As Xenophon's Cyrus illustrates, a good king could draw men to him and persuade them to support him without exerting any real effort. Because of his charm, Xenophon's Cyrus was able to cement the loyalty of his troops and consequently strengthen his political position.[9]

In order to appear as regal and impressive as possible, a king would do well to become cultured and urbane. In particular, he should study philosophy and poetry and be proficient in skills such as music and rhetoric. The study of philosophy and poetry made the king wiser, more just, and

9. Xenophon, *Cyro.* 5.1.24-30. Personal charisma was extremely important for kings who did not have natural and long-standing claims to legitimacy. One way they could enhance their legitimacy was by connecting themselves with a previous source of legitimacy. Alexander the Great set the standard for Hellenistic numismatic propaganda. Although rulers prior to him had put their images on coins, he brought this practice to new levels of activity, and it continued after his death. Symbols on Diadoch coins advertised their authority, power, and legitimacy. Additionally, wishing to draw legitimacy from their association with Alexander, they used his image or other typically Alexandrine motifs. For a discussion of the coins of Lysimachus, see Norman Davis and Colin M. Kraay, *The Hellenistic Kingdoms: Portrait Coins and History* (London: Thames and Hudson, 1973), 33-36 (coins 1-6); R. A. Hadley, "Royal Propaganda of Seleucus I and Lysimachus," *JHS* 94 (1974): 55-57, 63-65, plate 7; Lund, *Lysimachus*, 162-64. For a discussion of the coins of Ptolemy I, see Davis and Kraay, *Hellenistic Kingdoms*, 37 (coin 17).

more moral. For instance, Isocrates advised Nicocles to learn all he could because such knowledge is the foundation of his rule. Both philosophy and poetry taught important lessons. Such knowledge enabled the king to judge properly and to emulate other wise kings. Excelling at the musical arts was also important. It was not necessary to be an expert, but Dio Chrysostom encouraged the good king to at least learn to play the lyre or cithara in order to sing hymns to the gods or chant the praises of brave men. Rhetorical skill enabled the king to defend himself against accusations from his enemies. It also permitted him to speak in front of audiences and persuade them of his opinions.

The good king physically dominated his court with his beauty and refined nature, but he also impressed and awed his subjects with his wealth and benevolence. One of the most visible methods of advertising such wealth was the coin portrait. The Diadochs had struck portraits of themselves that stressed their physical strength and legitimacy. Later kings, especially the later Seleucids and Ptolemies, were less concerned with establishing legitimacy. Instead, they used their coin and clay seal portraits to stress their enjoyment of *tryphē* (the good life of pleasures and luxury). These kings appeared on their coins and seals as well-fed, corpulent monarchs enjoying the great prosperity that their kingdom provided for themselves but also for their subjects. This image of the slightly obese monarch applied even in the divine sphere. For instance, a portrait of Tyche of Seleucia Pieria has the same plump facial features as Antiochus VIII Grypus (125-96 BCE). The use of these features for both monarchs and gods suggests that such characteristics were viewed positively. Robert Fleischer hypothesizes that these images were promulgated precisely to counter the increasing instability experienced by the later Seleucid and Ptolemaic kings.[10]

One of the most frequent and praiseworthy uses of this immense wealth was as a tool of royal benevolence or *euergetism*. A king's obligation to be benevolent arose from his position as the highest patron of the state. Sthenidas the Locrian (ca. 400 BCE) argued that the king imitated the highest deity when he was magnanimous. Royal benefaction is widely attested during the Hellenistic period, and archaeologists have uncovered a myriad of inscriptions praising kings for donating large sums of money

---

10. Fleischer, "Hellenistic Royal Iconography," 34-36 (figures 17-19). See also M. M. Austin, "Hellenistic Kings, War and the Economy," *CQ* 36 (1986): 459-61, where he discusses the importance of wealth for the Hellenistic king.

to cities throughout the eastern Mediterranean. For instance, the city of Iasos praised Antiochus III for his continued support and benefaction to Greeks as a larger group and to Iasos in particular.

On a larger scale than donations for specific buildings was the construction of new cities or the rebuilding of old ones. City-founding was a centerpiece of Hellenistic royal activity because it enabled a king to demonstrate his wealth and power while simultaneously enabling him to acquire the heroic status of *ktistēs* (founder). Especially popular was the construction of cities named after the monarchs themselves or their relatives or friends. By the end of the Hellenistic period, the eastern Mediterranean was littered with such cities, including Alexandria, Antioch, Arsinoe, Seleuceia, and Eumenea. This practice continued into the first century BCE among Herod's royal contemporaries. Archelaus of Cappadocia (36 BCE–17 CE) refounded the ancient Hittite city of Garsaoura and renamed it Archelais. On the Black Sea coast, Polemo I of Pontus (ca. 37-7 BCE) constructed the city of Polemonion, ultimately making it his capital.

With Roman client kings, however, the situation was slightly different than during the reigns of the Diadochs. Because Rome had become the dominant power in the Graeco-Roman world, client kings had to include Rome and its leaders in their urban construction programs. To this end, a number of client kings constructed cities named in honor of the Caesars. These *urbes Caesarae* include Iol-Caesarea, built by Juba II of Mauretania (25 BCE–ca. 23 CE), as well as Sebaste in Pontus, which Polemo built on the site of Mithridates VI Eupator's royal residence at Cabeira. Archelaus of Cappadocia constructed Sebaste-Elaeussa in Cilicia, and on the old Cappadocian capital of Mazaca he erected Caesarea Mazaca. By creating new cities, Hellenistic kings illustrated their power and wealth. They also transformed themselves into heroic figures like those from the mythical past, and, as such, they could expect to receive heroic honors. Moreover, by naming these new cities after themselves or their relatives, these kings physically stamped their respective kingdoms with signs of their royal presence and majesty.

The King as Protector and Defender of His Subjects

Perhaps the most important duty and role of the good king was that of protector and savior of his people. Indeed, several kings chose to adopt the title of *Sōtēr* (savior) as part of their nomenclature, and this designation appears prominently on inscriptions and coins. For instance, both Ptolemy I of Egypt (ruled 323-283 BCE) and Antiochus I (ruled 281-261 BCE) received this title, which emphasized their power to protect their people from danger and harm.[11]

Political philosophers developed several images to evoke the centrality of this obligation, including the image of the king as a shepherd who tended to his subjects as a shepherd watches over his flock. Like a shepherd the good king oversaw his people and kept any danger away. Plato called the king "the herdsman of a herd devoid of horns" (*Politicus* 265d). Dio Chrysostom asserted that any ruler not concerned with "becoming a guide and shepherd of his people" could not justly call himself king, only despot. The good king, on the other hand, "takes thought for the shelter and pasturing of his own flock, and, besides, keeps off the wild beasts and guards it against thieves."[12] A further image invoked to describe the relationship between king and people was that of a father and his children. Philodemus urged the good king to be "gentle like a father" by ruling with a stern, yet kind and generous, demeanor. The king should feel able to punish subjects when they broke the law or endangered others in the same way that a father punished wayward children. However, just as a father would show restraint and compassion for his offspring, so too was it necessary for the king to restrain his anger and deal justly with even the worst offenders. A final image evoked to describe the role of the king was that of a bull. Dio Chrysostom remarked that when a predator appears, the bull, like the good king, fights "in front of the whole herd," and brings "aid to the weak in his desire to save the dependent multitude from dangerous wild beasts."[13] If the king were strong and secure, his enemies would fear him so much that they would not wish to attack him or his subjects.

---

11. For Antiochus III bearing the title *Sōtēr* on inscriptions, see *OGIS* 239; *SEG* 41.1003. For Ptolemy I bearing the title, see *OGIS* 19. For the Soter Era, see R. A. Hazzard, *Imagination of a Monarchy: Studies in Ptolemaic Propaganda* (Toronto: University of Toronto Press, 2000), 25-46. For Ptolemy and his wife Berenice as the *Theoi Soterēs*, see *OGIS* 54, 56. Other kings who did not use *Sōtēr* in their official titulature were sometimes hailed as *Sōtēr* by their subjects. A number of petitions to Ptolemy III Euergetes and Ptolemy IV Philopator ask them to grant the petitioner's request. One of the standard formulas addresses the king as the "savior of all people." See *P. Ent*[1] 2.12, 9.11, 11.6, 37.11, 75.15, 77.7, 78.16, 88.7, 90.7, and 101.8. Cf. Alan E. Samuel, *The Shifting Sands of History: Interpretations of Ptolemaic Egypt* (Lanham: University Press of America, 1989), 76-77. See also *OGIS* 253, where Antiochus IV Epiphanes is praised as *Sōtēr tēs Asias* ("savior of Asia").

12. Dio Chrysostom, *Or.* 1.13, 17; 3.40-41.

13. Dio Chrysostom, *Or.* 1.24-25; 2.68-71.

Strong and capable kings defended their subjects from both internal and external threats. Internally, the most obvious way in which a king could protect his people was to strive actively to create and maintain peace and prosperity within the kingdom itself. Isocrates hoped to see Philip of Macedon become an instrument of peace and stability who would unite the squabbling Greek city-states. To further this goal he exhorted the Macedonian king by comparing him to his mythical ancestor Herakles, who also brought peace and stability to Greece. Philodemus used the example of Nestor as peacemaker between Achilles and Agamemnon to illustrate the need for the king to heal internal division and create a stable monarchy. It was also incumbent on the good king to end internal disputes and squabbling. Philodemus depicted Zeus acting as mediator between Athena and Aphrodite. Just as Zeus acted as an arbitrator, healing internal conflict and creating order, so too must the good king, who was supposed to imitate Zeus in his rule.

External threats were an equally important concern. During the Hellenistic period, a major anxiety was the threat of barbarian (i.e., non-Greek) invasion. Thus, a king who could successfully defend his kingdom's and his allies' borders received praise and loyalty. For instance, the Antigonids were famous as defenders of northern Greece. The Attalid dynasty of Pergamum also received praise for its campaigns against non-Greeks. In a victory inscription erected in ca. 167/166 BCE, King Eumenes II accepted the honors bestowed on him by the Ionian league for his successful conquest of the barbarian armies that threatened Greek cities in Asia Minor. The Attalid dynasty even erected a giant altar (the Pergamene altar of Zeus) celebrating its wars against the barbarian Galatians. The reliefs on the altar depict the Attalids as champions of Greek civilization against the barbarian hordes. Such propaganda images reinforced the status of this dynasty as defenders and guardians of order and stability.[14]

As the primary protector of his people, the good king was of necessity an active military leader. This role implied not only commanding one's armies but also leading the soldiers into battle. Good kings inspired their soldiers with rousing speeches before battle, drew up clever battle plans, and then joined the men in the ranks. In their speeches, kings often recalled past glories and encouraged their soldiers to surpass their ancestors'

---

14. For the Antigonids as defenders of northern Greece see Polybius 9.35.2; 18.37.9. Cf. Livy 33.12.10. For the Ionian League's inscription in honor of King Euemenes II see *OGIS* 763. Also see Walbank, "Monarchies," 82.

and even their own accomplishments. At the battle of Raphia in 217 BCE, both Antiochus III and Ptolemy IV exhorted their troops before the battle. However, because both had recently come to power, they could not discuss any major accomplishments of their own. Instead, they inspired their troops by each recalling the glory and deeds of their respective ancestors. Such inspiration calmed the soldiers' fears, raised their morale, and increased their enthusiasm for battle.

Once the battle had been engaged, the good king's place was with his men in the ranks. Both of Xenophon's heroes, Agesilaus and Cyrus, displayed great bravery on the battlefield. Even when he was an old man Agesilaus led his army into battle, most notably against the Persian army near Sardis. In the midst of battle, he sent word to his cavalry that he was personally leading the infantry and that they should attack immediately in full knowledge that he would be following them. His bravery inspired his troops, and they crushed the Persian forces (Xenophon, *Ages.* 1.30-32). Xenophon also depicted Cyrus consistently leading his troops into battle. In his skirmish with the Assyrians, Cyrus charges into the fray with his soldiers and fights alongside them (*Cyro.* 3.3.57-63). In his narration of Evagoras's return from exile, Isocrates states explicitly that the king led his followers, who only numbered about fifty, in an attack on the palace at Salamis. He praises Evagoras's courage and asserts that it was fundamental to the success of his venture (*Evag.* 29-32).[15]

15. For the early Diadochs, legitimacy was a primary concern since none of them had natural claims to power. As such, these men stressed their right to rule through the notion of spear-won territory; that is, their power rested on their military strength and skill. For example, Lysimachus used the lion motif throughout his propaganda program to emphasize his military might and skill. For versions of a story glorifying Lysimachus as a "lion-killer," see Seneca, *Ira* 3.17.2; *Clem.* 1.25.1; *Q. C.* 8.1.11-19; Pliny, *HN* 8.21; Pausanias 1.9.5; Plutarch, *Demet.* 27.3; Justinus, *Epit.* 15.3.7-8. For Lysimachus's flagship being named the *Leontophorus* see Memnon in *FGrH* 434, fragment 8.4-6. For the lion *protomē*, facing left or right, appearing regularly on Lysimachus's coins throughout his reign, see Lund, *Lysimachus,* 6-8, 160-61. For a discussion of the portraits and statues of Hellenistic kings and their emphasis on military strength and physical vigor, see Smith, "Kings and Philosophers," 202-11. Cf. Roy, "Masculinity," 112-17. Ptolemaic court poetry also emphasized martial valor. Theocritus praises Ptolemy II Philadelphus as *warrior Ptolemy* who "knows how to throw a spear" in addition to possessing other martial virtues. See Theocritus, *Id.* 17.56, 103. Ironically, Ptolemy was not really a brave warrior and never actually fought in battle. However, the image of the mighty warrior was so important to royal legitimacy that he had to appear as such. For discussions of his reign, see Eric Turner, "Ptolemaic Egypt," in *CAH*² 7.133-59; H. Heinen, "The Syrian-Egyptian Wars and the New Kingdoms of Asia Minor," in *CAH*² 7.412-20. Cf. Samuel, *Shifting Sands,* 51-76.

Once a king emerged victorious in battle, he could advertise his achievement through both courtly poetry and physical monuments. Ptolemy II Philadelphus's court poetry advertised his military successes. Theocritus praised his king in his panegyric by declaring that, during Philadelphus's reign, "No foe crosses the Nile full of monsters to raise by land the battle cry in others' villages, and no enemy in armor leaps to the shore from a swift ship to harm the cattle of Egypt."[16] Military victories, in either defensive or offensive war, were physical manifestations of the strength and power of the king. Since Hellenistic monarchies often based their legitimacy on the individual strength of the monarch or his dynasty, it was essential that royal conquests be advertised actively throughout the kingdom. Thus, victory inscriptions and monuments became an important part of a Hellenistic king's self-presentation. In the Adulis inscription (*OGIS* 54), Ptolemy III Euergetes glorifies his victories in the Third Syrian War (246-241 BCE). In this inscription, the focus is entirely on Ptolemy and his martial valor, with only brief mention of his army and navy and no mention of any other individuals. An inscription commissioned by the city of Ilion expresses its goodwill and loyalty to Antiochus I and extols his triumphs, which were gained due to the support of the gods. Such inscriptions stressed the personal power and strength of the king as well as his ability to secure victory and protect his people.

Behaving Piously toward the Gods[17]

The final mandatory area of royal activity was in the realm of religion. In his position as king, the monarch also represented the community before its gods. If he wanted to fulfill his religious duties, he had to act piously toward them and secure their favor. A natural assumption underpinning this obligation of piety was the belief that monarchy on earth was a reflection of the reign in heaven and was therefore sanctioned by the gods. As a symbol of this relationship, the king was seen as the gods' anointed, chosen one, in par-

---

16. Theocritus, *Id.* 17.98-101.

17. As we will see in the next chapter, the expectations of Jewish rulers in the Second Temple period were quite similar to those of contemporary Hellenistic monarchs except that the Jewish kings were expected to behave piously toward one god, Yahweh, as opposed to the many gods of non-Jewish religious systems. Nevertheless, an analysis of typical Hellenistic royal behavior is still useful because it provides a clear illustration of the larger cultural milieu in which Jewish kings like Herod existed.

ticular the chosen of Zeus, the god of kingship. The king's powers and royal prerogatives derived from the gods, especially Zeus, and the gods taught the king how to govern effectively. For example, the Ptolemaic poet Theocritus stresses Ptolemy II Philadelphus's identity as the gods' anointed king when he stated that Zeus sent omens of Philadelphus's reign and loved and cared for him from birth (*Idylls* 17.74-75). Another way in which a king could stress his special status was by claiming descent from a god. The Seleucids claimed that their dynasty ultimately descended from Apollo Didymus. In support of this claim, a story circulated that Seleucus I had an anchor-shaped birthmark on his thigh, which indicated his divine parentage.[18]

Since the monarch was the chosen representative of the gods on earth, he was in the same relationship to them as his subjects were to him. A natural outgrowth of this belief was the evolution of the king into a demigod. Although this process reached its culmination only during the middle and late Roman imperial period, we see the beginnings of this belief in the Graeco-Roman world as early as the Hellenistic period.[19] Aristotle believed that if in a kingdom there should exist a man who surpassed all others in virtue, he would become like a god among men.[20]

On a slightly more practical level, the good king was expected to act piously toward the gods and encourage their worship. Sacrifices to the gods

---

18. For the Seleucid claims and the stories of Seleucus's birthmark, see *OGIS* 219, 227; Diodorus 19.90.4.

19. Hellenistic kings, in particular the Ptolemies, actively advertised themselves as gods on earth through royal cults and divine nomenclature. For the appearance of Ptolemaic royal cults and divine titulature such as *Theoi Sōterēs* (Ptolemy I and Berenice), *Theoi Adelphoi* (Ptolemy II Philadelphus and Arsinoe II), *Theoi Euergetai* (Ptolemy III Euergetes and Berenice of Cyrene), and *Theoi Epiphanai* (Ptolemy V and Cleopatra I) see *OGIS* 54, 56, 98; *SEG* 20.467. Cf. Walbank, "Monarchies," 82-99. See *OGIS* 90 (the Rosetta Stone) for Ptolemy V adopting the title *Epiphanēs*. Court poetry was also used to advertise a monarch's special nature. Theocritus explicitly calls Ptolemy II Philadelphus a demigod. He also expounds on Ptolemy's divine lineage and relation to Herakles. See Theocritus, *Id.* 17.13-52, 135-37. Coins advertised divine associations as well through use of divine attributes and assimilation of kings' facial features into those of various gods. See Fleischer, "Royal Iconography," 32-38 (figures 1, 19, 25, 37, 38). For the assimilation of Apollo and Zeus into Antiochus IV, see Robert Fleischer, *Studien zur Seleukidischen Kunst* I: *Herrscherbildnisse* (Mainz: von Zabern, 1991), 50-51, plates 22f-g, 23a. For deities taking on the features of Mithridates VI Eupator see W. Wroth, *A Catalogue of Greek Coins in the British Museum: Pontus, Paphlagonia, Bithynia and the Kingdom of Bosporus* (London: Longmans, 1889), 17-18 (numbers 51-58), plates 3.7-10 (Dionysus), 17 (number 46), 3.6 (Ares), 18 (number 61), 3.12 (Perseus).

20. Aristotle, *Pol.* 1284a-84b. Cf. Plato, *Min.* 3193-3206 where Plato depicts King Minos as in constant communion with Zeus and, as a result, like Zeus.

were essential if the king wanted them to favor him and his kingdom. The relationship between the gods and humanity was clear: people offered sacrifices to the gods, and the gods returned success and prosperity. Since the king was the leader of the community, it made sense that he also frequently functioned as the high priest of the kingdom, worshipping the gods and setting an example for his subjects. According to Xenophon, Cyrus was always careful to offer sacrifices to the gods before starting out on a campaign or before an actual battle. Such sacrifices, he hoped, would persuade the gods to help him and allow him to be victorious. When Plutarch's Agesilaus set off for his expedition against the Persians, he was extremely careful to sacrifice to the gods. He even risked angering the Thebans by personally conducting the sacrifice.[21] Historical Hellenistic monarchs frequently advertised this piety visually. The Ptolemies were especially active at such displays, perhaps because of the long-standing Egyptian tradition of depicting the king making offerings to the gods. Throughout her kingdom, Cleopatra VII consistently depicted herself making offerings to the gods.[22]

When a king respected the gods and cultivated their worship, they in turn would grant him and his kingdom success, prosperity, and security. Philodemus claimed that the pious king would ensure that his land was fertile, that the trees would blossom, that the livestock would multiply, and that the seas would be full of fish (col. 4.30). Dio Chrysostom predicted happiness and a long reign for a king who behaved piously toward the gods (*Or.* 2.74-77; 3.51). If a king were not mindful of the gods, however, he could expect instability and trouble. They would revoke their protection and strip him of his throne. On a more mundane level, failure to act piously toward the gods could anger a king's subjects and increase the likelihood that they would revolt against him and replace him.

Of all of the myriad ways that kings could demonstrate their piety to their people (and presumably to the gods), the most common and best-attested

---

21. Xenophon, *Cyro.* 1.5.6, 14; 3.3.21-22, 34; 7.1.1. Cf. 8.1.23. Omens and signs were one way the gods communicated with humans, and it was incumbent on humans to read and obey these divine messages. One of the topics that Cambyses and his son Cyrus discuss in book 1 of the *Cyropaedia* is omens and divine guidance. Cambyses advises his son never to act contrary to omens seen or auspices taken, especially regarding military affairs. To do so is to court disaster since it is to disregard the expressed desire of the gods. See *Cyro.* 1.6.44-46. For Agesilaus's actions before his campaign against the Persians see Plutarch, *Ages.* 6.4-6.

22. Diana E. E. Kleiner, *Cleopatra and Rome* (Cambridge: Harvard University Press, 2005), 85-87, 122, 138-39, 192, 268; Dieter Arnold, *Temples of the Last Pharaohs* (Oxford: Oxford University Press, 1999), 213-16.

was protection of existing sanctuary sites and construction of new ones. Sanctuary sites and temples were holy ground and thus inviolate. It was the ultimate act of blasphemy to violate their sanctity by destroying them or committing acts of violence within them. Xenophon praised his hero Agesilaus for his piety, and he offers the Spartan king as a model worthy of emulation. Agesilaus revered holy sites, even those of his enemies, and he refused to desecrate them by harming any suppliants of the gods. For example, after his battle with the anti-Spartan alliance led by Athens, Argos, and Thebes, he was told that a group of eighty enemy soldiers had taken refuge in a nearby temple. Although wounded and exhausted, Agesilaus did not forget his duty to the gods. He ordered that the enemy soldiers be given free passage wherever they chose to go. He even supplied an escort of cavalry to conduct them safely (Xenophon, *Ages.* 2.13; 11.1). Such behavior was both just and prudent, since attacking these men likely would have angered the gods whom Agesilaus respected and shown him to be an impious and unjust king.

Along with a strong respect for sanctuaries and other holy sites, kings often initiated building programs in honor of the gods and in hope of gaining a reputation for piety. This agenda would have provided physical evidence of the piety of a king and illustrated his power, wealth, and organizational skills. It also pleased the gods, who supported him and granted him and his kingdom success and prosperity. For a monarch to prove not only his connection to the gods but also their approval, he had to provide physical evidence. Nothing spoke as powerfully as gigantic temples dedicated to heaven. Many kings and even dynasties had patron deities, whose temples they constructed and maintained. The Attalid dynasty of Pergamum (282-133 BCE) cultivated the worship of the goddess Cybele and constructed several temples dedicated to her in Asia Minor, including the sanctuary site at Pessinous and the temple at Mamurt Kale, which was constructed by the Attalid founder Philetaerus (282-263 BCE). The Ptolemies created their own syncretic Hellenistic-Egyptian patron deity, Serapis, and actively patronized his worship. The most prominent example of such activity was the Serapeum in Alexandria. Begun by Ptolemy I Soter but significantly enhanced by Ptolemy III Euergetes, the Serapeum became the largest and most lavish temple in the Greek quarter of the city. In addition to a temple housing the cult statue, the Serapeum also contained a supplemental collection of scrolls from the city's great library.[23]

---

23. For the Attalid construction of Cybele sanctuaries at Pessinous and Mamurt Kale, see Strabo, *Geog.* 12.5.3. Cf. Lynn E. Roller, *In Search of God the Mother: The Cult of Anatolian*

Conclusion

Was a king a *good king* only if he fulfilled all of these characteristics and obligations? Of course not. It is not as if ancient philosophers or subjects carried an agreed-on checklist and graded their monarchs. Nevertheless, there does seem to have been a consensus among ancient thinkers about what exactly made a king good or bad, moral or immoral. There was also an active response by Hellenistic kings to these philosophical rules and criteria. Historical rulers attempted to fulfill these criteria, and, in return, they expected honor, praise, and loyalty. We cannot be sure exactly what Herod was reading while he was studying philosophy with Nicolaus. However, as we will see later, he was aware, at least in a general sense, of his royal duties and responsibilities, and he actively strove to appear as the just and virtuous Hellenistic king to his courtly elite, who would have been familiar with and well versed in the very philosophical treatises we have just surveyed.

In the next chapter, I will discuss the final cultural component of Herod's political milieu, Jewish kingship. As we will see, the obligations incumbent on Jewish rulers in the Second Temple period were quite similar to those of their contemporary Hellenistic monarchs. However, there were a few notable exceptions, such as the prohibition of figural images and piety to one god as opposed to many. As will become clear, these exceptions played a significant role in Herod's own self-presentation.

Cybele (Berkeley: University of California Press, 1999), 187-94, 210-12. For the foundation tablets of the Serapeum see *I. Alex. Ptol.* 13. Cf. Judith S. McKenzie, Sheila Gibson, and A. T. Reyes, "Reconstructing the Serapeum in Alexandria from the Archaeological Evidence," *JRS* 94 (2004): 73-121. Although not welcomed by many Jews, Antiochus IV's attempts to turn the Temple in Jerusalem into a temple to Olympian Zeus were consistent with his worship of this deity. For Antiochus's attempts, see 1 Macc 1:41-55; 2 Macc 6:1-6. Also see 2 Macc 6:2 for Antiochus's transformation of the temple on Mount Gerazim to the worship of Zeus Xenios (the Hospitable).

CHAPTER 3

Judaean History from the Maccabees to Herod

By the time Herod conquered Jerusalem and became de facto king in 37 BCE, Judaea had experienced more than one hundred years of independent Jewish rule. Prior to this independence, the region had been the province of successive empires — from the Assyrians and Babylonians to the Persians, to Alexander the Great, and finally to the Macedonian successors to Alexander, the Ptolemies and Seleucids.

After the death of Alexander in 323 BCE, his generals, known as the Diadochs (from the Greek word for successors), fought over the succession and ultimately splintered his empire into several smaller kingdoms, all vying for supremacy. Among these kingdoms were those which Alexander's generals Ptolemy and Seleucus established. Ptolemy carved out a kingdom in Egypt, while Seleucus's kingdom ultimately extended from Asia Minor (modern Turkey) in the west to the Indus River in the east. From ca. 312 until 198 BCE, the Ptolemies controlled Palestine. In 200 BCE, the Seleucid king Antiochus III Megas defeated the army of the Ptolemaic king, Ptolemy V Epiphanes, at the Battle of Panion. This victory put Ptolemaic forces on the run, and subsequent coastal victories over Sidon (199) and Gaza (198) confirmed Seleucid control over the region. According to Polybius (apud *AJ* 12.136), Antiochus conquered Jerusalem itself when the Jews assisted the Seleucid king in expelling the city's Egyptian garrison.

In return for their support, Antiochus III granted the Jews of Judaea several privileges including royal financial support for the Temple service and repair of any damages suffered during the war. Antiochus also guaranteed that the Jews could live according to their traditional

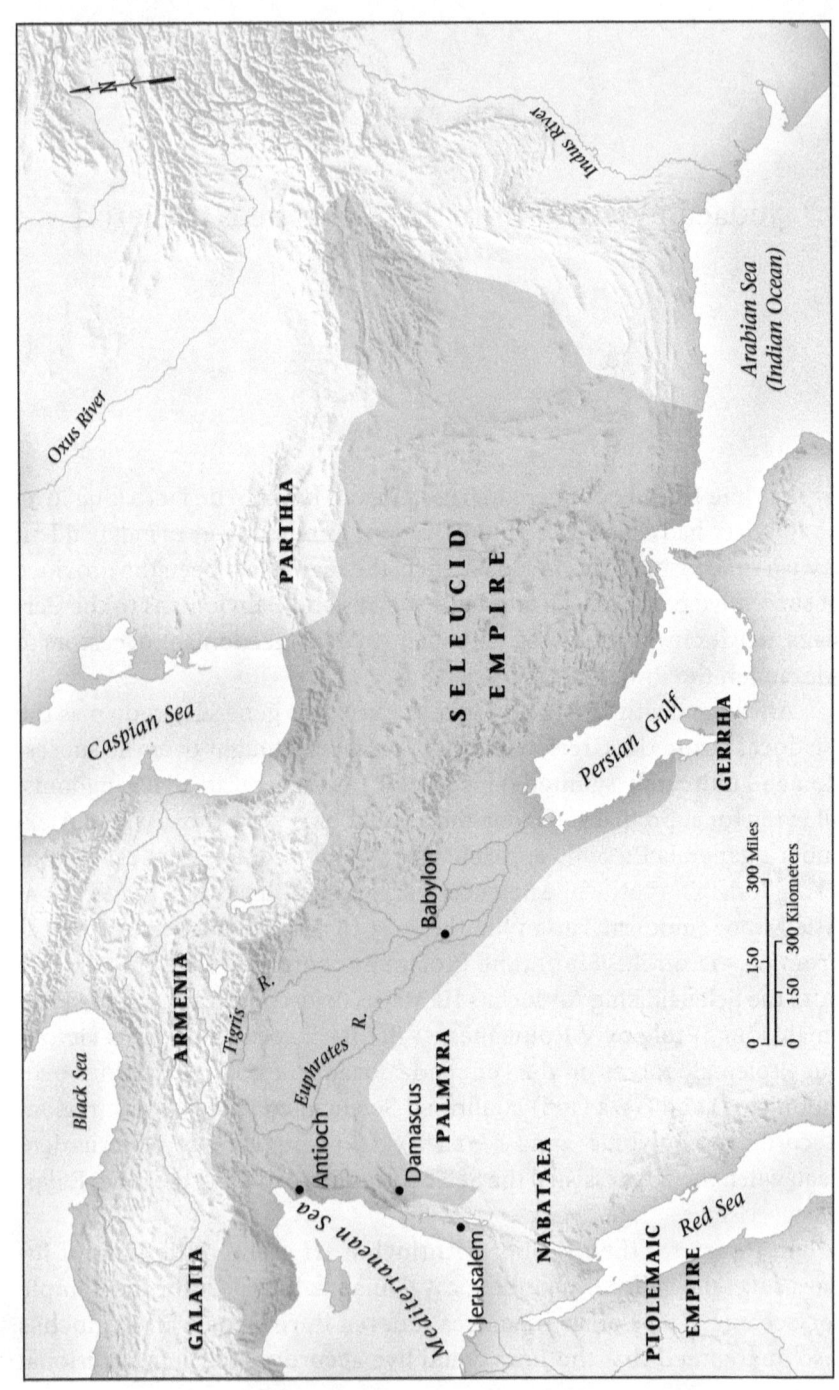

The Near East under the Ptolemies and Seleucids

laws, and he exempted Temple personnel and other Jewish elites from certain taxes.[1]

Seleucid rule must have seemed like a benevolent proposition, but only a decade after Antiochus's triumph over the Ptolemies, he suffered a tremendous defeat at the hands of the Romans. The resulting Peace of Apamea (188 BCE), whose terms included a sizable indemnity, strained Seleucid resources and may have forced the increase of taxation in the provinces and even the plunder of local sources of money, such as the Jerusalem Temple. The need to raise money to pay this indemnity might also have resulted in a greater willingness to accept and solicit money from members of the Jewish priestly elite who desired to become high priest, a position filled by the Seleucid king's appointees. A final consequence of Antiochus's defeat by the Romans was an increase in political instability within the Seleucid royal family. The Peace of Apamea required a royal Seleucid heir to be held as a hostage in Rome. This practice created increased dynastic rivalry and plotting. In such an environment, Seleucid claimants would naturally solicit support from subject territories. The history of the Hasmonean revolt and dynasty is one of Jewish elites attempting to play one Seleucid rival off another.[2]

In 175 BCE, Antiochus IV seized the throne after the death of his elder brother, Seleucus IV. Almost immediately, he became embroiled in local Judaean politics and, in particular, the conflict between two high priestly rivals, Jason and Menelaus. According to 2 Maccabees, Jason became high

---

1. For a complete listing of the privileges that Antiochus granted, see *AJ* 12.138-44. Josephus quotes a second decree (*AJ* 12.145-46) which states that Jerusalem and the Temple were sacred. This decree also upheld purity regulations as defined by ancestral law and mandated fines if anyone violated these regulations. The historicity of this second decree, however, is questionable. For a discussion of this decree, see Chris Seeman and Adam Kolman Marshak, "Jewish History from Alexander to Hadrian," in *Early Judaism: A Comprehensive Overview*, ed. John J. Collins and Daniel Harlow (Grand Rapids: Eerdmans, 2012), 44-45.

2. A decade after the Peace of Apamea, which ended Antiochus's war with Rome, his son and successor Seleucus IV attempted to plunder the Temple in Jerusalem, possibly to raise money to pay the Roman indemnity. For a narration of this incident, see 2 Maccabees 3. For a discussion of the Maccabean revolt and Hasmonean attempts to enhance their power by exploiting Seleucid weakness, see Seeman and Marshak, "Jewish History," 36-48. The term "Maccabee" appears as a title for Judah, son of Mattathias the Hasmonean, in the early days of the Hasmonean revolt (1 Macc 3:1; 2 Macc 8:1). There are several possibilities for the origin of the term. It might have been derived from Aramaic *maqqaba* ("hammer") in honor of Judah's ferocity in battle. It is also possible that it is an acronym for *Mi khamokhah ba'elim YHWH* ("Who is like you, YHWH, among other gods?" Exod 15:11).

priest after promising Antiochus "three hundred sixty talents of silver, and from another source of revenue eighty talents." Jason also sought to establish a gymnasium and an *ephebeion* and to "enroll the Antiochenes in Jerusalem."[3] Once he secured such permission, Jason then openly promoted a Hellenistic lifestyle among Judaea's secular aristocrats and priestly elite. Although the author of 2 Maccabees strongly disapproves of these reforms, it is not entirely clear that Jerusalem's population shared this view. Indeed, three years later, Menelaus supplanted Jason as high priest because he outbid Jason for the office, not because of unrest due to unpopular initiatives. After losing his office, Jason fled into exile in the Transjordan and plotted his revenge.[4]

Meanwhile, Antiochus had decided to invade Egypt. Having defeated the Egyptian army, Antiochus conquered all of Egypt except Alexandria and placed his young nephew Ptolemy VI Philometor on the throne. He then returned home. On his way back, he stopped by Jerusalem and took the opportunity to help himself to the adornments of the Temple. This raid was probably meant to replenish his purse after his expensive incursion into Egypt. The money became useful when his Egyptian settlement soon broke down, and he decided to return to Egypt in 168 BCE to settle the situation. This time, his army was stopped by the direct intervention of the Romans, who warned Antiochus to turn around or face war with them.[5]

While Antiochus was in Egypt in 168 BCE, a rumor spread that he had

---

3. 2 Macc 4:7-9. It is not entirely clear what "Antiochenes in Jerusalem" meant. Bickerman argued that Jason was establishing a Greek corporation in the Jewish city of Jerusalem. See Elias J. Bickerman, *The God of the Maccabees: Studies on the Meaning and Origin of the Maccabean Revolt*, trans Horst R. Moehring (Leiden: Brill, 1979), 38-42. Tcherikover argues instead that Jason was interested in replacing Jerusalem's existing political structures with new Greek structures. See Victor Tcherikover, *Hellenistic Civilization and the Jews* (reprint, Peabody: Hendrickson, 1999), 161-65, 404-9, for the argument that Jason wanted to create a Greek *polis* within the older city of Jerusalem.

4. 2 Macc 4:23-25. When, according to 2 Maccabees, Menelaus could not pay the promised sum of money, he resorted to handing over Temple vessels as gifts for Seleucid officials and neighboring cities. He also orchestrated the murder of the ex-high priest Onias III, who had taken refuge in Daphne, Syria. See 2 Macc 4:27-34.

5. Dan 11:29-30; 1 Macc 1:16-19. Polybius recounts that the Roman ambassador, Gaius Popilius Laenas, confronted Antiochus outside Alexandria and told him to evacuate Egypt and Cyprus or face war with Rome. When Antiochus asked for time to consider the ultimatum, Popilius drew a circle in the sand around the king and told him to decide before he stepped outside it. See Polybius 29.27; cf. Livy 45.11-12; Appian, *Syr.* 66.

been killed. Jason saw this as his opportunity to retake the high priesthood. He promptly invaded Jerusalem with a small force and attempted to assume control of the government and the high priesthood. Menelaus took refuge in the citadel, and Jason could not dislodge him or seize control. In the end, Jason returned to the Transjordan, ultimately spending the rest of his life as an exile in Egypt.

Unfortunately for Jerusalem, Antiochus, who had just been humiliated by the Romans, was in no mood to tolerate civil disturbances in his provinces. He was either unable or unwilling to distinguish the defenders of the city (Menelaus's forces) from those who had attacked it (Jason's army). Instead, Antiochus unleashed his army on the city, a decision that resulted in a bloody slaughter of the local population. Soon after, he sent a sizable force to Jerusalem to permanently garrison the city. Menelaus was allowed to remain in power. In order to protect him and his supporters, Antiochus built the fortress known as the Akra just to the north of the Temple Mount.

At this point in Judaean history, the only sources that still exist are 1 and 2 Maccabees, which are clearly hostile to the Seleucids and favorably disposed to the Hasmoneans. We must, therefore, be somewhat hesitant to accept their versions of events fully, especially the lament in 1 Macc 1:36-40 and the stories of the Jewish martyrs in 2 Macc 6:18–7:42. These accounts strongly contrast the piety and innocence of the local inhabitants, especially the Jewish martyrs, with the cruelty and barbarity of the Seleucid soldiers and officials.

According to both 1 and 2 Maccabees, immediately after placing the garrison in the Akra, Antiochus decided to actively suppress Jewish cultic and religious practices. Both texts describe at length a long list of repressive measures including the profanation of the Temple and its worship, the rededication of the Temple to Olympian Zeus, the construction of altars all over Judaea, and the prescription of cultic practices in honor of Dionysius and the birthday of the king. Seleucid officials also burned Torah scrolls and put faithful Jews to death. According to 2 Maccabees, the coastal town of Ptolemais also enacted such measures.

It is important to note that the accounts told in 1 and 2 Maccabees never offer a credible explanation for Antiochus's unprecedented behavior (in general, Seleucid rulers had been rather tolerant of native cultures and religions). In 2 Maccabees, Antiochus is the biblical tyrant, unknowingly ravaging the Jews as part of God's punishment of his rebellious people. 1 Maccabees asserts that Antiochus enacted his persecution through a royal decree addressed to all his subjects and sought their abandonment of ancestral custom and unification as one people (1 Macc 1:41-42). However, no evidence for such a decree exists outside 1 Maccabees, and there is no hint that the oppression felt in Judaea applied to Jews living elsewhere in the Seleucid kingdom (e.g., in Babylon, where a large number of Jews resided). It would seem, therefore, that the persecution and suppression of Judaism occurred only in Judaea.

Jews reacted to this persecution in a variety of ways, ranging from outright collaboration to passive noncompliance and to, as in the case of the Hasmoneans, open and violent resistance. This resistance began with small-scale guerrilla warfare and progressed to the recapture, purification, and rededication of the Temple a year after the initial revolt. The resistance continued sporadically for decades more as the Hasmoneans transformed from a local group of rebels to the legitimate rulers of Judaea.

Antiochus himself did not live long after the initiation of the persecution. The need to acquire more money and reassert Seleucid control in the East forced Antiochus to lead a campaign against the Parthians in 165 BCE. Before he left, he named his minor son Antiochus V Eupator as co-ruler under the guardianship of the Seleucid general Lysias. Antiochus was initially successful in his campaign, but in 164 BCE he became sick and died. His death precipitated a succession struggle that consumed the Seleucid kingdom for approximately one hundred years. During this turmoil, Judaea was able to break away from Seleucid control and achieve independence under the leadership of the Hasmonean dynasty.[6]

From Rebels to Rulers: The Rise of the Hasmoneans

The Hasmonean dynasty first appeared as an aristocratic family led by the patriarch Mattathias, a priest living in Modein in the Judaean lowlands. Mattathias and his sons refused to capitulate to Seleucid suppression of the Jewish cult and fled into the wilderness in order to raise an armed resistance. Some scholars have seen these actions as an attempt to gain

---

6. For the campaign against the Parthians and the death of Antiochus IV, see Appian, *Syr.* 66; 1 Macc 3:27-37; 6:1-17; 2 Macc 9:1-29; *BJ* 1.40; *AJ* 12.293-97, 354-61. The Cuneiform Babylonian king list of the Hellenistic period (*King List* 6) establishes 164 (Year 148 of the Seleucid calendar) as the year Antiochus IV died. See A. Sachs and J. Wiseman, "A Babylonian King List of the Hellenistic Period," *Iraq* 16 (1954): 202-12.

Judaean History from the Maccabees to Herod

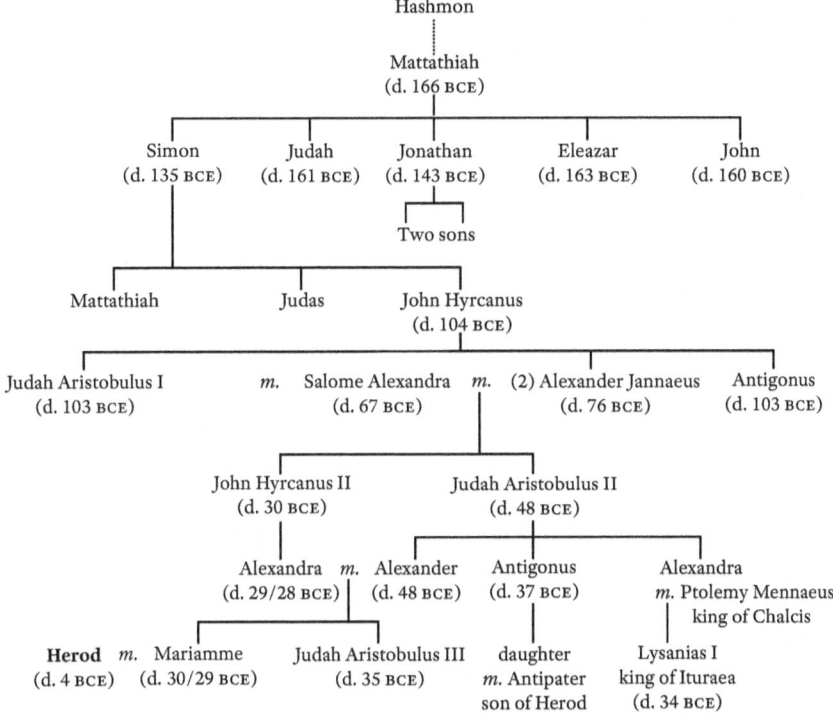

Family Tree of the Hasmonean Dynasty

power and influence within their region and throughout Judaea as well as a way to resist Seleucid persecution.[7]

---

7. Seth Schwartz, "A Note on the Social Type and Political Ideology of the Hasmonean Family," *JBL* 112 (1993): 305-17; Brent Nongbri, "The Motivations of the Maccabees and the Judean Rhetoric of Ancestral Traditions," in *Ancient Judaism in Its Hellenistic Context*, ed. Carol Bakhos (Leiden: Brill, 2005), 99-105. Nongbri essentially agrees with Schwartz's analysis, though he believes that the Hasmoneans were more likely "Jerusalem insiders" as opposed to Schwartz's view of them as village strongmen. Cf. Schwartz, *Imperialism and Jewish Society: 200 B.C.E. to 640 C.E.* (Princeton: Princeton University Press, 2001), 32-36, esp. 33-34. For an analysis of the Hasmonean revolt and its aftermath from a Seleucid perspective, see Thomas Fischer, "Hasmoneans and Seleucids: Aspects of War and Policy in the Second and First Centuries B.C.E.," in *Greece and Rome in Eretz-Israel*, ed. Aryeh Kasher, Uriel Rappaport, and Gideon Fuks (Jerusalem: Jerusalem Exploration Society, 1990), 6-10.

CULTURAL AND INTELLECTUAL MILIEU

Whatever their motivations, the Hasmoneans and their allies, the *Hasidim* (righteous ones), began a low-grade insurgency from the Judaean wilderness. Following the death of Mattathias in ca. 166 BCE, leadership passed to his son Judah Maccabee. Over the next two years, Judah successfully fought local Seleucid commanders. In 164 BCE, the Seleucid regent Lysias undertook a full-scale military expedition to quash the Hasmonean revolt. He besieged Judah and his men at Beth-Zur but failed to take the town. Instead, Lysias withdrew to Antioch, leaving Judah free to enter Jerusalem and recapture the Temple. Judah fortified Jerusalem and Beth-Zur and garrisoned both the Temple and Jerusalem. He also ordered the cleansing and rededication of the Temple and appointed priests to carry out this task. Such decisions, along with the move to commemorate the event as an annual festival, a decision supposedly approved by "Judah and his brothers and all the assembly of Israel" (1 Macc 4:59), testifies to a significant level of local recognition and support for Judah's insurgency by the end of 164 BCE.[8]

The news of Antiochus IV's death in Persia forced Lysias to spend most of the next year consolidating his status as royal regent. Judah and his rebels used this lull to launch a series of expeditions against neighboring Gentile communities under the guise of protecting the Jewish minorities living in or near these communities. Besides increasing their financial resources through plunder, these expeditions resulted in the relocation of some Jewish populations and thus the increase in size of Judah's army. In 163 BCE, Antiochus V executed the high priest Menelaus because of his failure to control Judaea. His death left a vacancy in the high priesthood which was not filled for another two years. This removal of a Jewish faction opposed to the Hasmoneans may also have aided Judah's attempts to increase his support in Judaea. By 162 BCE, Judah felt strong enough to launch an attack on the Akra, the Seleucid fortress in Jerusalem. This attack, however, failed and shows that Judah was not as powerful as he had believed. It also provoked Lysias into sending a new army to deal with the Hasmonean insurgency. This army was extremely successful and might have eliminated the Hasmonean rebels had Lysias not been distracted by the arrival in Antioch of a rival general, which forced him to make peace with Judah and return to Syria.[9]

---

8. 1 Macc 2:1–4:60; 2 Macc 8:1-29; 10:1-9; 11:1-34. Here 2 Maccabees disagrees with 1 Maccabees about chronology. According to 1 Maccabees, Lysias's first campaign occurred before the death of Antiochus IV, while 2 Maccabees places it after his death.

9. 1 Macc 5:1-6:63; 2 Macc 10:14-38; 12:2–13:26. 2 Maccabees claims that King Antiochus V formally received Judah in conjunction with the truce (2 Macc 13:24), but it also

Judaean History from the Maccabees to Herod

In 161 BCE, the Hasmoneans experienced additional setbacks. A new rival claimant to the Seleucid throne, Demetrius I (son of the former king Seleucus IV), arrived in the Levant, seized power and executed both Lysias and his rival Antiochus V. This coup had significant reverberations in Judaea. A local Jewish faction that was hostile to the Hasmoneans sent a delegation to the new Seleucid king and secured the appointment of a certain Alcimus to the high priesthood. Alcimus, with the military support of the Seleucid kingdom, then attempted to subjugate and suppress Judah and his men through a series of military engagements, which ultimately culminated in Judah's death at the Battle of Elasa (Spring 161 BCE).

During these internal Jewish struggles, Judah began a relationship that would have far-reaching consequences for Judaea. Immediately following his victory over Demetrius's general Nicanor at the Battle of Adasa, Judah sent an embassy to Rome seeking friendship and an alliance. The Roman Senate agreed and confirmed a treaty of mutual assistance. It also sent a letter of condemnation to Demetrius for his treatment of the Hasmoneans. Such a treaty would have been useful to Judah even though the Romans never sent any military aid, and Judah probably did not expect such aid. The propaganda coup that Judah achieved through Roman recognition would have helped him gain local support in opposition to Alcimus and position himself in the role of protector of and representative of the Jewish people. Although Judah's embassy did not change the situation in Judaea in any real way, it did initiate a relationship with Rome that his successors would use frequently in their quest for autonomy and legitimacy.[10]

With the loss of Judah at Elasa, the Hasmoneans and their followers were forced to withdraw and regroup under the leadership of their new leader, Judah's brother Jonathan. Jonathan spent the first years of his leadership in the wilderness near Tekoa, a town southeast of Jerusalem. Meanwhile, Alcimus died (ostensibly of natural causes), but Demetrius made no attempt to fill the high priestly office. No candidates presented themselves as his replacement, which suggests that the internal divisions among the Jews had resulted in a political stalemate. In 159/158 BCE, Jonathan's Jewish enemies broke this stalemate by calling in a Seleucid army led by the general Bacchides in order to wipe out Jonathan and his supporters.

---

claims that Judah was not defeated in battle, and thus the reliability of this section of the text is suspect.

10. 1 Macc 8:23-31. Judah had already lost a significant part of his support when the *Hasidim* ended their rebellion following the election of Alcimus to the high priesthood. Unfortunately for them, Alcimus betrayed and executed sixty of their leaders. See 1 Macc 8:12-16.

However, the campaign did not go according to plan, and Bacchides made peace with Jonathan and returned to Syria. Jonathan then moved to Michmash, a town north of Jerusalem and settled there. Although his tenure as Hasmonean leader did not begin so promisingly, Jonathan would revive the Hasmonean cause and, more importantly, achieve greater recognition, power, and status than Judah had achieved. He would successfully play one Seleucid dynast off of another.

His chance came in 153 BCE, when a new pretender to the Seleucid throne, Alexander Balas, landed in Ptolemais and challenged Demetrius for control of the kingdom. Judaea was ideally situated as a strong asset to either contender. Recognizing this opportunity, Jonathan elicited offers from both sides but ultimately sided with Balas, who appointed him high priest and *philos* (friend) of the king. When Balas defeated Demetrius in 150 BCE, Jonathan's position became even stronger, and he became the dominant figure in Judaean politics. Throughout the next decade, this scenario, in which rivals for the Seleucid throne solicited support from Jonathan, replayed itself several times. For Jonathan, each new rival presented an opportunity for new honors and positions. Local Jewish opponents occasionally caused problems, but he was able to deal with them without significant difficulty.

However, Jonathan soon became a victim of his own game. In 143 BCE, he was captured and executed by Diodotus Tryphon, who was the regent to the boy-king Antiochus VI, the son of Alexander Balas. Tryphon had decided to murder his ward and claim the throne himself, and he viewed Jonathan as a threat to this ambition. Leadership of the Hasmonean family fell to Simon, who quickly obtained the high priesthood from Tryphon's rival Demetrius II. Demetrius II was the son of Demetrius I, one of the Seleucid kings against whom Simon and his brother Judah had fought. Thus, in less than twenty years, the Hasmonean family had achieved official recognition from the Seleucid house, against which they had first waged war.[11]

Following the pattern set by previous Seleucids, Demetrius had offered Simon additional honors and privileges in order to gain his support. These included initiating a general peace between Demetrius and

---

11. 1 Macc 12:39–13:41. Cf. *AJ* 13.187-213. In *AJ*, Josephus claims that the Jews appointed Simon high priest, whereas 1 Maccabees makes it clear that Demetrius II appointed him. Given that the previous high priests, such as Jason, Menelaus, and Jonathan, had all been appointed by a Seleucid king, 1 Maccabees' version is more credible.

Simon, canceling all tribute and any taxes collected in Judaea such as the crown tax, recognizing Simon's possession of any fortresses constructed in Judaea, and enrolling Jewish soldiers in the royal bodyguard. 1 Maccabees is so pleased with these concessions that it boldly proclaims 142 BCE as the year that Simon removed "the yoke of the Gentiles" from Judaea (1 Macc 13:41). As an additional honor to Simon, the people began dating their contracts and official documents according to a calendar marking 142 as "the first year of Simon the great high priest and commander and leader of the Jews" (v. 42). Nevertheless, Demetrius did not cede control over the hated Akra, but Simon dealt with this irritation quickly and by June 141 BCE had starved the fortresses' inhabitants into surrender and expulsion. Thus, by 141, Simon had removed all traces of Antiochus IV's persecution.

Simon ruled as high priest and military leader for the next six years. During that time, he renewed treaties of friendship with Rome and Sparta and strengthened his hold over Judaea. In 140 BCE, a great assembly of the Jewish people passed a resolution declaring that, because Simon had "fought off the enemies of Israel and established its freedom,"

> Simon should be their leader and high priest indefinitely until a trustworthy prophet should arise, and that he should be their general, and that he should be given custodianship of the sanctuary and that he should appoint men over its functions and over the countryside and over the weapons and over the fortresses, and that he should be obeyed by all, and that all contracts in the country should be written in his name, and that he should wear purple and gold. And it shall be forbidden for anyone of the people or of the priests to abrogate any of these things or to oppose things said by him or to convene an assembly in the country without him or to wear purple or to put on a golden buckle, and whoever acts contrary to these things or abrogates any of them shall be liable for punishment.[12]

1 Maccabees, which is a pro-Hasmonean court document, claims that this decree was a spontaneous expression of popular support for Simon and that his rule and leadership was beloved by all. However, the authoritarian nature of the document itself, especially the limitations on criticism and disobedience of the regime, as well as the extradition clause in the Roman-

---

12. 1 Macc 14:16-49, esp. vv. 25-49.

Hasmonean treaty (1 Macc 15:21), suggests the existence of internal dissent and opposition to the Hasmonean regime. With this decree, however, Simon and the Hasmoneans have clearly transitioned from rebel leaders to de facto monarchs.

Simon was not able to enjoy his new power for very long. In 135 BCE his son-in-law Ptolemy son of Abubus, who was the *stratēgos* of Jericho, conspired with Antiochus VII Sidetes to murder Simon and his sons. Ptolemy invited Simon and two of his sons to a banquet in the fortress of Docus, and he killed them while they were drunk. Because he had not been present at the banquet, the eldest son, John Hyrcanus, survived and ultimately assumed his father's position as high priest and military leader.

The Hasmonean Dynasty

Seleucid recognition of Hasmonean control of Judaea did not preclude Seleucid interference in Judaean affairs. Nevertheless, by the reign of John Hyrcanus (135-104 BCE), the objective of such interference had changed from elimination and suppression of insurgency to reduction and limitation of Hasmonean power in Judaea and the surrounding regions. At the same time, the continued dynastic instability of the Seleucid kingdom as well as the increasing belligerence of the Parthians to the east distracted successive Seleucid kings and weakened their influence over the fledgling Jewish state. John Hyrcanus and his sons made the most of this distraction and effectively used it to expand their kingdom.

The death of Antiochus VII Sidetes in 128 BCE marks the end of effective Seleucid control of Judaea. For the next sixty-five years, the Hasmoneans would rule independently, first as high priests and then as high priests and kings. During his reign, which lasted from 134 to 104 BCE, John Hyrcanus I initiated a period of significant military and political expansion into the surrounding areas. He first moved east, capturing the city of Medeba and annexing the Transjordan to his kingdom. To the south, he conquered the region of Idumaea, including the cities of Adora and Marisa. He also conquered the region of Samaria, destroying the Samaritan temple on Mount Gerizim (ca. 112-111 BCE) and the cities of Shechem (112/111 BCE) and Samaria (112-107 BCE). He also substantially changed the makeup of the Hasmonean army. Unlike previous leaders, who had relied on a local levy to supply troops, he hired foreign mercenaries to fight alongside the

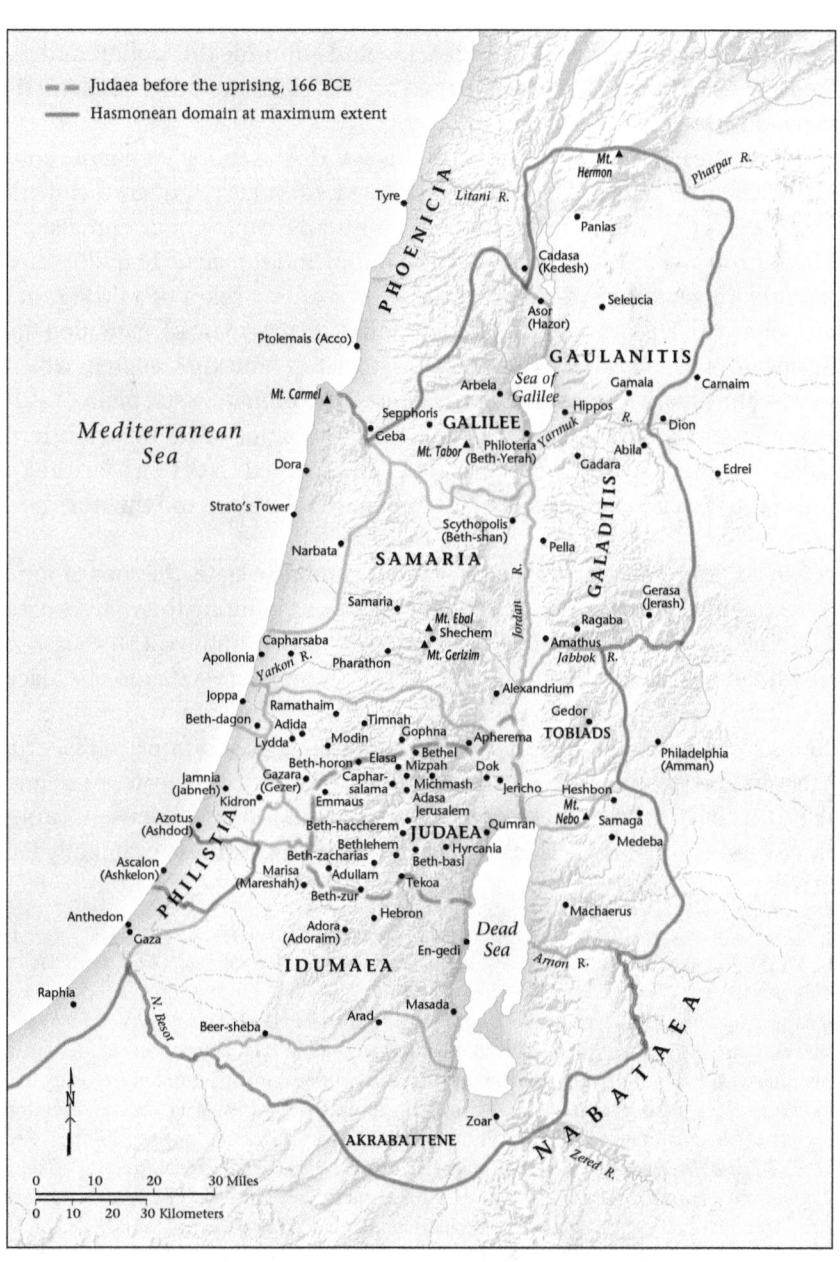

Hasmonean Judaea (ca. 166–40 BCE)

local Jewish soldiers. His descendants would continue this policy, and ultimately the Hasmonean army began to look like any other Hellenistic army in the region.[13]

Hyrcanus's sons, Judah Aristobulus I and Alexander Jannaeus, continued their father's policy of expansion. Aristobulus conquered and annexed a large portion of Ituraea and instituted a policy of circumcision, which probably resembled his father's policy in Idumaea. He might have extended his conquests further, but he died after a reign of a little more than one year. His brother, Alexander Jannaeus (103-76 BCE), extended the Hasmonean kingdom to its greatest territorial size during a reign in which he was almost always at war. He conquered the entire coastal plain of Palestine except for Ashkelon. This included the cities of Raphia (modern Rafah), Anthedon, Strato's Tower (later to be called Caesarea Maritima), and Gaza. He also conquered western Samaria, Galilee, and the northern Transjordan.

In addition to their expansion of the Hasmonean state, the sons of John Hyrcanus also radically changed their status by appointing themselves king while still retaining the office of high priest. Aristobulus was the first to crown himself, and with his coronation the Hasmonean state took its place as a recognizable Hellenistic monarchy. Like all Hellenistic monarchies, the Hasmoneans soon developed dynastic struggles and internal discord. Aristobulus I executed or imprisoned all his brothers, and between 67 and 63 BCE a civil war raged between the sons of Alexander Jannaeus, Aristobulus II and Hyrcanus II. This conflict between the brothers ultimately led

---

13. For Josephus's narrative of the wars of John Hyrcanus I, see *BJ* 1.62-66; *AJ* 13.254-55, 275-81. According to Josephus, Hyrcanus also forced the Idumaeans to circumcise or emigrate (*AJ* 13.257-58; cf. *BJ* 1.63). However, this conversion of the Idumaeans may have been less forced and more complicated than Josephus suggests. Scholars such as Aryeh Kasher, Peter Richardson, and Shaye Cohen have argued in their discussions of Idumaean relations with Judaea that, prior to the conquest of Idumaea, many Idumaeans already had adopted several aspects of Jewish religion and culture voluntarily. If so, their conversion might have been about realigning political loyalties more than religious sensibilities. See Aryeh Kasher, *Jews, Idumaeans and Ancient Arabs: Relations of the Jews in Eretz-Israel with Nations of the Frontier and the Desert during the Hellenistic and Roman Era (332 BCE–70 CE)* (Tübingen: Mohr, 1988), 44-77; Peter Richardson, *Herod: King of the Jews and Friend of the Romans* (Columbia: University of South Carolina Press, 1996), 54-62; Shaye J. D. Cohen, *The Beginnings of Jewishness* (Berkeley: University of California Press, 1999), 110-18. For the dating of the conquest and destruction of Samaria see Dan Barag, "King Herod's Royal Castle at Samaria-Sebaste," *PEQ* 125 (1993): 3; cf. Barag, "New Evidence on the Foreign Policy of John Hyrcanus I," *INJ* 12 (1992-93): 1-12.

to the direct intervention of Rome, the end of the independent Hasmonean state, and the rise of Herod the Great.[14]

We have seen that Jewish opposition to the Hasmoneans existed from the very beginning. We can imagine that a significant faction surrounded first the high priest Menelaus and then Alcimus. Both of these men rejected the Hasmoneans' claim to supremacy and actively opposed their goals. Even after the Hasmoneans achieved the high priesthood, resistance to them persisted, most notably the Pharisaic opposition to the Hasmoneans during the reign of John Hyrcanus I. With the Hasmoneans' revival of the Jewish monarchy and subsequent appropriation of both titles, opposition increased even further, reaching its pinnacle under Alexander Jannaeus. Besides overt demonstrations against Jannaeus's rule, a significant faction within the Jewish populace appealed to King Demetrius III Eucaerus, asking him to overthrow Jannaeus and presumably restore Seleucid control of Judaea. This attempted coup failed, and Jannaeus suppressed the opposition with cruelty and brutality. He not only crucified 800 rebels, but he also cut the throats of their wives and children as they watched. To make matters worse, all this was done while he and his concubines ate and observed the proceedings. It is no surprise, therefore, that the Qumran Pesher on Nahum refers to him as "the Lion of Wrath."

The death of Alexander Jannaeus and the ascension of his wife Salome Alexandra (76-67 BCE) seems to have improved the situation. According to Josephus, Salome succeeded primarily because she cultivated a close relationship with the Pharisees and involved them in her government. However, even her mild and peaceful rule could not fully reconcile all the opposition. When her sons appealed to Pompey to arbitrate their dispute (63 BCE), a delegation of more than 200 prominent men of Judaea also visited the Roman general and requested the removal of the Hasmonean monarchy and the restoration of a government ruled solely by a high priest. Though the Hasmoneans created an independent Jewish monarchy for the first time in five hundred years and extended that kingdom farther perhaps than any previous kingdom of Judah, a significant portion of the Jewish population never accepted them as monarchs and may never have accepted them at all.[15]

14. For Aristobulus I's treatment of his brothers, see *BJ* 1.71-84; *AJ* 13.301-18. Aristobulus also imprisoned and killed his own mother in order to deny her control over the kingdom as his father Hyrcanus I had wished. See *BJ* 1.71; *AJ* 13.302. For the civil war between Aristobulus II and Hyrcanus II, see *BJ* 1.120-58; *AJ* 14.4-79.

15. For opposition to the Hasmoneans during the reign of John Hyrcanus I, see *BJ*

With such opposition, it was essential for the Hasmoneans to present themselves as positively as possible. Moreover, they had to be extremely clever in utilizing those images and messages that would resonate the most with the greatest number of people. Because of the influence that this self-presentation would have on Judaea, but especially on a young courtier such as Herod, it is essential that we understand how it functioned. Therefore, it is to this self-presentation that we now turn.

Hasmonean Political Ideology

By far the most important royal Jewish models for Herod were his immediate predecessors, the Hasmoneans. In order to understand fully Herod's actions as a Jewish king, it is necessary to examine a few key aspects of Hasmonean kingship, specifically its expression of Jewish tradition and the high priesthood as well as its adoption of Hellenism and Hellenistic kingship. An understanding of how these two aspects functioned within the Hasmonean court will enable us to comprehend how Herod could simultaneously be both a Hellenistic and Jewish king and how he adapted and appropriated past Jewish tradition in fashioning his own royal persona.

Hasmonean Use of Jewish Tradition and the High Priesthood

Although both 1 and 2 Maccabees argue that the Hasmoneans began their public life as pious rebels responding solely to the anti-Jewish policies of

---

1.67; *AJ* 13.288-99. For opposition to Alexander Jannaeus, see esp. *BJ* 1.90-98; *AJ* 13.372-83. For the Qumranites using the term "Lion of Wrath" see 4Q169 3-4 i:6-9. Despite the arguments of some scholars, most notably Gregory Doudna, the scholarly consensus is that the term was indeed used for Jannaeus. See Gregory L. Doudna, *4Q Pesher Nahum: A Critical Edition* (London: Sheffield Academic, 2001). For a discussion of the scholarly consensus, see Shani L. Berrin, *The Pesher Nahum Scroll from Qumran: An Exegetical Study of 4Q169* (Leiden: Brill, 2004), 87-164, 220-34, 301-5. Cf. Hanan Eshel, *The Dead Sea Scrolls and the Hasmonean State* (Grand Rapids: Eerdmans, 2008), 117-31. Later rabbis, especially in the Babylonian Talmud, depict Jannaeus as the model of the wicked tyrant. For some examples of this portrayal, see *b. Berakhot* 48a; *b. Sanhedrin* 107b. For a discussion and analysis of the legitimacy problems facing the Hasmonean dynasty see Monika Bernett, *Der Kaiserkult in Judäa unter den Herodiern und Römern. Untersuchungen zur politischen und religiösen Geschichte Judäas von 30 v. bis 66 n. Chr.* (Tübingen: Mohr, 2007), 32-40.

Antiochus IV Epiphanes, we have seen that the situation was much more complex. While resistance to religious suppression may well have been one of the goals of the Hasmonean revolt, another important goal was the advancement and enhancement of their own power. From the beginning, the Hasmoneans faced significant internal opposition, which they were never able to suppress entirely.

Hasmonean Defense of Tradition

In order to increase their power and support while dealing with local opposition, the Hasmoneans skillfully clothed their political ambitions under the guise of defending and protecting the Judaean *patrios politeia* (ancestral constitution). Through this lens, the brave and pious Hasmoneans "rescued the Law out of the hands of the Gentiles and kings, and they never let the sinner gain the upper hand" (1 Macc 2:48). On his deathbed, Mattathias commands his sons to "show zeal for the Law and give your lives for the covenant of our ancestors" (v. 50). Such a claim was an attempt to garner support for their military activities and later to legitimate their preeminence in Judaean political society.[16] As a comparison, after the Peloponnesian War various Athenian factions made similar claims in pursuit of similar objectives. The Athenian example is useful because both rival

---

16. Also see 1 Macc 3:1-9, 21, 43; 4:36-59. Presenting themselves as defenders of *patrios politeia* provided them with a justification to murder many of their own countrymen who opposed them and whom they accused of being "lawless men who hate their own nation" (11:21). See Nongbri, "Motivations of the Maccabees," 105-10. For Rajak's examination of the Hasmoneans' use of invented tradition see Tessa Rajak, "Hasmonean Kingship and the Invention of Tradition," in *Aspects of Hellenistic Kingship*, ed. Per Bilde, et al. (Oakville: Aarhus University Press, 1996), 99-115. Cf. Seth Schwartz, "Israel and the Nations Roundabout: 1 Maccabees and the Hasmonean Expansion," *JJS* 42 (1991): 16-38; Bernett, *Kaiserkult*, 33, 35-36, 50, where she argues that the Hasmoneans depicted themselves as champions and defenders of Torah. As we have seen, the Hasmoneans certainly had rivals for control of Judaea. For example, the high priest Alcimus was their most formidable local opponent. Not only did he have official support from the Seleucid government (1 Macc 7:5-9; *AJ* 12.385), but he also used this support to persuade the *Hasidim* (and perhaps other groups) to abandon the Hasmoneans (1 Macc 7:13-14). Further, 1 Maccabees makes periodic mention of rivalries and factions within the Hasmonean alliance. Even though the author strongly criticizes such groups (5:55-62), their existence suggests that the Hasmoneans' hegemony was not as secure as the author would like us to believe. Cf. *AJ* 12.350-52, although Josephus minimizes the providential nature of the Hasmonean family and instead emphasizes Judah's martial acumen.

claims to *patrios politeia* have been preserved. A close reading of the two factions' arguments reveals the term's ambiguity and usefulness to those trying to grab power. In both the Hasmonean and the Athenian cases, ancestral traditions were used as a means to acquire power and legitimate authority while hiding true innovation. The Hasmoneans' appeal to *patrios politeia* cloaked their political ambition and enabled them to cast their own position as ancestral law and their opponents as wicked innovators. We do not have the literature of the Hasmoneans' opponents, but it is possible that they too portrayed themselves as preserving the ancestral traditions in contrast to the Hasmoneans. This trope, therefore, was a propaganda tool designed to assure the Hasmoneans of popular support and deny it to their rivals. As we will see below, Herod too evokes tradition and connection with the Jewish past in order to legitimate his regime.[17]

Hasmonean Use of Paleo-Hebrew

Besides invoking defense of the *ancestral customs* the Hasmoneans further connected themselves with tradition by subtly referencing the united monarchy of David and Solomon through their use of paleo-Hebrew script on their coins. All the Hasmoneans utilized this script on their coinage, even though it had not been commonly used since the end of the Davidic monarchy and the majority of Judaeans could not read it. Instead, the Aramaic

[17]. It is apparent that this invocation of the defense of traditionalism was a rhetorical strategy given the revolutionary ideas and reforms initiated by the Hasmoneans once they seized power. First and most importantly, while the Hasmoneans may have been Aaronides, even high-ranking Aaronides, they were certainly not Zadokites. For the priestly background of the Hasmoneans (priests of the course of Joarib) see 1 Macc 2:1; *AJ* 12.265. Cf. *AJ* 7.365-66; *Vita* 2. Instead, they were the first non-Zadokites to claim the high priesthood. Further, although the earlier Hasmoneans were content with only the high priesthood, after Aristobulus I, each Hasmonean ruler was both king and high priest. Such an innovation was extremely revolutionary and not universally popular. Both Josephus and the rabbis preserved a story in which critics of the regime protested the dual office of the Hasmoneans. While Josephus attributes the episode to the time of John Hyrcanus, the king in the rabbi's story is Alexander Jannaeus. Nevertheless, the accounts are similar enough to argue that they represent the same events, with one of the versions confused about the identity of the king. Regardless of which it was, the importance of the story is the internal dissent and criticism of the combination of the two offices, which were never before held simultaneously. For the rejection of Hasmonean possession of both the high priesthood and the monarchy, see *AJ* 12.288-96; *b. Qiddushin* 66a. Cf. Joshua Efron, *Studies on the Hasmonean Period* (Leiden: Brill, 1987), 143-218.

script, also known as square script or Syrian script, was the most common script during the first century BCE. It was used for writing both Hebrew and Aramaic, which was the lingua franca of Judaea. It is certainly true that some scrolls written in paleo-Hebrew had survived the destruction of the first Temple, and some of the priests and scribes knew how to read it. Furthermore, in some of the first-century scrolls written in Aramaic script scribes wrote the Tetragrammaton (the four letters that spell the name of God) in paleo-Hebrew letters, which suggests that they had preserved the script and used it for special purposes.

It is initially surprising that the Hasmoneans would have used a script not commonly used since the united monarchy, especially considering that the Hasmoneans did not seem interested in connecting themselves with the Davidic monarchy in other forms of public presentation. Moreover, if anything, they would have wished to avoid any associations with the Davidides, given that they had usurped David's throne illegitimately and had received their position from a foreign Seleucid king and not by the divine promise.

Brent Nongbri's discussion of *patrios politeia* may provide an answer. As stated above, he suggests the Hasmoneans were legitimizing themselves by claiming to fight for ancestral traditions and customs. What better way to advertise such a campaign than by minting coinage that used the archaic script of ancient Israel? While most Judaeans, including the elite, might not have been able to read paleo-Hebrew with any great ease, they might have been able to read the simple legends on the coins. More importantly, even if they were not able to read the coin legends, they might have recognized the script as archaic and one that harkened back to the glory years of the Davidic past. Thus, the Hasmoneans were able, on their coinage as well as in their propaganda, to claim ownership of the past and defense of its reinterpreted reality.[18]

---

18. As an interesting comparison, the coinage of the Bar Kochba revolts also used paleo-Hebrew for their coin legends. In both cases, coins that evoked the majesty and legitimacy of the ancient Jewish past and the Davidic dynasty would have been extremely appropriate and even inspiring for revolts that sought the liberation of Judaea from foreign rule. For discussion of the Bar Kochba coinage, see Meshorer, *TJC*, 115-65, 132, 163, 240-56 (plates 61-72); David Hendin, *Guide to Biblical Coins* (4th ed.; New York: Amphora, 2001), 262-71, 283-302 (plates 20-26). For a brief overview of Hasmonean ideology see Samuel Rocca, *Herod's Judaea: A Mediterranean State in the Classical World* (Tübingen: Mohr, 2008), 29-34. Like me, Rocca believes that the Hasmoneans drew on the traditions of both the Jewish high priesthood and Hellenistic monarchy.

Hasmonean Use of the High Priesthood

The Hasmoneans' use of the high priesthood was also a central facet of their legitimization campaign and an important precursor for Herod. Like them, he used the office to further his own power and ambition. The office was ideal for such use because of its authority and status in Judaean society. Beginning at the end of the Persian period and throughout the Second Temple period, the most powerful figure in the Judaean state was the high priest, who functioned for all intents and purposes as a priestly monarch.[19] Evidence of this situation appears, for example, in the Tobiad story in *Jewish Antiquities*. Joseph ben Tobiah and his son Hyrcanus may have been powerful and influential tax farmers, but the high priest was clearly the most senior official in Judaea. Indeed, Joseph needed permission from the high priest Onias to negotiate with King Ptolemy.[20] Furthermore, from the period after the death of the high priest Simeon, son of Onias, and Jonathan Maccabee's assumption of the high priesthood in 152 BCE, the high priest seems to have been the highest-ranking official in Judaea. Before the Hasmonean revolt Onias III, Jason, Menelaus, and Alcimus all ruled Judaea through the priestly office. Only the Seleucid officials outranked them. Thus, when the Hasmoneans replaced the descendants of Zadok as high priests, they did not change the Judaean constitution, merely the officeholders.

After ruling as high priests for more than fifty years, the Hasmoneans decided to claim the kingship as well while retaining the high priesthood.[21]

---

19. As David Goodblatt shows, primary sources ranging from Pompeius Tragus to the Aramaic *Testament of Levi* attest to the primacy of priestly monarchy as the ruling political theory of Judaea. Non-Jewish authors consistently described the Judaeans as being ruled by priests, which suggests that the high priesthood was the preeminent position. That is not to say that other powerful and influential offices did not exist. There likely were groups who favored the restoration of a monarchy or who wished to be ruled by a diarchy of high priest and king or who wished some other form of rule. However, the evidence in material written by both Jews and non-Jews indicates that those supporting the rule of the priests, and especially the high priest, were more influential. See David Goodblatt, *The Monarchic Principle: Studies in Jewish Self-Government in Antiquity* (Tübingen: Mohr, 1994), 1-130. For non-Jewish authors referring to the Judaeans as ruled by priests see Strabo, *Geog.* 16.2.46; Tacitus, *Hist.* 5.8.3; Justinus, *Epit.* 36.2.16; Dio 37.15.2.

20. *AJ* 12.160-236. Cf. Goodblatt, *Monarchic Principle,* 13-15. It is not entirely clear to which Ptolemy the story refers, although some scholars have suggested Ptolemy V, who married Cleopatra I in 193 BCE.

21. The importance of the high priesthood and the status associated with it likely ex-

Both Hyrcanus I and Alexander Jannaeus contemplated the notion of separating the high priesthood from the monarchy since both nominated their wives to succeed them as monarch.[22] This might suggest that the later Hasmoneans based their rule on the kingship, not on the high priesthood. However, Josephus's description of Mattathias Antigonus's exchange with the Roman commander Pompaedius Silo suggests that he and others regarded the high priesthood as a prerequisite for kingship. In the exchange, Antigonus argues that it was contrary to Roman notions of justice to give the kingship to Herod. If he himself (Antigonus) was unacceptable to Rome, there were other Hasmoneans of priestly rank more worthy than Herod.[23] It would seem then that the Hasmoneans never completely abandoned their reliance on the high priesthood, even as they also adopted other ruling models, such as Hellenistic kingship.

Why was the high priesthood so important? The centrality of this office to Judaea and its people is clear. High priests had ruled Judaea for hundreds of years, whereas a Jewish king had not existed since the sixth century BCE. Thus, it is not surprising that the Hasmoneans would want to monopolize the office and retain it even after they had claimed the title of king. The status that came with the high priesthood undoubtedly served to legitimize the Hasmoneans in the eyes of the people. Furthermore, with the status accorded to the high priesthood, the Hasmoneans

---

plains why Alexandra was so insistent that her son Aristobulus III become high priest (*AJ* 15.23-24, 36), seeing this as a way for the Hasmonean family to revive its fortunes and eventually eclipse Herod. Unsurprisingly, Herod eliminated Aristobulus as soon as he became a threat (*BJ* 1.437; *AJ* 15.49-56). For Aristobulus I claiming the title of king, see *BJ* 1.70; *AJ* 13.301. All of the Hasmoneans who minted coins refer to themselves on all or at least some of their coins as high priest. See Meshorer, *TJC*, 23-57, 201-20 (plates 5-43); Hendin, *Biblical Coins*, 130-33, 136, 140-43, 146-47, 154-55 (plates 8-9). For Hasmonean bullae advertising Alexander Jannaeus as both king and high priest, see *TJC*, 57-58. Cf. Nahman Avigad, "A Bulla of Jonathan the High Priest," *IEJ* 25 (1975): 8-12; "A Bulla of King Jonathan," *IEJ* 25 (1975): 245-46.

22. *BJ* 1.71, 107; *AJ* 13.302, 407. For Salome Alexandra's appointment of her son John Hyrcanus as high priest, see *BJ* 1.109; *AJ* 13.408.

23. We do not know whether Antigonus ever sent this exact message to Silo. Even if he did, we cannot know how sincere he was since he was desperate to save his dynasty. See *AJ* 14.403-4. This view of the high priesthood as a prerequisite to kingship is also implied by Josephus in *AJ* 14.77-78, where he blames Aristobulus II and Hyrcanus II for the dissension that led to Pompey's conquest in 63 BCE. In this section, Josephus bemoans the transfer of royal power from those of high priestly backgrounds to commoners. Such an attitude testifies to the survival of the theory of priestly monarchy down to Josephus's time. Cf. Goodblatt, *Monarchic Principle*, 23-25.

could increase their influence among Jews living outside Judaea, either in the neighboring regions of Palestine or in the Diaspora.[24] On a more local level, by occupying the high priesthood the Hasmoneans were able to control the vast system of Temple tithes. Through such management, they could control the priests as well as the Levites who relied on the Temple tithes for support.[25]

Hasmonean Adoption of Hellenism and Hellenistic Kingship

Every year in synagogue, young Jewish children learn of the story of the valiant Maccabees resisting the evil Greeks who wanted to prevent the Maccabees from being Jewish. As we have seen, this image is not really accurate. Although the first Hasmoneans began their revolt in response to the religious violence ordered by Antiochus IV, even these early Hasmoneans were not isolated from the larger world and the influences of Hellenism. Indeed, far from being universally hostile and antagonistic toward Hellenism, the Hasmoneans actually openly embraced several aspects of Hellenism and incorporated them into their self-presentation and identity. As such, the Hasmoneans were both Jewish and Hellenistic. Herod continued this process of Hellenization, while adding other influences to his identity. Herod, like the Hasmoneans, was both a Jewish king and a Hellenistic monarch.

As we have seen, the Hasmoneans initially secured their power by serving as vassals to the Seleucid state. This relationship between the Seleucid overlord and the Hasmonean vassal was always fraught with tension as various Seleucid kings tried to limit Hasmonean expansion. However, it was also the primary means by which the early Hasmoneans

---

24. As we will see later, during the first century BCE and especially during the reign of Herod, pilgrimages undertaken by Jews from the Diaspora increased tremendously. With their control of the high priesthood and therefore the Temple, the Hasmoneans would have been in an excellent position to exert their influence over the pilgrims who flocked to Jerusalem.

25. For Julius Caesar's decree, which indicates that the high priest collected the priestly gifts and then redistributed them, see *AJ* 14.203. For Schwartz's theory about the Hasmoneans using the collected priestly gifts to secure priestly support, see Seth Schwartz, "Herod, Friend of the Jews," in *Jerusalem and Eretz Israel: The Arie Kindler Volume*, ed. Joshua Schwartz, Zohar Amar, and Irit Ziffer (Tel Aviv: Eretz Israel Museum and Ingeborg Center, 2001), 71.

secured international and local recognition. Jonathan Maccabee even received an invitation to the wedding of Alexander Balas and Cleopatra Thea in ca. 150 BCE. At this wedding, both the Seleucids and Ptolemies publicly confirmed his claim to the high priesthood and leadership of Judaea.[26]

Additionally, from the time of Judah Maccabee down to Mattathias Antigonus, the Hasmoneans actively participated in international diplomacy by befriending far-away Gentile cities and states, including Rome and Sparta.[27] Along with these interactions the Hasmoneans also engaged in local diplomacy and friendship with neighboring dynasts. Most of the information about these friendships comes from the period of the Hasmonean civil wars (67-37 BCE), but it is reasonable to assume that similar such relationships occurred between earlier Hasmoneans and their neighbors.[28] During the Roman civil wars, Aristobulus II sought the aid of his friend the Ituraean dynast Ptolemy son of Mennaeus, who even married Aristobulus's daughter. When Hyrcanus II needed help retaking Jerusalem, he called on his friend and ally Aretas III, the king of Nabataea.[29] These friendships with local non-Jewish elites illustrate well how integrated the Hasmoneans were into the circle of regional elites and how they established and maintained friendships with their neighbors like every other Hellenistic monarchy.

---

26. Although Jonathan's invitation to the wedding of Alexander Balas and Cleopatra Thea was a great honor, his subordinate status was also clear. He went to the wedding as a Seleucid vassal, as one summoned by Alexander. The king granted him honors and status, but these grants also made him dependent on and subordinate to Balas. See Erich Gruen, *Heritage and Hellenism: The Reinvention of Jewish Tradition* (Berkeley: University of California Press, 1998), 17. Cf. Fischer, "Hasmoneans and Seleucids," 11-15.

27. For Hasmonean embassies to non-Jewish cities such as Rome and Sparta, see 1 Macc 8:17-32; 12:1-23; 15:15-24; *AJ* 12.415-19; 13.163-70. See *AJ* 13.259-66 for John Hyrcanus I's renewal of the treaty with Rome.

28. We know that prior to the Hasmoneans there were relationships and friendships between the Judaean elite and their neighbors. There is evidence from the fifth century BCE and following for marriage alliances between Jerusalem high priests and elite Ammonites and Samarians (*AJ* 11.302-12; 12.160ff.). Simon the Oniad fled to Daphne, Syria and sought sanctuary there (1 Macc 4:33-34). Around 170 BCE, the Oniad high priest Jason fled to his Nabataean friends for support (4:26; 5:6-10).

29. For Aristobulus's friendship with Ptolemy son of Mennaeus, see *AJ* 14.126. For Hyrcanus's friendship with the king of Nabataea, see *AJ* 14.14-21, 29-33. Unfortunately, Hyrcanus's friendship with the Nabataeans, specifically their new king, Malichos II, was the pretext Herod used to execute Hyrcanus in 30 BCE. For Herod's use of Hyrcanus's friendship with Nabataea as a pretext for his execution, see *AJ* 15.165-78.

CULTURAL AND INTELLECTUAL MILIEU

Hellenistic Motifs in Courtly Literature and Inscriptions

At the same time that the Hasmoneans were engaging with neighboring Hellenistic monarchies, they were also accommodating and adapting to the political norms and self-presentation of contemporary kingship. Such accommodation is hardly surprising considering that Hellenism had already made significant inroads in Judaea prior to the Hasmonean revolt. This accommodation to Hellenism is clearly illustrated by the decree of honors presented to Simon Maccabee in 143 BCE. This decree, which appears in 1 Macc 14:25-49, was an innovation in the Jewish context, but, according to Jan Willem Van Henten, it is quite comparable to other Hellenistic royal honorary decrees. He compares this decree with four Hellenistic priestly decrees: the Canopus decree of 238 BCE, the Raphia decree of 217 BCE, the Rosetta Stone of 196 BCE, and the Alexandria decree of 186 BCE. According to Van Henten, all four have the same five-part structure: date, reference to the issuing assembly, motivation for the decision, the decision itself, and provisions for publication of the decision.[30] Furthermore, like the rulers in these decrees, Simon was honored because of his deeds. Like a typical Hellenistic king, his status was dependent on his actions and accomplishments; his legitimacy rested on his ability to fulfill his obligations as ruler.

For instance, 1 Maccabees emphasizes the personal sacrifice that Simon and his family have undertaken "in order that their [the Judaean] sanctuary and the Law might be preserved" (14:29). In other words, they fought in defense of the *patrios politeia* of the Judaeans. The decree also praises Simon for his personal benefactions to the public good. He, acting the role of the royal patron, funded numerous building projects and other public works out of his own money.[31] He also fortified several towns and cities along the Judaean borders, and, most importantly, he fortified

---

30. Jan Willem Van Henten, "The Honorary Decree for Simon the Maccabee (1 Macc 14:25-49) in Its Hellenistic Context," in *Hellenism in the Land of Israel,* ed. John J. Collins and Gregory E. Sterling (Notre Dame: University of Notre Dame Press, 2001), 122-45. Van Henten also suggests that the extension of the mentioned honors to Simon's sons may be an adaptation by the author of 1 Maccabees designed to legitimize the position of Simon's successor John Hyrcanus. Cf. Edgar Krentz, "The Honorary Decree for Simon the Maccabee," in Collins and Sterling, *Hellenism,* 146-53, who finds similarities between Simon's inscription and contemporary honorary inscriptions from Syria and Asia Minor.

31. 1 Macc 14:32. Cf. Van Henten, "The Honorary Decree for Simon the Maccabee," 127, where Van Henten compares the mentions of Simon's financial subsidizing of the army to similar comments on the Rosetta Stone about Ptolemy V.

Jerusalem and increased the height of the walls (vv. 33-34, 37). Lastly, he defeated the enemies of the people, expelling them from Judaea (vv. 31, 36). For all this, the Seleucid king Demetrius granted him power and authority and made him a *philos* (vv. 38-39). The decree also established Simon as an autocrat, who held both religious and political power. His decrees could not be revoked, he was entitled to wear special clothing available to no other person, and contracts were made in his name (vv. 41-49). The decree depicts Simon as a father to his people and the Jewish state as his familial estate.[32]

This decree, which appears toward the end of 1 Maccabees, may derive from an actual decree, although the text has probably been adapted and then embedded into the narrative. If the text has been faithfully preserved, it offers us a clear example of the Hasmoneans using an honorary inscription rife with Hellenistic language and motifs to legitimate their autocratic control of Judaea. Even if the text is not a faithful reproduction of a historic decree but a thoroughly redacted work, it still testifies to the Hellenization of the Hasmoneans, since the larger text in which the inscription is embedded (i.e., 1 Maccabees) was written by a Hasmonean courtier in the early years of John Hyrcanus's reign. Its use of language and tropes that would appear normal in an inscription or royal decree from Hellenistic monarchies all over the eastern Mediterranean speaks to the Hasmoneans' active engagement with the larger Greek world.

Use of Greek Names

Given their high level of accommodation and adaptation to Hellenism, it is not surprising that the Hasmonean family eventually took Greek names in addition to their Hebrew names. In his historical narratives, Josephus often uses only the Greek names to identify particular Hasmoneans, although this might be because he wrote in that language. This naming pattern began with the sons of John Hyrcanus I, who were named Antigonus, Judah Aristobulus I, and Alexander Jannaeus. After them, there was at least one Alexander, two men named Aristobulus, and one Antigonus (Mattathias Antigonus). There were also at least three women named Alexandra. Moreover, these are only the names that appear in the written record. It would not be surprising if there were even more unattested cases in

---

32. Van Henten, "The Honorary Decree for Simon the Maccabee," 132.

the Hasmonean family. Some of these names, in particular Alexander and Antigonus, also appear on Hasmonean coins along with their Hebrew and Aramaic counterparts. The use of these names was not viewed negatively. The last Hasmonean, Mattathias Antigonus, inscribed his Greek name on the obverse of his most Jewish coin, which depicted the menorah and the showbread table. It is entirely possible that the use of such names in public and as a part of official titulature was meant to allude to famous rulers of the past, such as Alexander the Great and the Antigonids. It also may have been a conscious move by the Hasmoneans to situate themselves within the milieu of Hellenistic kingship through the use of common Greek names and thus to argue for inclusion of their dynasty within the larger Greek world.

In addition, several high-ranking members of the Hasmoneans' inner circle bear obviously Greek names. Two of Judah's trusted lieutenants and ambassadors to Rome bore the names Eupolemus and Jason. Two of the men leading Judah's army were named Dositheus and Sosipater. Jonathan and Simon employed two ambassadors named Numenius son of Antiochus and Antipater son of Jason. This catalog means that less than twenty years after the Hasmoneans' revolt, their inner circle contained men with Greek names whose fathers also bore Greek names. Such examples prove that the taking of such names by the Hasmoneans and their court did not represent a significant change in attitude or ideology. At least one, Aristobulus I, even adopted a Greek epithet as part of his titulature. According to Josephus, he was known as the Philhellene (Greek-lover). It is unclear whether this epithet was part of his official titulature or whether others used it merely to describe him. Nevertheless, the title does suggest an active interest in and promotion of Hellenism by him and his family.

Bronze Prutah of John Hyrcanus I
Obverse: *Yehohanan the High Priest and the Council* (hever) *of the Jews* in Paleo-Hebrew within wreath. Reverse: Double cornucopias adorned with ribbons, pomegranate between the horns, small A to lower left

Judaean History from the Maccabees to Herod

Silver Tetradrachma of Cleopatra Thea
Obverse: Portrait head of Cleopatra Thea. Reverse: Parallel double cornucopia
Basilissēs Kleopatras Theas Euetērias (Of Queen Cleopatra, Goddess of Plenty)
ZΠP (Year 187 of the Seleucid era = 126/125 BCE) (Wikimedia Commons)

Use of Greek Symbols

Names and titles were not enough. The Hasmoneans also utilized Hellenistic symbols on their coinage. For instance, one of the most common symbols on Hasmonean coins was the crossed double cornucopia. This image appears on at least one coin of each Hasmonean who minted coins, and it is the most prominent image on the coins of John Hyrcanus I, Judah Aristobulus I, and John Hyrcanus II. The cornucopia was one of the most commonly used symbols in the Greek world, and it was often associated with Tyche or Demeter. As a symbol of plenty, it was frequently paired with a poppy head, another symbol of fertility.

A double cornucopia coin type appeared on coins earlier than those of the Hasmoneans. The Ptolemaic queen Arsinoe II (ca. 316-270 BCE) used the image on a number of her coins as a heraldic symbol. Most likely, the Hasmonean double cornucopia type was borrowed and adapted from the Egyptian coins. Egypt played a central role in the political life of Hasmonean Judaea and was a frequent ally of the Hasmoneans, specifically during the reign of Alexander Jannaeus. As noted above, Jonathan Maccabee's legitimacy as ruler was confirmed at the wedding of Alexander Balas and Cleopatra Thea. Interestingly, there is a rare tetradrachma of Cleopatra Thea, minted in 126/125 BCE, which depicts parallel double cornucopias on the reverse. While we do not know precisely when John Hyrcanus first began minting coins, we do know that he became much more politically assertive after the death of Antiochus VII Sidetes in 129 BCE. It is tempting to see this coin of Cleopatra Thea as a possible model for Hyrcanus's coin, although such a theory is entirely speculative.

Bronze Prutah of Alexander Jannaeus
Obverse: Lily with Paleo-Hebrew Yehonatan the king around it
Reverse: Upside-down anchor within circle, *Of King Alexander*
in Greek surrounding (courtesy of Yehoshua Zlotnik, Archaeological Center, Jaffa)

Unlike those of Cleopatra Thea, the Hasmonean cornucopias were crossed, not parallel, and included a pomegranate, not a poppy head. The only known crossed double cornucopia coin type that precedes the Hasmonean period is a very rare civic issue of the city of Lebedos, but on this coin an owl, not a pomegranate, sits between the cornucopias. It would seem, therefore, that the crossed double cornucopia with a pomegranate in the middle was an original Hasmonean creation, which was ultimately copied in a civic issue of Ascalon from the time of Augustus and on Nabataean coins from the reigns of Obodas III (30-9 BCE) to Rabbel II (70-106 CE). Nevertheless, the use of a double cornucopia, even a modified one, does suggest a familiarity and comfort with Hellenistic symbolic language.

Perhaps the most conspicuous Greek symbol on Hasmonean coinage was the anchor, an extremely common symbol on coins of the Hellenistic East. Indeed, it was the dynastic symbol of the Seleucids, which traces back to a story about the dynasty's founder, Seleucus Nicator, who had an anchor-shaped birthmark on his thigh. The anchor was often used to advertise maritime interests, events, conquests, or simply sea power in general. The first anchor to be used on a Hasmonean coin appears on the lily-anchor coin of Alexander Jannaeus, which is likely a copy of the similar coin of Antiochus VII Sidetes. Jannaeus later used the anchor on about half of his coin types. Perhaps he was trying to connect himself visually with the Seleucids. This association would make sense because it was a Seleucid, Alexander Balas, who first bestowed political power and legitimacy on the Hasmoneans. Either way, Jannaeus's and other Hasmoneans' open use of coin types with clear Greek influences speaks to their desire to adapt to the norms of Hellenistic kingship and to take full part in the wider political environment of the Hellenistic world.

Judaean History from the Maccabees to Herod

What picture is emerging from this discussion? It would seem that almost from the beginning, the Hasmoneans were fully engaged with the Hellenistic world. Whatever their conflict was with Antiochus IV, it was not a war between isolated Judaism and Hellenism. This priestly family surrounded itself with people who had Greek names. It befriended Greek cities, and it used typical Hellenistic symbolic language to present itself to its audiences, both local and foreign. However, not all Jews embraced and accepted Hellenism and the Hasmoneans. Like all cultural forces, Hellenism had its share of critics and opponents, and, like all political leaders, the Hasmoneans had their detractors and critics.[33] Nevertheless, given the importance of this dynasty, especially during Herod's early reign, it is not surprising that he would mimic and imitate its self-presentation. Its thorough engagement with the wider Greek world had paved the way for him and helps explain why few, especially from the elite, objected when he continued its policy of openly embracing Hellenism.

For Herod, though, there was a significant problem with Hasmonean ideology: he was not a priest. Additionally, since he was not a Davidide, he could not easily claim a biological and thus dynastic connection to the Davidic monarchy, the only other significant native ruling class in Judaea in nearly one thousand years. As such, Herod's legitimacy was questionable

---

33. One of the clearest examples of critique of the Hasmoneans is *PssSol* 17. The author lambastes the Hasmoneans for usurping the throne of David. After narrating the fall of the Hasmonean house and the oppression wrought by Herod, the author describes his messianic ideal. This ideal king is first and foremost a Davidide (vv. 4, 22) who is expected to rule justly and righteously (vv. 26-27, 29, 32, 43), to be a powerful warrior and military commander who will humble the Gentiles so that they serve him, and to behave piously toward God and trust in God's strength and power (vv. 22-25, 30, 37-40). There has been significant debate over the dating of *PssSol,* especially psalm 17. While most scholars, such as Martin Hengel, Elias Bickerman, and Joshua Efron, date this psalm to shortly after Pompey's campaigns in the East (65-62 BCE), Kenneth Atkinson argues that this psalm actually describes the siege of Jerusalem by Gaius Sosius and Herod the Great in 37 BCE. Psalm 17 sees Herod as God's agent in punishing the Hasmoneans and later the Jewish people. For discussion of the chronology of the psalms, see Kenneth Atkinson, "Herod the Great, Sosius and the Siege of Jerusalem (37 B.C.E.) in Psalm of Solomon 17," *Novum Testamentum* 38 (1996): 313-22. Cf. Kenneth Atkinson, "On the Herodian Origin of Militant Davidic Messianism at Qumran: New Light from *Psalm of Solomon* 17," *JBL* 118 (1999): 435-60. For the generally accepted view that *PssSol* dates to Pompey's campaigns, see Martin Hengel, *The Zealots: Investigations into the Jewish Freedom Movement in the Period from Herod I until 70 A.D.*, trans. David Smith (Edinburgh: Clark, 1989), 20ff.; Elias Bickerman, *From Ezra to the Last of the Maccabees: Foundations of Post-Biblical Judaism* (New York: Schocken, 1962), 176ff.; Efron, *Studies on the Hasmonean Period,* 219-86.

in the eyes of many of his Jewish subjects. Indeed, this issue of legitimacy within the context of Jewish monarchy was one with which he contended throughout his reign. His solution, as we will see in the next chapters, was to accept his status as a non-priestly commoner, weaken the authority and influence of the high priesthood, and attempt to gain legitimacy with his Jewish subjects through his fulfillment of the duties and responsibilities of the ideal Hellenistic Jewish king. In this way, even if he could not actually be an ideal Jewish king, he could at least act like one.

We can now proceed to a comprehensive analysis of this attempt to create and maintain legitimacy through a complex and multivalent political self-presentation. This discussion will occupy the rest of the book, which I have divided chronologically into Herod's early reign (46-30 BCE) and his later reign (30-4 BCE). As we will see, as Herod's political needs changed, so too did his self-presentation. Further, it was this conscious program of expression, much more than a consistent policy of oppression and suppression, that enabled him to secure his throne and thrive for over thirty-five years.

SECTION II

From Hasmonean to Antonian

CHAPTER 4

Herod's Rise to Power (47-42 BCE)

Herod was born a commoner, but he was far from being a nobody. Rather, he was born in and grew up at the heart of the Hasmonean court, first under Salome Alexandra and then under Hyrcanus II. During this period, Herod's family, the Antipatrids, led one of the most powerful factions at court. His grandfather Antipas was the governor of Idumaea under Alexander Jannaeus and Salome Alexandra, and it is likely that Herod's father Antipater assumed the same position before moving to Jerusalem and becoming the most powerful courtier in Hasmonean Judaea. Thus, the young Herod matured into adulthood within the very epicenter of Judaean power and intrigue. During this period, his father was the preeminent man in Judaea. Although Herod's elder brother Phasael was the older of the two sons, Herod still played an important role at court, and the successes and influence he achieved during these early years became the foundation for his future rise to the throne.

Herod in Galilee

Herod's political career began when he was about twenty-five years old. His father Antipater appointed Herod and Phasael *stratēgoi* (governors) of Galilee and Jerusalem respectively. Josephus does not specify what Phasael's duties and responsibilities were, but we can assume from his title and from the description of his brother's actions that his job was primarily military, though he may have had political duties as well.[1]

---

1. For the career of Herod's grandfather Antipas, see *AJ* 14.10. Josephus uses a variety of terms for the offices the Antipatrids held and is not entirely consistent in his usage. He uses

Herod immediately proved the wisdom of his father's appointment by successfully repressing an outbreak of banditry in Galilee. Soon after his appointment, he learned that a group of bandits were ravaging the districts on the Syrian frontier that bordered Galilee. The leader of these bandits was a certain Hezekiah. Unfortunately, Josephus does not describe this group in any real detail, simply referring to them as "bandits." However, he does connect them to the "Fourth Philosophy," a revolutionary sect led by Judah of Galilee which arose in the first century CE and insisted on no ruler but God. Specifically, Josephus claims that Hezekiah was Judah's father. It is therefore possible that this group's banditry may have had explicit anti-Roman aims as well as those of more general social protest. However, if this were the case, it is surprising that anyone at the pro-Roman court of Hyrcanus would have objected to the summary execution of the bandits. Herod's difficulties with these outlaws and the fallout from his execution of them, which will be discussed in greater detail below, suggests that they were not mere brigands. Perhaps they were remnants of Aristobulus II's faction and as such were of relatively high social class or had allies at court.

In response to this outbreak of banditry, Herod deployed his army throughout the region and apprehended and killed the bandit chief and many of his men. His actions were extremely popular among the inhabitants of Syria, who had suffered the most from the bandits' activities. Herod also earned the appreciation and goodwill of his superior, Hyrcanus, and the Romans in the region, both of whom disliked the instability that such outlaws created. In particular, Herod's successes brought him to the attention of the proconsul of Syria, Sextus Julius Caesar, who later appointed him *stratēgos* of the Roman territory of Coele Syria. Josephus does not describe the reaction in Galilee. However, since large outlaw groups often had the tacit and even explicit support of the local population, and given the high probability that Hezekiah and his men were Jewish bandits attacking non-Jewish Syrians, it is likely that Galileans were less supportive of the official response.[2]

---

two terms for Antipater's office, *epitropos* (*BJ* 1.199; *AJ* 14.143) and *epimelētēs* (*AJ* 14.127 and quoting Strabo in 14.143). Josephus also uses these terms for Herod and Phasael, choosing the verb form of *epitropos (epitrepōn)* for both brothers at *BJ* 1.244 and *epimelētēs* for Herod at *BJ* 1.225 (contra *AJ* 14.280). Josephus most consistently uses *stratēgos* for Herod and Phasael prior to the death of their father. Perhaps the Antipatrid offices were not official and thus carried no formal title. Whether formal or informal, it is likely that their offices carried military, financial, and political responsibilities and powers.

2. For Josephus's discussion of Judah the Galilean and the Fourth Philosophy, see *BJ*

Herod's Rise to Power

How did the Antipatrids in Judaea capitalize on the news of Herod's actions? While Galilean bandits may have been popular in Galilee, we have no reason to believe that the urban population of Jerusalem had as positive an opinion of them, since bandit activity would have hampered trade and other commercial activities on which the urban population depended. Further, the local elites, who were heavily involved in these commercial activities, would certainly have approved of police action against brigandage. Herod's actions gained him fame, which increased his status at court and his reputation as a courtier and government official who could execute the tasks assigned to him. Antipater's status at court would also have risen because of his son's accomplishments, especially since he had appointed his son. However, status in this courtly society was a zero-sum game. In order for Herod to rise in the court, other courtiers had to fall from favor. Such a shift in relative status for both Herod and his family would therefore have incited the anger and enmity of rival courtiers. This enmity and hostility would ultimately lead to a charge of murder against the young Antipatrid.[3]

2.118; *AJ* 18.23-25. Cf. Richard A. Horsely and John S. Hanson, *Bandits, Prophets, and Messiahs: Popular Movements in the Time of Jesus* (Harrisburg: Trinity, 1999), 190-99; James S. McLaren, *Turbulent Times? Josephus and Scholarship on Judaea in the First Century* CE (Sheffield: Sheffield Academic, 1998), 158-62. For Herod's encounter with the bandits, see *BJ* 1.204-5; *AJ* 14.158-60. Both *BJ* and *AJ* emphasize the admiration and gratitude felt by the Syrians (*BJ* 1.205; *AJ* 14.160). For Sextus Caesar's appointment of Herod as governor, see *BJ* 1.213; *AJ* 14.180. Both *BJ* and *AJ* say Herod's territory was Coele-Syria, but *BJ* says the grant also included Samaria, though this is unlikely because Samaria was under the control of Hyrcanus and not Sextus Caesar. Sextus was the first cousin of Julius Caesar, who appointed Sextus governor of Syria (see Caesar, *B. Alex.* 66; Dio 47.26.3-7). Cf. T. Robert S. Broughton, *The Magistrates of the Roman Republic* (New York: American Philological Association, 1952), 2:289, 297. For discussions of bandits in Galilee and their support among local populations, see Benjamin Isaac, "Bandits in Judaea and Arabia," *Harvard Studies in Classical Philology* 88 (1984): 171-203; Martin Goodman, "The First Jewish Revolt: Social Conflict and the Problem of Debt," *JJS* 33 (1982): 417-27; Martin Goodman, *The Ruling Class of Judaea: The Origins of the Jewish Revolt against Rome, A.D. 66-70* (Cambridge: Cambridge University Press, 1987), 60-64; T. L. Donaldson, "Rural Bandits, City Mobs and the Zealots," *JSJ* 21 (1990): 19-40; Brent D. Shaw, "Tyrants, Bandits and Kings: Personal Power in Josephus," *JJS* 44 (1993): 176-204.

3. For the economic activities of the local Jewish elite during the first century CE and their dependence on trade and commerce, see Goodman, *Ruling Class*, 55-75. Although Goodman's analysis is of first-century CE elites, there is no reason to think that first-century BCE Jewish elites were not engaged in similar activities. For Josephus's narration of the enmity Herod earned because of his successes in Galilee, see *BJ* 1.208-9; *AJ* 14.163-65. *BJ*'s depiction of the following events is much more positive toward the Antipatrids. *BJ* accuses

Trial for Murder

The success of Antipater's youngest son in Galilee, coupled with the elder son's efficient governance of Jerusalem, threatened a number of rival courtiers who distrusted this family and sought their removal from power. These courtiers approached Hyrcanus and tried to create a breach between him and his subordinates by accusing Herod of overstepping his authority and executing the Galilean bandits without trial. Josephus provides us with two versions of this episode. *Jewish War* 1.209 states that the courtiers accused Herod of executing the bandits without trial. On the other hand, *Jewish Antiquities* 14.167 depicts them accusing him of executing the bandits even though the Sanhedrin had not first condemned them to death. The two accounts are not mutually exclusive since both emphasize that Herod was accused of murder and depict the charges as stemming from rival courtiers hostile toward Herod and his family.

What can we make of these two accounts? Which, if either, is more credible? Before we can begin to answer that question, we must first examine the charge of murder itself. As *stratēgos,* Herod likely would have had the authority to execute ordinary bandits without the delay of a formal trial. However, if, as I have suggested, these bandits were not mere outlaws but in fact remnants of Aristobulus II's faction, then it might have been necessary to seek Hyrcanus's permission. Thus, it is possible that the real charge in this case was usurpation of royal power. That Herod did not seek official permission to execute high-status individuals was proof, according to his rivals, that he sought greater power than he currently possessed, perhaps even royal power. *Jewish War's* account supports this hypothesis when it depicts Herod's rivals as saying that if he was only an official and not the king, he still needed permission to execute the bandits. Of course, the real reason behind their accusations was a desire to discredit and damage Herod's position at court. This attack on Herod was also directed at Antipater, since he would have been guilty by association. We should, therefore, see these accusations as part of a larger struggle for influence and dominance within the Hasmonean court. Interestingly, neither account mentions the ethnic identity of Antipater's family or their relative newness to the Hasmonean court. Apparently, the Idumaeans were integrated enough

---

the rival courtiers of being malicious and slanderous, while *AJ* only states that they were concerned about the power and recklessness of Herod.

into Hyrcanus's court that an attack on their ethnicity was not seen as strategically beneficial.[4]

Further complicating our understanding of Herod's trial is the significant difference between the two accounts of the event, particularly the depiction of Hyrcanus's role in the affair. While *Jewish War* shows him actively working to secure Herod's acquittal, *Jewish Antiquities* states that he merely aided him in fleeing the jurisdiction. In *Jewish War,* Herod stands trial in front of Hyrcanus. In *Jewish Antiquities,* however, Herod's trial is before the Sanhedrin. Which narrative is correct? Is either one accurate?

Let us deal first with the differences between the two narratives, particularly the question of the presence of the Sanhedrin at the trial. *Jewish War* does not mention this governmental body at all, but that is not conclusive evidence of its absence, especially because the account in this section of *Jewish War* often presents an abridged version of the one that appears in the corresponding section of *Jewish Antiquities.* Nevertheless, other evidence suggests that it is doubtful that *the* or even *a* Sanhedrin was involved in the affair. Some scholars, such as David Goodblatt, have argued against the existence of a permanent council body in Judaea throughout the Second Temple period, and indeed, the evidence for such a body is questionable. Josephus himself never uses the Greek word *synedrion* until this point in his narrative, and in his texts the word generally refers to an ad hoc advisory council. In this case, Hyrcanus might have called together a group of nobles to help hear the case against Herod, but the ethnarch himself would have had the final decision of guilt or innocence.

If there was no formal Sanhedrin at the trial, then Josephus's story of Herod overawing the entire Sanhedrin with the exception of one brave individual is also a fiction. In *Jewish Antiquities* 14.171-76 this lone dissenter is named Samias. Later, though, when Josephus alludes to this incident, he refers to the lone dissenter as Pollion and claims that Samias was Pollion's disciple. Moreover, the story of a king (or future king) threatening the Sanhedrin has a close parallel in the rabbinic story of King Yanni and Shimon ben Shetach. In this rabbinic story, a slave of King Yanni is on trial for murder, but Yanni intimidates everyone in the Sanhedrin except Shimon ben Shetach. Elsewhere, the Talmud refers to Herod as "the slave

---

4. For a discussion of the integration of Idumaeans into the Hasmonean and early Herodian courts, see Adam Kolman Marshak, "Rise of the Idumaeans: Ethnicity and Politics in Herod's Judaea," in *Jewish Identity and Politics between the Maccabees and Bar Kokhba,* ed. Benedikt Eckhardt (Leiden: Brill, 2012), 117-29.

of the Hasmonean house." Hence, it is possible that this story is referring to the actual trial. However, such a conclusion is unlikely because of the legendary nature of the Talmudic story. Additionally, it does not make sense that Herod would execute those who submitted to his intimidation but spare the one man who refused to do so and who threatened his life.[5]

In both accounts Hyrcanus is disinclined to try and convict Herod. So why did he try Herod at all? The texts state that he was stirred up either by his own jealousy *(Jewish War)* or by the arguments of courtiers hostile to Herod and his family *(Jewish Antiquities)*. Another possibility is that he was using the trial as a way to humble and control his ambitious subordinate. Such a maneuver, if successfully accomplished, would have required considerable political dexterity. However, the general depiction of Hyrcanus in both *Jewish War* and *Jewish Antiquities* is not of an astute and capable leader but of an indolent and lazy one. Furthermore, Josephus explicitly contrasts this indolence with the energy of his brother Aristobulus and claims that this difference in the two brothers resulted in the civil war

---

5. For the two accounts of the trial, see *BJ* 1.208-15; *AJ* 14.163-84. For the difference in Hyrcanus's role between the two accounts, see especially *BJ* 1.211; *AJ* 14.177. An additional detail that appears in *AJ* but not *BJ* is the appearance in Jerusalem of the executed brigands' mothers and their demand for justice (*AJ* 14.168). With no additional evidence it is hard to know whether this detail is credible or not. However, if this protest did occur, Hyrcanus's willingness to listen to the mothers' pleas supports my contention that Hezekiah and his men were not riffraff but higher status individuals whose female relatives could sway the monarch. For the relationship between the accounts in *BJ* and *AJ*, see Shaye J. D. Cohen, *Josephus in Galilee and Rome: His Vita and Development as a Historian* (Leiden: Brill, 1979), 48-58, 65-66. For arguments against the existence of a formal Sanhedrin at Herod's trial, see James S. McLaren, *Power and Politics in Palestine: The Jews and the Governing of Their Land, 100 BC–AD 70* (Sheffield: JSOT, 1991), 67-79. Cf. David Goodblatt, *The Monarchic Principle: Studies in Jewish Self-Government in Antiquity* (Tübingen: Mohr, 1994), 77-130, esp. 111-14. For the story of Pollion and his disciple Samias, see *AJ* 15.3-4 and cf. 15.370. For the story of King Yanni and Shimon ben Shetach, see *b. Sanhedrin* 19a-b. In the story, ben Shetach rebukes his colleagues, and the archangel Gabriel promptly strikes them dead. For Herod being called a "slave of the Hasmonean house" who commits murder, see *b. Bava Batra* 3b-4a; cf. *b. Qiddushin* 70. For an analysis of the Talmudic parallels to Herod's trial, see Joshua Efron, *Studies on the Hasmonean Period* (Leiden: Brill, 1987), 190-238, where Efron argues that the version in Josephus is fictional and based on Jewish sources. Cf. McLaren, *Power and Politics*, 67-79. In particular, McLaren calls the Samias-Sanhedrin story "an apocryphal anecdote" (77). Tamar Landau argues that Josephus uses Samias's speech to emphasize Herod's tyrannical tendencies. In her opinion, Herod's decision to spare Samias's life despite the man's opposition is a rhetorical trope common in Greco-Roman historiography. See Tamar Landau, *Out-Heroding Herod: Josephus, Rhetoric, and the Herod Narratives* (Leiden: Brill, 2006) 136-37.

between them. Nevertheless, Hyrcanus might have been not so hesitant and politically obtuse as he is portrayed. In *Jewish Antiquities* 14.138-39, Josephus quotes Strabo and states that Hyrcanus ordered Antipater to aid Julius Caesar and himself took part in Caesar's campaign in Pelusium in 48 BCE. Moreover, in both depictions of the trial, Hyrcanus is the main actor. He makes the decision to put Herod on trial, and he is ultimately the final authority who decides Herod's fate. If Hyrcanus was not actually politically inactive and incompetent, he might have instigated the proceedings as a way of thwarting his young courtier's ambition while simultaneously reasserting authority over his court by encouraging such courtly intrigue. Only when Sextus Caesar intervened to protect Herod and his rights as a Roman citizen did Hyrcanus relent.

Why did Sextus Caesar intervene in what should have been an internal Judaean matter and urge Hyrcanus to acquit Herod? Perhaps he was acting in his capacity as an advocate for Roman citizens. Herod had received Roman citizenship from his father and so had the right to a trial before a Roman magistrate. Sextus Caesar's actions, therefore, could be seen in the context of a proconsul's duty to protect Roman citizens living abroad. We could also see his actions in light of the Roman patron-client system. He was the preeminent Roman in the East at the time, and it would be only natural for him to forge ties of patronage between himself and the local elites. As a patron his duty would have been to protect his client (Herod) from unjust and unreasonable persecution. In this case, he successfully fulfilled these obligations.[6]

---

6. For Hyrcanus's supposed indolence, see *BJ* 1.120; *AJ* 14.13, 158. Daniel R. Schwartz has argued that Nicolaus of Damascus portrays Hyrcanus as incompetent in order to justify Herod's seizure of power and that Josephus echoed this motif in his own treatment of the Hasmonean ethnarch. Unlike Nicolaus, whose main literary goal, at least for the early part of Herod's reign, was praise of that regime, Josephus was interested in blaming the *stasis* (civil strife) of Hyrcanus and Aristobulus for the fall of the Hasmoneans and the rise of the Antipatrids. See Daniel R. Schwartz, "Josephus on John Hyrcanus II," in *Josephus and the History of the Greco Roman World: Essays in Memory of Morton Smith*, ed. Fausto Parente and Joseph Sievers (Leiden: Brill, 1994), 210-32, esp. 217-32. For Josephus's claims that Nicolaus wrote to please Herod, see *AJ* 14.9; 16.183-86. For a discussion of Nicolaus's authorial intentions, especially for his discussion of Herod's early reign, see Mark Toher, "Herod, Augustus, and Nicolaus of Damascus," in *Herod and Augustus: Papers Presented at the IJS Conference, 21st-23rd June 2005*, ed. D. M. Jacobson and N. Kokkinos (Leiden: Brill, 2009), 65-80, esp. 67. For Josephus's depiction of the Pelusium campaign, see *AJ* 14.127, 138-39. Interestingly, *BJ* presents a different version of these events, showing an active Antipater and an absent Hyrcanus. See *BJ* 1.187-92 and cf. 1.194, where Caesar confirms Hyrcanus as high priest in

With his acquittal achieved, Herod resumed his duties as governor of Galilee. Unfortunately, the Roman civil war between Julius Caesar and Pompey, which had not yet directly affected the Hasmonean kingdom, now engulfed the region. In 46 BCE Quintus Caecilius Bassus, a partisan of Pompey, assassinated Sextus Caesar and took control of his army. In response, Antipater (possibly on Hyrcanus's order) sent his two sons with an army to reinforce the Caesarians, who were besieging Bassus in Apamea, Syria. This siege began in the autumn of 45 BCE, and by early 44, Julius Caesar had sent Lucius Statius Murcus to Syria to oppose Bassus as well. In both accounts, Josephus states clearly that Antipater sent his sons out of deference to Julius Caesar and because of the favor Sextus Caesar had shown his family. In this way, the Antipatrids could reaffirm their loyalty and fulfill their obligations as Julius Caesar's (and Sextus Caesar's) clients.[7]

Herod and Cassius

On March 15, 44 BCE, a small conspiracy of Roman senators assassinated Julius Caesar. For Herod and his family, the death of their patron required a quick shift in political allegiance to the new preeminent Roman in the East, Gaius Cassius Longinus, who had been one of the main conspirators against Caesar. When Cassius became proconsul of Syria in 43 BCE, he immediately began raising an army to protect himself from the Caesarian faction. Cassius turned to his provinces to provide the necessary capital. In Judaea alone, Cassius exacted 700 talents. Antipater apportioned the collection to each of his two sons, Herod and Phasael, and to a rival courtier, Malichos. Because Herod was the first of the group to raise his portion of 100 talents, he earned Cassius's gratitude and respect.

Who was Malichos, and what does his rivalry with the Antipatrids tell us about the Hasmonean court in the 40s BCE? Although Josephus

---

order to please Antipater. For Sextus Caesar's intercession, see *BJ* 1.211-13; *AJ* 14.170. For an analysis of Caesar's motives, see A. Gilboa, "The Intervention of Sextus Julius Caesar, Governor of Syria, in the Affair of Herod's Trial," *Scripta Classica Israelica* 5 (1979-80): 185-94. For a discussion of patronage in general and patronage of foreign aristocrats, see p. 5 n. 2 above.

7. For multiple narrations of the Roman civil war between Caesar and Pompey, see Dio 47.26-27; cf. Livy, *Per.* 114.1; Strabo 16.2.10; Appian, *B. Civ.* 3.77. For Josephus's versions of the events see *BJ* 1.216-17; *AJ* 14.268-69. Cf. Emil Schürer, *The History of the Jewish People in the Age of Jesus Christ (175 BC–AD 135)*, ed., trans., and rev. Geza Vermes and Fergus Millar (Edinburgh: Clark, 1973-87), 1:248-50.

never makes his origins explicit, we can hypothesize Malichos's probable identity based on other clues. For instance, we know that he shared his name with three Nabataean kings. Further, through epigraphic analysis, Abraham Schalit has shown that the name is Nabataean in origin. Thus, it is likely that our Malichos had some connection to Nabataea.

If we accept that he was of Nabataean origin, then what was he doing in a Judaean court? While Nabataea and Judaea were certainly allies during the reign of Hyrcanus II, there is no indication of any other Nabataean aristocrats at court. But Nabataeans had begun making inroads into Idumaea during the Persian period, and it is possible that Malichos and his family were among that group of migrating ethnic Nabataeans. If so, then the rivalry with Antipater and his clan would have been a longstanding fight for power and influence between two Idumaean aristocratic families. Interestingly, Herod's mother, Cypros, was also Nabataean, and *Jewish Antiquities* even suggests that her family might have resided in Idumaea as well. Hence, there is a very real possibility that Antipater, Cypros, and Malichos represent three aristocratic families, all from Idumaea, two of which were allied through marriage. Even if Cypros was not an Idumaean Nabataean, the identification of Malichos as Idumaean — at least by geography — means that during the 40s BCE the two preeminent factions in the court of Hyrcanus II were Idumaean, not native Judaeans.[8]

Meanwhile, in the larger world, tensions among various Roman factions were increasing. Early in his tenure as proconsul, Cassius decided to

---

8. For Cassius as proconsul in 43 BCE, see T. Robert S. Broughton, *The Magistrates of the Roman Republic* (New York: American Philological Association, 1952), 2:343-44. For Cassius's raising of an army and his exaction of money from Judaea, see *BJ* 1.218-22; *AJ* 14.271-76; cf. Dio 47.28. For the first appearance of Malichos in the literary sources, see *BJ* 1.162; *AJ* 14.84, where Josephus depicts him leading Jewish soldiers against Alexander, son of Aristobulus II. For a discussion of Malichos's origins, see Abraham Schalit, *König Herodes. Der Mann und Sein Werk* (rev. ed.; Berlin: de Gruyter, 2001), 749-50. For the influx of Nabataeans into Idumaea in the sixth century BCE, see Aryeh Kasher, *Jews, Idumaeans and Ancient Arabs: Relations of the Jews in Eretz-Israel with Nations of the Frontier and the Desert during the Hellenistic and Roman Era (332 BCE–70 CE)* (Tübingen: Mohr, 1988), 6-10. For Hyrcanus's friendship with the Nabataean king Aretas III and their alliance against Aristobulus II, see *BJ* 1.123-27; *AJ* 14.14-33. For Cypros's ethnic identity, see *BJ* 1.181; *AJ* 14.121. *BJ*'s account is much more straightforward than *AJ*. Both state that Cypros was from a distinguished Arab family, but *AJ* adds the detail that she was also Idumaean. As I will discuss below, such an identity was entirely possible since there were several families of Nabataean (Arab) origin who lived in Idumaea. See also below and Marshak, "Rise of the Idumaeans," 117-29, for further discussion of the Idumaean dominance within the Hasmonean and early Herodian courts.

shore up his flank and attack the Caesarian Publius Cornelius Dolabella, who had taken control of Asia Minor. Although Judaea was peaceful when Cassius was in Syria, as soon as he left to besiege Dolabella at Laodicea, Hyrcanus's court again erupted into conflict. In particular, Malichos conspired to kill Antipater. Josephus provides two contrary reasons for this plot. According to *Jewish War,* he plotted murder so that he could be free to practice his injustices *(adikēmates),* while in *Jewish Antiquities* he is attempting to protect Hyrcanus. The truth probably lies somewhere in between the two. He might have wanted to eliminate his rival in order to neutralize an enemy and increase his own power and influence at court. In response to this new threat, Antipater crossed the Jordan and recruited an army of Arabs and Transjordanian Jews, with which he prepared to march on Jerusalem. Malichos realized that he was in a weaker position and successfully negotiated a truce. Josephus even states that Antipater again intervened on behalf of his rival, this time with Lucius Statius Murcus, one of Cassius's deputies, who had been ready to execute Malichos as a revolutionary.

Antipater's clemency was in vain. Apparently his enemy was only biding his time. Ignoring the truce to which he had recently agreed, he succeeded in bribing one of the royal butlers to poison Antipater in 43 BCE. When Herod heard of his father's death he wanted to retaliate immediately, but his brother Phasael advised caution. Perhaps the loss of their father and their relative youth made their position at court too weak to risk an open attack. Meanwhile, Malichos denied any involvement and raised a private army to protect himself from the negative fallout from the incident.

At first glance, this story is a little confusing. Why would Antipater spare a dangerous enemy not once but twice? There are several possibilities. The first is that these details are part of a highly stylized and dramatic narrative created by either Nicolaus of Damascus or Josephus to portray Antipater as a noble and clement individual eventually murdered by the man whom he had saved. The model for such a presentation might have been Julius Caesar, who pardoned those who ultimately murdered him. Another possibility is that Antipater spared his rival because he no longer perceived him to be a threat. This scenario is possible but unlikely. Why would Antipater, who was otherwise an astute political actor, not take the opportunity to eliminate his enemy and, moreover, go out of his way to spare him? I would like to submit a third possibility, which, as we will see, better explains the events: Hyrcanus ordered Antipater to spare Malichos.

There is no smoking gun for this theory in either *Jewish War* or *Jewish*

Antiquities. Nevertheless, it fits well with generally accepted models of courtly rivalry, such as those described by Peter Burke and Norbert Elias. According to these models, most monarchal systems of government have a ruler surrounded by a group of aristocrats, who together form a cohesive unit called the court or *courtly society*. Within these courts, factions inevitably form around leading courtiers and officials. Since the monarch doles out all social and political capital, any courtiers wishing to advance socially and politically must compete with each other for the monarch's approval and affection. The monarch can show such approval through ritual gestures or appointing favored courtiers to offices or transferring authority to them. Regardless of how the monarch indicates affection, the important feature of this model for our discussion is the total dependence of courtiers on the monarch for advancement. The relationship is not entirely one-sided. While the courtiers are certainly dependent on the king, he is also dependent on them for support and manpower. No king, even one in an autocratic system, can make every decision and be everywhere at once. Therefore, the aristocracy supplies an indispensable service by providing the personnel to carry out the king's wishes and actually govern the kingdom.

And yet, despite the mutual and beneficial relationship between king and aristocracy, there is always the danger that one aristocrat or a group will decide to remove the monarch in order to achieve more power. How can the monarch prevent such a revolt? Barry Weingast, a senior fellow at the Hoover Institution, has argued that an astute sovereign can remain in power by playing one faction against another and thus balancing the courtiers and their power. At the same time, such maneuvering on the part of the monarch distracts the courtiers from uniting and overthrowing the monarch. In a very real sense, a monarch's ability to create courtly instability actually bolsters the monarch's stability and security. A successful monarch excels at channeling the ambitions of his courtiers into productive avenues while simultaneously distracting them with the promotion of courtly rivalry.[9]

---

9. For the conspiracy to murder Antipater see *BJ* 1.223-24; *AJ* 14.277-79. In *BJ* Josephus does not mention the composition of Antipater's army, but in *AJ* he does. For the assassination of Antipater, see *BJ* 1.227-28; *AJ* 14.283-84. For a discussion of Julius Caesar's *clementia*, see Cornelia Catlin Coulter, "Caesar's Clemency," *CJ* 26 (1931): 513-24; David Konstan, "Clemency as a Virtue," *CP* 100 (2005): 337-46; Melissa Barden Dowling, *Clemency and Cruelty in the Roman World* (Ann Arbor: University of Michigan Press, 2006), 20-26. For coins of *Clementia Caesaris*, see Michael Crawford, *Roman Republican Coinage* (Cambridge: Cambridge University Press, 2001), 491, coin 480/21. Cf. Herbert A. Grueber, ed., *Coins of*

How does such a model play out in the world of Herod and Hyrcanus and lead us to conclude that the third scenario is the most plausible? I am suggesting that Hyrcanus was trying to maintain a balance of power within his court by preventing one prominent individual from disposing of another. If Malichos had been executed, presumably there would have been no other courtier willing or able to check Antipater's power. With both leaders still alive, neither side could claim total ascendancy, an outcome that would have endangered Hyrcanus's position on the throne. The maneuvers by both Antipater and Malichos, therefore, are examples of two factions jockeying for political power and prominence within the Judaean court. Hyrcanus, as the sovereign and ultimate arbiter, stood back and allowed both of his subordinates to strike at each other but never eliminate the other. With the assassination of Antipater, however, the balance of power collapsed. Hyrcanus found himself in a precarious position. Only swift and dynamic action could restore the equilibrium at court.

Fortunately for Hyrcanus, Herod was willing to act. He and his brother waited for the right opportunity and then wrote to Cassius, seeking his permission to kill Malichos. Presumably, they decided that it was wise to get Roman approval for their action, which would undoubtedly stir up unrest among Malichos's supporters. Although we do not know exactly what they wrote, they likely recounted Antipater's loyalty and the loyalty of his family. The brothers also probably reminded the Roman that Herod had procured money for him while Malichos was delinquent in his payment.

---

the Roman Republic in the British Museum (London: British Museum, 1910) 1:549, coins 4176-77. For Josephus's use of drama and pathos in his narratives, see Landau, *Out-Heroding*, 162. For models of courtly rivalry, see Norbert Elias, *The Court Society*, trans. Edmund Jephcott (New York: Pantheon, 1983); Peter Burke, *The Fabrication of Louis XIV* (New Haven: Yale University Press, 1992). Both Elias's and Burke's analyses focus on the court of Louis XIV at Versailles, but their conclusions can be extended to court societies in general. For Elias's discussion of the living arrangements of the French nobility, see *Court Society*, 41-65, 78-81. For the necessity of an aristocracy, see *Court Society*, 3, 35, 42-43. For analysis of how sovereigns can control their aristocracies, see Barry Weingast, "The Political Formations of Democracy and the Rule of Law," *American Political Science Review* 91 (1997): 245-46. For Weingast's discussion of elite pacts, see 252-53, 258-60. The central purpose of Weingast's article is to examine political foundations of democratic systems. Nevertheless, as he clearly states, his analysis is also applicable to autocratic forms of government because of their need for elites to help manage government and society. Indeed, in Weingast's estimation elites are an essential need because no king can rule alone. However, a sovereign who has the support of his elites both has a far more stable hold on power and can even violate the rights of his people with a high degree of success. Without such elite support, Weingast argues, a sovereign will quickly fall from power.

Herod's Rise to Power

In the end, the brothers received both permission for the assassination and the tribunes who carried out the murder.

According to Josephus, Malichos uncovered the plot against him and sought to forestall it by seizing the throne from Hyrcanus. In order to accomplish his plan, he traveled to Tyre to collect his son, who was being held hostage there. He hoped that with Cassius being distracted by his war with Antony and Octavian, he could take control of Judaea with little difficulty. However, Herod outmaneuvered him by inviting him and Hyrcanus to a banquet. While Malichos was on his way to the banquet, the Roman tribunes sent by Cassius ambushed and killed him.

On its face, Josephus's account of these events seems a little unbelievable. Why would Malichos attend a banquet planned by Herod when he knew Herod was plotting against him? I think Nicolaus or Josephus created this episode of execution at a banquet as a just and fitting parallel to Malichos's murder of Antipater at a banquet. As to who killed Malichos, Herod was too smart to move against his rival without Cassius's assent. It is, therefore, possible, and perhaps even likely, that Roman soldiers, acting under orders from Cassius, murdered Malichos. What was Hyrcanus's reaction to the assassination? Josephus states in *Jewish War* 1.234-35 that he initially fainted from fright and, when he had recovered, praised Cassius for saving his life and preserving the stability of his kingdom. In *Jewish Antiquities* 14.293, Hyrcanus is a little less effusive and only says that Malichos was a bad man and a traitor. While we cannot know for sure, I assume that Hyrcanus, regardless of whether he personally approved of his courtier's assassination, accepted the reality of the situation, even if with resignation. He really did not have much choice. Malichos was dead, and Cassius appeared to have sanctioned his death.

When Malichos's partisans in Judaea heard of his murder, they waited for Cassius to leave Syria for Greece (42 BCE), and then they openly attacked Phasael while simultaneously occupying several Hasmonean fortresses, including Masada. At this time, Herod was in Damascus but was unable to come to his brother's aid because of an illness. Josephus's narrative states that Hyrcanus provided some support and encouragement to these partisans of Malichos, so perhaps he was again playing politics within his court in an attempt to check the power of the now dominant Antipatrids. Nevertheless, Phasael managed to repel an initial attack, and once Herod had recovered from his illness he returned to Judaea and expelled the rival faction from the fortresses they had occupied.

This entire story of the rivalry between the Antipatrids and Malichos is one of intense courtly maneuvering that disintegrated into armed conflict and ultimately political murder. The Hasmonean dynasty had long depended on local *philoi* as a link between annexed territories and the Hasmonean center. The family of Malichos and the Antipatrids are two examples of these *philoi*, and it possible that they had been feuding and struggling for power even before Idumaea came under the control of the Hasmoneans. Their rivalry was thus transferred from a local Idumaean context onto the Judaean political stage, and victory by one faction over the other meant more than just control of Idumaea: it meant domination of the entire Hasmonean kingdom. Each side sought greater power and influence within the court of Hyrcanus. As we have seen, the Antipatrids triumphed in the end primarily because of their ability to obtain Roman support. As we will see, this support, more than any other factors, ultimately determined the winning faction in every major courtly conflict in Judaea within the next decade. The pattern was clear: whoever befriended Rome controlled Judaea.[10]

Finally, this episode also highlights one of the main features of the court of Hyrcanus II, the preeminence and dominance of Idumaean aristocrats. While there certainly were native Judaeans at court during the reign of Hyrcanus, the two preeminent factions were led by men of Idumaean origin. This integration of Idumaeans had begun during the reign of his father Alexander Jannaeus, but it seems to have accelerated after the death of his mother Salome Alexandra. Many of these nobles, most notably Antipater and Malichos, supported Hyrcanus. In contrast, Hyrcanus's brother Aristobulus, whom Josephus depicts as the more conservative of the two, seems to have drawn his support primarily, although not exclusively, from

---

10. For Herod's request to kill Malichos, see *BJ* 1.229-30; *AJ* 14.285-88. At the same time as he was seeking permission from Cassius, Herod returned to Samaria to quell a small localized revolt. See *BJ* 1.229; *AJ* 14.284. For Herod's appointment as *stratēgos* of Galilee, see *BJ* 1.225; *AJ* 14.280. *BJ* states that Cassius appointed him *epimelētēs* of all of Syria, but this assertion contradicts Appian's explicit statement that Cassius left his nephew in charge of Syria before leaving for Philippi. See Appian, *B Civ.* 4.63. *AJ*'s account, which states that Herod became governor of only Coele-Syria, is the more probable of the two narratives, especially since Herod had already occupied that position under Sextus Caesar. Moreover, such an appointment would not undermine Cassius's nephew, who would have been Herod's superior. For the murder of Malichos, see *BJ* 1.231-35; *AJ* 14.289-93. For the revolt of Malichos's partisans in the aftermath of his death, see *BJ* 1.236-38; *AJ* 294-96. For the Hasmoneans' use of local elites to govern annexed territories, see Seth Schwartz, "Herod, Friend of the Jews," in *Jerusalem and Eretz Israel: The Arie Kindler Volume*, ed. Joshua Schwartz, Zohar Amar, and Irit Ziffer (Tel Aviv: Eretz Israel Museum and Ingeborg Center, 2001), 70-72.

native Judaean Sadducees. These Judaean priests had long been the preeminent men in the kingdom, despite the recent gains made by the Pharisees and their allies under Salome Alexandra. It is easy to imagine that they were not happy with any change in the social makeup of the court, especially one that displaced them from their previous preeminence. Consequently, the fratricidal Hasmonean civil war may not have had its origins in the contrast between the energetic Aristobulus and the indolent Hyrcanus, as Josephus claims. Instead, it might have developed because of enmity between ethnic factions within the Hasmonean court. Whatever their motivations, Hyrcanus ultimately triumphed over his brother, and his new Idumaean nobility, who had now achieved preeminence at court, turned on each other. The cycle of violence and political murder thus continued.

Herod and Antigonus

Herod and his brother were now firmly in control of Hyrcanus's court. But as soon as Cassius and his army left Syria, the Hasmonean Mattathias Antigonus, the son of Aristobulus, assembled an army in an attempt to oust Hyrcanus and his Idumaean backers. Ptolemy, son of Mennaeus, who was tetrarch of Ituraea and Chalcis and Antigonus's brother-in-law, supported him in this attempt. At the same time their ally Marion, the despot of Tyre, invaded Galilee and captured three strongholds. In response, Herod marched an army into Galilee and expelled Marion's garrisons. Nevertheless, he consciously chose to spare all the prisoners his army captured, even making a point of sending them home with presents. Through this gesture, Herod may have sought to gain favor with the Tyrians and to emphasize his magnanimity and generosity. Engendering good relations between Tyre and himself, and by extension Hyrcanus, could only enhance his position in Jerusalem. Tyre was a large neighboring city and huge commercial center in the Levant, and Judaea would benefit from having friendly relations with the city. If Herod could secure such relations, his status within the court and his usefulness to his superiors would increase substantially. Additionally, maintaining good personal relations with neighboring cities made him a much more attractive ally for Rome. As I have discussed in previous chapters, the Roman system depended on client states cooperating with Rome and with each other. If Herod could personally ensure such cooperation, his utility to Rome would increase accordingly.

After settling affairs in Galilee, Herod then proceeded to the border between Judaea and Galilee (Josephus does not specify the exact location) and forced Antigonus to retreat with his army, presumably back to Ituraea. Herod returned to Jerusalem in triumph, whereupon he was betrothed to the Hasmonean princess Mariamme, the only granddaughter of both Aristobulus and Hyrcanus. While his brother Phasael may have been older and thus previously in a higher position, Herod's accomplishments had advanced his career. He was now the preeminent man at court and, by marriage, the natural successor to Hyrcanus, who had no sons of his own.[11]

Conclusion

Throughout his early years as a Hasmonean courtier, Herod was a loyal, albeit ambitious, servant of Hyrcanus and his regime. He was also a competent administrator and military leader. His actions against bandits in Galilee and against the Hasmonean usurper Antigonus proved that he could effectively govern his territory. Moreover, he consistently sought Roman approval and cultivated friendship with the succession of Roman senators who governed the neighboring province of Syria. This ability to ingratiate himself with Rome and advertise his effectiveness would help him immensely, especially over the next twelve years, when he would encounter two of the greatest threats to his own safety and power: the civil war between Octavian and Antony and the ambitious expansionism of Cleopatra.

In the next chapter, we will examine the subsequent period (42–30 BCE), which began with Herod's appointment as tetrarch, proceeded to his nomination as king of Judaea, and ended with the monumental defeat of his patron Marc Antony at the Battle of Actium. During this period, Herod

---

11. For the familial relationship between Mattathias Antigonus and Ptolemy, son of Mennaeus, see *AJ* 14.126. For Herod's war with Marion of Tyre and Antigonus, see *BJ* 1.238-41; *AJ* 14.298-300. We know that Herod's relations with Tyre improved later in his reign, enough that he built halls, porticoes, temples, and marketplaces there. See *BJ* 1.422. Despite the triumphant language in Josephus's narrative, it appears that Herod was not entirely successful in his campaign to reconquer the territory that Marion had seized. A few years later, in 41 BCE, Marc Antony was forced to issue a decree ordering the Tyrians to return territory they had seized during Marion's invasion. For the decree, see *AJ* 14.319-22. *BJ* 1.241 states that Herod married Mariamme after his successful defense of Judaea against Antigonus's army. However, Josephus later states that Herod married her in 37 BCE in Samaria during his war with Antigonus. Most scholars conclude that Josephus's first statement refers to the couple's betrothal, not their marriage. For Herod's marriage to Mariamme in 37 BCE, see *BJ* 1.344; *AJ* 14.467. I will discuss Herod's acquired Hasmonean identity later, in chapter 6.

skillfully transitioned from a loyal Hasmonean official to Antonian king to astute political dealmaker, who jumped ship at just the right moment and thus survived a civil war that claimed many contemporary monarchs and allies.

CHAPTER 5

Herod and Antony (42-30 BCE)

Herod's early career as a courtier under Hyrcanus II had been a tremendous success. Although still a young man, he had successfully governed Galilee, suppressed bandit activity within the region, and withstood invasions from abroad. When Cassius left for Greece to confront Marc Antony and Octavian, Herod had every expectation that he would soon be receiving even greater rewards from his new patron. Unfortunately, Cassius lost the Battle of Philippi (42 BCE) and subsequently committed suicide. Consequently, Herod found himself in the dire situation of trying to convince the new master of the East, Marc Antony, that he could be as loyal a client to him as he had been to Cassius and as his family had been to both Caesar and Pompey. Herod would succeed at this endeavor, and the next twelve years saw his continued rise from preeminent courtier to valued king and ally. It is to this story that we now turn.

Negotiating the World of the Second Triumvirate

The real victor at Philippi was Marc Antony. Although Octavian was present, he had contributed little to the Caesarians' victory. Indeed, he had been absent from the first battle — Pliny accuses him of hiding in the marshes — and Brutus's army had ransacked his camp. It was Antony's maneuvers that had forced a battle, and it was his generalship and bravery that sealed the victory. After Philippi, the triumvirs (Antony, Octavian, and Marcus Aemilius Lepidus) divided up the Roman world. Antony received the responsibility of the reorganization of the East. He also received control of Transalpine Gaul and Narbonensis (modern-day southern France), which had formerly been under the purview of Lepidus. Octavian was to control Italy and the West while continuing the war against Sextus Pompey. Lepidus himself was left with only western Spain and Africa.

Antony's most important task now was preparation for an upcoming Parthian campaign. The Parthian king Orodes II (ruled 57 to 38 BCE) had helped Brutus and Cassius, and the victorious triumvirs were looking to avenge this treachery. Furthermore, Julius Caesar had been planning a Parthian campaign before he was assassinated, and Antony could easily claim to be following his wishes. Additionally, such a campaign was a good way for Antony to win glory for himself by avenging the Roman defeat at Carrhae. Finally, a triumphant Parthian campaign would have enhanced Antony's glory and status significantly and enabled him to portray himself as the Roman version of Alexander the Great, the conqueror of the East.[1]

In preparation for his campaign, Antony spent the winter of 42-41 BCE in Greece. In the spring, he crossed over to Asia to raise money for his campaign and settle political affairs. On arriving in Tarsus, he summoned the Egyptian queen Cleopatra and demanded that she explain her actions during the recent conflict with Brutus, Cassius, and the other Liberators. Plutarch (and later Shakespeare) immortalized Antony's fateful meeting with Cleopatra as her gilded barge sailed up the Cydnus River, but this encounter was not merely about sex and charm. It was also about business and politics. Antony was in the process of establishing a new Roman system in the East and levying troops for his campaign. To this end, he excused those cities which had suffered most from the Liberators' exactions, including Lycia, Rhodes, Laodicea, and Tarsus. He also enlarged the territory of major cities such as Rhodes and Athens.[2]

All these efforts were designed to solidify his position as the new Ro-

---

1. For the various accounts of the Battle of Philippi, see Appian, *B. Civ.* 4.105-35; Dio 47.35-49. Cf. Plutarch, *Ant.* 22; *Brut.* 38.1-53.4. For the Triumvirs' division of territory see *B. Civ.* 5.3; Dio 48.1-2. For Parthian support of Brutus and Cassius see *B. Civ.* 4.59, 63, 88, 99. For Julius Caesar's intention to launch a Parthian campaign, see *B. Civ.* 2.110; Dio 43.51–44.1. Cf. Cicero, *Att.* 13.27.1; 31.3.

2. For Plutarch's narration of this fateful meeting, see *Ant.* 25-26. Christopher Pelling argues that Antony was displaying "ostentatious philhellenism" by supporting the great Greek cultural centers. Perhaps he was also imitating past Hellenistic monarchs who had shown their enthusiasm for these cities through similar conspicuous benefaction. He might have hoped that such benevolence would be rewarded with the same excitement that these cities had displayed toward those kings. For Pelling's discussion of Antony's dispensations after Philippi, see his "The Triumviral Period," in *CAH*², ed. Alan K. Bowman, Edward Champlin, and Andrew Lintott (Cambridge: Cambridge University Press, 1996), 10:11-12.

man in charge of the East and to bind eastern cities to him in a patron-client relationship. Cleopatra, as sovereign of the wealthy Ptolemaic kingdom, was one of the most important clients for him to acquire. In turn, she wanted Antony's support in her own dynastic struggles with her siblings. Antony spent the winter of 41-40 BCE in Alexandria with Cleopatra, and, in exchange for her loyalty, he ordered her sister, Arsinoë, dragged from sanctuary in the temple of Artemis at Ephesus and murdered. He also eliminated Serapion, the admiral who had given Cleopatra's fleet to Cassius and Brutus. Finally, he forced the town of Aradus to give up a pretender to the Egyptian throne who claimed to be Cleopatra's dead brother Ptolemy XIV. In addition to their mutual political benefit to each other, Antony and Cleopatra apparently also began a romantic relationship that resulted in the birth of twins (Alexander Helios and Cleopatra Selene) only a year later.[3] Once she had secured her control of Egypt, Cleopatra looked to expand and reclaim the Ptolemaic empire of old. This empire included Judaea and Syria, and the Hasmonean regime in Jerusalem was a serious obstacle to her goal. She used her influence with Antony to seize territory from Judaea and other neighboring kingdoms. In the *Donation of Alexandria*, Antony gave her control of the plain of Jericho and all the territory of Syria south of the Eleutherus River except Tyre and Sidon.[4]

In 41 BCE, however, Cleopatra was still one of many monarchs who traveled to Asia to pay court to the new Roman magistrate in the East. Herod too proceeded to Asia to meet Antony, catching up to him in Bithynia. At the same time, a rival embassy of Jewish leaders also arrived in Bithynia to greet Antony and lodge complaints against Herod and his brother.[5]

Josephus never explicitly specifies who these Jewish leaders were, and

---

3. Appian, *B. Civ.* 5.9; Dio 48.24.1-3. Cf. *BJ* 1.360; *AJ* 15.89. While later authors have emphasized Antony's infatuation with Cleopatra as an explanation for his actions, it is just as likely that he believed Cleopatra to be the person most capable of ruling Egypt and wanted to eliminate any potential rivals.

4. *BJ* 1.361; *AJ* 15.88-96; Plutarch, *Ant.* 36.2; Dio 49.32.5. It seems that Cleopatra also appropriated the cities of Gadara, Hippos, and Samaria. Her gains clearly weakened Herod by shrinking his territory. Nevertheless, he must have realized that he could not fight her directly, although he would not have wished to relinquish actual control of the disputed territory. Instead, choosing to minimize his conflicts with her, he agreed to lease the plain of Jericho from her. While he may have acquiesced to the loss of formal control over the land, he still retained a presence on it as the lessee.

5. *BJ* 1.242 refers to them as *Ioudaiōn hoi dynatoi* (the powerful men of Judaea), while *AJ* 14.302 calls them *Ioudaiōn hoi en telei* (the leading men of Judaea).

there is little external evidence to clarify their identity. One possibility is that they were simply an unknowable (at least now) embassy of wealthy citizens. However, by looking closely at the text, we can perhaps peel back the layers of time and arrive at an idea of who they were. Josephus uses two phrases to describe the embassy, *Ioudaiōn hoi en telei* in *Jewish Antiquities* and *Ioudaiōn hoi dunatoi* in *Jewish War*. Josephus uses the phrase *hoi en telei* approximately thirty-two times, but it appears to be a stock description of a nation's or group's elite. In particular, Josephus uses it with other partitive genitives for part or all of an elite group (e.g., *hoi en telei tōn Rōmaiōn, Surōn*, etc.). He also seems to use it interchangeably with other phrases indicating elite status such as *hoi gnōrimoi, hoi prōtoi, hoi episēmoi*, and *hoi dynatoi*. Thus, a simple concordance search seems unable to reveal the identity of this embassy.

But we might find some fruitful avenues if we examine the language the embassy uses when addressing Antony, first in Bithynia and then later in Antioch and Tyre. In Bithynia the embassy accuses Herod and his brother of usurping royal control and authority and leaving Hyrcanus with merely the pretense of kingship. Such claims almost exactly mirror the complaints raised in the Hezekiah affair. In each case, Herod's enemies accuse him of overstepping his authority and acting like a king even though he is merely a royal official.[6] Although certainly not conclusive evidence, the similarity of these two sets of accusations raises the possibility that some or even all of the embassy was composed of the same people who had secured Herod's indictment in 47/46 BCE (i.e., rival courtiers). If so, this episode serves as another example of courtly rivalry within the Hasmonean kingdom and an attempt to use Rome and its influence to curtail Herod's ever-increasing power.

Whatever the identity of the embassy, Antony refused to hear their complaints and summarily dismissed them. Josephus tells us that Herod had arrived in Bithynia around the same time as the embassy, and his presence had helped sway Antony's decision. This encounter seems to be the beginning of a patron-client relationship between Herod and Antony. As a good patron, Antony had sided with his client Herod and protected him. In return, Herod had offered Antony a financial gift as a token of his esteem.[7] While Antony may not have felt any powerful loyalty to Herod and

---

6. For the complaints made in Bithynia see *BJ* 1.242; *AJ* 14.301-2. For the complaints made to Hyrcanus during the Hezekiah affair see *BJ* 1.208-9, 242; *AJ* 14.163-67, 302.

7. *BJ* 1.242; *AJ* 14.303.

Phasael, he did have firsthand experience of the Antipatrids' political skill and acumen since he had been an officer during the Roman campaign in Judaea in 57 BCE.[8]

Moreover, Antony would have known that Herod was an effective governor and would have remembered the Antipatrids' loyal service to Rome. It thus seems as if Antony sided with Herod for purely utilitarian reasons: Herod was the most effective governor in Judaea, and Rome should support him.

After Bithynia, Antony continued his tour of the East and traveled to Syria. While in Daphne, a suburb of Antioch, another embassy of elite Jews approached him and leveled charges against Herod and his brother.[9] We do not know for certain what these charges were, but it seems reasonable to assume that they were similar to the ones leveled in Bithynia, namely that Herod and Phasael were overstepping their authority and presuming to wield royal power. In this case, Marcus Valerius Messala Corvinus spoke in defense of Herod and his brother. After listening to the arguments for each side, Antony asked Hyrcanus his opinion, and he sided with Herod. Thereupon, Antony appointed Herod and Phasael tetrarchs of the whole of Judaea.[10]

Although Herod's opponents are never explicitly named, the text provides us with a clue as to their identity and larger motive. Both *Jewish War* and *Jewish Antiquities* depict Antony asking Hyrcanus who was most qualified to rule. Such a question implies that the unnamed Jewish leaders were seeking to have Antony support their claim to higher office within Hyrcanus's administration at the expense of the Antipatrids. This goal in turn suggests that the unnamed Jewish embassy was again a rival group of courtiers. Given the status and influence of the recently-executed Malichos, I suspect that they were his supporters. In any event, Hyrcanus's sup-

---

8. *BJ* 1.162-66; *AJ* 14.82-88. Cf. Plutarch, *Ant.* 3.

9. *BJ* 1.243 states that the embassies made accusations against Herod and his brother, while *AJ* 14.324 says the charges were leveled against Herod and his associates. I think it is more likely that the embassy focused their attention on Herod and Phasael, since at this point Phasael was still an equal to Herod in rank and status. *AJ* seems to be anachronistically putting Herod forward as the leading courtier.

10. *BJ* 1.243-44; *AJ* 14.324-26. Neither *BJ* nor *AJ* offers a concrete date, though *AJ* speaks of Antony's famous meeting with Cleopatra in Cilicia before narrating this encounter in Daphne. We know from Plutarch that Antony and Cleopatra met in late summer 41 BCE, so we should assume that the embassy met Antony at Daphne after this, probably some time in early fall of 41. For Plutarch's chronology, see Plutarch, *Ant.* 26.

port ensured that Herod and Phasael prevailed, and Antony imprisoned fifteen members of the rival group and dismissed the rest.[11]

Josephus relates another episode of complaint in Tyre in which an even larger group complained to Antony about Herod and his brother. In this instance, Antony either dispatched the governor of Tyre to arrest the protesters (*BJ* 1.245) or sent a squad of Roman soldiers to attack the crowd (*AJ* 14.327-29). In both versions, Antony reaffirms his support for Herod and his brother. This story is historically suspect for a number of reasons. It seems unlikely that Tyre, which had a long and friendly relationship with Herod, would have supported his opponents even in the early part of his career. Moreover, it is unlikely that Antony, who had only recently arrived in the East, would risk outraging the local population by slaughtering a large crowd. It seems more likely that this story, which seems little more than a more dramatic doublet of the previous story, is a fiction of Nicolaus or Josephus. In all likelihood, it was designed to highlight either Antony's support of Herod or Jewish opposition to Herod.

Through all of these episodes, how did Herod portray himself to Antony and his Roman audience? Since Josephus does not tell us explicitly, we can only speculate. Nevertheless, given what we already know of Herod, it is likely that Herod appealed to Antony's practical needs. Being the new power in the East, Antony needed to gain approval and support for himself among the local rulers and elites. He may have established relationships with the various ruling families in the East while serving under Aulus Gabinius (57-55 BCE). But he would have needed to renew these relationships and establish new ones.

Herod would have been a useful ally in this endeavor. He was a powerful figure at the court of Hyrcanus II and had already proved himself an able administrator and governor who was unambiguously pro-Roman in his allegiance. His past support of Cassius was no obstacle since it merely reflected Herod's loyalty to Rome and its preeminent representative in the East. Loyalty and political acumen made Herod valuable and paved the way for his ultimate rise to the throne of Judaea.

---

11. *BJ* 1.244; *AJ* 14.325-26. Both narratives agree that Hyrcanus supported Herod because of his betrothal to Mariamme. In *AJ*'s account, a variant reading substitutes *stasiōtōn* for *antistasiastōn*. But both terms were used of a member of a faction or political party, which would add credence to my hypothesis. If the embassy were composed of elites who were merely seeking redress of grievances and not political power, then its members would not have been called "opposing partisans" *(antistasiastes)*.

FROM HASMONEAN TO ANTONIAN

Herod and Rome: Becoming King

Herod and his brother did not have a long time to enjoy their new status. Hyrcanus's nephew Mattathias Antigonus was planning a new offensive to wrest control of Judaea from his uncle and his Idumaean courtiers. In 40 BCE, he enlisted the support of Lysanias, the tetrarch of neighboring Ituraea and Chalcis, who induced the Parthians to support Antigonus's invasion. Lysianias's father Ptolemy had married Antigonus's sister Alexandra, and Ptolemy had supported Antigonus's failed invasion a few years before. After Lysanias (or Antigonus in *Jewish Antiquities*) promised the Parthian satrap Barzapharnes one thousand talents and five hundred women for his harem, the Parthians, who had already invaded Syria, agreed to support Antigonus. The Parthian army, under the command of Barzapharnes and Pacorus, the Parthian prince, accompanied Antigonus and invaded from the coast. This army marched south from Tyre, which refused them entry, to Ptolemais, and then on to Sidon and Judaea. According to Josephus, as the Parthians, under the command of a royal cupbearer also named Pacorus, progressed into Judaea, a large number of Jews flocked to Antigonus's camp.[12]

Antigonus sent his supporters to attack Jerusalem, and they managed to enter the city and fight their way up to the royal palace. However, Phasael and Herod successfully defended the palace and trapped Antigonus's supporters in the Temple. This stalemate lasted until Shavuot (Pentecost), when Antigonus proposed that Pacorus the cupbearer mediate the conflict. Phasael agreed to meet with the Parthian and even agreed to accompany Hyrcanus on an embassy to Barzapharnes in Galilee in the hopes that he might end hostilities between the two sides. When Hyrcanus and

---

12. Josephus does not specify who these Jews were, but we can speculate that they may have been the Galilean Jews who had supported the bandit Hezekiah and had been forcibly suppressed by Herod. See *BJ* 1.204-5; *AJ* 14.158-60. Kasher rightly notes that the Parthians' alliance with Antigonus served their interests quite well. If they wished to control Syria, they needed allies from the South to check any possible counterattack from Egypt. Antigonus and his Ituraean allies would have provided a useful buffer zone. The Parthians might also have been relying on Jewish sentiment to make their conquest easier. Within Parthian territory Babylon had the largest concentration of Jews, and a desire to reconnect Babylon with Judaea, as had occurred during the highpoint of the Hasmonean monarchy, may have influenced some Jews to support Antigonus instead of Herod. See Aryeh Kasher, *Jews, Idumaeans and Ancient Arabs: Relations of the Jews in Eretz-Israel with Nations of the Frontier and the Desert during the Hellenistic and Roman Era (332 BCE–70 CE)* (Tübingen: Mohr, 1988), 122-23.

Herod and Antony

Phasael arrived in Galilee, they discovered that Barzapharnes had no intention of ending the hostilities but merely wished to install Antigonus as king. After Barzapharnes left Galilee to rejoin Pacorus the prince, the Parthians imprisoned Phasael and Hyrcanus. In one version of events, Phasael killed himself rather than becoming a bargaining chip for Antigonus and the Parthians, while Antigonus mutilated Hyrcanus so that he could no longer be high priest.[13]

Meanwhile, Herod realized that his position in Jerusalem was hopeless. So, he gathered up his family (including his mother, his fiancée Mariamme, and her mother Alexandra) and his followers and fled to Idumaea. Realizing that the Parthians were pursuing him, Herod sent the women in his party ahead and secured his retreat. After fending off the Parthians, Herod pressed on to Masada, but throughout the journey a group whom Josephus identifies simply as "Jews" harassed Herod's party. Most likely, they were simply bandits who saw an opportunity to plunder Herod's party as they fled or who were trying to ingratiate themselves with Antigonus by attacking Herod. Either way, Herod and his party fought them off, and later he built Herodium on the site of their skirmish.[14]

On reaching the fortress of Rhesa in Idumaea, Herod met up with his brother Joseph.[15] Joseph provided Herod with valuable military reconnaissance and advised him to dismiss most of his followers since Masada could not support the approximately 9,000 who were in Herod's company. Herod dismissed the majority of his followers, and they dispersed throughout Idumaea, while he and 800 of his followers pressed on to Masada. Herod's

---

13. *BJ* 1.248-60, 268-73; *AJ* 14.330-47, 363-69. Josephus provides two accounts of the death of Phasael. In one (*BJ* 1.271; *AJ* 14.367) Phasael kills himself by dashing his head on a rock. In the other (*BJ* 1.272; *AJ* 14.368) Phasael survives the initial wound but is later poisoned by Antigonus. In a third account, from Sextus Julius Africanus, Phasael dies in battle with the Parthians. See Julius Africanus, *Chron.* 17.

14. *BJ* 1.263-65; *AJ* 14.352-60. In *AJ*, Herod stays with his mother and his fiancée, but *BJ*'s account is more believable because it would make sense for Herod to send the women of his party ahead if he was preparing to fight the pursuing Parthian army. *AJ*'s account enhances the drama of the episode, but it is likely more fiction than fact.

15. Kokkinos connects the fortress of Rhesa with the biblical Horesh(ah) in the Wilderness of Ziph, where David was hidden during his flight from Saul (1 Sam 23:19). It is possible that the narrator of this event (Nicolaus or Josephus) made this place the meeting spot of the brothers in an attempt to link Herod and David. On the other hand, Rhesa (if, as has been suggested, it was on the site of modern Khirbet Khureisa) would have been on the route to Masada and so would have made a logical meeting place. See Nikos Kokkinos, *The Herodian Dynasty: Origins, Roles in Society and Eclipse* (rev. ed.; London: Spink Academic, 2010), 162.

ability to hide his followers throughout Idumaea suggests that his support in this region was unsurprisingly high. Such support for Herod might explain why the Parthians destroyed Marisa, the regional capital of Idumaea.[16]

After depositing his family in Masada and garrisoning it, Herod traveled to Petra, hoping to raise money to ransom his brother, whom he did not know was already dead. *Jewish Antiquities* indicates that Herod and his father had lent large sums of money to King Malichos in the past, and Herod may have hoped to recover some of that money or at the very least borrow funds from Malichos. He may also have thought that his mother's Nabataean background would engender a warm welcome. Unfortunately for Herod, the Nabataean court saw the Parthian conquest of Judaea as an opportunity to renounce their debts to the Antipatrids. Perhaps Malichos also saw this as a chance for him to free himself of Roman control. Additionally, it is possible that the Parthians threatened him with reprisal if he should help Herod. For all these reasons, King Malichos ordered Herod to leave Nabataea immediately.[17]

Realizing that he lacked support in the region, Herod turned westward and made his way to Egypt in hopes of catching a ship to Rome. He soon reached Pelusium, but he could not secure passage to Alexandria aboard an Egyptian naval vessel. Instead, he managed to persuade the local officials to escort him on a private ship to Alexandria. Josephus states that Herod relied on his fame and rank to persuade them. When he arrived in Alexandria, Cleopatra briefly detained him before he finally sailed to Rhodes.

Because of the rough winter sailing weather, Herod was almost shipwrecked off the coast of Pamphylia, but he managed to arrive in Rhodes safely. In Rhodes, he reunited with two of his supporters, Sapphinius (Sappinius in *Jewish Antiquities*) and Ptolemy.[18] *Jewish Antiquities* states that Herod gave money to Rhodes to rebuild the city, which had been damaged during the most recent civil war, and constructed a large trireme for his journey to Brundisium. *Jewish War* does not mention the benefaction, only the trireme he commissioned to take him to Rome. There is no reason to doubt the account in *Jewish Antiquities* since it agrees with Herod's later benefaction to Greek cities. A possible motivation for his gift was that,

---

16. *BJ* 1.266-69; *AJ* 14.361-64. Cf. Kokkinos, *Herodian Dynasty*, 162-63.
17. *BJ* 1.274-76; *AJ* 14.370-72. Cf. Kasher, *Idumaeans*, 124.
18. For Herod's trip from Nabataea to Rhodes see *BJ* 1.277-80; *AJ* 14.375-77. Both Sapphinius and Ptolemy later became major figures in the court of Herod. Ptolemy would also become the royal treasurer. For a brief description of each man, see Duane W. Roller, *The Building Program of Herod the Great* (Berkeley: University of California Press, 1998), 63-64.

despite his dearth of funds, Herod was still interested in portraying himself as a kingly figure while he was traveling to Rome to secure Roman support. He probably did not actually present the Rhodians with the money at that time, especially since Josephus explicitly states that Herod had secured much of his wealth in Idumaea. Instead, he probably promised the city a certain amount and hoped that once he was named king he could raise the necessary capital.[19]

Continuing his trip, the refugee courtier arrived in Brundisium, probably in the middle of winter 40-39 BCE, and from there made all haste to Rome.[20] After telling Antony of the tragedies and setbacks he had suffered, he solicited the Roman's support in helping him claim the throne of Judaea. According to Josephus, he also received the aid of Octavian. It is certainly possible that both triumvirs actively supported Herod's bid to the throne. However, given that Antony was the preeminent Roman in the East, it seems more likely that Herod would have approached him exclusively. The mention of Octavian is more likely an anachronism, placed in the narrative to show Herod having friendly relations with Octavian even prior to Actium.[21]

Why did Antony support Herod even though he had no natural claim to the Judaean throne? In his narration of the events, Josephus implies that Antony admired Herod's nobility and enterprising character and had fond memories of the Antipatrids' past hospitality when Antony had served in the East. These factors must have been a part of Antony's calculations. However, there were other more basic and practical reasons for his decision. First, Herod was a personal client of his and as such could call on his patron to defend his interests in a time of crisis. Moreover, Antony was preparing for his ill-fated Parthian campaign, and having a friendly mon-

---

19. For Herod hiding his wealth in Idumaea see *BJ* 1.268; *AJ* 14.364. For Herod's promise to the Rhodians see *BJ* 1.280-81; *AJ* 14.377-79.

20. *BJ* 1.281; *AJ* 14.379. For the possible date of Herod's arrival in Rome, see *BJ* 1.281. Cf. Emil Schürer, *The History of the Jewish People in the Age of Jesus Christ (175 BC–AD 135)*, ed., trans., and rev. Geza Vermes and Fergus Millar (Edinburgh: Clark, 1973), 1:281; Peter Richardson, *Herod: King of the Jews and Friend of the Romans* (Columbia: University of South Carolina Press, 1996), 127; Roller, *Building Program*, 10. The storm that nearly shipwrecked Herod must have been one of the late autumn to early winter storms that effectively ended the sailing season for all but the most desperate seafarers. Perhaps Herod built his trireme (*BJ* 1.280; *AJ* 14.378) because he could not find passage on another ship.

21. *AJ* 14.383 states that Octavian supported Herod's bid for the throne of Judaea as a favor to Antony. This support is certainly possible and more believable than the claim in *BJ* 1.283 that Octavian was even more supportive of Herod than Antony was.

arch controlling Judaea would help him immensely, especially as it would make moving supplies and troops from Egypt into Syria much easier. Josephus mentions Antigonus's pro-Parthian leaning as a motivating factor for Antony, but he only connects this political alignment to the Parthian campaign in an oblique and ambiguous way.

Instead, I would suggest that Herod's potential usefulness to the Parthian campaign and his staunch loyalty to Rome were foremost in Antony's mind, and it would be surprising if he did not play on these factors when petitioning for Roman support. Moreover, we should view his appointment within the larger context of Antony's continued realignment of the Roman East. Beginning in 40 BCE and continuing for the next few years, Antony radically altered the political landscape of the eastern Mediterranean. He replaced old kings with new ones who were entirely loyal to him. For example, he expanded the kingdom of Pontus but replaced the king, Darius, with Polemo I (37-8 BCE). Amyntas (36-25 BCE) replaced Castor as king of Galatia, and Archelaus (36 BCE–17 CE) took the throne from Ariarathes. Antony thus built up a network of loyal client kings who were dependent on him for support and for their very thrones. Herod was a beneficiary of this process, and his appointment should be seen within this context. By highlighting his usefulness as a friendly client king, Herod secured Antony's support and thereby the support of the Roman Senate.[22]

In order for Herod to become king, he needed the support and confirmation of the Roman Senate and therefore needed an introduction to the Senate and an *appellatio* (formal recognition). Marcus Valerius Messala and Lucius Sempronius Atratinus introduced him to the Senate, emphasized the loyalty of the Antipatrids, and argued that he was a better candidate for the throne of Judaea than Antigonus, who was a client of the Parthians. The Senate agreed and formally appointed Herod king of Judaea. Accompanied by Antony, Octavian, and other magistrates, the new king then climbed the Capitoline Hill and offered sacrifices in the temple of Jupiter Capitolinus before the decree of his appointment was deposited in the public records.[23]

---

22. For Josephus's opinion on why Antony supported Herod's claim to the throne of Judaea see *BJ* 1.282-85; *AJ* 14.381-85. Josephus mentions Antony's Parthian campaign at the end of his description (*BJ* 1.284; *AJ* 14.385) and merely states that Herod's rule would be an advantage in Rome's war with Parthia. For Antony's realignment of the East, see Appian, *B. Civ.* 5.7; Dio 49.32.3. Cf. Pelling, "The Triumviral Period," 28-30.

23. *BJ* 1.284-85; *AJ* 14.384-88. Given what we know about other kings, it is likely that the Senate also named Herod a *rex sociusque et amicus* (allied and friendly king). See p. 6 above.

Herod and Antony

What was a Jewish king doing offering sacrifices at a Roman temple? Scholars such as E. Mary Smallwood and Gideon Fuks have criticized Herod for this action and seen it as an example of Herod's superficial Judaism at best and his open disdain for the religion at worst. Fuks further criticizes Herod for attending a banquet Antony threw in his honor after the Senate had appointed him.[24] In their criticism, both Smallwood and Fuks demonstrate a rather simplistic and dogmatic understanding of cultural interaction. Specifically, they insist that Herod could not have violated Jewish Law on a particular occasion and still retained some level of religiosity and religious identification. In response, we must realize that he was a refugee with few options open to him. At this stage in his career, he needed the Romans far more than they needed him. This was not the time or place for strong declarations of religiosity and exclusivity, especially when Herod was on the other side of the Mediterranean and far from his domestic audience. While it is true that he was technically violating Jewish Law, we cannot conclude from this violation alone that he had no notion of Jewish piety. Further, piety and cultural assimilation are multivalenced and complex concepts that cannot be summarized in one action alone. At this exact moment, Herod had to choose between respecting his religious sensibilities and ingratiating himself with those who were about to put him into power. He chose the latter; this decision may not have made him an exemplary Jew, but it hardly classifies him as an apostate or even as a bad Jew.[25]

---

24. E. Mary Smallwood, *The Jews under Roman Rule: From Pompey to Diocletian* (Leiden: Brill, 1976), 55-56; Gideon Fuks, "Josephus on Herod's Attitude towards Jewish Religion: The Darker Side," *JJS* 53 (2002): 242. For Josephus's narration of the event see *BJ* 1.285; *AJ* 14.389. Cf. Fuks, "Herod's Attitude," 242. Fuks is at a loss for why Josephus does not criticize Herod for what Fuks sees as a clear violation of Jewish law. He speculates that Josephus either did not understand the implications of Nicolaus's account or had something similar to hide in his relationship with the Flavians. Also see Monika Bernett, *Der Kaiserkult in Judäa unter den Herodiern und Römern. Untersuchungen zur politischen und religiösen Geschichte Judäas von 30 v. bis 66 n. Chr* (Tübingen: Mohr, 2007), 47-48, where, like me, she critiques modern scholars, such as Smallwood and Fuks, who see Herod's piety as superficial and inimical to Judaism.

25. For discussions of Herod's piety, see pp. 284-309 below. Cf. Peter Richardson's discussion in "Religion and Architecture: A Study in Herod's Piety, Power, Pomp and Pleasure," *Bulletin of the Canadian Society of Biblical Studies* 45 (1985): 3-29, and "Law and Piety in Herod's Architecture," *Studies in Religion* 15 (1986): 347-60. For a discussion of the complexity and multiple levels of cultural assimilation among Jews in the ancient world, see John M. G. Barclay, *Jews in the Mediterranean Diaspora: From Alexander to Trajan (323 BCE–117 CE)* (Edinburgh: Clark, 1996). As we will see below in chapter 10, Herod actively promoted his Jewish connections and clearly thought of himself as a Jewish king.

Herod played the role of the good client king, who dutifully traveled to Rome and received official recognition from the Senate for his royal title. He relied on the patron/client system to acquire Antony's support as well as the fact that he was a Roman ally while Antigonus was a Parthian supporter. By tapping into the cultural mindset of his Roman audience, Herod the refugee was transformed into Herod *rex sociusque et amicus*. He could now return to Judaea, defeat Antigonus, and claim his kingdom with the help of Roman military might.

Resourceful King, Useful Ally

Throughout his relationship with Antony, Herod unfailingly played the role of the useful client king, supporting his patron and publicly honoring him. For instance, in 38 BCE, Antony besieged the city of Samosata and its king, Antiochus I Theos (ruled 70-38 BCE). Herod left his own civil war with Antigonus to lead an army to reinforce the siege. Antiochus was an ally of the Parthians and had refused to surrender Parthian soldiers who had fled to Samosata. The siege of the city was thus part of Antony's larger, generally ill-fated, Parthian campaign. Initially, Antiochus proposed to pay one thousand talents and submit to Antony's authority, but Antony refused and would not permit his deputy to make peace. Although Josephus credits Herod and his army with securing the victory, Plutarch offers a less enthusiastic report stating that the siege dragged on until Antony finally accepted an indemnity of only three hundred talents. Regardless of the actual outcome, however, Herod had fulfilled his obligation to the man who had made him king and demonstrated his willingness to help when called on.[26] He would not receive another request for military aid for another seven years, and by that time civil war had once again erupted within the Roman world. Herod would now have to choose to be a loyal client and support Antony or switch sides and support Octavian. His choice was completely in line with his prior actions and demonstrated his commitment to the mutually beneficial relationship that had enabled his rise to power.

26. For Josephus's description of the siege, see *BJ* 1.320-22. Cf. Plutarch, *Ant.* 34.2. For a modern description of Antony's campaign, see Pelling, "Triumviral Period," 21-24. For client kings such as Deiotarus of Galatia providing troops to their Roman allies see Cicero, *Att.* 6.1.14. For the combination of Roman legions with client kings' forces see Livy 22.37. Cf. Tacitus, *Ann.* 12.15. For Rome subsidizing royal forces, see David Braund, *Rome and the Friendly King: The Character of the Client Kingship* (New York: St. Martin's, 1984), 183.

Herod and Antony

By the mid-30s BCE, tensions between Antony and Octavian had reached a critical point. The two triumvirs had never really had a good relationship, but mutual need and usefulness had bound them together before the Battle of Philippi (42 BCE) and afterward. Nevertheless, rivalry and distrust had led them to the brink of open hostilities more than once. Two pacts, one signed at Brundisium (40 BCE), the other at Tarentum (37 BCE), and the marriage of Antony to Octavian's sister, Octavia, had eased tensions. However, Antony's dalliances with Cleopatra and his weakness after his disastrous Parthian campaign only encouraged Octavian, who was steadily building support in the West. At Tarentum, Antony promised to send 120 warships from his navy to Octavian. In exchange he was supposed to receive four legions for the war with Parthia and a bodyguard of one thousand picked men for Octavia. While Antony sent the ships, Octavian reneged on the legions. In 36 BCE, Octavian finally defeated Sextus Pompey, who had been waging a guerilla war against the Triumvirate since its inception. Once Octavian had successfully forced Lepidus into retirement in 35 BCE, only the two remained.[27]

As hostilities increased between the two remaining triumvirs, and especially once Antony divorced Octavia in 32 BCE, war became inevitable. When it finally began, each side assembled armies composed of both Roman legions and allied soldiers. Kings from around the Roman world suddenly had to choose sides in the next bloody civil war for control of the Mediterranean. Herod loyally offered an auxiliary force to Antony and would have presented this army to Antony in person, but he was detained by his war with Nabataea. In particular, Cleopatra had persuaded Antony to send Herod against the Nabataeans because their king, Malichos, had reneged on rent that he owed the queen. Her real reason, according to Josephus, was to remove one of the two kings (either Herod or Malichos) and thus make the annexation of both kingdoms easier. Either way, Herod was not present at Antony's defeat, but he had done what he was supposed to do: he had provided soldiers when his patron had called on him. It is this loyalty and ability to please that Herod relied on when he met Octavian, the new master of the Mediterranean. Indeed, this pattern of supplying

---

27. For two modern discussions of the disintegrating alliance between Antony and Octavian, see Pelling, "Triumviral Period," 17-21; Ronald Syme, *The Roman Revolution* (rev. ed.; Oxford: Oxford University Press, 2002), 217-21. For ancient accounts of the Pact of Tarentum, see Appian, *B. Civ.* 5.92-95; Dio 45.54.3-4; Plutarch, *Ant.* 35.1-4. For Octavia's role as intermediary between the two triumvirs, see Eleanor G. Huzar, "Mark Antony: Marriages vs. Careers," *CJ* 81 (1986): 105-6.

royal troops as auxiliaries continued into the Augustan period, but, as we will see, Herod expanded the scope of his activities and found new and innovative ways to support his Roman patrons.[28]

Military and financial support was the focus of Herod's relationship with Antony, but Herod also used his position as king to publicly honor his patron and assert his allegiance both to him as an individual and to Rome as an allied government. The site he chose for his first architectural expression of loyalty was the most central one in his kingdom: in what was probably his first major building project he constructed a massive fortress to the north of the Temple Mount. This apparently superseded a Hasmonean fortress, the Bira (or *Baris*) and was built to guard the Temple. Herod named this fortress the Antonia after Marc Antony. Even after Actium, the name remained. Apparently, Augustus never considered it worthwhile to demand a name change, nor did he believe he would benefit from such a decision.[29]

Because of its size and location, the Antonia dominated the Temple and the city skyline. From its towers, one could look out across the entire Temple Mount and the city itself. As Josephus states, "If the Temple lay as a fortress over the city, Antonia dominated the Temple, and the occupants of that post were the guards of all three." What did this giant of a fortress look like? Although little physical evidence survives, archaeologists have attempted to reconstruct the fortress based on the descriptions found in Josephus and the little material evidence that remains. According to Josephus, the fortress was located on a steep rock about 72 feet (50 cubits) high in the northwest corner of the Temple Mount.[30] At the point where the facade met the Temple porticos, there was a flight of stairs connecting the fortress to the Temple esplanade. The rock on which the fortress stood was covered from bottom to top with smooth flagstones for both decoration and defense. In addition, there was a wall approximately two feet high in front of the actual fortress. The central part of the Antonia rose about 60 feet (40 cubits) above the top of the precipice and had four towers, three of which rose an additional 72 feet (50 cubits). The fourth tower, which was located in the southeast corner of the fortress, was taller, rising a total of 102 feet (70 cubits) above the top of the rock. Its interior, Josephus states,

28. *BJ* 1.364-65; *AJ* 15.108-11; Plutarch, *Ant*. 56.4; 61.1-2. Cf. Dio 51.5-6.

29. *BJ* 1.401; *AJ* 15.409. Cf. *BJ* 1.75, 118; *AJ* 15.292. For a description of the Antonia see *BJ* 5.238-46.

30. Josephus uses the *pēchys* (cubit) as his unit of measurement, which is equal to about one and a half feet.

had the appearance of a town but was like a palace in terms of its conveniences, including residential apartments, bathrooms, and courtyards.³¹

Based on this description, archaeologists have concluded that the Antonia fortress was a *tetrapyrgion* style fort, which means that it was a square or rectangle with the basic form of a tower surrounded by four secondary towers at the corners and protected by steep surrounding slopes on three sides (the side bordering the Temple Mount was presumably not as steep). Also, like the fortress Herodion located near Bethlehem, the Antonia had three towers of equal height and one (the southeastern in the Antonia and the southern in Upper Herodion) of greater height. Ehud Netzer speculates that these towers were divided into floors of slightly more than five meters each. In all likelihood, the Antonia was a partial model for the later construction at Herodion, although Herod modified the design slightly and expanded it, building the mountain fortress as a raised dome instead of a parallelogram.³²

While reconstructing Antonia's design may be an interesting archaeological puzzle, for our purposes it is more important that Herod chose to name this conspicuous building, which was located right next to the Temple, after Antony. He must have decided that such a visible display of public honor and friendship would both please his patron and advertise his close friendship with Rome to his internal audience. Such a display could only have enhanced his strength and authority since the fortress's presence looming over the Temple Mount would remind visitors daily that king had powerful supporters.

Nevertheless, it is noteworthy that this is the only known building Herod named after Antony, while he constructed entire cities named in honor of Augustus. Either his relationship with Antony did not last long enough for him to build more structures in his honor or there were other reasons keeping him from doing so. We certainly possess less information about Herod's relationship with Antony than about his relationship with Augustus. Such an imbalance is probably the result of the scarcity of inde-

---

31. For Josephus's description, see *BJ* 5.238-47.

32. Ehud Netzer, *The Palaces of the Hasmoneans and Herod the Great* (Jerusalem: Yad Ben-Zvi, 2001), 123-25. Also see Marie Ita of Sion, "The Antonia Fortress," *PEQ* 100 (1968): 139-43; Pierre Benoit, "L'Antonia d'Hérode le Grand et le Forum Orientale d'Aelia Capitolina," *HTR* 64 (1971): 135-67; Eric W. Cohen, "The Appendix of the Antonia Rock in Jerusalem," *PEQ* 111 (1979): 41-52; Gregory J. Wightman, "Temple Fortresses in Jerusalem Part II: The Hasmonean *Baris* and Herodian Antonia," *BAIAS* 10 (1990-91): 7-35; Roller, *Building Program*, 175-76, for further discussion of the Antonia.

pendent sources. Since Josephus relied on the work of Nicolaus of Damascus, and since Nicolaus did not enter Herod's employ until after Actium, it is not surprising that Josephus's account would be more complete for the Augustan period. However, the archaeological evidence also argues for Herod's greater activity during the principate. While evidence of building activity from 30 BCE onward litters Judaea, most especially Herod's cities and temples in honor of Augustus, there is a general paucity of material from the Antonian period.

How are we to explain this phenomenon? I suggest that from 43-30 BCE several factors combined to limit Herod's activities vis-à-vis Rome to little more than providing a monetary and military supply depot. In particular, the political situation of the triumviral period was one of great instability and almost constant civil war. In such an environment, it is only natural that Antony would want mostly military aid or financial support. As a resourceful and astute client king, Herod would have identified this focus and targeted his efforts to it. Further, in such a fluid and volatile political situation, making permanent statements of political loyalty by constructing huge and permanent monuments in honor of one patron or another was probably not the most judicious decision.

And yet, this instability cannot explain entirely the lack of permanent monuments to Antony. Rather, I would suggest that we cannot ignore the rapacious specter of Cleopatra looming over the entire Levant. The Egyptian queen had been making significant inroads into the region for a number of years prior to Actium and had managed to partially regain the old Ptolemaic empire. Because Herod knew that Cleopatra wanted his kingdom, he was best served by consistently showing his usefulness to Antony.[33] Further, in such an environment, the less attention he drew to himself the better. Only after the defeat of Antony and Cleopatra could Herod begin to assert himself more openly, and, as we have seen from the vast increase in activity during the Augustan period, he did exactly that. Without a doubt, he aggressively positioned himself as the client king par

33. Josephus's narration makes it clear that Herod knew Cleopatra wanted his kingdom and that he feared she might be able to persuade Antony to give it to her. See *BJ* 1.360, 362; *AJ* 15.97-103, 106. Josephus's story of Cleopatra's failed seduction of Herod fits too well with the various sexual calumnies made against her to be believable, and it is more probable that this story was created by Nicolaus of Damascus to further impugn her after her death. It is likely that Herod simply saw the benefit of placating Cleopatra and attempting to charm her with gifts and displays of friendship. See Tal Ilan, "Josephus and Nicolaus on Women," in Tal Ilan, *Integrating Women into Second Temple History* (Tübingen: Mohr, 1999), 111-13.

excellence of the Augustan principate, the client king who outperformed everyone else in his display of allegiance and friendship with Rome, who built not one but two cities in honor of Augustus, not one but three temples to Augustus and Roma, and the largest artificial harbor in the ancient world and named it Sebastos (Greek for Augustus).[34]

The evolution of Herod's self-presentation toward and in response to Rome is a transformation from a useful but unassertive client king, who was afraid of the shadow of the Egyptian queen and interested primarily in supplying his patron with money and soldiers, to a self-aggrandizing ally who openly advertised and asserted his special relationship with Rome, especially its leaders Augustus and Agrippa. Herod became the model of client kingship within the new principate, a man who could honor Augustus through city building and coin issues and simultaneously see his own standing increase as knowledge of his special status was made manifest in stone and bronze. It is to this relationship that we now turn.

---

34. All these honors are even more impressive because of the great care that Herod had to take not to offend the religious sensibilities of his Jewish subjects. It is noteworthy that none of these temples or cities was located in Jewish regions of Herod's kingdom, although Caesarea did have a Jewish population.

CHAPTER 6

Herod the New Hasmonean

In a few short years, Herod had managed to advance from dependable courtier to steadfast client king. He had manipulated and maneuvered his way to the top of the Judaean court, and ultimately entrenched himself as a firm and reliable Antonian. His Roman audience was indeed satisfied with him. His royal neighbors — many of whom were recent client kings themselves and with whom he had become familiar as a high-ranking courtier — also may have accepted him as a legitimate member of their circle. However, he still had to persuade his internal Jewish audience. His claim to the throne was tentative at best, and his only real legitimacy came from an external source, Rome. His family had long served as able administrators and regional governors. However, Herod was an Idumaean with a Nabataean mother, and thus some Judaeans did not even consider him entirely Jewish. If he was going to hold his kingdom for long, he needed to solidify his local base of power. Therefore, almost immediately upon receiving his crown, Herod began establishing his credibility and legitimacy as king of the Jews. In this attempt, he naturally turned to the most recent source of authority, the Hasmoneans. Through his use of dynastic maneuvering, architecture, and coins, he linked himself with this dynastic family and asserted his legitimacy as a quasi-Hasmonean and, perhaps more importantly, their rightful successor.[1]

---

1. For Herod's mother being a Nabataean see *BJ* 1.181; *AJ* 14.121. For Antigonus's denigration of Herod as a *hemiioudaios* ("half-Jew") see *AJ* 14.403. For a discussion of what Antigonus might have meant by this slur see Benedikt Eckhardt, "'An Idumean, That Is, a Half-Jew': Hasmoneans and Herodians between Ancestry and Merit," in *Jewish Identity and Politics between the Maccabees and Bar Kokhba*, ed. Eckhardt (Leiden: Brill, 2012), 91-115. While Antigonus's assertion reflects his view and possibly that of others, as Shaye

Herod the New Hasmonean

Marriage, Family, and Hasmonean Blood

By the late 40s BCE, and despite being a relatively new ruling dynasty, the Hasmoneans had managed to secure a certain legitimacy as both high priests and kings. Herod could not secure the high priesthood for himself, but if he was to become a legitimate king it would have to be as a Hasmonean or at least as the legitimate successor of the Hasmoneans. To achieve such status, Herod used both his marriage and the children he produced from it to further insinuate himself into the ruling family and to bind his family closer to it. This process began while Herod was still a young man with his marriage to the beautiful Hasmonean princess Mariamme. Hyrcanus may have made the match to stabilize his regime by ensuring the loyalty of the Antipatrids, but the real winner in this arrangement was Herod. Besides her reputed beauty and intellect, Mariamme was a unique prize because she was the granddaughter of both Hyrcanus II and Aristobulus II through Hyrcanus's daughter Alexandra and Aristobulus's son Alexander. As the only granddaughter of the two sons of Alexander Jannaeus, Herod's marriage to her in 37 BCE was a powerful signal that he was claiming the position of Hasmonean heir, especially since Hyrcanus had no sons. Once Herod had married Mariamme, his war against Aristobulus II's other son, Mattathias Antigonus, became a civil war for control of the Hasmonean family and thus the kingdom that this family legitimately ruled.

Herod's marriage to Mariamme may have been a political godsend for him, but the relationship itself was tempestuous and turbulent from the beginning. Josephus claims that Herod was madly in love with his wife, but this passion, if it existed and was not the invention of a dramatic narrator,

---

Cohen persuasively argues, it does not reflect the opinion of all Jews in the first century BCE. For a discussion of the authenticity of Herod's Jewish identity, see Shaye J. D. Cohen, *The Beginnings of Jewishness* (Berkeley: University of California Press, 1999), 13-24. Cf. Monika Bernett, *Der Kaiserkult in Judäa unter den Herodiern und Römern. Untersuchungen zur politischen und religiösen Geschichte Judäas von 30 v. bis 66 n. Chr.* (Tübingen: Mohr, 2007), 43-47, where she agrees with Cohen on Herod's membership in the Jewish community. For a brief overview of Herod's Hasmonean connection, specifically his link with Alexander Jannaeus, see Samuel Rocca, *Herod's Judaea: A Mediterranean State in the Classical World* (Tübingen: Mohr, 2008), 34-35. I will take up a number of the issues raised by Rocca and elaborate on them in greater detail below. For an abbreviated version of my conclusions, see Adam Kolman Marshak, "Glorifying the Present through the Past: Herod the Great and His Jewish Royal Predecessors," in *Christian Origins and Hellenistic Judaism: Social and Literary Contexts for the New Testament*, ed. Stanley E. Porter and Andrew W. Pitts (Leiden: Brill, 2012), 51-65.

soon turned to paranoia and jealousy, especially when Mariamme began to disdain her husband and his family as little more than presumptuous upstarts. In addition to this disdain and conflict with her Idumaean in-laws, Mariamme may also have been involved in various conspiracies against her husband. Regardless of her guilt, he suspected her and ultimately ordered her arrest and execution in 29 BCE. It is noteworthy, however, that Herod did not order her death until Octavian had confirmed him as king in 30 BCE after most major members of the Hasmonean family were dead. One interpretation, therefore, is that he used his marriage for political gain. When he achieved his goal, he no longer needed his wife. Indeed, in many ways, she had already served her usefulness since she had given him access to the Hasmonean name and, perhaps most importantly, Hasmonean children with whom he could construct a united Hasmonean/Herodian dynasty.[2]

These children by Mariamme had a distinct advantage over their father in the right to succession. Unlike Herod, his sons Alexander and Aristobulus (born ca. 36-35 BCE) could reasonably claim Hasmonean blood and thus both royal and high priestly legitimacy. Herod actively advertised this dynastic claim through the names he chose for his sons. Alexander recalled Alexander the Great, perhaps the most famous and idolized king and conqueror of the ancient world. More immediately it also evoked Alexander the father of Mariamme and King Alexander Jannaeus. Jannaeus had ruled Judaea for almost thirty years (103-76 BCE), and, although he had died forty years earlier, his memory still loomed large. He had been king when Judaea reached its greatest territorial expansion. His coins are the most numerous and widespread of all Jewish coinage and were still in circulation during the reign of Hyrcanus II and possibly into Herod's

---

2. For Herod's betrothal to Mariamme see *BJ* 1.241; *AJ* 14.300. For Mariamme's distinguished pedigree see *BJ* 1.241, 344, 432; *AJ* 14.467. As an additional bind between his family and the Hasmoneans, Herod married his brother Pheroras to Mariamme's sister. Citing Josephus (*BJ* 1.483), Kokkinos suggests that the marriage must have occurred after Herod's conquest of Jerusalem in 37 BCE but before the execution of Costobar in 26. See Nikos Kokkinos, *The Herodian Dynasty: Origins, Roles in Society and Eclipse* (rev. ed.; London: Spink, 2010), 164-66. Cf. Bernett, *Kaiserkult,* 42. For Mariamme's arrest and execution, see *BJ* 1.436-44; *AJ* 15.65-87, 202-36. For Josephus's (and possibly Nicolaus's) assessment of Mariamme's character, see *AJ* 15.237-39. In her article "Josephus and Nicolaus on Women" (In Tal Ilan, *Integrating Women into Second Temple History* [Tübingen: Mohr, 1999], 105-24), Ilan argues that the portrayal of Mariamme in Josephus's texts is taken directly from Nicolaus, who depicted her as a tragic heroine who fell prey to the wiles of Alexandra and the even more wicked Salome. While I find Ilan's hypothesis rather persuasive, it does not change the fact that Herod did execute her, and it seems likely that he did so because he feared her plotting.

reign as well. The name Aristobulus also resonated with royal Judaean symbolism. In particular, it was the name of three Hasmoneans, most notably Aristobulus I and II. Aristobulus I was the first Hasmonean to claim the title of king, and Aristobulus II was the grandfather of Mariamme and rival to Hyrcanus II.[3]

From a symbolic perspective, Herod had linked his sons and by extension himself with the Hasmoneans as their rightful successors and the progenitor of a legitimate Hasmonean/Herodian royalty. He had also appropriated the popular following and authority of this family. To this end, he relied on popular sentiment surrounding them and hoped that if his subjects did not see him as legitimate they would at least see his sons as such. It is true that Herod ultimately executed Alexander and Aristobulus. Nevertheless, we must remember that in the early years of his reign, nobody could have predicted such an internecine tragedy. Indeed, his hopes for dynastic succession fell squarely on the sons of Mariamme and their Hasmonean and Roman relationships.[4]

---

3. For Aristobulus I claiming the throne of Judaea, see *BJ* 1.70; *AJ* 13.301. For the career of Aristobulus II, see *BJ* 1.109, 117-84; *AJ* 13.407, 416-18, 422-29, 14.4-124. For Josephus's account of Jannaeus's reign, see *BJ* 1.85-106; *AJ* 320-404. For the coins of Jannaeus, see Meshorer, *TJC*, 37-42, 45-46, 209-17, plates 25-39. Meshorer argues that the coins of groups S and T were struck by John Hyrcanus II, whose Hebrew name, Meshorer believes, was Yonatan as opposed to Yehonatan (Alexander Jannaeus). See Meshorer, *TJC*, 26-27, 45-46. Although this theory is interesting, no conclusive evidence exists to support it, and it remains merely conjecture.

4. For a detailed analysis of Herod's dynastic plan, which rested on his identity as a Jewish king and thus required succession by one or more of his sons, see Rocca, *Herod's Judaea*, 78-82. See esp. pp. 80-82 for the planned succession of the sons of Mariamme and their crucial status as members of both a royal family (Herodian) and a high priestly family (Hasmonean). Peter Richardson claims that initially Herod named his older son Alexander as heir at first, even though he also trained his younger son Aristobulus to be a king as well. Unfortunately, there is no conclusive evidence to support Richardson's claim, and it must remain no more than a speculation. See Richardson, *Herod: King of the Jews and Friend of the Romans* (Columbia: University of South Carolina Press, 1996), 34. For a discussion of the popular support enjoyed by the Hasmoneans in the late first century BCE see Gedalyahu Alon, *Jews, Judaism, and the Classical World: Studies in Jewish History in the Times of the Second Temple and Talmud*, trans. Israel Abrahams (Jerusalem: Magnes, 1977), 1-15. Cf. Martin Goodman, *The Ruling Class of Judaea: The Origins of the Jewish Revolt* AD 66-70 (Cambridge: Cambridge University Press, 1987), 121. Additionally, several factors illustrate the high level of support for the Hasmonean family: (1) the continued status and prestige of Hyrcanus II in Judaea even though he was mutilated and living in exile in Babylon (*AJ* 15.5); (2) continued Judaean and Diaspora celebration of Hanukkah, the festival commemorating the Hasmonean purification of the Temple and seizure of power (2 Macc 1–2:18); (3) the

And yet, while Mariamme and her children may have been the keystone in Herod's construction of a Hasmonean identity, his connection to other members of the family was also vital, in particular his relationship with Hyrcanus II. First of all, as we have already discussed, Herod rose to prominence through the benevolence and patronage of the aging Hyrcanus. However, the old man's usefulness persisted even after the Parthians' invasion and capture of Hyrcanus. Once the war ended, the Parthians allowed Hyrcanus to return to Judaea, and Herod enthusiastically welcomed him back, ostensibly to share power (as we will see, such a scheme was furthest from Herod's mind). Bringing the old man back from exile would have been an extremely magnanimous gesture with little to no cost. In the first place, Hyrcanus's acceptance of the offer would necessitate his subordination and loyalty to his new patron as well as his approval for the new regime.

At the same time, Hyrcanus was no real threat to the new ruler. Having been mutilated by the Parthians and their ally Antigonus, Hyrcanus could not return to his former position as high priest. He could have tried to reclaim his other former position of ethnarch. However, since the Romans had given him this title, it would have been difficult, if not impossible, for him to recover it without their support, and it seems unlikely that they would have transferred their backing from a young, vibrant, and extremely loyal prince to an old and weakened one. Additionally, even with Roman support, without the high priesthood it would have been difficult for Hyrcanus to claim the ethnarchy. While Herod claimed his throne by right of conquest and foreign alliance, the Hasmoneans had always based their kingship and rule on their occupation of the high priesthood. Without this honor, Hyrcanus had no power base from which he could have attempted to regain his former influence and authority.

---

difficulty Herod experienced in conquering and pacifying Judaea. The campaign against Mattathias Antigonus took three years and bankrupted Herod. Surely if the Hasmoneans, and Antigonus in particular, had no popular following, Herod's campaign would have been much simpler. For the campaign, see *BJ* 1.264-357; *AJ* 14.352-491. For Herod's financial difficulties, see *AJ* 14.378, where Josephus mentions that Herod donated money to Rhodes even though he was in need of money. See also *BJ* 1.358, where Josephus states that Herod had little money left over after he took Jerusalem. Moreover, Josephus cites Strabo as claiming that the Judaeans were especially attached to Antigonus and his family (*AJ* 15.8-10). Also, (4) Aristobulus III's threat to Herod precisely because he was the only male Hasmonean remaining and was immensely popular (*BJ* 1.437; *AJ* 15.50-56); (5) Herod's efforts to be seen as a quasi-Hasmonean; and (6) Josephus's own appeal to his familial connections to the Hasmonean family (*Vita* 2-6), which suggests remaining nostalgic affection for the dynasty even a hundred years after the demise of the last Hasmonean.

As such, the old and now mutilated former ruler, who had survived both his own and others' civil wars, returned to Judaea at the bequest of the man who had replaced him to live in relative comfort, albeit political irrelevance. However, like so many of his family, he soon found himself on the wrong side of the new king's anxiety and insecurity. Having backed the loser at Actium, Herod no doubt felt that there was a chance, however unlikely, that the new ruler of the Mediterranean would replace him with another candidate, and the Caesarian former high priest was certainly a potential option. Therefore, before setting out for Rhodes to meet Octavian, Herod discovered Hyrcanus's plot to flee to the Nabataeans. He arrested him on charges of treason and ordered his execution.[5]

Another Hasmonean whom Herod used and then ruthlessly eliminated was Mariamme's brother Aristobulus III, who was only a young man when Herod became king in 37 BCE. Nevertheless, Herod appointed him high priest to succeed Hananel the Babylonian, whom he had appointed to succeed Hyrcanus in the priesthood. His hope must have been that the appointment of his brother-in-law would ease any tension resulting from his coup and perhaps appease those who had supported his rival Antigonus but were willing to be reconciled to the new political reality. Like his decision to invite Hyrcanus back to Judaea, this appointment at first seemed to come with no real cost. Aristobulus was a young and impressionable man, and Herod probably thought he could control him.

Unfortunately, Aristobulus's popularity became a significant threat during the Feast of Tabernacles in 35 BCE, when the crowd responded positively to his offering of the sacrifice. Even more alarmingly for the usurper Idumaean, the crowd focused on the youth's regal appearance and Hasmonean bloodlines. Fearing competition and internal strife so soon

---

5. For Herod's invitation to Hyrcanus to return and share power with him, see *BJ* 1.433-34; *AJ* 14.365-66; 15.11-22. Cf. Bernett, *Kaiserkult*, 43-44. For Hyrcanus's possession of the title ethnarch as evidenced by the various decrees and letters that Josephus quotes, see *AJ* 14.148, 151, 191, 196, 200, 226, 306. On the other hand, all these decrees and letters also describe him as the high priest of the Jews. Further, Josephus states that Pompey and Caesar confirmed Hyrcanus as high priest, but no mention is made of also appointing him ethnarch. See *BJ* 1.153, 194; *AJ* 14.73, 143. The Jews themselves, however, seem to have called him king (*AJ* 14.157, 172). The evidence suggests that Hyrcanus first inherited the titles of king and high priest that his father Alexander Jannaeus had held. After Pompey's settlement in 63 BCE, Hyrcanus was only high priest, even though his subjects still referred to him as king. This choice is hardly surprising given the high priest's political role as chief magistrate. After defeating Pompey, Julius Caesar confirmed Hyrcanus as high priest and added the office of ethnarch. For the execution of Hyrcanus II, see *BJ* 1.433-34; *AJ* 15.161-78.

after his conquest had been completed, Herod decided that he needed to eliminate his rival as soon as possible. After the festival, he invited him to the palace at Jericho and there had him drowned in the swimming pool. He then reappointed Hananel high priest, and never again appointed another high priest who could rival him for power or influence.[6]

Were marriage, family, and naming patterns really enough to transform Herod from a non-royal Idumaean usurper into a legitimate Hasmonean king, especially when he so violently discarded these familial ties? By themselves, probably not. However, these maneuvers were but part of a larger plan to smooth the transition of power. Architecture and other aspects of his self-presentation were equally important, and in these areas, as in his family planning, Herod was careful to emphasize continuity rather than change.

Herod's Architecture and the Hasmoneans

Of all of the aspects of Herod's reign, none has captured more scholarly attention or popular interest than his architecture. Indeed, the number of articles, monographs, and documentaries concerned with Herod's building program dwarfs any other subject in Herodian scholarship. This interest dates back to antiquity. Josephus devotes an extended passage in *Jewish War* to the building program. Even the rabbis marveled at the splendor of his architectural creations, asserting emphatically "He who has not seen the Temple of Herod has never seen a beautiful building" (*b. Bava Batra* 4a).

Desert Fortresses and Palaces

While the renovation of the Temple and the construction of Caesarea Maritima are far more famous, in his early reign Herod was more concerned

---

6. For the appointment of Hananel as high priest, see *AJ* 15.22. Herod must have known that the Judaeans would never have accepted him if he had tried to claim the high priesthood. For Herod's deposition of Hananel and appointment of Aristobulus as high priest, see *BJ* 1.437; *AJ* 15.31-40. *BJ* offers no reason that Herod appointed Aristobulus high priest, but *AJ* states that he did so to appease his wife and mother-in-law. Josephus claims that Herod appointed Hananel the Babylonian because he wanted to avoid giving the high priesthood to somebody who could be a political threat to him. For Hananel's reappointment after the death of Aristobulus, see *AJ* 15.56. For a discussion of the advantages for Herod of appointing non-Judaean high priests, see Goodman, *Ruling Class,* 29-50.

with strengthening his hold over the country and asserting continuity with the previous dynasty. To achieve these goals, he initially focused on a string of desert fortresses and fortified palaces, many built on existing foundations. Although Herod had a far more extensive building program, the Hasmoneans had been active builders in Judaea at least since the time of Jannaeus. Besides constructing several desert fortresses, they also renovated parts of the Temple Mount and constructed a fortress adjacent to the Temple. Herod thus had a model of building activity that he could follow and even some sites that already had structures on them. As we will see, he took this model and extended it greatly in terms of both quantity of sites and architectural innovation. These fortresses, built high atop rocky plateaus, dominated the surrounding plains and valleys while simultaneously offering strategic places of refuge in times of trouble. While these fortresses were the bulk of Herod's early constructions, he also commissioned a few large original palaces. In both cases, we can see clear attempts to evoke continuity with the Hasmoneans through architectural design and details.[7]

The heartland of the Judaean kingdom, specifically Jerusalem and the coastal cities, flank the western end of the Jordan Valley and the Dead Sea. This buffer zone is extremely dry, desolate, and mountainous. However, these same conditions provided several isolated hilltops and plateaus on which to construct a string of structures which merged defensive walls and palatial wings into palace fortresses. These hybrid outposts served a variety of functions including securing the kingdom's border against neighboring nations, controlling commercial traffic arteries, storing royal valuables, imprisoning important political enemies, and, perhaps most importantly,

---

7. For detailed discussions of the individual desert fortresses, see Adam Kolman Marshak, "Herod the Great and the Power of Image: Political Self-Presentation in the Herodian Dynasty" (Ph.D. diss., Yale University, 2008), 192-203. In *Herod's Judaea*, 153-90, Rocca analyzes the entire network of Herodian defensive fortifications and divides them into separate categories including (1) fortified cities, (2) the city acropolis and the tetrapyrgia, (3) static defense, and (4) military colonies. He also divides the construction of these fortifications into three phases. During the first phase (37-31 BCE), Herod concentrated mainly on rebuilding Hasmonean fortifications that had been destroyed in past wars. His primary defensive concerns were the Parthians, Cleopatra, and the Nabataeans. In the second stage (31-10 BCE) he moved beyond restoration and into dramatic modification. During this stage, his main defensive concerns still included the Parthians, but no longer Cleopatra. The Nabataeans were still a threat and, indeed, seem to have been Herod's primary concern. The final stage (10-4 BCE) is marked by a slow completion of the projects that Herod had undertaken during the second stage. See Rocca, *Herod's Judaea* 158-59.

providing safe havens of refuge in times of crisis and internal turmoil. We even have evidence that some of these sites functioned as cemeteries for members of the royal family who had fallen afoul of the monarch. Because of their location in the middle of desert, each of these fortresses possessed a sophisticated system of water collection that trapped and gathered runoff flowing down adjacent hills and mountains. Running from north to south, this system of palace fortresses included Alexandrion, Doq/Dagon, Cypros, Hyrcania, Machaerus, and, most famously, Masada.

Most of these fortresses were begun under the Hasmoneans, specifically John Hyrcanus and Alexander Jannaeus, and survived the civil war mostly intact. But Herod was not content simply to rebuild the walls and add a new coat of plaster. Instead, he substantially refurbished the defenses and embellished the amenities by adding pools, peristyles, reception rooms, and baths. He transformed these simple fortresses into lavish and luxurious fortified palaces. The strategic value of these fortresses — both their ability to guard the nearby region and their defensibility in times of crisis — is obvious and was probably the major reason for the renovations. But, while modernization of defenses was the first priority, the king's orders also included a significant enhancement of the living quarters to be more suitable for royal visitors and other important guests.

Perhaps most interestingly, he made no move to rename the fortresses. In the ancient world, naming was a vivid way of making political statements. As we see in Herod's later reign, he consciously used the renaming of cities to honor important individuals such as Augustus, Agrippa, and members of the Herodian family such as his brother Phasael, his father Antipater, and his mother Cypros. Herod's decision not to change the names of the fortresses Hyrcania (named for Hyrcanus I) and Alexandrion (named for Alexander Jannaeus) suggests a desire to honor these Hasmoneans and connect himself to them as their legitimate successor.

Who would have seen these structures and to whom was this architectural presentation directed? Fortresses such as Alexandrion were located on hilltops at the edge of the desert. However, Alexandrion was also in sight of the Jericho to Samaria road that ran along the Jordan valley below the fortress. Travelers along the road would have seen the fortress with its impressive monumental walls, high towers, and extensive water transportation facilities. These fortresses, looming over the valleys below, would have reminded passersby of the power and strength of the mighty king who built them. More importantly perhaps, the traveler would have seen in these fortresses an architectural continuity with Hasmonean building traditions. Finally, through their use as a line of strategic outposts, these citadels would also have reinforced royal control over the kingdom and discouraged most from resisting such control.

And yet, while we cannot disregard the effect these fortresses might have had on the average traveler, the more important audience must have been Herod's own court. He clearly updated these desert fortresses to house the royal court, and it is certainly possible that, while traveling to and from Samaria, he and his retinue would stop at some of these fortress palaces. The members of his court, therefore, would have been able to see the architecture up close, and from this view it would have been even more impressive. The massive walls and imposing fortifications would have reiterated to them the scale of the king's power and the extent of his control over his kingdom. Additionally, from their vantage point both from outside and inside the fortresses these courtiers would have had a unique opportunity to appreciate the architectural symbolism and continuity for which Herod was aiming. Having survived the recent civil war and thus having been part of the Hasmonean court of Hyrcanus II, they would have seen the new and impressive Herodian fortifications rising above what they previously had known as Hasmonean sites. And yet, these new structures looked Hasmonean in style and appearance, even if they had received substantial improvements. In essence, the political reality of Judaea, the outcome of the recent war, was visible in mortar and stone. Herod had conquered and defeated the Hasmoneans, and now his buildings were also victorious. Moreover, just as his buildings incorporated and succeeded their predecessors, so too was he was a rightful member of and successor to the preceding dynasty, albeit a more powerful and successful one.[8]

It is worth focusing our attention on two early sites, Masada and Jericho, both because their renovations involved significant original con-

---

8. For Josephus's commentary on Herod's building program, see *BJ* 1.401-21. For the rabbis' appreciation of it, see *b. Bava Batra* 4a, *b. Sukkah* 51b. For Herod's use of the desert fortresses as a secure place to store royal treasure, see *BJ* 1.528; *AJ* 13.417; 16.317. Salome Alexandra had also used the fortresses for such purposes. For the symbolic importance of physical reminders of royal power, see Clifford Geertz, "Centers, Kings, and Charisma: Reflections on the Symbolics of Power," in *Local Knowledge: Further Essays in Interpretive Anthropology* (3rd ed.; New York: Basic, 2000) 125. Geertz particularly stresses the importance of "the ceremonial forms by which kings take symbolic possession of their realm. In particular, royal progresses (of which, where it exists, coronation is but the first) locate the society's center and affirm its connection with transcendent things by stamping a territory with ritual signs of dominance."

struction and because they highlight the process described above in which Herod upgraded Hasmonean sites but was careful not to deviate too much from their architectural models. It is altogether fitting that we begin with Masada. No other site except perhaps the Temple Mount has captured so many people's attention and received so many visitors. Its symbolic importance continued long after the first century, even up to the modern period, when it became a symbol of aspirations and resolve first in Yitzhak Lamden's poem "Masada" and then later when Israel army recruits swore their oath of allegiance atop the mountain. According to Josephus, Jonathan Maccabaeus built the first structures at Masada, but most modern scholars disagree, and Herod is usually credited with the first substantial fortifications of the plateau. Most important for our purposes, however, is the strong architectural similarity that Herod's new structures atop the plateau bore toward earlier models. In particular, they closely resembled older Hasmonean palaces, especially the building style of the Twin Palaces at Jericho. Indeed, the nucleus of the Western Palace at Masada so strongly resembles the Twin Palaces that excavators, such as Ehud Netzer, once believed that the Hasmoneans had constructed some of the buildings on Masada.

What are these similarities? The nucleus of the Western Palace and that of the Twin Palaces at Jericho share a similar layout with a central interior courtyard, which lacks flanking colonnades, and an open *triclinium* (dining room) at the courtyard's southern end. The *triclinium* in both cases was accessed via an entranceway with two columns in front *(distylē in antis)*. Both complexes also make use of a main entrance with benches as well as a side entrance. At the northern end of each palace site is a service block and smaller rooms. Both sites also have bathhouses that contain an entrance, which also functioned as a dressing room, a bathroom, which was entered via a narrow corridor and through a narrow, low doorway with arched lintels, and a bathtub. Each of these bathrooms also has a stepped pool, which may have been used as a *mikveh,* and a sort of built-in chair in the bathroom. Even some of their wall decorations are similar. For example, both buildings have triangular niches for oil lamps and red-painted decorative grooves in the wall plaster about six feet above the floor. Finally, both employ a similar system of pilasters (rectangular half columns) on the ground floor to support the walls of an upper floor. Three other palace structures at Masada (buildings 11-13) have a similar layout as the Western Palace. They also were built around an inner courtyard with an open reception room accessed via a *distylē in antis* portico. Because of this similar

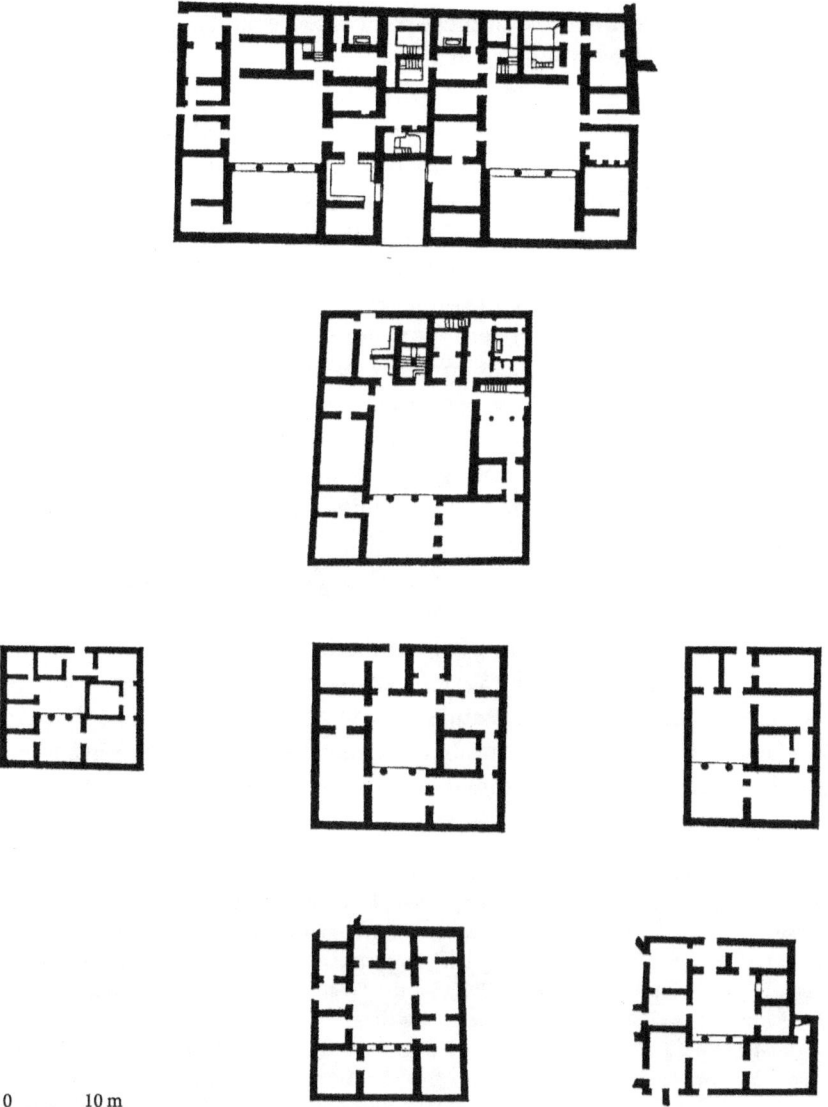

Comparison of Hasmonean and Herodian palaces
Herod's earliest palaces share several architectural features with their Hasmonean predecessors. As a result, they would have looked "Hasmonean." The Hasmonean Twin Palaces at Jericho (top), the core of the Herodian Western Palace at Masada, and five smaller associated buildings at Masada, including the guards' wing of the Western Palace.

layout, excavators believe that these palaces were built at the same time as the Western Palace (around 35 BCE).⁹

Herod's first palace in Jericho, which he built around 35 BCE, also has architectural features that look Hasmonean. The palace itself is a rectangular building (285 × 150 feet), which is built around a central peristyle courtyard and includes two interior bathing complexes. The bathing complex located east of the entrance room, which may have served as a ritual bath, looks remarkably similar to some of the *mikva'ot* in the Hasmonean palaces nearby. It is also the only *mikveh* found in a Herodian palace that contains an *'oṣar* (storage cistern for water).

Each of these palaces was constructed in a similar manner and displays similar architectural features. However, those similarities alone do not prove that Herod was mimicking the Hasmoneans. Both he and they may very well have been imitating somebody else. It is certainly true that Hasmonean palaces contained several elements adopted from typical Hellenistic royal architecture, such as the use of open and central peristyle courtyards with abutting rooms all around. Furthermore, like other royal examples of the late Hellenistic period, Hasmonean palaces contained multiple wings, open spaces, pools, and gardens to form a complex that integrated in one area all the various spatial needs of the king — administrative, ceremonial, leisure, and residential. They also made full use of impressive and dramatic natural landscapes to highlight their grandeur, a feature that would be expanded on and elevated in Roman architecture

---

9. For Josephus's attribution of the foundation of Masada to Jonathan Maccabee see *BJ* 7.285. For Netzer's discussion of the original Hasmonean settlement at Masada, which consisted of a garrison living in tents, see Joseph Aviram, Gideon Foerster, and Ehud Netzer, *Masada* 3: *The Buildings: Stratigraphy and Architecture* (Jerusalem: Israel Exploration Society, 1991), 615-23. For his initial belief that the Western Palace was Hasmonean see his *The Palaces of the Hasmoneans and Herod the Great* (Jerusalem: Yad Ben-Zvi, 2001), 80; *Masada* 3:646-49. For his analysis of the Twin Palaces, see his *Hasmonean and Herodian Palaces at Jericho: Final Reports of the 1973-1987 Excavations* (Jerusalem: Israel Exploration Society, 2001), 1:310-11. See also *Palaces,* 87; Achim Lichtenberger, *Die Baupolitik Herodes des Grossen* (Wiesbaden: Harrassowitz, 1999), 23-24. The relevant pilasters were found in the northwestern corner of the western mansion of the Twin Palaces, the northeastern corner of the eastern mansion (the kitchen), and in two rooms that were part of and adjacent to the bathhouse in the Western Palace at Masada. For the site reports on the Western Palace at Masada, especially the core of the palace, see *Masada* 3:235-63. For those on Buildings 11-13, see *Masada* 3:319-59, 599-604. Cf. Netzer, *Palaces,* 85-87; Sarah Japp, *Die Baupolitik Herodes des Grossen. Die Bedeutung der Architektur für die Herrschaftslegitimation eines Römischen Klientelkönigs* (Rahden: Leidorf, 2000), 144.

in both the late Republican and imperial periods. Herod's palaces took all these elements to a new level of creativity and brilliance, but ultimately they originated in Hellenistic royal architecture.[10]

However, since the Hasmoneans were the local ruling dynasty, the Judaean audience would have associated such architecture with the Hasmoneans rather than with some distant Hellenistic monarch. While determining the precise Hellenistic antecedents of Herodian palace architecture is perhaps an interesting project, what is more important is that the buildings looked Hasmonean to a local audience.

It is certainly possible, and perhaps even probable, that the architects who constructed the Western Palace and other early buildings had previously served in the Hasmonean court, thus partly explaining the architectural similarities. Nevertheless, we cannot entirely rule out Herod's own desire to connect himself visually to the Hasmoneans by building similar palaces. Architecture is a reflection of culture and taste, and a king, even one who is not entirely secure on his throne, can choose to design his palaces in a number of ways. While individual architectural similarities may not articulate political statements by themselves, Herod's choice to construct his first palaces at Masada and Jericho in such a way that they looked Hasmonean speaks to his desire to link himself visually with the Hasmoneans. These similarities in design make sense if we remember that Herod was still married to Mariamme and still sought to associate himself with the Hasmoneans at the time these palaces were constructed (mid 30s BCE). In 36 BCE, Antony gave Cleopatra control of Jaffa and the Plain of Jericho. Herod in turn leased the land and its estates from her. It is likely that he did not want to lose the potential wealth of Jericho, but an additional motivation might have been his desire to have a palace on the Jericho plain near the Hasmonean winter palaces. This possibility is

10. For analysis of the first Herodian palace at Jericho, especially the similarities between it and earlier Hasmonean palaces, see James B. Pritchard, "The Excavations at Herodian Jericho, 1951," *Annual of the American Schools of Oriental Research* 32-33 (1958): 1-13, 56-58; Netzer, *Palaces*, 40-42, 58. Cf. Netzer, *Hasmonean and Herodian Palaces at Jericho* 1:332, 338-39; *Palaces*, 40-42; Lichtenberger, *Baupolitik*, 59-60; Japp, *Baupolitik*, 121. Pritchard mistakenly identified the First Palace as a gymnasium. Subsequent work on the nearby palaces and comparisons with other Herodian and Hasmonean palaces has confirmed that this structure was indeed an early Herodian palace. For a discussion of the stylistic antecedents drawn from late Hellenistic royal architecture, see Inge Nielson, *Hellenistic Palaces: Tradition and Renewal* (Aarhus: Aarhus University Press, 1995), 14, 187. Cf. Rocca, *Herod's Judaea*, 106; Eyal Regev, "Inside Herod's Courts: Social Relations and Royal Ideology in the Herodian Palaces," *JSJ* 43 (2012): 185-87.

strengthened by the location of his first palace in the vicinity of the older Hasmonean complexes. Such a location suggests a desire to connect himself architecturally with the Hasmoneans. Visitors to Jericho would have seen the two complexes near each other and could visually connect Herod with his in-laws.

Building in Honor of Mariamme: A Tower and Possibly a City

The architectural similarities between the Herodian desert fortresses and their older counterparts were a subtle yet powerful statement of familial ties, but Herod did not stop there. He also made more explicit architectural statements, such as naming a prominent building in his capital after his Hasmonean wife Mariamme.[11] This building, a prominent tower on the Jerusalem skyline, was one of three towers built to protect the western side of the city of Jerusalem and Herod's palace in the Upper City. According to Josephus the king named the three towers Phasael, Hippicus, and Mariamme, for three individuals of whom he was exceedingly fond, his brother, his friend Hippicus, and his wife. Josephus states that the Tower of Mariamme was a square, multi-level tower and was more magnificent and luxurious than the others because Herod thought that a tower named after his wife should be more beautiful than one named after a man. With this prominent tower, Herod made a powerful public statement of his affection for his wife and reiterated his connection with her and thus with the Hasmonean family.

Herod may also have built a city in Ituraea and named it after his wife. According to Nikos Kokkinos, eighteen miles west-northwest of Homs, Syria, is a village called *Mrymyn* (Marjamīn or Mariamin), which was known in antiquity as *Mariamme*. Such a female name in a Syrian context is surprising, especially given its almost exclusive use within Jewish culture as the name Miriam. Kokkinos argues that this city might be named after the Hasmonean queen Mariamme. While his hypothesis remains speculative, circumstantial evidence suggests that it is at least possible.

We know that Herod had strong, friendly connections with the elites of Syria dating back to his tenure as *stratēgos* of Galilee when he defeated

---

11. As far as we know, the Hasmoneans did not have a habit of naming buildings after relatives or friends. The only two Hasmonean structures clearly named after individuals are Hyrcania (for John Hyrcanus I) and Alexandrion (for Alexander Jannaeus).

the brigands ravaging the Syrian frontier. When he became king, his influence in this neighboring region would have only increased. Further, we also know that he was an active benefactor in the region, and such activities would have increased his standing among Syrian elites. According to Josephus Herod built, among other things, a gymnasium in Damascus, a colonnade and pavement of the broad street in Antioch, a gymnasium in Ptolemais, marketplaces in Tyre, a theater in Sidon, and a basilica in Berytus. He also seems to have lightened the tax burden for the inhabitants of Balanaea, which belonged to the same region as Mariamme. It is possible that his euergetism resulted in a local commemoration in honor of him such as naming a town after his wife.

It is also possible that Herod owned the land that became the city of Mariamme, and thus a renaming would have a more personal flavor to it. We know that Hyrcanus II owned estates in Syria and Phoenicia, which no doubt passed to Herod, either when he became king in 40 BCE or when he executed Hyrcanus in 30. Further, he might have acquired lands either by purchasing them or by receiving them from wealthy friends and minor dynasts. Josephus indicates that Herod donated groves and meadows and made other types of land grants to many foreign cities, and it is possible that the area that later became the town of Mariamme was one such donation. If so, the town must have been named before 29 BCE, the year Herod executed Mariamme.

Although the evidence for this identification must remain somewhat speculative, it would fit well into Herod's pattern of founding cities and naming them after individuals important to him. In his later years, he renamed a number of cities after members of his family, including Antipatros and Phasaelis. More importantly, he named two cities after Augustus and one, Agrippias, after Marcus Agrippa. If Herod did indeed build and name a city in honor of his Hasmonean wife, it may have been another attempt to both honor his wife and highlight his Hasmonean credentials through his connection to her.[12]

---

12. For Herod's renaming of cities after his family, see *BJ* 1.417-18; *AJ* 16.142-45. For Herod's renaming of cities after Augustus and Agrippa, see *BJ* 1.416; *AJ* 13.357. This practice of naming cities after important individuals was extremely common among Hellenistic kings, and it is likely that Herod was influenced directly by their practices. See p. 15 above. For Hyrcanus's ownership of estates in Syria and Phoenicia, see *AJ* 14.209. For Kokkinos's hypothesis and analysis see Nikos Kokkinos, "The City of 'Mariamme': An Unknown Herodian Connection?" *MedAnt* 5 (2002): 715-46. For Josephus's description of the Tower of Mariamme see *BJ* 5.161-62, 170-75. For scholarly discussion of the towers, see Lichtenberger, *Baupolitik*, 93-95; Netzer, *Palaces*, 127-28. Also see pp. 256-57 below.

Thus, we have a multitude of early building projects designed to reference the previous dynasty, either implicitly or explicitly. Combined with his matrimonial and familial maneuverings, these early building projects suggest Herod was drawing on his connections, real or argued, with the Hasmonean dynasty. His numismatic program provides further evidence that this connection was a conscious move, and thus we should now examine his early coins in greater detail.

Herod's Coins and the Hasmonean Family

As we have already discussed, ancient coinage was an extremely useful medium for spreading political messages, because of its ability to be disseminated widely and to reach multiple audiences of all socioeconomic levels. The use of coins to articulate public policy and political presentation is a feature of Jewish coinage from the Hasmoneans until Agrippa II. For example, as mentioned earlier, the Hasmoneans used an archaic paleo-Hebrew script on their coins to recall the glories of the monarchic period and to associate the Hasmoneans with the kings of the Jewish royal past. The Herodians acted similarly, striking coins to advertise important events such as the founding of the city of Tiberias ca. 20 CE, Agrippa I's signing of a treaty with the emperor Claudius, and Agrippa II's promotion to kingship in 67/68 CE.

Dating and Interpretation of the Inscription-Anchor Coins

Was Herod using his coins to evoke a connection to his predecessors? To prove such an intention, we must first establish the relative dating of his coins and then focus on those coins, which represent the period or periods in which Herod was actively promoting his Hasmonean credentials. The coins that offer the best avenue of investigation for Herod's early reign are those with an inscription on the obverse (heads) side and an anchor on the reverse (tails). These coins are part of a larger group of Herodian coins known to numismatists as the "undated coin issues" because they lack a specific marking indicating their date of minting. For simplicity's sake, I will refer to these coins as the inscription-anchor coins. I believe that they were struck in the early part of Herod's reign and that they primarily, but not exclusively, advertise his connection to the Hasmoneans. To prove this theory, we must first show that these coins are, in fact, from this early period.

In a series of articles, Donald T. Ariel of the Israeli Antiquities Authority has established a relative chronology for the Herodian undated coin issues in which he argues that the inscription-anchor coins are the second (*TJC* 60) and third (*TJC* 61-64) issues of the undated coins, following the diadem-table series. In addition to a relative chronology, he also proposes a few possible absolute dates for the various coin types of this group. In the past, scholars have associated the inscription-anchor coins with the construction and inauguration of Caesarea Maritima. Ariel suggests two other possibilities, first, that these coins might be associated with Herod's annexation of the coastal ports of Gaza, Anthedon, Joppa, and Strato's Tower (the future Caesarea Maritima). These coins' status as some of Herod's earliest coin issues support such a theory. If these coins were struck in 30 BCE, we can use them as evidence for our assessment of Herod's political self-presentation at this crucial moment in his reign. The other possibility is that they were minted in 27-24 BCE when Herod was engaged in extensive economic activity, including establishing a city (Samaria/Sebaste) as well as famine and plague relief. If this date is correct, there was a break in minting following the execution of Mariamme in late 30/29 BCE with a resumption soon thereafter. Until further evidence materializes, I am inclined to defer to Ariel on the absolute dating, and thus we can assign a minting for this series in the years from 27-24 BCE. As we will see in the next chapter, the earliest of these issues would be contemporary with the dated coins from Samaria/Sebaste.[13]

Turning to the images on the coin type, we see that Herod used these

---

13. The first issue of undated coins, the diadem-table series, was struck in 30 BCE. For the evolution of Ariel's relative chronology see Donald T. Ariel, "The Jerusalem Mint of Herod the Great: A Relative Chronology," *INJ* 14 (2000-2002): 99-124; "A Numismatic Approach to the Reign of Herod the Great" (Ph.D. diss., Tel-Aviv University, 2006), 337-40. Cf. Donald T. Ariel and Jean-Philippe Fontanille, *The Coins of Herod: A Modern Analysis and Die Classification* (Leiden: Brill, 2012), 174-76. For his most recent suggestion of possible dates for the inscription-anchor coins, see "Numismatic Approach," 347-51, 361. Cf. Ariel and Fontanille, *Coins of Herod,* 180-81. See "Jerusalem Mint," 123, for his earlier suggestion of 30 BCE. In this earlier article, he also proposed that this series could have commemorated the beginning of construction work at Caesarea (22 or 20 BCE). Such a suggestion seems unlikely to me given how early these coins were in Herod's overall minting program and how late the construction of Caesarea was in his reign. If the coins were from 22 or 20 BCE, we would have to assume that Herod minted few if any coin types for the first eighteen years of his reign. It is possible, but it seems unlikely.

Inscription-anchor coins of Herod the Great
Herod used the anchor on his coins to connect himself visually to his Hasmonean and Seleucid predecessors.

coins to connect himself visually with his predecessors the Hasmoneans, and specifically with Alexander Jannaeus, by using the anchor image. As we have said, the anchor had been an extremely common symbol on coins of the Hellenistic East dating back to the early years of the Seleucid dynasty. Besides a specific reference to Seleucids, the anchor also was used to advertise maritime interests, events, conquests, or simply sea power in general.

Given the role that the Seleucids played in early Hasmonean history, it is not surprising that the anchor also appeared on Hasmonean coins, specifically those of Alexander Jannaeus, who used it on about half of his coin types. The anchor is also a central image for Herod's undated issues. Seven of his nineteen undated issues (37%) have an anchor on either the obverse or the reverse, making it the single most common motif. Their specific orientations differ: Jannaeus's anchors, like the Seleucid dynastic emblem, were inverted, but Herod's were upright. Still, Herod's anchors, especially the earliest ones (*TJC* 60-64), bear a close resemblance to the anchors on Jannaeus's coins, specifically his Aramaic anchor-star coin and his anchor-lily coin (*TJC* groups L and N).[14]

14. For the Seleucid claims and the stories of Seleucus's birthmark see *OGIS* 219, 227; Diodorus 19.90.4; Justinus, *Epit.* 15.4. For Herod's anchor coins see Meshorer, *TJC,* 221-24

How are we to explain these similarities? It is possible that Herod, or his mintmasters, simply used a common numismatic symbol and that there was no attempt to allude to the Hasmoneans or to Alexander Jannaeus. Perhaps this symbol was one of only a few with which the coin die carvers felt proficient. However, it is just as likely, if not more, that Herod was consciously connecting himself to Jannaeus and the other Hasmoneans through his coinage and was using symbols that would resonate with his internal audience. We must remember that this anchor symbol was by far the most common Jannaean motif, and it is hard to believe that Judaeans would not, at the very least, have recognized Herod's anchor coins as looking like Hasmonean coins. Moreover, from the familial evidence discussed earlier, we know that Herod connected himself with the Hasmoneans, especially with Jannaeus, through his naming of his children. Therefore, it seems likely that Herod was attempting to use the coins and their symbols to assert for himself the role of legitimate successor to the Hasmoneans. He also may have been trying to make a connection with the Seleucids in a larger sense. This strategy would make sense because it was a Seleucid, Alexander Balas, who first bestowed political power and legitimacy on the Hasmoneans. Moreover, the original Hasmonean anchor coins of Jannaeus were imitations of Seleucid anchors. Through a connection to both the Hasmoneans and the Seleucids, Herod would have been strengthening the image of his legitimacy as one in a long line of rulers of Judaea.

But why was Herod connecting himself with a family whom he had recently decimated? The answer may lie in the very act of decimation. Herod had certainly murdered several prominent Hasmoneans, including

---

(coins 59-65; plates 45-46). Cf. David Hendin, *Guide to Biblical Coins* (4th ed.; New York: Amphora: 2001), 167-68 (H498-500, 502); Ya'akov Meshorer, "Maritime Symbols on Ancient Jewish Coins," *INJ* 2 (1964): 8-10. For Jacobson's discussion of the anchor on Judaean coins see David M. Jacobson, "A New Interpretation of the Reverse of Herod's Largest Coin," *ANSMN* 31 (1986): 162-63, n. 69; "The Anchor on the Coins of Judaea," *BAIAS* 18 (2000): 73-81, esp. 74. For descriptions of Jannaeus's and Herod's anchors, see Meshorer, *TJC,* plates 25-27 (Alexander) and 45-46 (Herod). For Ariel's analysis of Herod's anchor images, specifically comparison to those of Jannaeus and the Seleucids as well as their typological significance, see Ariel, "Numismatic Approach," 127-30, 141, 225-26, 327. Interestingly, the anchor coins that Ariel dates as the earliest (*TJC* 60-64) do not have a ring on the top of their anchors, like Jannaeus's anchor coins. Thus, although the orientation of the Herodian anchors differs from that of Jannaeus's anchors, they do have some iconographic similarities. Additionally, as Ariel himself admits, the nuance of orientation probably was lost on most, if not all, viewers. In essence, the anchors would have appeared Hasmonean to the average viewer.

his grandfather-in-law Hyrcanus II (30 BCE), his wife Mariamme (30/29 BCE), and his mother-in-law Alexandra (28/27 BCE). However, there were still members of the family alive, namely, his two Hasmonean-Herodian sons. Moreover, the Hasmonean family still retained a high degree of popularity and prominence. To fully break from it would have been counterproductive, especially since Herod had spent the last ten years creating a Hasmonean identity for himself. Instead, Herod doubled his efforts to depict himself as an extension and continuation of the Hasmoneans, in much the same way as Octavian depicted himself as a continuation of the Roman Republic. Herod's use of an anchor, which connected him with the Hasmoneans (and also the Seleucids), articulates a message of continuity with the past, which could have helped counterbalance his obvious and violent break from it.[15]

The Anchor-Double Cornucopia Coins: Revisiting the Hasmoneans?

Among Herod's undated coin types, none is more numerous than the anchor-double cornucopia. At first glance, this type seems to fit seamlessly into Herod's visual program of promoting himself as a Hasmonean, and indeed Meshorer proposes such a hypothesis. The two symbols on the coin, the anchor and particularly the double cornucopia, are instantly recognizable as Hasmonean. Indeed, the double cornucopia is the most common symbol on Hasmonean coinage, and Hasmoneans from John Hyrcanus I to Mattathias Antigonus used this image.

Nevertheless, the case may not be as straightforward as Meshorer supposes. Like the anchor, the double cornucopia is not unique to Judaea or Judaeans. On the contrary, it was extremely common, especially in the Levant and Egypt. It first appears on coins of Ptolemy II Philadelphus as a reverse complementing the portrait of Philadelphus's sister/wife Arsinoe II on the obverse. R. A. Hazzard even speculates that it was the

---

15. This minting date of ca. 27-24 BCE also coincides with Herod's elimination of the somewhat mysterious sons of Baba, Idumaean members of the Hasmonean family who were supporters of Antigonus and who had fled Jerusalem after his defeat (*AJ* 15.260-66). Most scholars date their execution to 26/25 BCE. With their execution, Josephus states in *AJ* 15.266, "none of the family of Hyrcanus remained alive." Although this statement is somewhat inaccurate since some Hasmoneans did in fact survive this purge, it does attest to Herod's decimation of the family. With all prominent Hasmoneans eliminated, Herod could monopolize the family name for himself and, most importantly, his sons.

Herod the New Hasmonean

Bronze anchor-double cornucopia prutah of Herod the Great
By far the most common of the undated coins, the anchor-double cornucopia
coin marked the highpoint of Herod's reign.

dynastic symbol of Arsinoe. The Ptolemies continued to use the symbol afterward, and Herod's neighbor and rival Cleopatra struck numerous coins with the double cornucopia on the reverse.[16] Herod may have been referencing the Ptolemies (a gesture to Cleopatra perhaps?), or simply using a common numismatic symbol. And yet, the Ptolemaic double cornucopia is not exactly the same image as the one that appears on Herod's coins. In particular, the Ptolemaic double cornucopia are parallel and not crossed, as appear on Hasmonean and Herodian coins. Moreover, there is no central emblem between the Ptolemaic cornucopias, as there is on both the Hasmonean and Herodian coins, a pomegranate and a caduceus (staff of Hermes) respectively. But given the similarities in specific appearance, Meshorer concludes that Herod was consciously referencing the Hasmonean double cornucopia and thus the coinage of the Hasmoneans.

Meshorer also argues that Herod was alluding to his Roman connections through use of this coin. He reaches this conclusion through an analysis of the central emblem between the crossed cornucopias. A coin issued

---

16. For Meshorer's theory on the anchor-double cornucopia type see *TJC*, 67. For a discussion of the Hasmoneans' use of the double cornucopia see *TJC*, 33-34, plates 5-24, 28-43. For Hazzard's interpretation of the double cornucopia, see R. A. Hazzard, *Imagination of a Monarchy: Studies in Ptolemaic Propaganda* (Toronto: University of Toronto Press, 2000), 93-99. For the use of the double cornucopia by the Ptolemies, especially on coins with Arsinoe II's portrait on the obverse see J. N. Svoronos, *Ta Nomismata tou Kratous ton Ptolemaion (Ptolemaic Coinage)* (Athens: Sakellariou, 1904-1908), numbers 460, 475, 938, 947, 959, 961, and 1498. For Cleopatra's double cornucopia coins see Svoronos, numbers 1160 and 1161. Numbers 1871 and 1872 in Svoronos have a double cornucopia on the reverse, but it is a smaller image to the left of the main image, an eagle. Cf. David Sear, *Roman Coins and Their Values* (4th ed.; London: Seaby, 1988), numbers 7952 and 7955.

Gold Oktadrachma of Arsinoe II
Obverse: Portrait head of Arsinoe II, lotus-tipped scepter in background, K to left. Reverse: Parallel double cornucopia with grapes hanging at the sides, *Arsinoēs Philadelphou (Of Arsinoe, Brother-lover)*. Struck during the reign of Ptolemy VI-VIII (ca. 180-116 BCE)
(courtesy of Classical Numismatic Group, Inc. www.cngcoins.com)

by Marc Antony in summer 40 BCE, the year Herod was in Rome and appointed king, has on the reverse a double cornucopia with a caduceus in the middle. Herod, Meshorer argues, used a similar image to allude to Antony's coin and thus his close relationship with the triumvir. He might also have changed the symbol as a way of showing his individuality as king while still connecting himself with the Hasmoneans. Coins of the Diadochs illustrate this behavior. For example, Lysimachus, Seleucus Nicator, and Philip III copy the Alexander coin almost exactly except for some slight modifications that reflect their individuality and personal emblems.

With such a flexible image, Herod might have hoped his coin issue would articulate multiple messages to different audiences. On the one hand, his internal audience would have seen a Hasmonean double cornucopia and hopefully a Hasmonean king. On the other hand, his Roman allies, particularly Marc Antony, would have seen an Antonian symbol and would have interpreted it as a gesture of loyalty and support for both Rome and Antony.

While this hypothesis is interesting and certainly possible, there is one significant problem with it: the chronology of the anchor-double cornucopia coin does not seem to support this theory. In particular, through analysis of coin finds, comparisons of typological connections, and examination of epigraphic style, Ariel has persuasively proven that the anchor-double cornucopia series was struck quite late in Herod's reign (the absolute date he proposes is ca. 15 BCE). Unless we assume that late in his reign, and with the Augustan principate firmly established, Herod still wanted to allude to the disgraced and long-dead Antony, we must either reject or substantially modify Meshorer's theory.[17]

17. For the double cornucopia coins of the Hasmoneans and Herod see Meshorer, *TJC*,

Ariel's absolute date has its problems, though. Specifically, there does not seem to have been a need for new coinage in that year, so, while accepting the relative chronology (minted late in Herod's reign and after the inscription-anchor coin), we need to seek another more credible date. Looking at the symbols on the coin may provide a clue. Both the anchor and the double cornucopia are Hasmonean symbols, so it might be fruitful to find a date in some way associated with the Hasmoneans. Moreover, both symbols are associated with maritime events and as such might reference an important maritime event in Herod's reign.

Is there a year that can fit both criteria? As it turns out, a date slightly earlier than Ariel's, namely 17 BCE, fulfills both criteria well. In the early part of that year, Augustus adopted his grandsons Gaius and Lucius and made them his heirs. He also celebrated the Secular Games *(Ludi Saeculares)* May 31 through June 12. Herod's sons Alexander and Aristobulus, who were nineteen and eighteen years old respectively, were in Rome receiving an education and staying with the imperial family. In one visit, Herod paid his respects to his patron, attended the Secular Games, and collected his sons, whose education was now complete and who could now return to Judaea and play their role as Romanized client-princes. On their return to Judaea they received a rousing welcome from the populace, who hailed them as worthy heirs to the Judaean throne. What better time to strike a new coin? Not only was Herod in the middle of his two most ambitious projects, the Temple and Caesarea Maritima, but his Hasmonean sons had returned home and been received positively by the Judaean people. Herod finally had what he most wanted: legitimacy, if not for him, then at least for his sons. His new anchor-double cornucopia coins would both advertise his Hasmonean sons and allude to the new urban masterpiece he was completing at Caesarea, especially the massive harbor, which if not com-

---

201-9, 211-20, 222-23; plates 5-24, 28-43, 45-46. For Meshorer's hypothesis about Herod's imitation of Hasmonean coins see *TJC*, 67. For Antony's coin from 40 BCE see Michael Crawford, *Roman Republican Coinage* (London: Cambridge University Press, 2001), 1:100-101, numbers 520 and 521. For coins of the Diadochs, see Norman Davis and Colin M. Kraay, *The Hellenistic Kingdoms: Portrait Coins and History* (London: Thames and Hudson, 1973), 33-36 (coins 1-6); R. A. Hadley, "Hellenistic Royal Iconography on Coins," *JHS* 94 (1974), 55-57, 63-65, plate 7; Helen S. Lund, *Lysimachus: A Study in Early Hellenistic Kingship* (London: Routledge, 1992), 162-64. For Ariel's analysis of the relative chronology of the anchor-double cornucopia coin, see "A Numismatic Approach," 339-40, 351-53, 361; cf. Ariel and Fontanille, *Coins of Herod*, 174-76. Cf. "Relative Chronology," 99-124, esp. 107, 109, 111-22; Ariel and Fontanille, *Coins of Herod*, 181-82, where Ariel argues for a slightly later absolute chronology (ca. 12 BCE).

pleted by 17 BCE, was completed shortly afterward. This new coin, which would eventually be Herod's most numerous, marked what must have been a high point for the Idumaean courtier made king: his regime was stable. His friendship with Rome had never been better, and now his future and that of his dynasty were secure. He had, at least in his sons, finally achieved what he most desired: the status as rightful continuation and succession to the Hasmonean dynasty. Now he could solidify his place in Judaean history.[18]

Conclusion: Herod the Hasmonean

How do the major aspects of Herod's political self-presentation (dynastic maneuvering, architectural imaging, and numismatic advertisement) fit into the larger historical picture we are creating? Herod's victory over Mattathias Antigonus in 37 BCE enabled him to seize the throne of Judaea and eliminate his major rival, but it did not solve his legitimacy issues. Although he quickly purged the country of many of Antigonus's supporters through confiscation and execution, he understood he could not eliminate all the Hasmoneans, nor was it even desirable to do so. No doubt some had defected to his side, while others had supported him throughout the war. Perhaps the most obvious examples of this latter category are Hyrcanus, Mariamme, and her mother Alexandra, but there were others. Josephus himself also claimed maternal descent from Jonathan Maccabee, and his family also survived Herod's rise to power. They too may have either switched sides or always been supporters of the Idumaean faction. Herod

---

18. For Augustus's adoption of Gaius and Lucius and his holding of the Secular Games in 17 BCE see Dio 54.18.1-2. For Herod's visit to Rome to collect his sons and their triumphant return to Judaea see *AJ* 16.6-7. Recently, Bieke Mahieu has suggested that Herod's sons traveled to Rome to receive an education in 27 BCE and stayed there for ten years, thereby completing a traditional Roman education. Josephus's comment in *AJ* 16.6 seems to support such a hypothesis. For Mahieu's analysis and discussion of the education of Herod's sons, see Mahieu, "The Foundation Year of Samaria-Sebaste and Its Chronological Implications," *Ancient Society* 38 (2008): 190-94. For the completion of the Sebastos harbor at least by the time of Agrippa's visit in 15 BCE, see *AJ* 16.5D; Philo, *Legat.* 297. Cf. Kokkinos, *Herodian Dynasty,* 370. When attempting to read the symbolism of these coins, it is essential that we always stay in the historical present. In other words, although we now know that Herod would eventually execute both Alexander and Aristobulus, in 17 BCE such an outcome was not even on the horizon. He needed and wanted his sons to succeed him, and his anchor–double cornucopia coins reflect those feelings and his pride at achieving the stability and legitimacy he so craved.

even spared some of his Hasmonean opponents. In particular, his son Antipater married an unnamed daughter of Antigonus. This princess also had two unnamed brothers who seem to have survived the civil war, although they likely fled to Ituraea and the protection of their aunt Alexandra.[19]

Despite the chaos of the mid-first century BCE, and especially the fraternal struggle between Hyrcanus and Aristobulus, the Judaean populace retained a positive memory of the Hasmoneans. They were the family who had led Judaea to political and religious autonomy and independence. Herod could have tried to destroy that memory, but it was far better to co-opt it and modify it to suit his own needs. He thus depicted himself as the logical successor to the Hasmoneans, indeed as a quasi-Hasmonean king in his own right.

So, to whom was he speaking? Although we cannot be certain, given the political realities of the ancient world, it is likely that he directed this self-presentation primarily toward his own court, which was composed of his own partisans as well as some of his opposition who had managed to change sides or assure the new king of their loyalty. The family of Dositheos is a prime example. Although this family was connected to Herod through his uncle Joseph, some of its members actively agitated against Herod's appointment as tetrarch. Consequently, they were among those executed at Tyre. Nevertheless, this family's fortunes rose again, especially when Joseph married Herod's sister Salome, thereby becoming even more influential and powerful. However, after a short period, Salome turned on her husband and accused him of impropriety with Mariamme. As a result of her accusations, he was executed. Dositheos survived this fiasco and remained at court, though Joseph's execution probably left him out of favor and rather discontented. It was only natural, therefore, that Alexandra and Hyrcanus turned to him to negotiate between Hyrcanus and the Nabataean king Malichus. Dositheos saw this entreaty as an opportunity to regain the favor he had lost with the execution of his brother, and he revealed the plot to his king. It is likely that he thus regained Herod's trust, but he was himself soon plotting again, this time with the Idumaean *stratēgos* Costobar and the Hasmonean Sons of Baba. In the end, Dositheos was executed along with Costobar for treason.[20]

---

19. For Antipater's marriage to Antigonus's daughter see *AJ* 17.92. Cf. *BJ* 1.619. See *AJ* 14.489 for a mention of Antigonus's sons. Cf. *BJ* 1.185-86; *AJ* 14.126 for Alexandra's marriage to Ptolemy, son of Mennaeus and tetrarch of Chalcis.

20. See Menahem Stern, "Social and Political Realignments in Herodian Judaea," *Jerusalem Cathedra* 2 (1982): 44-45, for his discussion of the family of Dositheos. Stern claims

Although Herod ultimately turned to other forms of legitimacy besides his quasi-Hasmonean identity, in his early years, when legitimacy was a serious concern, he actively promoted his connection to his predecessors. In the process, he attempted to persuade those with political agency that his war with Mattathias Antigonus was not between a usurper and a rightful king but between two potential candidates from the same family. Even after Herod himself ceased to advertise his Hasmonean connections, he still evoked them for his sons Alexander and Aristobulus. The crucial difference, however, is that these young heirs to the throne were not just Hasmonean princes: they were Herodian princes as well.

---

that Dositheos and Joseph were brothers, but there is no real evidence for such an assertion. Josephus speaks of them only as relatives without specifying the particular tie. See *AJ* 16.169. Nikos Kokkinos has theorized that the two were brothers-in-law, Joseph having married Dositheos's sister prior to his marriage to Herod's sister Salome. For Kokkinos's discussion of this puzzle see *Herodian Dynasty*, 150-52. For the execution of members of Dositheos's family at Tyre, see *AJ* 15.169. For the marriage of Joseph to Salome see *BJ* 1.441. Cf. *AJ* 15.169. For Joseph's execution see *BJ* 1.441-43; *AJ* 15.68-69, 72, 81-82, 86-87, 168. For Dositheos's betrayal of Alexandra and Hyrcanus see *AJ* 15.168-72. If I am correct that those who opposed Herod at Tyre were in fact partisans of the Hasmonean courtier Malichos and part of a Nabataean faction, it would make even more sense for Hyrcanus to turn to Dositheos to negotiate with the Nabataeans. See pp. 82-83 above. For the conspiracy of Costobar and its ultimate failure, see *AJ* 15.252, 260. Interestingly, the name Dositheos, which first appears in a Jewish context during the Maccabean revolt, is also archaeologically attested at Marisa, the same Idumaean city where the name Baba appears. It is possible, therefore, that Dositheos was related or somehow connected to the sons of Baba even before his conspiracy with them and Costobar. Such a relationship might explain why he allied with these other Idumaean conspirators. It would also strengthen my contention that the Hasmonean court of the mid-first century BCE was full of extremely powerful Idumaean aristocrats and courtiers who had been battling each other for supremacy for decades, first in Idumaea and then, after the Hasmonean conquest under Hyrcanus I, in Judaea as well. For the appearance of the name Dositheos during the time of Judah Maccabee, see 2 Macc 2:19, 24, 35. For its appearance at Marisa in a Hellenistic era tomb see Warren J. Moulton, "An Inscribed Tomb at Beit Jibrin," *AJA* 19 (1915): 67 (number 3). For my analysis of this Idumaean courtly dominance and struggle see my "Rise of the Idumaeans: Ethnicity and Politics in Herod's Judaea," in *Jewish Identity and Politics between the Maccabees and Bar Kokhba*, ed. Benedikt Eckhardt (Leiden: Brill, 2012), 117-29. Cf. Kokkinos, *Herodian Dynasty*, 151-52, 155, 180-81.

SECTION III

Client King in an Augustan World

CHAPTER 7

Herod the Augustan Client King

September 2, 31 BCE, was a fateful day for Herod and the entire Mediterranean. For nearly twenty years, the Roman world had convulsed and teetered as bitter rivalry among Rome's elites exploded into almost constant civil war and unrest. For both Rome and Judaea, Octavian's victory over Mark Antony at Actium brought an end to the instability and chaos and ushered in a new era of peace and prosperity. However, Rome itself would never again be a republic. Instead it would transform, albeit slowly, into what its citizens supposedly feared the most: monarchy. For Herod and Judaea, such a change would have been entirely insignificant and unimportant. What was significant was that Herod now found himself on the losing side of this monumental conflict, and he needed to change sides quickly or sink as Antony's fortunes already had done.

Fortunately, this dangerous situation was nothing new. Over the same period that Rome had staggered under the weight of successive civil wars, Herod had changed patrons not once but three times, and now Actium required his fourth and final shift in alliance. For the rest of his reign, Herod would be the loyal and reliable client of the new *princeps,* Octavian, later called Augustus Caesar. Herod's relationship with Augustus would fluctuate over the years, but he would always remain useful to the *princeps* and adept at fulfilling most if not all of the obligations incumbent on him as a client king. It is primarily because of this utility that Augustus, despite whatever temporary doubts he may have had about the son-killing, paranoid monarch in Jerusalem, consistently supported him and, in a last gesture of gratitude and benevolence, upheld Herod's will and deposition of his kingdom. It is this story of the dynamic and productive relationship between these two men, both about the same age (Herod was ten years older), which we will examine for the rest of this book. Before we can carefully examine why the relationship between these two men was so productive, we must first look carefully at their initial encounters, in which the fate of the Judaean kingdom and the beginning of a new friendship were formed.

News of Antony's defeat and subsequent flight to Egypt spread throughout the Roman world. When Herod received the news, he quickly traveled to meet Octavian in the hope of salvaging his political career and his very life. Josephus tells us that he was extremely anxious about his prospects, especially because his claim to the throne was not as strong as the claims of others, most notably the Hasmoneans. In order to rectify this situation, Herod eliminated his potential rivals, most notably the elderly John Hyrcanus II. He then hastened to Rhodes to meet the victorious Octavian and persuade him to maintain the status quo in Judaea. In a scene vividly depicted by Josephus, Herod removed his diadem as a sign of humility and respect but refused to play the part of the terrified supplicant. Instead, speaking frankly, Herod pleaded his case and concluded by stating "I share in Antony's defeat, and with his downfall I lay down my diadem. I have come to you, resting my hopes for safety upon my integrity and presuming that it will be asked what kind of friend, not whose friend, I have been." In essence, Herod asserted that he could be just as good a friend to Octavian as he had been to Antony.[1]

What persuaded Octavian? It was probably some combination of what Herod said and what Octavian knew Herod capable of achieving. In other words, Octavian's decision probably rested on Herod's status as the most capable and reliable option. He would have taken into consideration the

---

1. For Herod's elimination of Hyrcanus immediately following Actium see *BJ* 1.433-34; *AJ* 15.163-78. It is unlikely that Octavian would have deposed the younger and more capable Herod in favor of the elderly Hyrcanus. However, knowing the Roman habit of favoring native dynasties, Herod may have thought that Octavian would nullify his appointment, regarding it as an unlawful usurpation sanctioned by the newly dead Antony. Interestingly, Herod's anxiety suggests that his appointment as king in 40 BCE did not actively involve Octavian. See *BJ* 1.441-43; *AJ* 15.162, 183-86 for Herod's concerns. For Herod's attempt to meet with Octavian as quickly as possible after Actium see *BJ* 1.387; *AJ* 15.187-88. For his speech before Octavian see *BJ* 1.388-90; *AJ* 15.189-93. It is unlikely that Josephus accurately recorded Herod's speech, especially because Nicolaus of Damascus (Josephus's primary source for this period) was not present at the time. In all likelihood, Josephus is following the practice, first described by Thucydides, by which the historian records speeches as best as possible, but where memory fails writes what the person should have said at that particular moment. See Thucydides 1.22.

friendship that the Antipatrid family had enjoyed with Julius Caesar and remembered Herod's friendship with Sextus Caesar and his successful reign as tetrarch of Galilee. More immediately, he would have recalled that Herod had been a consistent ally of Rome against Parthia and had helped secure Rome's eastern frontier. Finally, and perhaps most importantly, Herod had already shown his willingness to abandon Antony and help Octavian's campaign. After Actium and Antony's defeat, Herod betrayed Antony by assisting Quintus Didius, the new governor of Syria, and sending royal forces against a group of gladiators who were rushing from Cyzicus in Asia Minor to aid Antony in Egypt. Octavian needed kings who were more loyal to the Roman system than to any particular individual, who were familiar with and had shown the ability to control their own people and kingdoms. Herod was precisely that type of individual, and this trait, more than any other reason, was why Octavian confirmed Herod's authority. In so doing, he also restored to him the cities seized by Cleopatra and expanded his territory to include Gadara, Hippos, Samaria, and the coastal cities of Strato's Tower, Anthedon, and Gaza.

Over the next twenty-six years Octavian would have ample evidence that he had not made a mistake at Rhodes.[2] Indeed, Herod would show himself to be an extremely useful client king, one who fulfilled most, if not all, of the obligations incumbent on him, namely, (1) providing military support, (2) seeking approval for major decisions, (3) publicly honoring his patron, and (4) acting as an agent of Romanization. In this chapter, we will examine the first three of these obligations before turning in the next chapter to what was possibly Herod's greatest long-term influence: his transformation of Judaea into a kingdom fully involved in the larger Roman cultural world.

Military and Financial Support for Rome and Its Leaders

While he had many talents, Herod was never a glorious military conqueror. If we look at his entire reign, he achieved only a few clear military victories, his defeat of Antigonus notwithstanding. In particular, his pre-Actium

---

2. Plutarch, *Ant.* 71; *BJ* 1.392; *AJ* 15.195-96. Cf. Dio 51.7.1-6. Herod had thus quickly shifted his allegiance. As G. W. Bowersock says, Herod "understood the folly of loyalty to the dead." See Bowersock, *Augustus and the Greek East* (Oxford: Clarendon, 1965), 55. For Augustus's reorganization of the East after Actium see Bowersock, 42-61.

campaign against the Nabataeans was inconclusive, and his later campaign against them in 8 BCE did not lead to any real gains and even angered Augustus. Nevertheless, while perhaps not a magnificently successful conqueror, he still provided important military support to Augustus and Rome. This support mostly took the form of action against bandits and supplying royal forces to supplement the Roman army.

Starting in his tenure as *stratēgos* of Galilee, Herod consistently proved his ability to control banditry, which was important because such banditry disrupted the lucrative trade routes that ran through Judaea. During his reconquest of Judaea in 37 BCE Galilean bandits were again a problem, this time near Arbela. Additionally, these particular bandits may have had greater motives than simple plunder. They may actually have been partisans of Antigonus and their banditry no more than an attempt to wage a guerilla war against Herod and his Roman allies. Still, these brigands needed to be suppressed, as they were thwarting Herod's attempts to take control of the countryside. Herod's army thus attacked and successfully drove most of them out of Galilee and across the Jordan River.[3]

Ten years later, in 27 BCE, bandits were once again wreaking havoc on trade, this time in the territories of Trachonitis, Batanaea, and Auranitis, northeast of Judaea. The former ruler of these territories, Zenodorus, had leased the land from Lysianus, the tetrarch of Chalcis and Ituraea, who had been killed by Antony in 36 BCE. In order to enrich himself further, Zenodorus had incited local bandits to raid the nearby territory of Damascus and give him a share in their booty. The Damascenes had complained to the governor of Syria about these raids, and he had sent these complaints on to Augustus, who ordered the governor to campaign against the bandits. As a more permanent solution, he gave the territory to Herod specifically so that he could contain the menace. Josephus reports that the Judaean army successfully suppressed the outlaws and brought security and stability to the region. Additionally, when Zenodorus died seven years later in 20 BCE, Augustus gave Herod Zenodorus's land, including the territories of Ulatha and Panias.[4]

---

3. *BJ* 1.304-13; *AJ* 14.421-30. The only remaining resistance was a group who lived in a series of caves probably near Arbela. Herod's army attacked this group by lowering soldiers down into the caves in baskets. The soldiers then threw torches into the caves to flush them out. According to *BJ*, the brigands remained defiant, preferring death to surrender. *AJ* asserts, on the other hand, that most of the brigands surrendered.

4. For Zenodorus as the ruler of Trachonitis, Batanaea, and Auranitis see *BJ* 1.398; *AJ* 15.344. For Antony's decision to execute Lysanias see *BJ* 1.440; *AJ* 15.92. For Herod's mandate

Bandits continued to remain a constant problem in this part of Herod's kingdom, so much so that in 9 BCE he settled a group of Jewish Babylonians in Ulatha. He entrusted them and their leader Zamaris with the job of defending Ulatha and neighboring Batanaea against incursions by Trachonitide bandits. He also settled a group of Idumaean veterans in Trachonitis to patrol the region and maintain peace. These efforts suggest a coordinated effort and plan to police the realm, especially in those areas that were sparsely populated and were on or near the major trade routes. Josephus explicitly states that Zamaris's duties included guarding the pilgrims on their way to Jerusalem, and it is reasonable to assume that he was also meant to guard caravans of merchants as they passed near Trachonitis and through the other unsettled regions of the kingdom. Although it is not explicitly stated, the Idumaean soldiers presumably had similar duties.[5] For Herod, such protection meant increased trade and pilgrimage and thus increased tax revenues. In addition, he benefited politically because his actions were a visible demonstration of his ability to control bandit activity and protect commerce. With these successes, Herod could reasonably have

---

against banditry and his subsequent annexation of Trachonitis, Batanaea, and Auranitis see *BJ* 1.398-400; *AJ* 15.343-48. There has been some disagreement about exactly when this grant occurred. According to Josephus, the grant occurred "after the first Actiad" (*BJ* 1.398), meaning after the first four-year period between Actian games. Traditionally, most scholars have followed Schürer's dating of the first Actian games to 28 BCE and the first Actiad to 28-24 BCE. However, recently, Mahieu has persuasively argued that the first Actian games were held in 31 BCE, and therefore the first Actiad was 31-27. Augustus's grant to Herod, then, would have occurred at the end of 27 BCE. See Emil Schürer, *The History of the Jewish People in the Age of Jesus Christ (175 BC–AD 135)*, ed., trans., and rev. Geza Vermes and Fergus Millar (Edinburgh: Clark, 1973-87) 1:291, n. 10; Bieke Mahieu, "The Foundation Year of Samaria-Sebaste and Its Chronological Implications," *Ancient Society* 38 (2008): 183-96, esp. 185-88. For Augustus's decision to add Ulatha and Panias to Herod's territory see *BJ* 1.400; *AJ* 15.359-60. Cf. Dio 54.9.3. All the territories that Augustus granted to Herod had been part of the province of Syria since Pompey's conquest in 63 BCE. Augustus must have decided that these areas were still too unstable to govern as part of a settled province. Farming out the task of border patrol and policing to a local king would be cheaper and probably more effective. See Samuel Rocca, *Herod's Judaea: A Mediterranean State in the Classical World* (Tübingen: Mohr, 2008), 54.

5. For the settlement of the Babylonian colonists in Ulatha see *AJ* 17.23-26. For Herod's decision to settle Idumaean veterans in Trachonitis see *AJ* 16.285. For a discussion of the composition and duties of the Babylonian and Idumaean veterans see Israel Shatzman, *The Armies of the Hasmoneans and Herod* (Tübingen: Mohr, 1991), 170-80. For a discussion of the importance of military colonies such as the Babylonian and Idumaean ones see Rocca, *Herod's Judaea*, 188-89.

hoped for even more territory and responsibility. While his kingdom never grew larger — mostly because of his domestic troubles and his conflicts with the Nabataeans — his ability to suppress lawlessness and control trade routes was essential to the long-term economic growth of his kingdom and the Roman East. He may not have been a military hero, but he was an extremely effective policeman, and the new principate of Octavian needed more of the latter than anything else.

Rome and its armies also needed allies to gather necessary supplies and provide valuable local intelligence. Herod fulfilled this essential role and thus continued to provide ample evidence that his claim at Rhodes had not been erroneous. When Octavian and his army traveled to and from Egypt in pursuit of Antony and Cleopatra, Herod was the main supplier of food and material. Six years later he was instrumental in planning an expedition to Arabia in order to annex it. Aelius Gallus led this expedition, but Herod provided large amounts of supplies, 500 members of his bodyguard, and valuable information about the land. Although the expedition did not achieve its goals, his donation again demonstrated his ability and willingness to provide support for Roman military campaigns.[6]

In 14 BCE, Herod and a number of ships from his royal navy sailed from Caesarea Maritima to join Marcus Agrippa's expedition to the Black Sea. Agrippa had initiated this expedition in order to subdue the revolt of the Cimmerian Bosporus, and Herod's ships were an extremely useful addition. Given the importance of this campaign, it is likely that he provided a significant fleet, not just a symbolic contribution. Indeed, if the fleet was large and sufficiently equipped, that may partially explain why Rome did not build a fleet in the East until much later, relying instead on the ships of its client kings. We know from Josephus that Herod was extremely proud of his role in the campaign. Immediately on his return to Caesarea, he assembled the people and recounted his journey, emphasizing his role as the protector of the Jews of Asia (and no doubt the indispensable services he provided to Agrippa while on campaign). He then remitted a fourth of the people's taxes, which only further increased their goodwill to him.

Herod benefited greatly from his involvement in this campaign. By offering Agrippa the use of his fleet he proved his loyalty to Rome and

---

6. For Herod's supplying of Octavian's troops see *BJ* 1.384-95; *AJ* 15.198-201. For his role in the Arabian campaign see *AJ* 15.317. Cf. Strabo 16.4.22-24; Dio 53.29; Pliny, *HN* 6.160-62; *Res Gest. Divi Aug.* 26.5.

more importantly his usefulness to its goals in the eastern Mediterranean. Moreover, as discussed in greater detail below, he was able to show himself as a successful defender of Jewish interests within the Diaspora. He proved that he had the ear of the second most powerful man in the Roman world, and such visible proof of his power and influence could only strengthen his control over his own kingdom and subjects.[7]

Rome and its new masters needed financial as well as military support. Earlier in his career, Herod had demonstrated that he could raise money quickly and efficiently. When he switched his loyalty, he simply continued his old policy of presenting gifts to his patron. By doing so, he showed his adaptability and proved that a change of patron did not mean a change of behavior. After being confirmed as king by Octavian, Herod presented his new patron with large monetary gifts, specifically 800 talents to help fund the invasion of Egypt. Similar gifts followed at various intervals for the rest of Herod's reign. These gifts included 300 talents to celebrate Herod's reconciliation with his sons and a final testimonial bequest of 15 million pieces of silver to the imperial family. These gifts were certainly financially useful, but they functioned more significantly as concrete declarations of loyalty and fidelity. Because of the distance between Rome and Judaea, it was of paramount importance for Herod to repeatedly show Octavian that he was a reliable and dependable client. If that meant raising vast sums of money, it was a small price to pay for the trust of the most powerful man in the Mediterranean.[8]

Herod's financial involvement with the imperial family extended beyond mere gifts and into commercial enterprises, specifically the copper industry on Cyprus. In exchange for the gift of 300 talents in 12 BCE, Augustus granted Herod management of the Cypriot copper mines and half of their revenue. This was a huge windfall. Copper and its alloys, most notably

---

7. For Agrippa's Bosporus campaign see *AJ* 16.16-23. Cf. Strabo 11.2.3; Dio 54.24.4-7; Eutropius 7.9; Orosius 6.21.28. Clear evidence for when the Romans established a permanent fleet in the East does not exist. However, according to Shatzman, the earliest clear attestation for the existence of a permanent navy appears during the reign of Hadrian, which is also around the time that client kingship as a system became obsolete. See Shatzman, *Armies*, 187. For Herod's decision to remit the taxes of his subjects see *AJ* 16.62-65.

8. For Herod's gifts in the aftermath of Actium see *BJ* 1.393; *AJ* 15.196, 199, 200. For his gift after his family's reconciliation see *AJ* 16.121-29. For Herod's final will and his legacy to the imperial family see *BJ* 1.646; *AJ* 17.190. The existence of a bequest to Augustus and his family would probably have been publicized long before Herod died. Such advertisement would have reminded Judaeans of the close relationship between the royal family and Rome.

bronze, were vital to several industries in the ancient world, including the manufacture of arms and armor and the minting of coinage. On Cyprus Herod had at his disposal the largest known supply of copper for both trade and his own use. The revolt in Trachonitis necessitated a large minting of new coins to pay the royal army. Moreover, as discussed later, this period was also one of frenetic Herodian building both in Judaea and elsewhere, requiring huge expenditures, and control of the Cypriot mines enabled Herod to pay his expenses.[9]

This transaction is the only formal commercial relationship between Herod and Augustus mentioned by the literary sources. Nevertheless, it is highly probable that more existed. We know that Herod personally owned vast estates in Judaea and neighboring regions. He inherited some of these estates from his Idumaean and Hasmonean families, and some he no doubt purchased or confiscated from others. Some percentage of the crops raised on these estates went to local consumption, but a portion undoubtedly was exported. We know of at least one crop that Judaea exported in large quantities: dates grown in and around Jericho, and Herod owned most, if not all, of those date farms. We also know that Herod himself was a major importer of luxury items from the West. From amphora inscriptions found at Masada, which will be detailed below, we know that, in addition to exporting goods, Herod also imported several luxury items from Italy and the West. In both cases, interaction with imperial estates and members of the imperial family would have been unavoidable. Augustus and the imperial family, including all their slaves and freedmen, consumed large amounts of goods and owned massive amounts of land all over the Mediterranean, including Egypt with all its grain. Strong commercial ties, therefore, were yet another way in which Herod and his kingdom could integrate with and be essential to the larger Roman world.[10]

---

9. For Augustus's grant of the Cypriot mines to Herod see *AJ* 16.128. For the revolt in Trachonitis see *AJ* 16.271-74.

10. For a discussion of Herod's wealth see Emilio Gabba, "The Finances of King Herod," in *Greece and Rome in Eretz-Israel*, ed. Aryeh Kasher, Uriel Rappaport, and Gideon Fuks (Jerusalem: Jerusalem Exploration Society, 1990), 160-68. Cf. John W. Welch, "Herod's Wealth," in *Masada and the World of the New Testament*, ed. John F. Hall and John W. Welch (Provo: Brigham Young University Studies, 1997), 74-83.

Honoring Rome's New Masters

In the famous opening to *The Godfather*, Don Corleone admonishes the undertaker Bonasera for not paying him the proper homage and deference. For Don Corleone, money is not his objective. Instead, what he really wants is respect and thus loyalty and submission. The Roman patron-client system rested on a firm belief that clients were subordinate to their patrons, and one of the most tangible ways to reinforce this subordination was through the client's obligation to honor his patron publicly. By doing so, he openly acknowledged and acquiesced to his subordination. The relationship between client king and Roman patron was no different than that of a plebeian client to his patrician patron or of Bonasera to Don Corleone. Herod played the Bonasera part to perfection, first as a client to Caesar, then to Cassius, then to Antony. Now his new patron, Octavian, expected and demanded similar behavior, and Herod was quick to satisfy. He even accelerated and intensified this behavior as he discovered new and creative ways of honoring his new patrons. One way he publicly and concretely honored them was by consulting them on significant decisions pertaining to his kingdom.

Travel and information moved slowly in the ancient world. It could take a month or even longer for news from Judaea to reach Rome. It was essential, therefore, that Rome trust its allies, especially in the East, which bordered on the hostile kingdom of Parthia. Thus, a wise client king ensured that his patrons never doubted his loyalty or faithfulness. Herod recognized early this need for reliability, and he was consistently careful to solicit approval from Rome and its leaders before embarking on a major decision or course of action. As a result Antony and later Augustus were able to exercise a reasonable amount of control over decisions in Judaea that concerned them. For example, as we saw earlier, Herod wanted to kill Malichos immediately after discovering his role in Antipater's death. Nevertheless, before taking any action, he waited to receive permission from Cassius, who was in charge of the East at that time. When Herod began to suspect his sons Alexander and Aristobulus of treason, he took them to Rome with him and laid his claims before Augustus. This visit and the decision to solicit Rome's approval was an intelligent one, because Herod could shield himself from any culpability by depicting himself as merely following his patron's advice. Further, by bringing the matter to Rome, he could show his willingness to consult Augustus before taking any action. Such prudence would have pleased Augustus because it would have enabled him to control succession within the Judaean kingdom, an issue of central importance.[11]

During the inquiry, Alexander persuaded Augustus that he and his brother were guilty not of treason but merely of speaking ill of their father. Augustus reproved the youths and then reconciled them with their father. This reconciliation was short-lived, and in the end it was in vain. Nevertheless, when Herod finally executed the two princes, he first secured written approval from Rome. He followed a similar procedure prior to executing another son, Antipater. Indeed, not only did Herod inform Augustus, but he also invited the governor of Syria, Quinctilius Varus, to represent Rome at the trial and to give his opinion on the matter. In this way, he received official sanction for his actions not only from Varus, but also from Augustus, who wrote back approving any action that might be taken.[12] Deferring to Rome may have been the central obligation for a client king, but one with little downside. More often than not, Augustus permitted his client kings to act however they chose. Thus Herod ingratiated himself with his Roman patron at little cost, since he retained his freedom of action.

Consultation on significant matters was important, but there were other ways to honor Rome and its leaders publicly. Of all of the media available to him, Herod favored none so much as monumental architecture. It enabled him simultaneously to fulfill his obligations and indulge his creativity, to advertise his loyalty to the new regime visibly and mark the landscape concretely with his own glory and magnificence. He used monumental architecture to connect himself to Rome, and the monuments he created in honor of Augustus and his principate dwarf his early projects in number, size, and scope. Additionally, he expanded the repertoire he had utilized as an Antonian client to include extensive palaces, magnificent temples, and full-scale urban construction.

Herod dedicated rooms in his palaces to Augustus and Agrippa. For example, the Main Palace in Jerusalem's Upper City was a complex of two buildings. One was called the Caesareum after Augustus, while the other was named after Agrippa. Herod also named rooms in the Third Herodian Palace at Jericho after Augustus and Agrippa. Almost certainly, his decision to name his most important and lavish reception halls after Augustus and

---

11. *BJ* 1.452; *AJ* 16.90-92. A further benefit for Herod would be that he appeared as a just judge by delaying the executions pending trial in Rome.

12. For Herod's use of Augustus as a mediator between him and his sons see *BJ* 1.452-54; *AJ* 16.90-126. For Herod's letter to Augustus before executing Alexander and Aristobulus see *BJ* 1.535-37; *AJ* 16.356. For Herod's request to execute Antipater see *AJ* 17.89-145.

Herod the Augustan Client King

Agrippa would have been known throughout his court and by important visitors as well. Through the dissemination of this information, Herod could advertise his close relationship with the *princeps* and his current successor. His alliance and friendship with Rome as well as his desire to position his kingdom entirely within the Roman sphere were made manifest in stone and stucco. At the same time, he was fulfilling his obligations as a client king by honoring his patrons and showing his respect for and gratitude toward them. For the gesture to have its full effect, Augustus and Agrippa would have had to know about the namings, and we can imagine that when each visited Judaea (Augustus in 20 BCE and Agrippa in 15 BCE), they each saw their namesake rooms in the Main Palace personally. Given the timing of his visit, Agrippa might also have seen their counterparts at Jericho.[13]

While palace rooms were a great way to advertise gratitude and loyalty, Herod usually thought that bigger was better, and there was no better way to honor Augustus and Agrippa than by building cities and naming them after his two patrons. The first of these cities was Samaria/Sebaste. In 27 BCE, the Roman Senate voted to give Octavian the new name Augustus. Lucius Munatius Plancus (consul in 42 BCE) was responsible for the renaming proposal. Plancus, who was a former governor of Syria, was a long-time associate of Herod, and it is conceivable that he notified Herod of his intentions in advance. This would have given Herod time to plan a suitable response to the Senate's decision. Even if Plancus did not inform Herod beforehand, news of the decision spread quickly, and the title *Sebastos* (the Greek equivalent of Augustus) quickly became popular.[14]

---

13. For Josephus's description of these structures see *BJ* 1.402, 407; *AJ* 15.318. For an archaeological summary of the rooms at Jericho see Ehud Netzer, *The Palaces of the Hasmoneans and Herod the Great* (Jerusalem: Yad Ben-Zvi, 2001), 126. Netzer divides Herod's building program into five stages beginning in 37 BCE (although his table seems to have six, beginning in 40 BCE), some of which might overlap. He places the construction of the Main Palace in the Upper City in the latter part of the second stage (ca. 25-20 BCE). Since Augustus visited Judaea in 20 BCE and Agrippa visited in 15, it is entirely possible that both men saw the rooms named after them. As for the Third Herodian Palace, Netzer places it in the fourth stage (ca. 15-10 BCE). Depending on how construction proceeded at Jericho, Agrippa might have seen the reception halls during his visit, or at least their construction. Even if the rooms were still being constructed, it is possible that Herod told Agrippa about his plans to name the rooms after his Roman patrons. See Ehud Netzer, *The Architecture of Herod, the Great Builder* (Tübingen: Mohr, 2006), 303. Cf. Achim Lichtenberger, *Die Baupolitik Herodes des Grossen* (Wiesbaden: Harrassowitz, 1999), 176-78 and 176 n. 929, for Lichtenberger's chronology, which generally agrees with Netzer, though he uses only three phases: 37-28/27 BCE, 28/27-14 BCE, and 14-4 BCE.

14. For Herod's renaming of Samaria as Sebaste see *BJ* 1.403; *AJ* 15.296. Cf. Strabo

Herod may have decided to rebuild Samaria before 27 BCE. However, according to most scholars, construction began in 27, soon after the Roman Senate's decision. Rebuilding Samaria/Sebaste allowed Herod to fulfill several political needs at once. First and perhaps most importantly it enabled him to display his loyalty to and friendship with Augustus to both his internal and external audiences. Samaria/Sebaste also served as a strategic stronghold because Herod had settled the city with his loyal veterans. Finally, his decision to populate the city primarily with non-Jews minimized the disruption caused by the construction of a pagan temple in the center of town. The location of this temple complex was no accident. He positioned it over the site where the royal palace of the kingdom of Israel once stood. This positioning was a literal and metaphorical declaration of Herod's intent to transform the city from Samaria, former capital of the kingdom of Israel, into Sebaste, a model Graeco-Roman *polis* and an urban symbol of his position within the new political order.[15]

At roughly the same time that he was rebuilding Sebaste, Herod also participated in the construction of Octavian's victory city Nikopolis, which was located on the site of Octavian's military camp near Actium. As Jose-

---

16.2.34. For the renaming of Octavian as Augustus see Suetonius, *Aug.* 7.2; Dio 53.16.6-8; *Res Gest. Divi Aug.* 34. For Plancus as governor of Syria in 35 BCE see Broughton, *MRR* 2:593. Plancus was also proconsul in Asia in 40-38 and might have had contact with Herod at that time.

15. For a detailed analysis of the city of Sebaste and its function as Herod's first *urbs Caesarae*, see Monika Bernett, *Der Kaiserkult in Judäa unter den Herodiern und Römern. Untersuchungen zur politischen und religiösen Geschichte Judäas von 30 v. bis 66 n. Chr.* (Tübingen: Mohr, 2007), 67-98. Sebaste became the first city to be rebuilt and named in Augustus's honor. By the end of the first century BCE the eastern part of the empire was littered with cities named Sebaste, Sebasteia, or Sebastopolis. For the archaeological evidence that dates the reconstruction of Sebaste to 27 BCE see D. Barag, "King Herod's Royal Castle at Samaria-Sebaste," *PEQ* 125 (1993): 3-18, here pp. 4 and 13 nn. 6-7; Mahieu, "Foundation Year of Samaria-Sebaste," 183-84. Cf. Duane W. Roller, *The Building Program of Herod the Great* (Berkeley: University of California Press, 1998), 209-12, esp. 210. For Herod's fortifying of the city and settling it with non-Jewish veterans see *BJ* 1.403; *AJ* 15.292-93, 296-98. For Shatzman's discussion of the *Sebastenoi,* an elite unit or units in Herod's army levied from the inhabitants of Sebaste, see Shatzman, *Armies,* 185-86, 187, 191, 193-94, 211, 215 n. 188, 256. Cf. A. Kasher, *Jews, Idumaeans and Ancient Arabs: Relations of the Jews in Eretz-Israel with Nations of the Frontier and the Desert during the Hellenistic and Roman Era (332 BCE–70 CE)* (Tübingen: Mohr, 1988), 198-203, 210, 213-14. For Samaria being the site of the capital of the kingdom of Israel see Barag, "King Herod's Royal Castle," 16. The importance of this city is attested by the series of coins Herod minted in honor of the rebuilding. These coins will be discussed in greater detail below.

phus records, Herod contributed money to assist in the construction of the city, including funds for most of the public buildings. What better way for Herod to conceal his former status as a loyal Antonian and assert his current loyalty to the new regime than to finance the construction of its urban war monument? The pairing of this project with that of his own at Sebaste was even more fortunate. With these two ventures Herod could wipe away recent history and concretely forge a fresh identity for the new world in which he was living. Simultaneously, the location of Nikopolis offered additional benefits by giving Herod an opportunity to practice his *euergetism* on the Greek mainland. In essence, he could assert his identity as a Hellenistic monarch (a subject we will discuss in greater detail in a later chapter) while still maintaining his status as a client king of Rome.[16]

Herod's use of large-scale urban architecture continued after 28-27. Indeed, we see a tremendous expansion in this program, culminating in the construction of Caesarea Maritima and the rebuilding and expansion of the Temple in Jerusalem. While the Temple is probably Herod's most famous project, Caesarea Maritima was also a jewel in his architectural empire. His motives for building Caesarea include a desire to ingratiate himself with Augustus and to strengthen his position as a loyal ally and client king. He also wanted to use the city to stake his own claim on the international stage and enhance his position in world affairs. Further, a new port city would increase the prosperity of his kingdom by improving international trade and commerce. All these goals were achieved without too much direct Roman interference. In return, Rome gained an artificial all-weather harbor on the Mediterranean shore, which had a shortage of natural or safe anchorages, all for little or no cost to Rome. Herod bore the cost of construction and maintenance of this harbor and city, while Rome and its leaders could benefit from its use whenever they wanted. Between 25 and 22 BCE, Herod began construction of the city, which would become his urban masterpiece. He situated the city on a stretch of coastline that had recently belonged to Cleopatra but which Octavian had given to him

---

16. For Roman sources on the founding of Nikopolis see Dio 51.1.2-3; Pausanias 7.18.9, 10.38; Seutonius, *Aug.* 18.2; Strabo, *Geog.* 7.7.6. For Josephus's account of Herod's *euergetism*, see *BJ* 1.425; *AJ* 16.147. Ehud Netzer argues that such benefactions outside Herod's kingdom served two purposes, to assert his loyalty and to improve his ties with other areas of the empire. See his discussion in "Herod the Great's Contribution to Nikopolis in Light of His Building Activity in Judea," in *Proceedings of the First International Symposium of Nicopolis (23-29 September, 1984)*, ed. Evangelos Chrysos (Preveza: Demos Prevezas, 1987), 121-28, esp. 127.

after their first formal meeting in Rhodes in 30 BCE. The extensive building program for this city (completed ca. 12 BCE) also included a completely artificial harbor, which Herod named Sebastos. On its completion, the triple-harbored Sebastos, with its orientation toward the West and Rome, became the largest port on the Leventine coast and rivaled Alexandria as a port city, perhaps even stealing some of her trade.

Both literary and archaeological evidence attest to the magnificence of Caesarea's civic, financial, and residential buildings. Besides a stadium, a theater, and a palace complex, the city also boasted another temple to Augustus and Rome, which was located at the center of the city. This edifice, with foundations of huge ashlar masonary, contained gigantic statues of Augustus and Rome, rivaling, according to Josephus, the Olympian statues of Zeus and Hera at Argos. Moreover, although located at the intersection of the two main city roads (the *decumanus maximus* and the *cardo maximus*), the temple's orientation is turned slightly and thus is not parallel to either street. Instead, it looks west toward and is aligned with the true masterpiece of the city, the Sebastos harbor.[17]

---

17. For Josephus's discussion of Caesarea and its construction see *BJ* 1.408-14; *AJ* 15.331-41. For a description of the cult statues see *BJ* 1.414. The archaeological literature on Caesarea Maritima is quite extensive and cannot all be listed here. However, see especially Lee I. Levine and Ehud Netzer, eds., *Excavations at Caesarea Maritima: 1975. 1976. 1979 Final Report* (Jerusalem: Institute of Archaeology, Hebrew University of Jerusalem, 1986); Robert Bull, Edgar Krentz, and Olin J. Storvick, eds., *The Joint Expedition to Caesarea Maritima: Excavation Reports* (Lewiston: Mellen, 1987-2000); Kenneth G. Holum, Robert L. Hohlfelder, Robert J. Bull, and Avner Raban, *King Herod's Dream: Caesarea on the Sea* (New York: Norton, 1988); John P. Oleson, ed., *The Harbours of Caesarea Maritima: Results of the Caesarea Ancient Harbour Excavation Project* (Oxford: BAR, 1989-94); Robert Lindley Vann, ed., *Caesarea Papers: Straton's Tower, Herod's Harbour, and Roman and Byzantine Caesarea* (Ann Arbor: Journal of Roman Archaeology, 1992); Avner Raban and Kenneth G. Holum, eds., *Caesarea Maritima: A Retrospective after Two Millennia* (Leiden: Brill, 1996); Kenneth G. Holum, Avner Raban, and Joseph Patrich, eds., *Caesarea Papers 2: Herod's Temple, the Provincial Governor's Praetorium and Granaries, the Later Harbor, a Gold Coin Hoard, and Other Studies* (Portsmouth: Journal of Roman Archaeology, 1999). Cf. Kenneth Holum, Avner Raban, Avraham Negev, Antonio Frova, and Michael Avi-Yonah, "Caesarea," in *The New Encyclopaedia of Archaeological Excavations in the Holy Land (NEAEHL)*, ed. Ephraim Stern (Jerusalem: Israel Exploration Society, 1993), 270-91; Bernett, *Kaiserkult*, 102-12, 117-21. Also see Robert Hohlfelder, "Beyond Coincidence? Marcus Agrippa and King Herod's Harbor," *JNES* 59 (2000): 241-53. Cf. Byron R. McCane, "Simply Irresistible: Augustus, Herod, and the Empire," *JBL* 127 (2008): 725-35, esp. 733-35, for a discussion of Caesarea's value as a symbolic assertion of Herod's Romanization. For a discussion of Herodian international trade see Rocca, *Herod's Judaea*, 234-39, esp. 236-39. According to Josephus, Caesarea was either a ten-year or twelve-year project. If the dedication occurred in 12 BCE, work must have begun

Herod the Augustan Client King

The Sebastos harbor, which functioned as a physical port of entry into Judaea but also a symbolic gateway to the wider Roman world, was constructed of *pozzolana*, a hydraulic cement, composed of volcanic sand and hydrated lime, which hardens in water. This enabled the builders to construct massive blocks as large as 39 × 49 × 5 feet and weighing more than 50 tons. The harbor, which was actually comprised of three separate harbors, was big enough for a large fleet to lie at anchor. Its breakwater extended more than 1,500 feet into the water, and its 500-foot-long quay contained numerous anchorages at which ships could unload their goods before they were transported to the extensive warehouse district nearby. At the mouth of the harbor was an immense lighthouse tower, which Herod called the Drusion after Augustus's recently deceased stepson, Drusus. To celebrate the completion of the project, Herod held a huge festival, culminating with games in honor of Augustus. Herod also decreed that these games would occur every five years. This festival brought important visitors and guests from all over the Roman world and provided a perfect stage for Herod to display his wealth, magnanimity, and royal greatness. No doubt he hoped that his Caesarian games would soon rival other famous athletic meetings such as the Olympics.[18]

Herod's urban building projects also extended to rebuilding a city in honor of his friend Marcus Agrippa. His choice was the Gazan city of Anthedon, which he renamed Agrippias. The history of Anthedon in Gaza prior to the first century BCE is rather vague. There is no documented evidence of its existence before the Hellenistic period, but its name suggests that it might have been founded as a colony of the Boiotian city of Anthedon, which is mentioned by Homer in the *Iliad*. It first appears in the historical record as one of the cities annexed to Judaea when Alexander Jannaeus conquered Gaza at the beginning of the first century BCE. Jannaeus's conquest must have damaged the city severely because it was one of the many that Aulus Gabinius rebuilt in the 50s BCE. Unfortunately, these repairs would be short-lived because the city was destroyed in the civil war between Herod and Antigonus. After Actium, Octavian annexed Anthedon and other depopulated coastal towns of Gaza to Judaea. As with

---

at some time between 25/24 and 22 BCE. For a discussion of the chronology and a refutation of Schürer's chronology of 22-10/9 BCE see E. Mary Smallwood, *The Jews Under Roman Rule: From Pompey to Diocletian* (Leiden: Brill, 1976), 80, n. 62; Bernett, *Kaiserkult*, 99-100.

18. For the construction of the harbor and its tower see *BJ* 1.412; *AJ* 15.336. See pp. 218-21 below for a detailed discussion of the use of Roman hydrotechnology by Herod's engineers. For Herod's establishment of a quinquennial festival in honor of Augustus see *BJ* 1.415; *AJ* 16.136-41.

Sebaste, Herod resettled Agrippias with his veterans, which also gave it the dual function of honoring a patron and securing the countryside. The exact chronology for this reconstruction and resettlement is unclear. Roller suggests a date after Agrippa's death in 12 BCE, although there is no real evidence to privilege a post-mortem reconstruction over one before 12. Indeed, if anything, it would have made more sense to build a city in honor of Agrippa while he was still alive and thus able to appreciate the gesture. However, the reconstruction could still have had meaning even if Agrippa were dead. In this case, the primary audience would have been Augustus, whose friendship with Agrippa was so close that he had made Agrippa his heir. Either way, the reconstruction shows Herod publicly acknowledging one of his great Roman friends and patrons by attaching his name and memory to a resettled community.[19]

Public Inscriptions to Honor Augustus and Herod Himself

Herod also actively advertised his close ties to the imperial center through other permanent media such as dedicatory inscriptions and coins. The attractiveness of these modes of communication lies in their ability to speak to large groups of people simultaneously. Perspective audiences could see inscriptions in the public square and hold coins in their hands. It is no accident that inscriptions and coins are some of the most numerous examples of material culture that survive from antiquity. In Herod's case, we have a few

---

19. For Herod's rebuilding of Anthedon and renaming of it as Agrippias see *BJ* 1.87, 118, 416; *AJ* 13.357. For an unknown reason, Josephus refers to the city in *BJ* 1.416 as Agrippeum. Ptolemy mentions the city of Anthedon in *Geog.* 5.15. Boiotian Anthedon is mentioned in Homer, *Iliad* 2.508. For the annexation of Gaza into Judaea see *BJ* 1.87; *AJ* 13.357, 395. For the Gabinian rebuilding of Gazan Anthedon see *BJ* 1.166; *AJ* 14.88. For Anthedon's destruction in the civil war between Herod and Antigonus see *BJ* 1.416. Roller suggests that it might also have been damaged in the earthquake that struck Judaea in 31 BCE. See Roller, *Building Program,* 129. For Anthedon's annexation to Herod's kingdom after Actium see *BJ* 1.396; *AJ* 15.217. For Roller's theory on the chronology of the rebuilding of Anthedon see *Building Program,* 129. For Herod's decision to repopulate Agrippias with veterans see *BJ* 1.416. A final honor that Herod bestowed on Augustus was a festival held in Jerusalem every four years for which he constructed an amphitheater and a theater. In the amphitheater he held typical Roman spectacles. He further honored Augustus by placing dedicatory inscriptions all around the theater. As Josephus described, "All round the theatre were inscriptions concerning Caesar and trophies of nations which he had won in war, all of them made for Herod of pure gold and silver" (*AJ* 15.272). See *AJ* 15.268-73.

surviving inscriptions that mention him by name. Most of these inscriptions appear on honorary statue bases. Two in particular speak of his relationship with Rome and openly declare his loyalty to and friendship with Rome and its leaders. I will be discussing the concept of *euergetism* (elite generosity and benefaction) as represented by these inscriptions later, but for now we should focus on the specific political allegiance that they publicize.

The two dedicatory inscriptions that mention Herod's friendship with Rome both come from the Acropolis in Athens. This location is hardly accidental. As we will discuss later, Herod actively tried to promote himself as a typical Hellenistic monarch. What better way than to make donations and erect statues at the most Greek site in the ancient world, the Acropolis? Indeed, the first of these inscriptions was found directly behind the Parthenon, the famous temple to Athena on the Acropolis. It reads as follows: "the people to King Herod, friend of the Romans *(Philorōmaios)*, because of his good works and good will toward the city." The second inscription was found west of the Erechtheion. It reads "the People to Herod, the pious King and friend of Caesar *(Philokaisaros)* because of his moral excellence and good works."[20] Besides these two dedicatory inscriptions, archaeologists also have discovered two weights — one of lead from Ashdod and one of limestone of an unknown provenance — that have inscriptions mentioning Herod and his relationship with Rome. The limestone weight's use as an official weight and its mention of Herod's reign suggest that it was created and used in a Judaean market. On the reverse of the lead weight is a small anchor within a wreath, and on the obverse is a five-line inscription that says "In the time of King Herod, Pious and Friend of Caesar *(Philokaisaros).*"[21] The limestone weight's legend, which has one line running around the field on top and two

---

20. *OGIS* 414, 427. *OGIS* 414 reads as follows: *Ho Dēmos Basilea Herōdēn Philorōmaion euergesias heneken kai eunoias tēs eis eauton.* *OGIS* 427 reads: *Ho Dēmos Basilea Herōdēn eusebē kai Philokaisara arētes heneka kai euergesias.* Scholars disagree over which Herod the inscriptions refer to. Wilhelm Dittenberger, the editor of *OGIS*, believes they refer to Herod Agrippa I, but I believe that Herod the Great is more likely because he and not Agrippa was active in Athens, because many of Agrippa's inscriptions identify him as *basileus megas* ("great king") while his grandfather used only *basileus* ("king"; see Arie Kindler, *Coins of the Land of Israel* [Jerusalem: Keter, 1974], 29-33, 42-43), and Agrippa did not normally refer to himself only as Herod but as Herod Agrippa. Cf. P. Richardson, *Herod: King of the Jews and Friend of the Romans* (Columbia: University of South Carolina Press, 1996), 207-8.

21. *Basileuontos Herōdou Eusebous kai Philokaisaros.* For a discussion of this inscription see Alla Kushnir-Stein, "An Inscribed Lead Weight from Ashdod: A Reconsideration," *Zeitschrift für Papyrologie und Epigraphik* 105 (1995): 81-84.

horizontal lines within, reads "Year 32 [9/8 BCE] of King Herod, the Pious, Friend of Caesar *(Philokaisaros)*. Inspector of the Markets. Three minas."[22]

All four of these inscriptions testify to the importance that Herod attached to his relationship with Augustus and Rome. Although we do not know exactly why the Athenians erected two statues for Herod on the Acropolis, they probably were commissioned to honor him for some benefaction to the city. The Athenians may have chosen the wording of the inscription, but surely they would have carved something of which they thought Herod would approve. The two weights functioned similarly, even though their audience — not visitors to the Acropolis but local Judaeans using local markets — and function as official measurements of weight differed from the Acropolis inscriptions, which were meant to honor Herod's generosity to the city of Athens. In both cases, the presence of the term *Philokaisaros* testifies to the importance that Herod's regime attached to this title. Connection to Augustus, the source of all legitimacy in the post-Actium world, was essential. It reassured a king's subjects that he was of importance to the *princeps* and his regime, and consequently so was his kingdom. Such status was extremely important to Herod immediately following Actium, when his former connection to Antony would have been a real liability. However, the continued appearance of this title as late as 9/8 BCE (the approximate date of the limestone weight) indicates that close connection to Augustus and Rome never lessened in importance. Rome had put Herod on the throne in 40, and it was still ensuring his legitimacy more than twenty-five years later.

Herod's Dated Coins: Donative and Advertisement

In the previous chapter, we discussed how Herod used coins to link himself to his Hasmonean predecessors. As we discussed, coins were useful because of their volume and wide dispersion throughout the kingdom. Did Herod also strike coins to connect himself with Augustus? The answer may lie in four coin types which modern numismatists refer to as the

---

22. *L LB* ("Year 32") *Basileōs Herōdou Eusebous Philokaisaros agoranomou mna tria.* Meshorer originally published this inscription, but instead of *Eusebous* he suggested *Euergetou*. Kushnir-Stein's reconstruction of the stone weight from Ashdod and her comparison of the two weights suggests that Meshorer's reconstruction is incorrect. See Ya'akov Meshorer, "A Stone Weight from the Reign of Herod," *IEJ* 20 (1970): 97-98 (plate 27). Cf. Kushnir-Stein, "Inscribed Lead Weight," 83-84.

Herod the Augustan Client King

Herodian dated series. These four coin types all have the same date, "Year 3," and mintmark (ᛦ). In addition, every coin of this series has the same inscription, ΒΑΣΙΛΕΩΣ ΗΡΩΔΟΥ, "of King Herod," and uses the same style of neat and orderly lettering, starting at the top and moving clockwise to form a closed circle. There are four combinations of coin types in the dated series:

OBVERSE	REVERSE
1. a tripod with a *lebēs* (bowl)	a military helmet surmounted by a star
2. a crested helmet with cheek pieces	a decorated shield
3. a winged caduceus	a poppy head on a stem with leaves
4. an *aphlaston* (decoration on a ship's stern)	a palm branch with a fillet.[23]

In the past, several scholars have attempted to date these coins and explain their symbolic significance. For our purposes, it is not necessary to go into an exhaustive investigation of the previous theories and their deficiencies. Such analysis appears in previous publications of mine as well as of others. For now though we can briefly indicate that the existing theories do not adequately explain the evidence.

First, regarding the ᛦ symbol:[24]

---

23. For a general discussion of the coins of the Herodian dated series see Meshorer, *TJC*, 61-65, 221 (plate 44). Cf. D. Hendin, *Guide to Biblical Coins* (4th ed.; New York: Amphora, 2001), 161-62 (plate 9); A. K. Marshak, "Herod the Great and the Power of Image: Political Self-Presentation in the Herodian Dynasty" (Ph.D. diss., Yale University, 2008), 214-15. For discussion of Herod's largest coin and the images on it see David Hendin, "Confirmation of Herod Coin Motif Now Possible," *The Celator* 6 (1992): 38; "The Helmet on Herod's Large Coin," *The Celator* 12 (1998): 30. Cf. Meshorer, *TJC*, 64, 220, where Meshorer argues that the image is both a Roman auger's ceremonial cap (64) and a military helmet (220). For Sandy Brenner's theory about the image see "Coin of Herod the Great: Star or Crest?" *The Celator* 14 (2000): 40-47; "Herod the Great Remains True to Form," *Near Eastern Archaeology* 64 (2001): 212-14; Jean-Philippe Fontanille, "The Largest Herodian Coins: The Very First Dies," *The Celator* 19 (2005): 18-25. For the Greek *stater* from Orthagoreia see D. Sear, *Roman Coins and Their Values* (4th ed.; London: Seaby, 1988), numbers 1435 and 1436. For the coins of John Hyrcanus I and Herod Archelaus see Meshorer, *TJC*, 36, 79-80 (plates 18 and 48); Hendin, *Biblical Coins*, 133, 170-71 (plates 8-10).

24. The recent monograph by Donald Ariel and Jean-Philippe Fontanille contains an extremely well-organized and articulated critique of the following theories on the mintmark

Baruch Kanael suggests that the symbol is an abbreviation for "year 3" *(tritō etei)*. But there are no Palestinian or even Mediterranean precedents for using symbols on a coin to designate the same year a second time. While it is possible that Herod's dated coins are unique in this way, it is unlikely.

Josef Meyshan regards the symbol as an abbreviation for the city of Tyre. But these coins have been found far more commonly in and around the city of Samaria/Sebaste and thus were most likely minted there, not in Tyre. Furthermore, Tyre had a well-established symbolic vocabulary for its coins, including a club, a palm tree, ambrosial stones, and a conch. When not using one of those symbols, Tyrian coins used a ⊅ monogram surmounting a club. There is no indication that Tyre ever used a ⊉.

According to Michael Krupp and Shraga Qedar (echoed by Nikos Kokkinos), ⊉ is actually a cross and the Greek letter *rho* and is meant to evoke an *ēta* and a *rho* *(ēr)*, which is an abbreviation of the name Herod *(Herōdēs)*. They base their theory on one variant diadem-table coin, and Kokkinos, while using this one variant, finds only one more variant coin (an anchor-double cornucopia coin) with a cross standing in for *ē*. If ⊉ was the Herodian family's "standard mintmark,"[25] why does another symbol, ⊢P, appear on the king's official stone weight?[26] Additionally, Herod's name already appears on the coin, and, while possible, it would certainly be abnormal for the name to appear twice. It is far more likely that these two variant coins were created simply through errors in striking.

Ya'akov Meshorer regards ⊉ as an abbreviation for "tetrarch" *(tetrachēs)*. He reached this conclusion by connecting Herod's ⊉ coins with a coin of Ptolemy son of Mennaeus, tetrarch of Chalcis, struck in 63/62 BCE, that also has ⊉. But it predates the Herodian dated series by decades. Moreover, none of Ptolemy's other coins make use of this monogram, and it does not appear on coins of other contemporary tetrarchs. As an isolated occurrence, it is less likely that Herod would adopt it for his own symbolic vocabulary. Additionally, Meshorer

---

and dating of the dated series. See Donald T. Ariel and Jean-Philippe Fontanille, *The Coins of Herod: A Modern Analysis and Die Classification* (Leiden: Brill, 2012), 90-92, 124-26.

25. N. Kokkinos, *The Herodian Dynasty: Origins, Roles in Society and Eclipse* (rev. ed.; London: Spink, 2010), 130.

26. Meshorer, "A Stone Weight," 97.

The dated series of Herod the Great
These four coin types are distinguished from all of Herod's other coins by their inclusion of a date and a mintmark.

incorrectly calculated the year Antony appointed Herod tetrarch (see below).

According to Jodi Magness, ₱ is an abbreviation for Latin *tribunicia potestas* ("tribunician power"). But there is no precedent for Jewish coins with Latin inscriptions, and even the Roman procurators who ruled Judaea after its annexation in 6 CE did not strike coins that used Latin. It is also unlikely that Herod used Latin on his coins since the lingua franca of the Herodian court was Greek.

Second, among theories concerning the date, "Year 3," of the coins:

Kanael, Meyshan, and several others identify the date as 37 BCE, in commemoration of Herod's conquest of Judaea and establishment of his de facto control of the kingdom. But coin-find evidence suggests that the dated coins were minted in Samaria/Sebaste, which did not officially become part of Herod's kingdom until Augustus's confirmation of his rule in 30 BCE (*BJ* 1.396; *AJ* 15.217). How and why would Herod have struck coins in a city he did not rule? Archaeological evidence suggests that prior to Herod's rebuilding of Samaria/Sebaste in 27 BCE the city had not yet fully recovered from its destruction by John Hyrcanus I in ca. 108 BCE.[27]

Meshorer identifies the date as 40 BCE, in commemoration of Herod's

---

27. For the numismatic evidence that Samaria was destroyed ca. 108 BCE and not substantially rebuilt until the Herodian period see Ilan Shachar, "The Historical and Numismatic Significance of Alexander Jannaeus' Later Coinage as Found in Archaeological Excavations," *PEQ* 136 (2004): 5-33. Cf. Dan Barag, "New Evidence on the Foreign Policy of John Hyrcanus I," *INJ* 12 (1992-93): 1-12. Josephus complicates this issue slightly by reporting various events in Samaria that suggest some settlement activity prior to Herod's rebuilding of the city. He reports in *AJ* 14.75 that Pompey restored Samaria to its original inhabitants in his settlement of 63 BCE, in *AJ* 14.88 that Samaria was among the cities Gabinius restored during his proconsulship of Syria, in *AJ* 14.284 that Herod repaired the city of Samaria soon after the death of his father, in *AJ* 14.413 that Herod also left members of his family, including his mother, in Samaria before setting out against pro-Antigonus guerillas operating out of Galilee, in *AJ* 14.431, 457 that Samaria was the site of skirmishes between Antigonus's forces and Herod's, in *AJ* 14.437 that Herod set out from Samaria to Samosata in summer 38 BCE to aid Antony's siege of that city, and in *BJ* 1.344; *AJ* 14.467; 15.240-46 that Herod chose to marry Mariamme in Samaria and recuperated there after executing her in 29 BCE. It is certainly possible that some rebuilding had occurred prior to Herod's rebuilding of the city. However, the coin-find evidence is rather conclusive, and Josephus is not always the most reliable source. More likely than not, some people had already started moving back and rebuilding, but, prior to Herod's rebuilding, the city was nowhere near its former glory and size.

appointment as king of Judaea in the third year of his tetrarchy. This would require Herod's appointment as tetrarch to have occurred in 42 BCE, but literary evidence suggests that he did not become tetrarch until 41. This theory would also require that Herod minted his most elaborate coins at the beginning of his three-year quest to secure the throne of Judaea, a time when he was low on funds and supplies. Meshorer argued that the coins were struck in Samaria/Sebaste, but, again, Samaria/Sebaste did not officially become part of Herod's kingdom until 30 BCE.

Magness regards "year 3" as a reference to the third year of tribunician power of either Augustus (20 BCE) or Agrippa (15 BCE). But again the unlikelihood of the mintmark referring to *tribunicia potestas* removes any real reason to privilege 20 or 15 BCE over any other year.

If these "Year 3" coins are not from 40, 37, 20, or 15 BCE, then when were they minted? To answer that question we should begin by observing that they were minted in Samaria/Sebaste, that they have some connection to the city itself, and that they were struck in a limited series (hence their relative scarcity in proportion to other Herodian coins) to commemorate an event in Herod's reign that had some importance to his identity as king of Judaea and that occurred in the third year after some other significant event, which itself had ushered in a new era for Herod. The year that best fits these observations is 27 BCE, three years after Herod's confirmation in his kingship and neighboring Syria's becoming a "province of Caesar" controlled by a legate appointed directly by the *princeps*. And 27 BCE was itself when Octavian received the name "Augustus" and Herod began work on the reconstruction and expansion of Sebaste, his first city in honor of Augustus, and the beginning of its settlement by military veterans.[28] ⸋ sim-

---

28. For a detailed discussion of my proposed chronology see A. K. Marshak, "The Dated Coins of Herod the Great: Towards a New Chronology," *JSJ* 37 (2006): 212-40. Cf. Marshak, "Herod the Great and the Power of Image," 234-52. In this theory, "Year 3" refers not to the third year of Herod's reign but to the third year of his new era as a client king in the Augustan principate. We see this notion of a new era in Augustan propaganda as well. An astute politician like Herod would have understood this concept and quickly used it in his own propaganda. Unlike Augustus's new era, which began September, 31 BCE, Herod's new era began in the spring of 30 BCE, after his confirmation at Rhodes. It would thus not have been an Actian era per se, even though it was associated with Augustus. Instead, it would be better to refer to it as a "Rhodian" era in reference to Herod's confirmation at Rhodes. For the establishment of Augustus's Actian era see E. J. Bickerman, *Chronology of the Ancient World* (London: Thames and Hudson, 1968), 73. Cf. "Actium," *OCD,* 10. For an era of Pharsalus

ply represented the name of the mintmaster, so that we do not need an overly complicated explanation of the mark.

Many of the symbols on the four coins (e.g., the Apollo tripod, the star atop the military helmet, the shield, and the aphlaston) make more sense in an Augustan context than in an Antonian context.[29] Some of the symbols (e.g., the poppy stalk, the Macedonian-style helmet, and the Macedonian-style shield), along with the coin-find evidence, connect the coins with Sebaste more than with any other city in Judaea. Sebaste was the first major urban project in Herod's kingdom, and he began it three years into this new era in his reign. In an attempt to outdo other neighboring dynasts in highlighting his distinctive relationship with Augustus, he thus minted special coinage that was more aesthetically pleasing and significantly heavier than his previous issues.

In this new Augustan era, Herod stepped out of the shadow of Cleopatra and the Hasmoneans and asserted himself as a glorious Hellenistic Jewish king in his own right. For a decade, from his appointment as king

---

beginning in June 48 BCE see Bickerman, *Chronology,* 73. For a Caesarean era beginning in 49/48 BCE see B. V. Head, *Historia Numorum* (Oxford: Clarendon, 1911), 778, 782. For a Caesarean era beginning in 47 BCE see Head, *Historia Numorum,* 716, 781, 793. Ptolemy II Philadelphus (285-246 BCE) is another example of a monarch who began a new era, the "Soter Era" in the twenty-third year of his reign (263/62 BCE). For the Soter era see R. A. Hazzard, *Imagination of a Monarchy: Studies in Ptolemaic Propaganda* (Toronto: University of Toronto Press, 2000), 25-46. One possible problem with my proposed chronology is that none of the written sources ever mention an Actian era for Herod or his reign. While it is true that Josephus mentions two systems for reckoning Herod's reign, they are not based on Actium. Instead, they are reckoned from (1) Herod's 40 BCE coronation and (2) his conquest of Jerusalem in 37 BCE. However, we know of other monarchs having calendars that do not appear in the literary record. For instance, Herod's contemporary and rival Cleopatra used two dating systems — one for her reign in Egypt and a second for her "Syrian era" — and the second of these appears only on her coins. Like Cleopatra, then, Herod may have used another system of reckoning, one based on an Actian calendar, but only his coins record it. I am indebted to Donald T. Ariel for informing me of the two chronologies of Cleopatra. For these chronologies see Ariel, "The Coins of Herod the Great in the Context of the Augustan Empire," in *Herod and Augustus: Papers Presented at the IJS Conference, 21st-23rd June 2005,* ed. D. M. Jacobson and N. Kokkinos (Leiden: Brill, 2009), 113-26, here p. 122. Cf. Ariel, "Numismatic Approach," 192.

29. For the connection of the symbols on the dated series with Augustan imagery see Ariel, "A Numismatic Approach," 208-12 (general discussion), 214-15 (the star on *TJC* 44 with the *sidus Iulium*), 219-20 (the shield on *TJC* 45 with the *clipeus virtutis* presented to Augustus by the Senate in 27 BCE), 223 (the *aplaston* on *TJC* 47 with the Augustan symbol for victory at Actium). Cf. Paul Zanker, *The Power of Images in the Age of Augustus,* trans. Alan Shapiro (Ann Arbor: University of Michigan Press, 1990), 82-84, 92-97.

in 40 BCE until Actium, Herod had been primarily an ally of Antony. Now Antony was dead and disgraced. Herod, along with the rest of the Roman world, had to show Augustus that he could still be useful to the new regime and could adapt to the new political situation. An impressive new coinage commemorating the first *urbs Caesarae* was a rather conspicuous but nonetheless effective way of advertising Herod's change in allegiance and the simultaneous change in the political environment of the Roman world.

To whom were these coins and their messages directed? It is certainly possible that Herod was directing these coins to an outside audience, specifically the imperial court. By referencing Augustan images such as the Apollan tripod and the Actian aphlaston, Herod would be offering symbolic nods to Augustus's recent victory at Actium. Nevertheless, the material used for these coins (bronze) suggests a much more local scale of circulation and thus an internal audience, specifically one in or around the minting city of Sebaste. For which internal audience in Sebaste could these coins have been meant? The only real possibility is the coins were given to the colony of military veterans whom Herod was beginning to settle in the city.

Are there examples for this kind of royal donative with which Herod would have been familiar? Suetonius notes that Augustus repeatedly distributed gifts of money to the Roman people. Augustus himself mentions seven such instances in his *Res Gestae*. In both documents, the term used for these distributions is *congiarium,* which connects them to the periodic Republican practice of general donations to the people of oil, wine, grain, money, or some other commodity. A specific example of Augustus's *congiaria* occurred at the beginning of his career in 44 BCE. Julius Caesar's will stipulated that on his death each Roman citizen should receive 300 *sesterces* (seventy-five *denarii*). Augustus, then a young politician trying to secure the goodwill of the plebeians, determined that he would honor this proviso, even though Marc Antony had delayed the release of Caesar's property and created all sorts of obstacles to Augustus securing the funds. Not one to be frustrated in his plans, he used his own money and that of his supporters to make up the difference and thereby increase his support among the lower classes.[30]

---

30. For a general discussion of the Roman practice of *congiarium*, see William Smith, ed., *Dictionary of Greek and Roman Antiquities* (2nd ed.; Boston: Little, Brown, 1870), 350-51. Also see Ariel, "Numismatic Approach," 68-70. For a discussion of the various sizes of Roman imperial *congiaria,* see Richard Duncan-Jones, *Money and Government in the Roman Empire* (Cambridge: Cambridge University Press, 1994), 248-50. For Augustus's first

Herod was most likely present for a *congiarium* mentioned in the *Res Gestae* that took place in 12 BCE and may even have participated in it. He was in Rome seeking help in settling his domestic problems, specifically a fight with his two sons Aristobulus and Alexander. As a token of his appreciation for ending this family squabble, Herod gave 300 talents to Augustus, who, Josephus records, was at that time "offering spectacles and handouts to the people of Rome" (*AJ* 16.128). This passage refers to a *congiarium* that coincided with Augustus's assumption of the office of *pontifex maximus* and commemorated the death of Marcus Agrippa.[31] A variant reading of the particular verb used in the quoted clause *(poioumenos* instead of *poioumenon)* suggests that Herod himself participated in the *congiarium*. If nothing else, his gift of 300 talents paid for some of the cost of this large-scale benefaction to the people of Rome. While this example is not a precedent for a distribution in 27 BCE to the veterans of Sebaste, it does provide us with a specific example of Herod connecting to and even participating in a Roman *congiarium*.

The historical picture is now coming into focus. When Herod began rebuilding the city of Samaria in the spring of 27 BCE, he populated it with a detachment of non-Jewish military colonists, whose job was to police and guard the region from both foreign and domestic enemies. Because these colonists were so important to the defense of the region, it was essential that they remain loyal. One way to ensure this loyalty was to pay them. Thus, Herod's officials struck a special limited series of coins in 27 BCE, which were then distributed to these colonists as part of a royal *congiarium* to celebrate the rebuilding of the city and its renaming as Sebaste in honor of Augustus. However, these coins did more than just line the pockets of these new military colonists. They also articulated a carefully calibrated message of political allegiance and proximity: they spoke to and advertised

---

congiarium in 44 BCE see *Res Gest. Divi Aug.* 15. Cf. Appian, *B. Civ.* 3.17-24, 28; Plutarch, *Ant.* 16.1-2; Dio 45.5. Plutarch says Augustus paid the people in *drachmae,* but in all probability his reference to that denomination reflects his Greek background rather than reality. It would have been unusual for Augustus not to pay the legacy in Roman coinage *(sesterces* or *denarii)*. For Suetonius's comment on Augustus's *congiaria,* see *Aug.* 41. I am indebted to Donald T. Ariel for his talk at a 2005 conference in London in which he connected the *congiaria* and Herod's possible distribution in 12 BCE. See Ariel, "Coins of Herod the Great," 117-18, 122-24. Cf. Ariel, "Numismatic Approach," 70-71.

31. For Josephus's account of Herod's trip to Rome see *AJ* 16.90-129. For Augustus's assumption of the office of *pontifex maximus,* see *Res Gest. Divi Aug.* 10; Suetonius, *Aug.* 31; Dio 54.27.2-3.

the close relationship of Herod, Augustus, and the new principate. Through their use of symbols associated with and used by Augustus, they asserted a close friendship between king and *princeps* and the respect Herod had for his patron. As instruments of political self-presentation, they fashioned a double message that reverberated inside Judaea as well as throughout the Roman world. They depicted a confident monarch who had the power, wealth, and ability necessary to plan and construct a new city, the first of its kind. Perhaps more importantly, they loudly proclaimed Herod's new allegiance to Augustus and the principate at a time when he needed to distance himself from his prior loyalties and relationships. He was no longer an Antonian client, cowed into submission by fear of Cleopatra. He was now Augustus's man in the East, a king capable of constructing massive urban monuments to his new patron.

Herod's Undated Coins and Rome

Besides the dated series, other Herodian coins reference the close relationship between Herod and the principate. In the previous chapter, we discussed two such coins (the inscription-anchor and anchor-double cornucopia coins), although there we focused on their symbolic allusions to Herod's Hasmonean status. Here we will discuss two more coins whose iconography suggests a Roman connection, the diadem-table series (*TJC* 48-54) and the anchor-galley coin (*TJC* 65). I will discuss the final undated coin, the single cornucopia-eagle coin (*TJC* 66) in the penultimate chapter. Before beginning such a discussion, it is worth recalling the possible allusions to Rome on the anchor-double cornucopia coins, which were initially struck ca. 17 BCE and referenced the return of Herod's heirs Alexander and Aristobulus, who had just spent more than a decade in Rome with Augustus and his family, which might also reference the ongoing construction at Caesarea Maritima and its harbor Sebastos, and which were used, at least initially, to pay the workers building the city and the harbor.

Diadem-Table Coins

Both the diadem (an ornamental headband worn as a crown) and the three-legged table seem to have been important numismatic symbols for Herod and his regime. These images appear on coins in all three denomi-

Bronze diadem-table series of Herod the Great
This multi-denominational series of bronze coins was probably the first minting series during the reign of Herod the Great.

nations (small, medium, and large). Moreover, these two symbols appear individually or together on ten distinct coin types. As a pair they appear on seven. In comparison, the anchor, the other frequently used image, appears on seven coin types. The relative importance of the diadem and the table demands an explanation of their significance and the chronology of the coins on which they appear.

Examinations of the archaeological contexts in which these coins have been found suggest a minting early in Herod's reign. Epigraphic analysis agrees with the archaeological evidence. In particular, the coins' use of classical omegas (Ω) also suggests an earlier dating. Earlier coins of Alexander Jannaeus and Mattathias Antigonus only use the classical omega, while Judaean coins that postdate Herod, specifically those of Archelaus, Agrippa I, and the procurators, only use the cursive omega. Finally, the existence of two denominations for the diadem-table coins shows a degree of continuity with the coins of Herod's predecessor, Mattathias Antigonus, as opposed to Herod's successor in Judaea, Herod Archelaus, who lacked coins of similar types but different denominations. This denominational continuity with Antigonus also supports an earlier minting. Both its status as a denominational series and its epigraphic style also connect these diadem-table coins with the dated series, which we have already established was relatively early. Given all this information, it seems reasonable to conclude, as Ariel does, that the diadem-table series are the earliest of the undated Herodian coins.[32]

32. While most of Herod's undated coins appear in the material from the buildings of Area E in the Jewish Quarter in Jerusalem, the diadem-table coin is one of only two types that appear in the stratum below the buildings, the other being one of the inscription-anchor types (*TJC* 61). Since we have already established that the inscription-anchor coins are relatively early, it would make sense that the diadem-table coins are early as well. For the appearance of the diadem-table coins in the lowest strata of Area E (Strata 3 and 4) see Ariel, "Numismatic Approach," 257-58. Cf. Donald T. Ariel, "The Coins," in *Jewish Quarter Excavations in the Old City of Jerusalem: Conducted by Nahman Avigad, 1969-1982*, vol. 3, ed. Hillel Geva (Jerusalem: Israel Exploration Society, 2010), 192-217. The appearance of only one diadem-table coin in the Kadman Pavilion Horde and the absence of any of these coins from a horde discovered in Antipatris, which Herod founded only after 12 BCE, suggests that these coins were early. See Ariel, "Numismatic Approach," 249-52 on the lone appearance of this coin series in the Kadman Pavilion Hoard and the significance of this scarcity, 252-53 on the absence of diadem-table coins in the Antipatris hoard, and 242-44, table 9, 329-31, 337-38 on the epigraphic style of letter on the diadem-table coins and this style's significance. For the founding of Antipatris after the dedication of Caesarea see *AJ* 16.142. Although some examples of the diadem-table coins use the cursive omega (ω), many do not. On the other hand, the latest of Herod's issues, specifically the anchor-double cornucopia

If these coins were early, indeed the earliest of the undated coins, then for which event or accomplishment did Herod strike them? The diadem offers a possible clue: diadems were a symbol of kingship and legitimacy, and in 30 BCE Herod's legitimacy was in question. He had supported the loser in the civil war between Octavian and Antony, and in the spring of that year he rushed to Rhodes to persuade Octavian to retain him as client king of Judaea. Although in retrospect Herod was the obvious choice to rule Judaea, at the time his hold on power was insecure enough that he decided to eliminate his potential rival, the elderly Hyrcanus II, and to arrange a place of refuge for his family in the event that the outcome of his meeting should be unfavorable. According to Josephus, when Herod met Augustus, he made a point of removing his diadem as a sign of submission and deference. When Augustus had confirmed Herod's position, he signaled his status by placing the diadem back on his head. Along with his confirmed status, Herod also received additional territories and was able to return to Judaea with "more honor and freedom" than he had possessed before. All told, the meeting at Rhodes was a resounding success. There could be no better way to commemorate such a political triumph than the minting of coinage, a physical sign of a king's autonomy and freedom. It is no surprise, therefore, that on the obverse face of this new coin series was the diadem, the symbol of Herod's new legitimacy as king.[33]

Although these coins were extremely important to Herod's legitimacy, they seem to have been minted only for a brief span of time. Such brevity, coupled with the significance of their date of minting, has led Donald T. Ariel to speculate that they may have been used for a royal *congiarium* to celebrate Herod's reconfirmation. The use of a *congiarium* to mark the be-

---

(*TJC* 59), the single cornucopia-eagle (*TJC* 66), and the anchor-galley (*TJC* 65), only use the cursive form of the letter. The diadem-table coins' use of the angular sigma (Σ) also may suggest an early minting, but this evidence is not conclusive. The dated coins — whether 37 or 27 BCE, they are relatively early Herodian issues — all use only angular sigmas, which suggests that this letter might be indicative of earlier coins. However, Antigonus's coins use the lunate sigma (C), and thus this feature cannot conclusively fix relative chronology. For the denominational continuity with Antigonus's coins see Ariel, "Numismatic Approach," 338. After Herod's diadem-table coins, the Jerusalem mint lacked a denominational series until the middle of the Jewish War (69 CE) some one hundred years later.

33. For Herod's meeting with Augustus at Rhodes see *BJ* 1.386-97; *AJ* 15.198. For his removal of his diadem before meeting Augustus see *BJ* 1.387; *AJ* 15.187. For Augustus's placing the diadem on Herod's head after reconfirming his rule see *BJ* 1.393; *AJ* 15.195. Also see *AJ* 15.162-78, 184-86 for Herod's insecurity immediately after Actium and the steps he took to solidify his position, including the execution of Hyrcanus.

ginning of a ruler's reign was frequent among later Roman emperors, and, as discussed before, Augustus himself provided one to the Roman people to mark his acceptance of Julius Caesar's name and the stipulations of his will. It would not be unreasonable for Herod to behave similarly and to mark the beginning of a new era in his reign with a distribution of money using a new coin that highlighted his legitimate and confirmed status as king of Judaea.

In that same year (30 BCE) Herod also celebrated his *decennalia* as king of Judaea. It is possible, therefore, that the symbols on the coin allude to this moment as well. Most of the diadem-table series depict a symbol inside the diadem which has at various times been called a + or an X. One explanation is that it is the Roman numeral X, ten. If true, it would then be an ideal symbol for the king's *decennalia*, which would have been 31/30 BCE. However, given the turbulence with which the year 31 BCE ended, with Herod closing out the year unsure of his status within the new regime, it would not have been surprising if he postponed any celebration until he had met with Augustus at Rhodes. Once assured of his place in the new regime, Herod could have returned home to celebrate his *decennalia* and to welcome Augustus as he traveled on to Egypt. The main weakness in this theory is that it requires Herod to have used a Latin numeral on a Jewish coin, something that does not happen on any other Jewish coins before or after Herod's reign.

Another possible interpretation for the symbol within the diadem, first proposed by Ya'akov Meshorer, is that it is the Greek letter X *(chi)*, symbolizing the high priesthood. Meshorer connected the X with the high priesthood by referencing a pericope in the Babylonian Talmud, *b. Keritot* 5.2, which discusses the anointing of kings and priests. According to this pericope, kings were anointed by tracing the shape of the diadem on their foreheads. Priests, on the other hand, were anointed by tracing the shape of the letter X. According to Richardson, Herod appointed a new high priest, Joshua ben Phiabi, in 30 BCE. If Meshorer's interpretation is true, then the composite symbol of a X within a diadem would reference Herod's control over the high priesthood and his appointment of a new high priest, an act he achieved in the same year that the coins began to be minted.

Meshorer's theory is a tempting one, especially because it provides a clear link between one of Herod's coins and a concrete attempt by him to assert control over the high priesthood. However, while we cannot rule out the historical reliability of the Talmudic passage and its relevance to the diadem-table coins, we should be wary of using the rabbinic material without reservations, especially given the often ahistorical nature of rabbinic texts. Thus, it would seem that the most credible explanation at this time is that Herod struck the coins in 30 BCE, possibly as the vehicle of a royal *congiarium,* but certainly as a commemoration and celebration of his confirmation as king of Judaea by Augustus.[34]

Anchor-Galley

Given the importance of Caesarea Maritima and its significance for his political self-presentation, it is reasonable to assume that Herod might have struck a coin to mark the completion and dedication of the city. As we discussed in the previous chapter, he had already minted coins celebrating the Caesarea project and used them to pay its workers. Nevertheless, the completion of this decade-long project was monumental enough that Herod had established a great quinquennial festival in honor of Augustus, complete with athletic and musical competitions as well as gladiatorial combat, horse races, and beast hunts. Might Herod have wanted to strike a new coin to celebrate this event in an even more conspicuous way? Is there a coin that could have been this special issue?

One of the undated coins, specifically the anchor-galley coin (*TJC* 65), is a potential candidate, and a detailed analysis of it, including its scarcity, fabric, and style, seems to support such a hypothesis. In the first place, an examination of the relevant coin finds suggests that it was relatively rare and comprised less than one percent of provenanced Herodian coins. Such scarcity supports the notion that it was a special and limited minting. As for its place in the general chronology of Herodian coinage, there is conflicting

---

34. For Ariel's discussion of the minting motivations for the diadem-table series see Ariel, "Coins of Herod," 117-18; "Numismatic Approach," 343-47. For Meshorer's theory about the symbols on the obverse of these coins see *TJC,* 65-66. For a discussion of the symbol within the diadem see Ariel, "Numismatic Approach," 247-48. For Joshua ben Phiabi as high priest see *AJ* 15.322. For Richardson's dating of the appointment of ben Phiabi to 30 BCE see Richardson, *Herod,* 243, n. 13, 244-45. Richardson sees the appointments of ben Phiabi and his successor, Simon ben Boethos, both of whom may have been Egyptian, as connected to Herod's decision to rebuild the Temple and his attempt to integrate Diaspora Jews — in this case Egyptian Jews, specifically Jews worshiping at the temple in Leontopolis — into the Temple cult in Jerusalem. For Hananel's initial appointment to the high priesthood see *AJ* 15.22. For his reappointment following the murder of Aristobulus III see *AJ* 15.56.

 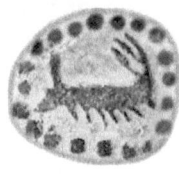

Bronze anchor-galley lepton of Herod the Great
Both the anchor and the galley were symbols often associated with maritime events or accomplishments.

evidence. On the one hand, the style of anchor, specifically its lack of a ring at the top, suggests an earlier minting. On the other hand, the style of the lettering and the outward reading inscription suggest a later date. Moreover, in terms of style and fabric, this coin is similar to the anchor-double cornucopia issue and thus was probably contemporaneous or nearly so. If we accept that the anchor-double cornucopia issue came later in Herod's reign (ca. 17-15 CE), then it makes sense that the anchor-galley coin was struck in the same period. However, a late date does not necessarily mean a minting in 12 BCE.[35]

In addition, another factor against connecting the anchor-galley coin to the inauguration of Caesarea is its small denomination and relatively poor quality. As such, it would have made a somewhat unimpressive vehicle for a royal *congiarium*. One would expect Herod to create a more impressive coin to commemorate his urban masterpiece. If not a *congiarium* coin, then what? Another possible interpretation for this coin is that it references Herod's involvement in Agrippa's Bosporus campaign. Josephus

---

35. For Herod's establishment of a festival in honor of Augustus see *BJ* 1.415; *AJ* 16.136-41. The idea that the anchor-galley coin had a connection to Caesarea Maritima first appeared in Ya'akov Meshorer's *Ancient Jewish Coinage* (New York: Amphora, 1982), in which he proposes dating this coin to the founding of the Sebastos harbor at Caesarea. However, it is not entirely clear whether "founding" means the beginning of construction (ca. 22 BCE) or the dedication (ca. 12 BCE). As I have shown, numismatic analysis of the coin suggests that the coin more likely comes from the dedication than the commencement of work on Caesarea. For Meshorer's discussion of the coin see *Ancient Jewish Coinage*, 2:13. For the relative scarcity of this issue see Ariel, "Numismatic Approach," 142, table 7. For analysis of the anchor image as well as the epigraphic style of the coin see "Numismatic Approach," 242-44, table 9, 339-40. For the similarity in style and fabric between the anchor-galley and the anchor-double cornucopia coins see J. Meyshan, *Essays in Jewish Numismatics* (Jerusalem: Israel Numismatic Society, 1968), 58. Cf. Ariel, "Numismatic Approach," 332, 340.

reports that on Herod's return from the Pontus he assembled the people, reported his accomplishments, and remitted a fourth of their taxes. If he wished to celebrate these accomplishments, a new coin, decorated with naval images, might work. These naval images led scholars such as Meyshan and Richardson to such a conclusion.

While there is no definitive argument against such an attribution, further investigation suggests 12 BCE is still the preferable date. As we have discussed above, in that year Herod received control of the copper mines on Cyprus and faced a revolt in the northeastern province of Trachonitis. Thus, in one year he received a large supply of raw materials for bronze coinage and developed a need for coinage to pay soldiers. Finally, in that same year, he named his three eldest sons, Antipater, Alexander, and Aristobulus, co-heirs and successors. These details, together with the completion of Caesarea Maritima, indicate that 12 BCE was an incredibly eventful year for Judaea, one in which a new coin issue had both a practical use (paying soldiers) and a symbolic one (celebrating the completion of a city and the naming of heirs). Taking all this historical information together with the sheer grandeur and scope of the Caesarea project as well as its importance to Herod's political self-presentation, it would seem that a minting in 12 BCE, while perhaps not as a *congiarium*, would still be credible and more probable than one in 14 BCE.[36]

Conclusion

We thus have uncovered multiple vehicles by which Herod advertised his status as a loyal and dutiful client king of Rome. Through gestures and actions ranging from simple financial support to grandiose urban projects

---

36. For Meyshan's and Richardson's initial attribution see Meyshan, *Essays*, 58; Richardson, *Herod*, 213. For Ariel's rejection of their hypothesis see "Numismatic Approach," 359. For Augustus's gift of the Cypriot copper mines see *AJ* 16.128. For the outbreak of rebellion in Trachonitis see *AJ* 16.130, 271-76; cf. 15.343-48. For Ariel's analysis of the anchor-galley coins and their chronology see "Numismatic Approach," 339-40, 359. The anchor-galley coin is absent from the Kadman Pavilion Hoard and from Area E in the Jewish Quarter, both of which date to the penultimate decade of the first century BCE. Because of its relative scarcity, its absence is not conclusive proof of its minting in 12 BCE. However, the absence does support the theory that it is a later issue than both the single cornucopia-eagle and the anchor-double cornucopia, both of which are present in the hoard and Area E. See "Numismatic Approach," 250, table 11, 258, table 15.

honoring Augustus, Herod strove to make his mark in a crowded political arena. In the next chapter, we will see another aspect of Herod's client kingship, namely his efforts to bring Judaea more fully into the Roman sphere through a deliberate and decisive program of Romanization.

CHAPTER 8

Bringing Judaea into the Roman Sphere: Herod and Romanization

Of all the obligations incumbent on Herod as a client king of Rome, none had more long-lasting and far-reaching consequences for his kingdom than his consistent policy of cultural assimilation and Romanization. Although some degree of Romanization (and certainly a fair amount of Hellenization) had already occurred in Judaea during the Hasmonean period, Herod significantly accelerated the process. By the end of his reign, Judaea was fully within the Roman sphere, and Roman influences could be seen everywhere from buildings to bathing practices.

There is significant evidence that Herod maintained an active program of Romanization within the life and activities of his court. This included, among other things, the education of his children in Rome, the importation and consumption of Roman products, and the increasing use of Roman military tactics in the royal army. All these behaviors integrated a client king and his family into the Roman world culturally, but also politically. A more Romanized king would find it easier to interact with Roman elites because they would share the same aesthetic and cultural tastes.

A Roman Education

One of their first steps in this process of Romanization was education. Since the third century BCE, Roman client kings had been sending their sons to Rome to receive a formal education and introduce them into Roman elite society. Specifically, client princes made contacts with both leading Romans and fellow client princes and developed ties of friendship and patronage that would aid them later in life and make the transition from prince to successor as seamless as possible. Just as important, however, was the acculturation that these princes must have undergone while in the capital. During their stay, they would encounter Roman customs and behaviors. Undoubtedly they adopted many of these customs, including perhaps a familiarity with Latin. The end result was that these young princes became increasingly Romanized and, when they returned home, they brought their new Romanization with them. Finally, but no less important, while in Rome these princes represented their fathers and protected their fathers' interests.

Herod was no exception to this custom, and he sent eight sons to Rome, which illustrates well the importance he placed on establishing relationships with powerful Romans and other client princes and kings. The first to go were Alexander and Aristobulus, who arrived in Rome in 22 BCE as the heirs apparent to the throne of Judaea. While in Rome, these princes initially stayed in the home of "a certain Pollio" before moving into the home of Augustus himself. Although there are other possibilities, it is most likely that this Pollio was the famous poet, historian, and ex-consul Gaius Asinius Pollio.[1] Like Herod, he had been a loyal Antonian who had successfully switched allegiances. Moreover, he also seems to have had an interest in Jews and Judaism since he surrounded himself with writers such as Marcus Terentius Varro, Timagenes of Alexandria, and Alexander Polyhistor, all of whom were familiar with Judaism or had even written about Jews. As an ex-consul and one of the leading intellectuals of the era,

---

1. For the arrival of Alexander and Aristobulus in Rome see *AJ* 15.342-43. Cf. Samuel Rocca, *Herod's Judaea: A Mediterranean State in the Classical World* (Tübingen: Mohr, 2008), 80. Seven of Herod's nine sons traveled to Rome for an education. He sent Antipater, son of Doris, who was already an adult when he returned to court, to Rome to make connections but not to be educated. Josephus dates the voyage of Alexander and Aristobulus to Rome with one of his more common phrases, *epi toioutois* ("at this time"). In this case, it refers to the completion of the rebuilding of Samaria/Sebaste. For the scholarly debate about the identity of the Pollio with whom the princes stayed see Louis H. Feldman, "Asinius Pollio and His Jewish Interests," *TAPA* 84 (1953): 73-80. David Braund debates Feldman in "Four Notes on the Herods," *CQ* 33 (1983): 240-41, and Feldman replies in "Asinius Pollio and Herod's Sons," *CQ* 35 (1985): 240-43. For other discussions see Ronald Syme, "Who Was Vedius Pollio?" *JRS* 51 (1961): 22-30; Michael Grant, *Herod the Great* (New York: American Heritage, 1971), 145; E. Mary Smallwood, *The Jews under Roman Rule: From Pompey to Diocletian* (Leiden: Brill, 1976), 89 n. 103; Emil Schürer, *The History of the Jewish People in the Age of Jesus Christ (175 BC–AD 135),* ed. Geza Vermes and Fergus Millar (Edinburgh: Clark, 1973-87), 1:321 n. 132; 231 n. 49; Duane W. Roller, *The Building Program of Herod the Great* (Berkeley: University of California Press, 1998), 26-28.

his home would have been an ideal place for the princes to enter Roman elite society and meet important Romans. He may very well have offered the princes their formal introduction to Augustus. The further boon of residing in the *Domus Augusti* not only enabled the princes to become further involved in the Roman aristocratic social scene, but also indicates the importance of Herod and his kingdom to the regime, since presumably not every prince stayed in Augustus's somewhat modest home. Additionally, the princes' presence there would have further strengthened the bonds between Augustus and the Herodian family.

Besides making political and social connections, the two princes became culturally Romanized. They were at the appropriate age (about thirteen or fourteen) for learning grammar and rhetoric, and although there is no explicit evidence for a specific course of study, it is likely that they learned at least some Latin. They also probably learned Roman army techniques and training, something that would have been of great value to the future kings of Judaea. Apparently the youths valued their education greatly because they boasted to their aunt Salome about it and used it as an example of how they were superior to her and her children, who did not have this Roman education.[2]

Although we do not hear of Alexander and Aristobulus promoting their father's interests while in Rome, it may well have occurred. However, we do have evidence that when Herod's eldest son Antipater was in Rome he advocated for his father and attacked his father's enemies. Specifically, when Herod made Antipater co-heir with his stepbrothers, he promptly sent him to Rome. By this time, Antipater was an adult, so his stay in the capital was not for the purposes of education; he was there to be the Judaean mouthpiece. When Herod was feuding with the Nabataean minister Syllaeus, it was Antipater who defended his father before Augustus and accused Syllaeus of murdering several notables in Petra and of plotting to assassinate Herod.

---

2. For client kings sending their sons to Rome to learn Latin see Polybius 27.15 (32.5-6 for the case of Charops of Epirus). Jugurtha of Numidia is perhaps the best example of a client prince who learned Roman military tactics. See Sallust, *Jug.* 7; 9.3; 101.6. Cf. Dio 51.15.6 for Juba II serving in the army under Julius Caesar. See also the discussion below of the Romanization of the Judaean royal army. For Alexander and Aristobulus's boasting of their education to their aunt see *AJ* 16.203. Interestingly, the two princes had a tutor named Gemellus who accompanied them to Rome. Presumably, he was their Latin teacher, although he might have taught them other subjects as well. See *AJ* 16.242-43. Cf. Rocca, *Herod's Judaea*, 91.

Bringing Judaea into the Roman Sphere

For all these reasons, it was essential for Herod to send as many of his sons as possible to Rome. They would reestablish ties with old friends and supporters, make contacts with new friends, defend their father's interests before Augustus, and acculturate themselves to Roman culture and social norms. In this way, Herod's princes became the glue that bound the Judaean kingdom ever more tightly to the Roman center. They were Herod's link to the *princeps* and, on their return to Judaea, the most capable agents of Romanization.[3]

Importation of Roman Luxury Goods

Herod's pattern of increased Romanization extended beyond merely sending his sons to Rome to be educated. He was also an active importer of Roman luxury goods. For instance, in the storerooms at Masada, excavators discovered sixty-five amphorae with Latin *tituli picti* (commercial inscriptions) and six amphora stamps in Latin. Seventeen of the sixty-five inscribed amphorae contain distinct dates, specifically the years 27, 26, 19, and 14 BCE. What about the undated amphorae? Since Masada was primarily used during Herod's reign, it is likely that the majority of the supplies found there, especially the luxury items, date to that period. Additionally, because the dated amphorae all come from Herod's reign, it stands to reason that many, if not all, of the undated ones also come from the same period, especially if they share other common features or contents. Both the dated and undated amphorae contained imported luxury products, which suggest more of a Herodian dating than any other. It is unlikely that a Roman army garrison stationed at Masada before 66

---

3. For Herod's naming of his three sons as co-heirs see *BJ* 1.459; *AJ* 16.134. For Antipater's visit to Rome see *AJ* 16.273. He no doubt benefited from his father's suspicions of his half-brothers. For Antipater's advocacy on behalf of his father see *AJ* 17.54-57. While Nicolaus of Damascus credited himself with persuading Augustus of Syllaeus's guilt and perfidy (*AJ* 16.335-55) and reconciling Augustus with Herod, it is possible that he deliberately ignored Antipater's contribution out of hatred for him. From fragments of Nicolaus we know that the two men did not have a friendly relationship (*FGrH* 90, fragment 136). Moreover, Nicolaus would have wanted to monopolize the credit for this successful embassy to Augustus. However, it is unlikely, especially given his status as royal heir, that Antipater had no role in soliciting Augustus's favor and support. For Herod's sending of Nicolaus to Rome see *AJ* 16.299. A potentially negative result of Herod sending his sons to Rome was that they were free to plot against him while away from his oversight. For Antipater's plots against Herod while in Rome see *AJ* 17.6.

and after 73 CE purchased luxury items from Italy and imported them to the fortress. The local garrisons lived off local products, and the Roman army did not normally supply its soldiers with oil and wine, the products most often carried in amphorae. Thus, we can reasonably infer that many, if not most, of the undated amphorae also come from the Herodian period.[4]

So, what was in these Herodian amphorae? Among the items indicated by the inscriptions are numerous types of wine including Aminean, Caecuban, Massic, Philonianum, and Tarentian, as well as honey, apples from Cumae, and *garum,* a ubiquitous Roman fish sauce. In addition, excavators also found 125 grams of a sandy material at the bottom of a locally-produced jar, which they determined was *allec,* another Roman fish sauce. While the jar was locally produced, the excavators determined that the *allec,* as well as the *garum* from the amphorae, was imported, most likely from Spain. The absence of evidence for *garum* production in Palestine during the Herodian period supports this conclusion.[5] *Garum, muria,* and *allec* were fish sauces that the Romans popularized and that were widely consumed for about a millennium. Besides being a tasty condiment, they preserved the nutritional elements in fish meat for prolonged periods of time and were used to preserve fish, meat, vegetables, and other perishable food items. High quality *garum* usually contained only one type of fish, while the lowest quality product was a mixture

---

4. For analysis of the *tituli picti* and the Latin amphora stamps see Hannah M. Cotton and Joseph Geiger, "The Latin and Greek Documents," in *Masada,* vol. 2 (Jerusalem: Israel Exploration Society, 1989), 8. See also Cotton and Geiger, "The Economic Importance of Herod's Masada," in *Judaea and the Graeco-Roman World in the Time of Herod in the Light of Archaeological Evidence,* ed. Klaus Fittschen and Gideon Foerster (Göttingen: Vandenhoeck and Ruprecht, 1996), 167-68.

5. For the contents of the amphorae see Cotton and Geiger in *Masada,* 2:149-67. Two other amphorae inscriptions (numbers 820 and 821) might refer to *muria,* a fish sauce related to *garum.* The inscriptions are fragmentary, so the reconstruction is speculative at best. For analysis of the contents of the locally-produced jar as well as the provenance of the contents see Hannah Cotton, Omri Lernau, and Yuval Goren, "Fish Sauces from Herodian Masada," *JRA* 9 (1996): 223-31. Cotton, along with Lernau and Goren, took a two-gram sample of the sandy material and analyzed it using a binocular microscope. Based on their observations, they determined that the fish material was composed of a large number of fish scales, broken fin spines, vertebral processes, ribs, and neurocranial fragments. They estimate that the fish whose bones make up the material were about four to five centimeters long. For a discussion of *garum* production and its geographic distribution see Robert I. Curtis, *Garum and Salsamenta: Production and Commerce in Materia Medica* (Leiden: Brill, 1991), 142ff.

Bringing Judaea into the Roman Sphere

of leftover fish with no real market value as well as some small marine invertebrates. The use of different additives and the details of the curing process were also important factors in determining the quality of the *garum, allec,* and *muria*.[6]

Cotton, Lernau, and Goren argue that the fish sauces found at Masada were of high quality and expense. They may even have been kosher. The only way that a fish sauce could have been kosher was if it was composed only of fish with fins and scales. Pliny the Elder provides a clue that kosher *garum* did exist. In his discussion of fish sauces, he speaks about a type of *garum* which Jews used. Although he confuses Jewish dietary laws — he states that the *garum* used by Jews was composed of scaleless fish or invertebrates — he may be correct that kosher *garum* was available to Jews. Another clue comes from the rabbinic corpus. The rabbis speak of a food item, *ḥileq*, which might be the Hebrew pronunciation of *allec*. Further, they provide a criterion for how a fish sauce can be made kosher: it must be made of kosher fish that are not mixed with non-kosher fish or shellfish. Jews, then, could have purchased and consumed *garum* and *allec* as long as the sauces were clearly not a mixture of kosher and non-kosher fish. In other words, kosher fish sauces had to be of higher quality than regular ones, which could be adulterated with all sorts of extra ingredients. Since the *allec* found in the local jar was high quality and was composed of only two kinds of fish, herring and anchovy (both of which are kosher), it is entirely possible that Herod specially ordered this *allec* or received it as a gift precisely because it was kosher. The original amphora in which it arrived at Masada might have contained a label advertising the quality of

---

6. *Garum* was a by-product of salteries along the southern and northern shores of the western Mediterranean, especially Spain and North Africa. It consisted of small, fresh, ungutted fish — although fish intestines and gills were sometimes added — which were placed in the sun for 1 to 3 months in closed earthenware vessels and mixed with large amounts of salt to suppress putrefaction. Intestinal enzymes broke down the fish meat into a fluid-like substance, which was then removed and sieved to make a salty, spicy, clear liquid seasoning. *Muria* was a salty liquid similar to *garum* used mostly for its preservative characteristics. *Allec* was the residue of *garum* and was a thick, semi-liquid mash that contained the macerated parts of the fish (bones, meat, scales, etc.). Initially, *allec* was seen only as an inexpensive spice. Indeed, Cato the Elder recommended it for slaves (Cato, *De Agricultura* 58). However, by the first century BCE it had become an expensive food additive. Pliny the Elder describes *allec* and its manufacture in his *Natural History*. He emphasizes that the higher quality *allec* used smaller fish (*HN* 31.95), probably because bones could be swallowed by accident. For the chronology of these fish sauces and their assignment to the Herodian period see Cotton, Lernau, and Goren, "Fish Sauces," 232-36.

the *allec* and its kosher status. Since the *garum* inscription is fragmentary, it is possible that this amphora's inscription had a similar message.[7]

Garum and *allec,* along with imported wine, apples, and honey, were all luxury items imported from Italy and the western Mediterranean to Masada and the royal table. Herod's decision to import these luxuries speaks to his desire to further place himself within a Roman cultural sphere. Wine was produced all over the Mediterranean, and there were plenty of vineyards in Judaea and neighboring regions, but Herod chose to import specifically Italian vintages as well as other Italian luxury goods despite the cost and inherent difficulties in transporting perishable items across the sea. Perhaps he had adopted the Roman custom of eating apples at desert. If so, this culinary choice would be yet another example of his increasing Romanization at court. This Romanization was not in conflict with his Jewish identity. The existence of kosher *garum* and *allec* enabled him to keep Jewish dietary laws while still enjoying the latest in Roman culinary delights. Herod could be both Jewish and Roman simultaneously.[8]

Herod's importation of fish sauces and other luxury items from Italy also illustrates the financial relationships he had with Romans in the West. A number of amphorae containing Philonianum wine came from the vineyards of a certain Lucius Laenius. Other amphorae inscriptions suggest that Herod imported more products from the farms of this Roman. It is possible that some or all of these amphorae were gifts from Laenius instead of traded items and, as such, reflected personal ties between the Judaean royal family and the Italian aristocracy more than economic activity within the kingdom. However, the scale and diversity of the provenance of the finds suggests that these amphorae were not exclusively gifts and that their acquisition was not solely a matter of personal relationships. However, regardless of their precise

---

7. For Cotton, Lernau, and Goren's conclusion that the fish sauces found at Masada were of high quality and could have been kosher see "Fish Sauces," 232, 236-37. For the biblical rules of *kashrut* see Lev 11:9-11; Deut 14:9-10. For Pliny's discussion of "kosher" *garum,* see *HN* 31.95. The Mishnah mentions ḥileq among the "things of the Gentiles" that are forbidden, although apparently this prohibition was not absolute (*m. 'Avodah Zarah* 2.6). The rabbis seem to have been confused about what ḥileq was and why it was forbidden. In *b. Avodah Zarah* 39a, Hanan bar Rabah identifies it as a type of kosher fish called "the Sultanith," which by itself is kosher but is forbidden because it is often caught along with non-kosher fish. In *y. Avodah Zarah* 32a, Rabbi Yehohanan says that it is "minced Tarith," which also, although a kosher fish, is prohibited for the same reason.

8. For apples as a Roman dessert see Horace, *Satires* 1.3.6-7. For the cultural and economic significance of Herod's gastronomic imports see Cotton and Geiger in *Masada,* 2:133-77. Cf. Cotton and Geiger, "Economic Importance," 169.

Bringing Judaea into the Roman Sphere

economic status — whether as gifts or purchases — the Laenius amphorae provide evidence for a close relationship between Judaea and Italy, a relationship that was accelerated by Herod after his accession to the throne.[9]

Romanization of the Army

Romanization did not just happen at the dining table. Herod also demonstrated a desire to bring his kingdom more fully into the Roman sphere through a reorganization of the Judaean royal army along Roman lines. We have relatively little knowledge of the preceding Hasmonean army. However, we do know that it began as an all-Jewish or mostly Jewish army and that John Hyrcanus I was the first ruler to recruit Greek mercenaries. By the reign of Hyrcanus II the Hasmonean army was a mixture of Jews and Greeks. Given the long association between the Hasmoneans and Seleucids, it is probable that the Hasmoneans used a military colonist system as well as a levy of some kind. They also seem to have absorbed the existing units that had previously served under the Seleucids.[10]

Neither Josephus nor any other literary source tells us what happened to the Hasmonean army during the civil war between Antigonus and Herod. It is possible that the majority of the army stayed loyal to Antigonus, although some of it must have defected to the other side. Either way, it did not survive the war, and Herod built his army largely from scratch.[11] Israel Shatzman has divided the Herodian royal army into two

---

9. For a discussion of the wine and other products produced by Lucius Laenius see Cotton and Geiger in *Masada*, 2:149-58. For a discussion of the economic ties between Judaea and Italy as illustrated by the Masada amphorae see Cotton and Geiger, "Economic Importance," 170. For a general overview of the Judaean economy see Rocca, *Herod's Judaea*, 227-34. Among the major export products were dates, balsam, and bitumen. Rocca, *Herod's Judaea*, 234-39, discusses Judaean internal and external trade.

10. For the makeup of the Hasmonean army see Israel Shatzman, *The Armies of the Hasmoneans and Herod* (Tübingen: Mohr, 1991), 11-35; Jonathan P. Roth, "Jews in the Roman Service during the Great Revolt" (paper presented at the annual meeting of the Society of Biblical Literature, San Antonio, Texas, November 20-23, 2004), 4.

11. It seems that the Herodian royal army remained relatively static from the reign of Herod, through his successors, right up to the outbreak of the Great Revolt. Even the Roman garrison was actually a collection of Herodian units under Roman command. Because of this general lack of change, it is possible to use evidence from after Herod's reign to gain some idea of how the army functioned during his reign. See Roth, "Jews in the Roman Service," 5. For a good overview of the composition of the Herodian army see Shatzman, *Armies*, 170-91.

main groups: (1) military colonists, that is, those given land in exchange for the performance of certain military duties, including both settled veterans and those still in active service, and (2) the regular standing army. Josephus records the existence of several Herodian military colonies. The first and perhaps most important was the colony at Sebaste, which initially consisted of 6,000 men. There were also colonies at Bathyra in Batanaea, Heshbon (Esbonitis), which was east of the Dead Sea in the Peraea, Gaba, which was north of Mount Carmel, Trachonitis, and Idumaea.[12]

The soldiers in the standing army garrisoned the string of fortresses running north-south along the Judaean desert, including Masada, Alexandrion, Hyrcania, and Cypros. There was also a garrison of regular soldiers in the Antonia in Jerusalem. The commander of each of these fortresses was called a *Phrourarchos*. Herod's defenses also included fortified towers *(pyrgoi)* and fortified positions, especially along the Negev border. Additionally, there were royal arsenals *(hoplothēkai)* guarded by garrisons. Other soldiers in the standing army included the royal bodyguard *(doruphoroi)*, which was composed of Thracians, Germans, and Gauls. Shatzman estimates that the size of the royal guard was about 2,000 men. Another elite unit in Herod's standing army was the *Sebastēnoi*, who first appear in Josephus's description of the revolts after Herod's death. The *Sebastēnoi* may have received their name because they garrisoned Sebaste, or, more probably, because the majority of the unit was recruited from the citizen body of the city.[13]

---

12. For Josephus's discussion of the military colony at Sebaste see *BJ* 1.403; *AJ* 15.293. Cf. Roth, "Jews in the Roman Service," 5-6. For Josephus's mention of the colony at Bathyra in Batanaea see *AJ* 17.23-27. For his discussion of the colonies at Heshbon and Gaba see *AJ* 15.294. Shatzman notes that, unlike the military colonies in Batanaea and Trachonitis, the colonies in Heshbon and Gaba were made up of discharged soldiers whom Herod settled in the area to provide security. The settlers at Sebaste were also veterans. See Shatzman, *Armies*, 180-82. For the colony in Trachonitis, which was composed of Idumaeans, see *AJ* 16.285, 292. Roth believes that the Idumaean garrison was destroyed in the Trachonitide revolt of 10/9 BCE. He further argues that Josephus's mention of Idumaeans fighting against the rebel Simon in the revolt following Herod's death (*BJ* 2.58) is proof that military colonies, if destroyed, were later rebuilt. See Roth, "Jews in the Roman Service," 7. However, he misreads Josephus, who never states that the Idumaean colony was destroyed, merely that their territory was despoiled. See *AJ* 16.292. Herod also settled 2,000 veterans in Idumaea. These veterans initially revolted after Herod's death, and their numbers swelled to 10,000. Eventually, Achiab, a royal cousin, persuaded them to surrender without a fight. See *BJ* 2.55, 75-77; *AJ* 17.270, 297.

13. For a discussion of the *pyrgoi* in Herod's realm see M. H. Gracey, "The Armies of the Judaean Client Kings," in *The Defense of the Roman and Byzantine East*, ed. Philip Freeman and David Kennedy (Oxford: BAR, 1986), 318. Josephus mentions one of these fortified

Bringing Judaea into the Roman Sphere

This new and reorganized army fluctuated in size but contained between 15,000 and 20,000 men and was similar to its predecessor in that it was a multi-ethnic force. The non-Jews included Syrians, Ituraeans, Nabataeans, and, as we will see later, Romans. However, the majority of the army seems to have been Jewish. Some of these Jews had joined up at the beginning of the reconquest of Judaea, while others probably were holdovers from the Hasmonean army.[14]

How was the army organized? Did it use a Hellenistic or Roman model? Was it based on the phalanx or legion? Scholars differ on the answer to these questions, with some, such as Schalit, claiming that Herod used a Hellenistic model and others, such as Shatzman, arguing for a legionary template. In order to answer this question, we must examine not only the terms Josephus himself used for these armies, but also the ethnic identities of the commanders, the size of the units, and the uses to which these units were put. Once we have established a comprehensive picture of the Herodian army, we can then compare it to existing models. Through such analysis, it may be possible to settle the issue and offer a clearer view of one of Herod's most important and loyal institutions.[15]

---

towers (in Malatha) in the episode where a despondent Herod Agrippa I plots suicide (*AJ* 18.147). He also mentions a royal armory when he discusses the revolt of Judah the Galilean (*BJ* 2.56). On the royal bodyguard see *BJ* 1.397, 672; *AJ* 15.217; 17.198. Cf. Shatzman, *Armies*, 183-85. As a comparison, the royal guard of Ptolemy IV had 3,000 infantry and 700 cavalry (Polybius 5.65.2, 5), and Juba, king of Numidia, had a guard of 2,000 Gallic and Spanish cavalry (Caesar, *B. Civ.* 2.40.1). For Josephus's discussion of the *Sebastēnoi* see *BJ* 2.52, 58, 63, 74; *AJ* 17.266, 275-76, 283, 294. Eventually this elite unit was absorbed into the Roman army (probably after the annexation of Judaea in 6 CE) and made up the bulk of the Roman garrison until the outbreak of the Great Revolt. See *BJ* 2.236; *AJ* 20.122. Cf. Acts 27:1. For Shatzman's discussion of the origin of the unit's name see *Armies*, 185-86.

14. For Jews, including Idumaeans, making up the core of the Herodian army see Shatzman, *Armies*, 163-65, 186. See also Rocca, *Herod's Judaea*, 134-35, 195. Although Rocca concurs with Shatzman, he is unsure whether Jews made up a small or vast majority. Additionally, he emphasizes that the royal army was probably the single most cohesive force within the realm, binding the various ethnicities together. For estimates on the size of the army see Shatzman, *Armies*, 193-94; Rocca, *Herod's Judaea*, 135-40. Rocca generally agrees with Shatzman, although he has a slightly different method of calculation and reaches slightly different numbers. However, his estimates also fall in the 15,000 to 20,000 range, and thus I think it reasonable to stay within that estimate. As Rocca concludes, Herod's army was smaller than that of the late Hasmoneans and certainly those of the Ptolemies and Seleucids. However, it was significantly larger than those of his fellow client kings.

15. For Abraham Schalit's theory about the organization of the Herodian army and whether it was based on a Hellenistic or Roman model see his *König Herodes. Der Mann*

One of the most frequent terms Josephus uses for units in Herod's army is *speira*. Twice he uses it when narrating the civil war between Herod and Antigonus. In 39 BCE Herod tried to secure his supply lines for the siege of Jerusalem. He therefore set out to Jericho with ten *speiras*, five Roman and five Jewish, as well as a mixed unit of mercenaries and a few mounted cavalry. In 38 BCE, Herod's brother Joseph took five *speiras* from the Roman commander Machaerus and pitched camp near Jericho. During the battle there, he and his entire force were killed. According to Shatzman, Josephus usually uses *speira* to refer to both Roman legionary cohorts and infantry cohorts of the Roman auxiliary forces during the imperial period. When Plutarch narrates Herod's defection after Actium, he writes that Herod transferred his allegiance to Octavian *echōnta tina tagmata kai speiras* ("with a certain number of legions and cohorts"). Since there was no Roman army in Judaea in 30 BCE, these troops must have been royal forces. Consequently, if we can determine precisely what Josephus meant when he used this term, we can answer our question of what Herod's army looked like.[16]

---

und Sein Werk (rev. ed.; Berlin: de Gruyter, 2001), 167-69. The main problem with Schalit's conclusions is that they ignore the significant evolution of and diversity among armies from the early Hellenistic period (Alexander the Great and his immediate successors) to the late Hellenistic period of the Ptolemies and Seleucids. Moreover, it is important to note that Herod had close interaction with actual Roman forces from an early age. As early as 46 BCE he and his brother Phasael had led an auxiliary force to Apamea to help the Caesarians avenge the murder of Sextus Caesar and besiege Caecilius Bassus (*BJ* 1.216-17; *AJ* 14.268-69). In 43 BCE Cassius entrusted both infantry and cavalry to Herod in his capacity as *stratēgos* of Galilee (*BJ* 1.225; *AJ* 14.280). Cassius's role in this appointment raises the possibility that at least some of these soldiers could have been Romans or men organized in Roman-style legions. Such an opportunity undoubtedly gave Herod the chance to become familiar with Roman military organization and tactics. Finally, since we know that other contemporary client kings used the Roman army as a model (Caesar, *African War* 48.1 [Juba II] and Cicero, *Att.* 6.1.14 [Deiotarus of Galatia]), it is possible that Josephus's use of terms is not so straightforward. Specifically, he might be using Greek terms for what was actually Roman organization. See also Rocca, *Herod's Judaea*, 140-47, who argues that Herod's army was essentially a Hellenistic one with many Roman features.

16. For Herod's march to Jericho in 39 BCE with ten *speiras* as well as other forces see *BJ* 1.301; *AJ* 14.410. For Josephus's description of the massacre of Joseph and his soldiers see *AJ* 14.448-49. For Josephus's use of *speira* to describe the unit who suppressed the Passover riot following Herod's death see *BJ* 2.11; *AJ* 17.215-16. Cf. *BJ* 1.323-24. For Josephus's consistent use of *speira* to refer to a basic unit of a Roman auxiliary force see Shatzman, *Armies*, 205-6, n. 134. When Josephus describes the massacre of Joseph and his troops, he mentions six cohorts. This inconsistency in the narrative might be merely the result of Josephus's carelessness. However, it is peculiar that Joseph did not use his own soldiers but instead took

Bringing Judaea into the Roman Sphere

Complicating the picture is that Josephus does not use the term *speira* exclusively. On at least three occasions, he describes Herod's army using the terms *telos* and *ilē*, which are words commonly referring to cavalry and infantry forces in a Hellenistic army. Two of the passages describe Herod's campaigns in Galilee in the winter of 39/38 BCE (*BJ* 1.305; *AJ* 14.415), and one narrates his attempts to procure supplies for his army in 37 (*AJ* 14.472). The term *ilē*, which appears in *Jewish War* 1.305 and *Jewish Antiquities* 14.415, could refer to a Hellenistic cavalry squadron, but it is also the Greek equivalent of *ala*, the standard cavalry unit in a Roman auxiliary force. If *ilē* in these passages refers to an *ala*, then it should be paired with the Greek equivalent of *cohort*, which is usually *speira*, not *telos*. However, in two passages clearly referring to a Roman army (the army led by Gaius Sosius), Josephus uses the term *telos* instead of *speira* to specify military units. Thus, we can conclude that at least in the first two passages *telos* could be a substitute for *speira*. In the third passage, it is unclear exactly what type of unit Herod was sending out.[17]

This linguistic analysis suggests that words such as *speira*, *telos*, and *ilē*, which usually refer to Hellenistic military units, can, at least in Josephus, also refer to an army organized along Roman military patterns. Such a hypothesis seems even more probable when we examine the words Josephus uses to describe Herodian officers. These include the *stratēgos*, *hēgemōn*, *hipparchos*, *lochagos*, *stratopedarchēs*, and *taxiarchos*. As we will see, all of these terms could refer to Roman-style military officers. From our previous discussion, we have seen that Josephus uses the term *stratēgos* to describe Herod's position in Galilee as well as Costobar's position in Idumaea. However, it also appears as the word for a myriad of other positions and offices, some purely military, some purely political, and some a combination of both. Similarly, the term *hēgemōn* appears in the narratives in a variety of contexts. Nevertheless, it is especially noteworthy that Josephus uses both terms to designate Roman officers of various ranks from junior to most senior. It is thus possible that when he uses these terms to describe an officer in the royal army, he is using them as the Greek equivalent of a Roman military office.[18]

Roman forces. Shatzman theorizes that this extra cohort was in fact a unit of Jewish soldiers. For Plutarch's depiction of Herod's defection to Octavian see *Ant.* 71.1.

17. For the appearance of the term *ilē* in the Josephan corpus see *BJ* 2.67, 236, 500, 544; 3.66, 97; 6.68, 172; 7.5, 225; *AJ* 17.286; 19.365; 20.98, 122; *Vita* 121, 214. For the appearance of *ilē* paired with *telos* see *BJ* 1.345-46; *AJ* 14.468-69. Also see Shatzman, *Armies*, 207.

18. For a select appearance of *stratēgos* and *hēgemōn*, see Shatzman, *Armies*, 208,

In Josephus's texts, the title *hipparchos* appears four times: once in reference to two Herodian cavalry officers, once for a cavalry officer in the army of Agrippa II, and twice for Roman officers commanding auxiliary mounted units. The office of *lochagos* appears twice, once to refer to a Roman officer and once to an officer in the royal army. *Stratopedarchēs,* which is the Greek equivalent of *praefectus castorum,* appears as a designation for officers in both the royal army and the Roman army. These officers' main duty was to oversee the construction and use of siege equipment and to supervise the construction of temporary military camps *(castra).* When Herod informed Augustus that he had imprisoned his sons Alexander and Aristobulus, he sent his *stratopedarchēs,* Volumnius, to deliver the message. Finally, Josephus uses *taxiarchos* seven times, four times to refer to commanders in Herod's army or those of his successors and three times to refer to Roman officers. In sum, therefore, as with his descriptions of royal military units, Josephus's terminology for officers in the royal army is varied and somewhat unclear. Nevertheless, it is apparent that he uses terms that he also applied to Roman officers. As such, it is reasonable to conclude that the royal army may have been organized to follow Roman military patterns.[19]

---

n. 146. Another term that appears prominently in the Herodian narrative just after Herod's death is *chiliarchos*. During the riots after Herod's death, Archelaus sent a cohort of soldiers led by a *chiliarchos* to quell the disturbance. As stated above, this troop of soldiers seems to have been part of the royal army. One might argue that the term derives from Hellenistic military terminology, but Josephus's use of the term, especially throughout *BJ* and in *AJ* 14–20, makes it clear that he uses it specifically of Roman military tribunes. See *BJ* 1.230, 233, 235; 2.244, 335, 544; 3.87, 122, 324, 325, 344, 346; 4.636, 640; 5.48, 503; 6.131, 238; *AJ* 14.229, 238, 288, 291; 19.18, 23, 46, 85, 91, 122, 148, 189-90; 20.132, 136, 152.

19. For Josephus's use of the title *hipparchos,* see *BJ* 1.527 (a Herodian commander); 2.310 (a commander in Agrippa II's army), 291, 531 (Roman officers). The name of the *hipparchos* in 2.291 is Iucundus. 2.544 mentions a cavalry commander with the same name, but then the term is *eparchos ilē,* and the man has a cognomen as well (Aemilius). If this officer were the same individual, it would further illustrate the fluidity of Josephan military terms. For Josephus's use of *lochagos,* see *AJ* 17.199 (the royal army); *BJ* 3.83 (the Roman army). For Josephus's use of *stratopedarchēs* in reference to Roman soldiers see *BJ* 2.531; 6.238. He also uses the term to designate a Parthian officer (*AJ* 18.333). Cf. Rocca, *Herod's Judaea,* 142-44. For Volumnius's mission to Rome see *BJ* 1.535. As another example, Herod Agrippa II's *stratopedarchēs* (*BJ* 2.556; *Vita* 407) was Philip ben Iakimos, the grandson of Zamaris and the man responsible for training Agrippa II's army (for the latter: *AJ* 17.30-31). Cf. *Vita* 46-61, 177-80. An inscription from Sur al Laja' in southern Syria was dedicated to a certain Herod, son of Aumos, who was also a *stratopedarchēs* in the army of Agrippa II. See *OGIS* 425. For the appearance of the term *taxiarchos,* see *BJ* 1.369, 461, 491, 673 (in the Herodian army);

Bringing Judaea into the Roman Sphere

Besides a linguistic analysis of Josephan terms, an examination of the ethnic identity of known Herodian officers suggests that Roman influence was significant. In particular, Herod's army contained several men of high rank who seem to have had Roman backgrounds. At the time of Herod's death in 4 BCE, a certain Gratus was the commander of the royal infantry, and a certain Rufus was in charge of the royal cavalry. Josephus does not give their military titles on this occasion or any other when he speaks of them. However, judging by their names, it is possible that they were in fact Roman citizens either by birth or by later acquisition. This possibility is also true for the *stratopedarchēs* Volumnius mentioned above. A final Roman name that appears in the service of the Herodians is *Ioukoundos*, or *Iucundus* in Latin, for two different men. One served as a bodyguard for Herod while the other was a cavalry officer in the royal army just before the outbreak of the Great Revolt. It is possible that these men were not in fact Roman by ethnicity but merely had Latin names. Alternatively, some or all of these men could have been Jews who received Roman citizenship and adopted Latin names or nicknames. However, it is just as likely that these men were in fact Romans. If so, they would have been excellent conduits for the transfer of Roman military tactics to the royal army. If they were Romans, given their skill set, it would not be surprising that they would have obtained high rank in Herod's service.[20]

Close examination of the size and composition of royal military units also suggests Roman influence and models. Shatzman examined the strength of various army units in the royal army and concluded that the numbers suggest multiples of the basic Roman military units. For example, in 39 BCE, Herod entrusted to his brother Joseph an army of 2,000 infantry

---

BJ 3.83, 87; 5.121 (in the Roman army). Josephus even uses the term for officers in his own army, which he organized along Roman military lines. See *BJ* 2.577; *Vita* 242. Cf. *AJ* 12.301 for a *taxiarchos* in the army of Judah Maccabee. For Rocca's analysis of Josephus and his use of military terms see *Herod's Judaea*, 136-37, where he also states that Josephus's terminology is somewhat inconsistent.

20. For the appearances of Gratus and Rufus see *BJ* 2.52, 58, 63-64, 74; *AJ* 17.275-76, 283-84, 294. For the bodyguard named Iucundus see *AJ* 16.314-16. After falling out of favor with Herod, he became a bodyguard for Alexander, Herod's son. Eventually, he fell under suspicion, was arrested, and ultimately tortured. During his torture, he claimed that Alexander had bribed him to murder the king. For the *hipparchos* Iucundus see *BJ* 2.291. A Lucius Caecilius Iucundus was a wealthy banker in Pompeii in the first century CE. It would be an immense stretch of the evidence to suggest that the two men were related. However, the existence of a family, the Caecilii Iucundi, in Italy supports the notion that Herod's officer could have been a Roman.

and 400 cavalry. Herod himself took an army of 3,000 infantry and 600 cavalry to Samaria in 38 BCE. In 25 BCE, he sent a division of his bodyguard (500 men) to help Aelius Gallus and his expedition to Arabia Felix. Herod's elite unit, the *Sebastēnoi,* had a total of 3,000 men. All these infantry totals are multiples of 500, which was close to the ideal number for one cohort in a Roman legion (the ideal number being 480). Hence, Joseph's army had four cohorts, and Herod's army had six. He sent one cohort to aid Gallus, and the *Sebastēnoi* had six cohorts. It is more difficult to detect a pattern in the cavalry figures, but Shatzman suggests that this might be the result of the greater difficulty in assembling trained cavalry.

Herod also seems to have mimicked Roman military strategy in his use of siege tactics and his construction of Roman *castra* (military camps). During the siege of Jerusalem in 37 BCE, Herod's army cut down all the trees in the area and surrounded the city with three lines of fortifications. It also erected siege towers to batter the walls and force entrance into the city. The engineers operating the siege equipment would have been under the command of a *stratopedarchēs*. This strategy is reminiscent of Julius Caesar's siege of Alesia in 52 BCE, and it is tempting to imagine Herod reading Caesar's commentaries on the Gallic wars, which had been published only a few years before. Herod also seems to have employed the Roman military camp *(castrum)* during his first Nabataean war in 31/30 BCE. Although Josephus does not refer to it explicitly as a Roman-style camp, his description of a temporary camp protected by palisades suggests a Roman *castrum*. We do not know for sure if the Judaean royal army used *castra* prior to this campaign, but it would make sense, especially given the king's familiarity with the Roman army.

We also must remember that Herod's armies periodically served in an auxiliary capacity alongside Roman legions. Further, after Archelaus's deposition, the royal army was absorbed into the Roman provincial military. Both situations suggest close interaction between Roman legions and the Herodian royal army, and such close interaction would have been easier if the two forces were organizationally and tactically integrable. As such, it would not be surprising if Roman patrons encouraged their client kings to train their armies according to Roman military practices.[21]

21. For the size of the army of Herod's brother Joseph during the reconquest of Judaea see *BJ* 1.303; *AJ* 14.413. For the size of Herod's army at the same time see *BJ* 1.314-16; *AJ* 14.431-32. For Herod's decision to send Aelius Gallus 500 men for his Red Sea expedition see *AJ* 15.317. For the size of the *Sebastēnoi* see *BJ* 2.52; *AJ* 17.266. Cf. Shatzman, *Armies,* 210-11. For Herod's use of Roman siege tactics see *AJ* 14.466. For his use of Roman *castra*

Bringing Judaea into the Roman Sphere

From Herod's perspective, too, an army modeled on the Roman legion was preferable. Since the royal army was one of the main bulwarks of Herod's regime, it needed to be as effective and intimidating as possible. Who better to imitate than the most powerful army in the Mediterranean, an army that had proved its effectiveness against the Greek phalanx? Moreover, Herod's early years as a *stratēgos* had provided him the opportunity to become familiar with the Roman army. As king, he could put this knowledge to good use, especially if he received the assistance of discharged Roman veterans. Furthermore, his early years as a courtier had proven to him that he could win the support and favor of powerful Romans by presenting them with a strong and efficient army that they could use. There would be no better way to present such an army than to have trained, organized, and disciplined it according to Roman military standards.

And yet, Herod did not discard Hellenistic styles and techniques entirely. Indeed, it would be more accurate to say that certain features from the Hellenistic world persisted and sometimes blended with newer Roman features. Despite there being clear Roman alternatives, Herod consciously chose to use the four-towered *tetrapyrgion*, a structure originating in the Hellenistic world, for his fortified palaces, including the Antonia and Upper Herodion. His military colonies also seem to have followed the Seleucid model more than the Roman model. He settled military colonists together in villages within the royal domain. In the case of the colony in Batanaea, he followed the established Hellenistic precedent by awarding Zamaris the Babylonian an estate and enclosing a colony within that estate. He also seems to have clung to a Hellenistic emphasis on cavalry. In particular, the army with which he conquered Judaea in 37 BCE generally had a ratio of cavalry to infantry of one-to-five. So, for example, we see his brother Joseph leading 400 cavalry and 2,000 infantry into Idumaea. The percentage of cavalry declined during Herod's skirmish with the brigands hiding in the caves of Arbela in Galilee (38 BCE). During this battle he had a force of 200 cavalry and 1,500 infantry. Nevertheless, the proportion was back to one-to-five when Herod arrived in the city of Samaria in 37 BCE. There he had an army of 600 cavalry and 3,000 infantry. This proportion is far more similar to a Hellenistic army than a Roman army, which would

---

during the first Nabataean war see *BJ* 1.367; *AJ* 15.112. Also see Rocca, *Herod's Judaea*, 143-44. For the royal army's service in an auxiliary capacity see *BJ* 1.217, 320-22; *AJ* 14.269, 439-47; 15.317. For the absorption of the Herodian army after annexation see Schürer, *History of the Jewish People,* 1:363-64.

have a much higher percentage of infantry, specifically heavily-armored legionnaires.

In other areas, however, Herod seems to have blended Hellenistic and Roman styles together to create a new hybrid. Herodian city walls and towers are a good example of his utilization of the best elements of both the Hellenistic and Roman worlds. While the walls and towers themselves seem to have derived more from the Hellenistic than Roman world, the gates of these walls borrowed from Rome. Like their Roman counterparts, Herodian gates had three arched entrances, the middle larger than the two side entrances. These entrances were protected by two flanking towers, which were circular, octagonal, or square in shape. If desired, the inner court of this style of gate could be reinforced with additional gates also using a tripartite entryway.[22]

There is no irrefutable evidence that Herod's army was organized and trained according to Roman military patterns. It is certainly possible that the royal army, like the Hasmonean army before it, was based on a Hellenistic model. Josephus's military terminology refers to both Hellenistic and Roman military offices and units. Additionally, there do seem to have been clearly Hellenistic prototypes that persisted into the Herodian period. However, the presence of officers who likely were Romans, Herod's own experience with Roman armies, the royal armies' later seamless absorption into the procuratorial army, and most importantly the greater utility in organizing the army according to a Roman model, all suggest the use of a Roman template for the organization of the royal army.

As a blended Hellenistic-Roman army which contained Roman veterans, it would have been an extremely useful conduit for Romanization and the increasing accommodation of Judaean citizens to Roman cultural values and norms. Within the multiethnic mixture of Herod's kingdom,

---

22. For a discussion of Herod's preference for the Hellenistic *tetrapyrgion* and military colony see Rocca, *Herod's Judaea*, 156-57, 188-90. Cf. Getzel M. Cohen, "The Hellenistic Military Colony: A Herodian Example," *TAPA* 103 (1972): 83-95, for an analysis of the military colony in Batanaea and its Hellenistic antecedents. For the size and composition of Herod's army during his conquest of Judaea see *BJ* 1.303; *AJ* 14.413 (Joseph's army in Idumaea), *BJ* 1.314-16; *AJ* 14.415 (Arbela), *AJ* 14.431-32 (Samaria). For a discussion of the proportion of Herod's cavalry to his infantry see Rocca, *Herod's Judaea*, 145-46. These proportions are all from Herod's first campaign as king, and they may only represent the composition of his army during his early reign. It is possible that these proportions changed, especially as more Romans and Romanized individuals began serving in his court and army. For Herod's construction of hybrid city fortifications see Rocca, *Herod's Judaea*, 155-57, 163, 165-67.

this royal army, unified by its common discipline and organization, could have served as an extremely powerful source of social cohesion. Such unity would have increased Herod's internal security and simultaneously aided his ability to fulfill his obligation as a client king to provide a stable and peaceful friendly kingdom to Rome and its leaders.

Constructing Roman Buildings

The army was not the only conduit for Roman culture and society, nor is it the only evidence of Romanization. Another clear indicator of an active process of Romanization was the construction and use of uniquely Roman and Italian structures within Judaea. In Herod's kingdom, we can see numerous examples of Roman buildings, ranging from the more private and religiously inoffensive, such as private baths and palatial residences, to the public and potentially explosive, such as theaters, amphitheaters, and temples. Although, as we will see, Judaea contained several examples of each, the architecture of these structures is sometimes slightly modified from the standard, thus reflecting Herod's own flair and style. Nevertheless, although not rigidly Roman in all aspects, these modified structures and the importation of Roman building types vividly illustrate an active decision to adopt Roman cultural norms.

Roman Baths

Bathing and immersion in water had been a central aspect of Judaean life for centuries before Herod's reign. Nevertheless, his introduction of Roman bathing culture was a prominent avenue through which he directed his kingdom ever further into the larger Graeco-Roman world. Within his realm he constructed over twenty-seven individual bathing facilities in seven of his excavated palaces and fortresses. In contrast, all of his Jewish contemporaries built a total of twenty-seven bathing facilities. In other words, in the one hundred-fifty-year period during the mid-first century BCE to mid-first century CE, Herod constructed half of all bathing facilities built in Judaea. Although he certainly inherited a local tradition of bathing construction from the Hasmoneans, close examination of the Herodian facilities shows clear Roman influence that moves beyond his immediate predecessors and their influences. For example, the overrepresentation of Herodian bathing facilities in comparison to those built by other Jews becomes even more pronounced when considering only the bathing facilities with a hypocaust heating system, a hallmark of the Roman bath. Of the eleven facilities with hypocausts, eight are Herodian, meaning that he built almost seventy-five percent of the Roman type bathing facilities.[23]

The well-preserved bath complex next to the Northern Palace at Masada is a clear imitation of the standard Romano-Italic bathhouse down to even the finest details of decoration and the *Reihentyp* (row-type) floor plan, which required the bather to retrace his steps to finish the entire bathing cycle. Further, the complex also contained the latest Roman hypocaust system, remains of which are still visible today. Slightly different in layout but still clearly influenced by Roman designs is the bath suite in Herod's Third Palace at Jericho. It has an axial row design with a pair of *caldaria* (hot rooms) on the eastern end and a rotunda with apsidal niches for benches on the western end. This rotunda was probably a *laconicum* or sweating room, and its design conforms to the characteristic architecture for such a room. Similar designs appear in the bathhouses of Campania in the first century BCE such as the Stabian and Forum Baths of Pompeii. Agrippa's Thermae, which he commissioned in 26-19 BCE, provide another good comparison, since the Thermae also had a similarly designed large chamber.[24]

---

23. For comparisons of Herodian bathing facilities in Judaea to non-Herodian complexes see Danielle Steen Fatkin, "As the Romans Do? Bathing in Herodian Palestine" (paper presented at the annual meeting of the Society of Biblical Literature, San Diego, CA, November 17-20, 2006); "Royal Power and Bathing in Herod's Palestine," chapter 3 in "Many Waters: Bathing *Ethe* of the Roman Empire" (Ph.D. diss., Stanford University, 2007), 12-13, Appendix C. Cf. Inge Nielsen, *Thermae et Balnea: The Architecture and Cultural History of Roman Public Baths* (Aarhus: Aarhus University Press, 1990), 1:98, 103-4, 111, 114.

24. Another Roman-style bathhouse that contained all the expected rooms was built in the basement of the lowest terrace of the Northern Palace at Masada. This Roman influence can be seen at other sites as well. At Upper Herodion, builders constructed another bath complex with a similar layout, in which the *apodyterium, frigidarium, tepidarium,* and *caldarium* were arranged in a circuit. In both of these baths, as in the bathing complex on the summit of Cypros, the *caldarium* contains a circular apse at its eastern end for an *alveus* (hot water bath). For the classification of bathhouses by type see Daniel Krencker, "Vergleichende Untersuchungen romischer Thermen," in *Die Trierer Kaiserthermen. Ausgrabungsbericht und grundsätzliche Untersuchungen römischer Thermen* (Augsburg: Filser, 1929), 174-305; Nielsen, *Thermae et Balnea,* 2:50-52. For analysis of the bathhouse next to the Northern Palace at Masada see Joseph Aviram, Gideon Foerster, and Ehud Netzer, eds., *Masada: The Yigael Yadin Excavations 1963-1965, Final Reports* (Jerusalem: Israel Exploration Society, 1989-95), 3:76-101; Gideon Foerster in *Masada,* 5:193-205. Cf. David M. Jacobson, "Placing Herod the Great and His Works in Context," *PEQ* 134 (2002): 87. Because of space

Bringing Judaea into the Roman Sphere

Would Herod's Jewish elites have objected to the introduction of Roman bathing complexes and practices? While we cannot know precisely what these individuals thought of these new bathhouses, it is noteworthy that despite Herod's enthusiasm for Roman bath complexes, other Judaean elites were less interested, as evidenced by their decision not to build their own Roman-style bathing facilities. Nevertheless, in spite of this hesitance, Jewish elites could not have remained untouched by Roman influence. Given its centrality for Herod, courtly life and political advancement would have required some acquaintance with and participation in Roman bathing culture. Further, if Roman baths were really so unpopular with his court, Herod probably would not have built so many. Just as he did not use figurative art that violated his subjects' religious sensibilities, so too it is unlikely that he constructed bathing complexes that offended a significant number of his courtiers.

As was common in other areas in which Herod adopted Roman construction techniques and styles, he modified his buildings to suit his local needs and environment. For instance, he placed Judaean immersion pools in Roman style bathhouses. Perhaps this blending of the two traditions made the adoption of some elements of Roman bathing customs more palatable to a local elite audience that might have initially been skeptical of their king's innovative building. Either way, his decision to build bathhouses that utilized Roman architectural forms speaks to his desire to Romanize both his court and his kingdom.[25]

---

constraints, the bathhouse in the basement of the lowest terrace of the Northern Palace was slightly modified. The *frigidarium* was only a stepped pool, and the *apodyterium* was located in the cellar below the eastern portico, outside the central hall of the lower terrace. See Netzer in *Masada* 3:164-70. Cf. Ehud Netzer, *The Palaces of the Hasmoneans and Herod the Great* (Jerusalem: Yad Ben-Zvi, 2001), 118. For Netzer's analysis of the baths at Herodion and Cypros see *Greater Herodium* (Jerusalem: Hebrew University of Jerusalem, 1981), 84-85 (Herodion); Netzer, *Hasmonean and Herodian Palaces at Jericho: Final Reports of the 1973-1987 Excavations* (Jerusalem: Israel Exploration Society, 2001-08), 2:251-57 (Cypros); Jacobson, "Placing Herod the Great and His Works," 87-88. Cf. Arthur Segal, "Herodium," *IEJ* 23 (1973): 27-29. Vitruvius recommends a similar layout for bathing complexes (*De Architectura* 5.10.5). While I do not think that Herod's architects were literally using Vitruvius as their guidebook on building, his text does at least provide a model with which we can compare Herodian architecture to Roman designs. For a discussion of the bathing complex in Herod's Third Palace at Jericho and a comparison with the Stabian and Forum Baths of Pompeii as well as Agrippa's thermae see Nielson, *Thermae et Balnea*, 26-34, 43-45, 158-59. Cf. Jacobson, "Placing Herod the Great and His Works," 87-88.

25. For Fatkin's analysis of Jewish elites' acceptance of Roman bathing practices see

Roman Residences as Models for Herodian Palaces

On a slightly larger scale than bathing facilities, Herodian palaces are an ideal area in which to see the development from Hellenistic paradigms to Roman models. During the early years of his reign, Herod commissioned palace residences that incorporated Hellenistic palatial elements. His predecessors, the Hasmoneans, had taken these elements and modified them to suit their particular needs, and Herod modeled his own palaces after theirs in an attempt to connect himself visually with their dynasty and thus appropriate their legitimacy. However, toward the middle of his reign (ca. 20s BCE), Herod sought new architectural influences for his palaces, which he found in Roman Republican villas. The vast complex at Herodion, which occupied an area of approximately fifty acres, is equal in size to some of the larger estates of the late Republic and early empire such as the villa of Vedius Pollio at Posillipo. On the other hand, Herod's other royal estates, such as Masada and Heshbon, were large but not oversized in comparison to contemporary villas. Size and grandeur were important, but it was equally vital that Herod not irritate his Roman patrons by building estates that were too grandiose.

Besides comparable size, there are other similarities between Herod's later estates and Roman villas. A distinctive feature of Herodian estates such as those at Jericho, Herodion, and Masada was the conscious refashioning of the original landscape. That is to say Herodian builders transformed the landscape in order to emphasize particular topographical features or to highlight the builders' ability to conquer nature. At Jericho, for instance, Herod's Third Palace straddled both sides of the Wadi Qelt and thus symbolically overcame the obstacle of a flowing wadi (river valley). Similar designs (i.e., building on both sides of a river or moving body of water) appear at a villa near Sperlonga that dates to the first half of the first century BCE as well as the later Neronian era villa outside Subiaco. The ability to conquer nature, which could be displayed through the conscious choice of difficult landscapes on which to construct one's buildings, elevated them from simple constructions to visual symbols of power and conquest over nature. The most famous example of this conquest of nature in the Herodian portfolio is perhaps the Northern Palace at Masada, which, perched on a series of three narrow terraces, seems to dangle in mid-air.

"Many Waters," 33. For a chart detailing the overwhelming propensity of large bathing facilities to include an immersion pool see "Many Waters," Appendix C, figure 14b.

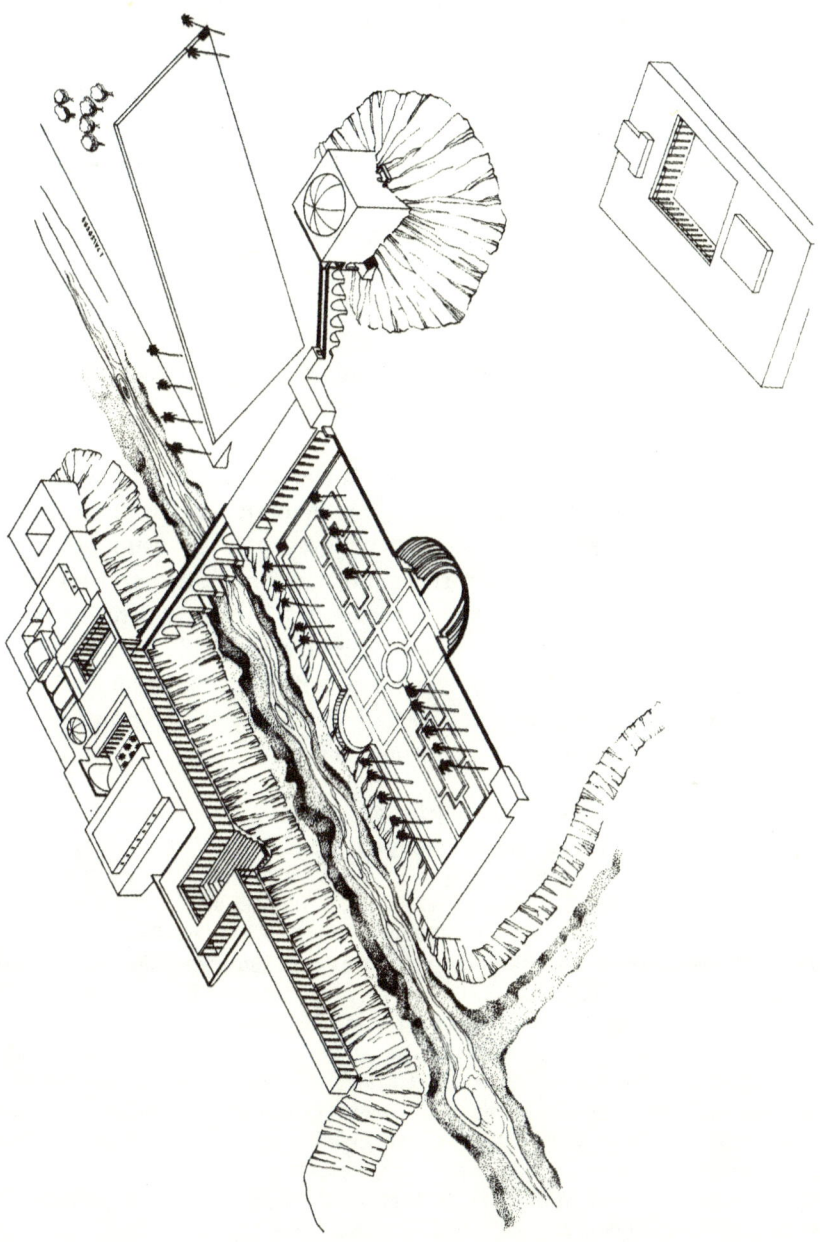

Isometric view of Herod's First and Third Palaces at Jericho
Herod's Third Palace at Jericho straddled both sides of the Wadi Qelt and thus symbolically "conquered" the surrounding terrain.

The Promontory Palace at Caesarea, with its lower wing jutting out into the sea, is another example of this type of construction.

Villas of the late Republic and early empire also used extreme landscape construction. The Villa of Manilius Vopiscus at Tibur (modern Tivoli), which is mentioned in a poem of Statius, contained rooms that straddled the gorge of the Anio waterfall. Because of the steepness of the cliff, these rooms were accessible only through a tunnel. From the inside of these rooms, one had an unspoiled view of the waterfall and of the Tiburtine Acropolis. Construction on the edge of a cliff also appears in the early imperial Villa Iovis and Villa Damecuta on Capri as well as in the villa on the Punta della Campanella outside Sorrento. These imperial era structures all postdate the Herodian Northern Palace, but they are all perched on the edge of steep precipices.[26]

In addition to general characteristics, Herodian palaces contain numerous architectural details that show Roman influence. For instance, the Northern Palace at Masada created its hanging effect by using extensive terraces built on massive supporting substructures. Such construction evokes the terracing of Roman villas such as the Villa dei Misteri at Pompeii (second century BCE), which was built on a raised platform, the Villa of Diomedes (first century BCE), which was constructed on multiple levels, or the villa of Quintilius Varus at Tivoli (first century BCE). Pompey's villa at Albano (first century BCE) is another example.[27]

---

26. For a comparison of the size of Herodian estates to contemporary Roman villas see Reinhard Förtsch, "The Residences of King Herod and Their Relations to Roman Villa Architecture," in Fittschen and Foerster, eds., *Judaea and the Graeco-Roman World in the Time of Herod*, 74-75. For the conscious refashioning of landscape in both Herodian and Roman estate planning see Jacobson, "Placing Herod the Great and His Works," 86. Cf. Förtsch, "The Residences of King Herod," 75-78. For a detailed analysis of Masada's Northern Palace and its architectural daring see Gideon Foerster in *Masada*, 5:170-93. Cf. David M. Jacobson, "The Northern Palace at Masada — Herod's Ship of the Desert?" *PEQ* 138 (2006): 99-117. For discussion of the Promontory Palace at Caesarea see Kathryn Gleason, "Ruler and Spectacle: The Promontory Palace," in *Caesarea Maritima: A Retrospective After Two Millennia*, ed. Avner Raban and Kenneth G. Holum (Leiden: Brill, 1996), 208-12; Achim Lichtenberger, *Die Baupolitik Herodes des Grossen* (Wiesbaden: Harrassowitz, 1999), 122-24; Netzer, *Architecture*, 106-12. For Statius's description of the Villa of Manilius Vopiscus see *Silvae* 1.3. For a discussion of Roman villas perched on steep precipices see Förtsch, "The Residences of King Herod," 77-78.

27. Harald Mielsch, *Die Römische Villa. Architektur und Lebensform* (Munich: Beck, 1987) 39-41, figures 15 and 16 (Villa dei Misteri), 41-43, figure 17 (Villa of Diomedes), 43-44, figure 18 (Villa of Quintilius Varus at Tivoli). Foerster (contra Mielsch) does not believe that the concept of a terraced palace is Roman. Instead, he sees this form as a transitional

Bringing Judaea into the Roman Sphere

In Upper Herodion, one can recognize a modified Roman atrium complex in the suite of rooms west of the main peristyle (rooms 19-23). Aside from differences in the side wings and the lack of an *impluvium* (central depression designed to collect rainwater), the layout of this suite is almost identical to one in the Villa Settefinestre, which dates to around 30 BCE. It is unlikely that Herod received visitors in his atrium, as a typical Roman patron would. However, from an architectural point of view, there was no other room that embodied *Romanitas* quite like the atrium, and this may explain its presence in the mountain palace.

Another Roman room-type, the *vestibulum* (waiting room), exists in three instances at Masada: the entrance to the Western Palace, a room at the gate at the end of the Snake Path, and the waiting room of the Northern Palace. There are no other contemporary examples of this type of room known in the eastern Mediterranean. These three rooms have typical masonry benches and are decorated in First Pompeian Style wall paintings (another Roman influence). In terms of the layout and size they seem to be direct imitations of Italian *vestibula,* though they are slightly larger than most *vestibula* in Roman townhouses and villas. Since they do not seem to have been used in connection with the meeting of clients or the *salutatio* (morning greeting), more likely they served a symbolic role as emblems of Roman construction and style. In other words, they displayed Herod's Romanization through their mere existence.[28]

Roman influences also extended to the dining and entertaining areas

---

phase, a late Hellenistic building with strong Italian overtones. I do not think we need to be so concerned about exactly what type of classification the terraced palace fits into. As we will see, terraced temples were a feature of Hellenistic architecture. However, it also was part of the repertoire for late Republican villas, and, as such, Herod's use of it in his palace represented the influx of Roman architectural culture into Judaea. He may not have been using it to demonstrate his loyalty to Rome, as Mielsch suggests (*Die Römische Villa,* 44), but his use did indicate an adoption of Roman culture and Romanization, something Augustus and Rome's elites would have appreciated. See Gideon Foerster, "Hellenistic and Roman Trends in the Herodian Architecture of Masada," in Fittschen and Foerster, eds., *Judaea and the Graeco-Roman World in the Time of Herod,* 59-60.

28. For a discussion of the atrium complex at Upper Herodion and its comparison to the Villa Settefinestre see Netzer, *Greater Herodium,* 98-99, illustration 107; *Palaces,* 102. Despite its lack of use to receive clients, the appearance of the atrium would have been a visual symbol of Herod's own *Romanitas* and his connections with the larger Roman world. For a discussion of the *vestibula* at Masada see Netzer in *Masada* 3:36 (vestibule of the Northern Palace), 308-12 (vestibule of the Western Palace), 562-63 (vestibule of the Snake Path Gate). See Förtsch, "The Residences of King Herod," 80, for a discussion of the significance of the *vestibula* at Masada.

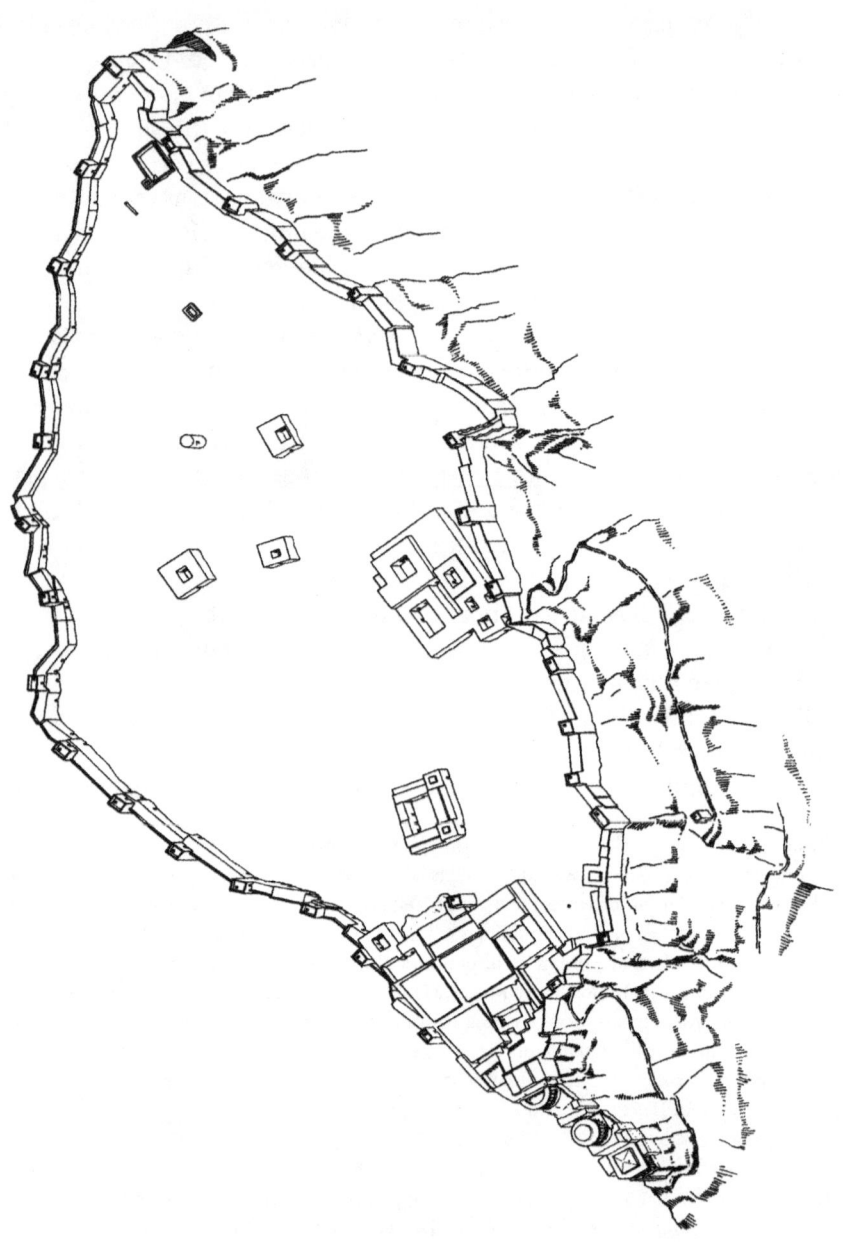

Isometric view of Herod's palace complex at Masada
The total area of the Masada plateau was about thirty-seven acres, which, while substantial, was well within the acceptable range for contemporary villas.

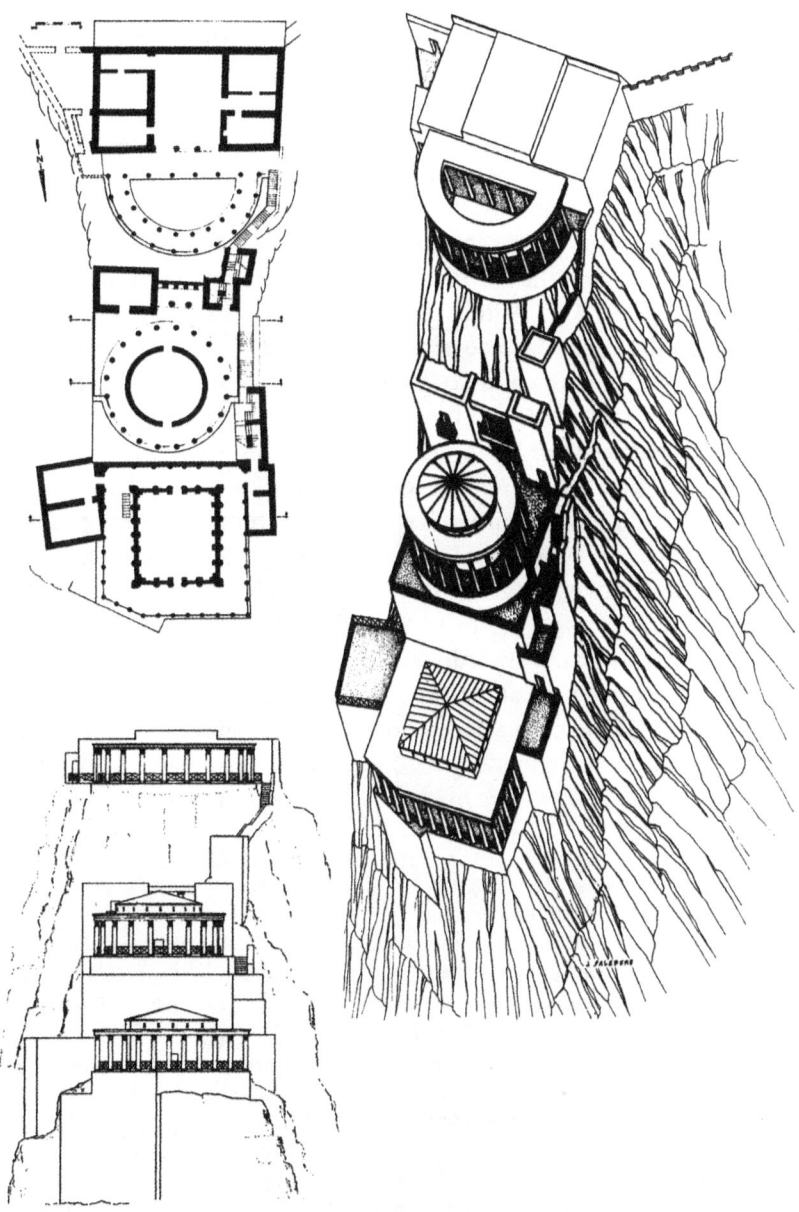

Reconstructed plan, elevation, and isometric view of the Northern Palace at Masada
The palace's "hanging" effect evoked the terracing of contemporary Roman villas.

of Herod's palaces, specifically his formal dining rooms *(triclinia)*. In palaces such as Herodion, Herod constructed large *triclinia,* whose layouts seem to have their origins in late Republican villa architecture such as that at the Villa Boscoreale. Another Roman-inspired *triclinium* was built in Herod's Third Palace at Jericho. This dining room, which also had a small antechamber *(procoeton)* typical in Roman villa architecture, belongs to an architectural tradition that includes the so-called Maecenas Auditorium (built ca. 40 BCE) and the *triclinium* in the Villa Imperiale, which was built between 20 and 10 BCE. A final example of Herod's Roman dining rooms is the one in the upper terrace of the Northern Palace at Masada. Besides being decorated with Second Style wall paintings, this suite also contained several small rooms, axially arranged around a semicircular porch and portico that overlooked the Dead Sea valley. The design of this semicircular portico resembles the reception rooms of the Augustan-era Villa of the Punto Eolo on the island of Pandateria (Ventotene). More importantly, perhaps, it also resembles the viewing galleries of the late Republican Villa Farnesina, which may have belonged to Herod's friend and patron Marcus Agrippa. If it did, it is possible that Herod visited Agrippa's residence and was influenced by its construction. Either way, the appearance of identifiably Roman architecture at the top of Masada and at other Herodian sites is illustrative. Herod could have chosen to build his palaces in any style he desired; he chose to make them Roman, albeit not rigidly so, and this choice speaks to his embrace of both Roman architecture and culture.[29]

29. The *triclinium* at Herodion was paved with colored stones arranged in an *opus sectile* pattern and was entered from the courtyard. See Netzer, *Greater Herodium,* 84, 98-99. Cf. Segal, "Herodium," 27-29; Lichtenberger, *Baupolitik,* 102; Netzer, *Palaces,* 102; Netzer, *Architecture,* 186. This *triclinium* is similar to the main one at the Villa Boscoreale. For a discussion of this main reception room (*Oecus* H) at the Villa Boscoreale see Valentin Kockel, "Archäologische Funde und Forschungen in den Vesuvstädten II," *Archäologischer Anzeiger* (1986): 557. For a discussion of the Herodian *triclinium* in the eastern corner of the North Wing of Herod's Third Palace at Jericho see Netzer, *Jericho* 1:260-61, 320. Cf. Lichtenberger, *Baupolitik,* 62-64. According to Förtsch, the *procoeton-triclinium* at Jericho is the only known example in which the *procoeton* is augmented with rectangular niches in the walls (Förtsch, "The Residences of King Herod," 80). For the use of a small antechamber *(procoeton)* next to the main *triclinium* in villa architecture see Kockel, "Archäologische Funde und Forschungen," 521-22. This design also appears in the much later villa at Perl-Nennig, south of Trier. See Förtsch, "The Residences of King Herod," 80. For a discussion of the *triclinium* of the Northern Palace at Masada and its similarities with the Villa of the Punto Eolo and the Villa Farnesina see Netzer in *Masada,* 3:137-47, 584-85; Foerster, *Masada,* 5:171-74; Lichtenberger, *Baupolitik,* 25-27; Netzer, *Palaces,* 90-92; Jacobson, "The Northern

Bringing Judaea into the Roman Sphere

Roman Entertainment in Judaea: Amphitheaters and Theaters

So far we have discussed private buildings, or at least buildings that few outside the royal court and its guests would have been able to access. For Herod to adopt and use Roman styles and forms in his private residences shows his personal level of acculturation but not necessarily a desire to Romanize his kingdom. However, if we examine some of the more public buildings he constructed — those buildings to which many of his subjects would have had access — we see this same enthusiasm for and embrace of Roman architecture and culture. The first category of buildings we will examine is one of the most identifiably Roman: the amphitheater.

In total, Herod commissioned at least three amphitheaters in his kingdom, one in Jerusalem, one in Jericho, and one in Caesarea. Although archaeological remains exist only at Jericho and Caesarea, these ruins unmistakably testify to the adoption of Roman forms of entertainment, such as *venationes* (animal hunts) and even gladiatorial combat, by Herod and his court. Interestingly, these complexes are not amphitheaters in the classical Roman sense. Indeed, Herod seems to have modified them so that they were able to accommodate both athletic and equestrian events. It would appear then that he was not really borrowing the architectural form of the amphitheater from the Romans. He was far more creative, combining the hippodrome, amphitheater, and stadium into one multi-use complex, J. H. Humphrey's so-called "amphitheatrical hippostadium."[30]

Palace at Masada," 100-103, figures 2-4. Cf. Foerster, "Hellenistic and Roman Trends in the Herodian Architecture of Masada," 58.

30. Josephus does not always refer to these structures as amphitheaters, and indeed, as we will discover, they are not true amphitheaters like that in Pompeii or the Flavian Amphitheater in Rome. See *BJ* 1.414; *AJ* 15.268, 341; 17.194 for his use of the term "amphitheater." See *BJ* 1.659; *AJ* 17.175, 193 for his references to the structure at Jericho as a hippodrome. He also mentions a hippodrome in Jerusalem during his narration of the disturbances after Herod's death in 4 BCE (*BJ* 2.44; *AJ* 17.255). This hippodrome is probably the amphitheater mentioned in *AJ* 15.268. For a discussion of the possible location of the Jerusalem amphitheater see Bernett, *Kaiserkult*, 54, 56. She places the amphitheater outside the city to the south, perhaps in the Hinnom Valley. As J. H. Humphrey rightly observes contra Roller, it was not until the Hadrianic period that a true Roman-style amphitheater was constructed by truncating the larger Herodian structure. Further, separate Roman-style hippodromes did not appear in the Greek East until the second century CE. See John H. Humphrey, "'Amphitheatrical' Hippo-Stadia," in Raban and Holum, *Caesarea Maritima*, 121-29. Cf. Roller, *Building Program*, 91-92; Joseph Patrich, "Herodian Caesarea — the Urban Space," in *The World of the Herods: Volume 1 of the International Conference The World of the Herods and*

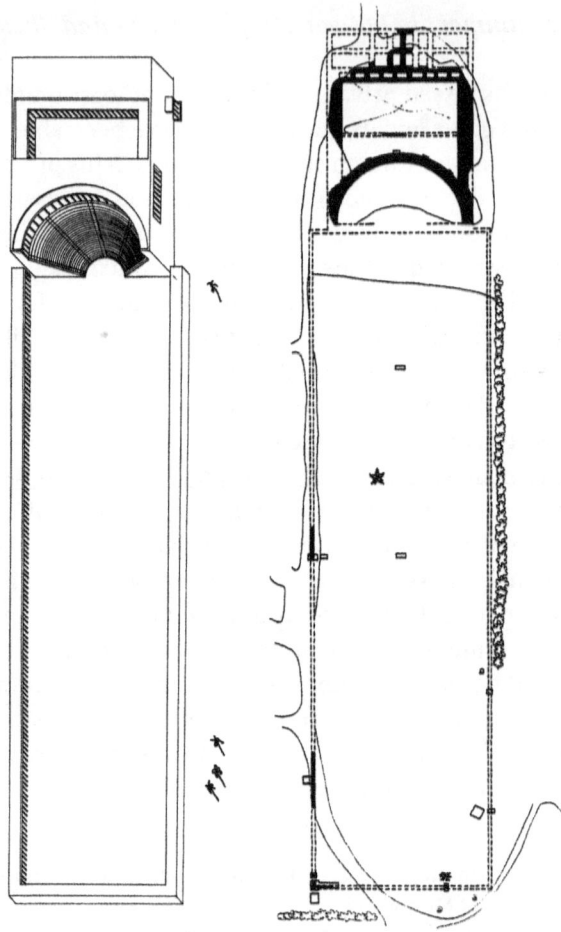

Isometric view and plan of the Jericho hippostadium

Nonetheless, the mere institution of Roman blood sports was in itself an innovation for Judaea and an adoption of Roman customs. By putting on such games during his Caesarian festivals, Herod displayed his *Romanitas* as well as his desire to orient his kingdom more fully within the larger Roman world. Simultaneously, by not adhering to strict Roman standards

---

the Nabataeans Held at the British Museum, 17-19 April 2001, ed. Nikos Kokkinos (Stuttgart: Steiner, 2007), 116-20.

Bringing Judaea into the Roman Sphere

of construction, Herod was also demonstrating his own architectural flair and autonomy.[31]

During his reign, Herod also commissioned at least two theaters inside his kingdom (Roller suggests there might also have been theaters at Jericho and Sebaste) and two outside his kingdom at Damascus and Sidon. The theater in Jerusalem, which was probably constructed for the games Herod hosted in 27 BCE to honor Augustus, appears in Josephus's narrative, although no remains survive.[32] Achim Lichtenberger and Joseph Patrich have proposed a new hypothesis concerning this theater,

---

31. As Bernett suggests, the Caesarian games in Jerusalem would have seemed exciting but a little strange for all the different groups attending it. Specifically, Herod's desire to mix Roman and Hellenistic festival elements (e.g., musical performances and *venationes*) while also avoiding any overt offense to Jewish sensibilities would have resulted in a unique and novel festival, unfamiliar to all parties attending. Even Herod's Roman guests would have noticed key omissions. In particular, there is no evidence that Herod's first Caesarian games, the ones held in Jerusalem, featured gladiatorial combat. According to Josephus, they were limited to *venationes* (animal hunts) and *damnatio ad bestias* (execution of criminals by animal fight, *AJ* 15.275). The festival held in Caesarea Maritima, on the other hand, does seem to have had gladiatorial combat in addition to *venationes* (*AJ* 16.137). It is possible that the longer Herod's kingdom was within the Roman sphere, the more accustomed it became to Roman forms of entertainment. For Bernett's analysis of the festivals see *Kaiserkult*, 59-61. For a discussion of the offense that *damnatio ad bestias* might have caused among certain Jews see *Kaiserkult*, 61-64.

32. Since it is likely that the passage describing the theater in Jerusalem was an insertion into an otherwise continuous narrative, we cannot determine the chronology simply by examining the location of the passage describing the games in Josephus's narrative. However, the passage describing the construction of Sebaste is part of the same narrative chunk as the passage describing the Caesarian games in Jerusalem. Since we know that Sebaste was begun in 27 BCE, we can date the games in Jerusalem to the same year. See Schürer, *History of the Jewish People,* 1:289-90 for a discussion of the chronology. For a discussion of the possible locations of the Jerusalem theater see Bernett, *Kaiserkult,* 53-56. Many scholars argue that the games held in Jerusalem were in imitation of the *Actia,* a festival inaugurated by Octavian to celebrate his victory at Actium. Disputing this theory, Bernett observes that Josephus's narrative makes no mention of the presence of Apollo at these games, an absence which, given the prominent place Octavian accorded the god in his victory, is peculiar if the games were indeed Actian. Moreover, she also notes that, unlike Herod's games, the *Actia* did not have gladiatorial combat. Instead, they had gymnastic events, musical competitions, and horseraces. In Bernett's opinion, the Herodian games in Jerusalem commemorated the three victories (Illyricum, Actium, and the annexation of Egypt) that Augustus had celebrated in his triple triumph in Rome in 29 BCE. In Bernett's opinion, Herod's decision to inaugurate games in Jerusalem was inspired by Octavian's refashioning of Alexandria into a Caesarian city. See Bernett, *Kaiserkult,* 56-57.

that it was not a monumental stone structure but rather a temporary wooden one.[33]

Although Greeks had always built permanent theaters out of stone, the Romans had a long tradition of temporary wooden theaters, many of which were nonetheless monumental and lavish. Indeed, some of these temporary structures had a *scaena frons* (decorated backdrop) that included columns, marble revetments, mosaics, and frescos. Two of the most elaborate examples appeared in theaters constructed by Lucius Mummius in 144 BCE and Lucius Pulcher in 99 BCE. The most elaborate theater was perhaps the one constructed by Marcus Aemilius Scaurus during his aedileship in 58 BCE, which had a three-story *scaena frons*. Even Pompey's stone theater had a *scaena frons* made of wood, and Augustus erected the last documented wooden theater in Rome, near the Tiber, for the *Ludi Saeculares* in 17 BCE.[34]

---

33. For Lichtenberger's and Patrich's theories see Achim Lichtenberger, "Jesus and the Theater in Jerusalem," in *Jesus and Archaeology*, ed. J. H. Charlesworth (Grand Rapids: Eerdmans, 2006), 286-99; Joseph Patrich, "Herod's Theater in Jerusalem: A New Proposal," *IEJ* 52 (2002): 231-39. Cf. Netzer, *Architecture*, 112-15. The Italian theater, which was freestanding with an elaborately decorated *scaena* and a semi-circular orchestra, seems to have developed first in southern Italy and Sicily during the second and early first centuries BCE. The large stone theater at Pompeii, which dates to the 70s BCE, is a good example, but it is somewhat unique in that Rome did not have a stone theater until the theater of Pompey was constructed in 55 BCE. The next stone theaters in Rome were the theaters of Balbus, which was not completed until 13 BCE, and of Marcellus, which was not finished until 11 BCE. There had been a long tradition of wooden theaters in Rome, and when the censors Valerius Messala and Lucius Crassus tried to build a stone auditorium in Rome in 154 BCE they encountered strong resistance. Eventually, the consul Publius Cornelius Scipio Nasica passed a decree requiring the destruction of the partially built structure, because he felt that it would become a source of corruption. For Roman resistance to stone theaters see Livy, *Per.* 37; Velleius Paterculus, *Roman History* 1.15.3; Appian, *B. Civ.* 1.28; Augustine, *City of God* 1.31, 33. Cf. Tacitus, *Ann.* 14.20, where Tacitus states that initially people watched the show standing up so as not to spend the entire day in idleness. Also see Vitruvius, *De Architectura* 5.5.7 for his comments on theaters and their composition. Vitruvius wrote ca. 16-13 BCE and thus was a witness to the erection of both the Balbus and Marcellus theaters. For the scholarly discussion of Roman-style theaters and the stone theaters in Rome see Axel Boëthius, *Etruscan and Early Roman Architecture* (New York: Penguin, 1978), 198-206; Amanda Claridge, *Rome: An Oxford Archaeological Guide* (Oxford: Oxford University Press, 1998), 214 (theater of Pompey), 220 (theater of Balbus), 243-45 (theater of Marcellus).

34. In 52 BCE, Gaius Scribonius Curio introduced an innovative structure: two wooden theaters that could revolve to become one circular amphitheater. For Curio's theaters see Pliny, *HN* 36.116-20. For the theaters of Lucius Mummius and Lucius Pulcher see Tacitus, *Ann.* 14.21; Pliny, *HN* 35.23. For the theater of Aemilius Scaurus see *HN* 34.36; 36.5, 50, 113-

Bringing Judaea into the Roman Sphere

Given this long tradition of wooden theaters, many of which were contemporaneous with Herod's life and building program, it would not be surprising if his theater in Jerusalem were also wooden. Support for this theory comes from an examination of the later theater at Caesarea. As we will see below, this theater was more akin to a Roman theater than a Greek theater. If Herod were using Roman models for the construction of his theater complexes, he would have constructed his first theater of wood. Moreover, Josephus emphasizes that the theater at Caesarea was made of stone. Such a comment would not have been necessary if the theater in Jerusalem were also a stone building.

Even Josephus's narrative of the trophies incident suggests that the structure was wooden. According to the narrative, Herod decorated the *scaena frons* of the theater in Jerusalem with the trophies of gold and silver that commemorated his victories in war. Such decorations, probably shields and body armor on wooden skeletons, were popular throughout the Graeco-Roman world during the principate. As Patrich rightly observes, however, if the theater had been made of stone instead of wood, we would expect the decorations to have been stone reliefs carved into the theater itself rather than precious metals covering wooden skeletons. Consequently, it seems most probable that Herod's theater in Jerusalem was constructed of wood. This composition does not mean that it was a simple affair. Rather, we can imagine that Herod, like Mummius, Pulcher, and Aemilius Scaurus, spared no expense in decorating his building. In addition to the gold and silver we know about, there were probably other lavish architectural decorations such as marble columns, architectural statuary, and colorful frescos.[35]

Herod may have had several motivations for constructing his theater in Jerusalem, none perhaps more important than to depict himself as a

---

15, 189. In this theater, the lowest story was decorated with marble, the middle story was covered in glass mosaics, and the top story was plated with gold. Numerous marble columns and bronze statues decorated the stage as well. For Pompey's and Augustus's theaters see Lichtenberger, "Theater," 294; Patrich, "Herod's Theater," 234.

35. For Josephus's comment that the theater at Caesarea was made of stone see *AJ* 15.341. For a stylistic comparison of Jerusalem's theater to the one at Caesarea see Patrich, "Herod's Theater," 235. Comparison with the composite theater-hippodrome complex at Jericho yields further support. Even though this structure is a uniquely Herodian creation, the *scaena frons* and the stage of the theater part of the complex were made of wood. See Netzer, *Palaces*, 67. For Josephus's description of the trophies in the Jerusalem theater see *AJ* 15.272, 277-79. For Patrich's analysis based on this description see Patrich, "Herod's Theater," 236.

modern (and thus Roman) man. At the time that he constructed this first theater, wooden structures were the norm. Herod's evolution from building wooden to stone theaters mirrored a similar change occurring in Rome. By the time he inaugurated the theater at Caesarea, stone theaters had become more common, although wooden ones still existed. Herod not only adopted Roman culture but also helped its diffusion, particularly in the Levant, where his Jerusalem theater was one of the first constructed.

At the same time, however, the erection of a massive and magnificent temporary theater would also have connected him with Hellenistic royal practice, since there also was a tradition in the classical and Hellenistic worlds of temporary festival architecture, especially temporary tents or ships to commemorate victories and holidays. As with coins, Herod used his architecture as a means of disseminating political messages that could be understood differently depending on the audience. Herod wanted to seem Roman to the Romans and Greek to the Greeks. Constructing a magnificent and lavish wooden theater would have accomplished both desires simultaneously. Finally, by building a temporary wooden structure, which could be assembled or disassembled when necessary, he may have been attempting to minimize the possible antagonism among his Jewish subjects caused by the erection of a theater in the capital.[36] Through all these maneuvers, he was walking a fine line between being an agent of cultural change and being an antagonist to traditional Jewish society. If he wanted to have true architectural freedom, he needed to build outside the traditional Judaean heartland. Herod found his opportunity in the next decade at the site that became his masterpiece of urban architecture, Caesarea Maritima.

At Caesarea, Herod was able to move from wood to stone and erect a freestanding structure just south of his promontory palace that was on the cutting edge of Roman architecture. This theater, which could seat approximately 3,500 to 4,000 spectators, vividly demonstrated both his enthusiasm for Roman culture and his desire to seem modern and daring. Theater performances and musical contests were of course held in this

---

36. For the use of wood in theater construction as evocative of Roman culture see Lichtenberger, "Theater," 295. For Jewish antagonism toward the trophies see *AJ* 15.272-79. Apparently, there were some in Jerusalem who believed Herod was violating the Second Commandment against graven images. Although Herod eventually proved he was not, the incident shows that Jewish sensibilities were an issue vis-à-vis the theater. Cf. Lichtenberger, "Theater," 290.

theater, but it is also possible, using the theaters in Rome as a model, that gladiatorial matches were held in the theater.[37]

Perhaps the most obvious influence of Roman architecture is the design of the theater itself. Instead of utilizing the Hellenistic theater design, in which seating was set into the hillside and an open arrangement of stage buildings enabled mobs to gather with no means of control, Herod chose to use the Roman style of theater, which was freestanding and accordingly enabled the portals to be guarded at the ground level. Like Roman theaters, such as the Theater of Pompey, the theater at Caesarea merged the *cavea* and the stage building into one structure that could only be entered from the portals on the ground floor, thereby controlling ingress and egress. The area behind the *scaena* at Caesarea has not been entirely excavated, and it may have contained a *quadriporticus* (four-sided covered walkway), which would also have controlled access.[38]

Like his amphitheaters, which were Roman but not rigidly so, Herod's theater at Caesarea was actually part of a larger public hippodrome–palace–theater complex. Such a combination had Hellenistic antecedents, especially in the great cities of the Hellenistic East such as Alexandria and Pergamum. Herod may also have received some inspiration from the city of Rome itself, principally from the buildings he saw during his first two visits to Rome (40 and 17 BCE), most impressive of which was the great Pompeian public complex in Rome (the Opera Pompeiana), which included, among other buildings, a temple and a theater.

37. From the Herodian period, remains survive of the orchestra of Caesarea's theater, which was cut into the bedrock, as well as its *cavea* and stairways, which were built on substructures. Remains of the *euripus,* the channel for removing water from around the orchestra, are also visible. The floor of the orchestra was covered in multiple layers of plaster painted with colorful floral, geometric, and fish-scale patterns. The orchestra's walls were decorated with frescos of imitation marble panels. The *scaena frons,* which was built in the Hellenistic style, had a square exedra flanked by smaller concave niches. It was decorated with fine plasterwork frescoes designed to imitate marble revetment. Excavators also found several architectural pieces of stucco-coated stone in the theater as well. The estimated seating capacity is based on the diameter of the orchestra (ca. 56 feet) and that of the *cavea* (ca. 220 feet). See Kenneth G. Holum, Robert Hohlfelder, Robert J. Bull, and Avner Raban, *King's Herod's Dream: Caesarea by the Sea* (New York: Norton, 1988), 82-85; Holum, "Caesarea," in *NEAEHL,* 273; Arthur Segal, *Theatres in Roman Palestine and Provincia Arabia* (Leiden: Brill, 1996), 64ff.; Lichtenberger, *Baupolitik,* 124-25. Cf. Patrich, "Herodian Caesarea — the Urban Space," 113-16. For the possible uses for the theater at Caesarea see John H. Humphrey, "'Amphitheatrical' Hippo-Stadia," 126.

38. Antonio Frova, et al., *Scavi di Caesarea Maritima* (Rome: Bretschneider, 1966), 173; Kathryn Louise Gleason, "Ruler and Spectacle," 217-18; Barbara Burrell and Ehud Netzer, "Herod the Builder," *JRA* 12 (1999): 705.

While we should not attribute too much to Herod's first visit to Rome in 40 BCE — he was there only seven days and in the midst of his quest to secure backing for his possession of the throne of Judaea — it is likely that the city made some impression on him and the development of his architectural tastes. During this first visit, Herod spent most of his time in and around the Opera Pompeiana, mostly because Antony lived there and had an office in the adjacent Porticus Minucia Vetus. Moreover, it is entirely possible that the theater at Caesarea was not begun until after Herod's second, more leisurely visit to Rome in 17 BCE, and at that time he could have toured the city and the Theater of Pompey. We cannot be sure how this complex influenced Herod's thinking, but the combination of public buildings grouped together in a coherent and connected area is suggestive.

Additionally, the visual relationship between the theater and the promontory palace at Caesarea may have been influenced by the layout of the Opera Pompeiana. Specifically, the palace was placed in such a way as to be visually connected to the theater and vice-versa. Such visual association and connection is similar to those seen in the various elements of the Opera Pompeiana, which was designed to appear as one large and unified complex instead of several separate structures. By creating such an identifiably Roman theater, which also had certain Hellenistic elements to it, Herod was able to express his Hellenized and Romanized identities simultaneously, an act entirely appropriate for a region in which Roman culture and ideas had only recently begun to make inroads against the far more dominant Hellenistic culture of the Greek East.[39]

39. For the prevalence of combined palace-entertainment complexes in the Hellenistic East see Gleason, "Ruler and Spectacle," 209-12. For the existence of a *domus* (house) owned by Pompey adjacent to his theater see Plutarch, *Pompey* 40.5. For Roller's discussion of Herod's visits to Rome see Roller, *Building Program*, 33-42. See also *BJ* 1.281-85; *AJ* 14.379-89. For Antony's seizure of Pompey's house see Dio 48.38. For a visual connection between the Caesarea theater and the Promontory Palace see Gleason, "Ruler and Spectacle," 213. If the *scaena frons* of the Caeasarea theater were not present, a spectator seated in the *cavea* of the theater would have been able to gaze directly at the Promontory Palace as if it were a part of the stage scenery. With the *scaena frons* present, audience members saw an articulated architectural facade. There is no conclusive evidence whether the stage building of the Herodian theater was permanent, but Gleason suggests that the upper section of the *scanae frons* was temporary during the Herodian period. See Gleason, "Ruler and Spectacle," 223. One problem with Gleason's theory about the visual link between the theater and the palace is that they are not located on a single axis, but slightly off one. That incongruence might be a reflection more of the topography of the site than anything else. However, it may also have existed because of other architectural concerns, such as the desire to have a palace

Bringing Judaea into the Roman Sphere

Roman Temples

Perhaps even more potentially explosive than his theaters and amphitheaters were the three temples Herod constructed at Caesarea, Panias, and Sebaste in honor of Rome and Augustus, as well as others he built outside his kingdom. These *Augustea* were clear violations of Jewish Law, and their sheer inflammatory nature makes their opulence and grandeur that much more striking. They speak to the lengths to which Herod was willing to go to integrate himself into the larger Roman world, which was beginning to develop and embrace the ruler cult. In particular, they highlighted Herod's relationship with the principate through their dedications and visually through their architecture.

The first of these temples to be constructed was the one at Samaria/Sebaste, which was begun around 27 BCE. This *Augusteum,* which had a hexastyle Corinthian facade, was approximately 115 feet long and 80 feet wide with a portico 23 feet deep in front. In front was a large forecourt, which measured about 20 feet by 170 feet and was accessed by a flight of twenty-four steps, divided into two equal levels. The temple stood 1450 feet above sea level and was erected on a podium 14 feet above the forecourt. Corner pilasters decorated the southern facade of the temple, and the *cella* was divided into a broad nave and two narrow side aisles.[40]

Besides the temple, Herod may have made another architectural gesture

---

dramatically jut out west into the ocean, a feature that emphasized Herod's links to the West and his ability to conquer the natural topography.

40. At the northeastern and northwestern corners of the complex were two rectangular towers. Between the forecourt and the flight of steps was a narrow space (72 × 18 feet), and a similar space (72 × 15 feet) lay between the top of the steps and the temple facade. Herod's builders also constructed two parallel retaining walls shaped like a letter Π on the northern slope, and this addition almost doubled the available space. A central row of square piers or columns divided subterranean corridors, which were formed by the parallel retaining walls around the forecourt. Each row of piers supported a pair of arches spanning the breadth of the corridor. Wooden roofs, which were the floors of colonnades 26 feet in breadth, covered the corridors. These colonnades were supported by two rows of columns, one along the edge of the forecourt and a central row situated above the supporting piers of the substructures. The two major excavations at Sebaste were the Harvard Expedition of 1908-10 led by George Andrew Reisner, and the Joint Expedition of 1931-35 led by J. W. Crowfoot. For the site reports see George Andrew Reisner, et al., *Harvard Excavations at Samaria, 1908-1910,* vol. 1 (Cambridge: Harvard University Press, 1924); John W. Crowfoot, K. M. Kenyon, and E. L. Sukenik, *Samaria-Sebaste I: The Buildings at Samaria* (London: Palestine Exploration Fund, 1942); John W. Crowfoot, G. M. Crowfoot, and K. M. Kenyon, *Samaria-Sebaste III: The Objects from Samaria* (London: Palestine Exploration Fund, 1957).

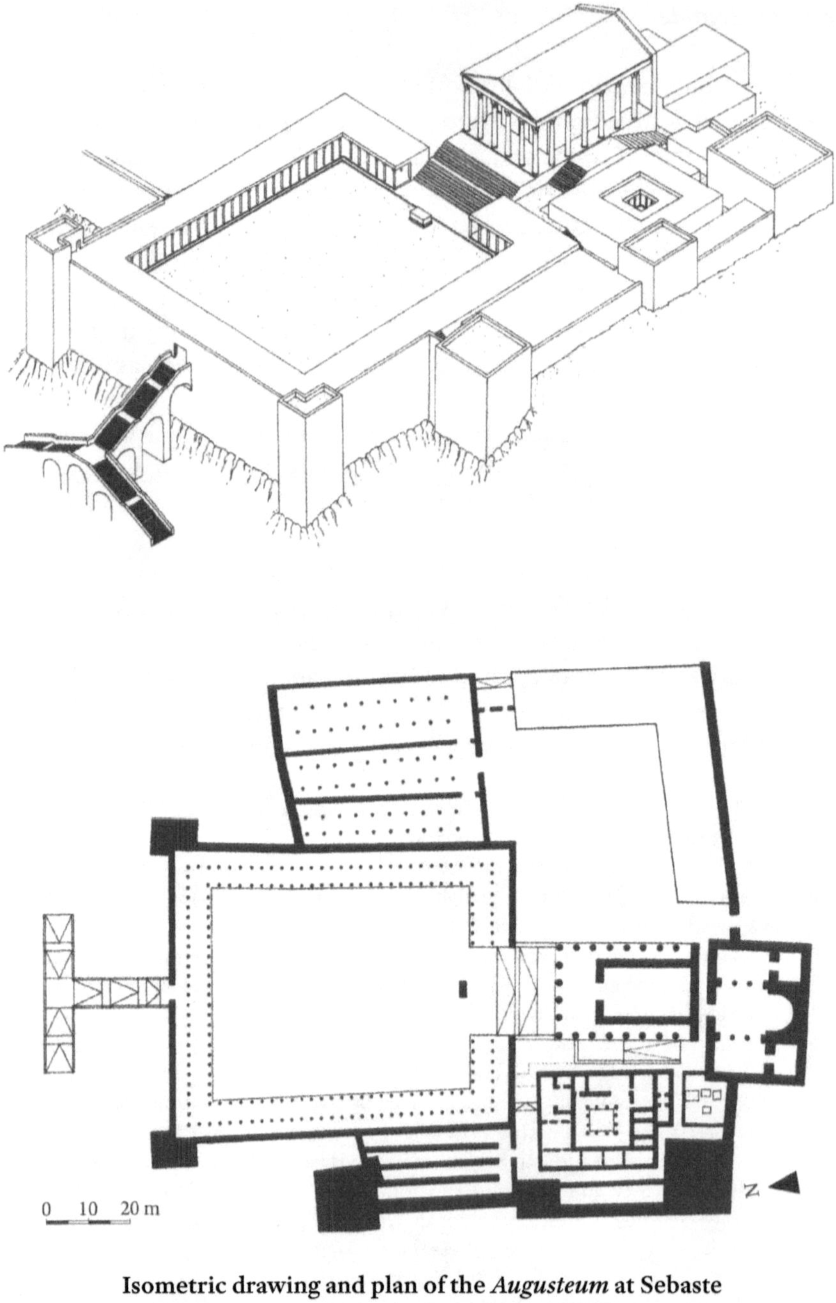

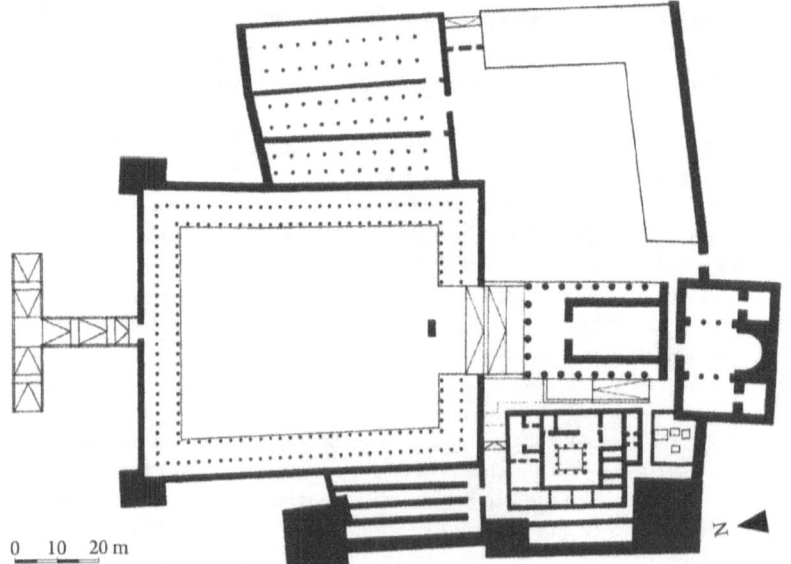

Isometric drawing and plan of the *Augusteum* at Sebaste

toward his Roman patron at this site. In the southwestern corner of Sebaste's acropolis sits a large peristyle residence of about 8500 square feet that abuts the *Augusteum*. This building stood below both the level of the temple's podium and that of the forecourt and thus did not block the view from either one. Only the eastern side of the building is well preserved. As a result, the arrangement of its rooms is only clear on that side. What remains have been uncovered, though, reveal a luxurious building with stuccoed and fluted columns and mosaic floors, including one whose black-and-white pattern is similar to those of floors in the Northern Palace at Masada and the First Palace at Jericho. In the northeastern part of the house, excavators discovered a bathroom with a tub. The walls of the house were stuccoed and painted with polychrome frescoes of the Second Pompeian Style. Given the architectural and decorative styles of the building as well as its construction during the Herodian period, it was most likely a royal residence.

In her analysis of Sebaste, Monika Bernett raises the possibility that a larger and grander palace stood on the eastern side of the acropolis. If so, what was the function, symbolic or practical, of this peristyle building on the western side of the plateau? Bernett suggests that whatever the practical uses of the peristyle building were, its symbolic use was as an architectural statement of political loyalty and honor. Specifically, the building was an imitation of the Hellenistic royal pattern of constructing palaces next to sanctuaries of one's patron god. The most famous Roman example of this practice, of course, was the *Domus Augusti*, the home Augustus constructed on the Palatine Hill, which was adjacent to and connected with his temple of Apollo Palatinus. As Bernett argues, even if the residence was somewhat modest in scale, its location next to the *Augusteum* gave sanction to Herod's reign and granted him special status, since he alone could live atop a mountain and *with* a god.

Herod could not have constructed this palace-temple complex with direct knowledge of Augustus's plans for the Palatine. After 40 BCE, Herod did not visit Rome again until 17 BCE, and by that time, the complex had already been built. It is more likely that he (and Augustus) were drawing on the Hellenistic model of royal residences adjacent to the temples of patron deities as seen in cities such as Attalid Pergamum and Ptolemaic Alexandria. He thus expressed his loyalty to Rome and acceptance of its protective power and imperial cult using Hellenistic symbolic language, a hybrid response, which was typical of the contemporary eastern Mediterranean.[41]

---

41. Netzer believed that the residence was not a royal palace because, in his opinion, a

The *Augusteum* at Caesarea, which also had a hexastyle Corinthian facade, was built on a high, partially artificial platform overlooking the harbor. Today, the platform rises just over 43 feet above sea level and is approximately 344 feet north to south and 295 feet east to west. The temple itself rose another 80 to 100 feet above the platform and was 152 feet by 94 feet. Josephus remarked on its impressive size and splendor. Indeed, he claimed, it was so large that it could be seen from a great distance as one entered the harbor. Josephus also states that the entire city including the temple was constructed of white marble. However, archaeology has revealed that Herod was more interested in the appearance of marble than the actuality of it. Rather than import such expensive building materials, he had his architects create the illusion of it by plastering local kurkar to give the appearance of marble. This method also appears at other Herodian sites such as the palaces at Herodion, Jericho, and Masada.

In each *Augusteum* were two cult statues, one to Roma and one to Augustus. Josephus remarks that the cult statues were modeled on the statue of Hera at Argos and on Phidias's Zeus at Olympia. Herod's use of these models raises the possibility that the Roma statue was meant to honor Augustus's wife Livia. As Bernett argues, the Augustan period saw a revival of classical art and imagery, and Herod's imitation of two famous statues from Classical Greece is not surprising. What is a little peculiar, however, is his fashioning of the goddess Roma as Hera and not Athena. Surely, Bernnet argues, Roma would have been better represented as Athena, the triumphant warrior goddess and patron of peace. Such a depiction also would have made a great deal of sense for a king like Herod, who was famous not for his military victories but for his prosperity and wealth.

---

royal palace would have had a better location and more advanced bathing facilities. Instead, he suggests that the building could have been the home of the city's governor or perhaps that of the priest in charge of the temple, or that it could also have been the residence used by Herod's family and friends when visiting the city. However, the style of the building and its decorations as well as the chronology of its construction suggests that the simplest explanation, namely that it was a royal residence, is probably the correct one. For discussion of the peristyle building as well as his identification of it as Herod's palace see Reisner, et al., *Harvard Excavations at Samaria*, 180-85; Dan Barag, "King Herod's Royal Castle at Samaria-Sebaste," *PEQ* 125 (1993), 8-9; Netzer, *Architecture*, 90-91. For the analysis of this building as an imitation of the *Domus Augusti* on the Palatine and a statement of Herod's subordination to and protection by Augustus as "living god" see Bernett, *Kaiserkult*, 84-89. For Paul Zanker's analysis of the *Domus Augusti* and the Temple of Apollo Palatinus see *The Power of Images in the Age of Augustus*, trans. Alan Shapiro (Ann Arbor: University of Michigan Press, 1990), 50-53.

Bringing Judaea into the Roman Sphere

Why Hera and not Athena? We know that in many parts of the Roman world, especially the Roman East, Livia received divine honors in her own right or in association with Olympian gods, particularly Hera and Juno. Furthermore, Livia seems to have had her own relationship with Herod and his family. She especially seems to have developed a relationship with Herod's sister, Salome, who left Livia significant property in her will. If Herod wished to honor Livia as well as Augustus, it would have made sense to depict her as Hera. Moreover, in a temple at the heart of his greatest *urbs Caesarae,* the veneration of Augustus and Livia as the Olympian spouses would have been far more fitting than anything else. Indeed, as Bernett suggests (citing the work of Ulrike Hahn), such a depiction was popular and common. However, as Josephus states quite explicitly, the female statue in the *Augusteum* at Caesarea was Roma, not Hera. If Bernett is correct that Herod was honoring Livia with the statue, then there must be a reason why he would not do so as openly as possible.

As we know from Suetonius and Cassius Dio, Augustus was extremely hesitant to accept divine honors for himself and his family. He probably feared that accepting such honors without reserve would destroy the illusion of republicanism that he was trying to maintain. When he finally consented, his stipulation was that he could be worshiped in the East (where such practice was common) as long as the temple was consecrated jointly to him and Rome. In Rome itself, he permitted no such temples. To a typical Hellenized monarch, such reluctance was unnecessary: kings had received divine honors for centuries. However, as a king who had to be discreet and ambiguous at times to avoid offending his subjects, Herod probably would have seen Augustus's provision as sensible and prudent. He was thus happy to represent Livia in the guise of Roma to satisfy the restriction and yet not miss an opportunity to honor his patron and his patron's wife. If the cult were in honor of both Augustus and Livia, then the quinquennial games introduced by Herod would have been in honor of the imperial couple as well. Livia's significant contribution to the inaugural games makes much more sense in this context.[42]

---

42. For the size and scale of the temple see Lisa C. Kahn, "King Herod's Temple of Roma and Augustus at Caesarea Maritima," in Raban and Holum, *Caesarea Maritima,* 141-45. For Josephus's discussion of the scale and size of the cult statues see *BJ* 1.414; *AJ* 15.339. For his claims that the temple was entirely "white stone" see *BJ* 1.408; *AJ* 15.331. For the archaeological reality of plastered kurkar see Kahn, "King Herod's Temple," 131-32. Cf. Ehud Netzer, "Herod's Building Projects: State Necessity or Personal Need?" *Jerusalem Cathedra* 1 (1981): 58; Moshe L. Fischer and Alla Stein, "Josephus on the Use of Marble in Building Projects

The third of these *Augustea* is the one about which we know the least. There is not even a consensus about its location. While some scholars believe that the structure at the entrance to the Cave of Pan is the *Augusteum*, others such as Ehud Netzer suggest that the *opus reticulatum* edifice about 330 feet west of the caves on a prominent terrace is in fact the temple. Still others, such as J. Andrew Overman, Jack Olive, and Michael Nelson, argue that Panias was not the site at all. Instead, they argue that the temple was in nearby Omrit. While there is no conclusive evidence for any of these identifications, Josephus clearly states that the temple was in Banias (Panias). Therefore, until clear evidence to the contrary appears, it is best to agree with the literary record. Whether the temple is the building in front of the cave mouth or the *opus reticulatum* site nearby is still an open question, although my inclination is to agree with Netzer. His candidate seems a better option because it was built on a prominent terrace and uses *opus reticulatum* covered in plaster. We know that Herod used these exact building techniques in other later constructions (e.g., the Third Palace at Jericho), and, wherever this shrine was, it was completed during the latter part of his reign. Further, the white plaster would explain Josephus's description of a temple built from "white marble" (*BJ* 1.404) or "white stone" (*AJ* 15.363).[43]

---

of Herod the Great," *JJS* 45 (1994): 79-85. For an analysis of the facade platform masonry see Kahn, "King Herod's Temple," 134. Cf. Avraham Negev, "Caesarea," *IEJ* 11 (1961): 81-83 and 13 (1963): 146-48; Kenneth G. Holum, "The Temple Platform: Progress Report on the Excavations," in Holum, Raban, and Patrich, eds., *Caesarea Papers 2* (Portsmouth: Journal of Roman Archaeology, 1999), 12-26; Farland H. Stanley, Jr., "The South Flank of the Temple Platform," in *Caesarea Papers 2*, 35-41; Patrich, "Herodian Caesarea — the Urban Space," 105-10. For Bernett's theory on a cult of Livia at Caesarea as well as Augustus at Caesarea see *Kaiserkult*, 112-17. She credits Herod with one of the first, if not the first, depiction of a seated Hera/Livia. Other known depictions of this kind date to after Augustus's death. Caesarea's games in honor of both Augustus and Livia would not have been unique. We know of other examples of games in honor of the imperial couple and other members of the *domus Augusta* in cities such as Aizanoi (Anatolia), Gytheion (Laconia), and Pergamum.

43. For the various positions on the location of the third *Augusteum*, see Ze'ev Maov, "Banias, Temple of Pan — 1989," in *Excavations and Surveys in Israel* 9 (1989-90): 85; J. Andrew Overman, Jack Olive, and Michael Nelson, "Discovering Herod's Shrine to Augustus," *BAR* 29.2 (2003): 40-49, 67-68; Andrea M. Berlin, "Debate: Where Was Herod's Temple to Augustus? Banias Is Still the Best Candidate," *BAR* 29.5 (2003): 22-24; J. Andrew Overman, Jack Olive, and Michael Nelson, "Debate: Where Was Herod's Temple to Augustus? The Authors Respond," *BAR* 29.5 (2003): 24; Ehud Netzer, "Debate: Where Was Herod's Temple to Augustus? A Third Candidate: Another Building at Banias," *BAR* 29.5 (2003): 25; J. Andrew Overman, Jack Olive, and Michael Nelson, "A Newly Discovered Herodian Temple at Khirbet Omrit in Northern Israel," in Kokkinos, ed., *World of the Herods*, 177-95. Cf. Bernett,

Bringing Judaea into the Roman Sphere

Since we have little to no evidence about what the *Augusteum* at Panias looked like, we will only consider the other two when examining the several important archaeological connections between them. For example, both are hexastyle and have similar Corinthian columns with molded abacus and channeled volutes. Furthermore, both seem to have had grand central stairways leading from the base of the platform to the temple itself. In the case of the Caesarea *Augusteum,* the central stairway rose from the city's inner harbor up to the platform. A further architectural connection can be made with the temple at Suwēda, about one hundred miles east of Caesarea in the Haurān region of southwest Syria, which was constructed between 50 and 28 BCE. In 23 BCE, Herod received this region from Augustus, and it is possible that he had sponsored the construction of the temple. Like Caesarea, the capitals at this shrine show a widely sloping volute stem, although at Suwēda they are decorated with a cable pattern instead of a more traditional composite Corinthian capital.[44]

Additionally, both temples — and the third *Augusteum* if we conclude that it was the *opus reticulatum* building at Panias — were centerpieces of their cities and seem to have been built following Roman patterns of

---

Kaiserkult, 127-28, 130-46. She agrees with Berlin and Netzer that Omrit was not the site of the *Augusteum* built by Herod but could have been the site of one built by Agrippa II. She also agrees with Netzer that the *opus reticulatum* building is the remains of the *Augusteum.* Indeed, she argues that this temple was the orientation point for Herod Philip's later city. The literary record is actually quite explicit. For instance, in *BJ* 1.404-6, Josephus states that the temple was at Banias. Moreover, in both there and in *AJ* 15.359, 363-64 he describes a site at the base of a cliff which had a large cavern. The site also had a large spring at it, which some people believed was the source of the Jordan River. These descriptions fit Banias much better than Omrit, which is nowhere near a large spring. For the chronology of the temple see *AJ* 15.363. According to this passage, Herod begins construction of the temple after Augustus's visit to Syria, so the *terminus post quem* is 20 BCE. *BJ* 1.404's description appears within a general panegyric of Herod's building program, and thus is not useful for determining the chronology of the site. For the likelihood of the "white marble" being plastered stone see Fischer and Stein, "Josephus on the Use of Marble," 79-85.

44. For the similarities in the columns at the two temples see Kahn, "King Herod's Temple," 138. Cf. Reisner, *Harvard Excavations at Samaria,* 191-92. Excavators also found a similar capital in the Sebastean basilica. See Crowfoot, *Samaria-Sebaste I,* plate 84, numbers 2, 3, and 5. For the appearance of a central staircase in each *temenos,* see Kahn, "King Herod's Temple," 135-36; Barag, "Herod's Royal Castle," 4-8. The staircase remains at Caesarea appear to be Byzantine in date, but they may reflect an older Herodian-era scheme. For Herod's annexation of the Haurān region see *BJ* 1.398; *AJ* 15.344. For a discussion of the temple at Suwēda see H. C. Butler, *Architecture and Other Arts: Publications of the American Expedition to Syria 1899-1900,* vol. 2 (New York: Century, 1903), 327-35.

construction. In particular, each was constructed on a high platform towering over the rest of the city. Like other Italian temples, the platform was constructed using a giant substructure. Moreover, Herod constructed these platforms so as to make them dwarf everything else in the city and appear to be removed and separate from the rest of the city. In contrast, classical and Hellenistic temples, while somewhat separate from the rest of their cities, were more fully integrated into the city plan. Another sign of Roman influence is that all three *Augustea* (if Caesarea's did have a central stairway) were reached by climbing a large and monumental stairway. This hallmark of Roman sacred architecture focused attention on the front of the temple and controlled access to the interior.

And yet, as was typical in the Eastern Mediterranean, these temples did not completely reject past architectural features and styles. Instead, they embraced certain aspects of Hellenistic sacred architecture and modified them to fit the new Roman context. The *temenos* at Sebaste, for instance, was constructed on an artificial platform supported by terracing and massive substructures. A grand stairway on the north side of the complex was probably the ceremonial entrance to the sacred precinct. Once visitors climbed this stairway, they had to proceed through a series of additional grand stairways and a courtyard with porticos surrounding it before they reached the temple itself. Such a layout emphasized the vertical and horizontal aspects of the complex as well as the ever-increasing grandeur of the view. All these features are typical of the Hellenistic hanging temple, examples of which include the Asklepieion at Kos, the temple of Athena at Lindos, and the Demeter complex at Pergamum. In Italy, the best examples of this type of architecture are the late second to early first-century BCE temples of Fortuna Primigenia at Praeneste and Hercules Victor at Tivoli.

At Caesarea Maritima, Herod also created a hybrid structure. While the *Augusteum* there contained several Roman elements, it also contained a *peristasis,* a four-sided porch of columns, which surrounds the *cella* (sanctuary) of a Greek peripteros-style temple. This covered walkway enabled the priests to perform cultic processions inside the temple itself. As Bernett observes, the *Augusteum* at Caesarea Maritima seems to have been one of the first (if not the first) Roman temple with a *peristasis,* and it is possible that its construction influenced similar structures.[45]

---

45. Duane Roller has argued that the influences for Herod's *Augustea* were the *Caesarea* at Alexandria and Antioch (*Building Program,* 92-93). However, even while acknowledging the Roman influence on Herod's temples, it is important that we permit him some degree of

Bringing Judaea into the Roman Sphere

In sum, there seem to be several clear similarities between the three shrines Herod constructed in honor of Augustus and Rome and between these *Augustea* and other traditional Roman temples. As one of the first builders of cult sites dedicated to Augustus — other contemporary examples include those at Ancyra in Turkey, at Philae in Egypt, and at Vienne in France — it is no surprise that Herod would draw on the traditions of Roman sacred architecture. Nevertheless, his buildings moved beyond mere Roman copies, combining Roman and Hellenistic elements into new compositions that reflected his hybrid identity as a ruler straddling multiple worlds and cultures. Interestingly, since Herod was one of the first (if not the first) to construct a temple in honor of Augustus, it is possible that his architecture actually led and influenced the field as opposed to following it.

Using Roman Building Technology and Decoration

In addition to the utilization of Roman buildings, Herod's architects also employed Roman technology and building techniques, such as the use of *pozzolana* for harbor installations and the appearance of *opus reticulatum* and *opus sectile*. Native Judaean building traditions were long established by the end of the first century BCE, and Herod's decision to use new and innovative means of construction speaks to his desire to position his kingdom more fully into the emerging Roman world of the principate.

---

creative autonomy. As Netzer and Burrell insightfully note ("Herod the Builder," 706-7), it is extremely questionable whether these temples, which honored Julius Caesar, were founded by him at all. Further, not all imperial cult complexes were laid out according to the rigid pattern of temple-in-forum propagated by Rome. Indeed, none of Herod's *Augustea* follows this pattern, as even Roller admits. Like Netzer and Burrell, I believe that Roller overstates his case. However, as they acknowledge, Herod clearly integrated several Roman architectural features into his designs, and such integration testifies to a significant level of Romanization. For the integration of classical and Hellenistic temples into city plans see Henner von Hesberg, "The Significance of the Cities in the Kingdom of Herod," in Fittschen and Foerster, *Judaea and the Graeco-Roman World in the Time of Herod*, 11-14. For a detailed discussion of the sacred precinct at Sebaste see Barag, "Herod's Royal Castle," 4-16; Netzer, *Architecture*, 85-92. Cf. Bernett, *Kaiserkult*, 74-89, esp. 83 for the Hellenistic architectural influences on the precinct. For the *Augusteum* at Caesarea Maritima as the first Roman-style temple with a *peristasis* see *Kaiserkult*, 109. The temple of Jupiter Heliopolitanus at Baalbek is another example of a Roman temple that incorporates the Greek *peristasis* into its architecture.

Pozzolana *and Roman Hydrotechnology*

Perhaps the most conspicuous and intricate example of Herod's adoption of Roman technology was in the area of hydroconstuction (building on and in water). The coastline of Judaea lacked any large natural harbors, and, if Herod wanted a city to compete with the other major metropolises of the eastern Mediterranean, namely Antioch and Alexandria, he would have to construct it, a task that was an enormous financial and logistical undertaking. His use of *pozzolana* cement to build his Sebastos harbor at Caesarea Maritima enabled him to create a capstone harbor for his urban monument, but it also demonstrates an enthusiastic embracing of Roman technology.

The Sebastos harbor had three basins — inner, middle, and outer — and relied on the use of large piers built in the open water and protected by massive breakwaters. At the mouth of the outer harbor, which was located in the northwest corner of the harbor, were large structures that were probably towers. One of these large towers likely was the Drusion that Josephus mentions (*BJ* 1.412; *AJ* 15.336). Underwater excavations have discovered stone pavement and huge ashlars which suggest that storage vaults with a paved promenade in front may have existed along the inner quay in addition to the anchorage points. The overall length of the harbor

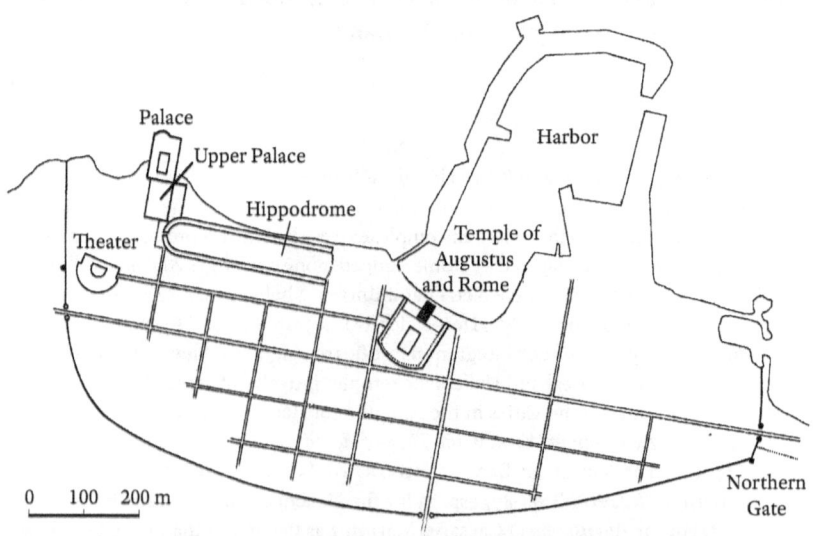

Plan of Caesarea and the Sebastos harbor

piers was about 3200 feet, and thus the total area of the harbor was about 100,000,000 square feet. In comparison, the Kantharos harbor in Piraeus was about 7,500,000 square feet, and the military harbor at Rhodes was about 2,000,000 square feet.[46]

Building a harbor at Caesarea was not an easy task. There were no offshore islands to afford a partially protected anchorage, and there was no natural bay. Furthermore, the area lacked a navigable river, which could have been used for constructing a safe docking space along its banks. Instead of these ideal conditions, there simply was a straight sandy coastline exposed to the waves. Additionally, a south to north longshore current carried huge quantities of sand and silt from the Nile. Any construction along this coast would thus have resulted in a significant deposit of material to the south and coastal erosion to the north. Moreover, any constructed enclosed basin would begin to silt up almost immediately. Finally, the ocean floor at the proposed site was predominantly sand, which made building moles on it an extremely challenging task.

Local architects and hydroengineers did not have sufficient experience for such a project, so Herod imported builders and architects from Rome, who had extensive experience with constructing marine structures. To get these experts he would have needed permission, and he probably turned to his close friend and fellow builder Marcus Agrippa. Agrippa had been responsible for a number of civil structures in Rome already and had also reorganized the navy and built the appropriate infrastructure to support it. Further, in the 30s BCE he had built a fleet in the Bay of Naples and constructed the Portus Iulius, a secure anchorage for it. Such experience with naval fleets and hydroengineering would place him in a good position to advise Herod. Most importantly, he would have known the men capable of building the harbor; if they were not in his entourage, he could summon them from Italy.

To construct his massive harbor complex under these less than ideal conditions, Herod utilized the most modern building methods and materials, including hydraulic cement, composed of *pozzolana,* a volcanic ash imported from Italy around the Bay of Naples. Vitruvius, whose treatise

---

46. Avner Raban et al., "The Under Water Excavations 1993-1994," in *Caesarea Papers 2*, 152-68; Eduard G. Reinhardt, "Stratigraphic Excavations of Outer Harbour Deposits: Preliminary Report (1994)," in *Caesarea Papers 2*, 189-97; Avner Raban, et al., "Land Excavations in the Inner Harbour (1993-1994)," in *Caesarea Papers 2*, 199-217; Brian Yule and Anthony J. Barham, "Caesarea's Inner Harbour: The Potential of the Harbour Sediments," in *Caesarea Papers 2*, 263-84. Cf. Netzer, *Architecture*, 100.

on architecture was completed just before work began on Sebastos (ca. 25 BCE), had written about and recommended the use of *pozzolana* in marine structures. Its use at Caesarea was essential in order to compensate for the poor quality local kurkar stone. Builders at Caesarea used large concrete blocks — many of more than 1,000 cubic feet in volume and 90 tons of weight — in concert with stone blocks, which had been the main building material in earlier harbors. To create these concrete blocks, the builders erected a series of double-walled wooden frames shaped like rectangular boats to construct the harbor quays. These frames were floated into position and sunk. Workers then poured concrete into the molds once they were submerged and anchored in their proper place.

Herod would have provided the money to pay for the massive importation of *pozzolana,* but he also needed approval to arrange transport for the massive amount of material needed. Agrippa could have facilitated the acquisition and transport of the raw materials needed on grain ships diverted from their normal east-west route (Rome to Alexandria) to Caesarea. These grain ships would have carried the supplies as ballast in their holds and, once they had unloaded their cargo at Caesarea, would have taken on local ballast for the rest of the trip. To use the grain ships in such a way would have required the permission of either Augustus or Agrippa, since only they could have tampered with the transportation of the grain supply or made a decision that might impact its orderly transport. It is unlikely that Herod would have circumvented Agrippa and asked Augustus directly, nor would he have had the temerity to suggest the plan in the first place given his status as a client king. Agrippa could have suggested such a scheme while Herod was visiting him on Lesbos; he might have even suggested that some of his builders visit the Caesarea site and survey it.

If this hypothesis is true, and it does seem possible, the construction of Caesarea would represent a successful synergy of Roman technology and organization with Judaean ambition and manpower. Construction had proceeded rapidly, especially considering that winter conditions prohibited any significant work in the sea for about four or five months a year. Assuming construction began immediately, Sebastos was completed in seven years (22-15 BCE). Agrippa's visit in 15 BCE (*AJ* 16.13) might even have been timed to celebrate the completion of the harbor. Through his use of Roman technology and architects, Herod had conceived of a grand harbor that would increase trade and commerce while simultaneously advertising his and his kingdom's increasing Romanization and deeper involvement in the larger Graeco-Roman world. He had successfully merged two of his worlds, and the result was the new maritime jewel in his commercial crown.[47]

Herod's reliance on Roman building techniques continued above the water as well. *Opus reticulatum* and *opus sectile* were both building techniques readily identifiable as Roman, and both appear for the first time in Judaea in Herodian buildings. *Opus reticulatum* involved the use of uniformly cut small tufa bricks placed in diagonal rows. Behind the lattice-like outer facing was a core of concrete. The finished patterns resembled a net, hence the term *reticulatum* (Latin for "net"). This building technique first came into vogue in Rome during the first century BCE. Although rarely seen east of the Adriatic, it also appears at two capitals of Herod's contemporaries, Caesarea-Iol, the capital of Juba II of Mauretania, and Sebaste-Elaeussa, the winter residence of Archelaus I of Cappadocia.[48] Scholars usually date the arrival of *opus reticulatum* in Judaea to the late part of Herod's reign, since the buildings where it appears all date to that period.

One of the examples of this Herodian use of *opus reticulatum* is at Panias, where the technique appears in the walls of a structure that may be the temple to Augustus.[49] At Jericho the technique appears in the large sunken

---

47. For the difficulties of building at Caesarea see Robert L. Hohlfelder, "Beyond Coincidence? Marcus Agrippa and King Herod's Harbor," *JNES* 59 (2000): 249. For Vitruvius's discussion of *pozzolana,* see *De Architectura* 5.12.2-6. For the size of the large blocks constructed at Caesarea see Netzer, *Architecture,* 100. For a discussion of how the concrete blocks were built see Christopher Brandon, Stephen Kemp, and Martin Grove, "*Pozzolana,* Lime, and Single-Mission Barges (Area K)," in *Caesarea Papers 2,* 169-78. For the speculation on Agrippa's role in the Caesarea harbor see Hohlfelder, "Beyond Coincidence?" 249-51. For Herodian international trade see Rocca, *Herod's Judaea,* 236-39.

48. For the appearance of *opus reticulatum* at Caesarea-Iol see Philippe Leveau, "Caesarea de Maurétanie," *ANRW* 2.10.2 (1982): 712-13. For its appearance at Sebaste-Elaeussa see Eugenia Equini Schneider, et al., *Elaiussa Sebaste I. Campagne di Scavo 1995-1997* (Rome: L'Erma di Bretschneider, 1999), 103-14. For its use in Judaea see Jacobson, "Placing Herod the Great and His Works," 88; Hazel Dodge, "The Architectural Impact of Rome in the East," in *Architecture and Architectural Sculpture in the Roman Empire,* ed. Martin Henig (Oxford: Oxford University Committee for Archaeology, 1990), 109, 112.

49. As stated above, these walls are set on a broad natural terrace overlooking the nearby pools of the spring. The northern wall of the pair seems to have been a retaining wall, while the southern one was freestanding. They are approximately 8 feet apart and seem to have been the foundation walls for a colonnade that stood between them. Despite the poor state of preservation, Netzer was still able to excavate the site. To the north of the two walls are the remains of a hall (39 feet wide and at least 49 feet long) entered from the south. Within the area excavated by Netzer, the hall is entirely hewn from the rock. For

garden south of the Wadi Qelt. This formal garden was set within a large rectangular structure (475 × 130 feet) whose southern facade contained 48 niches of alternating semicircular and rectangular shapes separated by small half-columns. Between the niches is a wall of *opus reticulatum* mixed with *opus quadratum*. In the middle of this facade was a series of tiered benches shaped like a theater *cavea* and containing flowerbeds.[50]

The final example of *opus reticulatum* in Herodian Judaea was found on a rocky hill in Jerusalem near the Damascus Gate. This round building, first excavated by Konrad Schick in 1878 and then again in 1893, was initially thought to be a burial site, but since the initial digs did not find a tomb it was concluded that it had served as an open courtyard. New excavations in 1977 determined that the building was larger and taller than initially thought. Its facade was built of ashlar masonry, while the inner face was constructed using *opus reticulatum*. Its location on the principal axis of entry into and exit from Jerusalem and its prodigious height meant that it would have been extremely visible and prominent along the skyline. Pottery found at the site dates the building to the first century BCE and the Herodian period in particular. In addition, the use of Herodian style ashlars (comb-dressed margins and a large central boss) also supports such a date.

But was it one of Herod's constructions? The building's location provides a clue to its identity. Twice in his narrative, Josephus mentions a structure that he calls "Herod's monument" *(Hērōdou mnēmeion)*. This structure stood between Mount Scopus and the third wall, which coincides with the location of the round structure. Its design as a round structure also connects the building with Herod, since it resembles the Etruscan and Roman *tumulus* tombs. Perhaps the most influential of these *tumuli* was the mausoleum of Augustus, which the *princeps* built for himself and his family in 28 BCE. Who would think to model a tomb after Augustus's tomb in

---

instance, builders cut as much as 15 feet of rock out of the cliffside on the north end of the structure. A 3-foot-wide rock-hewn wall projected above ground level on the eastern side prior to excavation. Furthermore, in the course of excavations, archaeologists discovered the bottom of the parallel wall on the western side. Small holes for marble slabs appear on both walls, which suggests that they were covered with marble on their inner faces. See Netzer, *Architecture*, 218-21.

50. As Netzer observes, it is unlikely, given Herod's consistent observance of the Second Commandment, that these niches contained statues. More likely, they contained vessels such as decorated flowerpots or ornamental plants. See Netzer, *Architecture*, 66. Cf. Netzer, *Jericho* 1:288-93, 323-24.

Rome? Herod is the most obvious choice. Such mimicry would have been politically useful, as it would have demonstrated both his Romanization and flattery of Augustus. While Josephus refers to it as Herod's monument, most scholars believe that Herod's tomb is actually at Herodion. This structure, then, could have been either a monument to him in Jerusalem or the Antipatrid family tomb, which is what Ehud Netzer and Sarah Ben-Arieh concluded when they excavated it. The construction of this structure was probably contemporary with that of the Third Palace at Jericho and the *Augusteum* at Panias, probably by the same Roman engineers who worked at those sites.[51]

We have now cataloged three examples of Herod's use of *opus reticulatum* within his kingdom, and there may have been more that have not survived. Clearly, this technique was one that he employed enthusiastically in his buildings. How then would its use add to his self-presentation, especially since walls constructed using this technique would have been plastered over and painted? It seems clear that he imported Roman engineers and architects during the latter part of his reign, and that these men were responsible for the *opus reticulatum* walls. While these walls would not have been visible after being plastered, members of the royal court surely

---

51. For Josephus's discussion of the location of Herod's monument in Jerusalem see *BJ* 5.108, 507. Although Suleiman the Magnificent constructed the current Damascus Gate in the sixteenth century, there are remains of an older and equally impressive gate below the current one dating to the Herodian period. For the initial excavation of the *opus reticulatum* building near the Damascus Gate see Konrad Schick, "Neue Funde im Norden von Jerusalem," *ZDPV* 2 (1879): 102-4, plate 3. For the later excavations and analysis see Ehud Netzer and Sarah Ben-Arieh, "Remains of an Opus Reticulatum Building in Jerusalem," *IEJ* 33 (1983): 163, 170-75. Archaeologists also discovered another concentric circular wall (with an outer diameter of 41 feet and an inner diameter of 29 feet) inside the other wall. See Netzer, *Architecture,* 132-34. Cf. Ehud Netzer, "Herod's Family Tomb in Jerusalem," *BAR* 9.3 (1983): 52-53; Rocca, *Herod's Judaea,* 356-57. For a discussion of the mausoleum of Augustus in Rome see Claridge, *Rome,* 181-94. There is a tomb on the hillside west of the Old City in the public garden next to the King David Hotel that also has been identified as Herod's tomb (Netzer, *Architecture,* 134, n. 24, and cf. Netzer, "Herod's Family Tomb," 59). This subterranean tomb is composed of a central room with a barrel-vaulted ceiling and four burial chambers branching off from the central room. Herodian ashlars decorate the walls of these rock-cut chambers. There is also a courtyard north of the entrance to the tomb, which was sealed in antiquity by a large rolling stone (ca. 6 feet in diameter). Within the courtyard is a structure composed of heavy ashlars that form an L and may have originally been the base of a monument. Although this tomb is quite impressive, there were many wealthy families in Jerusalem who could have constructed it. It is unlikely to be the monument mentioned by Josephus because it is in the wrong location.

would have known of their construction and the presence of these Roman artisans who had brought such new technology. Advertisement of these Roman architects and their use of the latest building techniques would have reinforced the king's image as an architectural innovator and Romanized client king. We can also imagine him showing off his new buildings to important guests and explaining the use of *opus reticulatum*, which, as we said before, was somewhat rare in the eastern Mediterranean. In the end, his use of this new building technique was yet another example of his adopting Roman norms and customs, a habit that was well known to his subjects and friends.

Besides *opus reticulatum*, Herod's builders also used another common Roman building technique, *opus sectile*, to decorate the floors of his palaces, such as at Masada, Jericho, and Herodion. *Opus sectile*, which developed during the late Republic, involves the use of various materials such as marble, mother of pearl, and glass, which are cut or inlaid into walls and floors to make a picture or form a pattern. At Masada, *opus sectile* floors dating to ca. 25 BCE can be found in all three major rooms of the bathhouse, and these floors are extremely Roman in appearance. In particular, the two shapes of tiles used in Masada pavements, square and triangular, are two of the shapes Vitruvius mentions in his discussion of *opus sectile* (*De Architectura* 7.1.4), and the measurements of the tiles are generally multiples of a Roman foot. For example, the triangular tiles found in the *apodyterium* (dressing room) have a base and height of three-fourths of a Roman foot (slightly more than eight inches). The Masada floors also use different-colored limestone and slate, the same materials that appear in the earliest Roman *opus sectile* pavements, which date to the second to first centuries BCE. Finally, the floor patterns at Masada are seen in other first-century BCE Roman floors in Italy such as those at Pompeii and the Casa di Livia in Rome. A similarly impressive *opus sectile* floor was uncovered at Jericho in the large reception hall in the north wing of the Third Winter Palace. Additionally, *opus sectile* floors also appear in the *Augusteum* at Panias as well as in the palace-fortresses of Cypros and Machaerus. There also is evidence for at least two *opus sectile* pavements at Herodion, one in the *triclinium* of Upper Herodion and one in the *caldarium* of the pool complex in Lower Herodion.

In contrast to the *opus reticulatum* walls, the *opus sectile* floors in Herod's palaces and fortresses would have been visible to any guest. Thus, it is no surprise that many of these floors appear in several of his Roman-style structures, such as bathhouses. Nor is it surprising that he would also place a Roman floor in the large reception hall, one of his most conspicuous and public rooms at Jericho. Visitors to the palace would be visually reminded of his Romanization each time they entered the room, and, if Netzer is correct that this hall was a main reception room, these reminders would be frequent and public.[52]

The artisans who decorated Herod's palaces and other buildings also utilized Roman styles and techniques in their stone decoration and relief, especially the scroll ornamentation. These decorations are of two types, neo-Attic and neo-Pergamene. The former is characterized by a general lack of vegetal elements and a tendency toward abstraction, while the latter displays a more naturalistic appearance. In Herodian architecture, the neo-Attic style appears in a large mosaic in one of the salons *(oecus)* of the Western Palace at Masada and in sarcophagus panels from Mount Scopus and the Tomb of the Kings. This style also appears in a scroll composed of tendrils and trifoliate crowns that decorated a sarcophagus from the Mount of Olives. The neo-Pergamene style, on the other hand, includes examples

---

52. For a general discussion of *opus sectile,* see Federico Guidobaldi, "Pavimenti in Opus Sectile di Roma e dell'Ara Romana. Proposte per una Classificazione e Criteri di Datazione," in *Marmi Antichi. Problemi d'Impiego, di Restauro e d'Identificazione,* ed. Patrizio Pensabene (Roma: "L'Erma" di Bretschneider, 1985), 226-30. For a discussion of the beginnings of *opus sectile* in Italy during the post-Sullan period see Marian E. Blake, "The Pavements of the Roman Buildings of the Republic and Early Empire," *MemAmAc* 8 (1930): 40-41. For an overview of mosaic decoration in Herodian Judaea see Sarah Japp, "Public and Private Decorative Art in the Time of Herod the Great," in Kokkinos, ed., *The World of the Herods,* 237-38. Masada excavators found fragments of tile as well as tile imprints and thus were able to reconstruct these pavements even though most of them are totally dismantled. For a discussion of the *opus sectile* floors at Masada and their connection with floors found in Roman buildings in Italy see Foerster, *Masada,* 5:158-61; Netzer, *Masada,* 3:78-93, illustrations 132-35, 137, 149, 140, 144, plan 5. For a discussion of the *opus sectile* floor patterns in the Casa del Fauno see Blake, "Pavements of the Roman Buildings," 106 (plates 22.1 and 24.2). For a discussion of the relevant *opus sectile* patterns at Herculaneum see Guidobaldi, "Pavimenti in Opus Sectile," 186 (plates 2.1-2, 23). For the impressive *opus sectile* floor at Jericho see Netzer, *Jericho* 1:238-39. Cf. Netzer, *Palaces,* 65-66, Netzer, *Architecture,* 64. All the tiles at Jericho were looted in antiquity, but the impressions they made in the mortar are still quite visible, except in the southwest, where the floor has completely eroded. In addition, fragments of the tiles that adhered to the bedding have enabled scholars to determine some of the types of stone used in the floor. These include a local black bituminous stone, a local white to pale red limestone, and a marble that was probably imported from Asia Minor or Cyprus. For discussions of the other Herodian *opus sectile* floors see Netzer, *Architecture,* 220-21 (Banias); *Jericho* 2:255-56 (Cypros); Virgilio Corbo, "Macheronta. La Reggia-Fortezza Erodiana," *Liber Annuus* 29 (1979): 322 (Machaerus); Netzer, *Architecture,* 192, n. 51 (Herodion). Cf. Foerster, *Masada,* 5:161.

such as the sarcophagus pen from the so-called Tomb of Herod and the decorated pediment from the Tomb of the Judges.[53]

Herodian borrowing of Roman decorative styles extended to wall painting as well, and these Roman frescoes are some of the most ubiquitous of Herodian ornamentation. For example, one of the rooms of the large bathhouse at Masada and all three of the terraces of the Northern Palace were decorated with frescoes painted in the Late Pompeian Second Style, which utilized architectural features and *trompe l'oeil* (trick of the eye) compositions. Besides Masada, Second Style wall paintings also appear at Caesarea, Samaria, Jerusalem, Jericho, Cypros, and Herodion. At Upper Herodion, for instance, archaeologists found several walls in the bathhouse complex decorated in Second Style.

Most of these Italic style wall decorations appear in buildings constructed during the later part of Herod's reign. This chronology is not at all surprising, since we know that Herod imported several Italian artisans and engineers to design and construct Caesarea Maritima as well as his other later palaces, such as the Third Winter Palace at Jericho. Nevertheless,

---

53. Originally, scholars, such as Carl Watzinger, proposed that the local Herodian scroll ornamentations were Alexandrian in origin. He believed that the combination of stylized and naturalistic plant motifs was characteristic of the artwork of the Ptolemaic capital. See Watzinger, *Denkmäler Palästinas. Eine Einfürung in die Archäologie des Heiligen Landes* (Leipzig: Hinrichs, 1933-35), 2:60. Also see Marion Malthea-Förtsch, "Scroll Ornamentations from Judaea and Their Different Patterns," in Fittschen and Foerster, *Judaea and the Graeco-Roman World in the Time of Herod*, 177-97, esp. 179, 185. Malthea-Förtsch emphasizes that both of the scroll ornamentation styles are relatively contemporary and can be traced back to the late Republican and early Augustan periods. She also concluded that the Herodian scroll styles were imported from Rome, even if they ultimately derived from Asia Minor. Cf. Japp, "Public and Private Decorative Art," 227-34. See Jacobson, "Placing Herod the Great and His Works," 86, where he notes that the Augustan age was especially marked by a drawing of Hellenic culture into Italy from Greece and Asia Minor and then a diffusion of this hybrid across the entire Mediterranean.

For the neo-Attic scroll ornamentation in the Western Palace at Masada see Netzer, *Masada* 3:249-50, illustrations 393-95; Foerster, *Masada* 5:140-43, 148-49 (plates 13a and b). Also see Netzer, *Palaces*, 84 (figure 105); Rina Talgam and Orit Peleg, "Mosaic Pavements in Herod's Day," in Netzer, *Architecture*, 381. For a discussion of the sarcophagus panels from Mount Scopus and the Tomb of the Kings see Malthea-Förtsch, "Scroll Ornamentations," 188-89 (figures 2, 4, and 6), 193 (figure 16). For the discussion of the neo-Attic scroll ornamentation on a sarcophagus from the Mount of Olives see "Scroll Ornamentations," 190-91 (figures 9 and 10). For a discussion of the neo-Pergamene scroll ornamentation on the "Tomb of Herod," see "Scroll Ornamentations," figure 17. In reality, this tomb is probably not Herod's, nor that of his family. For the "Tomb of the Judges," see Nahman Avigad, "Jerusalem: Description of the Tombs," in *NEAEHL*, 750-53.

his decision to decorate his palaces using the latest Roman wall painting designs and techniques speaks both to his Romanization and his desire to advertise this acculturation to his visitors and guests.[54]

Conclusion: Herod, Client King and Cultural Transmitter

What picture has emerged from the discussion in the last few chapters? An already successful and resourceful king, having realized that the political tides had changed dramatically, sought to ingratiate himself with the new power in the Mediterranean and then energetically devoted himself to proving that his survival was not a mistake but an excellent decision. With the defeat of Antony and Cleopatra at Actium, Herod had to change patrons and self-presentation for a third time. He accomplished this metamorphosis by relying on Rome and its leaders' expectations of client kingship. Specifically, he drew on the notions of how the good client king was to behave and fulfilled those obligations admirably.

Given its strategic significance and somewhat restive population, Augustus required a strong and loyal ally in Judaea, so Herod took pains to emphasize his ability to provide such services. He provided the *princeps* with supplies, troops, and financial aid. He suppressed banditry. He consulted his patron before making important decisions, and he reasserted his loyalty time and again through architecture, coinage, and cultural assimilation. These actions enabled Augustus to exercise control over Judaean pol-

---

54. For discussions of the wall paintings at Masada see Netzer, *Masada,* 3:158-62, 166, illustration 257; Foerster, *Masada,* 5:13-18, figures 32-36. Cf. Silvia Rozenberg, "Wall Paintings of the Herodian Period in the Land of Israel," in Netzer, *Architecture,* 356-57; Japp, "Public and Private Decorative Art," 238-42. Other Second Style fragments were also found in the upper terrace. These were decorated with painted designs such as floral motifs, parts of garlands, and fluted columns. See Netzer, *Masada,* 3:137-47; Foerster, *Masada,* 5:28-33 (plates 6b-c, 7-9, 15b). For a comparison of Herodian wall paintings to those in Greece and Italy see Klaus Fittschen, "Wall Decorations in Herod's Kingdom: Their Relationship with Wall Decorations in Greece and Italy," in Fittschen and Foerster, *Judaea and the Graeco-Roman World in the Time of Herod,* 139-62. Fittschen concludes that Herod borrowed heavily from outside Judaea and that his wall paintings are thoroughly Graeco-Roman in style. For an analysis of the wall paintings at Jericho see Silvia Rozenberg, "The Wall Paintings of the Herodian Palace at Jericho," in *Judaea and the Graeco-Roman World in the Time of Herod,* 121-38. Also see Marshak, "Herod the Great and the Power of Image: Political Self-Presentation in the Herodian Dynasty" (Ph.D. diss., Yale University, 2008), 221-22, for a detailed discussion and analysis of Herodian frescoes and their Graeco-Roman influences and antecedents.

itics without formally involving himself in such affairs. They also enabled Herod to bind himself to Rome ever more tightly. As the principate was stabilizing, Herod was finding his own place and niche in the new political landscape. All his actions were well advertised and designed to depict him as the most suitable client king both in Judaea and throughout the entire eastern Mediterranean.

Until his death in 12 BCE, Marcus Agrippa played the role of chief intermediary between Rome and Judaea and between their heads of state. While we cannot be entirely sure of the depth of the personal relationship between *princeps* and king, it seems that there was a real bond of friendship and mutual respect between Herod and Agrippa, a bond that enabled Herod to achieve his political goals while simultaneously honoring a genuine friend and fellow builder.

And yet, even if there was not a sincere friendship between Herod and Augustus, there at least was a profound appreciation of the other's utility. Indeed, throughout Herod's reign, and even despite some temporary setbacks in their relationship, Augustus maintained an alliance and friendship with him precisely because he was the most suitable candidate for the job. From the perspective of the *princeps,* his client king had fulfilled his obligations to Rome. Consequently, Augustus used Roman military and political power to support Herod and his claim to the Judaean throne. Without such support, it would have been much more difficult, if not impossible, for Herod to remain on the throne, die a natural death, and pass on his kingdom as he saw fit. Roman support, therefore, was essential to his success, and such support would not have been forthcoming if he had not realized what was expected of him and acted accordingly.

Besides political survival, Herod had plenty to gain from his loyalty and service to Rome. In particular, he gained privileged access to Roman technology, especially Roman building technology, by which he could construct elaborate and lavish buildings, further enhancing his own reputation and glory. Rome was thus as useful to Herod as he was to it, and such mutual benefit explains why the client king relationship worked so well.

In the next sections, we will examine how Herod behaved within the milieu of Hellenistic kingship and how he drew on the cultural expectations of his Hellenized, non-Jewish, courtly elites and neighboring dynasts to solicit their support for and approval of his regime. Support from these individuals was also crucial to his success. As king, he needed a royal court populated with loyal supporters who could perform the necessary functions of government and help solidify his internal power base and control over his own kingdom. He also needed to cultivate and maintain friendly relations with his non-Jewish neighbors. Augustus wanted a well-organized, stable, and friendly coalition of allied kingdoms, and any failure to create such harmony could and did result in one's deposition. As we will see, Herod took to the role of glorious Hellenistic monarch with great aplomb, skill, and, ultimately, success.

CHAPTER 9

Herod the Hellenistic King in an Augustan World

By the time Herod became king, Judaea had been immersed in the Hellenistic world for hundreds of years. More immediately, by the time of Aristobulus I (104-103 BCE), Herod's predecessors, the Hasmoneans, had become strong promoters of Hellenism and had adopted much of Hellenistic political ideology for their own monarchy. Nevertheless, although the Hasmoneans had fully engaged in the larger Hellenistic world, Herod increased this participation, elevating Judaea from a minor Hellenistic kingdom to a major one. In the process, he enthusiastically embraced the wider Greek East, energetically playing the role of patron and benefactor to numerous Greek cities around the Mediterranean. He also imported leading intellectuals, such as Nicolaus of Damascus, which infused the court in Jerusalem with a vibrant and Hellenized character. Finally, he actively advertised his piety, a quality, which, as we have seen, was valued highly by those inculcated in Hellenistic royal virtues. All these actions were attempts to appeal to the cultural expectations of both the Hellenized members of his court and his neighboring dynasts. These local rulers, being Hellenized themselves, would have responded favorably to such behavior and granted Herod status and friendship in the same way they would any other Hellenistic monarch. By appealing to its cultural expectations, Herod emphasized his membership in the larger monarchical community of the Hellenized East and also created a niche for himself and his kingdom within the new Greek East of the Augustan principate.

Unfortunately, no verifiable portraits of our elusive king survive. This absence is due, in part, to the luck of survival, but it is also the result of Herod's general avoidance of figural images, at least inside his own kingdom.[1] Con-

---

1. There have been several attempts to connect ancient portraits with our elusive

sequently, we have no real idea of what Herod actually looked like. Moreover, as we have suggested, Josephus's narrative, while certainly providing descriptions of Herod's physical appearance and character, is still a highly stylized presentation from an author immersed in Graeco-Roman culture and political philosophy. As such, we should focus less on Herod's physical appearance and personal character and more on those things we can more clearly observe, specifically his actions. While such an emphasis will, unfortunately, leave our picture somewhat incomplete, it will help us avoid being trapped in Josephus's rhetorical circle, where the same elite author who describes our main character's virtues is, himself, influenced by those virtues.

Herod and *Euergetism*

Of all of the Hellenistic royal virtues, the best attested for Herod is *euergetism*. It is, therefore, appropriate that we began our discussion of Herod's Hellenistic royal persona by discussing his patronage and benefaction. Philosophically, such activity was expected of every monarch as a way of displaying his wealth and virtue. Moreover, from a practical point of view,

---

king. Two statue heads, one from Jerusalem and one from Memphis in Egypt, have been identified by some scholars as depicting Herod. Furthermore, a head from Byblos, one from Ostia, and another from Naples have also been suggested as images of the king. Unfortunately, there is no way of verifying these theories, and as such they must remain only as possibilities. For a discussion of the head from Memphis and its identification as Herod see Duane W. Roller, *The Building Program of Herod the Great* (Berkeley: University of California Press, 1998), 273-75; Nikos Kokkinos, *The Herodian Dynasty: Origins, Roles in Society and Eclipse* (rev. ed.; London: Spink, 2010), 137-38; Samuel Rocca, *Herod's Judaea: A Mediterranean State in the Classical World* (Tübingen: Mohr, 2008), 127-29. Kokkinos also believes that Herod's portrait appears on coins, specifically on the obverse of Ascalonite coins dated to the years 63, 64, and 74, which correspond to 41, 40, and 30 BCE. While it is possible that these images are indeed of Herod, it seems unlikely. In 41 BCE, he was *stratēgos* of Galilee, but his brother Phasael was the more powerful and influential Antipatrid. In 40 BCE, he had been named king by Rome, but he had not yet even returned to Judaea. In 30 BCE, Augustus had either not yet confirmed Herod's reign or had just done so. Either way, Herod's control over Judaea was not entirely secure, and thus he would have made a poor subject for a coin from an autonomous city. For his interpretation of the coins see Kokkinos, *Herodian Dynasty*, 133-36. For persuasive refutations of this hypothesis see Alla Kushnir-Stein, "Review: Nikos Kokkinos, *The Herodian Dynasty: Origins, Role in Society and Eclipse*," *Scripta Classica Israelica* 18 (1999): 194-98, esp. 198; Rocca, *Herod's Judaea*, 127; Donald T. Ariel, "A Numismatic Approach to the Reign of Herod the Great" (Ph.D. diss., Tel-Aviv University, 2006), 245-46; Donald T. Ariel and Jean-Philippe Fontanille, *The Coins of Herod: A Modern Analysis and Die Classification* (Leiden: Brill, 2012), 93.

euergetism offered the Hellenistic monarch an opportunity to create and maintain friendly and patronal relationships between himself and those he patronized. Herod took up this challenge quite enthusiastically, and, by the end of his reign, he was one of the most prolific and active patrons in the eastern Mediterranean. These benefactions can be divided into four major categories: (1) buildings and urban structures, (2) endowments, (3) tax assistance and monetary gifts, and (4) personal intercession.

Instances of Euergetism

By all accounts, Herod's Judaea was extremely wealthy; he, personally, as the largest landowner in the realm, was also extraordinarily rich. This vast wealth enabled him to advance his political agenda through timely and benevolent donations to both cities and kingdoms. From both literary and epigraphic sources, we know that Herod was involved in a variety of *euergetism*. Specifically, we have evidence of his involvement in funding specific building projects and financing entire urban enterprises. We also know he endowed several athletic competitions and civic gymnasiums. We have records of him providing tax relief for grateful cities. Finally, we have evidence that he used his personal connections to act as a powerful intercessor, especially for Jewish populations in the Diaspora. Thus, Herod could say with great accuracy that he was an active patron doling out benefaction in exchange for loyalty and public honor.

What are some of the examples of Herod's patronal activities? According to lists that appear in Josephus's narratives, Herod donated a variety of buildings to cities all around the Levant. In particular, he gave gymnasia to the cities of Tripolis, Damascus, and Ptolemais. He also commissioned exedras, porticoes (*stoa* in Greek), temples, and marketplaces for Berytus and Tyre. Similarly, he endowed Sidon and Damascus with theaters, and Laodicea received an aqueduct. At Byblos, he constructed the city wall. Closer to his kingdom, he provided Ascalon with baths, fountains, colonnades, and possibly a palace. In Antioch, he paved the broad street that ran north to south through the city and donated the money for the colonnades that ran along it. This street, which Antiochenes had once shunned because of the prevalent mud, was now paved with marble. It may also have been the prototype for what would become a fixture in Roman urban architecture, especially in the eastern Mediterranean. By the second century CE, most eastern Roman cities in that region contained colonnaded streets as a main architectural feature.

Herod the Hellenistic King in an Augustan World

Herod was also active in the Greek islands. For instance, while on his way to see Marcus Agrippa in Asia Minor, he stopped over in Chios and gave the city enough money to rebuild its main *stoa,* which had been destroyed during the Mithridatic war seventy years prior. Rhodes received sufficient funds from him to rebuild its temple of Pythian Apollo on an even grander scale than before. He also contributed significant money to rebuilding the Rhodian shipyards. An inscription that archaeologists discovered on the island Syros but which might be Delian in origin raises the possibility of a Herodian donation to the nearby island of Delos. There is no record of Herod ever visiting Delos, but the island had had a large Jewish community since the second century BCE and was a major trading port and cultic center. It is unlikely that he would have passed up a chance to become a patron of such a center of Hellenic life and activity.

Perhaps the most politically astute building program Herod undertook was at Nikopolis, where he provided funds for many of the public buildings. Which buildings might he have constructed? Rocca suggests that Herod would have focused on the *temenos* of Apollo, the gymnasium, and perhaps the stadium, all of which were associated with the Actian Games supervised by Herod's friend Eurycles of Sparta. Why did Herod, and not Augustus or Agrippa, fund most of the building? Neither of the two Romans could have been the main benefactor of the city and its athletic games because such benefactions, specifically support of athletic competitions in a Greek city, would have connected them with the philhellenism of their defeated enemy Marc Antony. Herod, on the other hand, was an ideal patron, who would not suffer any serious political repercussions from his actions. Indeed, he had much to gain. Besides being the primary patron at the city constructed to commemorate Augustus's victory at Actium, the battle in which Herod had sided with the loser Antony, such patronage would also cement his status as the preeminent Hellenized client king in the new Augustan world. By providing the new city with public buildings, Herod both satisfied his obligations to his patron and created new clients for himself.[2]

---

2. For Herod's wealth see Rocca, *Herod's Judaea,* 209, 213-16, where he discusses the king's wealth and his real estate portfolio. Rocca concludes that most of the land in the kingdom was royal land worked by peasants and sometimes given to royal friends as either permanent or temporary gifts. Unlike most of the Hellenistic and Roman world, though, cities did not own their hinterlands: Herod did. For Herod's *euergetism* in the Greek islands, see *BJ* 1.422-25; *AJ* 16.146-49. For the donations to Chios, see *AJ* 16.16-19. Josephus emphasizes the great size and beauty of the Hellenistic portico on Chios as well as Herod's insistence that the money he donated be used immediately. For the donations to Rhodes, see *BJ* 1.424; *AJ*

Herod also made several financial endowments to cities throughout the Greek East. At Kos he endowed in perpetuity the annual office of gymnasiarch, one of whose primary duties was to pay for the oil and other necessaries of the gymnasium. According to Josephus, Herod supplied the necessary grain to all those who requested his assistance. Epigraphic evidence also testifies to his patronage of the island, and it is tempting to connect the

---

16.147. As a young man, Herod had visited Rhodes on his way to Rome to secure the support of the Senate in his civil war with Antigonus. Josephus recounts that while there, and despite his relative poverty, Herod donated funds for the rebuilding of the city, which had been damaged during the war against Brutus, Cassius, and their allies. Later, when Herod was securely on the throne, he gave money to the city to rebuild its shipyards and construct new ships. The city may not yet have fully recovered, and it would have needed the funds, especially considering the centrality of sea trade to its economy. For Herod's visit to Rhodes on his way to Rome in 40 BCE, see *BJ* 1.280; *AJ* 14.377-78. Unfortunately, Josephus is rather vague about which buildings Herod helped rebuild during his initial visit. For Ersie Mantzoulinou-Richards's analysis of the Delian marble slab found on Syros and her reading of the inscription see "From Syros: A Dedicatory Inscription of Herodes the Great from an Unknown Building," *Ancient World* 18.3-4 (1988): 87-99. Cf. Peter Richardson, *Herod: King of the Jews and Friend of the Romans* (Columbia: University of South Carolina Press, 1996), 205-6; Roller, *Building Program,* 225. Mantzoulinou-Richards speculates that the marble slab on which the inscription appears, originally came from a building on Delos but was transported to Syros later when Delos had become a "self-service" quarry for anyone interested in acquiring well-cut stones for building needs. For literary evidence of a Jewish community on Delos dating back to at least the mid-second century BCE, see 1 Macc 15:15-24. Cf. *AJ* 14.231-32 for a Delian edict upholding Jewish rights on the island. Archaeological evidence also attests to a thriving and old Jewish community on Delos. Indeed, one of the earliest known ancient synagogues was built on Delos. See Monika Trümper, "The Oldest Original Synagogue Building in the Diaspora: The Delos Synagogue Reconsidered," *Hesperia* 73 (2004): 513-98. For Herod's patronage at Nikopolis, see *BJ* 1.425; *AJ* 16.147. Even if Josephus's assertion that Herod funded most of the buildings at Nikopolis is a slight exaggeration, we can imagine that he would not have passed up an opportunity to be intimately involved in Augustus's victory city. Cf. Ehud Netzer, "Herod the Great's Contribution to Nikopolis in Light of His Building Activity in Judea," in *Proceedings of the First International Symposium of Nicopolis (23-29 September, 1984)* ed. Evangelos Chrysos (Preveza: Demos Prevezas, 1987), 121-28, esp. 127. For a description of the buildings at Nikopolis, see Strabo, *Geog.* 10.2.2. Also see Rocca, *Herod's Judaea,* 46-47, for his speculations about which particular buildings were Herodian donations and why Herod was the main donor and not Augustus or Agrippa. Two fragmentary inscriptions, one from Paphos and one from Selaema in the Hauran (ancient Auranitis), may also testify to Herodian *euergetism*. Unfortunately, in both cases, only the name *Herōdēs* remains, and thus it is not clear whether it refers to our Herod, one of his descendants, or another individual also named Herod. While the inscriptions' locations fit within the known purview of King Herod's *euergetism*, without additional information we cannot include these sites as definite instances of his royal benefaction. For the two inscriptions, see *CIG* 2.2628 (Paphos); Frederic D. Allen, "Greek and Latin Inscriptions from Palestine," *AJP* 6 (1885): 213, number 57 (Selaema).

literary and epigraphic evidence, although it is possible that each is talking about a separate benefaction. An inscription carved onto a cylindrical statue base of bluish marble states, "The *Damos* (people) honored King Gaius Julius Herod for his virtue and goodwill toward it." Although we do not have a explicit date, we can perhaps connect this inscription with Herod's 14 BCE visit to Agrippa, who was staying on Lesbos. While traveling to that island, Herod stopped at Chios and took the opportunity to restore a *stoa* there. On his way from Judaea to Chios, he would have passed by Kos, and it is possible that this benefaction was his perpetual endowment of the gymnasiarchy mentioned in Josephus. Even if it is not, it does testify to a royal patronage of a prominent community (Kos) in the eastern Mediterranean.[3]

And yet, the Kos endowment was a mere sideshow to Herod's grand gesture at Olympia. By the beginning of the Augustan period, the Olympic Games were a shadow of their former glory. Lack of money and a decline in the general prestige of Greece had led to a significant deterioration in the quality of the city and its games. The Augustan period brought a revival of athletics in Greece, and Herod was a part of this rejuvenation. In 12 (or possibly 8) BCE, he became the lifetime manager *(agōnothetēs)* of the Olympic Games. His duties and responsibilities were mostly financial, but he would also have lent his prestige and reputation to the games. In addition, he may have financed the opening ceremonies, official sacrifices, banquets, and possibly even the erection of statues for the victors. Richardson suggests that Herod may also have provided money to rebuild the temple of Zeus there, which had been damaged in an earthquake in 36 BCE.[4]

---

3. As Josephus states, "Many cities, as if they were a part of his kingdom, received from [Herod] grants of land" (*BJ* 1.423). For discussions of the Koan inscription, see Kerstin Höghammer, *Sculpture and Society: A Study of the Connection between the Free Standing Sculpture and Society of Kos in the Hellenistic and Augustan Periods* (Uppsala: Boreas, 1993), 43, 66, 77, figure 6; David M. Jacobson, "King Herod, Roman Citizen and Benefactor of Kos," *BAIAS* 13 (1993-94): 31-35. This inscription is also notable because its language almost exactly mirrors the texts of two Athenian inscriptions dedicated to Herod, which will be discussed in greater detail below. Höghammer suggests that the inscription was carved to honor Herod for his endowment of the gymnasiarchy. Jacobson, while acknowledging the possibility, also observes the lack of definitive evidence to connect the donation to the base. I agree with Jacobson that we should be cautious. Nevertheless, the inscription does offer concrete proof that Herod was an active patron on the island. See Höghammer, *Sculpture and Society*, 43, 66, 77; Jacobson, "Herod, Roman Citizen and Benefactor," 33. For Herod's journey to Chios, during which he may have visited nearby Kos, see *AJ* 16.18-19.

4. We reach a date of 12 BCE for two reasons. First, it is likely that Herod's grant to Olympia dates to around that year, the same time as his grants to other Greek cities. Those

CLIENT KING IN AN AUGUSTAN WORLD

Herod also gave monetary gifts to several cities, and these gifts took a variety of forms ranging from tax concessions to outright donations. In Syria, Herod eased the tax burden of the city of Balanaea. He offered similar benefaction to Phaselis in Lycia and various unnamed towns in Cilicia. Again, Josephus's lack of specificity when discussing these benefactions makes it difficult to determine precisely what occurred, but Herod could not have lightened the tax burdens of cities such as Balanaea unless he had been given the tax concession for them. He could then have collected less revenue from the city. This monetary loss would have been offset by the creation of strong bonds of patronage with the cities he favored.[5] Herod also actively gave gifts of money to cities all over the Greek East. In addition to rebuilding the damaged *stoa* at Chios, he provided the city with sufficient funds to repay a loan it owed Augustus and to pay the tribute it owed to the imperial treasury. He also donated money to Samos, Pergamum, and Sparta. The regions of Lycia and Ionia also were recipients of his generosity. Finally, and perhaps most symbolically for a king trying to play the part of a Hellenistic monarch, he actively patronized Athens, the

---

benefactions were concurrent with his passage through the Greek islands on his way to visiting Agrippa in 14 BCE. Moreover, Josephus explicitly states that Herod endowed the Olympic games and attended them as president at the same time as he was traveling to Italy to visit Augustus, who was staying in Aquileia at that time. Augustus was in northern Italy at the beginning of an Olympiad only in 12 BCE, when he was overseeing the transition of a province from senatorial to imperial governance. See Richardson, *Herod*, xix; Roller, *Building Program*, 74, 230, for discussions of the chronology. Cf. Ronald Syme, *The Roman Revolution* (rev. ed.; Oxford: Oxford University Press, 2002), 394. As Roller observes, it is not entirely clear what being perpetual *agōnothetēs* meant. He suggests that the position may have lasted only as long as Herod was alive since a certain Marcus Cocceius Timasarchos of Rhodes held the position ca. 200 CE. For Richardson's theory about Herod's involvement in the rebuilding of the temple of Olympian Zeus, see Richardson, *Herod*, 185, 272, n. 45. According to Monika Bernett, Herod's *euergetism* could also function as a public response to and expression of his gratitude for the benefits that Augustus conferred on him. Augustus had made Herod so wealthy and powerful that it was expected that he donate some portion of that wealth to the cities around the eastern Mediterranean. See Bernett, *Der Kaiserkult in Judäa unter den Herodiern und Römern. Untersuchungen zur politischen und religiösen Geschichte Judäas von 30 v. bis 66 n. Chr.* (Tübingen: Mohr, 2007), 117-26, 352-53.

5. For Herod's easement of various cities' tax burdens, see *BJ* 1.428. As discussed above (see p. 125), Balanaea was in the same region as the city of Mariamme, which Herod build in honor of his wife. For Herod's inability to lessen a city's taxes without first receiving its concession for tax collection, see Emilio Gabba, "The Finances of King Herod," in *Greece and Rome in Eretz-Israel*, ed. Aryeh Kasher, Uriel Rappaport, and Gideon Fuks (Jerusalem: Jerusalem Exploration Society, 1990), 160-68.

Herod the Hellenistic King in an Augustan World

city that most clearly symbolized Greek culture and life. Two inscriptions found on the Acropolis testify to his benefactions to that city. They praise Herod for, among other things, his "good deeds and goodwill" *(euergesias kai eunoia)* and his "virtue and benefaction" *(aretē kai euergesia)* respectively. Such praise presumably was because of gifts he presented to the city, although what exactly these gifts were is unknown. Suetonius informs us that during the reign of Augustus many of Rome's client kings cooperated in the completion of the still-unfinished temple of Olympian Zeus, which they dedicated to the *genius Augusti*. Given the high profile of such a project and its ability to advertise loyalty to the principate, it is extremely likely that Herod was involved in it. It is therefore possible that his statues on the Acropolis were related to this project, although if they were honoring his involvement in the temple project, one would expect some mention of the project on the statue bases. Alternatively, the statues may have been honoring Herod for providing funds for the restoration and maintenance of the Acropolis. Regardless of the reason for the statues, their presence testifies to his patronage of the seat of Greek culture and learning, which was ideal for a king trying to depict himself as a typical Hellenistic monarch.[6]

Royal munificence also took forms other than financial support. As a powerful and influential king, Herod also could act as an intercessor between a city and Rome. According to Josephus, he successfully interceded with Agrippa on behalf of several unnamed individuals while traveling with him during his Bosporus campaign. For example, in 14 BCE, while Agrippa was planning his expedition, his wife Julia, the daughter of Augustus, traveled to meet him. While en route, she was caught in a flashflood of the Skamandros River near Ilion and almost drowned. Agrippa

---

6. For Herod's payment of Chios's taxes, see *AJ* 16.26. Which tribute Chios was paying is unclear. Perhaps it had been levied on the city after it had closed its gates to the wrecked fleet of Eumenes II, a Roman ally during the Third Macedonian War (171-168 BCE). See Livy 44.28. For Herod's benefaction to Samos, Pergamum, and Sparta see *BJ* 1.425. Cf. *AJ* 16.23-24. For the Herodian inscriptions on the Athenian Acropolis, see *OGIS* 414, 427. See Suetonius, *Aug.* 60, for the completion of the Athenian temple of Olympian Zeus. See Roller, *Building Program,* 220, where he speculates that Herod might have built the temple of Rome and Augustus on the Acropolis. Also see Rocca, *Herod's Judaea,* 44. While such a project would certainly fit with the king's larger goal of playing both the loyal client king and the benevolent Hellenistic monarch, without additional evidence Roller's claim can only be speculative at best. Herod was not the only Judaean leader to have a statue in Athens. According to Josephus, the city of Athens erected a bronze statue of John Hyrcanus II in the precinct of the *Demos* (the People) and the *Charites* (Graces). See *AJ* 14.149-55. Cf. Roller, *Building Program,* 219; Rocca, *Herod's Judaea,* 44.

was furious with the city and levied a 100,000 drachmae fine for negligence against it. Although the fine was onerous, the city officials were afraid to appeal it before Agrippa. Instead, they petitioned Herod, seeking his help in their plight. According to Nicolaus, the king then spoke with Agrippa regarding the matter, noting the essential unfairness of the fine as well as Ilion's unique historical status as both the site of the Trojan War and the reputed ancestral city of the Julian clan (and indeed Rome). Herod then persuaded Agrippa to cancel the fine, reconciling him with the city, and subsequently permitted Nicolaus to deliver the good news to Ilion in person. In response, Ilion honored Agrippa and praised Herod for his intercession.[7]

Choosing the Cities outside His Kingdom

Why did Herod choose some foreign cities over others? At first glance, there seems to be no particular logic behind his choices for benefaction. It is certainly possible that many of these donations were solicited and offered on an ad hoc basis. However, on closer inspection, a pattern does emerge, delineated by four significant rationales: (1) connections to Herod and his family, (2) proximity to Judaea and prominence in the Greek East, (3) importance to Rome and its leaders, and (4) the presence of a large Jewish population.

Of all of the provinces in the eastern Mediterranean, none had a closer connection to Herod and his family than Syria, and no city in Syria was more important to him than Antioch. Aside from being an important city near Judaea and the capital of the Roman province of Syria, Antioch had played a large role in Herod's career from its beginnings. He was a frequent visitor, especially as a young man. Moreover, it was the site of his defense by Messalla and appointment as tetrarch along with his brother Phasael.

---

7. For Josephus's claim that Herod frequently advocated on behalf of his petitioners to Agrippa see *AJ* 16.24-25. Josephus even states that Herod was the primary cause of many of Agrippa's benefactions while the two were together. Although this claim is surely an exaggeration, it does suggest a prominent role for the Judaean king in Agrippa's *euergetism*. For Nicolaus's version of the intercession, an account in which he plays an extremely prominent role, see *FGrH* 90 fragment 134. Cf. *AJ* 16.26 for Josephus's version, in which Nicolaus does not appear at all. For the inscription from Ilion honoring Agrippa as "kinsman, father of the city, and benefactor" *(syngenēs kai patron tēs poleōs kai euergetēs)* see *SIG* 4:776. Cf. *IGR* 4:203. For Ilion's praise of Herod see *FGrH* 90 fragment 134.

After Actium, Herod visited Antioch again. This time, he was escorting Augustus as the victorious triumvir returned from Egypt to Rome. Several other cities in Syria also had personal connections to him and his family. Damascus, for instance, was where he fled when Hyrcanus put him on trial for the execution of the Galilean bandits. Herod's war against the bandits of Trachonitis, who had been harassing Damascene territory, pleased the city and likely strengthened relations between it and him. Such friendship made good political sense, especially given the proximity of Damascus to Herod's northeastern border. Finally, and perhaps most importantly, Damascus was the hometown of Nicolaus, his secretary and closest advisor. It is, therefore, not surprising that he should have offered his patronage to the city.

Along the Levantine coast, several cities had close connections with Herod and his family and thus were fitting beneficiaries of his royal magnanimity. Not only was Ptolemais an important port city on Herod's northwestern border, but it also had a close connection with Herod himself. It had been an important ally for him during his civil war with Antigonus, and he landed there in 39 BCE to begin his conquest of Judaea. He also used it as a staging ground for his attack on Galilee in 38 BCE. After Actium, he met Octavian there, accompanied him as he reviewed his troops, provided provisions for his army, and entertained him and his friends at a banquet in the city. Another Levantine city associated with Herod was Laodicea-on-the-Sea. Although we know of only one visit — in 35/34 BCE Antony summoned him there to answer accusations made against him by Cleopatra and the supporters of the murdered Aristobulus III — it was an important one because he was able to clear himself of these charges and return home with his rule confirmed. Far more important than this visit perhaps was his connection with the city through his friend Alexas, who was a native of Laodicea and an influential advisor to Antony. According to Plutarch, Alexas was also a close friend and advisor to Cleopatra and had persuaded Antony not to reconcile with his then wife Octavia, the sister of Octavian. Following Actium and the sudden defection of several formerly loyal clients and allies, Antony sent Alexas to Judaea to persuade Herod to remain loyal. This mission failed, however, and both men ultimately changed allegiances. This abandonment of Antony failed to save Alexas, however. Notwithstanding Herod's pleas for mercy, Octavian refused to spare him, perhaps because of his central role in Antony's abandonment of Octavia. Despite Alexas's eventual disgrace and execution, Herod's relationship with his Laodicean friend may have been deeper than mere political expediency. Perhaps this bond played some role in the decision to build an aqueduct for Laodicea.[8]

More than almost any other Levantine city, Tyre enjoyed extremely good relations with Herod and his family, and it leveraged these close ties extremely well. Even before his reign as king, Herod visited the city frequently. For instance, he eliminated his father's assassin and rival Malichos on the beach there. In 41 BCE, Herod, now a tetrarch, expelled the Tyrian tyrant Marion from Galilee, but chose to repatriate all the prisoners his army had captured, an act of goodwill that earned him the city's favor. Later that year, an embassy approached Antony while he was in Tyre and complained of Herod's misrule, but it was unsuccessful in dislodging him from power. During the civil war, Tyre seems to have supported him. Specifically, a group of Tyrians was willing to act as surety for the loan Herod attempted to secure in order to ransom his brother from the Parthians. Finally, unlike other Levantine cities such as Ptolemais and Sidon, Tyre refused entry to the Parthian prince Pacorus when he marched through the Levant in 40 BCE. Thus, friendship with Herod might have been part of a larger loyalty to Rome. This friendship seems to have been rewarded when he presented Tyre with a series of new public buildings.[9]

8. For Herod's landing at Ptolemais in 39 BCE see *BJ* 1.290; *AJ* 14.394. For its status as a staging ground for his invasion of Galilee see *AJ* 14.452. For Octavian's arrival there and Herod's reception for him see *BJ* 1.394-95; *AJ* 15.198-200. For Herod's visit to Laodicea see *AJ* 15.64-67, 75-76. Plutarch states that the philosopher Timagenes introduced Herod and Alexas of Laodicea, but the precise chronology of their relationship is unclear. More than likely they first met when Antony arrived in the East in 41 BCE, although it is possible that they encountered one another the next year when Herod was in Rome seeking recognition for his claim to the Judaean throne. Even if the two men had met in 40 BCE, it is unlikely, given the haste with which Herod left the capital, that they had much time to develop their relationship. See Plutarch, *Ant.* 72.2. For Antony's arrival in the East see pp. 93-97 above. For Alexas's role in Antony's rejection of Octavia see Plutarch, *Ant.* 72.2 and cf. 66.5, where Alexas is one of two friends to accompany Antony as he flees Actium. For the downfall of Alexas and his execution see *Ant.* 72.2-3; *BJ* 1.393-94; *AJ* 14.197. As discussed above, Octavian was willing to keep most of Antony's client kings in power to minimize disturbances and disorder. Lacking any official office, Alexas had no real bargaining chip to play. Anger and hatred also may have played roles in Octavian's refusal to spare him. In particular, it is possible that his role in persuading Antony not to reconcile with Octavia was the source of this hostility. Such a possibility is only speculative, but it would help explain why he was singled out for execution while other loyal Antonians were not.

9. For Herod's use of Tyrian citizens as guarantors of his loan see *BJ* 1.275. The account in *AJ*, on the other hand, mentions that Herod offered Phasael's seven-year-old son as security (14.371). It is possible that both are true, as Herod was certainly in desper-

Further to the south was the Idumaean coastal city of Ascalon. Although Kokkinos argues vehemently for an Ascalonite origin for the Antipatrids, there is little conclusive evidence for such a theory. Nevertheless, the city was an important Idumaean town and had played a prominent role in Judaean politics over the previous hundred years. Further, it had frequent interaction with members of the Antipatrid family. As *stratēgos* of Idumaea, Herod's grandfather Antipas had befriended the Ascalonites as well as the Arabs and Gazans by giving them many gifts. Later, Herod's father Antipater raised an army to support Julius Caesar's forces in Egypt, and he staged his attack from Ascalon. Additionally, after the murder of Aristobulus II and the execution of his son Alexander, Aristobulus's widow and her remaining children were sent into exile. The children were placed under the care of Ptolemy, son of Mennaeus and tetrarch of Chalcis, while the widow went to Ascalon. Apparently, Antipater believed his relations with the city were strong enough that he could leave her there without worry. Such a strong relationship, as well as the city's importance as a Levantine port, means that Herod's desire to continue good relations with the city through benefaction and public building is unsurprising and made good political sense.[10]

---

ate straits. Unfortunately for him, his brother was already dead, and the Nabataean king refused to loan him the money. For Tyre's refusal to admit the Parthians into its city in 40 BCE see *BJ* 1.249; *AJ* 14.333. For Herod's benefaction to Tyre see *BJ* 1.422. Relations between Herod and Tyre were so strong that scholars such as Meyshan have argued that Herod's dated coins were struck at the mint of Tyre. See p. 158 above for a refutation of this theory. Cf. Adam Kolman Marshak, "The Dated Coins of Herod the Great: Towards a New Chronology," *JSJ* 37 (2006): 217, 221.

10. For the interaction of Herod's grandfather Antipas with the city of Ascalon while he was a Hasmonean official see *AJ* 14.10. For Antipater's staging of an invasion of Egypt from Ascalon see *BJ* 1.187-89; *AJ* 14.127-30. Cf. *AJ* 16.52. For the exile of Aristobulus II's widow to that city see *BJ* 1.185-86; *AJ* 14.123-26. For Antipater's role in the exile of the family of Aristobulus see *BJ* 1.196; *AJ* 14.140-42. Cf. Kokkinos, *Herodian Dynasty*, 114. Among other evidence, Kokkinos has used the coin portraits described in n. 1 above to argue for an Ascalonite origin for the Antipatrids. See Kokkinos, *Herodian Dynasty*, 100-139. This hypothesis is certainly possible, and there is some evidence to support it. Nevertheless, several factors indicate that the family was not from Ascalon. When Josephus first introduces Herod's father Antipater in *AJ*, he notes that Antipater's father Antipas served the Hasmoneans well and maintained good relations with Nabataea, Gaza, and Ascalon (14.10). This narration, however, offers no sense that Antipas was from any of these three cities. If Antipas had been a native of one of them, Josephus likely would have noted the connection. Additionally, Kokkinos puts great stock in the friendly and frequent interactions between the Antipatrids and Ascalon to support his claim of an Ascalonite origin for the Antipatrids. However, simply because

Herod also drew on connections with the Greek city of Sparta, which held a special place in Judaea's esteem because of its long-standing historical relationship with the kingdom and its likely fictional ties of kinship. The friendship between the Spartans and Judaea allegedly dated back to the late fourth century BCE, when the Spartan king Areus supposedly wrote to the high priest Onias I, the son of Yaddua, desiring formal relations with Judaea and claiming to have discovered a common ancestor between the Spartans and the Jews, namely Abraham. Even though this letter of Areus is probably fictional, a tradition of kinship seems to have developed by the Hellenistic period, and there was an attempt by Jonathan Maccabee to initiate relations with Sparta by drawing on this connection. Additionally, it was well known that Romans had long admired Sparta and its martial discipline. It is thus no surprise that Herod chose to support this city. He may have been encouraged in this endeavor by his friend Gaius Julius Eurycles, one of the most colorful personalities of early Augustan Greece. A partisan of Octavian, he commanded the Spartan forces at Actium and was rewarded for his services with Roman citizenship and rule over Sparta. While we do not know when he first met Herod, we

---

a great deal of political interaction and friendship existed between the city and this family does not mean that they originated from the city. Moreover, if they did, why did it never become part of the Herodian kingdom? Surely the city would have wanted to be annexed by a king who was one of their own. Another problem with Kokkinos's hypothesis is that it relies on a tradition derived from three Christian authors: the second-century CE theologian Justin Martyr, the third-century CE historian Sextus Julius Africanus, and the fourth-century century CE polemicist Epiphanius of Salamis. Justin merely mentions an Ascalonite origin for Herod while Africanus and Epiphanius narrate a story in which Herod's father was a temple slave *(hierodoulos),* a story that has the tone of gossip and slander. This tradition's chronological distance from the Herodian period, as well as the malicious tone of Africanus's and Epiphanius's narratives, argue against their historical reliability. Even Justin's account has a whiff of gossip, and its inclusion as part of a larger theological dialogue makes it suspect as historical fact. If the tradition were more than just Jewish gossip circulating after Herod's death, why does it not feature in Josephus's discussion, especially when he actively attempts to refute Nicolaus's account of the Antipatrids' origins. For critiques of Kokkinos's hypothesis on the origin of the Antipatrids, see Peter Richardson, "Review: Nikos Kokkinos, *The Herodian Dynasty: Origins, Role in Society and Eclipse,*" *JJS* 50 (1999): 156-58; Joseph Sievers, "Review: Nikos Kokkinos, *The Herodian Dynasty: Origins, Role in Society and Eclipse,*" *JSJ* 32 (2001): 101-5, esp. 102-3; David J. Bryan, "The Herodians: A Case of Disputed Identity; A Review Article of Nikos Kokkinos, 'The Herodian Dynasty,'" *Tyndale Bulletin* 53 (2002): 223-38, esp. 227, 233-35. We would do better to look for the origins of the Antipatrids at Marisa, a possibility that Kokkinos also entertains, at least for Herod himself. See Kokkinos, *Herodian Dynasty,* 96.

do know that in approximately 10 BCE he traveled to Judaea, where, for somewhat obscure reasons, he stirred up trouble at the Herodian court and conspired with Herod's eldest son Antipater. Ultimately, because of his schemes and conspiracies, Augustus sent him into exile. Before all this trouble, however, Eurycles seems to have had a good relationship with Herod, and this friendship, coupled with the supposed kinship of the Jews and the Lacedaemonians, may have persuaded the king to donate to Eurycles' home-city.[11]

Herod also seems to have been concerned with the proximity and prominence of potential recipients of his royal benevolence. Unsurprisingly, the region that benefited most was the Levant, especially the coastal cities. Outside this region, his main centers of activity were the Aegean islands and the Cyclades. Mainland Greece was the third region that received significant benefaction. Interestingly, many recipients of his munificence, especially within the Levant but also outside it, were prominent cities in the Greek East. Why did proximity and prominence matter? Good relations with neighbors were essential for a successful client king, and Herod would have realized quickly that high status within this region would strengthen his position and make him a more desirable ally for Rome. Furthermore, the Greek East was the cradle of Hellenistic civilization, and he, who wanted to depict himself as a true and legitimate Hellenistic monarch, would have been best served by focusing on the Greek East and in particular on cities such as Athens, Antioch, Rhodes, and Delos. As the birthplace of Homer, Chios was another ideal location for Herod to make his mark. Creating bonds of clientage and friendship between himself and the most prominent Greek cities would have elevated him from a minor king to a major player within the Hellenistic-Roman world. More people would see his buildings, and his reputation would benefit.

An additional benefit for Herod and his kingdom would be increased trade and economic prosperity for both. This increased trade would have

---

11. For the embassy of Jonathan Maccabee to the city of Sparta and the probably fictional letter of King Areus to the high priest Onias see 1 Macc. 12:1-23. For the renewal of friendship between Sparta and Judaea during the reign of Simon Maccabee see 1 Macc 14:16-23. Cf. *AJ* 12.225-27; 13.165-70. For a good introduction to Eurycles of Sparta see G. W. Bowersock, "Eurycles of Sparta," *JRS* 51 (1961): 112-18. Cf. Bowersock, "Augustus and the East: The Problem of Succession," in *Caesar Augustus: Seven Aspects*, ed. Fergus Millar and Erich Segal (Oxford: Clarendon, 1984), 169-88. For Eurycles' command of the Spartan forces at Actium see Plutarch, *Ant.* 67. For his scheming at Herod's court see *BJ* 1.513-32; *AJ* 16.300-310.

been a natural byproduct of his patronage, and thus we see that many of the cities he chose to patronize, including Antioch, Delos, Rhodes, and Tyre, were important commercial ports and hubs. Furthermore, as commercial relations between Judaea and the rest of the Mediterranean increased, the number of caravans and merchants passing through the kingdom would also have risen. Thus, Herod stood to gain in the realm of tax and duty collection. Status was important, but so too were money and commerce.[12]

Since any royal benevolence would have elevated his status, it is notable that there is no evidence of any Herodian benefactions west of Greece. Rome, the capital of his greatest allies, does not contain irrefutable evidence of his benefaction, and it is extremely doubtful that he was active there. Egypt is also noticeably absent from the list of recipients, despite its proximity to Judaea and the importance of Alexandria in the Graeco-Roman world. Why did Herod thus limit himself? We cannot know for sure, but political considerations probably were foremost in his mind. In the first place, he would have derived little benefit from patronizing faraway cities in the West, such as those in Spain or North Africa. As for omitting Alexandria, in his early years prior to Actium, benefaction in the capital of Cleopatra's kingdom would only have drawn attention to himself and ire from her. Once she was dead, Egypt remained inaccessible because of its strategic importance as the grain basket of the empire and the jealousy with which Augustus controlled it. The disgrace and suicide of Cornelius Gallus, the prefect of Egypt who foolishly sought to exalt himself and his accomplishments, was lesson enough to politically astute men such as Herod. Similar considerations may have persuaded him to forgo activity in Rome and Italy: he may have seen them as being the exclusive domain of the *princeps* and his family.[13]

Another factor in Herod's decision to patronize certain cities over

---

12. For a detailed list of the recipients of Herod's benefaction see Richardson, *Herod*, 201-2. Cf. Rocca, *Herod's Judaea*, 42-45. For evidence of Herod's trading relationship with the rest of the Mediterranean see pp. 145-46 above. It is somewhat surprising that, as far as we know, Ephesus did not receive any attention from the king. As one of the major cities of the Greek East and indeed the Greco-Roman world, Ephesus would have been an ideal place for him to assert himself as a patron and benefactor. Perhaps his lack of personal contact with the city prevented him from establishing a patronal relationship with the city.

13. Even Roller, whose monograph finds Herodian/Roman connections everywhere, does not argue for Herodian benefaction in Rome outside of the 300 talents Herod presented to Augustus in 12 BCE after Augustus reconciled him with his sons Alexander and Aristobulus (*AJ* 16.128). See Roller, *Building Program*, 234-35. For the fall of Cornelius Gallus and its causes see Dio 53.23.5-7. Cf. Seutonius, *Aug.* 66.

others was their relative importance to Rome and, in the latter part of his reign, their relative importance to Augustus and Agrippa. For example, Rhodes long had been an important Roman friend and ally, especially during the series of wars with the Antigonids and the Seleucids (214-168 BCE). In 164 BCE, Rhodes signed a peace treaty with Rome, which effectively ended its political independence. In the Mithradatic Wars (88-81, 75-63 BCE), Rhodes sided with Rome against Mithradates VI of Pontus. Additionally, during the middle and late Republic, Rhodes was a major schooling center for Roman noble families, and its school of Stoicism included famous philosophers such as Panaetius and Posidonius. As a young man, Cicero studied there. For a young Herod, who first arrived in Rhodes in 40 BCE on his way to Rome, such a city provided an ideal setting for his first "royal" benefaction. It enabled him to establish a royal reputation in an important commercial city that was allied with the very people he needed to impress most. At the same time, his benefaction to Rhodes would have benefited Rome as well since Rome used Rhodian ships to combat Mediterranean pirates.

Cities such as Berytus and Nikopolis, which were personal projects of Augustus and his family, were also ideal candidates for royal benefaction. Berytus had achieved a brief period of prominence during the Hellenistic period. However, by the Augustan period, it had lost much of its former glory and was in need of restoration. Agrippa took up this task and established Berytus as the Roman colony *Colonia Julia Augusta Felix* in 15 BCE. The city's importance to Herod's friend and patron makes it unsurprising that he devoted a great deal of money and effort to it by financing a multitude of buildings including temples, government buildings, and marketplaces. As one of only two Roman colonies in Syria, Berytus offered Herod the opportunity to highlight his building skills while advertising his friendship with Agrippa and earning gratitude for his efforts.[14] Herod's involvement with Nikopolis fits the same pattern, except that it was Au-

---

14. We know that Agrippa visited Judaea at the same time that Berytus became a colony, and it is possible either that Agrippa requested Herod's assistance during his visit or, more probably, that Herod offered his aid while Agrippa was in his kingdom. For a general discussion of the history of Berytus in the Hellenistic and Roman periods see Jean Lauffray, "Beyrouth Archéologie et Histoire, Époques Gréco-Romaines I. Periode Hellénistique et Haut-Empire Romain," *ANRW* 2.8 (1977): 135-63. For Agrippa's visit to Judaea see *AJ* 16.12-15. For Herod's patronage of Berytus see *BJ* 1.422. Berytus also happened to be where Herod's sons Alexander and Aristobulus stood trial before Gaius Sentius Saturninus, the governor of Syria, and his legates. See *BJ* 1.538-51; *AJ* 16.356-72.

gustus's project. Moreover, since Herod had been on the losing side of the conflict commemorated by Nikopolis, he would have felt a special need to play a conspicuous role in the city's construction. Through his building program, he may have hoped to erase the memory of his former loyalty to Antony and to reaffirm his friendship with Augustus and his commitment to the *Pax Augusta*.

Catering to Rome and its interests was only part of the equation. Internal politics and domestic concerns may also have played a role in Herod's decision to patronize certain cities. Specifically, Herod seems to have targeted cities that contained large Jewish populations. Evidence for these communities comes from archaeological and literary material. Archaeologists have uncovered a synagogue at Delos, whose oldest levels date to before the First Mithradatic War (88-84 BCE). Additionally, Delos is one of the many cities whose edicts on Jews appear in *Jewish Antiquities*. Other cities whose edicts Josephus incorporates include Kos, Laodicea, Pergamum, Sidon, and Tyre. As king of Judaea, Herod was the most prominent Jewish figure in the ancient world. Through his influence as a patron and benefactor to many Greek cities he may have been able, or at least thought he was able, to improve the situation of Diaspora Jews living in those communities. In turn, this defense of Diaspora Jews would have enhanced his image as the patron and defender of the Diaspora, an image that would have played well inside his kingdom. Unfortunately, we cannot chart precisely the improvement of Jewish life within the Diaspora throughout Herod's reign, so his success in this endeavor must remain hypothetical until more evidence is discovered. However, it stands to reason that a city beholden to him through ties of patronage and clientage would try to avoid offending him by mistreating, at least in an official capacity, the Jews in their midst.[15]

Given all this data, can we deduce a series of motivations for Herod's benevolence to foreign cities? We cannot entirely eliminate the possibility of random chance in the disbursement of his benevolence. Perhaps some of the cities profited from his generosity simply because they were in the right place at the right time; in a sense, they were beneficiaries of royal whim. Nevertheless, there does seem to be enough of a pattern in his program of

---

15. For a discussion of the synagogue on Delos see Trümper, "Delos Synagogue." For the edicts in Josephus that attest to the existence of Jewish communities in cities such as Delos, Kos, Laodicea, Pergamum, Sidon, and Tyre see *AJ* 14.190-267. In detail, Delos's edict exempted Jews from military service. For Herod's defense of Jews in Ionia see pp. 301-2 below.

euergetism that we can deduce a wider goal and multiple motives for his activities. On the one hand, he wished to appear as a typical Hellenistic king, and royal *euergetism* was the norm for such monarchs. By bestowing benefaction on cities, Herod enhanced his own reputation vis-à-vis his fellow dynasts and neighbors. He also strengthened ties of loyalty and friendship between Judaea and other kingdoms and cities in the eastern Mediterranean. Such friendship and good relations would have enhanced trading relationships between the patronized cities and Judaea, thus increasing the wealth of both the kingdom and, perhaps most importantly, the royal purse. In addition, by choosing cities that were on good terms with or were important to Rome and its leaders, he certainly would have pleased his imperial patrons and further solidified his status as a useful client king. Finally, he may also have been seeking to improve the status of local Jewish communities. Benevolence from a Jewish king could only improve the local opinions of the Jews and consequently the lives of Jewish communities in the Diaspora.[16]

Benefaction within Judaea

Greece and the Greek East were not the only recipients of Herod's *euergetism*. Unsurprisingly, he was also an active patron within his own kingdom, especially during crises. In 25/24 BCE, a great drought afflicted Judaea and the neighboring regions, and this drought and the subsequent food shortage led to an outbreak of disease and widespread death. According to Josephus, Herod melted down several of his own silver and gold vessels and sent the precious metal to Egypt to buy grain, relying on his friendship with the prefect Gaius Petronius to ensure himself and

---

16. Lichtenberger argues that Herod's ostentatious display of *euergetism* was firmly in the tradition of Hellenistic monarchy and designed to earn him a glorious reputation within the Greek world. His strong desire for such a reputation came from his *philotimia* ("love of fame"), which is described quite vividly by Josephus (*AJ* 15.330; 16.150-60). Lichtenberger is certainly correct that Herod's vanity and *philotimia* played a role in his actions. However, as we have seen, there were several other motivations that also influenced his decisions. For his discussion of Herod's motivations see Achim Lichtenberger, *Die Baupolitik Herodes des Grossen* (Wiesbaden: Harrassowitz, 1999), 168-75. Cf. Aryeh Kasher and Eliezer Witztum, *King Herod, a Persecuted Persecutor: A Case Study in Psychohistory and Psychobiography* (Berlin: de Gruyter, 2006), 181-243, where they discuss the psychological motivations for Herod's building program, among which was the "euphoria of construction," a megalomaniacal joy at the good fortune he had achieved and the amazing triumphs he had accomplished.

his kingdom priority. Having procured sufficient grain to feed his people, he supervised its transport back to Judaea and distribution among the populace. He provided grain not only for his own kingdom but also for his neighbors in Syria, who also were suffering from drought and famine. Because many of his subjects' flocks had died or been completely consumed in the famine, he also provided wool for clothing during the winter. Finally, when the harvest approached again the next year, he sent approximately fifty thousand men into the fields to harvest the crop, feeding and supplying them the entire time they were at work. According to Josephus, this effort produced 100,000 bushels of grain for export out of Judaea and 800,000 bushels for use within the realm. All this coordination provided food and clothing for Judaea's population and consequently earned the king significant gratitude, even from those who had been hostile to him in the past. This incident shows Herod at his diplomatic best. Since Egypt was the personal property of Augustus, he must have approved any distribution. Augustus needed grain from Egypt as badly as Herod did, and his willingness to give some of his supply to Judaea is a clear testimony to Herod's powers of persuasion.[17]

---

17. For Josephus's narration of the drought and plague see *AJ* 15.299-304. For Herod's actions in response see *AJ* 15.305-16. From this same period, Strabo recounts an instance of Augustus aiding the city of Tralles after it suffered an earthquake in 26 BCE (*Geog.* 12.8.18). Josephus states that the drought occurred in the thirteenth year of Herod's reign, which was either 28/27 or 25/24 BCE (depending on whether Josephus was referring to the beginning of Herod's reign *de iure* or *de facto*). Most scholars count from 37 BCE, the beginning of Herod's *de facto* reign and thus date this event to 25/24 BCE. Richardson, counting from 40, the date of Herod's appointment as king, puts this event in 28/27 BCE and argues that the year before was a sabbatical year. See Richardson, *Herod,* 222-23. There does not seem to be any clear reason in the text to privilege one date over the other. However, we know from archaeological evidence that Herod began the construction of Sebaste in 27 BCE (Dan Barag, "King Herod's Royal Castle at Samaria-Sebaste," *PEQ* 125 [1993]: 4, 13). If there had been a famine that year or the year before, forcing Herod to melt down his precious vessels to pay for grain, it is unlikely that he would have been able to pay for such a large building project as Sebaste. Given this evidence, I would argue, contra Richardson, that the famine took place in 25/24 BCE. For the need to solicit Augustus's approval before receiving any grain from Egypt see Rocca, *Herod's Judaea,* 211, and see 40, n. 62, where Rocca connects Herod's assistance during the famine with the title *euergetēs* ("benefactor"). He cites as evidence a limestone weight first published by Meshorer in 1970. However, as we have discussed (see pp. 155-56 above), Alla Kushnir-Stein has persuasively shown that Meshorer incorrectly transcribed the legend on the weight: instead of *Euergetou* ("benefactor"), the relevant word is *Eusebous* ("pious"). Consequently, we should not relate the weight's title to Herod's gift of wheat to his subjects.

Herod's generosity toward his subjects also extended to tax relief. Around 20 BCE he chose to remit a third of the taxes owed by his subjects, and in 14 BCE he remitted a fourth of the taxes owed. In the section of *Jewish Antiquities* discussing the first remission, Josephus states that the king's public motive was to allow his people to recover from the drought. His real motive, however, was to gain popularity and earn back the goodwill of those who were dissatisfied with his regime. Tax relief would have achieved both goals simultaneously. Certainly, he would have achieved a public relations boon, but the general economic health of his kingdom would also have benefited him, since it would have decreased dissatisfaction and agitation, which could lead to rioting and other internal instability.[18]

Although there are no further explicit mentions of similar domestic benevolence in the literary sources, other brief instances of royal benevolence appear throughout the Josephan narratives. To commemorate the dedication of the Temple, Herod sacrificed 300 oxen. There is no explicit mention of a feast for the populace. However, it would have been odd for a king to pass up such an opportunity to display both his wealth and his magnanimity. Such a celebration also occurred at the dedication of Caesarea Maritima in 12 BCE. Like the good Hellenistic king that he aspired to be, Herod displayed the royal Hellenistic virtues of wealth and magnanimity on a grand scale within his kingdom. Judaeans, who had experienced long periods of domination by Hellenistic monarchs, would have recognized and been familiar with such behavior in their king and indeed may even have expected and demanded it from him. Herod's ability to fulfill their expectations enabled him to increase his popularity and persuade his subjects, even if temporarily, that he was indeed a good and benevolent king.[19]

---

18. For Herod's remission of a third of the taxes owed him see *AJ* 15.365. For his remission in 14 BCE see *AJ* 16.65. In the passage discussing the first remission the Greek word *tote* ("at this time") appears to connect this episode with Augustus's visit to Syria in 20 BCE. See *AJ* 15.354. Richardson argues that this event took place after the Sabbatical year 23/22 BCE, and thus it should be placed in 22/21 BCE. He also argues that Herod's decision to remit taxes was an imitation of Roman practice and would therefore have been unpopular among more conservative Judaeans who would have objected to his "tampering with the divine order of things" (Richardson, *Herod,* 236). However, it is hard to believe that any Judaean would have objected to tax relief, even if it was seen as a Roman innovation.

19. For Herod's sacrifice of 300 oxen to dedicate the reconstruction of the Temple see *AJ* 15.421-23. For Herod's sacrifice in honor of the completion of Caesarea Maritima see *AJ* 16.136-37. Monika Bernett proposes an alternative motivation for Herod's generosity toward his Jewish subjects, namely an attempt to assuage his "guilt" and the anger of his subjects over his establishment of an imperial cult in Judaea. It seems to me, however, that she oversimplifies

CLIENT KING IN AN AUGUSTAN WORLD

Urban Construction and the Hellenistic Herod: Building in the Royal Tradition

Royal benefaction was just one of the many pursuits in which Hellenistic kings were supposed to engage. Beginning with Alexander the Great and his string of eponymous cities, city-building and monumental architecture became centerpieces of Hellenistic monarchies, activities instantly associated with classic Greek heroes such as Herakles. As "founder" *(ktistēs)* of a new city, a king typically received heroic honors from the new citizens. Building on a massive scale thus advertised and highlighted a ruler's power and wealth. As the Hellenistic period progressed, certain notions of art and decoration crystallized. Any king who wished to be seen as a true and legitimate monarch had to adhere to these general standards, although local variation was possible and frequent.[20]

---

the complex relationship between Jews and Rome and thus overstates the level of inherent conflict between the two cultures. As we have seen, Romans such as Agrippa and Augustus respected the Jerusalem Temple and even patronized its cult (e.g., Agrippa's sacrifices during his visit and Augustus's willingness to pay for daily sacrifices on his behalf). As we will see in the next chapter, during the Herodian period the Temple became an international religious site open to non-Jews as well as Jews. Furthermore, as scholars, e.g., the research of Erich Gruen and Martin Goodman, have shown, the Jews living during the Herodian period and afterward were far more integrated into the larger world than Bernett would have us believe. In such an environment of cultural interaction, it is hard to see Herod facing such monolithic outrage from his Jewish subjects, especially since he seems to have made special efforts to avoid any clear-cut religious outrage and only build his cult temples in regions of his kingdom that were either not predominantly Jewish or not Jewish at all. While certainly there were those who rejected any form of honor directed toward Augustus, most Jews living under Herod probably accepted his actions as part of interaction and alliance with Rome. Finally, it is noteworthy that Josephus himself, who Bernett believes would not have passed up an opportunity to criticize Herod, describes all three *Augustea* in detail and yet says nothing negative about them. Surely, if Judaea's Jews, as represented by Josephus, really were as hostile to Herod's establishment of the imperial cult, some trace of this disapproval would remain in these descriptions. For Bernett's analysis of Herod's motivations for his *euergetism* toward his Jewish subjects see *Kaiserkult,* 146-70, esp. 152. For detailed studies of Jewish integration in the larger Graeco-Roman world and the absence of inherent, irreconcilable conflict between Rome and the Jews see Erich Gruen, *Diaspora: Jews amidst the Greeks and Romans* (Cambridge: Harvard University Press, 2002); Martin Goodman, *Rome and Jerusalem: The Clash of Ancient Civilizations* (New York: Vintage, 2008).

20. Several Hellenistic monarchs, including Ptolemy II Philadelphus and Seleucus I Nicator, constructed cities and named them after family members and friends. Ptolemy II built the Red Sea port of Berenike Troglodytica, naming it after his mother. Appian recounts that Seleucus Nicator established cities across the whole of his empire named after family

Herod the Hellenistic King in an Augustan World

Herod enthusiastically stepped into this arena of royal construction. In particular, he built or rebuilt several cities. He also commissioned towering edifices that dwarfed previous buildings and emphasized his dominance over nature and topography. Through these stone edifices he asserted his control over his kingdom, advertised his wealth, and increased his glory and reputation as one of the leading builders of the first century BCE. In a very real sense, he stamped his kingdom with physical signs of his rule and advertised his regime and power through stone and brick.

Eponymous Cities and Fortresses

While many Hellenistic monarchs had created cities named for themselves or for important family members, Herod did not limit himself merely to cities. Instead, he also named fortresses and even towers after those close to him. Naming was a powerful statement of affection between him and the recipient. It enabled him to decorate the landscape with physical reminders of the Herodian presence. On the Plain of Sharon, near the source of the Yarkon River, he rebuilt and expanded the ancient city of Aphek in ca. 9 BCE, renaming it Antipatris after his father Antipater. Little is known of the exact layout of the city, but archaeologists have uncovered a main north-south street, approximately twenty-five feet wide and paved with flagstones arranged in a herringbone pattern. Flanking both sides of this *cardo* were colonnades and several shops. The design of each shop was similar, with a front room opening onto the street and a backroom serving as a storehouse. In the shops, excavators found small clay casks, which were

---

members. He named sixteen of them Antioch after his father, five of them Laodicea after his mother, three of them Apamea after his first wife, and one Stratonicea after his second wife. He also established nine cities in honor of himself, calling them Seleuceia. For a discussion of the status accorded to a Greek *ktistēs,* see Wolfgang Leschhorn, *Gründer der Stadt. Studien zu einem Politisch-Religiösen Phänomen der Griechischen Geschichte* (Stuttgart: Steiner, 1984), 1-5. For a general background on Berenike Troglodytica see David Meredith, "Berenice Troglodytica," *Journal of Egyptian Archaeology* 43 (1957): 56-70; G. W. Murray, "Troglodytica: The Red Sea Littoral in Ptolemaic Times," *GJ* 133 (1967): 24-33; Steven E. Sidebotham and Willemina Z. Wendrich, "Berenike: Roman Egypt's Maritime Gateway to Arabia and India," *Egyptian Archaeology* 8 (1996): 15-18. For a discussion of other Ptolemaic eponymous cities see Leschhorn, *Gründer der Stadt,* 223-29. For Appian's discussion of the city-founding of Seleucus Nicator see Appian, *Syr.* 57. The Attalid dynasty was also heavily involved in founding eponymous cities, such as Attaleia, Eumenea, and Apollonis. See Esther V. Hansen, *The Attalids of Pergamon* (2nd ed.; Ithaca: Cornell University Press, 1971), 175-79.

used to store and display merchandise. In addition to the *cardo,* excavators also found a few large buildings constructed of ashlar masonry and a fortress built on the town's acropolis. This fortress was originally erected in the second century BCE, probably by Alexander Jannaeus as part of his defensive measures for the region around the Yarkon. Herod rebuilt the fortress, both to protect Antipatris and to control the road between Jerusalem and the Mediterranean Sea.[21]

Another Herodian city named after an important family member is Phasaelis. Named for Herod's beloved brother, who had died after being captured by the Parthians, it lies on the western edge of the Jordan Valley approximately fifteen miles north of Jericho. Like Antipatris, the demographic composition of the city is unclear. There does seem to have been a group of Idumaeans who emigrated to Phasaelis from neighboring Acrabatene. However, whether there were non-Jewish inhabitants is uncertain, as is whether the demographics of the city changed following Herod's death, when it came under the control of his sister Salome. Josephus's narrative places the founding of the city after the inauguration of Caesarea Maritima (12 BCE), but this dating is not entirely certain. Although originally a wilderness, Phasaelis became famous for its agriculture, especially its date palms, which are mentioned by Pliny and Horace. Ptolemy mentions

---

21. For the founding of Antipatris see *BJ* 1.417; *AJ* 16.142-43. Cf. Sextus Julius Africanus, *Chron.* 17.4. This site, originally known as Aphek, first appeared in nineteenth-century BCE Egyptian curse texts as a fertile region containing an abundance of water and large trees. In the Bible, it was one of the Canaanite cities that Joshua conquered, and later the Philistines attacked Israel from this city. During the Hellenistic period, it was known as Pegae. For the appearance of the name Aphek in a topographical list of Thutmose III, where it is placed between Lod, Ono, and Yehud to the south and Suocoh to the north see Sarah Japp, *Die Baupolitik Herodes des Grossen. Die Bedeutung der Architektur für die Herrschaftslegitimation eines Römischen Klientelkönigs* (Rahden: Leidorf, 2000), 99. Cf. Abraham Eitan, "Aphek," in *NEAEHL,* 62. For the appearance of Aphek in the Bible see Josh 12:18; 1 Sam 4:1; 29:1. For the change of Aphek's name to Pegae during the Hellenistic period see Moshe Kochavi, "The History and Archeology of Aphek-Antipatris: A Biblical City in the Sharon Plain," *BiblArch* 44 (1981): 75-86; Japp, *Baupolitik,* 99. Cf. Roller, *Building Program,* 131. No concrete evidence exists concerning the identity and demography of the local inhabitants, although, as Kasher suggests, it is likely that the citizenry was predominantly Jewish, as were most of the surrounding inhabitants at that time. On this question see Aryeh Kasher, *Jews and the Hellenistic Cities in Eretz-Israel: Relations of the Jews in Eretz-Israel with the Hellenistic Cities during the Hellenistic and Roman Era (332 BCE–70 CE)* (Tübingen: Mohr, 1990), 206-7. For discussions of the archaeological site of Antipatris and the finds there see Kochavi, "History and Archeology of Aphek-Antipatris," 83; Eitan, "Aphek," 70; Japp, *Baupolitik,* 99; Netzer, "Herod the Great's Contribution to Nikopolis," 126-27; Roller, *Building Program,* 131-32.

the city in his *Geography,* and it may even appear on the Madaba map, a sixth century CE mosaic map that contains the oldest surviving original cartographic depiction of Judaea and the surrounding area.

The city of Phasaelis is located about a half-mile from the base of the nearby foothills, thus occupying none of the arable land. Extensive ruins exist on the site, but they have not been excavated in great detail. Nevertheless, we can tell that the town was built on a Graeco-Roman orthogonal plan with a total extent of approximately two and one-half miles north to south. Remains of several Roman-style roads are still visible, complete with a central rib for effective water drainage, the longest visible example of which runs almost 1,000 feet in length. Foundations for several large buildings exist, and one of these may have been a palace. A possible agora also exists, as do the foundations of a building that might have been a temple. Remnants of a bathhouse can be seen in the northeastern part of the city. The visible remains of the city's buildings seem to be composed of rubble and fieldstone as opposed to the more impressive ashlar masonry. Nevertheless, the size of the ruin as well as the extent of the water facilities testify to the economic prosperity of this town that literally grew out of a barren landscape. These water facilities were fed by a spring in the nearby Wadi Fasajil. From the stream, an aqueduct stretches about five miles toward the ancient city. In direct proximity to the aqueduct are a series of plastered reservoirs and irrigation ditches, probably for the farms in the region. Other similar water facilities can be found throughout the region, testifying to the importance of water in the city's economic activities.[22]

---

22. For speculation on the ethnic identity of Phasaelis's inhabitants see Kasher, *Hellenistic Cities,* 207. For discussions of the archaeological excavations at Phasaelis see Lucetta Mowry, "Settlements in the Jericho Valley during the Roman Period (63 B.C.–A.D. 134)," *BiblArch* 15 (1952): 31-32; Günther Harder, "Herodes-Burgen und Herodes-Städte im Jordanangraben," *ZDPV* 78 (1962): 49-63; Roller, *Building Program,* 192, 209; Japp, *Baupolitik,* 146; Netzer, *Architecture,* 226. Josephus mentions Phasaelis in *BJ* 1.418; *AJ* 16.145. If the city had been founded soon after the inauguration of Caesarea, it would have coincided nicely with the construction of the somewhat parallel city of Antipatris, named for Herod's father. Bernett connects the founding of Phasaelis with the agricultural expansion of the date plantations of Jericho, fields that Herod recovered from Cleopatra in 30 BCE. As a result, she proposes that the city was founded at the same time as Sebaste (Bernett, *Kaiserkult,* 152-53). Unfortunately, we have only Josephus's narrative on which to base our chronology, and he clearly puts the founding of Phasaelis after the inauguration of Caesarea Maritima. For this reason, we should reject Bernett's hypothesis. For Phasaelis's famous date palms see Pliny, *HN* 13.44 (Horace, *Epistles* 2.2.184). Cf. Rocca, *Herod's Judaea,* 230. Phasaelis is mentioned in Ptolemy, *Geography* 5.15. See also Roller, *Building Program,* 192.

Antipatris was a strategically important and economically viable city, guarding an important road between Jerusalem and Caesarea. Phasaelis was a fertile agricultural city at the center of the lucrative Judaean date palm industry. Although neither of these cities was a major metropolis like Jerusalem or Caesarea, they each had a significant population. Moreover, as important centers of local production and trade, they would have been visited by many merchants. In such a context, renaming the cities after members of his family was a conspicuous way for Herod to honor them and, at the same time, to mark the region as a symbol of Herodian rule in Judaea. Such renaming also placed him within the norms of Hellenistic monarchy, which sought to recreate the landscape and designate it as personal property of the ruler.

A final group of eponymous cities are those named for important Romans, specifically, the two "Caesar-cities" *(urbes Caesarae)* of Herodian Judaea, Samaria/Sebaste and Caesarea Maritima. As we have seen, these cities functioned as public statements of loyalty and friendship to Rome. However, simultaneously, these cities also asserted Herod's own power, wealth, and majesty. Alexander the Great had built his magnificent capital on the seacoast, and Herod, his monarchical heir, did as well. Moreover, just as a harbor dominated Alexandria's landscape, so too did the Sebastos harbor dominate the area of Caesarea. The scale alone of a city like Caesarea Maritima, a new metropolis to rival Jerusalem, suggests such a desire for greatness: Herod could not be the *ktistēs* of Jerusalem, but he could be for Caesarea. As the founder of this new city, which contained the largest artificial harbor in the Roman world, he could take his place alongside the other Hellenistic royal builders of major cities such as Antioch and especially Alexandria. In a sense, therefore, and to a domestic audience, these cities could simultaneously serve as both *urbes Caesarae* and *urbes Herodei* (Herod-cities), highlighting his friendship with Rome, but also emphasizing his royal prerogative and city-founding capabilities. It is thus noteworthy that more than sixty years after its completion, the city was still closely associated with him. Indeed, during the procuratorship of Antonius Felix (52-60 CE), when a dispute arose in Caesarea over whether it was to be a Jewish or Greek city, *both sides* appealed to Herod's status as founder. The Jews claimed that his Jewish identity meant that the city should be Jewish, while the Greek citizens argued that he had given the city a Greek constitution and therefore meant for it to be Greek. It would seem then that his desire was fulfilled: even though the two sides disagreed about his intentions, his link with the city was clear and unmistakable.[23]

Herod used monumental architecture to honor important members of his family and court on a smaller scale as well. Throughout his kingdom, he sprinkled eponymous buildings, such as the desert fortress Cypros, which overlooked the city of Jericho and initially may have been a Hasmonean fortress (possibly either Threx or Taurus). However, during his reign Herod substantially rebuilt and improved the site. In the process, he changed its name, glorifying his mother, who was a Nabataean princess. This fortress offers wonderful views of the entire Plain of Jericho, the mountains east of the Jordan, and the northern part of the Dead Sea. It had a strategic function as well, being an ideal place from which to watch the main Jerusalem-Jericho road. Herodian Cypros was divided into two areas, one on the mountaintop and the other about 100 feet below it.

In Upper Cypros, which seems to have been two stories high, excavators found a palace containing approximately twenty rooms, several corridors and courtyards, two cisterns, and two bathhouses, the better preserved of which contains a clear Roman-style *caldarium* (hot room), a *tepidarium* (warm room), and a small *frigidarium* (cold room). Lavish architectural decorations, such as floors of *opus sectile* and walls decorated with colorful frescoes, appear in the bathhouse as well as throughout the palace. The palace also contained painted Corinthian capitals and well-executed stuccowork. In Lower Cypros, excavators discovered around forty rooms, corridors, and courtyards, some of which still contain their original stucco wall decorations. On the northern side is another Roman-style bathhouse with an *apodyterium* (changing room), a *laconicum* (sauna), two *praefurnia* (ovens for heating the *caldarium*), and cold-room and hot-room suites. All the floors in the bathhouse were paved with mosaics, and the walls were coated with white plaster. Stucco profiles also appear in the *caldarium*. At the southeastern corner of Lower Cypros, archaeologists revealed the basement of a structure whose upper floor was a magnificent hall (possibly a peristyle courtyard) complete with painted Corinthian columns and lavish stuccowork.

To provide a steady supply of water for all these bathing facilities in

---

23. For the similarities between Alexander the Great's founding of Alexandria and Herod's founding of Caesarea Maritima, as well as a discussion of some key differences, see Rocca, *Herod's Judaea,* 47-48. For the dispute that arose between the Jews and non-Jews of Caesarea see *BJ* 2.266-70; *AJ* 20.173-78. For a detailed discussion of Caesarea Maritima see pp. 151-53 above.

the hot and arid desert climate, an elaborate water supply system was created even before Herod's rebuilding. Nevertheless, concurrent with his renovations was the expansion of the water system, including a long conduit that conveyed water from the springs of the Wadi Qelt to the foot of the fortress. The luxury and decoration in this desert fortress, as well as its size and the presence of the two bathhouses, suggest that Cypros was not simply a military installation. In reality, like other Herodian desert fortresses, it was a fortified yet luxurious palace. Members of the royal court may even have stayed here when the king was in Jericho. Cypros was another physical reminder of the king's political control of the countryside. It also enabled Herod to mimic other Hellenistic monarchs, such as Ptolemy Philadephus and Seleucus Nicator, who named cities or buildings after their mothers.[24]

Other family members and close friends received eponymous buildings, and none were more prominent than the three main towers of Herod's palace in Jerusalem, which were named for his brother Phasael, his wife Mariamme, and his friend Hippicus. All three towers were multistory structures, composed of huge ashlar blocks and incorporated into the existing Jerusalem fortifications adjoining the palace. According to Josephus, Phasael's tower was tallest of the three structures at a height of ninety cubits or approximately 155 feet. In modern terms, then, the tower was about fifteen stories tall. Josephus states that it resembled the Pharos in design, although he also claims that its circumference was much larger than that of

---

24. For a thorough analysis and explanation of the archaeological site at Cypros see Netzer, "Cypros," in *Jericho* 2:239-80. Cf. Netzer, *Architecture*, 207-12; Lichtenberger, *Baupolitik*, 71-73; Japp, *Baupolitik*, 135-36; Netzer, *Palaces*, 72-75. According to Netzer, the details of the columns and capitals in this hall bear a striking resemblance to those unearthed at the Northern Palace at Masada, especially on the Lower Terrace, as well as the columns from the peristyle courtyard at Alexandrion. See Netzer, *Architecture*, 211. For a discussion of the water supply at Cypros see Ze'ev Meshel and David Amit, "The Water Supply Systems of Cypros Fortress," in *The Aqueducts of Israel*, ed. David Amit, Joseph Patrich, and Yizhar Hirschfeld (JRAS 46; Portsmouth: Journal of Roman Archaeology, 2002), 313-29. An interesting possibility is that the rebuilding and renaming of the fortress coincided with the death of Herod's mother. If so, it would have been a way for the son to honor his mother and preserve her memory. Archaeologists such as Netzer believe that Cypros was constructed in two stages (ca. 34 BCE and ca. 28 BCE), and it is possible that she died around that time. However, as we do not know her personal chronology, such a suggestion can only be speculative. If true, it would certainly offer us some insight into Herod's relationship to his mother. For the possible chronology of Cypros see Barbara Burrell and Ehud Netzer, "Herod the Builder," *JRA* 12 (1999): 708.

the lighthouse in Alexandria. Phasael's tower was actually two structures in one: the first part included defensive fortifications, in particular parapets and bulwarks, and the second tower contained lavish apartments, including a bath suite. The summit of this tower also had additional battlements and turrets, making the entire structure a strongly fortified palatial tower. Netzer argues that the three towers were multi-use structures, operating as bastions, watchtowers, and lookout posts. It is possible that they also served as part of a larger kingdom-wide signaling network — they were tall enough for such use. They certainly functioned as physical reminders of the royal presence. As imposing physical reminders of his power and technical skill, these towers cast a tall shadow over the city below. The guards who patrolled the parapets and bulwarks of these towers helped reinforce the notion that the king was in control.

Aside from being reminders of political dominance, these towers were also monuments and sources of prestige. Specifically, by naming one of the towers after his wife, the Hasmonean princess Mariamme, Herod could portray himself as a legitimate successor to the Hasmoneans. By naming a tower after his brother, who had earned a good reputation while *stratēgos* of Jerusalem and who valiantly died protecting Jerusalem from the Parthians, he could appropriate some of the dead man's popularity. Finally, by building a tower in honor of his dead brother he could gain both a reputation of filial piety and glory as a spectacular builder.[25]

25. For the appearance of the three towers in Josephus see *BJ* 5.161-71; *AJ* 16.144. For Phasael's ability to earn the goodwill of the Judaean people see *BJ* 1.206; *AJ* 14.161. Who was Hippicus? Kokkinos argues that he was Herod's male lover, but Rocca rejects this claim, arguing that their status as "friends," meaning men of the same age, does not correspond to the typical homoerotic relationship of the Hellenistic world, which consisted of an older man *(erastos)* and a younger one *(eromenos)*. For Kokkinos's theory see Nikos Kokkinos, "The Royal Court of the Herods," in *The World of the Herods: Volume 1 of the International Conference The World of the Herods and the Nabataeans Held at the British Museum, 17-19 April 2001*, ed. Nikos Kokkinos (Stuttgart: Steiner, 2007), 285. Cf. Rocca, *Herod's Judaea*, 95-96, for Rocca's response. Presently only the podium of one of these towers exists, and it is currently known as the "Tower of David." Which of the Herodian towers is it? While some scholars such as Hillel Geva believe it is the tower of Hippicus, most scholars agree with Netzer that it is Phasael's. Either way, both were extremely tall and imposing and towered above surrounding structures. According to Josephus the tallest tower in the Antonia fortress was seventy cubits (ca. 121 feet), while the Hippicus tower was eighty cubits (ca. 138 feet) and Mariamme's tower fifty-five cubits (ca. 95 feet). For the widely-accepted estimate on the length of a cubit (52.5 cm./20.67 in.) see Leen Ritmeyer, "Locating the Original Temple Mount," *BAR* 18.2 (1992): 64, n. 14. For the various arguments see Hillel Geva, "The 'Tower of David' — Phasael or Hippicus?" *IEJ* 31 (1981): 57-65; Netzer, *Architecture,* 127; Kokkinos,

CLIENT KING IN AN AUGUSTAN WORLD

Herod's Personal Monument: Herodion

The pinnacle of Hellenistic urban construction was the design and erection of a city named after and in honor of oneself. Alexander had dozens. Seleucus Nicator had nine. Why should Herod not have his own? In the desert, seven and a half miles south of Jerusalem, he constructed a villa/palace/city that would become his personal monument and largest palace. The background to the construction of this largest of Herodian palace complexes is dramatic. After the Parthians had captured Phasael and John Hyrcanus II, Herod abandoned Jerusalem and fled south into Idumaea with several members of his household, including his mother and his sister Salome. He also took his fiancée Mariamme and her mother Alexandra. Along the way, the party encountered hostile Jewish forces. At the site of what would become Herodion, Herod and his besieged companions defeated their enemies and managed to escape to safety.[26]

Although this victory may have seemed hollow at the time, especially given the beleaguered state Herod was in, it must have been important enough to him that years later he chose the exact site to build his largest palace and, ultimately, his tomb. Perhaps it was the symbolism of the site and its victory: it offered a stark contrast of his present fortunes with his past. As a young man he had fled Jerusalem a defeated and humbled fu-

---

Herodian Dynasty, 159, esp. n. 22. Herod utilized the multistory tower design at several sites around his kingdom. In the sense that the three eponymous towers had multiple stories and lavish apartments inside, they resemble the tall towers at both Herodion and the Antonia. For scholarly discussions of the towers see Roller, *Building Program*, 178; Lichtenberger, *Baupolitik*, 94-95; Netzer, *Architecture*, 125-29, 183-86.

26. For Josephus's narration of the escape from Jerusalem and fight with enemy forces see *BJ* 1.265; *AJ* 14.352-62. In *AJ* this flight becomes a moment of great pathos. Josephus describes the refugees as entirely pitiable, wailing and bemoaning their fate. Only Herod manages to keep his spirit high, and during their escape he attempts to revive his party's morale and inspire their courage. However, even he becomes despondent when the wagon in which his mother is traveling falls over and seriously injures her. According to Josephus, he is anxious both for her health and for her safety. Specifically, he fears the delay will enable their enemies to capture them. Because of the negative turn of events he becomes so depressed that he draws his sword as if to kill himself. However, he is restrained by his companions and urged not to abandon them. Chastised by his companions, Herod quickly regains his senses, sees to his mother, and reorganizes the party. They then continue on their way to Masada. While the version in *AJ* is certainly more exciting than the simpler narrative in *BJ*, it seems to be more of a dramatic retelling than historical reporting. It is certainly possible that Cypros was injured during the escape from Jerusalem. However, the scene is more likely a fiction composed by Josephus or Nicolaus, designed to evoke pathos and sympathy in the reader.

gitive. He had returned a mighty warrior, supported by the greatest army in the world, and now he was the glorious and powerful king of the entire realm.

Geographically, it was an ideal location for Herod's *hērōon,* his tomb and monument to his glory and greatness, since it was close enough to Jerusalem to be visible from the city on a clear day. Literary evidence, namely Josephus, asserts that the site did indeed become the king's tomb. When Herod died in 4 BCE, the funeral procession began in Jerusalem and proceeded to Herodion. In this procession, his sons and his relatives surrounded the funeral bier, which was of solid gold and imbedded with precious stones. A costly purple covering, embroidered with several different-colored threads, draped the bier. Upon it lay Herod's corpse, dressed in a purple robe, with a diadem and crown on his head. A scepter was also placed in his right hand. The royal army led the procession, arrayed in battle gear and led by their commanders. Five hundred royal servants and freedman followed the army, carrying spices to perfume the air. Behind the bier walked the royal bodyguard, followed by regiments of Thracians, Germans, and Gauls. Once the procession reached Herodion, funeral rites were performed, and the king's body was interred in his tomb.

Despite this vivid description and scholarly consensus, the actual tomb lay hidden for two thousand years. During that time most scholars agreed that the tomb was somewhere at Herodion. Strengthening the argument were several visible elements of a memorial complex. In particular, just below the large palace of Lower Herodion runs a massive flat platform (1150 × 100 feet), which is known as the Grand Course and may have been the straightaway on which Herod's funeral procession progressed once it reached the actual tomb. Along the northern side of the Grand Course was a colonnade approximately 130 feet long. On the southern side of the Course, opposite the colonnade, was a building containing a large stepped pool, partially cut into the natural slope, which may have been a *mikveh* (Jewish ritual bath). At the western end of the Grand Course and about nine feet below, excavators discovered the "Monumental Building," an elaborate hall with three entrances in the main (eastern) facade and two more located in the north and south walls. Inside, the building is decorated with niches all around the interior flanked by engaged columns on pedestals. The interior walls were probably plastered and then decorated with stucco and frescoes. The exterior walls were probably decorated similarly. The thickness of the northern and southern walls suggests that there was a vaulted ceiling and a monumental roof. The building is on the same axis as the Grand Course, suggesting that they were linked architecturally. A narrow reflecting pool was constructed in front of the building and parallel to it. All these structures may have been part of an elaborate funeral and memorial complex designed to memorialize Herod and serve as a monument to his memory.[27]

So where was the tomb itself? Some, seeing a connection between the tumulus-shape of Upper Herodion's mountain palace and the mausoleum of Augustus, argued that the tomb must be there. Others asserted that the tomb was to be found in Lower Herodion. In 2007, archaeological excavations under Ehud Netzer seemed to settle the dispute and confirm the descriptions in the literary sources. While digging in the vicinity of the "Monumental Building," Netzer and his team found a tomb structure and

---

27. For Josephus's narration of the royal funeral see *BJ* 1.670-73; *AJ* 17.196-99. For analysis of the Jewish-Macedonian hybrid nature of Herod's funerary rites see Rocca, *Herod's Judaea*, 352-54. For a description of the Grand Course see Netzer, *Architecture*, 195-96. In the past, some have suggested that the Grand Course was a hippodrome or racecourse. However, it is too narrow to have been a hippodrome and too long to have been a stadium. Furthermore, as Netzer points out, Herod built such structures either within or near established cities, such as Caesarea Maritima, Jericho, and Jerusalem (Netzer, *Architecture*, 195-96). See also Netzer, *Jericho*, 2:195-225; Joseph Patrich, "The *Carceres* of the Herodian Hippodrome/Stadium at Caesarea Maritima and Connections with the Circus Maximus," *JRA* 14 (2001): 269-83; "Herod's Theater in Jerusalem: A New Proposal," *IEJ* 52 (2002): 231-39. For a discussion of the Monumental Building and the possible *mikveh* nearby see Netzer, *Architecture*, 195-96; *Palaces*, 114-15; Lichtenberger, *Baupolitik*, 104; Japp, *Baupolitik*, 117. The entrance to the stepped pool passed through a double doorway, which is a characteristic feature of various ritual baths (Netzer, *Palaces*, 115). Excavators have found other elements that might have belonged to this memorial complex, including a large group of limestone ashlars with chiseled margins and projecting bosses similar to those on the Temple and at Machpelah (Hebron). These stones were discovered in secondary use in a Byzantine church built close to the Monumental Building. Netzer believes they formed part of a Doric frieze, containing either floral designs or triglyphs and metopes. Both types were common on Judaean tombs of the Second Temple period. This frieze could have come from a nearby monument, perhaps even Herod's actual tomb. Further, in the 1997-2000 excavations, archaeologists uncovered the foundation of a U-shaped building about 180 feet southeast of the Monumental Building. West of these foundations is a ritual bath composed of two pools. These foundations might have been the base on which the ashlar structure sat. Interestingly, this U-shaped structure rests on a diagonal axis that bisects the large pool in the pool complex, the *tholos* (circular building) at the center of this pool, and the round eastern tower of the Mountain Palace-Fortress of Upper Herodion. Netzer argues that this building might have been a vestibule for Herod's actual tomb. Until a detailed site report of his latest discoveries is published, it is hard to know exactly how this structure fits into his reconstruction of Herod's tomb. Nevertheless, its location on a significant axis suggests a relative importance in the overall structure of the memorial. See Netzer, *Architecture*, 198.

pieces of a limestone sarcophagus, which they believe is the royal sarcophagus. They also found two other intact sarcophagi, which they believed may have been the final resting place of important Herodian women such as Herod's fourth wife Malthace, mother of Archelaus, Herod's son and successor as ruler of Judaea. Unfortunately, Netzer's tragic accidental death while on-site has delayed the publication of these excavations. Nevertheless, despite some recent critiques, most notably by Joseph Patrich and Benjamin Arubas, the preliminary reports and subsequent elaborations by Roi Porat, the archaeologist who took over from Netzer, strongly suggest that Herod's tomb was indeed in Lower Herodion right where Josephus claimed it was.[28]

Ultimately, it seems as if Herodion was a unique combination of multiple functions including those of a fortified palace, a summer villa, the capital

---

28. For the theories of scholars such as Duane Roller and Jodi Magness that the tomb was somewhere in Upper Herodion see Roller, *Building Program,* 167; Jodi Magness, "The Mausolea of Augustus, Alexander and Herod the Great," in *Hesed Ve-Emet: Studies in Honor of Ernest S. Frerichs,* ed. Jodi Magness and Seymour Gittin (Atlanta: Scholars, 1998), 313-29. In her article Magness connects the three rulers' mausolea and uses this connection to argue for burial in Upper Herodion. Cf. Jodi Magness, "Where Is Herod's Tomb at Herodium?" *BASOR* 322 (2001): 43-44. For the analyses of scholars such as Ehud Netzer, Barbara Burrell, Achim Lichtenberger, and Sarah Japp who believed the tomb was in Lower Herodion see Ehud Netzer, *Greater Herodium* (Jerusalem: Hebrew University of Jerusalem, 1981), 41; Lichtenberger *Baupolitik,* 111, n. 540; Burrell and Netzer, "Herod the Builder," 709-11. Cf. Ehud Netzer, "Searching for Herod's Tomb: Somewhere in the Desert Palace-Fortress at Herodium, Palestine's Master Builder Was Buried," *BAR* 9.3 (1983): 31-51; Netzer, *Palaces,* 114-16; Japp, *Baupolitik,* 118. For newspaper articles discussing Netzer's 2007 find see Amiram Barkat, "Researcher: We Have Found Herod's Tomb," *Haaretz,* May 8, 2007; Associated Press, "Archaeologists Find Tomb of King Herod," *New York Times,* May 9, 2007. Cf. Barbara Kreiger, "Finding Herod's Tomb," *Smithsonian* 40.5 (2009): 36-43. For David M. Jacobson's hesitation to accept Netzer's interpretation of his excavations see Jacobson, "Has Herod's Place of Burial Been Found?" *PEQ* 139 (2007): 147-48. Although a detailed excavation report has not yet been published, Netzer provides preliminary data on his findings while also responding to Jacobson's critique. See Ehud Netzer, "In Search of Herod's Tomb," *BAR* 37.1 (2011): 36-70. For Joseph Patrich's and Benjamin Arubas's critiques of Netzer's theory, see Patrich and Arubas, "'Herod's Tomb' Reexamined: Guidelines for a Discussion and Conclusions," in *New Studies in the Archaeology of Jerusalem and Its Region,* vol. 7, ed. Guy D. Stiebel, Orit Peleg-Barkat, Doron Ben-Ami, Shlomit Weksler-Bdolah, and Yuval Gadot (Jerusalem: Israel Antiquities Authority, 2013), 287-300. Cf. Nir Hasson, "Archaeological Stunner: Not Herod's Tomb After All?" *Haaretz,* October 11, 2013; Hershel Shanks, "Was Herod's Tomb Really Found?" *BAR* 40.3 (2014): 40-48. For a persuasive rebuttal to these critiques, see Roi Porat, Yakov Kalman, and Rachel Chachy, "Herod's Tomb and the Memorial Complex at Herodium," in *New Studies in the Archaeology of Jerusalem and Its Region,* 7:257-86.

Reconstruction of Herod's tomb complex at Herodion

of a royal province (called a toparchy), a royal tomb, and a monument to Herod's victory over Antigonus and to his eternal glory. In this combination of functions, Herod was both drawing on Hellenistic influences and predecessors and staking out his own unique interpretation. As discussed previously, royal founders *(ktistoi)* were entitled to certain heroic honors, one of which was burial in one of their main foundations. Greeks and Romans normally placed their cemeteries outside city walls. Thus, to be buried inside the walls, contrary to normal custom, was a great honor reserved for heroes and *ktistoi*. In accordance with this practice, Alexander and some of his successors, such as Seleucus I Nicator, Lysimachus, and Demetrius I Poliorketes, were buried in their principal eponymous cities. Contemporary kings such as Antiochus I of Commagene continued this tradition. Antiochus constructed the vast complex of Nemrud Dagh, which consists of a massive tomb and colossal statues depicting various gods as well as Antiochus himself. Along with eponymous cities, Hellenistic kings were often also accorded founder-cults. As a Jew, Herod could not have such a cult, but there was no reason he could not have a monument to his greatness, a *nefeš*, at Herodion. What better site than the location of the battle between him

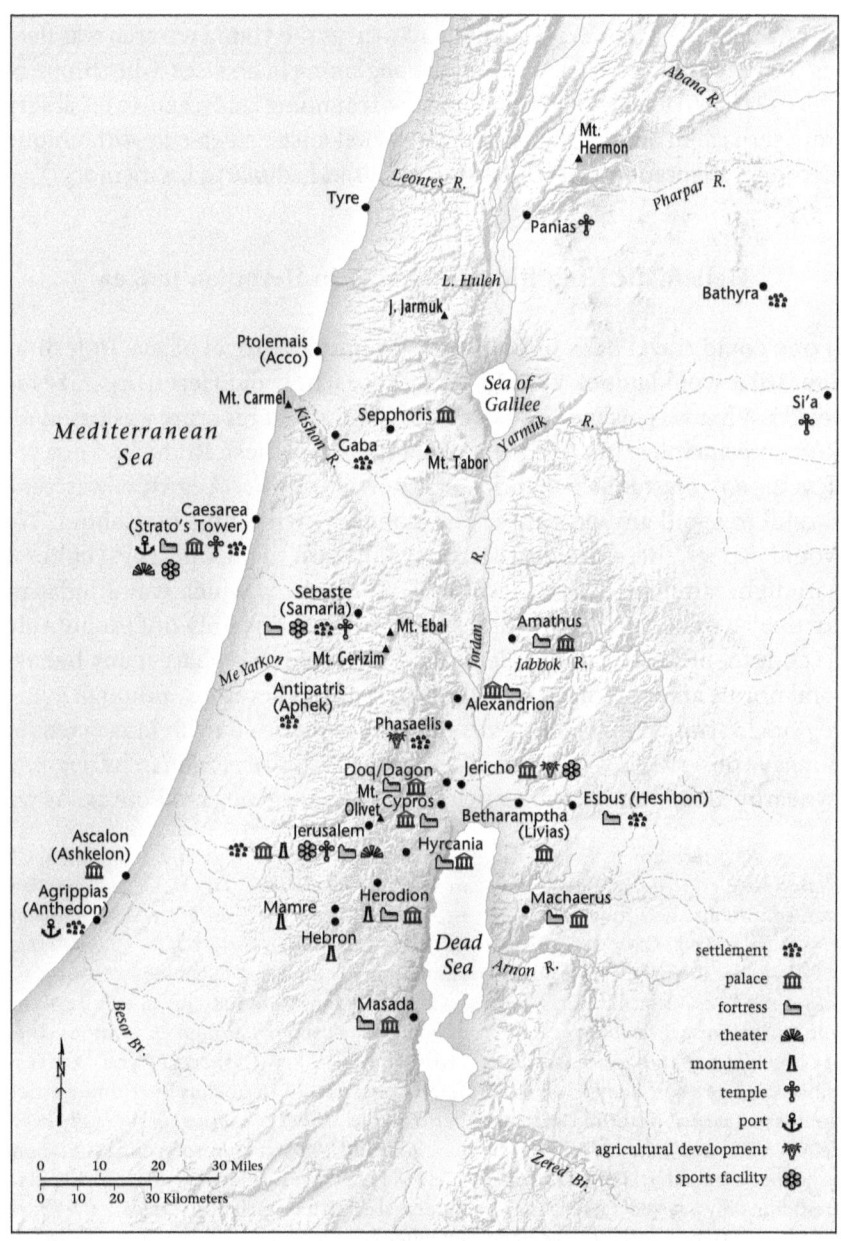

Herod's domestic building program (40-4 BCE)
Herod left almost no region of his kingdom without some architectural creation of his. Thus, he physically marked his kingdom with impressive monuments to his power, presence, and royal prerogative.

and Antigonus, which was fought in 40 BCE as the young tetrarch was fleeing Jerusalem, a battle that marked the beginning of his rise to the throne of Judaea? Due to its (1) domination of the surrounding landscape, (2) visibility from Jerusalem, and (3) combination of Hellenistic ruler-cult with unique Herodian adaptations, it was a fitting and grand edifice to his memory.[29]

Hellenistic Kingship and Virtues in Herodian Judaea

If one could travel back in time and step into the royal palace in Jerusalem, what would it look like? In other words, how did Herod organize his court? What was his model? We already know that his army was based on Roman principles, but his court could not be because Rome had not yet developed an established and fixed courtly routine: Augustus was very careful to avoid any appearance of monarchy within his household. We would expect, therefore, that Herod would turn to the only royal cultural paradigm familiar to him, Hasmonean monarchy, which was a Judaean particular subset of Hellenistic kingship. While certainly not monolithic or congruent in all aspects, Hellenized kingdoms did share many behavioral norms and organizational characteristics. Therefore, although some regional variation must have existed, visitors to the court in Judaea would not have observed a significant difference from those of monarchs reigning in nearby kingdoms such as Cappadocia, Commagene, and Pontus. As we

---

29. For Herodion as the capital of a toparchy see *BJ* 3.54-56; Pliny, *HN* 5.14.70. Cf. Netzer, *Greater Herodium*, 104-5; Abraham Schalit, *König Herodes. Der Mann und Sein Werk* (rev. ed.; Berlin: de Gruyter, 2001), 203-11; A. H. M. Jones, *The Cities of the Eastern Roman Provinces* (2nd ed.; Oxford: Clarendon, 1971), 272-73; Schürer, *History of the Jewish People*, 2:192-96. For the privilege of burial within the city walls being extended to heroes and *ktistoi*, see Simon Hornblower, *Mausolus* (Oxford: Oxford University Press, 1982), 255 and nn. 250-52. For a discussion of Hellenistic ruler-cults centered around eponymous cities see Leschhorn, *Gründer der Stadt*, 205-6 (Alexandria), 238-39 (Seleuceia Pieria), 257 (Lysimacheia), 262-68 (Demetrias). For a general overview of Antiochus I of Commagene's tomb-sanctuary at Nemrud Dagh see Alberto Siliotti, *Hidden Treasures of Antiquity* (Vercelli: VMB, 2006), 216-23. I do not believe Nemrud Dagh was a prototype for Herodion, as has been argued by Yoram Tsafrir and Netzer. I concur with Magness that it is related to Herodion only in a general sense as a monumental tomb for a Hellenistic ruler in the Greek East. As she rightly observes, the significant differences in design and architecture as well as the unrelated cultural contexts of the two sites make a direct influence unlikely. For Tsafrir and Netzer's hypotheses see Yoram Tsafrir, "The Desert Fortresses of Judaea in the Second Temple Period," *Jerusalem Cathedra* 2 (1982): 140; Netzer, *Greater Herodium*, 100. See also Magness, "Mausolea of Augustus, Alexander and Herod the Great," 317.

will see, Herod embraced Hellenistic royal culture even more enthusiastically than his Hasmonean predecessors and in the process moved Judaea culturally even closer to its Hellenized neighbors than it had been before.

One of the most apparent indications that the Herodian royal court continued in and deepened the Hellenistic tradition established by the Hasmoneans was its exclusive use of Greek. In contrast, the Hasmoneans used Greek along with the traditional languages of Judaea — Hebrew and Aramaic. For instance, all the coins struck during Herod's reign used Greek in their legends. In contrast, most Hasmonean coins (twenty-two out of twenty-eight coin types) have only Hebrew legends. Of the six that contain Greek, all have a combination of Hebrew and Greek. Even Judah Aristobulus I, the Hasmonean, who received the title *philhellene* ("Greek-lover"), used only Hebrew on his coins. Surely, if Greek had not been the courtly language of the Herodians, we would not see such an overrepresentation of it on the coinage. Furthermore, inscriptions found in Jerusalem that mention Herod are also exclusively in Greek.[30]

In addition to its use of Greek, the Herodian court also seems to have mimicked a number of Hellenistic royal practices. Specifically, like other Hellenistic kings, Herod and his court celebrated the anniversary of his ascension. Festive commemoration of royal anniversaries was a centerpiece of the ruler-cult in many of the major Hellenistic kingdoms and often occurred in the course of major festivals. While his subjects' religious sensibilities made it impossible for Herod to link his anniversary celebration with any explicit ruler-cult, there was no reason that he could not commemorate his rule with a festival in honor of his reign. Such a festival would have enabled him to remind his subjects of his authority, to reassert symbolically his legitimacy, and to delight the populace of Jerusalem with spectacles and games, during which there would have been free food and entertainment.

According to Josephus, just such a festival occurred in the same year that preliminary work finished on the sanctuary of the Temple (ca. 22/21 BCE). Indeed, he states that the work ended on the same day as the anniversary of Herod's ascension. Because of this coincidence, the anniversary festival was even larger and more spectacular than before. There is

---

30. For analysis of the coin legends on Hasmonean and Herodian coins see Meshorer, *TJC*, 201-20. For Aristobulus I's status as a *philhellene*, see *AJ* 13.318. For an analysis of Greek inscriptions found in Jerusalem see Benjamin Isaac, "A Donation for Herod's Temple in Jerusalem," *IEJ* 33 (1983): 86-92. For a discussion of the languages of Judaea during the first century BCE see Rocca, *Herod's Judaea*, 241-47.

CLIENT KING IN AN AUGUSTAN WORLD

no detailed description of this festival, although we could use Josephus's narration of the festivals in honor of Augustus, as well as descriptions of other Hellenistic royal festivals, to get some idea of what the Herodian anniversary celebration would have looked like. Most likely there would have been processions and parades, advertising both the strength of the army and the wealth of the kingdom. We know that the festival to commemorate the construction of Caesarea had musical contests as well as gladiatorial combat and *venationes* (animal hunts), and it is possible that Herod's anniversary celebrations did too. Feasts, both public ones and those reserved for special guests, would also have been a centerpiece of this celebration, providing the king another opportunity to display his wealth and generosity, two aspects central to Hellenistic ruling ideology.[31]

Herod's bureaucracy also followed typical Hellenistic patterns. In particular, like his predecessors and contemporaries in the Greek East, he created a close circle of advisors known as his *philoi* (friends). Nicolaus of Damascus was the most famous and prominent royal friend, but others included (1) Ptolemy the royal treasurer, (2) Nicolaus's brother Ptolemy of Damascus, and (3) Lysimachus, who was involved in the conspiracy of Costobar and Antipater Gadia and was ultimately executed. Many of Herod's inner circle were Hellenized non-Jews, although some of them, such as Alexas (the husband of Salome) and Dositheos, were Jewish. As was the case in other Hellenistic courts, ethnic background seems not to

---

31. For Josephus's discussion of the festival that celebrated the construction of Caesarea Maritima see *AJ* 16.136-41. For Herod's celebration of the anniversary of his accession to the throne see *AJ* 15.423. For a discussion of Hellenistic ruler-cult and anniversary festivals such as the *Ptolemaieia,* the *Antigoneia,* and the *Demetrieia,* which took place in honor of Ptolemy II Philadelphus, Antigonus III Doson, and Demetrius I Poliorcetes respectively, see F. W. Walbank, "Monarchies and Monarchic Ideals," in *CAH,* ed. A. E. Astin, M. W. Frederiksen, R. M. Ogilvie, and F. W. Walbank (2nd ed.; Cambridge: Cambridge University Press, 1984), 7:87-99, esp. 92-93. The Ptolemaic festival described by Kallixeinos of Rhodes is a good example of a royal procession designed to advertise the Ptolemies' great wealth and military might. See *FGrH* 627 fragment 2; Athenaeus, *Deipnosophistae* 196a-203b. For an analysis of this procession see E. E. Rice, *The Grand Procession of Ptolemy Philadelphus* (Oxford: Oxford University Press, 1983). Cf. Dorothy J. Thompson, "Philadelphus' Procession: Dynastic Power in a Mediterranean Context," in *Politics, Administration and Society in the Hellenistic and Roman World,* ed. Leon Mooren (Leuven: Peeters, 2001), 368-88. A more contemporary example was the procession of Antony and Cleopatra in 34 BCE to celebrate Antony's victory in Armenia. While this procession was a military triumph rather than an anniversary festival, the feasts and parades can provide some idea of what occurred at the Herodian festival. See Plutarch, *Ant.* 50.4; Dio 49.40.3-41.6. Cf. Diane E. E. Kleiner, *Cleopatra and Rome* (Cambridge: Harvard University Press, 2005), 137-41.

have hindered membership in Herod's inner circle of friends. Adoption of Greek culture and loyalty to the king were the most important elements for both Herod's court and those of other Hellenistic monarchs.³²

32. For a detailed discussion of Herod's court, both its physical makeup and its daily activities, see Kokkinos, "Royal Court of the Herods," 281-301; Rocca, *Herod's Judaea*, 70-72. Cf. Eyal Regev, "Inside Herod's Courts: Social Relations and Royal Ideology in the Herodian Palaces," *JSJ* 43 (2012): 181-82. In his catalog of those individuals serving at court, Rocca divides them into different groups according to their proximity to the king. He begins with Herod's family and then moves on to his *philoi* and his sons. He then proceeds to discuss foreign dignitaries residing in Judaea, and then the domestic staff who served in the royal court. See Rocca, *Herod's Judaea*, 73-94. Cf. Roller, *Building Program*, 57-65. Interestingly, Rocca asserts that Ptolemy of Damascus, the brother of Nicolaus, was only a minor figure at court, more of a *philos* of Herod's son Antipas. While it is true that Ptolemy only appears in the literary sources as a defender of Antipas's interests in the succession conflict following Herod's death, Josephus is explicit that Ptolemy was an honored courtier. Thus it seems unwarranted for Rocca to minimize Ptolemy's status, especially given his familial connection to Nicolaus, one of the most powerful men in Judaea. See Rocca, *Herod's Judaea*, 87. For the appearance of Ptolemy of Damascus as a supporter of Antipas's claim to the throne see *BJ* 2.21; *AJ* 17.225. While the ethnic and religious identities of some of the courtiers discussed by Rocca and Roller are clear, for others they are less so. One in particular whose identity has been disputed is Alexas, the courtier who announced the news of Herod's death to the army and thus probably had a high-ranking position such as commander of the army. See *BJ* 1.666; *AJ* 17.193-94. His marriage to Herod's sister Salome proves his Jewish identity since the king had refused the Nabataean minister Syllaeus's earlier marriage proposal because he wanted his sister to marry a Jew (*AJ* 16.220-26). On Alexas and his descendants see Kokkinos, *Herodian Dynasty*, 185-86. Cf. Rocca, *Herod's Judaea*, 86. Another courtier whose identity is unclear is the royal treasurer (and minister of the interior) Ptolemy. While Roller asserts that his name implies an Alexandrian and non-Jewish origin, Rocca disagrees, arguing for a Judaean and Jewish background. As Rocca suggests, Ptolemy had a deep knowledge of the Judaean socio-political and economic landscape and a longstanding relationship with Herod dating back to the king's days as a young courtier. Both factors support Rocca's hypothesis. While we cannot be entirely sure, I tend to agree with him. It certainly would make sense for Herod to have a Jew as one of his most trusted advisors, especially since the other, Nicolaus, was not Jewish. For Ptolemy as royal treasurer see *AJ* 16.191. For Ptolemy's receipt of large tracts of land as rewards for loyal service see *BJ* 2.69; *AJ* 17.289. For Ptolemy's active role in suppressing civil disturbances see *AJ* 16.321. Cf. *BJ* 1.280, 473, 667-69; 2.14-24; *AJ* 14.377; 16.191, 257; 17.195, 219-28. For Roller's discussion of Ptolemy see Roller, *Building Program*, 63. For Rocca's interpretation see Rocca, *Herod's Judaea*, 85. In a recent article in *Journal for the Study of Judaism*, Eyal Regev employed the theory of Access Analysis to examine the architectural outline of several of Herod's palaces throughout their various building stages. Specifically, he focused on the spatial layout of the palaces and the relative ease with which the public engaged with Herod. He concluded that Herod's court, at least until the latter part of his reign, was extremely social with relatively close interaction between the king, his courtiers, and his guests. Only after ca. 15 BCE, he

Some of these *philoi* were also leading intellectuals in the Graeco-Roman world and formed part of Herod's literary circle, a collection of scholars, thinkers, and writers whom he invited to Judaea and supported financially. The Ptolemies had set the standard for intellectual and cultural patronage; their capital, Alexandria, boasted two libraries, the Museum, an observatory, a zoo, and an anatomical institute. Other kings attempted to replicate such cultural amenities. Cities such as Antioch and Pergamum had public libraries, which aspired to rival those in Alexandria. Closer to Herod's Judaea and, indeed, extremely influential on him, was the group of intellectuals surrounding Marc Antony. This collection of scholars, poets, and philosophers included Asinius Pollio, Alexander Polyhistor, Strabo of Amaseia, Timagenes of Alexandria, and, prior to his service in Judaea, Nicolaus of Damascus, who was the tutor to the children of Antony and Cleopatra. Herod probably met many of these individuals through his relationship with Antony, and Actium provided him a perfect opportunity to poach members of this circle to create one of his own.

By 30 BCE, his hold over Judaea was secure enough that he could concentrate on other issues, such as enhancing his status vis-à-vis other neighboring monarchs and rulers. There could be no better way to highlight his Hellenism and royal credentials than to surround himself with leading intellectuals and artists. In so doing, he could mimic the royal patrons of the past and establish Judaea as a cultural and intellectual center in the Greek East.

Herod himself also participated. As the center of this literary circle he would have to engage in literary, historical, and philosophical activities. We read in Nicolaus's *Universal History* that the two men studied together frequently, with Nicolaus teaching Herod the finer points of philosophy as well as history. Indeed, it was during one of their periods of historical study that the king urged his advisor to write a history of his reign. What might have the king read? We cannot know for sure. However, his education under Nicolaus's tutelage likely would have included classical poetry such as Homer, classical history such as Thucydides, and classical philosophy such as Plato. An interest and knowledge of Jewish authors, as well as authors who wrote about Jews, would have been useful as well. All this education would have enabled him to participate fully in the intellectual life of his

---

concludes, did Herod start constructing palaces that limited access to him, although in this later period the scale of the palaces and the size of the royal court increased significantly. See Regev, "Inside Herod's Courts," 190-214.

court. Familiar with philosophy and guided by its wisdom, he would also have been able to depict himself to his courtiers and neighboring rulers as a wise and educated king.[33]

Herod not only spoke the part of a Hellenistic monarch, he also dressed it through both the style of clothing he wore and the symbols of royalty he used. The accoutrements his corpse was dressed in were standard for kings from the time of the Diadochs onward. Moreover, as befit his status as a ruler straddling multiple cultures, the purple robe also had a particular Jewish context and meaning, which started as early as the reign of Jonathan Maccabee and the Seleucid civil war between Alexander Balas and Demetrius I Soter (152-150 BCE). During this war, the two rivals each attempted to secure the friendship and support of Jonathan and the Hasmoneans by promising him power and other incentives. Alexander Balas offered to appoint him high priest and enroll him among his *philoi*. Additionally, he sent Jonathan a purple robe and a golden crown as symbols of his new status. Given the Hasmoneans' enthusiastic assimilation of the royal metaphors and visual vocabulary of their neighbors, it is unsurprising that both the robe and the crown became standard elements of their official costume. On his accession, Herod too continued the use of these accessories, probably both out of a familiarity with the visual vocabulary of Hellenistic monarchy and out of a desire to perpetuate Hasmonean royal custom, thus showing that little had changed from the Hasmoneans' reign to his.

Of the two items, the diadem seems to have been the more evocative

---

33. For a discussion of the libraries created by Hellenistic monarchs for their respective capitals see Walbank, "Monarchies," 73. Cf. Eric Turner, "Ptolemaic Egypt," in *CAH* 7:170-72. For a discussion of the intellectual circle surrounding Marc Antony see Roller, *Building Program*, 19-28. Although much later than Herod's reign, Pliny the Elder remarked that Jerusalem was "by far the most famous city of the East" (*HN* 5.70). Even if this statement is something of an exaggeration, it testifies to the expanded status of Judaea and Jerusalem during the first century CE. Herod's importing of intellectuals and artists contributed significantly to that enhanced reputation; without his patronage of the arts, Jerusalem would not have become the city so famous to Pliny. For Herod's urging Nicolaus to write a history of his reign see *FGrH* 90 fragment 135. For a discussion of the possible books in Herod's library see Ben Zion Wacholder, *Nicolaus of Damascus* (Berkeley: University of California Press, 1962), 81-86. Among the works in the library, according to Wacholder, were those of Eupolemos, a Hellenized Jewish author, and Alexander Polyhistor, a member of Antony's intellectual circle who wrote about the Jews. The works of Polybius may also have been in his library. For a detailed discussion of Herod's literary circle see Rocca, *Herod's Judaea*, 91-94. Cf. Roller, *Building Program*, 57-65.

since it appears as a prominent image on several Herodian coin issues. By the first century BCE and certainly earlier, it had become an easily recognizable symbol of royalty. It was usually a headband of white or purple and white, ending in a knot with two loose strips flowing behind. A king would wear it either on the head or over a helmet as a symbol of his authority and power. Evidence for Herod's use of it during his lifetime comes from the account of his meeting with Octavian at Rhodes. As a symbol of his obeisance to the victorious triumvir, he removed his diadem and clothed himself as a commoner. In the narrative, the overt symbol of his "commoner" appearance is the absence of his diadem. By removing it prior to this encounter, he demoted himself to his former station and symbolically enabled Octavian to reappoint him as king.

As we have discussed above, the diadem also appears quite prominently on the obverse of several of Herod's undated coins and refers specifically to his reconfirmation at Rhodes in 30 BCE. On coins minted just after his reconfirmation, it would have been an ideal and timely symbol. Circulating among the populace and in the court and tapping into their visual vocabulary, these coin types would remind them of their king's authority and control over the kingdom. They also offer us a window onto Herod's own conception of his identity as monarch. Choosing to use an image from Hellenistic royal iconography as opposed to one from another cultural context strongly suggests that he saw himself primarily as a *basileus,* as opposed to a *melech,* a king who was Jewish, but a Hellenized one like his immediate predecessors the Hasmoneans.[34]

---

34. For Alexander Balas's gifts to Jonathan Maccabee in order to secure his loyalty see 1 Macc 10:1-21, 62, esp. 10:20-21. Cf. *AJ* 13.35-57, esp. 45. For Simon Maccabee's use of purple as a sign of his high priesthood and hegemony over Judaea see 1 Macc 14:42. For a discussion of the Hellenistic diadem see Walbank, "Monarchies," 67. Cf. Polybius 30.2.4. For Herod's meeting with Octavian at Rhodes, where he removed his diadem before petitioning for clemency see *BJ* 1.387; *AJ* 15.187. Cf. *BJ* 1.390, where Herod explicitly connects his diadem with his royal status. For the appearance of the diadem on Herod's coins see Meshorer, *TJC*, 221-22, numbers 48-54 (plates 44-45). Cf. David Hendin, *Guide to Biblical Coins* (4th ed.; New York: Amphora: 2001), 490-94. There are actually small variations among this larger series. On the obverse some (*TJC* 48-50) have an open diadem and the others (51-54) have a closed diadem. Other stylistic variations include the use of an "x" (*TJC* 48) or a "+" (*TJC* 49-52), or neither (*TJC* 53-54). Variation also appears on the reverse: some have a flat bowl on top of the table and two bent palm branches flanking the table (*TJC* 48-49); others lack the palm branches (*TJC* 50-51); coins of another group lack the bowl (*TJC* 52-54). These variations in coin types are likely the result of individual variation of the obverse and reverse dies, and the images are close enough that we can group them as one larger series. See pp.

Herod the Hellenistic King in an Augustan World

Even allowing for local variation and adaptation, it seems quite clear that the Herodian royal court in Judaea was established along the lines of a Hellenistic monarchy, complete with all its internal organization and ceremonial and courtly rituals. Obviously the various monarchies around the Greek East were not monolithic. However, certain norms and characteristics were common among them, and Herod enthusiastically adopted these norms and customs for his own use. Such a choice is not surprising, considering that his predecessors acted similarly. The system established by the Hasmoneans would have been intimately familiar to Herod, since he had grown to adulthood entirely within it. By continuing these traditions, behaviors, and organization of the previous dynasty, he could project an image of continuity to his internal audiences, an image which was especially important to him in the early years of his reign. To the external world of his neighboring dynasts, Herod would appear a typical Hellenistic king, a monarch whom they could recognize and engage with as their equal. To Rome, such a kingdom was instantly recognizable as a suitable candidate for client kingship and status as a *rex sociusque et amicus,* an accomplishment Herod strongly desired and required if he were to retain his hold on power. Thus, the structure of his court was fundamental to his ability to engage with his elites, interact with his neighbors, and cooperate with Rome.

Herod and Hellenistic Piety

The ideal Hellenistic monarch needed to be generous not only to humans but also (and especially) to the gods who controlled his fate. In particular, he needed to construct temples in their honor and ensure that the proper religious practices were occurring. Otherwise, the gods would not bless the kingdom with fortune and success. Theoretically, for a Hellenized *Jewish* king, this obligation would have been slightly different: his duty was to God alone and no other gods. Indeed, he would be in violation of his obligation if he did patronize other deities. In practice, however, Herod reigned over a multiethnic kingdom including both Jews and non-Jews. Furthermore, he lived in a multicultural Roman Empire that encouraged assimilation and interaction among cultures. Unlike the Hasmoneans,

---

157-60 above for a summary of the various theories about the meaning of the cross and diadem on these coins. For Herod's mimicry of Hasmonean monarchy see p. 71 above. For his minting of the diadem-table series see pp. 165-70 above.

whose overwhelmingly Jewish power base enabled them to ignore the religious concerns of non-Jewish inhabitants of their realm, Herod's territory included several significant non-Jewish communities. In addition, his court included a number of powerful non-Jews, including Nicolaus of Damascus and his brother Ptolemy. Given the demographic composition of both his kingdom and his court, Herod was obliged to pay attention to Greek cultic sites in addition to the Temple in Jerusalem. Nevertheless, he had to be careful and avoid offending the religious sensibilities of his Jewish subjects. To this end, he avoided patronizing non-Jewish cultic sites within the Jewish regions of his kingdom, reserving his patronage to those areas in which few, if any, Jews resided.

This balancing act is most clearly demonstrated in his choice of locations for his three temples to Augustus and Roma — Sebaste, Panias, and Caesarea Maritima. All three stood in areas that, at least initially, had few, if any, Jewish residents. Sebaste, located in the heart of the region of Samaria, had been predominantly Samaritan before John Hyrcanus I destroyed it around 108 BCE. Besides Samaritans, though, there was also a significant non-Jewish population, some of whom had moved into the region during the Assyrian period. During the reign of Alexander the Great, a group of Macedonians emigrated and settled there. Following Herod's decision to rebuild the city, he populated it with non-Jewish veterans and Hellenized Samaritans, although a few Jews may have settled there as well. Still, the city was predominantly non-Jewish, and its numerous shrines to various pagan deities attest to the mostly non-Jewish character of the city. Panias was located in an entirely non-Jewish part of the kingdom; resultantly, building an *Augusteum* or patronizing the local Pan cult presented no problems. The coastal region, of which Caesarea (formerly Strato's Tower) was a part, was also predominantly non-Jewish, although in this case it was mostly Hellenized Phoenician as opposed to Samaritan. However, there was a significant Jewish population in Caesarea, which would have resented the patronage of a pagan shrine. Herod's solution to this demographic reality was to make the city a Greek *polis* but permit the Jewish community to organize itself as an autonomous political and legal body subject to his sovereignty alone.[35]

35. For the destruction of Samaria by John Hyrcanus I see *BJ* 1.64-65; *AJ* 13.275-81. For the settlement of Samaritans and Macedonians in the region of Samaria see Eusebius, *Chronicon* 123; Q. C. 4.8.9-11. Cf. Kokkinos, *Herodian Dynasty*, 69. For Herod's rebuilding of the city of Samaria and his settlement of non-Jewish veterans there see *AJ* 15.296. For a discussion of the identity of these settlers and the thoroughly Hellenized non-Jewish char-

Herod the Hellenistic King in an Augustan World

All these maneuvers reflect a careful political triangulation and suggest that Josephus was somewhat accurate when he distinguished between "Jewish territory" and "foreign territory" in terms of the king's ability to patronize non-Jewish cults and temples. The rule was simple: in non-Jewish areas, he had free rein to play the part of the pious Hellenistic king, respecting local gods and patronizing their cults. In Jewish territory, however, he had to either avoid such actions altogether or at least obscure them. Examples of this political calculus include all his religious benefactions to cities of the Greek East. Among these are his building of temples in Tyre and Berytus, his rebuilding of the temple of Pythian Apollo at Rhodes, and his endowment of the Olympic games. In addition, and closer to home, Herod was a patron of the temple to Baʻal Shamim at Siʻa near Canatha. Epigraphic evidence suggests that the temple was constructed between 33/32 and 2/1 BCE. In 1860 excavators found a statue base in the remains of the temple's porch. This statue base, which originally had stood in a prominent place to the right of the main door, contained an inscription that read, "To King Herod, Lord, I, Ovaisatos, son of Saudos, placed this statue at my own expense." It suggests the king had been a patron of the temple in some capacity. We know that he had been active in the region during his Arab campaign of 32-31 BCE and that he received Auranitis from Augustus in 23 BCE. The inscription probably dates to after he took control of the region, since his early activity in the area consisted of suffering defeat at the hands of the Nabataeans. W. H. Waddington argued that Ovaisatos son of Saudos was one of the three thousand Idumaean military veterans who settled in Trachonitis

---

acter of the city see Kasher, *Hellenistic Cities*, 199-203. Also see Mark A. Chancey, *The Myth of a Gentile Galilee* (Cambridge: Cambridge University Press, 2002), 153-55. For a general overview of Panias see John Francis Wilson, *Caesarea Philippi: Banias, the Lost City of Pan* (New York: Tauris, 2004), 9-17; John F. Wilson and Vasilios Tzaferis, "An Herodian Capital in the North: Caesarea Philippi (Panias)," in Kokkinos, *World of the Herods*, 131-43. Cf. Chancey, *Myth of a Gentile Galilee*, 123-25. Herod's son Philip received this territory as his tetrarchy in 4 BCE. During his reign he struck numerous coins with the heads of Augustus, Tiberius, Livia, and even himself on them. Had Jews made up a significant percentage of his subjects, it is unlikely he would have used such images, especially since his brothers, Archelaus and Antipas, whose territories were predominantly Jewish, avoided figurative imagery. See Meshorer, *TJC*, 78-90, 224-30, numbers 67-111 (plates 47-51). For a discussion of the demographic problems of Caesarea Maritima see Kasher, *Hellenistic Cities*, 202-4; Chancey, *Myth of a Gentile Galilee*, 143-48. For Josephus's division of Herod's realm into "Jewish" and "foreign" territory and his discussion of Herod's balancing act between the two segments of the population see *AJ* 15.328-30.

and policed the region. If so, it would mean that the donation to the Baʻal Shamim temple did not occur until about 9 BCE.

For our purposes, it is enough that the inscription dates to the latter part of Herod's reign. In this period, with his legitimacy established and his control over his kingdom secure, he could begin to concern himself with his presentation as a Hellenistic monarch and successor to Alexander and the Diadochs. Patronizing local cults and showing piety to the various gods worshiped by his subjects was a central obligation of such a king, and here in Auranitis, where few Jews lived, he could freely display his piety toward other deities besides God.

If Waddington is correct about his dating of the inscription, it could add an additional dimension to the donation. As we know, during the last decade of Herod's reign, Trachonitis and the nearby regions such as Auranitis were somewhat unstable due to rural banditry and rebellion. By patronizing the important cultic center at Siʻa, especially a temple dedicated to a god who had ties to both the indigenous population and the newly settled Idumaeans patrolling the territory, Herod could enhance his standing within the region and perhaps lessen the instability plaguing it. In other words, this benefaction to the Baʻal Shamim temple could have been meant, not only to display Herod's piety, a necessary and respected royal virtue, but also to earn the gratitude and goodwill of the inhabitants of the region, an astute political gesture with limited downside.[36]

---

36. For Herod's activity near Siʻa during his Arab campaign see *BJ* 1.366-68; *AJ* 15.112-20. For Herod's acquisition of Auranitis from Augustus see *BJ* 1.398; *AJ* 15.343. Baʻal Shamim was a principal god of Canaan, Nabataea, and Palmyra and also had Edomite and Israelite connections. Siʻa, which was in Auranitis, was an important cult center with temples dedicated to Baʻal Shamim and Seia (the local personification of Tyche). For a discussion of the temple and the statue base identifying Herod as a patron see Richardson, *Herod*, 184, 206-7; "Origins, Innovations and Significance of Herod's Temple," in *Building Jewish in the Roman East* (Waco: Baylor University Press, 2004), 279. Some scholars have argued that the temple dedicated to Seia was actually dedicated to Dushara, a Nabataean deity. For a refutation of this theory see Jane Taylor, *Petra and the Lost Kingdom of the Nabataeans* (Cambridge: Harvard University Press, 2002), 134-35. Cf. J. Dentzer, "A Propos du Temple Dit de 'Dusares' à Si," *Syria* 56 (1979): 325-32. For the inscription, which in Greek reads *Basilei Hērōdei kuriō Obaisatos Saudou ethēka ton andrianta tais emais dapanais*, see *OGIS* 415. Cf. *IGR* 3:1243. For Herod's settlement of 3,000 Idumaeans in Trachonitis because of the instability in that region and nearby Auranitis see *AJ* 16.283-85, 292; 17.23, 26. Cf. Israel Shatzman, *The Armies of the Hasmoneans and Herod* (Tübingen: Mohr, 1991), 170-80. See also pp. 142-43 above.

Conclusion: Herod the Hellenistic King

The Hellenistic world was a multiethnic and diverse one encompassing several kingdoms and cultural communities. Nevertheless, there was a high degree of cultural conformity resulting in shared norms and ideals. Within this environment, a generally accepted set of duties and obligations existed for kings and other political leaders. Far from being removed and at odds with this system, elite Judaea had enthusiastically embraced it by at least the second century BCE. Because of this acceptance, any king who wished to rule with a significant degree of consent and, as a result, stability needed to fulfill these duties and obligations, or at least fulfill enough of them to satisfy his courtiers and those with political agency. Moreover, by the end of the first century BCE the Greek East had come under the influence of Rome and existed within the larger Roman Empire. Kings living within this sphere needed to cooperate and coexist, despite personal rivalries and feuds. The ability to recognize another monarch and his style of rule was essential to such coexistence and cooperation.

Herod understood this political reality implicitly. Throughout his reign, he used multiple media to depict himself as a typical Hellenistic monarch. In his official presentation, he was the benevolent and generous patron, who supported both his own subjects and neighboring communities. Through this *euergetism,* he created and strengthened his relationships with those he benefited. He also solidified his reciprocal patron-client network and increased his reputation, glory, and status around the Mediterranean. Finally, his patronage stimulated trade and commercial business between Judaea and other communities around the eastern Mediterranean, enriching both him and his subjects. In another aspect of Hellenistic royal ideology, he presented himself as the wealthy and powerful builder who constructed massive edifices and thriving cities in honor of himself, his family, and his patrons Augustus and Agrippa. His building program highlighted his wealth, power, and organizational abilities, as he physically dotted the landscape with reminders of his presence and royal prerogative. Finally, he was the pious and dutiful king, who worshiped and respected the deities in the non-Jewish regions of his kingdom but honored and revered only God in the Jewish parts of his realm. All these parts combined to create one single image: Herod the glorious and ideal Hellenistic king, reigning over his realm with divine sanction. It was this fulfillment of cultural expectations that enabled Herod to satisfy his Hellenized audience and acquire their support for his regime. This was a king to whom neighboring monarchs could relate and to whom Hellenized courtiers could submit and be loyal.

Interestingly, Herod never really emphasized his martial prowess, despite the importance of this virtue and the notion of "spear-won territory" to earlier Hellenistic monarchs. While he clearly celebrated the anniversary of his ascension to the throne and thus his military victory over Antigonus, the victory itself does not seem to have been a centerpiece of his self-presentation. Perhaps this reticence stems from his status as a client king in a world where military conflict between allied kings was at odds with Roman foreign policy. Indeed, the only real military campaign in which he engaged during the latter part of his reign was against neighboring Nabataea. Besides achieving a very mixed result in that campaign, Herod suffered severe political repercussions, particularly in his relationship with Augustus, who did not approve of open warfare among his clients. It is no surprise, then, that military might would not have been a central tenet of Herodian self-presentation. Peace and prosperity were more becoming virtues in this new era.[37]

In the next chapter of this study, we will be examining Herod's presentation of himself as *Melech HaYehudim* ("king of the Jews") and his relationship with his Jewish subjects. As we will see, this relationship was perhaps his most ambivalent and complicated. As we already have seen, in his early years he concentrated on depicting himself as a legitimate successor to the Hasmoneans in order to win the support of his local audience and to stabilize his control over the kingdom. However, by the middle of his reign, his authority and control were secure, and he began to think of his place within Jewish history. The next chapter will examine his activities in this area and his interaction, not only with Jews in Judaea but also with those living in the Diaspora, to whom he became a benevolent patron and

---

37. For Herod's military campaign against the Nabataeans (ca. 12-9 BCE) and the political fallout from this expedition see *AJ* 16.270-99, 335-50. Cf. Richardson, *Herod,* 279-81, 286-87. Josephus does discuss Herod's physical prowess and his martial exploits as a young man in the court of Hyrcanus II. His narrations of the reconquest of Judaea (40-37 BCE) also contain praises of Herod's military expertise. Unfortunately, Josephus (along with his primary source, Nicolaus) was just as steeped in classical rhetoric as Herod was. Thus, it is difficult, if not impossible, to distinguish between the two authors' emphasis on Herod's military excellence and his personal presentation of this excellence. Given this difficulty, it seems best not to include this evidence in our discussion of the tangible and verifiable royal self-presentation. For Josephus's panegyric on Herod's physical and military magnificence see *BJ* 1.429-30. For the praise of his skill in battle, especially in his early years as *stratēgos,* see *BJ* 1.204-5, 236-41, 250-53, 290-353; *AJ* 14.159-60, 294-300, 335-39, 394-491.

defender. By the end of his reign, this Idumaean usurper, a commoner who had married into a royal and high priestly family, had been transformed into the most visible and powerful representative of ancient Jewry; he had become a ruler able to advocate successfully for Jews and Jewish interests around the Mediterranean, a position unrealized by any other ancient Jew after him.

CHAPTER 10

Herod, Melekh HaYehudim

Herod's most complex relationship was with his Jewish subjects. Throughout his reign, but especially in the early years, he was always acutely aware of his dubious claim to the throne of Judaea and his potentially problematic Idumaean lineage. Although by the outbreak of the Jewish Revolt in 66 CE the Idumaeans had become accepted members of the Judaean *ethnospoliteia,* in the first century BCE their membership was much more recent. While some considered them authentic Jews, others saw them as recent converts, who were not full members of the community. Further, Herod's lack of priestly standing and his status as a usurper of the Hasmonean dynasty made his claim to legitimacy even more tenuous. Thus, he spent the early part of his reign establishing his domestic credentials. By the middle of his reign, however, he had secured his throne and the goodwill of many, if not all, of his subjects. It was during this period of his reign (ca. 27-10 BCE) that he concentrated most on exalting himself to his domestic audience as a Jewish king in his own right. To this effect, he connected himself with the Jewish heroes of the biblical past in an attempt to appropriate their legitimacy and magnificence. He also promoted himself as a pious and glorious Jewish king who protected his people and served God by building shrines in God's honor. The culmination of this pious building program was the rebuilding and renovation of the Temple, a topic that we will discuss in the next chapter.

The Jewish Diaspora also was a target of his political self-presentation, and in his attempts to elicit its support he was perhaps more successful. Substantial Jewish populations lived all over the Mediterranean, and especially in areas of major commercial activity such as Delos, Ephesus, Rhodes, Tyre, and Sidon. Indeed, as we have seen in the previous chapter,

Herod, Melekh HaYehudim

he seems to have been extremely active precisely in the cities where large Diaspora communities resided. As we will see, his presence in the Diaspora extended beyond civic benefactions for the cities in which Jews resided. Indeed, Herod actively promoted these Diaspora communities and offered himself as a reliable and effective patron. In turn, these communities supported his kingdom by making pilgrimages to Jerusalem as well as paying the half-shekel tax to the Temple, an institution over which he exercised significant control. By the end of his reign, he had managed to bind the Diaspora and Judaean communities more tightly together, creating a larger and more connected Jewish *ethnos,* which extended throughout the Mediterranean and had him as its primary patron and spokesperson. In effect, he transformed from being king only of Judaea to being king of the Jews.

Herod, David, and Solomon

Association with the Hasmoneans had brought Herod relative peace and security, but he desired more. Specifically, he wanted a glorious reputation among the Jews to rival the status that he enjoyed among the Greeks. This standing required him to make a conscious effort to insert himself into Jewish history as a rightful and legitimate successor to the heroes of the Jewish past. It is during this latter part of his reign, when basic security needs had been satisfied, that he attempted to link himself with the Jewish paradigms of royal leadership, David and Solomon. He hoped that a close association with them would enable him to surpass his predecessors the Hasmoneans, who had not claimed connection with such biblical heroes, and that such an association would enshrine him in posterity as the most magnificent Jewish king of the post-biblical world.

For Jews, the term *Melekh HaYehudim* ("king of the Jews") was connected with the glorious past of the Davidic monarchy and the First Temple period. We have already seen how the Hasmoneans attempted to connect themselves with this glorious past through their coinage. Herod also tried to appropriate that past and place himself as its successor. He could already claim to have a kingdom that rivaled David's, as described in 2 Samuel. However, he must have decided he needed a more tangible and visible link. Accordingly, around 10 BCE, he constructed a memorial to David at the entrance of his tomb in Jerusalem. This edifice, reportedly built of white marble, was a costly and conspicuous monument on the Jerusalem skyline. According to Josephus, however, this building's origins were shrouded in a much baser action: tomb robbing. He asserts that the king, who was low on funds, decided to open the tomb of David and plunder it. When he opened it, in the dark of night to avoid detection and accompanied by only a few close friends, he did not find any money but did find several items of gold and other valuables, which he took away. Josephus then asserts that he would have gone deeper into the tomb and even opened the graves of David and Solomon, but suddenly a supernatural flame appeared and killed two of his bodyguards.

Josephus's story is not credible and is more likely an attempt by the historian to attack Herod and his biographer, Nicolaus, whom he accuses of covering up the true motives for this construction project. Even if David's tomb were still standing during the Herodian period, it is hard to believe that it would not have been plundered of all of its wealth during one of the many conquests of Jerusalem, beginning with Nebuchadnezzar's in 586 BCE. Secondly, a story of the plundering of David's tomb also appears during the reign of Hyrcanus I, and therefore this story of Herod's theft could possibly be a doublet. Further, the two mentions of the event seem to contradict each other. In the earlier section, *Jewish Antiquities* 7.394, Josephus says Herod opened a chamber of David's tomb and took away a large sum of money, but in *Antiquities* 16.179-82, he states that Herod found no money in the tomb. Moreover, in the earlier section, Josephus makes no editorial comment about Herod's actions. It is only when he wants to attack Nicolaus's bias and partiality that he concocts this dramatic story of divine punishment and warning. Finally, the charge of tomb robbing was a common slander of tyrants, who were thought to be greedy and prone to robbing temples and tombs.[1]

---

1. For Josephus's discussion of the monument see *AJ* 16.179-84. Cf. Samuel Rocca, *Herod's Judaea: A Mediterranean State in the Classical World* (Tübingen: Mohr, 2008), 27-28. The site of David's tomb was known to Nehemiah (Neh 3:16) and was still known during the first century CE (Acts 2:29). However, what was located at the site prior to Herod's construction is unknown. Textual evidence helps date the renovation of David's tomb to ca. 10 BCE. Josephus puts the discussion of this structure after his discussion of the completion of Caesarea Maritima (10/9 BCE) but before his narration of the palace intrigue of Antipater (10 BCE) and before Herod's war with the Nabataeans (9 BCE). Since the Nabataean minister Syllaeus was executed in 6/5 BCE (*AJ* 16.351-53), we can place the construction of the memorial between 10 and 5 BCE. See Achim Lichtenberger, *Die Baupolitik Herodes des Grossen* (Wiesbaden: Harrassowitz, 1999), 154.

Jacobson suggests that the monument might have looked similar to Herod's other monuments to Jewish heroes, such as the enclosures at Hebron and Mamre, which we will discuss below. See David M. Jacobson, "King Herod's 'Heroic' Public Image," *RB* 95 (1988):

Herod, Melekh HaYehudim

Instead, the story in Josephus probably reflects an actual historical program of renovation and reconstruction designed to physically and visually connect Herod to the glorious Jewish past. Jacobson has suggested that Herod might have built the monument as a Hellenistic *hērōon,* honoring David as the *ktistēs* of Jerusalem. According to this theory, his building was another expression of his desire to further Hellenize Judaea and to turn Jerusalem into a true Hellenistic metropolis. As Jacobson says, it was common practice for Hellenized cities to honor hero-founders and to fill the tombs of the hero-founders with treasure. This custom would explain how David's tomb managed to retain its treasures even after the destruction of the First Temple by the Babylonians. Without going into the possibility of the tomb still containing treasure — a hypothesis that seems unlikely — I think we can take Jacobson's theory and extend it slightly. In creating a *hērōon* for David, Herod is engaging with his Jewish past by using a Hellenistic cultural vocabulary. Specifically, in addition to honoring David as the *ktistēs* of Jerusalem, Herod also connects himself visually with his predecessor and sets himself up as the new model of Jewish kingship. In the Hellenistic world, kings who significantly rebuilt and refounded old cities were able to declare themselves the new *ktistoi* of the cities. While it is unlikely that he could have accomplished such a feat because of his subjects' sensibilities, he could adorn the sepulchre with costly decoration and thus suggest visually that he was a pious king and a worthy successor to the Davidic monarchy.[2]

---

399. For John Hyrcanus I's alleged robbery of David's tomb to bribe Antiochus VII Sidetes see *BJ* 1.61; *AJ* 13.249. For literary analyses of the tomb-robbing incident and its aftermath see Tamar Landau, "The Image of Herod in Josephus' *Bellum Judaicum,*" in *Josephus and Jewish History in Flavian Rome and Beyond,* ed. Joseph Sievers and Gaia Lembi (Leiden: Brill, 2005), 173-75. Lichtenberger, *Baupolitik,* 155, states that the story describes a prompt punishment for the grave robbers (death for two bodyguards) and, because of its placement before Antipater's palace intrigues, suggests that Herod's family problems were a result of his impiety. Such narrative traits, Lichtenberger argues, are typical traits of Jewish folklore and thus cast further doubt on the story's historicity.

2. For the filling of heroic tombs with treasure see Strabo, *Geog.* 17.1.8, where he recounts how one of the later Ptolemies, probably Ptolemy X Alexander I, stole the gold sarcophagus of Alexander the Great from his mausoleum in Alexandra. See Jacobson, "Herod's Heroic Public Image," 397-99, for his theory about Herod's renovation and expansion of David's tomb. Lichtenberger, *Baupolitik,* 155, argues that Jacobson's theory is a little farfetched. In his view, it is more likely that Herod's building was part of a larger contemporary trend in Jerusalem of decorating graves with Hellenistic motifs. In this case, Lichtenberger suggests, a motif in private representation was fastened onto a public building. He may be right to connect this decoration of David's tomb with the larger trend in funerary architecture. Nevertheless, I think he ignores the political and propagandistic possibilities offered by

Association with David was not enough for Herod. He also desired to be connected with David's son and successor Solomon, who in many ways was an even better model. Hellenized Jewish authors especially saw Solomon as the king who ruled over a golden age, the pinnacle of Jewish history. For them, he represented the Jewish equivalent of the ideal Hellenistic king: an absolute monarch who presided over a wealthy and magnificent court, a just, learned, and wise king, perhaps the wisest of his age, who ushered in an era of peace and prosperity, which enabled him to construct a magnificent temple to his god. Certainly Solomon had his problems. In particular, his numerous wives and concubines, along with his willingness to accept foreign cults in Jerusalem, had given him a reputation for decadence and corruption. However, in striving to emulate him, Herod could be seen as correcting his mistakes and thereby surpassing him in greatness. Simultaneously, Herod's conscious modeling could enable him to appeal to the Diaspora and its expectations of Jewish monarchy. He could also tap into the cultural expectations of Judaeans, who also revered Solomon as a glorious king from their past. Finally, he could model himself after a monarch who was recognized as an absolute ruler, a trait Herod would certainly have appreciated.

Perhaps the greatest evidence for Herod's desire to be the new Solomon was the rebuilding of the Temple. Indeed, this project would have enabled him to surpass the biblical king by expanding the size and grandeur of the Temple Mount, making it more lavish and beautiful than ever before. We can see this desire in Herod's speech to the Judaean populace before commencement of his grand project, which is recorded in Josephus. In this speech, the king explicitly compares himself to Solomon and asserts that his primary goal in his endeavor is to rectify the failure of the exiles from Babylon, namely their inability to rebuild a sacred precinct equal to and worthy of Solomon's. By fixing this inferior building, he will even surpass the glory and grandeur of the first one. He continues by emphasizing that the completion of this task will be the most notable of his accomplishments and the one that will earn him eternal fame. It will also be a tremendous and conspicuous act of piety. As a sign of his dedication to the project, Herod advertises that he will fund the entire enterprise, a decision that only further highlights his glory as king.[3]

---

the construction of a monument to Jerusalem's most famous king as well as Herod's frequent use of public building of all types to articulate political messages and motifs.

3. It is likely Josephus modified or even composed the speech in its entirety based

Herod, Melekh HaYehudim

In the end, the rebuilding was a major success. Since work on the Temple was never fully completed until 64 CE, it provided lifetime employment for tens of thousands of workers and their descendants. Therefore Herod could claim responsibility for a new "golden age" of economic prosperity. Indeed, in his speech before the rebuilding, Herod emphasized the prosperity and wealth of the kingdom under his stewardship and the piety of his project. Additionally, the project itself significantly enhanced Herod's status as a pious monarch and enabled him to emulate and even surpass Jewish biblical heroes while claiming legitimate and worthy succession to them. We cannot discount the symbolism of such a grand project at the most important and conspicuous site in his entire kingdom. No other initiative during Herod's reign accumulated more prestige and fame for him among his Jewish subjects than his work on the Temple Mount. It solidified his position as a Jewish king in his own right, elevated the status of that precinct in the Roman world, transformed it into the largest sanctuary site in the ancient world, and embellished it to such a degree that the rabbis would state, "He who has not seen the Temple of Herod has never seen a beautiful building."[4]

---

on what he thought Herod should have said, a common technique of ancient historians in the Thucydidean tradition. Nevertheless, it is still useful in revealing the king's intentions. If Josephus were echoing an authentic speech (perhaps recorded in Nicolaus's *Universal History*), then the speech gives us clear insight into Herod's motivations. If, however, Josephus created it based on what he thought was appropriate, it still is useful because it reveals that even decades after his death people still thought Herod was trying to emulate Solomon. For the advantages to a Jewish king of modeling himself after Solomon see Rocca, *Herod's Judaea*, 25-26. Cf. Monika Bernett, *Der Kaiserkult in Judäa unter den Herodiern und Römern. Untersuchungen zur politischen und religiösen Geschichte Judäas von 30 v. bis 66 n. Chr.* (Tübingen: Mohr, 2007), 163. For the Thucydidean method of historical writing see Thucydides 1.22. For Herod's speech to the Judaean people in which he explains his plans and his motives see *AJ* 15.382-87. For his desire for immortal glory and fame as the impetus for his rebuilding project see *AJ* 15.380. For an analysis of Herod's piety see Peter Richardson, "Religion and Architecture: A Study in Herod's Piety, Power, Pomp and Pleasure," *Bulletin of the Canadian Society of Biblical Studies* 45 (1985): 3-29; "Law and Piety in Herod's Architecture," *Studies in Religion* 15 (1986): 347-60. Cf. Jacobson, "Herod's Heroic Public Image," 391-93. For Josephus's claim that Herod funded the entire enterprise see *BJ* 1.401; *AJ* 15.387, 389. While it is unlikely that he paid for the whole project, he probably paid for much of it, especially since he would have wanted to monopolize credit for the rebuilding.

4. As Mark Toher suggested at the *Herod and Augustus* conference at University College in London in 2005, Herod's reconstruction of the Temple employed tens of thousands of laborers for life, and this massive public works project would have made him extremely

In light of this desire, it is interesting to examine the character of Solomon who appears in *Jewish Antiquities*. As Samuel Rocca has observed, although at first glance Josephus's Solomon looks similar to his biblical counterpart in 1 Kings, some of the modified passages might reflect a created Solomon whose narrative was inspired by Herod and his kingship. For example, Rocca notes that the Josephan Solomon sacrifices at Hebron and rebuilds Jerusalem's city walls, while such events do not appear in 1 Kings. Herod, on the other hand, constructed an enclosure at Hebron and rebuilt much of Jerusalem, including possibly the Second Wall. Further, Josephus's superlative-laden descriptions of the Solomonic Temple and the royal palace may also have been inspired by the sheer magnificence of Herod's Temple and Main Palace. It is possible that Josephus's depiction of Solomon owes its creation to Nicolaus or another court historian. In which case, Josephus's narrative, created more than eighty years after Herod died, could have been influenced by the king's propaganda without Josephus even being conscious of it.[5] In effect, Herod had achieved what he most desired: association and identification with the Davidic monarchy, particularly Solomon.

Herod and Jewish Piety

In the past most Herodian scholars accepted Josephus's assertion that Herod was more Greek than Jewish, at best ambivalent toward Judaism,

---

popular among the urban masses. I think we can go even further along this line of reason and argue that one of the practical goals of Herod's entire building program was to employ the unskilled laborers of Judaea and secure their support for his regime. Cf. Rocca, *Herod's Judaea*, 212. For Herod's emphasis on the wealth and prosperity of his kingdom and its enabling of the Temple project see *AJ* 15.384, 387. For the rabbinic view of Herod's Temple see *b. Bava Batra* 4a.

5. For Solomon's rebuilding of the city walls see *AJ* 8.21, 150. For Solomon's sacrifice at Hebron see *AJ* 8.22-25. For Herod's construction of an enclosure at Hebron see pp. 294-97 below. Although there is no consensus, many scholars attribute the construction of the "Second Wall" to Herod. See Hillel Geva, "Jerusalem," in *NEAEHL,* ed. Ephraim Stern (Jerusalem: Israel Exploration Society, 1993), 736. For Josephus's description of Solomon's Temple and palace see *AJ* 8.61-140. For Josephus's description of Herod's Temple and his palace in the Upper City see *BJ* 1.402; 5.176-81, 184-247. Cf. *AJ* 15.318, 391-402, 410-20. For Rocca's interpretation of the connections between Herod and Solomon see Samuel Rocca, "Josephus and the *Psalms of Solomon,*" in *Making History: Josephus and Historical Method,* ed. Zuleika Rodgers (Leiden: Brill 2007), 323. Cf. Rocca, *Herod's Judaea*, 28.

Herod, Melekh HaYehudim

and at worst antagonistic toward it. It is only recently that such a viewpoint has come to be seen as overly simplistic, failing to account for the diversity of religious practice and piety that was prevalent in first-century BCE Judaea. While his religious practices and sensibilities were not in alignment with those of all his subjects, and while he seems to have offended some of them with his actions, Herod did consider himself a Jew and accordingly felt himself bound by certain obligations and commandments. Moreover, as king of Judaea and as the most visible representative of his religion around the Roman world, he actively attempted to live a "Jewish" life within and in harmony with the larger Graeco-Roman world. In this regard, he seems to have been no different from many of his contemporaries who were attempting a similar sort of accommodation. It is worth investigating, therefore, how Herod's piety played a role in his success as king. Did he appear, at least to some of his Jewish subjects, as a pious and religious sovereign? Did his actions really garner as much criticism and anger as Josephus would have us believe? As we shall see, his public religiosity was as much a part of his self-presentation to his Jewish audience as it was to his Hellenistic and Roman audiences. He was not a Hellenized monarch who simply happened to be born a Jew. Instead, he was a fully Hellenistic, Romanized Jewish king, the first of a new breed of Jewish rulers who felt at home in each of these worlds.[6]

6. For Josephus's assessment of Herod's essential philhellenism see *AJ* 19.329. For his criticism of Herod for departing from "the ancestral customs" *(tōn patriōn ethōn)* and corrupting them through his cultivation of "foreign practices" *(xenikois epitēdeumasin)*, see *AJ* 15.267. Cf. *AJ* 15.328, where Josephus again accuses Herod of ignoring Jewish customs and changing its laws. For scholars who see Herod's attitude toward Judaism as ambivalent and his Judaism as superficial see Emil Schürer, *The History of the Jewish People in the Age of Jesus Christ (175 BC–AD 135)*, ed. Geza Vermes and Fergus Millar (Edinburgh: Clark, 1973-87), 1:311-14; E. Mary Smallwood, *The Jews under Roman Rule: From Pompey to Diocletian* (Leiden: Brill, 1976), 82; Jacobson, "Herod's Heroic Public Image," 392; Doron Mendels, *The Rise and Fall of Jewish Nationalism: Jewish and Christian Ethnicity in Ancient Palestine* (New York: Doubleday, 1992), 212; David M. Jacobson, "Herod the Great Shows His True Colors," *Near Eastern Archaeology* 64 (2001): 100-104; Aryeh Kasher and Eliezer Witztum, *King Herod, A Persecuted Persecutor: A Case Study in Psychohistory and Psychobiography* (Berlin: de Gruyter, 2006), 187-90, 410-17. Also see Peter Richardson, *Herod: King of the Jews and Friend of the Romans* (Columbia: University of South Carolina Press, 1996), 30-32, esp. 32, where he states that Herod encouraged "Torah disobedience." For Kokkinos's view of Herod as more of a Hellenized Phoenician than an authentic Jew see Nikos Kokkinos, *The Herodian Dynasty: Origins, Roles in Society and Eclipse* (rev. ed.; London: Spink, 2010), 86-139, 342-62. See esp. 96 n. 43, where Kokkinos asserts, "Herod practiced Judaism only in diplomacy." For the hypothesis that he was openly antagonistic toward Judaism see Gideon

Herod's coinage provides a clear indication of his personal piety. For a king as supposedly hostile to Judaism as he was, it is altogether surprising that no offensive images, and certainly no figural representations, appear on his coins aside from one dated coin that has a caduceus (staff of Hermes) on the reverse and an undated coin that has an eagle on the reverse. It is altogether even more noteworthy when we consider that his son Philip placed the heads of Augustus, Livia, and Tiberius as well as his own image on his coins. Herod's grandson Agrippa I (who was even king of Judaea) also put his own image, as well as that of his son Agrippa II and his wife Cypros, on his coins. Even the caduceus and eagle symbols may not be as offensive as they initially might appear. As for the caduceus, although it certainly had a pagan connotation and connection with a pagan god, it could just as easily have functioned as a symbol of trade or prosperity, particularly given its appearance on an economic instrument such as a coin. The eagle as well may not be as offensive as some believe, especially when one considers that the Tyrian shekel, the only coin accepted as legal tender in the Temple itself, had the head of Herakles-Melqart on the obverse and an eagle on the reverse. Indeed, the reverse image of a seated eagle looks very similar to the eagle on Herod's coin. If Jews paying the temple tax and purchasing sacrificial animals with a coin that had *two* figural images on it did not complain, then it is reasonable to assume that they would not have found a Herodian coin with an eagle any more offensive.[7]

Fuks, "Josephus on Herod's Attitude towards Jewish Religion: The Darker Side," *JJS* 53 (2002): 238-45. For a more positive view of his Jewishness see Eyal Regev, "Herod's Jewish Ideology Facing Romanization: On Intermarriage, Ritual Baths, and Speeches," *JQR* 100 (2010): 197-222. For an in-depth analysis of the wide range of Jewish reactions to the Graeco-Roman world, which ranged from rejection to full assimilation, see John M. G. Barclay, *Jews in the Mediterranean Diaspora: From Alexander to Trajan (323 BCE–117 CE)* (Berkeley: University of California Press, 1999).

7. For an overview of Herodian coinage see Meshorer, *TJC*, 221-24. For a discussion of the coin with a winged caduceus on the reverse see *TJC*, 64 (coin 46, plate 44). For an overview of the eagle coin see *TJC*, 67-69, 224 (coin 66, plate 46); David Hendin, *Guide to Biblical Coins* (4th ed.; New York: Amphora, 2001), 168 (H501, plate 9). For a general discussion of Tyrian shekels including their importance to the Temple cult see *TJC*, 72-74. For the lack of controversy surrounding eagles on Jewish coins see Donald T. Ariel and Jean-Philippe Fontanille, *The Coins of Herod: A Modern Analysis and Die Classification* (Leiden: Brill, 2012), 117-19. It is noteworthy that of the hundreds of Tyrian shekels and half-shekels discovered in Israel, only one (a half-shekel found at Masada) was deliberately vandalized. As a slightly later example of Jewish sensibilities, Jesus' objection to the moneychangers was not that they were using coins with images on them. Rather, it was that they were turning the Temple into a marketplace (Mark 11:15-19; Matt 21:12-13; Luke 19:45-48; John 2:13-16). For analysis of

It is also possible that the eagle on Herod's coin was associated with the eagle he placed atop a gate of the Temple Mount by at least 15 BCE, the year of Marcus Agrippa's visit to Jerusalem. Ariel and Fontanille have persuasively suggested that this coin type was minted in the middle of Herod's coin issues, following the inscription-anchor coins and immediately preceding but continuing concurrently with the anchor-double cornucopia issues. In terms of an absolute date, they propose a time frame of 20 to 15 BCE. In chapter 6 I proposed an absolute date of 17 BCE for the anchor-double cornucopia coin. If the single cornucopia-eagle coin is indeed slightly earlier, then we should assign a date of 20-18 BCE for the minting. This date seems to suggest some association with the Temple (its dedication perhaps?), which was the major construction project going on at the time, although the construction at Caesarea was also fully operational. Connections with both the Tyrian shekel and the golden eagle would fit such a chronology, but, given that both were commissioned by Herod, I think we should prefer the connection with the eagle above the Temple gate, even if, as Ariel and Fontanille suggest, the single cornucopia-eagle coin does not require a connection with the Temple's eagle.[8]

---

the inoffensive nature of a caduceus and its use as a generic symbol of trade and prosperity see Ariel and Fontanille, *Coins of Herod*, 100-101, 111. For the coinage of Herod's successors, specifically those who put figurative images on their coins, see *TJC*, 228-30 (Philip), 230-31 (Agrippa I). Philip ruled a territory that was largely devoid of Jews, and Agrippa's coins with human heads on them were struck not in Jerusalem but in Panias and Tiberias. Nevertheless, there still were Jews living in those two cities, and Tiberias was even the capital of Galilee, an extremely Jewish region. Additionally, some of both Philip's and Agrippa's coins must have made their way into Judaea and become known to the Judaean public. Herod's refusal to mint coins with portraits on them, even in areas of his kingdom with few or no Jewish inhabitants, speaks to his desire to uphold the Second Commandment.

8. For a discussion of relative and absolute chronologies for the single cornucopia-eagle coin see Donald T. Ariel, "A Numismatic Approach to the Reign of Herod the Great" (Ph.D. diss., Tel-Aviv University, 2006), 339-40, 353-57. Cf. Ariel and Fontanille, *Coins of Herod*, 159-76, 182-84. I arrived at a date of ca. 15 BCE for the erection of the golden eagle based partially on the chronology of the Temple rebuilding project. Josephus dates the beginning of this construction to either the fifteenth year of Herod's reign (*BJ* 1.401) or the eighteenth (*AJ* 15.380), which correspond to 23/22 BCE or 20/19 BCE. Josephus also states that there was a dedication ceremony a year after work had begun, "coincidently" on the same day as the anniversary of the king's accession (*AJ* 15.421-23). Since the beginning of construction seems to have occurred after Augustus's visit to Syria (20 BCE), it seems more likely that construction began in 20/19 BCE and the dedication ceremony in 18/17 BCE. For Augustus's visit see *AJ* 15.354; Dio 54.7. Fuks thinks that Herod would have wished to celebrate his restoration with the erection of a powerful symbol of his authority, and the eagle would

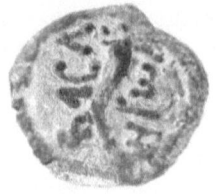 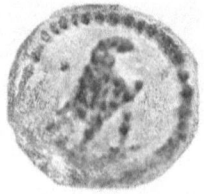

Bronze single cornucopia-eagle lepton of Herod the Great
This coin is the only one of Herod's that depicts an animal.

And yet, the bird did cause a problem, although it took more than a decade for it to develop. When in 4 BCE Herod became seriously ill, a rumor began to spread that he had died. In response, two Jewish teachers, Judah ben Sephoraeus and Mattathias ben Margalus, exhorted their students to help them cut down the eagle and destroy it. They and their students climbed up on the gate, knocked the eagle to the ground, and cut it up with axes. They were immediately caught, and ultimately Herod sentenced the teachers and their accomplices to death by burning. Now this episode might be evidence that an eagle was indeed an offensive symbol to Jews, especially since the two teachers cited its existence as a violation of the Second Commandment against graven images. However, assuming my date for the eagle is correct, it would have been perched above the Temple gate for more than ten years before this incident. In that time, tens of thousands of Jews must have walked through the gate and under the eagle without complaint and without considering the Temple defiled or polluted. Moreover, as we have suggested, the eagle had been a symbol on Tyrian shekels for years and on a coin issue of Herod's for more than a decade. Why, if the statue was such an issue for so many Jews, did it take a decade for any resistance to appear, and, when it did, why was that resistance limited in size and scope?

One might argue that the issue was not the eagle per se, but its presence within the sacred precinct. Indeed, Josephus raises this exact objection, stressing the illegality and immorality of placing a graven image within the Temple complex. However, the First Temple and possibly the Second con-

---

have served that function well. Such a motive is certainly possible, but another possibility is that he commissioned the eagle just before Agrippa visited in 15 BCE as a way of honoring his Roman patron. Josephus states that Herod engraved Agrippa's name on a Temple gate (*BJ* 1.416). It is tempting to link the two events, although such a conclusion must remain tentative without further evidence. See Richardson, *Herod*, 213, where he also argues that the eagle was erected over the gate in 15 BCE.

tained religious images within the precinct, specifically the cherubim who stood on either side of the Ark of the Covenant. Moreover, only a small group of Jews objected enough to act, and only when they believed Herod was dead. Their attack could, therefore, be seen not as a religious objection but as an attack on a symbol of Herod's regime, which they vigorously opposed.

Additionally, Jewish law *(halakah)* is not necessarily as clear as it initially seems. Exod 20:4 cites two prohibitions: "you shall not make yourself a graven image, or any likeness of anything that is in the heaven above, in the earth beneath or in the water under the earth." The first clause prohibits idolatry while the second proscribes figurative representations from the natural world. Richardson's analysis of the rabbinic material has shown that for the most part the rabbis emphasized the first prohibition but were surprisingly lenient on the second. There is even a passage in the Mishnah in which Rabban Gamaliel is seen bathing in the Bath of Aphrodite, in which there was a statue of the goddess. When confronted about the apparent illegality of his actions, Gamaliel replies, "I came not within her limits; she came within mine!" He adds, "Thus, what is treated as a god is forbidden, but what is not treated as a god is permitted." The most general prohibition on images, attributed to Rabbi Meir, is also relatively late. It says, "All images are forbidden because they are worshipped once a year." The rabbinic material seems to show a general evolution to greater and more inclusive prohibitions against the creation of images. Further, these opinions are not monolithic and represent a range of severity. Even if the rabbinic material does not represent first-century BCE attitudes, its diversity of opinion does suggest that a similar situation existed in that century. In other words, while there clearly was some objection to Herod's eagle and its location above a gate of the Temple, it seems that the majority of Jews were either not offended or not offended enough to act. What had first seemed like a major violation of *halakah* was actually at most another issue of interpretation.[9]

---

9. For Josephus's narration of the eagle incident see *BJ* 1.649-55; *AJ* 17.151-60, 167. For his objection to the eagle see *BJ* 1.650. For the existence of figurative statuary, specifically the cherubim, see Peter Richardson, "Law and Piety in Herod's Architecture," *Studies in Religion* 15 (1986): 354. Even Fuks, who is quite critical of Herod's attitude toward Judaism, acknowledges that the majority of Jews did not have a problem with the eagle. He even refers to Judah, Mattathias, and their students as "ultra-zealous Jews." See Fuks, "Herod's Attitude towards Jewish Religion," 242. For the prohibition of Rabbi Meir see *m. ʿAvodah Zarah* 3.1. For a discussion of the rabbinic material see Richardson, "Law and Piety," 351-54. For the story of Rabban Gamaliel in the Bath of Aphrodite see *m. ʿAvodah Zarah* 3.4. Cf. *m. ʿAvodah Zarah* 4.3.

Another related indication of Herod's personal piety is the almost total lack of figurative art in his private residences. Mosaics can be found in all of his palaces, but the designs are mostly geometric patterns along with a few depictions of designs prominent in Jewish art, such as olive branches, pomegranates, and fig and vine leaves. Masada provides the best examples of Herodian mosaics, and none of them contains pictorial images. Instead, they are of three types: (1) *opus sectile,* (2) black and white geometric patterns, and (3) polychrome geometric patterns. Further, while all of Herod's palaces were decorated with wall paintings, there is no indication that any of the paintings had designs that would have offended Jewish religious sensibilities. At Masada, for example, excavators have concluded that the wall paintings were executed in a variant of the Second Pompeian Style, which featured painted masonry elements meant to give the impression of drafted stonework. In other words, none of the artistic elements present in the wall paintings would have offended traditional Jews. Herod's villas were the most modern, most imaginative, and most Roman of his buildings. In addition, they were also private residences, which few outside his court and his honored guests would ever have visited. While we might perhaps expect him to respect his subjects' religious sensibilities in public buildings, if he really were such a radical Hellenist with no religious scruples, it is surprising that he did not choose to decorate his palaces with the latest sculpture or figurative wall paintings and mosaics. The fact that few such images have been found suggests that Herod demonstrated a real adherence to the Second Commandment's prohibition on figural representations.[10]

---

10. For a discussion of the three types of mosaics found at Masada see *Masada: The Yigael Yadin Excavations 1963-1965, Final Reports,* ed. Joseph Aviram, Gideon Foerster, and Ehud Netzer (Jerusalem: Israel Exploration Society, 1989-95), 5:140-61. For the mosaics at Cypros see Ehud Netzer, *Hasmonean and Herodian Palaces at Jericho: Final Reports of the 1973-1987 Excavations* (Jerusalem: Israel Exploration Society, 2001-08), 2:255-56. For an analysis of the wall paintings at Masada see Foerster in *Masada* 5:13-27. Cf. Silvia Rozenberg, "The Wall Paintings of the Herodian Palace at Jericho," in *Judaea and the Greco-Roman World in the Time of Herod in the Light of Archaeological Evidence,* ed. Klaus Fittschen and Gideon Foerster (Göttingen: Vandenhoeck and Ruprecht, 1996), 121-38. For Richardson's analysis of Herod's piety with regard to figural images see Richardson, "Law and Piety," 349-50. In his *Vita* Josephus recalls that as a general in the Great Jewish Revolt, he urged the destruction of one of Herod Antipas's palaces in Galilee because it contained pictures of animals. If Herod the Great's palaces had contained similar decorations, one would think that Josephus would have mentioned them. While it is true that some of his palaces were burned after his death, it is probably not because they contained offensive decorations. See *Vita* 65.

Herod, Melekh HaYehudim

It is in his palaces and private residences that we see another example of his adherence to Jewish law and custom, namely his concern for and participation in ritual bathing. As we have already discussed, Herod built elaborate bathing facilities in all his villas, palaces, and fortresses. These facilities were of the latest designs and followed Roman traditions of bathing. But they seem also to have been constructed with attention to Jewish ritual bathing. Archaeologists have uncovered a total of forty-one possible ritual baths, or *mikva'ot* in Herodian palaces and the buildings related to them. Of those, eighteen were directly connected to the palaces themselves. These figures suggest a strong concern for maintaining ritual purity at both court and in private life. Of particular interest in this subgroup are the thirteen that functioned as *frigidaria* in a Roman-style bathing complex. Were these actually *mikva'ot* or simply *frigidaria* plunge pools? Structural characteristics, such as the great depth of the Herodian pools and their relatively large size, equate these pools more closely with other ritual baths than with traditional Roman *frigidaria* pools. These close connections to *mikva'ot*, as well as the positive identifications of archaeologists such as Ronny Reich, Gideon Foerster, and Ehud Netzer, suggest that many of the eighteen *frigidaria* pools also functioned as ritual baths.

The implications of this conclusion are significant. In the first place, as Regev suggests, the Josephan portrait of a king more Greek than Jewish seems to fly in the face of this evidence. If Josephus's portrait were really accurate, one would not expect Herod and his court to have paid so much attention to Jewish ritual purity, especially in their private residences, where few non-courtly individuals would ever have stepped foot. Moreover, this concern for ritual purity outside the Temple occurred at a time when such preoccupations were more popular, but by no means the norm. Thus, Herod was not simply following popular practice, hoping to obscure his own private Greekness. Instead, he was actively asserting a particular and positive Jewish identity, one that was not even the norm. Secondly, his combination of Roman and Jewish bathing customs does not seem to have been simply a matter of convenience. Rather, it reflects a desire to merge the two bathing cultures together and create a hybrid acceptable and valid according to both Roman cultural norms and *halakah*. In other words, Roman bathing could be Jewish, and Jews could be Roman even while bathing.[11]

11. For Regev's analysis as well as a catalogue of the Herodian *mikva'ot*, see Eyal Re-

Marriage was another area in which Herod seems to have asserted an active and well-defined Jewish piety, which continued into the next generations of his family. Of his ten known wives, five were unambiguously Jewish. Although some or all of the others were not Jewish by birth, it is more likely that they adopted the religious customs of their husband than vice-versa. On the other hand, while Herod was alive, there are no documented cases of Herodian women marrying non-Jewish men. Indeed, when his sister Salome wished to marry the Nabataean minister Syllaeus, Herod insisted that the prospective groom undergo circumcision and conversion. When he refused, the betrothal was annulled. This pattern of Herodian men marrying non-Jewish women continued into the next generations, but the opposite generally did not occur. In total, we know of thirteen cases of marriage between Herodians and non-Jews. But of those thirteen only three involve Herodian women marrying non-Jewish men. Moreover, in two of those three cases, the men converted to Judaism. As we can see from the cases of both Syllaeus the Nabataean and Epiphanes, the son of Antiochus IV of Commagene, who was betrothed to Agrippa I's daughter Drusilla, refusal to undergo such a procedure disqualified one from marriage to a Herodian princess. The evidence suggests, then, that Herodian Jewish identity was patrilineal and not matrilineal, a principle at odds with rabbinic Judaism, but the norm from biblical times until the first century CE. Herod and his family seem to have resisted the urge and advantage of marrying their daughters off to non-Jewish husbands as a way of enhancing the family's status and cementing political alliances. It would seem that Jewish identity, at least the ethnic component of it, was of paramount importance. It may also be that the Herodians saw the potential backlash from their subjects as more costly to them than the benefits of such mixed marriages. Nevertheless, it is also just as likely that they per-

---

gev, "Herod's Jewish Ideology Facing Romanization: On Intermarriage, Ritual Baths, and Speeches," *JQR* 100 (2010): 207-12. He persuasively argues that concern for ritual purity outside the Temple reached its peak of adherence during the mid-first century CE, decades after Herod's death. It is possible that Herod was conforming to Jewish norms more as a matter of public policy than personal piety. As king of the Jews, it would have been important for him to be respectful of his subjects' religious sensibilities. However, given how few people would have ever seen the royal bathhouses, as well as the other cultural evidence we have discussed above, it seems more likely that the plethora of *mikva'ot* was a matter of personal concern, although one need not exclude all traces of political calculation. For a discussion of Herod's Jewish ideology, which saw close friendship and interaction with Rome as beneficial to Jews and Judaism, see Regev, "Herod's Jewish Ideology," 213-21.

Herod, Melekh HaYehudim

sonally felt it improper for the women of their family to marry outsiders and thus leave their people.[12]

Finally, it is worth recalling the famous quip of Augustus that he "would rather be Herod's pig than his son" (Macrobius, *Saturnalia* 2.4.1). Such a joke would only make sense if Herod actually did keep kosher and consequently did not eat pork. Support for this hypothesis comes from archaeologists, who have uncovered a significant amount of stone eating vessels at Herodian sites, such as Herodion, the Winter Palaces at Jericho, Machaerus, and Cypros. The advantage of this material, as opposed to ceramic, metal, or glass, is that it is immune to ritual impurity. While incredibly popular and plentiful at Jewish sites around Israel, they are not as plentiful at non-Jewish sites and indeed seem to be distinctively Jewish. As Regev argues, their near ubiquity at Herodian sites, specifically his private residences, suggests a strong desire on his part and that of his court to adhere to ritual purity, at least in regard to dining and *kashrut*, and thus an active Jewish identity.[13]

---

12. For a discussion of ancient Jewish views of marriage and conversion, as well as the conclusion that a non-Jewish mother would not have been an impediment to one being a full member of the Jewish community see Shaye J. D. Cohen, *The Beginnings of Jewishness* (Berkeley: University of California Press, 1999), 140-74, 239-307. Cf. Regev, "Herod's Jewish Ideology," 203-4. The lack of pre-rabbinic references to the necessity of female conversion or even to a conversion ritual strengthens this claim and suggests that marriage was enough of an acceptance of Judaism. For discussion and analysis of the Herodian paradigm of marriage see Tal Ilan, "Intermarriage in the Herodian Family as a Paradigm for Intermarriage in Second Temple Judaism" (paper presented at the Society of Biblical Literature Annual Meeting, University College London, November 23-26, 2002), 1-15; Regev, "Herod's Jewish Ideology," 202-6. Herodian acceptance of patrilineal descent is not surprising given its normative nature until the first century CE. Further, as we have seen, Herod himself was the product of a Jewish father and a non-Jewish mother. For the rejected engagements of Syllaeus the Arab and Epiphanes, son of Antiochus IV of Commagene, see *AJ* 16.225 (Syllaeus); 20.139 (Epiphanes of Commagene). For the marriage of Berenice to Polemo II of Cilicia and the two marriages of Drusilla (to Azizus of Emesa and Antonius Felix) see *AJ* 20.141-45. It is worth noting that there is a hint of scandal in the one case in which a Herodian woman married a non-Jewish man who did not convert. Josephus strongly disapproves of the behavior of Drusilla, daughter of Agrippa I, whom he accuses of transgressing the laws of her ancestors. He does not offer any such negative editorial comments in the other two cases. It is also interesting that the two women who married non-Jewish men were both daughters of Agrippa I, a man who had spent much of his life outside Judaea and at the imperial court. Culturally and chronologically both daughters were far removed from Herod's Judaea, and we should not use their behavior as an indication of his personal piety or religious sensibilities.

13. For the proliferation of stone vessels at Herodian sites see Regev, "Herod's Jewish

As we can see, the evidence suggests that in multiple ways and contexts, Herod actively chose a Jewish identity for himself and showed a willingness to embrace Jewish ritual and cultural practices, even if they did not benefit him politically. As we will see below, this desire to display an active Jewish piety extended beyond his private life and into his extremely public building program.

Piety and Abraham

As discussed previously, Herod used architecture and building to connect himself visually with the Hasmonean dynasty, with prominent men such as Augustus, and with Jewish heroes of the past such as David and Solomon. He also built edifices at both Hebron and Mamre, two sites closely linked with the patriarch Abraham. Hebron is where Abraham built a tomb for his wife Sarah in the Cave of Machpelah. Eventually it became the resting place of all the patriarchs and matriarchs except Rachel, who was buried near Bethlehem. Mamre was where Abraham pitched his tent, dug a well, built an altar, and learned of the birth of his son Isaac. Herod's aim was apparently to appropriate some of the popularity and legitimacy of Abraham, the patriarch of both Judaeans and Idumaeans, through veneration of his memory.

Both the enclosure at Hebron, which is built on the supposed site of the Cave of Machpelah, and the one at Mamre are large rectangular edifices. At Hebron, the ground slopes away from the southwest side, so the enclosed platform is elevated above the ground there. Both have outer facades decorated with courses of pilasters similar to the ones on the retaining walls of the Temple. The stones that make up both enclosures are Herodian in date with typically Herodian comb-dressed margins and coarse central bosses. Both seem to have been designed with great care and geometric precision. For instance, at Hebron, the six cenotaphs ded-

---

Ideology," 206-7. One group that especially would have been interested in stone vessels was the Pharisees, for whom it was essential to eat ordinary food in a state of ritual purity. Interestingly, Rocca has argued persuasively that the Pharisees, or the mainstream members, were supporters of the regime. It raises the question of whether this group religiously influenced the king or he was simply following a general Jewish predilection for stone dinnerware. For Rocca's analysis of Pharisaic support, especially that of the Pharisees Pollio and Samias, see *Herod's Judaea*, 254-59. For Herod's support among the Essenes see *Herod's Judaea*, 252-53.

icated to the six patriarchs and matriarchs (Abraham, Isaac, and Jacob, Sarah, Rebecca, and Leah) are laid in two parallel rows in a strict and regularly spaced symmetrical pattern, although two of them, those of Isaac and Rebecca, have been moved to accommodate later construction. This layout creates a series of geometric patterns within the space, composed of congruent triangles with angles of 30°, 60°, and 90°. The effect of these relationships produces an aesthetically pleasing building constructed to honor the memory of the founding figures of the Jewish people.[14]

There is some disagreement among scholars regarding Herod's motives in building the two enclosures. One theory is that Herod built them for the Idumaeans. We know that the Idumaeans had inhabited the surrounding area since the destruction of the First Temple, and at that time (early 6th century BCE) the two cities were a part of Edom (later Idumaea). Furthermore, even prior to John Hyrcanus I's conquest, many Idumaeans had already adopted some aspects of Jewish religion and culture voluntarily. Despite this cultural affinity, some persistence of older Idumaean religious traditions remained, in particular the cult of Qos *(Kōze)*, as ev-

---

14. For the importance of Hebron in the Bible see Gen 23:1-20; 49:29-32. For the importance of Mamre see Gen 13:18; 18:1-15. Cf. Gen 14:13, 24, where Mamre is the name of one of the three Amorite chiefs with whom Abraham allies in order to save Lot. For the original site reports on the enclosure at Hebron see L. H. Vincent and E. J. H. Mackay, *Hébron, le Haram el-Khalil. Sépulture des Patriarches* (Paris: Leroux, 1923). Cf. R. De Vaux, "Mambre" *Dictionnaire de la Bible Supplément* 5 (1957): 753-58. For an analysis of the ashlar masonry at Hebron see David M. Jacobson, "Decorative Drafted-Margin Masonry in Jerusalem and Hebron and Its Relations," *Levant* 32 (2000): 135-39, 145-46. Jacobson argues that drafted-margin ashlar masonry was used in Herodian religious enclosures because it looked like the masonry used in the older parts of the Temple's retaining walls, areas which were associated with Solomon, his Temple, and the biblical age. The use of this drafted-margin masonry was thus entirely appropriate for enclosures associated with Abraham. For a discussion and analysis of the layout and architectural design of the enclosure as well as the significance of this design see David M. Jacobson, "The Plan of the Ancient Haram el-Khalil at Hebron," *PEQ* 113 (1981): 74-77. Jacobson's detailed plan of the enclosure shows that the building can be divided into a basic rectangular grid with symmetrical axial lines oriented at 60° to the minor axis. Within this grid, the cenotaphs occupy points of intersection between the two grids. According to him, such a geometric relationship between the angles and the sides of the enclosure is similar to the geometric plan of the Herodian *temenos* at Jerusalem. It is also similar to the design of the *temenos* of the temple of Jupiter Damascenus, which also has an exterior enclosure wall decorated with pilasters. For a discussion of the enclosure at Mamre see Itzhak Magen, "Mamre," in *NEAEHL,* 939-42. See also the original excavation report, A. E. Mader, *Mambre. Die Ergebnisse der Ausgrabungen im Heiligen Bezirk Ramet El-Halil in Südpalästina 1926-1928* (Freiburg i. B.: Wewel, 1957). Cf. Ehud Netzer, *The Architecture of Herod, the Great Builder* (Tübingen: Mohr, 2006), 229-32.

idenced by the revolt of the theophorically-named Idumaean governor Costobar. These traditions, however, were probably quite similar to and possibly influenced by those of Judaea. The book of Genesis even provides a literary connection between Jews and Edomites: Esau, the brother of Jacob, is said to be the father of the Edomites. Finally, as Eusebius and Sozomen both relate, until the construction of a Constantinian basilica at Mamre there was a pagan cult at the site associated with the Oak of Abraham. Thus, it is possible that Herod was attempting to promote native Idumaean cult traditions and ingratiate himself with the Idumaean population. The major problem with this hypothesis is that Idumaeans were some of the staunchest supporters of the regime, and it is hard to see how a king who had his issues with some of his Jewish subjects would actively risk offending them by constructing pagan or semi-pagan religious shrines at locations connected to an important figure for Jews like Abraham. Another related possibility, advocated by Lichtenberger, is that Herod might actually have been attempting to suppress native Idumaean religious traditions in the hopes of ingratiating himself with his Jewish subjects.

There is a third possibility — a scenario that I consider more likely — namely, that Herod was appealing to both groups, Jews and Idumaeans, simultaneously. Since both considered Abraham their forefather, it is possible that the shrines would have satisfied both groups. As Kasher has noted, many Idumaeans already had voluntarily assimilated Jewish customs and religious beliefs. Further, Herod himself is evidence that a number of them considered themselves full-fledged Jews. Whatever his exact personal piety, he clearly considered himself king of the Jews and, as such, a Jew. If he could consider himself thus, we can assume that other Idumaeans did as well. Strikingly, only seventy years after Herod's death, they were some of the most enthusiastic defenders of Jerusalem and the Temple. It is certainly possible that some of that fervor existed during the first century BCE.

With respect to the Jews, although Hebron and Mamre are on the border of Judaea and Idumaea and certainly may have been settled by Idumaeans during the Persian and Hellenistic periods, it is hard to believe that the Jews would have completely renounced any religious claims over these two sites, especially since they were so important in the lives of the patriarchs. Rather, it seems more likely that they maintained religious ties with these sites and would therefore have appreciated royal patronage of them. Consequently, Herod's constructions at these sites expressed his piety and attempt to associate with Abraham, the patriarch of both groups. The effect of this association would be to strengthen his claim to be a legitimate king of the Jews and Idumaeans, one who venerated and honored the famous Jewish heroes of the past and as a result absorbed some of their legitimacy.[15]

15. For a discussion of the Idumaeans, their movement into the region around Hebron and Mamre, and their adoption of Jewish customs and practices see Aryeh Kasher, *Jews, Idumaeans and Ancient Arabs: Relations of the Jews in Eretz-Israel with Nations of the Frontier and the Desert during the Hellenistic and Roman Era (332 BCE–70 CE)* (Tübingen: Mohr, 1988), 44-77; Lichtenberger, *Baupolitik,* 146-47. For the persistence of native Idumaean customs, particularly worship of Qos, as well as Costobar's revolt and its quasi-nationalist goals see *AJ* 15.253-58. Cf. Adam Kolman Marshak, "Rise of the Idumaeans: Ethnicity and Politics in Herod's Judaea," in *Jewish Identity and Politics between the Maccabees and Bar Kokhba,* ed. Benedikt Eckhardt (Leiden: Brill, 2012), 125-29. For the biblical connection between Idumaeans and Judaeans see Gen 25:30. For early Christian discussion of the pagan cult at the Oak of Abraham near Mamre see Eusebius, *Onomasticon* 6.12-16; Sozomon, *Church History* 2.4. For Lichtenberger's theory about the significance of Hebron and Mamre see Lichtenberger, *Baupolitik,* 147-49. He proposes the possible existence of an Asherah tree cult associated with Mamre that was retroactively connected with Abraham in Genesis. For the rapid integration of Idumaeans into the Hasmonean kingdom see Marshak, "Rise of the Idumaeans," 117-29. For Herod's reference to the patriarchs as "our fathers" *(pateres hēmeteroi)* when speaking to the Judaean people, a term that suggests a conscious self-identification as a Jew, see *AJ* 15.385. For the formation of Jewish nationalism among Idumaeans, a trend that culminated in a large Idumaean contingent among the defenders of Jerusalem and the Temple see Israel Ronen, "Formation of Jewish Nationalism among the Idumaeans," in Kasher, *Idumaeans,* 214-39, esp. 224-39. Monika Bernett explicitly rejects the interpretation of Hebron and Mamre as bicultural sites (Idumaean and Judaean), arguing instead that any patronage of Idumaean religious traditions would have been more scandalous to Herod's Judaean subjects than his establishment of a Roman imperial cult, and the king would not have risked such rejection of Hasmonean ideology and the resulting disapproval, especially not in the period from 37 to 30 BCE, when he was trying to connect himself with the Hasmonean family. Furthermore, in Bernett's opinion, Josephus would not have passed up a chance to castigate Herod for such a scandal (Bernett, *Kaiserkult,* 158-61). Bernett's criticisms, however, rest on a false dichotomy between Idumaean religious sensibilities and those of Judaeans, as well as a continuation of an anti-Idumaean mentality within the later Hasmonean court. As we know, this divide between Idumaeans and Judaeans was not nearly as deep or neatly defined as Bernett supposes, even if there were some on both sides who retained the traditional animus (e.g., Costobar). Furthermore, as we have seen, Idumaeans were well integrated into the courts of the later Hasmoneans, and examples can be found in all the factions in the disintegrating Hasmonean court. For example, the Idumaean Malichos and his family violently opposed the Antipatrids. Additionally, the Idumaean Sons of Baba supported Antigonus against the Idumaean Herod. When we reject Bernett's stark view of religious diversity within the Hasmonean and Herodian kingdoms, we reach the conclusion that a bicultural monument may not have been scandalous at all. Her criticism also relies on a date for the enclosures at Hebron and Mamre in the 30s BCE, a time when, in her view, Herod would not have strayed from Hasmonean ideology to support Idumaean-Judaean

Herod's Religious Conflicts with His Subjects

Despite some success at avoiding offense and displaying an active Jewish piety, Herod still encountered problems over his handling of religion. In particular, Josephus records several episodes in which Herod ran afoul of his subjects' religious sensibilities. Between his descriptions of the execution of the Sons of Baba and the drought of 25/24 BCE, Josephus inserts a special section in which he discusses Herod's violation of Jewish ancestral customs. He specifically criticizes his institution of quinquennial athletic games in Jerusalem in honor of Augustus and his construction of a theater in the city and an amphitheater on the plain as introductions of foreign and unwanted elements into Jewish life. Furthermore, he strenuously objects to the practice of throwing condemned men to wild beasts for others' amusement, which he regards as a serious impiety.

Additionally, Josephus accuses Herod of upsetting his subjects by placing trophies in the theater, which supposedly violated the Jewish prohibition of graven images. In this account, while Josephus criticizes the king for his violation of *halakah,* he also depicts Herod as attempting to alleviate his subjects' concerns and to prove to them that he was not in fact disrespecting the Second Commandment, that the trophies were not in fact idols but merely wooden stands with weapons on them. Herod summons a group of leading Jews and strips the trophies of their arms, revealing the bare wood behind. With the trophies fully revealed, the delegation is mollified, and the situation ends peacefully. Perhaps Herod's only concern was keeping his aggrieved subjects quiet. But it is equally likely that he really did not see the trophies as violating *halakah,* and the disagreement between him and some of his subjects as depicted by Josephus was merely an argument over the proper interpretation of the Law, not a sign of antagonism toward Judaism on the part of Herod.[16]

---

religious cults. However, she offers no explanation for why she dates the construction of these enclosures to the 30s BCE other than that Richardson dates them to this period (Richardson, *Herod,* 61-62, 184, 199). Given the architectural similarity of these two enclosures to the Temple in Jerusalem as well as their role in Herod's self-presentation to his internal Jewish audience, their construction better fits the period of 20-10 BCE, when Herod was most interested in depicting himself as a pious Jewish king and hero. In this later period, Herod's ruling ideology was much more independent of Hasmonean ideology. Therefore, even if the enclosures represented a break from Hasmonean ideology (which I do not believe), such a break would not have been out of character.

16. For Josephus's comment about Herod's transgression of Jewish law and custom

Josephus also criticizes Herod for reforming the laws regarding theft in an attempt to reduce its occurrence. As a remedy, he made the penalties harsher so that one who was caught in the act of breaking and entering would be sold into slavery and deported from the kingdom. Josephus objects to this punishment, claiming that it contravened *halakah,* which demands fourfold restitution. If the thief could not pay, he was to be sold into slavery, but only to a Jew and only for a period of six years. Josephus presents his interpretation as the only correct one and argues that Herod's attempts to alter it illustrate his disdain for Jewish law. However, there are several problems with accepting Josephus's interpretation as normative for the Herodian period.

In the first place, Josephus's interpretation is not as clear and unimpeachable as he would have us believe. The prohibition against selling a Jewish slave to a non-Jew is connected to a biblical verse that concerns the sale of a Hebrew slave (Exod 21:2). This verse is not the one that discusses the proper punishment for theft (which is 22:1-2), nor is there any reason to assume a connection between the two verses. The actual verse states that a thief should make either fourfold or fivefold restitution, but only in the case of a sheep, and "if he has nothing, he shall be sold for his theft" (22:2), not specifying to whom he should be sold or where. Second, we have no contemporary sources for this law; neither the Qumranites, nor Apocrypha texts, nor the pseudepigraphic texts address this particular subject. While it is true that rabbinic law agrees with Josephus's objection to selling Jews to non-Jews, it is important to note that any rabbinic decision postdates

---

see *AJ* 15.267-70, 274-75. See also Fuks, "Herod's Attitude towards Jewish Religion," 239. For his specific criticism of both Herod's institution of games in honor of Augustus and his building program see *AJ* 15.268. Schürer notes the abrupt narrative shift between *AJ* 15.266 and 15.299 and thus postulates that a different source was inserted between these two sections. This source, which is rather hostile to Herod, criticizes him for his violation of Jewish ancestral rights. It might be Josephus or another Jewish author. It is certainly not Nicolaus, who would not have criticized his patron in such a way. See Schürer, *History of the Jewish People,* 1:290-91 n. 9. For the trophies incident see *AJ* 15.277-79. For a detailed analysis of this incident see Bernett, *Kaiserkult,* 64-65. Herod's performance in the theater did not satisfy all of his subjects, and some of them continued unsuccessfully to plot his assassination. Bernett suggests that Herod's failure to mollify his Jewish subjects completely during this first Caesarian festival resulted in his decision to forgo any repeat of the event in Jerusalem. It is noteworthy that Herod's other festival, which inaugurated his masterpiece Caesarea Maritima, was held in a city with a significant non-Jewish population. His other two temples dedicated to Augustus were also in parts of his kingdom that were totally or mostly non-Jewish. See Bernett, *Kaiserkult,* 65-66.

the Herodian period and thus may have been a reaction to Herod's reforms, not a clarification of an existing law. Moreover, other Jewish thinkers do not agree with Josephus's stated punishment. For example, Philo writes of a twofold restitution for theft. Therefore, Herod may simply have been proposing a new interpretation of the law in Exodus. He might have felt completely capable of reinterpreting the law in his position as king. He might even have received the support of certain priests and possibly even the high priest.

This is not to say that Josephus was lying about opposition to these reforms. Some Jews would not have agreed with Herod's interpretation and would have been upset because of this disagreement. However, such a disagreement does not indicate that Herod was contravening or disrespecting Mosaic Law, merely that there was a lack of consensus on the issue. Josephus's commentary represents a distinctive interpretative mode of thinking, which is in conflict with the one Herod chose, assuming he followed one distinct school of interpretation. It would be more accurate to state that he is presenting Herod's reforms and actions negatively in much the same way as a political candidate would present his opponents' ideas and policies.

Interestingly, Rocca has made a persuasive argument that Herod was influenced by Roman law in the creation of this rule. In particular, he cites the example of Augustus, who faced similar bandit problems and dealt with them by repressing the bandits, killing most of them, and sending the remainder to the amphitheaters. Moreover, a contemporary Roman jurist, Marcus Antistius Labeo, wrote the juridical definition of theft and the resultant penalties. If Rocca is correct, then this law would be another example of Herod's adoption of Roman culture and norms, and yet, such adoption does not necessitate a rejection of Judaism. For instance, the rabbinic corpus is rife with rulings that seem to mirror or be influenced by existing Roman law. One example is the change from patrilineal to matrilineal descent, a change that seems to mirror Roman rules of citizenship, which traced identity from the mother. If the rabbis can mimic Roman law and custom in their rulings without being anti-Jewish, then so too can Herod.[17]

17. For Herod's law against thieves see *AJ* 16.1-4. Josephus claims the law significantly increased the people's dislike of the king. For the rabbinical prohibition on sales of Jewish slaves to non-Jews see *Sifre Deut.* 118. For an alternative punishment for theft see Philo, *Special Laws* 4.11-12. Another example of a legal reform that received the backing of the priestly class was the first-century CE legal institution of the *prosbul,* which permitted the collection of a debt even after a Sabbatical year. See Martin Goodman, *The Ruling Class of Judaea:*

Herod, Melekh HaYehudim

Patronage and Inclusion of the Diaspora

Patronage and Euergetism *in the Diaspora*

Herod's performance for his internal audience was just one part of his Jewish political self-presentation. Just as important to his identity as a glorious Jewish king was the support and recognition of those Jews who lived not in Judaea but in the Diaspora. The sixth-century BCE conquest of Judah by the Babylonians had initiated an extensive dispersion of Jews across the Mediterranean world, and five centuries later Jews were living all over the Graeco-Roman world, although the largest populations were in the Eastern Mediterranean. These communities had acculturated to the larger non-Jewish world in which they were living, and yet, while not politically a part of Judaea, they had maintained religious and social relations with their homeland. By the middle of his reign Herod found himself in firm and stable control over his kingdom, which was peaceful and prosperous. This success enabled him to focus his attention on other goals, and he began to concern himself with his status as a glorious Jewish king. In this endeavor, he turned to the Diaspora as a crucial source of legitimacy and support. As a ruler who straddled the various cultural boundaries, he was able to function as a bridge between the Diaspora and Judaea, bringing the Diaspora more closely into Judaea's orbit and solidifying the ethno-religious bond that held these two communities together. Because of an active policy of supporting the Diaspora, by the end of his reign he could boast with good reason that he was not only king of Judaea but also king of the Jews.

In many ways, his interactions with the Diaspora were no different than those he had with other non-Jewish communities. In 14 BCE, while in Asia visiting Marcus Agrippa, he was approached by the Jews of Ionia. They complained to him that they were suffering mistreatment at the hands of their neighbors by being forced to participate in military service and civic duties, obligations from which the Roman government had ex-

---

The Origins of the Jewish Revolt AD 66-70 (Cambridge: Cambridge University Press, 1987), 57-58. For speculation that Herod's law concerning thieves only applied to the non-Jewish regions of his kingdom see Rocca, *Herod's Judaea,* 279. For the possibility of a multitude of legal interpretations on issues of *halakah,* see Ilan, "Intermarriage in the Herodian Family," 14-15. Cf. Rocca, *Herod's Judaea,* 277-29, where he also argues that Herod's law mimics the viewpoint of Roman jurisprudence. For an analysis of the similarities between rabbinic views of Jewishness and Roman citizenship laws see Shaye J. D. Cohen, "The Matrilineal Principle in Historical Perspective," *Judaism* 34 (1985): 5-13, esp. 11.

empted them. They were also being forced to appear in court on holy days and prevented from sending the money they had collected to pay the half-shekel Temple tax, a tax incumbent on all Jewish men. As the ruler of the Judaea and therefore the protector of the Temple, Herod was an ideal patron for these Jews. Many of them would have approved of his renovation and rebuilding of the Temple, which had begun several years earlier. Others would have seen him as a powerful king, friendly with Agrippa and likely to help out his coreligionists. Some of them might even have considered him to be king of all Jews everywhere and, logically, the person to assist them.

In any case, the Jewish embassy approached him and secured his services as well as those of his spokesman Nicolaus of Damascus. In his speech before Agrippa, Nicolaus emphasized the loyalty of the Jews and enumerated the abuses done to them. He reminded Agrippa that Herod and his family had been loyal supporters of Rome and that the king supported the Jews' petition. Agrippa then ruled in favor of the Ionian Jews and confirmed their rights of citizenship and self-rule *(isonomia)*.

A little later in *Jewish Antiquities* Josephus cites a number of Augustan-era edicts regarding religious freedom for Diaspora Jews. Among these are two edicts concerning the Jews of Ephesus in Asia Minor and Cyrene in Libya. Agrippa is the author of both edicts, and each of them addresses problems similar to the one experienced by the Ionian Jews, specifically the rights of *isonomia* and the freedom to practice the Jewish religion without restriction. Given the similarity of the conflict as well as Agrippa's role in solving them, it is tempting to link them with the case of the Ionian Jews and hypothesize a role for Herod in the positive conclusion of these conflicts. Both communities fit well into the model of Herodian *euergetism* which we discussed in the last chapter. In particular, both concerned major port cities with large and established Jewish communities. Indeed, Ephesus was one of the major metropolises of the Roman world, a group that also included Rome, Alexandria, Antioch, and Pergamum. Perhaps Herod also intervened in these matters, and it was his patronage of these two communities that persuaded Agrippa to issue the edicts.

If so, then we have at least three cases in which Herod personally advocated for and championed the rights of Diaspora Jews. His defense of these rights and of these Jews, particularly their right to collect money for the Temple, benefited him personally. Since the Temple was the main religious institution in his kingdom, it was to his benefit to have external dedications flowing into it. However, there were other motives involved as well. As a king who was trying to assert his presence on the international stage, such a vigorous defense of Jewish interest was only natural. Besides elevating his status vis-à-vis Diaspora Jews, it would also have earned him support from home, where his subjects would have approved of his actions on behalf of their coreligionists. Herod thus positioned himself as the king and patron of all Jews, not just the Judaean Jews.[18]

Inclusion of the Diaspora

Herod also sought to include the Diaspora in the cultic life of the Temple in Jerusalem. He accomplished this goal by promoting and supporting increased pilgrimage and opening up the ranks of the high priesthood to the Diaspora. By the end of his reign, Judaea and specifically Jerusalem had become significant pilgrimage sites for Jews all over the Mediterranean as well as those living as far away as Babylon. Moreover, the high priesthood, once the exclusive privilege of the Judaean priestly elites, became an office open to anyone of high priestly descent. In a sense, it was transformed from a Judaean priesthood to a Jewish priesthood.

One of the most visible transformations in Herod's kingdom was the metamorphosis experienced by the capital city. Prior to the first century BCE Jerusalem was a cramped and underdeveloped city, certainly not an ideal pilgrimage destination. Archaeological evidence suggests that at the end of the Persian period the development of the city was still slow and gradual. This stagnancy continued into the pre-Hasmonean period: the city remained within the fortified boundaries of the City of David into the third and second centuries BCE and occupied an area no larger than thirty acres. Population estimates are in the low-to-mid thousands, which means

---

18. For the Ionian Jews' complaints and Herod's agreement to help them see *AJ* 16.27-30. For Nicolaus's speech before Agrippa see *AJ* 16.31-65. Cf. 12.125-28. Although Josephus (and possibly Nicolaus) may be overstating things by asserting that Agrippa ruled in favor of the Ionian Jews because of Herod's goodwill and friendship — Agrippa and Augustus had favored the Jews on previous occasions — Herod's support and intercession at least ensured a prompt hearing. And yet, given the personal nature of power and politics in the Roman world, it is certainly possible, and perhaps even probable, that Herod's patronage of the Ionian Jews led to Agrippa's positive response. For the Roman edicts regarding religious freedom for Jewish communities see *AJ* 16.160-73, esp. 167-70. For the power of personal patronage in political decisions see Ernst Badian, *Foreign Clientelae, 264-70 B.C.* (Oxford: Clarendon, 1958), esp. 160.

that it was one of the smallest urban centers in the eastern Mediterranean. Real growth began during the Hasmonean period, during which the city expanded onto the whole of the southwestern hill, which had been uninhabited since the destruction of the First Temple. As the Hasmonean period progressed, the population of the city increased to approximately 30,000-35,000 and continued to spread outward, expanding up the Tyropoeon Valley. Along with this expansion came further fortification of the city with the restoration of the First Wall and the building of the Second Wall. By the end of the Hasmonean period, the fortified section of the city encompassed around 230 acres, and the population was around 40,000 people. Although now a much larger city, there were still limitations to its growth. For instance, the water system could not support a major metropolis, and the Temple Mount, which was significantly smaller than the present-day site, had fallen into disrepair over the centuries.

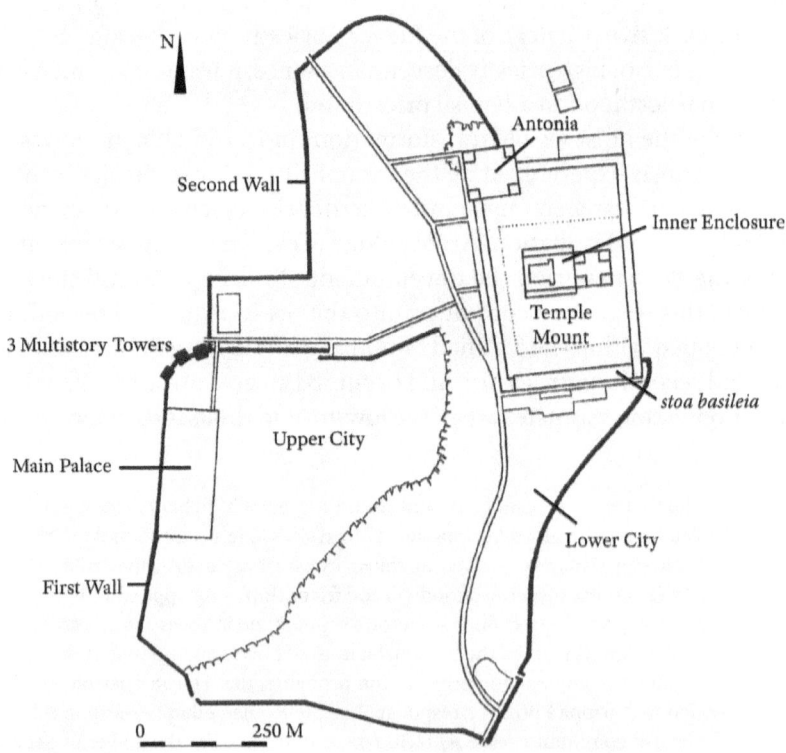

Partly reconstructed plan of Herodian Jerusalem

Herod, Melekh HaYehudim

Herod's extensive building program in Jerusalem completely changed the city and transformed it into one capable of being a major pilgrimage center. The city also contained many of the elements of a classical Greek *polis* including a theater, a hippodrome, and a gymnasium with a connecting *xystos* (a long portico often connected to a gymnasium). Although the city as a whole lacked a Hippodamian plan, Herod did redesign large parts of the city. The main thoroughfare of this new plan ran from the Upper City, where he built his palace (the present-day Citadel), to Wilson's Arch. He also gave Jerusalem a waterworks network large enough to support a large population of up to 75,000 people. Finally, as will be discussed in greater detail in the next chapter, he significantly enlarged the size of the Temple Mount, doubling the area of the esplanade and creating a *temenos* (forecourt) that, at about 1,550,000 square feet (thirty-five acres), was the largest sanctuary site in the ancient world and an ideal site for the thousands of pilgrims who now flocked to Judaea annually.[19]

19. For a discussion of the development of Jerusalem from the Persian to Hasmonean periods see Geva, "Jerusalem," 720-21; Dan Bahat and Chaim T. Rubenstein, *The Illustrated Atlas of Jerusalem,* trans. Shlomo Ketko (New York: Simon and Schuster, 1990), 34-40. Cf. Rocca, *Herod's Judaea,* 332-33. It is important to note that population estimates are speculations at best, and the archaeological evidence is not totally definitive. Thus, different authors have slightly different numbers, although those given here seem to have the most support. For the dilapidation of the Temple and its modest construction see Schürer, *History of the Jewish People,* 1:308; Smallwood, *Jews under Roman Rule,* 91. For Herod's rebuilding and enhancement of Jerusalem into a city capable of being a major pilgrimage site see John Strange, "Herod and Jerusalem: The Hellenization of an Oriental City," in *Jerusalem in Ancient History and Tradition,* ed. Thomas L. Thompson (London: Clark, 2003), 109-10. Cf. Seth Schwartz, "Herod, Friend of the Jews," in *Jerusalem and Eretz Israel: The Arie Kindler Volume,* ed. Joshua Schwartz, Zohar Amar, and Irit Ziffer (Tel Aviv: Eretz Israel Museum and Ingeborg Center, 2001), 68-69; Bahat and Rubenstein, *Illustrated Atlas,* 40-53. See Rocca, *Herod's Judaea,* 334-35, for a discussion of Herod's repair and expansion of Jerusalem's water supply system. For Herod's expansion of the Temple Mount see Lichtenberger, *Baupolitik,* 131-42; Sarah Japp, *Die Baupolitik Herodes des Grossen. Die Bedeutung der Architektur für die Herrschaftslegitimation eines Römischen Klientelkönigs* (Rahden: Leidorf, 2000), 126-30. For Jacobson's theories on the geometrical planning of the Temple see David M. Jacobson, "Ideas Concerning the Plan of Herod's Temple," *PEQ* 112 (1980): 33-40; "The Plan of Herod's Temple," *BAIAS* 10 (1990-91): 36-66; "Sacred Geometry: Unlocking the Secret of the Temple Mount, Part 1," *BAR* 25.4 (1999): 42-53, 62-64; "Sacred Geometry: Unlocking the Secret of the Temple Mount, Part 2," *BAR* 25.5 (1999): 54-63, 74; "Geometrical Planning in Monumental Herodian Architecture," *BAIAS* 17 (1999): 67-76. On the eve of revolt in 66 CE, Josephus estimates that there were 3,000,000 pilgrims. He also cites an estimate of 2,700,000 later in *BJ*. While his numbers may be gross exaggerations — the number, according to Rocca, was closer to 300,000 — the crowds now able to enter the city on the three

Just as central to Herod's transformation of Jerusalem and the Temple Mount into world-class pilgrimage sites was his radical alteration of the high priesthood, specifically its role, status, and membership. As far back as the Persian period, the high priesthood had been the most powerful local office in Judaea, and, at the same time, it was the only office recognized by all Jews throughout the Diaspora. Given the status of the office, it is no surprise that successive high priests served as liaisons between the Jewish people and their various foreign overlords. Although these foreign powers had reserved the right to appoint the high priest, the office had traditionally been limited to only the few families who were Zadokites (individuals who could trace their lineage patrilineally back to Zadok) and usually was passed from father to son. During the Hellenistic period, the Oniad family had held the office, and after it, the Hasmoneans.

When Herod took the throne, he knew that he could not be high priest and so sought to control the office and its holder. His first attempt was to maintain the illusion of continuity with the past by creating a diarchy with him as king and his Hasmonean brother-in-law Aristobulus III as high priest. Perhaps this arrangement was meant as a temporary bridge to a situation in which his sons by Mariamme would be both kings and high priests. In any event, this endeavor was a miserable failure, especially when it became clear that Aristobulus was more popular than Herod. His solution was to murder his brother-in-law and assume control over the office, if not in name then in practice. Thus Herod began a policy that revolutionized the high priesthood and had far-reaching consequences for both the office and Judaism. He asserted control over the high priesthood and radically changed the profile of those who occupied it.

The first hallmark of this policy was not new: high priestly candidates did not inherit their office. Instead, the king appointed them. What was novel was that their term of office now became relatively short: throughout his reign, Herod frequently deposed his high priests. Further, he consciously snubbed Jerusalemite families in favor of candidates from the Diaspora, particularly Egypt and Babylon. His motivation for such a policy was likely grounded in political expediency. By denying the highest religious position to native Jerusalemites, he was preventing any local elite from gaining enough power and prestige to challenge his authority. As foreign appointees, these new high-priestly families were entirely dependent on him for support and legitimacy.

---

pilgrimage holidays must have been massive. See *BJ* 2.280; 6.421 for Josephus's estimates. Cf. Rocca, *Herod's Judaea*, 235, esp. n. 141.

This pattern began with his first appointee, Hananel, who, according to Josephus, came from Babylon and reigned as high priest from 37 to 36/35 BCE and from 35 to 30 BCE. His appointment may have served other political needs as well. At the time of his investiture, Herod's patron Marc Antony was actively involved in a war with Parthia, and a Babylonian high priest under the control of a Roman client king would have been extremely valuable to Antony, especially as he moved into Parthian territory and closer to Babylon. He might have hoped for the support of the large Jewish community living in Parthia, or at least their neutrality. Although Herod deposed Hananel in favor of Aristobulus III, he quickly gave the job back to the Babylonian once Aristobulus was dead.

Hananel's successors also fit the pattern Herod had set whereby he was in full control of the high priesthood and its officeholder. Hananel's immediate replacement was Joshua (Jesus) ben Phiabi (30-28/27 BCE), whose family seems to have been Egyptian. Richardson even believes he was from Leontopolis. If that is the case, it is likely that Joshua was an Oniad, and thus Herod may have been attempting to appropriate whatever legitimacy the Oniads still possessed. Such an attempt would make sense in 30 BCE, primarily because of the relative instability of Herod's position after Actium. This time period (30-27 BCE) also marked his break with his Hasmonean persona and his murder of Hyrcanus II and Mariamme, two actions that, while ultimately necessary and successful, would have made his regime more unstable in the short term. An alliance with the Oniads would have done much to restore his credibility with both native Judaeans and Diaspora Jews. The next three appointments, Simon Boethus (ca. 28/27-5 BCE), Mattathias ben Theophilus (5-4 BCE), and Joazar ben Boethus (4 BCE) also fit the pattern, although Mattathias was of Jerusalemite origin. Simon Boethus had two selling points: he was from the Diaspora (specifically Alexandria), and he had a beautiful daughter, Mariamme, whom Herod married, although he divorced her in the same year (5 BCE) that he deposed her father. Given the divorce of the daughter and deposition of the father, it is surprising that Herod would again appoint a member of the House of Boethus, Joazar, the son of Simon Boethus, the very next year. Perhaps loyalty, his status as the uncle of one of Herod's potential heirs (Herod III), and his Alexandrian background were reasons to overlook his deposed father. Despite being a native Judaean, Mattathias did not serve as high priest for long and thus was unable to build up any significant power base from which he might threaten the king.

The background of the final person who served as high priest during

Herod's reign, Joseph ben Ellem, is unclear, although Rocca believes he was also a Jerusalemite. Even if he was, he was only a temporary substitute because the reigning high priest, Mattathias ben Theophilus, was temporarily impure. Because ben Ellem was not a royal appointee, his identity is less important than the others. In the aggregate, of the six men appointed high priest by Herod four were not Jerusalemites. This number is even more significant when we consider the length of time each man served. In total, Hananel and Simon Boethus were high priests for a total of almost thirty of Herod's thirty-three years as undisputed king of Judaea. Moreover, when we remember that Aristobulus III's elevation to the high priesthood was part of Herod's initial attempt to link himself to the Hasmoneans and therefore was meant only for a domestic audience, the disparity between Jerusalemite and non-Jerusalemite high priests becomes even starker.[20]

As we have suggested above, Herod's motivation for this replacement of Jerusalemite high priests with foreign ones may have been based on local political concerns and expediency. Nevertheless, we should not discount a larger motivation influencing his actions, namely using these ap-

---

20. For an overview and discussion of the high priesthood see Richardson, *Herod*, 243-47. His list of high priests includes a Boethus (who he argues is Mariamme II's father) and his son Simon (whom he sees as Herod's brother-in-law), although he acknowledges the possibility that the two are one person. Based on Josephus's narratives, I agree with Kokkinos that there is only one individual whose name was Simon ben Boethus. He was the father of Mariamme II and the later high priest Joazer ben Boethus. In this case, Boethus was a family name passed down from father to son. See Kokkinos, *Herodian Dynasty*, 217-20, for his argument about Simon Boethus as well as the dating of his appointment to 29/28 BCE. Because of the extensive period of mourning, described by Josephus in *AJ* 15.240-46, I have allowed for a gap between Mariamme the Hasmonean's execution in 29 BCE and Herod's marriage to Mariamme II (and appointment of her father to the high priesthood) in 28/27 BCE. Kokkinos also proposes that the house of Boethus may have been connected to the Oniads based on his reading of *AJ* 19.298. In this passage, Josephus mentions that Simon Boethus was high priest as were three of his sons. In the same way, Josephus states, Simon the Oniad was high priest as were three of his sons. While this identification is possible and would support my analysis of Herod's appropriation of Leontopolis and the Oniads, it seems more likely that Josephus is commenting on the power and prominence of the house of Boethus. In this commentary, he uses the Oniads as a comparison. See Kokkinos, *Herodian Dynasty*, 218. For Herod's appointment and deposition of high priests see *BJ* 1.437; *AJ* 15.22, 34, 39-41, 56 (Hananel); *BJ* 1.437; *AJ* 15.31-40 (Aristobulus III); *AJ* 15.322 (Joshua ben Phiabi); *AJ* 15.320-22; 17.78 (Simon ben Boethus); *AJ* 17.78, 164-66 (Mattathias ben Theophilus); *AJ* 17.164, 339 (Joazar ben Boethus). Cf. *AJ* 17.165-67 for the one-day replacement of Mattathias by Joseph ben Ellem. For the evidence of the Egyptian origin of the houses of Boethus and Phiabi see Menahem Stern, "Social and Political Realignments in Herodian Judaea," *Jerusalem Cathedra* 2 (1982): 49-52.

pointments of non-Jerusalemite high priests to further incorporate the Diaspora. As Seth Schwartz argues, these appointments may have been designed to weaken the connection of the high priesthood with Judaea, so that the office became connected with all Jews, not simply Judaeans. While leaders prior to Herod certainly had reached out to the Diaspora, he took this policy to a new level of engagement, reconfiguring the central Judaean institutions (Temple and high priesthood) and the capital city (Jerusalem) from their exclusive Judaean identity to one accessible to other Jews, such as Galileans and Idumaeans, as well as those living in the Diaspora. While Diaspora Jews could now receive numerous benefits from Herod and be welcomed more fully into Jewish religious life, they did not have to endure the less wholesome aspects of his rule, such as taxes and political repression. By including all Jews in his sphere of influence, Herod came closer to uniting the Diaspora and Judaea than any ruler since the Davidic monarch, an accomplishment that certainly helped him portray himself as the new David or Solomon, a ruler who was not just king of the Judaeans (along with his non-Jewish subjects), but truly king of the Jews.[21]

Conclusion: Herod, Melekh HaYehudim

Herod's metamorphosis from a Hasmonean successor to an independent Jewish monarch largely occurred because of the change in the political situation within Judaea. When he first ascended to the throne in 40 BCE, he was a non-royal, non-priestly Idumaean, who had no natural claim to legitimacy. Further, he was supplanting a royal and high priestly dynasty, which, although perhaps losing a little of its luster during the fraternal civil war between Hyrcanus II and Aristobulus II, nevertheless retained popular support and affection. Because of these very real challenges, he needed the status and legitimacy of the Hasmonean dynasty. Additionally, he needed to persuade the Jewish elites within his kingdom that he was not actually a usurper but was the rightful successor to Hyrcanus (as op-

---

21. For the motivation behind Herod's appointment of Diaspora high priests see Goodman, *Ruling Class,* 41-42, 111-12, 118-20; Schwartz, "Herod, Friend of the Jews," 68, 73-74; Rocca, *Herod's Judaea,* 282-85. Cf. Lichtenberger, *Baupolitik,* 139-40; Peter Richardson, "Origins, Innovations and Significance of Herod's Temple," in *Building Jewish in the Roman East* (Waco: Baylor University Press, 2004), 293-94. For a discussion of resistance to Herod's appointment of Diaspora high priests by native Jerusalemite Zadokites, as well as by a few of Herod's in-laws, most notably his mother-in-law Alexandra, see Bernett, *Kaiserkult,* 43.

posed to Mattathias Antigonus or even Aristobulus III). Through marriage, dynastic naming, architecture, and coins Herod asserted his Hasmonean identity to his subjects but primarily to the local Jewish elite whose support he needed to maintain control.

Simple legitimacy was not Herod's end goal. Once his authority was established and his control over his kingdom was secure, he shed his Hasmonean identity, refashioning himself into an independent Jewish monarch, the king of all Jews, both in Judaea and in the Diaspora. In this new guise, he sought to enhance his royal status by associating himself with the biblical heroes of the past. Through his architecture, he depicted himself as their worthy successor and an emulator of their greatness. Specifically, by building massive edifices at Hebron and Mamre, which were reminiscent of the Temple Mount, he visually connected himself with Abraham and depicted himself as a pious king who honored the Jewish heroes of the past. More important to him, perhaps, was an association with the paragons of Jewish royalty, David and Solomon.

In making these associations, Herod's primary audience was the local Jewish elite who would have understood the allusions and references. Moreover, this audience was perhaps his most difficult one to appease, especially given his non-royal, non-priesty background. Other non-elite Jews might have rightly interpreted his actions, but their political agency was quite weak, and thus Herod was not particularly concerned with gaining their approval. He made this task easier for himself by eliminating or marginalizing many of the traditional high priestly families and creating a new elite drawn from his supporters not only in Judaea but also in Idumaea, Babylon, and Egypt. He may even have attempted to appropriate the legitimacy of the Oniads by appointing some of their members to the high priesthood.

All these actions have an element of political expediency to them, but what made Herod's reign so revolutionary was his attempt to expand his influence outside Judaea and into the Diaspora. In particular, he established himself as the Diaspora's primary patron, one who intervened on its behalf and represented it in legal disputes. He also appointed its Zadokite families as high priests, binding them and other Diaspora Jews more closely to the Temple and simultaneously transforming it and the high priesthood from Judaean-specific institutions into Jewish ones. Finally, his rebuilding of Jerusalem, especially the Temple Mount, greatly enhanced the city and remade it into a world pilgrimage site of the first rank. Indeed, writing more than eighty years after Herod's death, the Roman author Pliny the

Elder even went so far as to call Jerusalem "by far the most famous city of the East" (*HN* 5.70). Because of this massive expansion of the *temenos*, it could now accommodate the huge flocks of pilgrims pouring into the city, and each of these visitors would be visually reminded of Herod's role as king of the Jews and patron of the Temple.

And yet, he was not entirely successful in his overall presentation. Periodically, his competing motivations and cultural outlook would conflict with the religious sensibilities of his subjects. The incident in the theater and the golden eagle episode are perhaps two cases in which Herod's notion of what was acceptable offended some of his subjects. All these confrontations, however, were relatively minor and transient. Furthermore, the religious disputes with his subjects seem to have been primarily between him and the lower classes, a group that did not have much, if any, political agency. Therefore, they did not represent a significant threat to the stability of his regime. In the end, by tapping into the cultural expectations of Jewish kingship and by succeeding, for the most part, in embodying these expectations, Herod persuaded Jewish elites, at home and in the Diaspora, that he was a glorious *Melekh HaYehudim* ("king of the Jews"), a king who could compare himself favorably with the paragons of Jewish royalty, David and Solomon. Obviously not everyone agreed with this assessment, but enough did for him to die a peaceful death at an old age and to pass on his kingdom to his chosen successors.

CHAPTER 11

Herod and the Temple

Throughout this study, we have seen Herod the Great play the political chameleon, appealing to each of his audiences by presenting the image that would be most desirable to each. It is fitting, therefore, to end our investigation with the building and institution that illustrates this flexibility and multi-faceted presentation better than all others, the Jerusalem Temple. No other institution in his kingdom was as important, and his involvement with it shows him playing each of the three roles we have discussed, often simultaneously.

Rebuilding the Temple in Jerusalem

As king of Judaea, Herod's primary religious duties and obligations were to God, and the focus of his religious program was Jerusalem and the Temple Mount. By the first century BCE, the Temple of Zerubbabel was rather dilapidated. Moreover, it had always been a lesser creation than the original Solomonic Temple. With his taste for the grandiose, Herod would not have been content with a shabby and rundown sanctuary site at the center of his capital. Further, renovating and rebuilding the Temple would have enabled him to dramatically illustrate his piety toward God and his commitment to Judaism and its cult. It also would have enabled him to surpass his predecessors, the Hasmoneans, who had made only slight additions and improvements to the Temple Mount. Herod's project far surpassed any completed by them and thus would enable him to successfully compare his piety to theirs, placing him in the upper echelon of Jewish monarchic heroes right next to David and Solomon.

Herod and the Temple

Before he could begin this project, he had to secure the consent and approval of the populace if he were to gain the maximum benefit for such a costly venture. To this end, according to Josephus, he assembled the Jerusalemites and announced his intentions. In the speech, which appears in *Jewish Antiquities,* Herod stressed the peace and prosperity experienced by the kingdom as well as his friendship with the Romans. He also emphasized his past experience with building and construction and how that would enable him to accomplish the reconstruction project. Most notably, he asserted that all those previous projects were nothing compared to this ultimate act of piety he was about to undertake. The response to this speech was one of disbelief and skepticism, and to placate his subjects Herod promised not to begin any demolition until all the materials had been assembled. To this end, he assembled one thousand wagons and hired ten thousand workers. He also trained over a thousand priests in masonry and carpentry since they would be needed to work on those parts of the Temple off-limits to non-priests. Although these numbers are probably estimates, they illustrate the size and scope of the project as well as the amount of expenditure Herod was willing to incur.[1]

When did the construction begin on the Temple and its esplanade?

---

1. In his speech to the people, Herod uses the word "piety" *(eusebēs)* twice to describe his rebuilding project. See *AJ* 15.384, 387. Schalit suggests that by rebuilding the Temple, Herod expected God's blessing on him and divine sanction for his rule. He also argues that he perceived himself to be the restorer of David's kingdom and the expected Messiah (Abraham Schalit, *König Herodes. Der Mann und Sein Werk* [rev. ed.; Berlin: de Gruyter, 2001], 471-74). Schalit may be correct that Herod thought his reconstruction of the Temple would bring divine blessing and sanction. However, perhaps more immediately, and certainly more tangibly, it would result in praise and support from his Jewish subjects, as well as glory for him as an enterprising and wealthy monarch who was expected to build temples for his god. As for Schalit's other hypothesis concerning David and the Messiah, I believe he is reading too much into the evidence. As I have discussed in chapter 10, Herod certainly wished to link himself to David, but such a connection did not carry messianic undertones. Instead, there was more of an attempt to appropriate some of David's legitimacy as a Jewish hero. Furthermore, any attempt by him to claim messianic status would have been entirely unsuccessful and would have gone against his own political agenda, especially his friendship with Rome. For his promise to his subjects and his preparations for the project, see *AJ* 15.388-90. Given the duration of the building project, especially the fact that it was not completed until 64 CE, it is unlikely that all the materials were assembled prior to the beginning of construction. What is more likely is that the king assembled a large amount of the initial construction materials, enough to placate the populace and prove to them that the project was feasible. Cf. E. Mary Smallwood, *The Jews under Roman Rule: From Pompey to Diocletian* (Leiden: Brill, 1976), 91-92.

Josephus offers two dates for the commencement of building activities on the Temple Mount, either in Herod's fifteenth regnal year (*BJ* 1.401) or in his eighteenth year (*AJ* 15.380). Further complicating this issue is that it is unclear whether he was counting from 40 (the beginning of Herod's *de jure* rule) or from 37 BCE (the beginning of his *de facto* reign). The two dates most accepted by scholars are 20/19 and 23/22 BCE. Schürer argues that 20/19 BCE is the correct date based on his reading of *Jewish Antiquities*. In the text, Josephus uses the word *tote* to connect Herod's speech to the populace (*AJ* 15.380) with an earlier passage describing Augustus's visit to Syria (*AJ* 15.354). Since we know that Augustus arrived in Syria in 20 BCE, construction must have begun the same year. Smallwood disagrees with Schürer and suggests that 23/22 is a better date for two specific reasons. First, Herod had just deposed the high priest Joshua ben Phiabi, replacing him with Simon ben Boethus, the father of Herod's wife Mariamme II, and he may have hoped that the reconstruction project would assuage the populace's anger over the deposition. Further, Josephus states that the construction of the sanctuary took eighteen months and courts and porticos took eight years. Smallwood interprets this to mean that the entire construction lasted eight years, with the first eighteen months being spent on the sanctuary. If so, then the Temple complex would have been completed in 15/14 BCE (or 16/15 by inclusive reckoning) in time for the visit by Marcus Agrippa. As Smallwood indicates, Agrippa's visit to Jerusalem and the Temple would have had more significance if the king's crown jewel had just been completed instead of being still under construction.[2]

---

2. For Schürer's chronology, see Emil Schürer, *The History of the Jewish People in the Age of Jesus Christ (175 BC–AD 135)*, ed. Geza Vermes and Fergus Millar (Edinburgh: Clark, 1973-87), 1:292 n. 12. Cf. Achim Lichtenberger, *Die Baupolitik Herodes des Grossen* (Wiesbaden: Harrassowitz, 1999), 131. For Smallwood's chronology, see her *Jews under Roman Rule*, 92 n. 112. For the date of Augustus's visit to Syria, see Dio 54.7. Roller argues for a commencement date of 20/19 BCE based on Augustus's visit. However, he suggests that preliminary surveying may have taken place for many years prior to the official initiation of work, thus explaining Josephus's two dates (Duane W. Roller, *The Building Program of Herod the Great* [Berkeley: University of California Press, 1998], 176-77). This explanation for the two dates seems to be more wishful thinking than reasoned analysis, and there is no indication in *BJ* 1.401 that Josephus was speaking merely about surveying and not actual construction work. Sarah Japp prefers 20/19 to 23/22 BCE, although her reasoning is based, not on any synchronization with Cassius Dio, but solely on the assumption that the two dates were counting from 37 and not 40 BCE. See Japp, *Die Baupolitik Herodes des Grossen. Die Bedeutung der Architektur für die Herrschaftslegitimation eines Römischen Klientelkönigs* (Rahden: Leidorf, 2000), 127 n. 1068. For Herod's deposition of Joshua ben Phiabi in favor

Herod and the Temple

Which should we prefer? A dedicatory inscription carved into a limestone plaque and discovered by Benjamin Mazar south of the Triple Gate helps provide an answer. This inscription was found among debris that had filled a pool located inside a Herodian-era palace. It records a donation made in the twentieth year of King Herod by a certain Paris (or possibly Sparis) son of Akeson, who was probably a Jewish resident of Rhodes. His donation was for a section of pavement. Although not found *in situ*, the provenance of the inscription suggests that it originally came from nearby, perhaps from the southern part of the Temple Mount, even from the Royal Stoa itself. Such a location makes sense especially because, as Josephus states, the open southern court of the Temple was "completely paved with a variety of all types of stones." Depending on which starting date Paris used (either 40 or 37 BCE), Herod's twentieth regnal year was either 21/20 or 18/17 BCE (counting either from 40 BCE or 37 BCE).

Schürer's chronology does not work regardless of which date was the twentieth regnal year. If it were 21/20 BCE, it would mean that Paris of Rhodes's dedication was offered one year *before* the reconstruction began. A twentieth year of 18/17 BCE would also not fit with a commencement of construction in 20/19 BCE. Josephus states that the entire construction took either eight years or nine and a half. Either way, for a project that lasted most of a decade, it would be unusual to place a dedicatory inscription marking the completion of a section of pavement only two years after the project had begun. Five years (more than half of the way through the project) is a much more reasonable time to place a dedicatory inscription for pavement for a courtyard on the southern part of the Temple Mount, and thus we should prefer Smallwood's chronology for the project (23/22-15/14 BCE).[3]

---

of Simon ben Boethus see *AJ* 15.320, 322. For Agrippa's visit to Jerusalem and the Temple see *AJ* 16.12-15.

3. For Josephus's comment on the stone pavement of the Temple esplanade see *BJ* 5.192. The inscription found by Mazar, which is eight inches high, ten inches wide, and five inches thick, was published by Benjamin Isaac in *Israel Exploration Journal*. It also appears in *Supplementum Epigraphicum Graecum*. See Benjamin Isaac, "A Donation for Herod's Temple in Jerusalem," *IEJ* 33 (1983): 86-92; *SEG* 1277. A fourth-century Byzantine city wall tower was later erected upon the site where the inscription was found. The inscription is dated according to a regnal formula that mentions both a ruler and a high priest. Thus, the ruler must have been an individual who reigned for at least twenty years but was not a king and high priest. The only candidate that fits this criterion is Herod the Great. In Herod's twentieth regnal year (20/19 BCE if counting from 40 BCE or 18/17 BCE if counting from 37 BCE), the high priest would have been Simon ben Boethus. See Nikos Kokkinos, *The Herodian*

The Physical Layout of the Temple

In its final form, the Temple Mount stretched from the Antonia fortress in the north to the City of David in the south, and from the Kidron Valley in the east to the Upper City in the west. Although the Mount had dominated the Jerusalem cityscape prior to Herod's rebuilding, by the time he was finished it was significantly larger and grander than ever before. Easily the tallest structure in the city, it dominated the urban landscape. At about 1,550,000 square feet (thirty-five acres), it was also the largest sanctuary site in the ancient world. Its walls were the walls of the city on the east, north, and part of the west, although in the mid-first century CE, Herod Agrippa constructed a new wall on the north side of the Temple Mount. Few remains exist of the buildings that once stood upon the plateau. Josephus and the Mishnah, in particular tractate *Middot,* describe it in detail, and other texts, such as Philo's writings, the Talmud, and the New Testament, provide additional details. Archaeology also helps fill in the gaps and even referee between the sources when they disagree.[4]

Dynasty: Origins, Roles in Society and Eclipse (rev. ed.; London: Spink, 2010), 217-20, for the dating of ben Boethus's high priesthood. The location where the inscription was found might also indicate that the pavement originally came from a section south of and below the esplanade. However, Isaac argues that the considerable sum Paris spent on the donation suggests a location on the Temple Mount itself as opposed to below it. See Isaac, "Donation for Herod's Temple," 87-89. A final possible date for the beginning of construction is 26/25 BCE (counting fifteen years from 41/40 BCE). The main problem with this date is that it is far too early to make historical sense. Herod had only recently begun building Sebaste, and his position in the Augustan principate was not yet fully stable. It is difficult to see him choosing this moment to begin the largest and most politically complex construction project of his reign. Moreover, the two events are far removed from each other in the Josephan narrative. One would have to conjecture that Josephus's discussion of the Temple is an extremely large *analepsis* (literary flashback) that actually belongs about 100 sections back from where it appears in the text. It is far simpler to place the event later in the decade when Herod's friendship with Augustus and Agrippa and his status within the principate were secure. So, how does one explain the two dates provided by Josephus? Thomas Corbishley attempted to synchronize these dates by arguing that the one in *AJ* was counted from 40 BCE while the one in *BJ* was counted from 37. We know that Josephus was aware of and made use of both possible dates for the beginning of Herod's reign (*BJ* 1.665; *AJ* 17.191). Further, the weight of the archaeological evidence strongly suggests that the Temple renovation was begun in 23/22 BCE, and this date can be both the fifteenth and eighteenth years of the king's reign depending on whether one is counting from 40 or 37 BCE. See Thomas Corbishley, "The Chronology of the Reign of Herod the Great," *Journal of Theological Studies* 36 (1935): 26-27.

4. For the most complete descriptions of the Temple see *BJ* 5.184-226; *AJ* 15.391-425; *m. Middot* 2.1–5.4. Descriptions of the First Temple are found in 1 Kings 6–8 and 2 Chroni-

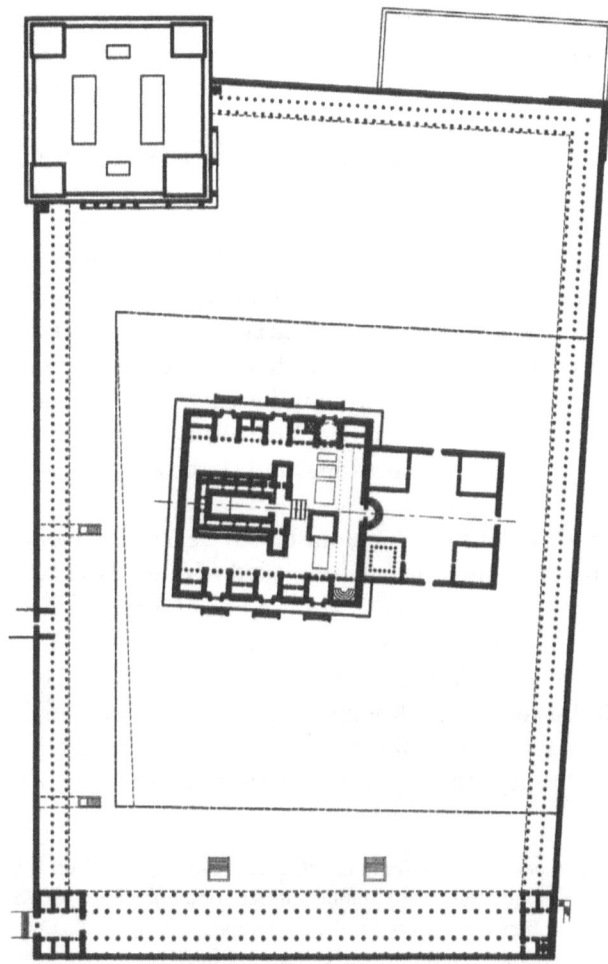

Reconstructed plan of Herod's Temple Mount
At just over thirty-five acres, Herod's Temple Mount
was the largest sanctuary site in the Roman world.

---

cles 2–4. A somewhat imaginary description of the ideal temple is found in Ezekiel 40–43. There is an entire subfield of biblical archaeology that focuses on the Second Temple and its construction. See especially Benjamin Mazar, *The Mountain of the Lord: Excavating in Jerusalem* (New York: Doubleday, 1975); Hillel Geva, "The Temple Mount and Its Environs," in *NEAEHL,* ed. Ephraim Stern (Jerusalem: Israel Exploration Society, 1997-93), 736-44; Lichtenberger, *Baupolitik,* 131-42; Japp, *Baupolitik,* 126-30; Ehud Netzer, *The Architecture of Herod, the Great Builder* (Tübingen: Mohr, 2006), 137-78. See also David M. Jacobson, "Ideas

The first stage of the Herodian reconstruction program was the expansion of the *temenos* to about double its original size. Using the latest engineering and construction techniques, Herod's builders removed and shaped massive amounts of earth and rock. About one million cubic feet were removed from the northwestern edge of the platform alone, leaving a steep scarp of more than thirty feet. The southwestern corner of the Mount was built on foundations that lay about one hundred feet below the esplanade, and the southeastern and northeastern corners were about 135 and 115 feet below respectively. The retaining walls supporting the massive platform were fifteen to sixteen feet thick and built of ashlars laid in courses averaging three to four feet high. This sheer size and gargantuan nature of merely the retaining walls gives us some idea of the visual effect the Temple would have had when it was standing. Hellenistic royal architecture reveled in the magnificent and awe-inspiring, and Herod's Temple would have fit nicely within this category.

In order to enter its precinct, one had to walk through one of its monumental gates. The more heavily trafficked of these gates were those on the west and south sides. On the western side of the Temple Mount were four gates, which today are named after the men who discovered them. Running north to south they are Warren's Gate, Wilson's Arch, Barclay's Gate, and Robinson's Arch. Robinson's Arch is the only remaining part of what once was a monumental stairway built on piers and arches that linked the Temple Mount to the roadway that ran along the base of the western

---

Concerning the Plan of Herod's Temple," *PEQ* 112 (1980): 33-40; Ruth P. Goldschmidt-Lehmann, "The Second (Herodian) Temple, Selected Bibliography," *Jerusalem Cathedra* 1 (1981): 336-59; M. Ben-Dov, "Herod's Mighty Temple Mount," *BAR* 12.6 (1986): 40-49; Katherine Ritmeyer and Leen Ritmeyer, "Reconstructing Herod's Temple Mount in Jerusalem," *BAR* 15.6 (1989): 23-53; David M. Jacobson, "The Plan of Herod's Temple," *BAIAS* 10 (1990-91): 36-66; Leen Ritmeyer, "Locating the Original Temple Mount," *BAR* 18.2 (1992): 24-45, 64-65; Dan Bahat, "Jerusalem Down Under: Tunneling along Herod's Temple Mount Wall," *BAR* 21.6 (1995): 31-47; David M. Jacobson and Shimon Gibson, "A Monumental Stairway on the Temple Mount," *IEJ* 45 (1995): 162-70; Brian Lalor, "The Temple Mount of Herod the Great at Jerusalem: Recent Excavations and Literary Sources," in *Archaeology and Biblical Interpretation,* ed. John R. Bartlett (London: Routledge, 1997), 95-116; Roller, *Building Program,* 176-78; David M. Jacobson, "Sacred Geometry: Unlocking the Secret of the Temple Mount, Part 1," *BAR* 25.4 (1999): 42-53, 62-64; "Sacred Geometry: Unlocking the Secret of the Temple Mount, Part 2," *BAR* 25.5 (1999): 54-63, 74; "Geometrical Planning in Monumental Herodian Architecture," *BAIAS* 17 (1999): 67-76; "Herod's Roman Temple," *BAR* 28.2 (2002): 19-27, 60-61. For Herod Agrippa's construction of a new city wall see *BJ* 2.218; *AJ* 19.326-27.

retaining wall. The gate itself opened onto the *temenos* directly west of the *Stoa Basileia* (Royal Stoa), and it may have been used primarily or even exclusively by Herod and his court when he visited the *Stoa* and the Temple.[5]

South of the Mount was the Ophel (City of David), and below it was the Lower City. Anyone ascending from these areas would have used the entrances on the south side. These entrances, now called the Double and Triple Gates, were originally both double entrances (the easternmost part of the Triple Gate was added during the Middle Ages), and are known as the Huldah Gates. Besides being the most direct way to enter the precinct from the south, they also seem to have had a certain popularity and significance. This significance might have been due to a long-standing tradition dating back to the time when the Ophel included the important parts of the city. It might also have been because of the large plazas south of the Temple in which large

---

5. The largest ashlar block used in the construction was more than forty-three feet long and ten feet high and weighed an estimated 300 tons. See Netzer, *Architecture*, 161-62. Cf. Shimon Gibson and David M. Jacobson, *Below the Temple Mount in Jerusalem* (Oxford: British Archaeological Society, 1996), 268-79; Lichtenberger, *Baupolitik*, 132-33; Japp, *Baupolitik*, 126-30. For a discussion of the drive toward immense size, height, and visual effect see Peter Richardson, "Origins, Innovations and Significance of Herod's Temple," in *Building Jewish in the Roman East* (Waco: Baylor University Press, 2004), 277. There is a discrepancy between the number of gates mentioned by Josephus and the number according to *m. Middot* 1.3. Archaeological excavations have generally supported Josephus over the Mishnah. Combining this support with Josephus's status as an eyewitness has led most scholars to privilege his account over the Mishnah's and conclude that *Middot*'s description of the entrances and exits describes a situation prior to the extension of the esplanade and not during Herod's reign. For the relevant sections see *m. Middot* 1.3; *AJ* 15.410-20. Above Barclay's Gate is a huge monolithic lintel, twenty-five feet long and seven feet high, that dates back to the Herodian period. Both Barclay's and Warren's Gates were apparently not connected to the main thoroughfare that ran parallel to the base of the western retaining wall. Instead, they connected with a narrower walkway adjacent to the wall. Below this walkway were rows of stores, some of which probably sold items to be used in the Temple such as animal and food sacrifices. See Netzer, *Architecture*, 172-73. Cf. Ritmeyer and Ritmeyer, "Reconstructing Herod's Temple Mount," 23-53. For Josephus's discussion of the Temple gates see *AJ* 15.410. In this passage, Josephus mentions four gates. The first gate is the one that stood above Wilson's Arch. It led to the Hasmonean palace, which was opposite the Mount and in which Agrippa II constructed his *triclinium*, which provided an uninterrupted view into the Temple courtyards (*AJ* 20.189-95). The two gates that "led into the suburb" are Warren's Gate and Barclay's Gate, and the final gate mentioned by Josephus in this passage is the one accessed by Robinson's Arch. For discussions of Robinson's Arch see Mazar, *Mountain of the Lord*, 13. Cf. Ritmeyer and Ritmeyer, "Reconstructing Herod's Temple Mount," 25-26; Bahat, "Jerusalem Down Under," 31-47; Geva, "The Temple Mount and Its Environs," 740-42; Lalor, "The Temple Mount of Herod," 100-106; Lichtenberger, *Baupolitik*, 133.

crowds could gather. To reach these gates, visitors could approach directly from a street built along the southern wall. However, the main accessway seems to have been via the plazas that were located south and below the gates. Leading up from these open spaces to the gates were two wide monumental stairways with easily ascendable stairs designed to accommodate the massive number of pilgrims who would use them at least three times a year during the pilgrimage holidays of Sukkot, Pesach, and Shavuot. The stairway leading up to the Double Gate was about four times as wide as the stairs ascending to the Triple Gate, and this difference in scale as well as the Double Gate's location directly opposite the center of the Temple Mount suggest that it was the more important of the two southern entrances.[6]

Once visitors passed through these entrances, they entered long, decorated passages that led them underneath the *Stoa Basileia*, through the superstructure of the Temple complex, and up onto the esplanade. Currently, only the passageway leading from the Double Gate is known to have survived. It is about forty feet wide and divided into two corridors separated by a colonnade. Four shallow cupolas, which survived *in situ* and are decorated with elaborate geometric and floral stone carvings, give some idea as to the original splendor of the passageways.[7]

---

6. For various theories about the popularity of the Huldah Gates see Netzer, *Architecture*, 171, 173-74. Cf. Ritmeyer and Ritmeyer, "Reconstructing Herod's Temple Mount," 23-53; Lichtenberger, *Baupolitik*, 133. Leen and Katherine Ritmeyer argue that the Triple Gate was used exclusively by the priests to reach the Temple platform and also to enter storerooms where supplies used in the Temple's rituals were housed. Although this theory cannot be entirely verified, it is certainly possible. The street leading up to the gates was paved with well-dressed rectangular flagstones. Visitors ultimately reached the gates by a short flight of stairs. The plazas that lay below the gates were not built on a system of supporting walls but were paved directly on top of a massive fill, which was retained by a broad wall on the southern border of the plazas. They were paved with huge stone slabs laid over a level of less finely worked slabs. Netzer suggests that these plazas may have been constructed during Herod's life, but they were probably finished after his death. See Ritmeyer and Ritmeyer, "Reconstructing Herod's Temple Mount," 35; Netzer, *Architecture*, 174. Cf. Jacobson and Gibson, "A Monumental Stairway," 162-70.

7. For a discussion of the passageway leading from the Double Gate to the *temenos*, see Charles Warren and C. R. Conder, *Survey of Western Palestine* (London: Palestine Exploration Society, 1884), 164-66; 231; Gibson and Jacobson, *Below the Temple Mount*, 235-59. Cf. Ritmeyer and Ritmeyer, "Reconstructing Herod's Temple Mount," 45-46; Dan Bahat, "The Western Wall Tunnels," in Hillel Geva, *Ancient Jerusalem Revealed* (Jerusalem: Israel Exploration Society, 1994), 182. The rest of the passageway and the corridors of the Triple Gate were probably decorated similarly. According to the Mishnah, visitors were supposed to enter on the right and leave on the left, unless they were mourners. In that case they

Herod and the Temple

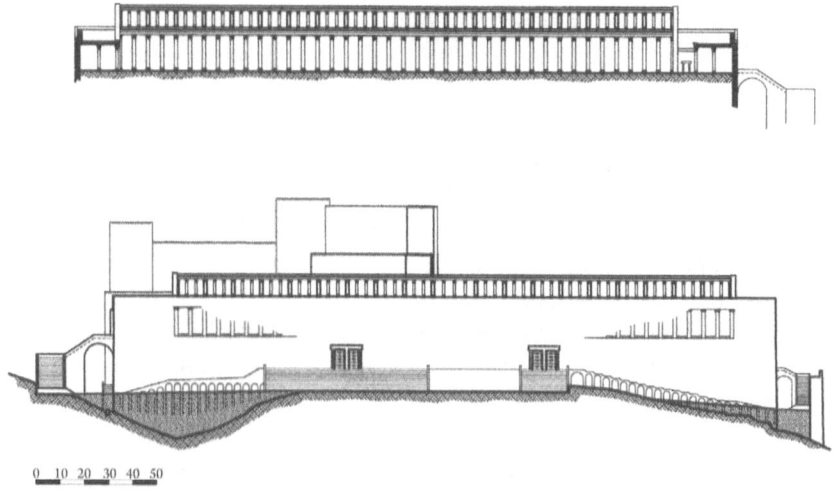

Reconstructed elevations of the south side of the Temple Mount including the Huldah Gates

During Herod's reign, the north and east retaining walls of the Temple Mount functioned as city walls, and thus the gates within these walls were also city gates. The Mishnah mentions the Shushan Gate, through which the high priest left as he traveled to the Mount of Olives to prepare the ashes of the red heifer. These ashes were then used to ritually cleanse those who had come into contact with a corpse. However, archaeologists have not found any irrefutable evidence for this gate's existence unless it stood at the site of the present-day Golden Gate, below which there are a few traces of an earlier gate, albeit one from the post-Second Temple period.

---

entered on the left, so as to receive special attention and comfort from those exiting. This arrangement suggests either that one gate was used for entrances and one for exits or, more likely, at each gate one corridor was used for entrances and the other for exits. See *m. Middot* 2.2, although we should again be hesitant to accept the Mishnah's view uncritically. Between and below the Huldah Gates, there seem to have been two buildings. The westernmost contained several *mikvaot*, which were cut into the bedrock, suggesting that it was a bathhouse used for purification prior to entering the Temple. The building east of the bathhouse contains many rock-hewn rooms and may have been a council house or one of the three courts of law located within the Temple precinct. According to the Babylonian Talmud, one of these courts sat in the "Chamber of Hewn Stone," located either at one of the gates of the sanctuary or at one of the gates of the city leading into the Temple Mount. See *b. Sanhedrin* 11. Cf. Ritmeyer and Ritmeyer, "Reconstructing Herod's Temple Mount," 47.

Remains of an arch have been found on the southern part of the eastern wall. This arch seems to be all that is left of what was once a monumental staircase similar in design and opposite in location to Robinson's Arch. It also provided access to the *Stoa Basileia* as well as the street running along and below the southern wall. The picture is even less clear on the north side, where it would have been difficult to have a gate at all since the Antonia occupied the hill on the west and the eastern side bordered the valley that descended to the Kidron Brook. Further, a large pool known as the Pool of Israel, which was built in this valley during the Herodian period, adjoined a section of the northern wall. The Mishnah mentions a gate called the Tadi Gate, but states that it was never used.[8]

Passing through one of the gates, visitors reached the Herodian *temenos* and the Temple sanctuary itself. Although bound by biblical descriptions of the First Temple regarding the sanctuary, Herod had significant freedom to design the rest of the site. He chose to construct double colonnades on the north, west, and east sides of the *temenos*. The older Temple probably had colonnades as well, although Josephus only mentions one, which was located on the eastern side and was known as Solomon's Stoa. According to Josephus, each of these colonnades, which were each about sixty-one feet (thirty cubits) wide, was built of white marble. Cedar beams and monolithic columns about forty-six feet high (twenty-five cubits) supported their roofs. Given Herod's building predilections, however, it is likely that these stoas were actually constructed of local stone and then plastered white to appear like marble. The total length of all of the

---

8. North of the Temple was the suburb of Bezetha, which may be identical to the section known as *Bēzeth*. The Seleucid general Bacchides pitched his tents there after leaving Jerusalem (1 Macc 7:19). Depending on the manuscript, Josephus calls it *Bērzēthō* or *Bēthzēthō* (*AJ* 12.397). Herod's grandson, Herod Agrippa I, enclosed this new suburb within the city when he constructed the wall known as the Third Wall. See *BJ* 2.218-19, 328, 530; 5.149, 151, 246; *AJ* 19.326-27. For a discussion of the Shushan Gate, which was on the east side of the Temple Mount, see *m. Middot* 1.3. For the ritual of the red heifer, whose ashes were used to purify one who had touched a corpse, see Num 19:1-22; *m. Parah.* Cf. Joseph L. Blau, "The Red Heifer: A Biblical Purification Rite in Rabbinic Literature," *Numen* 14 (1967): 70-78. The Golden Gate is also called the Gate of Mercy *(shaʿar harakhamim),* and the Gate of Eternal Life in Arabic. In Jewish tradition, the Messiah will come through this gate at the end of days. See Geva, "The Temple Mount and Its Environs," 743. For a discussion of the eastern and northern walls of the Temple, specifically the arch and monumental stairway on the eastern side of the Temple Mount and the Pool of Israel see Netzer, *Architecture,* 175 with n. 135. For the rabbinic discussion of the Tadi Gate see *m. Middot* 1.3, 9. No archaeological evidence for this gate has been discovered.

Herod and the Temple

colonnades was approximately 3,900 feet (3,360 feet if the Antonia fortress projected into the esplanade and there were no colonnades below it or around it). They provided an excellent architectural frame for the Temple's sacred precinct and offered shade from the sun and protection from the rain and wind. They also would have been ideal places for individuals to relax, congregate, and conduct the business necessary for the rituals taking place around them, such as money changing. Herod also used these stoas to house and display the spoils he had taken in his military campaigns, especially those against the Nabataeans.[9]

Enclosing the south side of the Mount was the *Stoa Basileia*. Because of his lack of priestly standing, Herod could not enter the innermost parts of the Temple. But as king he no doubt wanted to maintain his prestige and presence as much as possible. To that end, he constructed this stoa, a building so large and magnificent that it would be useful and appropriate for ceremonies and grand receptions, especially during national gatherings. It was still within the extended Temple platform, but because it was outside the bounds of the sacred precinct he had much more freedom in

---

9. For Josephus's discussion of Solomon's Stoa see *BJ* 5.185. Cf. *AJ* 20.219-21. Most scholars do not think that Solomon actually constructed this colonnade. Nevertheless, Josephus's testimony suggests that first-century BCE Jews regarded it as extremely old. Netzer believes it dates back to before the Hasmonean period. For Josephus's description of the porticos on the north, west, and east sides see *BJ* 5.190-92. Although such dimensions are relatively modest given the overall size and scale of the Temple Mount, Netzer is correct to remind us that these double colonnades were twice the width and height of the reconstructed double colonnades in the forecourt of the *Augusteum* at Sebaste. Also see Netzer, *Architecture,* 161 (Solomon's Stoa), 164 n. 96 (porticos on Herod's Temple Mount). Cf. Lichtenberger, *Baupolitik,* 137-38. For a discussion of Herod's use of marble see Moshe L. Fischer and Alla Stein, "Josephus on the Use of Marble in Building Projects of Herod the Great," *JJS* 45 (1994): 79-85. We see this pattern of using stone column drums covered in plaster throughout Herod's building program in places such as Caesarea Maritima, Herodion, and the Northern Palace at Masada. For the social and economic activities that probably occurred in the Temple's colonnades see Mark 11:15-19, 27-33; Matt 21:12-17, 23-27; Luke 19:45-48; 20:1-8. Cf. John 2:12-25. For Herod's use of them to display his war spoils see *AJ* 15.402. While the New Testament certainly puts a negative connotation on the moneychangers, they performed a necessary function, since the Temple accepted only certain forms of currency. Pilgrims who wished to make the half-shekel donation to the Temple needed to change their money in order to fulfill this obligation. For the commandment to pay the half-shekel tax see Exod 30:11-16. Cf. J. Liver, "The Half-Shekel Offering in Biblical and Post-Biblical Literature," *HTR* 56 (1963): 173-98. Cf. Donald T. Ariel and Jean-Philippe Fontanille, *The Coins of Herod: A Modern Analysis and Die Classification* (Leiden: Brill, 2012), 39-41, where they suggest that the Tyrian shekel may not have been the only permissible currency, even while it was the most desired.

its architectural design. It was built as a two-level triple colonnade, with the lower level containing a fourth wall of engaged columns, which probably were built into the southern retaining wall of the Temple Mount. The lower colonnades had column bases with double convex moldings of the Attic-Ionic type and Corinthian capitals. The upper colonnades consisted of smaller columns but the style of the bases and capitals is unknown. This upper level provided the interior with large amounts of natural light, which would have been ideal for viewing the beautifully carved wooden ceiling panels. The northern side of the stoa opened fully onto the rest of the Temple platform, allowing easy entrance and egress for visitors.

The *Stoa Basileia* was probably one of the most spectacular individual buildings Herod constructed throughout his reign. It is perhaps no surprise that it was located at the focal point of his kingdom, the Temple Mount. Lacking a priestly lineage, Herod was unable to obtain the office of high priest with its accompanying legitimacy and authority. The high priest was not only the chief administrator of the Temple but also the only individual who could enter the Holy of Holies. Thus, even if for only one day on Yom Kippur, he was closer to the divine presence than any other person. This fact gave him enormous spiritual and charismatic power, which Herod was never able to control fully. Although Herod could appoint and depose high priests, he could never be one. Moreover, he could not even participate in the priestly rituals, and he was even prohibited from entering the inner courts of the sanctuary itself. His consolation was the stoa. It enabled him to have a presence on the Mount at all times. During any occasion when the king decided to entertain guests there, it would have been closed to the general public, but at other times throughout the year it was probably open to anyone who visited the Temple Mount. Visitors could stroll through its colonnades, take shelter from the sun and heat, appreciate the architectural genius of the building, and marvel at its artistic embellishments, such as the ornamented ceiling with its high relief woodcarvings. Such a building would have advertised Herod's majesty to all. Further, because of its size and visibility on the Mount, visitors to the Temple would be visually reminded of his presence and his role as a pious benefactor and rebuilder of the Temple, the holiest site in Jerusalem and now an international place of worship.[10]

---

10. For Josephus's description of the *Stoa Basileia*, see *AJ* 15.411-16. According to Josephus, it had 162 columns, each with a circumference of the spread of three men's arms (*AJ* 15.414). Netzer proposes a diameter of about five feet. He also suggests a distance between

Herod and the Temple

The Temple as Culmination of Herodian Political Ideology

Our discussion of the Herodian reconstruction leaves no doubt as to the magnificence of this complex, and any ruler in the Graeco-Roman world would have been justifiably proud of such an accomplishment. And yet, what makes the Temple such a good illustration of Herodian presentation and ideology is its multiplicity of meaning, its ability to speak to several audiences using each one's vocabulary and cultural norms. Like most of the buildings in Herod's building program, the Temple combined architectural designs and influences from multiple sources, yet it retained many of the elements and measurements of the original, especially the sanctuary. It could thus look Hellenistic to the Hellenized non-Jews, Roman to the Romans, and Jewish to the Jews.

In the discussion that follows, it is important to remember that our

---

columns of approximately twenty feet, based on the average width of the corridors of the Double and Triple Gates, coupled with the distance (230 feet) between those two gates. If we accept a column total of 160 as opposed to 162, then the four column rows would easily divide into forty columns per row. Accepting a distance between columns of approximately twenty feet, there would have been twelve intercolumniations between the two gates. Netzer proposes twelve intercolumniations east of the Triple Gate and eleven west of the Double Gate. See Netzer, *Architecture,* 167-70. Other reconstructions also exist. See Thomas A. Busink, *Der Tempel von Jerusalem, von Salomo bis Herodes. Eine Archäologisch-Historische Studie unter Berücksichtigung des Westsemitischen Tempelbaus* (Leiden: Brill, 1970-80), 1200-1232; Ritmeyer and Ritmeyer, "Reconstructing Herod's Temple Mount," 23-53. Cf. Lalor, "The Temple Mount of Herod," 104. Netzer's reconstruction argues that the upper colonnades were composed of columns of about three feet in diameter and about thirty feet in height. According to this reconstruction, these columns were placed as pairs between two successive pillars with engaged columns on their edges. Each unit of two columns and two pillars took up the distance of two intercolumniations on the ground level, except in the central aisle where the units took up the length of three intercolumniations. In Netzer's scheme, these central units were also three columns and two pillars instead of the two column and two pillar unit seen throughout the rest of the structure. Such a design would enhance the stability of the structure while not detracting from its aesthetics. For modern estimation of the size of the *Stoa Basileia,* see Netzer, *Architecture,* 165-69. Cf. Roller, *Building Program,* 177; Lichtenberger, *Baupolitik,* 133-34; Japp, *Baupolitik,* 129. For the possible uses of the stoa as well as its symbolic value see Netzer, *Architecture,* 170-71. Cf. Ehud Netzer, "Herod the Great's Contribution to Nikopolis in Light of His Building Activity in Judea," in *Proceedings of the First International Symposium of Nicopolis (23-29 September, 1984),* ed. Evangelos Chrysos (Preveza: Demos Prevezas, 1987), 122; Netzer, *Palaces,* 129-130; Richardson, "Origins, Innovations and Significance," 276. For David M. Jacobson's discussion of the Roman influences on Herod's reconstruction see Jacobson, "Herod's Roman Temple," 18-27, 60.

separation of influences is somewhat artificial and meant as an analytical tool. In reality, the Graeco-Roman world was a delightful polyglot of cultures, a frenetic melding and mixing of influences. In such an environment, it would have been difficult, if not impossible, to identify separate and distinct influences.

One of the most important Hellenic influences on the Temple was the classical acropolis, of which the most famous was the Athenian Acropolis. While not slavishly dependent on the Athenian model, Herod seems to incorporate several aspects of its design, function, and layout. In particular, both structures utilize *entasis,* a design in which a slight convex curve or swelling is added to the middle of a tapering structure, so that it is wider than the top or bottom. In classical architecture, this application most often appears in columns of Doric-order temples, such as the temple of Aphaia on Aigina, as well as the temples at Agrigento, Paestum, Segesta, and, most famously, the Parthenon. According to most scholars, the purpose of this correction is to combat the illusion of straight lines and right angles, when seen at a distance against the sky, seeming to be thinner in the middle than on the top and bottom. Recently, Peter Thompson, among others, has argued that no such optical illusion exists. Instead, the real reason for using *entasis* is that it provides a greater strength-to-weight ratio than a parallel column. Regardless of the architectural motivation, its characteristic presence in exclusively Doric-order temples makes its use in the Temple's Corinthian order exterior walls surprising. As the southwestern corner of the Temple Mount clearly shows, Herod utilized *entasis* for the outer walls of his *temenos*. In particular, each course of Herodian ashlar blocks bulges out slightly more than one inch from the course below.

By itself, Herod's use of the *entasis* does not mean that he was consciously mimicking the Athenian Acropolis, especially since it was a common Hellenic architectural feature. However, similarities in function strengthen this connection. Besides being built high above the city, both structures were the central religious spaces of their respective cities. Even though the Temple also functioned as a pseudo-agora or forum, its primary purpose was religious. Additionally, we already know that Herod was an active patron at Athens and that there were at least two Herodian dedications on the Acropolis. Further, Josephus tells us that the statues of Roma and Augustus at his *Augusteum* in Caesarea resembled cult statues by Polykleitos (Hera of Argos) and Phidias (Zeus of Olympia), two of the most famous classical sculptors.

Another similarity between the Jerusalem Temple and major Hellenic

Herod and the Temple

sanctuary sites is the incorporation of *anathemata,* offerings donated *ex voto* (in fulfillment of a vow). These items mostly came from the government and were spoils of war. We know that Herod donated spoils from the Nabataean war, and it is likely that he made similar offerings throughout his reign. The most famous Hellenic example of a sanctuary site receiving such gifts is the Sanctuary of Apollo at Delphi, where modern visitors can walk past the myriad of treasuries that were constructed by the Greek cities to house their *anathemata.* Other sanctuary sites with massive amounts of *anathemata* include the Acropolis of Athens and Olympia, which Herod actually visited. While the practice of making offerings to a sanctuary site from the spoils of war predates the Greeks and is not unique to them, it certainly was fundamental to their religious world, and an individual as Hellenized as Herod would have been extremely familiar with such a practice.[11]

Despite these elements, the major architectural influence on Herod's Temple was Roman. This influence extended to almost all areas of the complex, even the sanctuary itself, although its design was severely limited by biblical injunction. Such influence is hardly surprising, given the contemporary political climate and Rome's dominance. Nevertheless, Herod's choice of influence went beyond mere expedience or even unconscious imitation. He could have chosen to rebuild the Mount using only Hellenistic architecture, a decision that still would have been fashionable and resulted in no less a grandiose structure. However, as we have already seen, he enthusiastically embraced the architecture of the Roman West and utilized its building techniques and styles in other parts of his building program to an extent that was unparalleled among his contemporaries. Moreover, just as he was on the cutting edge of modern technology in other buildings, so too was he on the Temple Mount. Such innovation can hardly be simply

---

11. For Herod's use of *entasis* on the outer walls of the Temple Mount in imitation of the Parthenon see Rocca, *Herod's Judaea,* 297-98. For an ancient discussion of *entasis,* see Vitruvius, *De Architectura* 3.3.10-13; 3.5.14. For its use on the Parthenon see Jeffrey M. Hurwit, *The Athenian Acropolis: History, Mythology, and Archaeology from the Neolithic Era to the Present* (Cambridge: Cambridge University Press, 2000), 167-68. For a refutation of the optical correction explanation in favor of one emphasizing engineering advantages see Peter Thompson, Georgia Papadopoulou, and Eleni Vassiliou, "The Origins of Entasis: Illusion, Aesthetics or Engineering?" *Spatial Vision* 20 (2007): 531-43. For Herod's *anathemata* see *AJ* 15.402. For discussion of the *anathemata* at Delphi and Olympia as well as a description of the Acropolis of Athens see Pausanias 10.9.1-17.1 (Delphi); 5.21.1-27.12 (Olympia); 1.22.4-28.3 (Athens). Cf. Rocca, *Herod's Judaea,* 298-99.

a matter of passive replication. Instead, we should see Herod's rebuilding of the Temple as similar to Augustus's program at Rome, which included multiple forums and temples at the heart of a capital city.

In order to complete his magnum opus, Herod utilized several central aspects of Roman architecture and technology and drew on well-defined architectural models, specifically those of the Roman temple and forum. To enlarge the public space available, he relied on a standard feature of Roman temple architecture, namely an elevated terrace with *cryptoportica* forming the substructure. The expansion of the southern side of the Temple Mount required a substantial removal of earth and rock and the construction of colossal retaining walls to hold up the incredible weight of the platform. In order to accomplish this herculean task, Herod lengthened the Temple's terrace and constructed a series of superimposed arches, which were covered by vaults. This layout was similar but not identical to the string of *cryptoportica* he constructed for the temple complex at Sebaste. The two main southern entrances to the Temple, the Huldah Gates, were part of this substructure, providing both support for as well as access to the platform.

As we saw in chapter 8, in constructing elevated terraces for temples, Herod could look to the precedent of sacred architecture in places such as Pergamum, Kos, and Lindos. In Italy, he could look to the precincts of Fortuna Primigenia at Praeneste (Palestrina) and Hercules Victor at Tibur (Tivoli). Both of these late second and early first centuries BCE temples consist of an expansive sanctuary on top of an elevated terrace built atop an artificially leveled plateau. They also utilize twin entrances, symmetrically placed on either side of a principal axis and ultimately leading to the temple platforms. Interestingly, both sanctuaries enjoyed elevated status during the Augustan period, since, as Suetonius tells us, they were two of Augustus's favorite sites. In Jerusalem, the Huldah Gates served this function, providing two symmetrical entries on either side of the midpoint of the southern wall of the Temple and facing the City of David. As we have already discussed, these gates seem to have been the most popular, and, therefore, we can compare them to those at Praeneste and Tivoli.

Although the elevated terrace was not new, the use of several *cryptoportica* to elevate a forum or public platform, which would become standard in Roman imperial architecture, was still an innovation in the first century BCE. There were no contemporary examples in the city of Rome itself, although we do see later examples in imperial forums such as those in Arelate (Arles) and Narbo (Narbonne). Herod was not responsible for this new architectural form, but he seems to stand at the vanguard of its development. Moreover, his blending of old and new Roman styles is entirely in line with his tastes in the other architectural genres that we have discussed previously and reflects the ethos of his time period: innovation going hand-in-hand with tradition.

While forced to comply with the biblical dimensions where they existed, Herod benefited from discrepancies between the descriptions in 1 Kings and 2 Chronicles and lacunae in these blueprints. He had a significant amount of freedom in his enlargement and reconstruction of the *temenos,* and it is not surprising that he would turn to his imperial patrons for inspiration and ideas. Just as the heart of the Roman city, the forum, was a multi-purpose space, providing an environment for religious rituals but also for economic transactions and political discourse, so too was the Jerusalem Temple precinct. Part marketplace, part political arena, this structure was a central influence on the layout and design of the Herodian *temenos.* The standard Roman forum was a large rectangular open space surrounded by colonnades. The two most important buildings in any forum were the basilica (the public administration building) and the temple of the primary deity of the town. Usually, the basilica would be on one of the short sides of the forum, and the temple of the patron deity would either be in the middle of the forum or in front of the basilica. In Jerusalem, these two essential buildings were represented by the *Stoa Basileia* and the Temple's sanctuary. Although the *Stoa Basileia* resembled a Hellenistic stoa in that its northern wing (the wing facing the rest of the *temenos*) was open, inside it looked like a standard Roman basilica, with an inner colonnade on all sides.

Did Herod have the *Forum Romanum* (the forum in Rome) in mind when designing his *temenos?* It does not seem so. Instead, scholars have looked to other specific forum models. John Ward-Perkins has proposed that Herod modeled his Temple Mount after the open spaces in Cyrene and Alexandria, which were eastern interpretations of the Roman model. The *Caesarea* at Alexandria and Cyrene were both large rectangular areas with a temple in the middle and a basilica on one of the short sides of the rectangle. The main problem with Ward-Perkins's proposal is that there is no evidence that Herod ever visited either of these sites, although it is possible that he would have had some knowledge of them given their relative proximity to Judaea. Rocca has proposed an alternative model, namely the forums of Augustan-era colonies in Gaul and Spain such as Glanum and Arelate (modern-day Arles) in Gaul and Tarragona in Spain.

These colonies, which were settled by the veterans of Agrippa and Augustus, all contain forums with a central or side temple and a basilica. Like the Jerusalem Temple, these precincts were the civic and religious centers of their towns, whereas the *Caesareum* in Alexandria was just one of many large precincts in the city. Moreover, as colonies created by his patrons, their architectural features might have offered a certain attraction for Herod and his architects. I would offer a third possibility, namely that the inspiration was more subtle and flexible than either Ward-Perkins or Rocca suggests. In other words, Herod did not need to be thinking of the forum of a particular city to be modeling his *temenos* after a Roman forum. Instead, given his predilection for mixing and melding influences while providing his own interpretation of them, it is more likely that he included the main architectural elements of the Roman forum and modified them to suit his needs and the space itself. The Jerusalem *temenos* was, therefore, both Roman and Herodian at the same time.[12]

Another extremely Roman element in the Temple's design was the dimensions of its buildings and their relationship to each other. Where he was free to do so, Herod utilized Graeco-Roman notions of harmony and aesthetics and merged them with the biblical model. As David Jacobson argues, the Herodian Temple Mount conformed to a rigorous geometrical scheme based on a set of equilateral (60°) triangles. This scheme of triangles forming a rectangular *temenos* also appears at the Machpelah enclosure at Hebron and in the Herodian forum at Sebaste. Ground plans based on equilateral triangles appear in great frequency in Graeco-Roman architecture. The Roman architect Vitruvius recommends that a Roman theater be designed using a series of four equilateral triangles, spaced at 30°

---

12. For Herod's use of elevated terraces and *cryptoportica* and the influence of sanctuary sites in Latium see David M. Jacobson, "The Jerusalem Temple of Herod the Great," in *The World of the Herods: Volume 1 of the International Conference The World of the Herods and the Nabataeans Held at the British Museum, 17-19 April 2001,* ed. Nikos Kokkinos (Stuttgart: Steiner, 2007), 157-58. Cf. Netzer, *Architecture,* 87-88, 163; Rocca, *Herod's Judaea,* 300. For the essential *Romanitas* of the Herodian Temple see Jacobson, "Herod's Roman Temple," 19-27, 60-61, where he argues that Herod's imitation of Roman models was somewhat unconscious and passive. See Rocca, *Herod's Judaea,* 300, for refutation of Jacobson's argument. For Augustus's affection for the sanctuaries at Praeneste and Tivoli see Seutonius, *Aug.* 72.1. For Herod's imitation of Roman forums see Jacobson, "The Jerusalem Temple of Herod the Great," 158, 164. For the debate about specific models for the Jerusalem *temenos,* see John B. Ward-Perkins, *Roman Imperial Architecture* (2nd ed.; New York: Penguin, 1981), 366; Rocca, *Herod's Judaea,* 301. Cf. Dan Bahat and Chaim T. Rubenstein, *The Illustrated Atlas of Jerusalem,* trans. Shlomo Ketko (New York: Simon and Schuster, 1990), 44.

intervals, the points of which would set the path of the stairways running between the seats of the *cavea* (seating area) and the stage (*De Architectura* 5.6.1-2). These mathematical and geometric aesthetics even shaped the design of the building most defined by biblical injunction, the sanctuary of the Temple. As per the biblical requirements, it contained the necessary tripartite divisions of porch *('ulam)*, main hall *(hekhal)*, and holy of holies *(devir)*. Behind the porch, the interior width of the sanctuary was seventy cubits (129 feet). However, Herod's builders enlarged the eastern facade of the sanctuary to a length of 100 cubits (184 feet) and raised the height to match the length. In reality, the building was T-shaped and resembled a reclining lion. However, from the front entrance, a visitor would see it as a flawless cube, a structure embodying the number ten, which the Pythagoreans believed was a perfect reflection of the proportions of the human body, specifically the number of fingers on each hand.

Interestingly, Vitruvius stresses the need for symmetrical aesthetics when constructing temples. He states emphatically, "The design of temples depends on symmetry *(symmetria)*, the principles of which must be most carefully observed by the architect." For him, "without *symmetria* and proportion, there can be no principles in the design of any temple; that is if there is no precise relation between its members, as in the case of those of a well-shaped man" (*De Architectura* 3.1.5). In the ancient world, *symmetria* had a much more profound meaning than our modern notion of symmetry. For Plato, it expressed "beauty and excellence" (*Philebus* 64E). There could be no better place for beautiful perfection than in a shrine to a god. Given the centrality and exceptionality of the Jerusalem Temple and its sanctuary, Pythagorean symmetry would have been a necessity.

And yet, however Hellenistic or Roman Herod's Temple was, it still retained many elements of its Solomonic predecessor as well as of the Near Eastern temples by which that structure was influenced. The location of the sanctuary and its eastern orientation remained unchanged. So too did the tripartite division of the sanctuary with its series of courtyards increasing in holiness as one moved toward the center. The massive altar in the Herodian complex remained on the same axis as the sanctuary and was composed of field stones untouched by iron tools, as required by biblical command. Like its predecessor, the Temple corners had horns, and its summit was reached by a ramp from the south side. In short, Herod's Temple, like the rest of his building program, was a seamless mixture of several cultural traditions, uniting the differing aspects of his personality and identity and integrating them into a unique and novel architectural expression.[13]

The Temple's status and function as the central religious institution of the Herodian state, and indeed of the Jewish people, enabled Herod to present himself as king and patron of all Jews everywhere. We already have seen how he expanded the high priesthood to extend the reach of the Temple and, by extension, his own influence further into the Diaspora. The expanded and renovated Temple Mount served a similar function, providing new incentives for religious pilgrimage and for the spaces these new visitors would need. While Jews had always made sacred visits to Jerusalem and the Temple — indeed such visits were obligatory for Jewish men three times a year, on Sukkot, Passover, and Shavuot — these sacred visits increased as the *Pax Augusta* made travel easier and safer. With a *temenos* of more than thirty-five acres, Jerusalem and its only sanctuary site could now take its place as a pilgrimage site of the first rank.

Along with a significant growth in Jewish visitors, the Herodian period

---

13. For a discussion of Herod's use of equilateral triangles and symmetry in the Jerusalem Temple see Jacobson, "Sacred Geometry Part 1"; "Sacred Geometry Part 2"; "The Jerusalem Temple of Herod the Great," 149-51. For the importance of *symmetria* in classical design see Jerome J. Pollitt, *The Ancient View of Greek Art: Criticism, History and Terminology* (New Haven: Yale University Press, 1974), 14-22, 160-62. For the popularity of geometrical designs, especially those exhibiting 60° angles, see Michael Avi-Yonah, *Oriental Art in Roman Palestine* (Studi Semitici 5; Rome: Università di Roma, 1961), 15-21. Cf. Jacobson, "The Jerusalem Temple of Herod the Great," 160. For a discussion of the circular geometric design of the Upper Palace at Herodion see Ehud Netzer, *Greater Herodium* (Jerusalem: Hebrew University of Jerusalem, 1981). Also see David M. Jacobson, "The Design of the Fortress of Herodium," *ZDPV* 100 (1984): 127-36. For the Temple's retention of local and Near Eastern architectural features see Jacobson, "The Jerusalem Temple of Herod the Great," 150, 153. As a comparison, it is worth examining other contemporary and near-contemporary sanctuaries, particularly those in Phoenician and Near Eastern sites. One example of a large urban Late-Hellenistic complex is the temple of Eshmun in Carthage. Like the Jerusalem Temple, it towered over the city below. It too mixed native and Hellenistic architectural elements together, though the native elements seem to have been preeminent. Around the Near East, there are also other contemporary examples of urban sanctuary sites that display features similar to the Jerusalem Temple. These include the sanctuary of Bel at Palmyra, the temple of Dushares (Qasr al Bint) at Petra, the sanctuary of Zeus at Damascus, and the temple of Jupiter Heliopolitanus at Ba'albek. Each of these has an immensely large *temenos* which is an expansion of an older and smaller sanctuary. Moreover, they all have a rectangular precinct with a temple in the middle and an adjacent central altar. See Rocca, *Herod's Judaea*, 299. Cf. Dan Bahat, "The Architectural Origins of Herod's Temple Mount," in *Herod and Augustus: Papers Presented at the IJS Conference, 21st-23rd June 2005*, ed. D. M. Jacobson and N. Kokkinos (Leiden: Brill, 2009), 236.

also saw an increased non-Jewish presence at the Temple. In order to accommodate these new tourists (both those religiously interested and those just curious), Herod's reconstruction created an identified space where non-Jews and foreigners could visit and even worship. They now could climb the Temple Mount and enter the *temenos* as long as they did not pass beyond the *Soreg,* the barrier and rampart that separated non-Jews from Jews. Large signs placed at regular intervals delineated the boundary of the *Soreg* and warned non-Jews against entering the inner courts of the sanctuary. When Marcus Agrippa came to Jerusalem in 15 BCE, he went up to the Temple Mount with Herod to offer sacrifices but must have only gone as far as the *Soreg,* as he would not have wished to cause offense or incite a disturbance. Nevertheless, by providing an area that non-Jews could enter and in which they could worship God — in the process allowing them to come closer to the sanctuary itself — Herod was, in a way, transforming the Jerusalem cult from a Judaean-specific and exclusive status to one more inclusive and worldwide, one that could be honored and reverenced by Jews and non-Jews alike. Such a transformation is completely in accord with the increased travel, communication, and peace of the *Pax Augusta.* Moreover, it is no surprise that this development occurred at the same time and even at the behest of a monarch who felt comfortable in multiple worlds. Jerusalem and the Temple, like their king, were asserting themselves on the Roman stage as objects of glory, respect, and veneration.[14]

14. For Herod's rebuilding and enhancement of Jerusalem into a city capable of being a major pilgrimage site see John Strange, "Herod and Jerusalem: The Hellenization of an Oriental City," in *Jerusalem in Ancient History and Tradition,* ed. Thomas L. Thompson (London: Clark, 2003), 109-10. Cf. Seth Schwartz, "Herod, Friend of the Jews," in *Jerusalem and Eretz Israel: The Arie Kindler Volume,* ed. Joshua Schwartz, Zohar Amar, and Irit Ziffer (Tel Aviv: Eritz Israel Museum and Ingeborg Center, 2001), 68-69; Bahat and Rubenstein, *Illustrated Atlas,* 40-53. For Herod's expansion of the Temple Mount see Lichtenberger, *Baupolitik,* 131-42; Japp, *Baupolitik,* 126-30. For pilgrimage as a religious obligation of all Jewish men see Exod 23:14-17; 34:23; Deut 16:16-17. Cf. *AJ* 4.203. For non-Jews' ability to visit the Temple Mount as long as they did not cross the *Soreg,* see *m. Middot* 2.3. Excavators have found two examples of the *Soreg* warning, both written in Greek. See *CIJ,* 1400. Cf. *BJ* 5.193; 6.125; *AJ* 15.417. The text of these prohibition inscriptions, which were hung around the boundary of the *Soreg,* read, "No foreigner shall enter within the balustrade of the Temple, or within the precinct. Whoever is caught doing so will have himself to blame for his death that will follow in consequence." For a discussion of the Court of the Gentiles and an analysis of its role in Herodian ideology see Richardson, "Origins, Innovations and Significance," 287-88, 292-94. When Agrippa visited Judaea in 15 BCE, he also visited the Temple and sacrificed a hecatomb (100 cattle) to God. Presumably, he entered the Court of the Gentiles and then the priests made sacrifices on his behalf. See *AJ* 16.13-15. Cf. Philo,

In the ancient world, no other building was as important to Jews and Jewish identity than the Temple in Jerusalem. It is not surprising that Herod would have wanted to leave his mark on this complex, the center of Jewish religion and cultic practice. Nevertheless, such a project would have been inconceivable in the early part of his reign. As an important but insecure client king, who was actively repelling the advances of a much more powerful Cleopatra, Herod would not have had the money, freedom, or agency to undertake such a project. Only once his reign had become secure and his coffers full could he attempt such a massive enterprise.

The result completely fits with Herod's grandiose sense of scale and bombast. The Temple Mount was not just a large religious complex, but the largest in the ancient world. It employed tens of thousands of his subjects and brought in untold amounts of money in sacrifices and donations. From Herod's perspective, it also enabled him to claim membership in an elite group of builders and patrons, of which Augustus and Agrippa were his only real rivals. At the same time, it provides us with the clearest image we have of a king who felt the tug of several cultural worlds and architectural tastes and responded appropriately. It shows Herod at his chameleon best, appealing simultaneously to the aesthetic and religious sensibilities of all three of his major audiences, Jewish, Roman and Hellenistic, without any significant hesitation or error. In the multicultural world of Roman Judaea, Herod and his Temple were right at home.

Leg. 157, where Philo states that Augustus made several dedications to the Temple and also paid for the daily sacrifices made on his behalf. See also *AJ* 16.163, 173 on Augustus's confirmation of the right of Diaspora Jews to send their half-shekel donation to the Temple.

CONCLUSION

The Political Self-Presentation of Herod the Great

We began this investigation with a question: Why and how did Herod the Great succeed as monarch despite a dubious lineage and a weak and ambiguous claim to legitimacy? As we have seen, he accomplished this herculean task through a combination of political skill and flexibility. He assumed public presentations and personae that would appeal to the expectations and demands of his audiences, and he shed them as soon as they became inadequate and obsolete. Put simply, he consistently morphed into the right king for the right situation.

We can identify three major stages in Herod's career. During each stage, he presented a distinct and explicit persona that matched his political needs and situation. These three stages are: his courtier stage (47-40 BCE), his early reign as king of Judaea (40-30 BCE), and his later reign as king (30-4 BCE).

Herod the Courtier

When Herod began his political career in the early 40s BCE, he was merely a talented and capable courtier among many similar ambitious individuals. It is true that he had a certain advantage over other courtiers in that his father was the *epimelētēs* of Judaea, the most powerful and influential of the officials within the court of the Hasmonean John Hyrcanus II. His brother Phasael was *stratēgos* of Jerusalem. Moreover, his grandfather Antipas had been *stratēgos* of Idumaea during the reign of Alexander Jannaeus and possibly that of Salome Alexandra. However, good lineage would not be enough to keep Herod and his family in ascendancy. As we have seen, the Antipatrids combined political acumen with efficiency to position themselves as the favorite Judaean courtiers in the eyes of Rome's leaders such as Sextus Caesar and Gaius Cassius Longinus.

On the assassination of his father Antipater in 43 BCE, Herod and his brother became the preeminent men at court, although their position was not entirely stable since they needed to repel actively the encroaching ambitions of rivals within the court. Continuing their successful governance of the kingdom and strengthening their friendly relationship with Rome, they rose to new heights of power and influence. When Marc Antony came to the East, it was only natural that he should appoint the brothers as tetrarchs of Galilee and Judaea and entrust them with the daily management of the kingdom. At this point in his career, Herod succeeded because he fulfilled the expectations of his Roman and Judaean superiors. To both audiences, he was a resourceful and efficient governor and courtier who suppressed banditry in his territory, kept the peace, and provided a strong measure of support to the reigning Jewish monarch, the ethnarch John Hyrcanus II. It is especially noteworthy that Hyrcanus betrothed his granddaughter Mariamme to Herod and not to Herod's elder brother Phasael. While we do not know the precise reasons behind this decision, it does suggest that even at this point Herod was able to demonstrate his political value and worth.

Herod's Early Reign as King of Judaea

This status quo might have continued with Herod and his brother Phasael dominating the royal court but ultimately remaining subservient to the Hasmonean family. However, the year 40 BCE brought both great fortune and great tragedy to the Antipatrids: Herod lost a brother but gained a kingdom. In the process, circumstances on the ground forced him to adapt his self-presentation from that of a resourceful and deferential courtier to that of an energetic and staunchly pro-Roman client king. Simultaneously, he needed to transform from an assistant of the Hasmonean family to the rightful and legitimate successor to the Hasmoneans.

After the death of Phasael and the mutilation of Hyrcanus during the Parthian invasion of 40 BCE, Herod became the logical choice to rule Judaea. However, when he received Judaea from the Roman Senate, he had an extremely tentative claim to the throne. Despite his competence in government and his family's long position as preeminent courtiers, he had no real royal connections. In addition, because he was an Idumaean with a Nabataean mother, some Judaeans did not even consider him entirely Jewish. His quest for legitimacy in the eyes of both Rome and Judaea was his primary focus in these early years, and it became the foundation on which he constructed his self-presentation. Almost immediately on receiving his crown, Herod began establishing his credibility and legitimacy as monarch. As we have seen, in order to accomplish this task, he further cultivated his friendship and clientage with Antony and strengthened his connections with the previous ruling dynasty, the Hasmoneans. During these early years, he actively assisted Antony by offering him military and financial aid and bestowing public honors on him. Through his architecture, coins, and familial maneuvers, Herod also presented himself as a legitimate successor to the Hasmonean dynasty, the family who had ruled Judaea for over one hundred years and still retained a popular following. By the time Antony had left the East on his ill-fated journey to Actium, Herod had managed to achieve enough legitimacy to solidify his control over his throne and kingdom.

Herod's Later Reign as King of Judaea

Augustus's triumph at Actium demanded a substantial and significant shift in Herod's political alignment and presentation. He was famous throughout the Graeco-Roman world as a staunch Antonian, and now his patron had been defeated and demoralized. Within a few months of his defeat at Actium, Antony was dead, and Herod needed a novel image to go with his new patron. He immediately began asserting his allegiance to the principate through multiple media, such as coins and architecture. By relying on Roman expectations of client kingship and fulfilling them admirably, he was able to transition from an Antonian to an Augustan client king with little or no difficulty. When Augustus needed military support for his Egyptian campaign, Herod offered troops, supplies, and guides. When Agrippa was beginning his Bosporus campaign, Herod provided ships and financial support. In addition, he knew how to praise his patrons and highlight his loyalty to them and Rome. By building physical monuments that honored Augustus and Agrippa, he bound himself even closer to these new masters of the Graeco-Roman world. He saw an opportunity to advance himself within the world of client kingship, and he exploited it to its utmost.

With his position vis-à-vis Rome secure, with his hold on Judaea stable, and especially with the death of his great rival Cleopatra, Herod could now assert himself in a way unimaginable only a few years before. He could finally step out of the Hasmonean shadow and portray himself as a powerful and glorious Hellenistic Jewish king, a monarch in close affinity to the famous Jewish heroes of the past, particularly David and Solomon. He asserted this identity most publicly and spectacularly through his architecture. In particular, he constructed a vast monument to David that was visible all over Jerusalem and visually connected Herod to his famous predecessor. Additionally, through his reconstruction and expansion of the Temple Mount, he also became the new Solomon, the pious Jewish king who constructed the house of God. This new complex was more than twice the size of the original and even grander and more magnificent. Herod's Temple articulated both Jewish piety and Hellenistic majesty. The enclosures at Hebron and Mamre were similar to the program on the Temple Mount in that they were attempts to connect Herod with the heroes of the Jewish past, specifically Abraham, and appropriate their legitimacy and popularity.

In the realm of politics, Herod also articulated an image of Jewish piety and patronage, but instead of merely benefiting his own kingdom, he sought a wider audience in the Jewish Diaspora. As the wealthy, powerful, and influential king of Judaea, he could protect and defend the interests and needs of this Diaspora. He could fulfill the Hellenistic royal obligation to practice *euergetism,* while simultaneously projecting an image as a benevolent Jewish king. Through his defense of Jewish interests abroad as well as his welcoming of the Diaspora into his kingdom and even into the Temple itself, he positioned himself as the king of not just Judaeans but of Jews all over the Roman world. While certainly not believing that he had actual political control over all Jews living in the Diaspora — Herod was wise enough to know that such an assertion would not have been appreciated by Rome, and especially Augustus — he realized that as the only significant Jewish monarch in the Graeco-Roman world, he naturally would be the individual other Jews would look to as a patron and defender.

In this later part of his reign, he was concerned less with creating legitimacy than he was in staking his claim to be remembered among the pantheon of Jewish monarchical heroes and glorious Hellenistic kings. More than anything he desired a splendid and magnificent reputation among both Greeks and Jews. His immediate predecessors and their political ideology no longer defined his public persona. Instead, during this latter stage, his major decisions and actions were guided by his persistent quest to ensure a lasting, celebrated, and glorious name for himself. He wished to be known as the most loyal Roman ally, the greatest Hellenistic king to rule Judaea, the benevolent patron of the Diaspora, and, perhaps most importantly, the fitting and rightful successor to the paragon of Jewish kingship, the house of David. He had come a long way from a resourceful and influential but non-royal Idumaean courtier. He was now, in every cultural world in which he resided, the king of the Jews: the *Melech HaYehudim,* the *Basileus Ioudaiōn,* the *Rex Iudaeorum.*

So what larger picture emerges from all of these historical vignettes and stages? Herod the Great faced a complex political situation on ascending the throne. He responded to this volatile and turbulent environment by presenting a sequence of images and identities that satisfied his present political needs. When he needed to maintain a low profile but still prove his usefulness, he focused on bankrolling his Roman patron. When he needed to establish legitimacy with his local elites, he focused on presenting himself as a Hasmonean. When his political objectives changed, so too did his presentation. With the establishment of the principate and the *Pax Augusta,* Herod was free to assert himself in a way previously impossible. He could aggrandize himself through lavish public displays of loyalty to and friendship with Rome and Augustus. In the realm of Jewish politics, he could shed his Hasmonean identity, an image which was no longer necessary and, with his violent removal of Hyrcanus and Mariamme, no longer suitable. He could transform himself into a Jewish king in the mold of the biblical heroes of the past.

In the end, what remained constant throughout Herod's reign was his astute ability to assess his political needs and present a public image that achieved his goals. Contrary to what many have emphasized previously, political oppression and repression were not the primary foundations of his success. To be sure, he used both quite effectively and ruthlessly, sometimes even excessively. However, suppression and violence were not the only tools he utilized to maintain control. Indeed, if we examine the Josephan narratives carefully, what quickly becomes clear is that official violence was not nearly as frequent or effective as some scholars have argued. Instead, Herod succeeded and thrived as king of Judaea precisely because he was able to depict himself as the best candidate for the job to those with political agency and power. In this way, he was the ultimate political chameleon: he identified his situation and crafted an image and persona that would best satisfy his current needs and obligations.

Was he successful? In the chaotic and bloody death throes of the Roman Republic, he not only survived three civil wars but ultimately ruled in relative peace for over thirty years and passed on his kingdom to his chosen descendants. Very few rulers of this time period (or any time period) could claim such a feat.

Kings and rulers of all stripes, whether client kings or imperial masters, have always needed legitimacy and authority to govern effectively. Their success or failure as rulers depends on how well they can elicit and maintain the support of those with political agency within their kingdoms. In that sense, therefore, our investigation of Herod, with its emphasis on authority creation and maintenance, provides a new method of examining how and why kings, ancient and more modern, have succeeded or failed.

This study is particularly valuable for the field of Roman client kingship, especially for those about whom we know significantly less. Ancient rulers such as Archelaus of Cappadocia, Juba II of Mauretania, and even Cleopatra can all be understood more completely by focusing on political self-presentation and its role in authority creation and maintenance. By focusing on how these monarchs depicted themselves in the public sphere, we can move beyond the rhetoric of the primary sources and past overly simplistic understandings of power dynamics to a more complete, more mature view of the mechanisms by and media through which these sovereigns exerted their power within their kingdoms. This approach will enable us to get closer to the heart of the political machinery that operated more than 2,000 years ago. It will enable us to focus on what really caused a ruler to succeed or fail, namely, his ability to persuade those with political agency to support him. Oppression and repression certainly had their roles and functions, but simple force was not enough to keep these kings, or any king for that matter, in power. They needed the consent of their elites, and how they presented themselves to these elites was fundamental to achieving that consent.

One example of the benefits of our approach will suffice: Archelaus of Cappadocia was the son of a Hellenized Cappadocian nobleman. Antony appointed Archelaus king of Cappadocia in 36 BCE in place of the deposed Ariarathes X, whose family had ruled Cappadocia since the death of Alexander the Great. Lacking any natural claim to the throne, Archelaus must have experienced the same instability and lack of legitimacy that Herod did in his early reign. Unfortunately, he did not have a Nicolaus or Josephus to write about him, and all we know about this dynamic king comes from scattered references in the Roman sources plus some archaeological evidence in Turkey. Nevertheless, if we focus on what these scattered pieces of evidence say about his presentation of himself and keep in mind the general milieus of client kingship and Hellenistic monarchy, we can better interpret the available evidence and material. Undoubtedly, Archelaus's court was composed of ethnically and culturally diverse individuals with competing interests and motivations. By appealing to their cultural expectations of what it meant to be a good king, he was able to maintain his hold on power. At the same time, he could never forget that it was Rome who put him into power, and Rome could always revoke that favor (as it did during the reign of Tiberius in 17 CE). Because of the ever-looming presence of his imperial patrons, he no doubt devoted much energy and attention to portraying himself as a loyal and friendly ally. If we examine the available material in this light, we can no doubt glean more from it than before. We can also better explain why Archelaus succeeded while other monarchs failed.

In the end, Herod provides an ideal template from which we can examine and assess other Graeco-Roman monarchs such as Archelaus of Cappadocia, not because he was necessarily the most adept or skilled (although he certainly excelled in the realm of power maintenance), but because he is the best documented. He provides a window onto this otherwise veiled world of politically proficient and agile kings, dominating turbulent forces within their own realms in a cruel and merciless game of thrones in which the winner survived and prospered and the loser was overthrown and killed.

Herod the Great proves that the *power of image,* and one's *political self-presentation,* more than physical force and violence, determines a king's fate. They enable the king to rise to the heights of power and glory or to sink to the depths of failure and ruin.

APPENDIX A

A Recent Critique of My Chronology for the Dated Coins

In their recent monograph Donald Ariel and Jean-Philippe Fontanille raise a few objections to my proposed chronology for Herod's dated coins. In particular, they object to the location of the dated coins' mint in Samaria and to my proposed time frame. Instead of Samaria/Sebaste, they propose Jerusalem as the more likely site of the mint and 37 BCE as the more likely minting year. While I would agree with them that the evidence for a 28/27 BCE minting of the dated series in Samaria/Sebaste is not completely unimpeachable, as I will show below, their critiques are not sufficient to invalidate my theory.

The Argument

In support of their hypothesis, they note that the dated coins used flans with beveled edges, and almost all of the Hasmonean coins, which were struck solely in Jerusalem, have beveled edges. Furthermore, they discount the conclusive nature of the coin distribution evidence favoring Sebaste as the mint by noting that the spatial distribution of the dated coins within the city is somewhat limited. One might expect the distribution within the city to be more widespread if it really were the minting site. They also note that the flan molds, which were found in 1968 by Ibrahim al-Fani and identified by Meshorer as Herodian, could also fit the larger denominations of undated coins, which Meshorer himself attributes to Jerusalem.

Finally, they suggest that the iconography on the dated coins, while seemingly pagan in appearance, does not preclude a minting in Jerusalem. In the first place, the images chosen were somewhat ambiguous and could have been read in multiple ways; pagan images to those who minted the coins and inoffensive coin types that either recycled Hasmonean coin images or utilized new symbols that had no obvious iconographic meaning and could be open to various interpretations (fruit, an aphlaston, a tripod, etc.). In addition, the supposedly Macedonian connection of the two helmets on the dated coins does not necessitate a link with Samaria, even though Alexander the Great settled Macedonian veterans in that city. It is possible, they suggest, that the Macedonian connection is more personal. Herod sought to link himself with Alexander, a man with whom he clearly felt some affinity, having named one son Alexander and another Philip. Moreover, it is possible, in their opinion, that the designers of the coin images had a sufficiently different point of view from those who viewed and used the coins. Specifically, the former saw pagan symbolism while the latter saw more general Hellenistic language. Thus, while not ruling out the possibility of Samaria/Sebaste as the minting site, Ariel and Fontanille argue that Jerusalem is also a possible site and indeed is more likely given the existence of a mint there for the undated coins.

But what about the minting year? Did Herod count his regnal years from the Jewish month of Nisan (March/April), and, if so, was Jerusalem not under Herod's control until the summer of 37 BCE, a date well into Herod's fourth year as *de iure* king of Judaea? Ariel and Fontanille cite studies by Ormond Edwards and Alla Kushnir-Stein that suggest that Herod might have counted his regnal years from Tishri (September/October) and not Nisan. If that is the case, then the conquest of Judaea and Jerusalem was in Herod's third year. As the year in which Herod finally achieved *de facto* control over his kingdom, 37 BCE would have been an ideal year for a royal *congiarium* for his soldiers, his subjects, or both, and the dated coins, in the opinion of Ariel and Fontanille, would have been ideal for such a benefaction. The creation of a mint and the striking of large coins would have taken a certain amount of time and organization, two things that might not have been at the top of Herod's agenda during those first busy and somewhat chaotic months after the conquest of Judaea. However, according to Ariel and Fontanille these problems do not present an obstacle to a 37 BCE date. As they note, citing C. H. V. Sutherland, the striking of coins dated to a particular year periodically extended beyond the year in question without any change to the coin legend. Thus, even if the Jerusalem mint was not finished minting the dated coins before the end of Herod's third year as king, it might still have struck Year 3 coins for a few months into Year 4 (37/36 BCE).

In addition to suggesting reasons that Jerusalem as the minting site and

APPENDIX A

37 BCE as the minting year are to be favored, Ariel and Fontanille raise a few objections to my chronology. In the first place they argue that to accept the 27 BCE chronology one must show that a regnal era beginning in 40 BCE is impossible. Specifically, they suggest that it is "methodologically dubious" to use any year other than an ascension year for a king whose minting authority and status as king are clearly indicated on a coin, unless that ascension year is impossible. They also argue that my proposed timeframe is a little tight, since Herod arguably would not have had time to find out about Octavian's renaming, begin work on Sebaste, and order the striking of special coinage all before the end of a Year 3 dated to 28/27 BCE. Instead, if construction on the city began in spring/summer 27 BCE, it would represent the era's fourth year, not its third.[1]

Response to Ariel and Fontanille's Critiques of Samaria/Sebaste as the Minting Site

While Ariel and Fontanille rightly observe that the case for Samaria/Sebaste as the minting site is not irrefutable, they still acknowledge it as a real possibility. Furthermore, as we will see, their objections to its candidacy are not as cogent as might initially appear. Regarding the beveled flans used in striking the dated series, it is true that the Hasmoneans also struck coins on beveled flans, and their coins were minted in Jerusalem. However, Kushnir-Stein, the author of the article they cite for their analysis of the beveled edges, excludes coastal cities such as Tyre and Ascalon as possible minting sites, since neither used beveled flans, and instead suggests Samaria as a more likely possibility. Additionally, as they themselves admit, the first clearly attested non-Herodian coins from Samaria/Sebaste are Domitianic

---

1. For Ariel and Fontanille's arguments against Samaria/Sebaste as the minting site and 28/27 BCE as the minting year in favor of Jerusalem as the minting site and 37 BCE as the minting year, see their *The Coins of Herod: A Modern Analysis and Die Classification* (Leiden: Brill, 2012), 90-91, 94-98, 103, 165-66, 174-77. For a discussion of the beveled flans used in the dated series, their use in earlier Hasmonean coinage, and the possibility of a Jerusalem mint for the dated series, see Alla Kushnir-Stein, "Some Observations on Palestinian Coins with a Bevelled Edge," *INJ* 14 (2000-02): 78-83. Cf. Alla Kushnir-Stein, "Coins of the Herodian Dynasty: The State of Research," in *The World of the Herods: Volume 1 of the International Conference The World of the Herods and the Nabataeans Held at the British Museum, 17-19 April 2001*, ed. Nikos Kokkinos (Stuttgart: Steiner, 2007), 55-56. For Sutherland's analysis of dated coins being struck after the date appearing on the coin see C. H. V. Sutherland, *Coinage in Roman Imperial Policy: 31 B.C.–A.D. 68* (London: Methuen, 1951), 182.

A Recent Critique of My Chronology for the Dated Coins

in date (about 100 years after Herod's death), and thus their use of regular non-beveled flans is somewhat irrelevant. They do mention Seleucid coins that might have originated in Samaria, but they are from the reign of Antiochus IV, which, besides being from a foreign royal house, also predates our era by more than 200 years. Clearly, there is enough time between Antiochus IV (175-164 BCE) and Domitian (81-96 CE) for Samaria to develop a mint that used beveled edges, a style favored by the Hasmoneans who ruled Judaea before Herod. Indeed, given Herod's connection to the Hasmonean court and the large amount of continuity between Hyrcanus's late era court and Herod's early court, it would not be surprising if the first Herodian mintmasters had worked in the Hasmonean mint. If so, it would make sense for them to use flans with beveled edges just as they had previously. Thus, while we cannot entirely eliminate Jerusalem as a mint site based on the flans used, we also cannot rule out Samaria/Sebaste.

Ariel and Fontanille's argument about the somewhat limited spatial distribution of dated coins at Samaria/Sebaste does weaken the strength of the coin find evidence. As they suggest, one would expect to see a more even distribution around the city. However, this limited spatial distribution could be explained by a number of causes and by itself (as they readily admit) does not preclude the possibility of Sebaste as they minting site. This same point applies to the flan molds that could also fit the larger denomination of the undated, Jerusalem-struck Herodian coins. While these flan molds do not eliminate Jerusalem as the minting site, they also do not eliminate Sebaste.

Ariel and Fontanille's observation about Herod's use of somewhat ambiguous iconography (images that could appear pagan to pagans and ambiguous to Jews) actually supports a mint site of Samaria/Sebaste better than Jerusalem. We should recall that while Samaria was initially inhabited by Samaritans, who probably shared the Jews' distaste for graven images, it also was inhabited by Macedonian veterans whom Alexander the Great had settled there during his lifetime. Indeed, as Ariel and Fontanille themselves admit, Samaria probably had a pagan majority with a Samaritan minority. If so, it would be easier to strike coins in Samaria with images that some could interpret as pagan than in Jerusalem, where a Jewish majority would be more troublesome if roused by a particular image or images. In short, Ariel and Fontanille's observations, while causing some initial hesitation about Samaria/Sebaste, do not, in the end, warrant rejecting that city as the source of the dated series.[2]

2. For Kushnir-Stein's suggestion that Samaria/Sebaste was a likely place for the strik-

APPENDIX A

What about the chronology? As we will see, my proposed timeline is not as tight as Ariel and Fontanille believe. As Suetonius and Cassius Dio report, on January 13, 27 BCE, Octavian ostensibly resigned all his offices, laid down all his official powers, and transferred control of Rome back to the Senate and People of Rome. In so doing, he claimed that he had achieved his goal of restoring the Republic and therefore no longer needed to hold office. Within three days, the Senate had responded to Octavian's resignation by showering him with praise, restoring his offices to him, and granting more honors and powers. The capstone to this senatorial capitulation was the renaming of Octavian as Augustus. If we were to take the ancient sources' accounts at face value, we would think that this entire spectacle was a spontaneous response to a serious offer of resignation. However, nobody seriously believes that any of this show was spontaneous. Political spectacles such as this one are carefully stage-managed in order for events to reach a predetermined outcome. For Octavian to pull off a spectacle of this magnitude, there must have been months of private negotiations and strategy-sessions in which he and his closest associates carefully orchestrated each stage of the performance. Political performances of this type and size also frequently involve coordinated leaks of information. These intentional disclosures pre-gauge public opinion and allow the actors to modify and amend the presentation before its unveiling.

There are indications within the ancient sources that such negotiations occurred. Suetonius records a discussion among Octavian and his advisors over what his new name should be. Some wanted Romulus, since they saw the *princeps* as a second founder of the city. According to Cassius Dio, Octavian himself preferred that name. Lucius Munatius Plancus, on the other hand, proposed the name Augustus. He probably saw it as more godlike and safer, especially considering Romulus's bloody career, reference to which would have been unseemly in the new era Octavian was hoping to establish. Given the importance of this new name and its centrality to the regime that developed out of the First Settlement, it is highly unlikely that the decision regarding the new name was made quickly or spontaneously.

But how would Herod have found out about the renaming before January in 27 BCE? We know that Plancus had a close connection with Herod, having served as governor of Syria in 35 BCE and governor of Asia

---

ing of the dated coins see "Some Observations on Palestinian Coins," 82. Cf. Kushnir-Stein, "Coins of the Herodian Dynasty," 55. For the demography of Samaria prior to Herod's reconstruction of the city see Ariel and Fontanille, *Coins of Herod*, 95.

in 40-38 BCE. As governor of two nearby provinces and a loyal Antonian, Plancus would have had ample opportunity to develop a relationship with Herod. Given the centrality of Plancus to the First Settlement, it is not entirely impossible that Herod obtained advance notice of the plan and began his own preparations for an appropriate response. Moreover, a king as politically astute and active as Herod would have had diplomats and informers in Rome to gather information and report back to him. If Plancus was not the source, it is possible that someone else provided such notice. Possible candidates include Marcus Valerius Messala Corvinus, a man who had defended Herod in Antioch before Antony and like Herod was an Antonian who had successfully switched sides. Marcus Agrippa is another. Although his friendship with Herod is better documented in the years following the First Settlement, it probably developed in these early years of the principate.[3]

Even if Herod did not receive advance notice from Plancus or any other Roman, news traveled quickly and would have reached Judaea by the spring. Plans for the new city and the settlement of veterans of the royal army could already have been well under way. All Herod needed to change was the name of the city. If, as I suggest, the coins were meant as a royal *congiarium* to commemorate the refounding of Samaria as Sebaste and to honor the *princeps,* actual construction need not have commenced before a ceremonial *groundbreaking* festival and commemorative coin minting were organized and initiated. The dated series, or at least some of them, could have been struck before the end of 28/27 BCE and thus been minted in Year 3. Even if minting of the coins persisted for some time, it would not have made sense to change the date on the new coins, especially because they were meant to honor two events that had occurred in Year 3 of Herod's new era. As we know from Sutherland, whom Ariel and Fontanille themselves cite in support of their chronology, the striking of coins dated to a particular year sometimes extended beyond the year in question without any change to the coin legend. If this analysis can support a 37 BCE dating, there is no reason that it cannot support a 27 BCE dating as well.

3. For the ancient sources' narratives of the First Settlement and the debate within Augustus's inner circle, see Suetonius, *Aug.* 7; Dio 53.16.6-8. See especially Dio 52.1-40 for the debate between Maecenas and Agrippa over whether Octavian should resign his offices. Cf. *Res Gest. Divi Aug.* 34. For Plancus as governor of Asia (40-38 BCE) and governor of Syria (35 BCE), see Broughton, *MRR* 2:381, 387, 391, 407. For a biographical overview of Messala Corvinus, see Ronald Syme, *The Augustan Aristocracy* (Oxford: Clarendon, 1989), 200-216.

APPENDIX A

The final criticism of Ariel and Fontanille is that my proposal of a 28/27 BCE minting is methodologically dubious because it relies on a dating system that does not begin in an ascension year for a king whose minting authority and status as king are clearly indicated on the coin. The main problem with this critique is that 30 BCE was an ascension year of sorts. It marked the end of Herod's tenure as an Antonian and the beginning of his new role as a client king of Octavian. As a sign of this new relationship, Octavian significantly enlarged Herod's kingdom, presenting him with several major cities, including Samaria, the city that would become Herod's first *urbs Caesarae*. Thus the reconfirmation at Rhodes in 30 BCE did not just save Herod's life. It also revitalized his fortunes and transformed his status within the Roman world. If not a bona fide ascension, this reconfirmation comes as close as possible.

There is even a close precedent for a monarch to use a second date for counting regnal years, as Ariel mentions in both his dissertation and a paper presented at the 2005 *Herod and Augustus* conference in London. Cleopatra counted her regnal years according to two eras. One, her Egyptian era, began with her ascension to the Ptolemaic throne in 69 BCE. The other, her so-called Syrian era, began in 37/36 BCE with her acquisition of territory in Syria, which had once been part of the Ptolemaic Empire but had been lost centuries before. If Cleopatra could have seen the expansion of her kingdom as grounds for a new dating system, it stands to reason that Herod could have seen the preservation and significant enlargement of his kingdom in a similar way. If the *Donations of Alexandria* marked a new era for Cleopatra, the settlement at Rhodes was in the same vein for Herod.

Thus, Ariel and Fontanille's hesitation on methodological grounds is unwarranted. Additionally, while sound methodology is important, we should not let it present too much of an obstacle to our reconstruction of the past. As Ariel himself suggests, "sometimes the historical truth does not follow good methodology."[4] We have not entirely ruled out 37 BCE as

---

4. For the two dating systems of Cleopatra, see Emil Schürer, *The History of the Jewish People in the Age of Jesus Christ (175 BC–AD 135)*, ed. Geza Vermes and Fergus Millar (Edinburgh: Clark, 1973-87), 1:288 n. 5. For Ariel's analysis of the two dating systems, see his "The Coins of Herod the Great in the Context of the Augustan Empire," in *Herod and Augustus: Papers Presented at the IJS Conference, 21st-23rd June 2005*, ed. D. M. Jacobson and N. Kokkinos (Leiden: Brill, 2009), 122; "A Numismatic Approach to the Reign of Herod the Great" (Ph.D. diss., Tel-Aviv University, 2006), 192. Cleopatra's Syrian era is not well attested by the ancient sources. It only appears on a few coin types and in a number of papyri and one fragment of Porphyry.

A Recent Critique of My Chronology for the Dated Coins

a possibility for the minting of the dated series, but this failure to eliminate it completely should not prevent us from proposing other dates. We should instead allow the evidence to take us where it will, and in this case it takes us to a chronology that I have laid out in both my dissertation and this book, namely, that Herod struck his dated coins in 28/27 BCE, the third year of his new *Rhodian* era, to commemorate the refounding of Samaria as Sebaste and to honor the *princeps,* who had recently been given the new name Augustus.

APPENDIX B

Did Herod Mint Silver Coinage?

One of the most glaring absences in our study of Herodian coinage has been any discussion of gold and silver coins. Indeed, the disparity between the pomp and grandiosity of Herod's reign as it appears in Josephus, and the relatively unimpressive bronze coinage minted by the king has led several scholars to look for supposedly missing Herodian coins. As Ya'akov Meshorer stated, "It is unlikely that such a colorful and powerful personality with economic and political ambitions would not have taken advantage of the opportunity to strike a prestigious coinage." Meshorer's answer to this disparity between an impressive building program and unimpressive coinage is to claim that Herod took over minting of the famous Tyrian shekel, the silver coin renowned in the ancient world for its purity (more than 90%) and the only coin permitted for use in the Temple in Jerusalem. In particular, Meshorer argues that Herod began minting these silver coins in 18/17 BCE, a date which, he asserts, coincided with the termination of minting operations in Tyre. According to most scholars, however, Tyre struck autonomous silver coinage continuously for more than two hundred years beginning in 126 BCE and ceasing around the time of the First Jewish Revolt (66 CE).

In support of his claim, Meshorer points to two episodes in Josephus's narratives in which Herod converts gold and silver ornaments and furnishings into silver coinage as proof that Herod struck his own silver coinage. In the first instance, he uses the precious metals to provide money for his patron Marc Antony (*BJ* 1.358) and to pay for grain from Egypt during the famine of 25/24 BCE (*AJ* 15.306-7).

Meshorer also supports his claim with analysis of the coins themselves. Stylistically, Meshorer divides the Tyrian shekels into two main groups

Did Herod Mint Silver Coinage?

The Tyrian shekel
One of the purest silver coins in the ancient world, the Tyrian shekel
was the preferred currency used at the Temple in Jerusalem.
(courtesy of Classical Numismatic Group, Inc. www.cngcoins.com)

based on chronology, die execution, and the nature of the flans used. The first group, he writes, was of much higher quality minting. The dies were smaller than the flans on which they were struck, which enabled the entire design and inscription to appear on the coin. In contrast, the second group used dies that were not executed as expertly. They also used smaller flans. As a result, on most of these coins either the inscription or the design does not appear on the flan. The presence or absence of a KP monogram also separates the two groups. This monogram first appears on the reverse of shekels struck in 18 BCE and continues to appear on them until the end of their minting in 66 CE. Meshorer theorizes that the KP signified a change in the mint, and he connects it with the penalty Augustus levied on Tyre in 20 BCE for civil disturbances within the city. Besides a stylistic dichotomy Meshorer also cites a geographical one: most of the early shekels were found in Lebanon, while almost all of the late shekels were found in Judaea, Samaria, and Galilee. Finally, Meshorer argues that the Mishnah clearly mandates the use of only Tyrian shekels to pay the head-tax to the Temple. Therefore, if, as Meshorer suggests, Tyre lost its ability to strike shekels in 20 BCE, it would have been necessary for someone else to issue them so that Jews could pay the tax. Given the importance of the coin to the Temple cult, the most logical person to continue such a coin series was Herod.[1]

---

1. For Meshorer's theory, see his "One Hundred Ninety Years of Tyrian Shekels," in *Studies in Honor of Leo Mildenberg: Numismatics, Art History and Archaeology*, ed. A. Houghten, et al. (Wetteren: Editions NR, 1984), 171-80. For the penalty levied by Augustus against the city of Tyre, see Dio 54.7.6. Although Meshorer argues that there was an apparent drop in the quality of the engraving of the shekels, he also observes there did not seem to have been a corresponding devaluation in the amount or quality of the silver

APPENDIX B

While this theory would explain the apparent disparity between Herodian coinage and architecture, it has a number of flaws and thus should be rejected. In the first place, it is possible that in both Josephan episodes cited by Meshorer the metals were turned into bullion and not coins. Since the payments were meant for people who were not in Judaea, it seems odd that Herod would have minted coins only to export them. In both cases, Antony and Petronius, the prefect of Egypt, would have accepted bullion as payment. Thus, while these episodes might refer to minting operations, the language in the narratives does not necessitate such an interpretation.

Approaching Meshorer's argument from a non-literary perspective reveals further problems. In general, the Romans tended to permit preexisting gold and silver coinage to continue in areas over which they exercised control, but they were generally loath to permit its initiation in areas where it had not existed previously. Therefore, it would have been strange (although not impossible) for Judaea to begin minting silver coins when it had no prior tradition of such minting. Regarding the penalization of Tyre in 20 BCE, Brooks Levy, among others, has noted that the loss of autonomy would have been short-lived and would not have resulted in the closing of the mint of one of the more prestigious coin series in the eastern Mediterranean. She also rejects Meshorer's stylistic argument as an oversimplification of a much more complicated series which saw a number of changing styles throughout the almost two hundred years of its existence (126 BCE–66 CE). Rather than seeing the changes as an abrupt degradation beginning in 18 BCE, we should view it as a gradual one involving both style and coin fabric. As for the KP monogram, it is more likely an abbreviation for *kata Rōmaious* ("under Roman permission"), the Greek equivalent of the Latin *senatus consultu* (by decree of the Senate). Meshorer's argument about the relative frequency of later shekels in

---

used in the coins. In support of his theory, Meshorer also points to Josephus's discussion of Herod's will as proof that the king struck silver coins. In his final will, Herod left 500,000 pieces of "coined silver" *(argyriou episēmou)* to his sister Salome (*AJ* 17.189). Meshorer argues that Josephus would have specified the currency if it were not royal coinage. He also cites the paraphrase of this section by the Byzantine writer Ioannes Zonaras, which uses the phrase "into currency" *(eis nomisma)*. See Meshorer, *Ancient Jewish Coinage* (New York: Amphora, 1982), 2:201 n. 7. Using Zonaras's paraphrase as an indication of what Josephus meant more than a millennium earlier is problematic. Moreover, Josephus usually does not specify the currency of coins he is mentioning. Given his lack of specificity, as well as the evidence discussed in this appendix, we should reject Meshorer's interpretation.

Did Herod Mint Silver Coinage?

Jerusalem is also flawed. Careful analysis of both coin hoards and isolated coin finds seems to contradict his proposed geographical distribution, according to which later shekels were more numerous in Jerusalem than in other places. There seems to be no noticeable difference in the distribution of isolated finds between the earlier and later shekels. Indeed, it seems that Meshorer's claim is largely unsubstantiated and based more on his impressions of the frequency of shekels in the Lebanese antiquities market.

Finally, while Meshorer is correct that the Tyrian shekel had a special relationship with the Temple tax, it is not clear that it was the only acceptable currency. The key passage for Meshorer is the statement from the Tosefta that "silver mentioned in the Pentateuch is always Tyrian silver. What is Tyrian silver? It is Jerusalemite." He also cites Mishnah *Bekhorot*, which speaks of a Tyrian *maneh* as an example of acceptable currency (*m. Bekhorot* 8.7). Given the frequent ahistorical nature of rabbinic material, we should always be hesitant to use it as unambiguous evidence for behavior during the first century BCE. However, even if we accept these passages as illustrative of the Herodian period, they do not make Meshorer's theory unassailable. The pericope in the Tosefta, while mentioning Tyrian shekels, is actually discussing wedding contracts and not taxes. Further, while Meshorer interprets the statement "it is Jerusalemite" as referring to a Jerusalem mint for shekels, this interpretation is not mandatory. The statement could be referring simply to the role these coins had played in the payment of the Temple tax rather than a transfer of the coin's mint from one city to another. Moreover, although Mishnah *Bekhorot* speaks of the head-tax, it mentions other financial obligations as well. More importantly, while it stipulates that the tax may be paid in Tyrian shekels, it does not require that currency. Other payments to the Temple did not need to be in coinage. Instead, one could pay them in the equivalent weight of silver bullion based on a Tyrian standard. A passage from Josephus shows a female proselyte sending the Temple a gift of "purple and gold" (*AJ* 18.82). While this gift may not have been seen as the equivalent of the head-tax, it does suggest that non-currency payments would have been accepted. It is likely, therefore, that at least some Jews did not pay the head-tax with coins and yet still felt that they had fulfilled their obligation. While the Tyrian shekel may have been the preferred coin for the Temple tax, it was not the only one permissible, which makes a transfer to a Jerusalem mint far less necessary.

Given all this evidence, we should reject Meshorer's theory about the

APPENDIX B

transfer of the mint from Tyre to Jerusalem. However, he may be correct that the popularity of the Tyrian shekel for payments to the Jerusalem Temple might have been extremely influential in keeping the mint that made the shekels open. In this vein, Herod may have played a vital role as patron of both the Temple and its worshipers. As for the monogram, it more likely refers to some conditions or additional control placed on Tyre after 18 BCE, as *kata Rōmaious* would accomplish.[2]

---

2. For critiques of Meshorer's theory, see Brooks Levy, "Tyrian Shekels and the First Jewish War," in *Proceedings of the 11th International Numismatic Congress (1991)*, ed. Tony Hackens and Ghislaine Moucharte (Louvain: Professor Marcel Hoc Association for the Promotion of Numismatics, 1993), 267-74; "Tyrian Shekels: The Myth of the Jerusalem Mint," *SAN* 19 (1995): 33-35. Also see Donald T. Ariel and Jean-Philippe Fontanille, *The Coins of Herod: A Modern Analysis and Die Classification* (Leiden: Brill, 2012), 36-40; Peter Richardson, *Herod: King of the Jews and Friend of the Romans* (Columbia: University of South Carolina Press, 1996), 223 n. 18. For Roman willingness to accept bullion as payment see Richard Duncan-Jones, *Money and Government in the Roman Empire* (Cambridge: Cambridge University Press, 1994), 10. For the interpretation of the KP monogram as an abbreviation for *kata Rōmaious* see Hannah Cotton and Wolfram Weiser, "Neues zum 'Tyrischen Silbergeld' herodianischer und römischer Zeit," *ZPE* 139 (2002): 235-50. For the statement about Tyrian shekels in the Tosefta see Tosefta *Ketubbot* 13.20. Although in support of his argument Meshorer also cites Mishnah *Sheqalim*, the tractate concerned with dedications to the Temple, it never specifically mentions Tyrian shekels. Indeed, the only coin it explicitly notes is a "gold dinar," which it mentions when discussing a contribution (*m. Sheqalim* 6.6).

Bibliography

Primary Sources

Supplementum Epigraphicum Graecum. Amsterdam: J. C. Gieben, 1923-2001.
Lettre d'Aristée à Philocrate. Edited by André Pelletier. Paris: Cerf, 1962.
Allen, Frederic D. "Greek and Latin Inscriptions from Palestine." *AJP* 6 (1885): 190-216.
Ammonius. *De Adfinium Vocabulorum Differentia.* Edited by Klaus Nickau. Leipzig: Teubner, 1966.
Aristotle. *Politica.* Edited by David Ross. Oxford: Oxford University Press, 1957.
———. *Ethica Nicomachea.* Edited by Ingram Bywater. Oxford: Clarendon, 1957.
Appian of Alexandria. *Historia Romana.* Edited by P. Viereck and A. G. Roos. 2 vols. Leipzig: Teubner, 1962.
Arrian (Lucius Flavius Arrianus). *Flavii Arriani quae Exstant Omnia.* Edited by A. G. Roos and G. Wirth. 2 vols. Leipzig: Teubner, 1967-68.
Athenaeus Naucratites. *Deipnosophistae.* Edited by Georg Kaibel. 3 vols. Leipzig: Teubner, 1965-67.
Berlin-Brandenburg Academy of Arts and Sciences, ed. *Inscriptiones Graecae.* 12 vols. Berlin: Reimer, 1873-1915.
Böckh, Philipp August, ed. *Corpus Inscriptionum Graecarum.* 5 vols. Berlin: Officina Academica, 1828-77.
Brunt, P. A., and J. M. Moore, *Res Gestae Divi Augusti: The Achievement of the Divine Augustus: Introduction and Commentary.* Oxford: Oxford University Press, 1970.
Cagnat, R., ed. *Inscriptiones Graecae ad Res Romanas Pertinentes.* 4 vols. Chicago: Ares, 1975.
Callimachus. *Callimachus.* Edited by Rudolf Pfeiffer. 2 vols. Oxford: Clarendon, 1949-1953.
Cassius Dio (Dio Cassius Cocceianus). *Historia Romanarum.* Edited by Philip Boissevain. 5 vols. Berlin: Weidmann, 2002.

Curtius Rufus, Quintus. *Historiarum Alexandri Magni Macedonis.* Edited by Theodore Vogel. Leipzig: Teubner, 1903.

Dietrich, Manfried, Oswald Loretz, and Joaquín Sanmartín, eds. *Keilalphabetischen Texte aus Ugarit.* 2nd ed. Münster: Ugarit, 1995.

Dio Chrysostom (Dion of Prusa). *Orationes.* Edited by Guy de Budé. 2 vols. Leipzig: Teubner, 1915-19.

Dittenberger, Wilhelm, ed. *Orientis Graeci Inscriptiones Selectae. Supplementum Sylloges Inscriptionum.* 2 vols. Leipzig: Hirzel, 1903-05.

———. *Sylloge Inscriptionum Graecarum.* 4 vols. Leipzig: Hirzel, 1915-24.

Ehrenberg, Victor, and A. H. M. Jones, *Documents Illustrating the Reigns of Augustus and Tiberius.* Oxford: Clarendon, 1955.

Flavius Josephus. *Opera.* Edited by Benedict Niese. 7 vols. Berlin: Weidmann, 1955.

———. *Life.* Edited by H. St. John Thackeray. London: Heinemann, 1926.

———. *Jewish War.* Edited by H. St. John Thackeray. 3 vols. Cambridge: Harvard University Press, 1999.

———. *Jewish Antiquities.* Edited by Louis H. Feldman, Ralph Marcus, and Allen Wikgren. 9 vols. Cambridge: Harvard University Press, 1997-2000.

Frey, Jean-Baptiste, ed. *Corpus Inscriptionum Iudaicarum: Jewish Inscriptions from the Third Century B.C. to the Seventh A.D.* 2 vols. New York: Ktav, 1975.

Frisch, Peter. *Die Inschriften von Ilion.* Bonn: Habelt, 1975.

Gelzer, Heinrich. *Sextus Julius Africanus und die Byzantinische Chronographie.* 2 vols. New York: Franklin, 1967.

Grenfell, Bernard P., Arthur S. Hunt, and J. Gilbart Smyly, eds. *The Tebtunis Papyri.* 4 vols. London: Oxford University Press, 1902-76.

Guéraud, Octave, ed. *Enteuxeis Requêtes et Plaintes Adressées au Roi d'Égypte au IIIe Siècle avant J.C.* 2 vols. Cairo: Société Royale Égyptienne de Papyrologie, 1931-32.

Hall, Clayton M. *Nicolaus of Damascus' Life of Augustus.* Menasha: Banta, 1923.

Head, Barclay V. *A Guide to the Principal Gold and Silver Coins of the Ancients: From circ. B.C. 700 to A.D. 1.* 3rd ed. London: British Museum, 1889.

Hill, G. F. *British Museum Catalogue of Greek Coins: Phoenicia.* London: British Museum, 1910.

———. *Catalogue of the Greek Coins of Palestine.* London: British Museum, 1914.

Höghammer, Kerstin. *Sculpture and Society: A Study of the Connection Between the Free-Standing Sculpture and Society of Kos in the Hellenistic and Augustan Periods.* Uppsala: Boreas, 1993.

Horace (Quintus Horatius Flaccus). *Opera.* Edited by Stephan Borzsák. Leipzig: Teubner, 1984.

Isocrates. *Discours.* Edited by Georges Mathieu and Émile Brémond. 4 vols. Paris: Belles lettres, 1928-66.

Jacoby, Felix. *Die Fragmente der Griechischen Historiker.* 3 vols. Berlin: Weidmann, 1926-57.

Bibliography

Justinus, Marcus Junianus. *Epitoma Historiarum Philippecarum Pompei Trogi*. Edited by Francis Ruehl. Leipzig: Teubner, 1915.

Malalas, John. *Ioannis Malalae Chronographia*. Edited by Johannes Thurn. Berlin: de Gruyter, 2000.

Martínez, Florentino García, and Eibert J. C. Tigchelaar. *The Dead Sea Scrolls Study Edition*. 2 vols. Leiden: Brill, 1997-98.

Moran, William L. *The Amarna Letters*. Baltimore: Johns Hopkins University Press, 1992.

Nepos, Cornelius. *Vitae Excellentium Imperatorum*. Edited by Alfred Fleckeisen. Leipzig: Teubner, 1884.

Nicolaus of Damascus. *Life of Augustus*. Edited by Jane Bellemore. Bristol: Classical, 1984.

No author. "A Hoard of Herodian Coins." *INJ* 2 (1964): 45.

Pausanias. *Graeciae Descriptio*. Edited by Frederick Spiro. 3 vols. Leipzig: Teubner, 1903.

Philodemus, *Il Buon Re Secondo Omero: Filodemo*. Edited by Tiziano Dorandi. Naples: Bibliopolis, 1982.

Philo Judaeus. *Opera*. Edited by Leopold Cohn and Paul Wendland. 7 vols. Berlin: Reimer, 1896-1930.

———. *Complete Works*. Edited by F. H. Colson and G. H. Whitaker. 10 vols. Cambridge: Harvard University Press, 1929-62.

Plato. *Platonis Opera*. Edited by John Burnet. Oxford: Clarendon, 1961-64.

Plutarch (L.[?] Mestrius Plutarchus). *Vitae Parallelae*. Edited by Konrat Ziegler and Hans Gaertner. 4 vols. Munich: Saur, 1998-2000.

Pritchard, James B., ed. *Ancient Near Eastern Texts Relating to the Old Testament*. 3rd ed. Princeton: Princeton University Press, 1974.

Propertius (Sextus Propertius). *Elegiae*. Edited by Paul Fedeli. Leipzig: Teubner, 1984.

Pseudo-Aristotle. *Rhetoricum ad Alexandrum*. Edited by W. S. Hett. Cambridge: Harvard University Press, 1957-61.

Rahlfs, Alfred, ed. *I Maccabees*. In *Septuaginta*. Stuttgart: Württembergische Bibelanstalt, 1935.

———, ed. *II Maccabees*. In *Septuaginta*. Stuttgart: Württembergische Bibelanstalt, 1935.

———, ed. *III Maccabees*. In *Septuaginta*. Stuttgart: Württembergische Bibelanstalt, 1935.

Rehm, Albert, ed. *Didyma II. Die Inschriften*. Berlin: Mann, 1958.

Sear, David. *Roman Coins and Their Values*. 4th ed. London: Seaby, 1988.

Seneca (Lucius Annaeus Seneca). *De Clementia*. Edited by F. Haase. Leipzig: Teubner, 1902.

Stern, Menahem. *Greek and Latin Authors on Jews and Judaism*. 2 vols. Jerusalem: Israel Academy of Science and Humanities, 1974-84.

Stobaeus, Joannes. *Anthologium*. Edited by Kurt Wachsmuth and Otto Hense. 5 vols. Berlin: Weidmann, 1958.

BIBLIOGRAPHY

Strabo of Amaseia. *Geographica*. Edited by August Meineke. 3 vols. Leipzig: Teubner, 1915-25.
Struve, Vasilii, ed. *Corpus Inscriptionum Regni Bosporani*. Moscow: Hayka, 1965.
Suetonius (Gaius Suetonius Tranquillus). *Divus Augustus*. Edited by John M. Carter. Bristol: Classical, 1982.
Svoronos, J. N. *Ta Nomismata tou Kratous ton Ptolemaion (Ptolemaic Coinage)*. 4 vols. Athens: Sakellariou, 1904-08.
Tacitus (P. [?] Cornelius Tacitus). *Historiae I-V*. Edited by C. D. Fisher. Oxford: Oxford University Press, 1922.
Theocritus. *Bucolici Graeci*. Edited by A. S. F. Gow. Oxford: Oxford University Press, 1958.
Virgil (Publius Vergilius Maro). *Opera*. Edited by R. A. B. Mynors. Oxford: Clarendon, 1972.
Wilmanns, Gustavus, ed. *Corpus Inscriptionum Latinarum*. 17 vols. Berlin: Akademie der Wissenschaften, 1881.
Xenophon. *Opera Omnia*. Edited by E. C. Marchant. 5 vols. Oxford: Oxford University Press, 1958-61.

Secondary Sources

Abel, F.-M. *Géographie de la Palestine*. 2 vols. Paris: Librairie Lecoffre, 1933.
Africa, Thomas. "Worms and the Death of Kings: A Cautionary Note on Disease and History." *Classical Antiquity* 1 (1982): 1-17.
Amiran, David H. K., E. Arieh, and T. Turcotte. "Earthquakes in Israel and Adjacent Areas: Macroseismic Observations since 100 BCE." *IEJ* 44 (1994): 260-305.
Amiran, Ruth, and A. Eitan. "Herod's Palace." *IEJ* 22 (1972): 50-51.
Amit, David. "What Was the Source of Herodion's Water?" *Liber Annuus* 44 (1994): 561-78.
———. "The Aqueducts to the Fortress of Alexandrium." In *The Aqueducts of Israel*. Edited by David Amit, Joseph Patrich, and Yizhar Hirschfeld. JRAS 46; Portsmouth: Journal of Roman Archaeology, 2002, 306-12.
———. "The Aqueduct of the Fortress of Dok (Dagon)." In *The Aqueducts of Israel*. Edited by David Amit, Joseph Patrich, and Yizhar Hirschfeld. JRAS 46; Portsmouth: Journal of Roman Archaeology, 2002, 330-35.
Ando, Clifford. *Imperial Ideology and Provincial Loyalty in the Roman Empire*. Berkeley: University of California Press, 2000.
Applebaum, Shimon. "Judaea as a Roman Province: The Countryside as a Political and Economic Factor." In *ANRW* 2.8. Berlin: De Gruyter, 1977, 355-96.
Arav, Rami. "Some Notes on the Founding of Straton's Tower." *PEQ* 121 (1989): 144-48.
Ariel, Donald T. "The Jerusalem Mint of Herod the Great: A Relative Chronology." *INJ* 14 (2000-02): 99-124.
———. "The Coins of Herod the Great in the Context of the Augustan Empire." In

Bibliography

Herod and Augustus: Papers Presented at the IJS Conference, 21st-23rd June 2005. Edited by D. M. Jacobson and N. Kokkinos. Leiden: Brill, 2009, 113-26.

———. "A Numismatic Approach to the Reign of Herod the Great." Ph.D. diss., Tel-Aviv University, 2006.

———. "The Coins." In *Jewish Quarter Excavations in the Old City of Jerusalem: Conducted by Nahman Avigad, 1969-1982.* Vol. 3. Edited by Hillel Geva. Jerusalem: Israel Exploration Society, 2010.

Ariel, Donald T., and Jean-Philippe Fontanille. *The Coins of Herod: A Modern Analysis and Die Classification.* Leiden: Brill, 2012.

Arnold, Dieter. *Temples of the Last Pharaohs.* Oxford: Oxford University Press, 1999.

Ashcroft, Bill. *Post-Colonial Transformation.* London: Routledge, 2001.

Ashton, Sally-Ann. "Identifying the Egyptian-style Ptolemaic Queen." In *Cleopatra of Egypt: From History to Myth.* Edited by Susan Walker and Peter Higgs. Princeton: Princeton University Press, 2001, 148-88.

Asmis, Elizabeth. "Philodemus's Poetic Theory and *On the Good King According to Homer.*" *Classical Antiquity* 10 (1991): 1-45.

Atkinson, Kenneth. "Herod the Great, Sosius and the Siege of Jerusalem (37 B.C.E.) in Psalm of Solomon 17." *Novum Testamentum* 38 (1996): 313-22.

———. "On the Herodian Origin of Militant Davidic Messianism at Qumran: New Light from *Psalm of Solomon* 17." *JBL* 118 (1999): 435-60.

———. "Herod the Great as Antiochus *Redivivus*: Reading the *Testament of Moses* as an Anti-Herodian Composition." In *Of Scribes and Sages: Early Jewish Interpretation and Transmission of Scripture.* Edited by Craig A. Evans. London: Clark, 2004, 134-49.

Austin, M. M. "Hellenistic Kings, War and the Economy." *CQ* 36 (1986): 450-66.

Avigad, Nahman. "A Bulla of Jonathan the High Priest." *IEJ* 25 (1975): 8-12.

———. "A Bulla of King Jonathan." *IEJ* 25 (1975): 245-46.

———. "Jerusalem: Description of the Tombs." In *NEAEHL.* Edited by Ephraim Stern. Jerusalem: Israel Exploration Society, 1993, 750-56.

———. "Samaria." In *NEAEHL.* Edited by Ephraim Stern. Jerusalem: Israel Exploration Society, 1993, 1306-10.

Aviram, Joseph, Gideon Foerster, and Ehud Netzer. *Masada: The Yigael Yadin Excavations 1963-1965, Final Reports.* 5 vols. Jerusalem: Israel Exploration Society, 1989-95.

Avi-Yonah, Michael. *Oriental Art in Roman Palestine.* Studi Semitici 5. Rome: Università di Roma, 1961.

———. "Caesarea." *IEJ* 13 (1963): 146-48.

———, ed. *The World History of the Jewish People.* Vol 1.7: *The Herodian Period.* New Brunswick: Rutgers University Press, 1975.

Badian, Ernst. *Foreign Clientelae, 264-70 B.C.* Oxford: Clarendon, 1958.

Bahat, Dan. "The Western Wall Tunnels." In Hillel Geva, *Ancient Jerusalem Revealed.* Jerusalem: Israel Exploration Society, 1994, 177-90.

———. "Jerusalem Down Under: Tunneling along Herod's Temple Mount Wall." *BAR* 21.6 (1995): 31-47.

———. "The Architectural Origins of Herod's Temple Mount." In *Herod and Augustus: Papers Presented at the IJS Conference, 21st-23rd June 2005*. Edited by D. M. Jacobson and N. Kokkinos. Leiden: Brill, 2009, 235-45.

Bahat, Dan, and Chaim T. Rubenstein. *The Illustrated Atlas of Jerusalem*. Translated by Shlomo Ketko. New York: Simon and Schuster, 1990.

Baines, John. "Kingship, Definition of Culture, and Legitimation." In *Ancient Egyptian Kingship*. Edited by David O'Conner and David P. Silverman. Leiden: Brill, 1995, 95-156.

———. "Ancient Egyptian Kingship: Official Forms, Rhetoric, Context." In *King and Messiah in Israel and the Ancient Near East*. Edited by John Day. Sheffield: Sheffield Academic, 1998, 16-53.

Barag, Dan. "A Silver Coin of Yohanan the High Priest and the Coinage of Judaea in the Fourth Century B.C." *INJ* 9 (1986-87): 4-21.

———. "New Evidence on the Foreign Policy of John Hyrcanus I." *INJ* 12 (1992-93): 1-12.

———. "King Herod's Royal Castle at Samaria-Sebaste." *PEQ* 125 (1993): 3-18.

Barker, Ernest. *From Alexander to Constantine: Passages and Documents Illustrating the History of Social and Political Ideas*. Oxford: Clarendon, 1956.

Bauckham, Richard J. "Josephus' Account of the Temple in *Contra Apionem* 2.102-109." In *Josephus' Contra Apionem: Studies in Its Character and Context with a Latin Concordance to the Portion Missing in Greek*. Edited by Louis H. Feldman and J. R. Levison. Leiden: Brill, 1996, 327-47.

Beebe, H. Keith. "Caesarea Maritima: Its Strategic and Political Significance to Rome." *JNES* 42 (1983): 295-307.

Ben-David, Aryeh. "The Hebrew Phoenician Cubit." *PEQ* 110 (1978): 27-28.

Ben-Dov, Meir. "Herod's Mighty Temple Mount." *BAR* 12.6 (1986): 40-49.

Benoit, Pierre. "L'Antonia d'Hérode le Grand et le Forum Orientale d'Aelia Capitolina." *HTR* 64 (1971): 135-67.

Ben Zeev, Mariam Pucci. "Seleukos of Rhosos and Hyrcanus II." *JSJ* 26 (1995): 113-21.

———. "Who Wrote a Letter Concerning Delian Jews?" *RB* 103 (1996): 237-43.

———. "Polybius, Josephus and the Capitol in Rome." *JSJ* 27 (1996): 21-30.

———. "Caesar's Decrees in the Antiquities: Josephus' Forgeries or Authentic Roman Senatus Consulta?" *Athenaeum* 84 (1996): 71-91.

Berlin, Andrea M. "Debate: Where was Herod's Temple to Augustus? Banias Is Still the Best Candidate." *BAR* 29.5 (2003): 22-24.

Bernett, Monika. *Der Kaiserkult in Judäa unter den Herodiern und Römern. Untersuchungen zur politischen und religiösen Geschichte Judäas von 30 v. bis 66 n. Chr.* Tübingen: Mohr, 2007.

Berrin, Shani L. *The Pesher Nahum Scroll from Qumran: An Exegetical Study of 4Q169*. Leiden: Brill, 2004.

Bickerman, Elias J. "La Coelé: Notes de Géographie Historique." *RB* 54 (1947): 256.

———. *From Ezra to the Last of the Maccabees: Foundations of Post-Biblical Judaism*. New York, Schocken, 1962.

Bibliography

———. *The God of the Maccabees: Studies on the Meaning and Origin of the Maccabean Revolt.* Translated by Horst R. Moehring. Leiden: Brill, 1979.

Bilde, Per. *Flavius Josephus Between Jerusalem and Rome: His Life, His Works and Their Importance.* Sheffield: Sheffield University Press, 1988.

———. "The Geographical Excursuses in Josephus." In *Josephus and the History of the Greco-Roman World: Essays in Memory of Morton Smith.* Edited by Fausto Parente and Joseph Sievers. Leiden: Brill, 1994, 247-62.

Billows, Richard A. *Antigonos the One-Eyed and the Creation of the Hellenistic State.* Berkeley: University of California Press, 1990.

Blake, Marian E. "The Pavements of the Roman Buildings of the Republic and Early Empire." *MemAmAc* 8 (1930): 7-159.

Blau, Joseph L. "The Red Heifer: A Biblical Purification Rite in Rabbinic Literature." *Numen* 14 (1967): 70-78.

Bloch, Maurice. "The Ritual of the Royal Bath in Madagascar: The Dissolution of Death, Birth and Fertility into Authority." In *Rituals of Royalty: Power and Ceremonial in Traditional Societies.* Edited by David Cannadine and Simon Price. Cambridge: Cambridge University Press, 1987, 271-97.

Boëthius, Axel. *Etruscan and Early Roman Architecture.* New York: Penguin, 1978.

Bomgardner, David L. "A New Era for Amphitheatre Studies." *JRA* 6 (1993): 375-90.

Bond, Helen. "Josephus in Recent Research." *Currents in Research: Biblical Studies* 8 (2000): 162-90.

Bowersock, G. W. "Eurycles of Sparta." *JRS* 51 (1961): 112-18.

———. "Augustus and the East: The Problem of Succession." In *Caesar Augustus: Seven Aspects.* Edited by Fergus Millar and Erich Segal. Oxford: Clarendon, 1984, 169-88.

Bowman, Alan K. *Egypt After the Pharaohs: 332 BC–AD 642.* London: British Museum, 1986.

Bowra, C. M. "Aeneas and the Stoic Ideal." In *Oxford Readings in Vergil's Aeneid.* Edited by S. J. Harrison. Oxford: Oxford University Press, 1990, 8-21.

Brandon, Christopher, Stephen Kemp, and Martin Grove. "*Pozzolana,* Lime, and Single-Mission Barges (Area K)." In *Caesarea Papers 2.* Edited by Kenneth G. Holum, Avner Raban, and Joseph Patrich. Portsmouth: Journal of Roman Archaeology, 1999, 169-78.

Braund, David. "Four Notes on the Herods." *CQ* 77 (1983): 239-42.

———. *Rome and the Friendly King: The Character of the Client Kingship.* New York: St. Martin's, 1984.

Braund, Susanna Morton. "Virgil and the Cosmos: Religious and Philosophical Ideas." In *The Cambridge Companion to Virgil.* Edited by C. A. Martindale. Cambridge: Cambridge University Press, 1997, 204-21.

Breasted, James H. *Ancient Records of Egypt.* Chicago: University of Chicago Press, 1906.

Brenk, Frederick E. "Antony-Osiris, Cleopatra-Isis: The End of Plutarch's *Antony.*" In *Plutarch and the Historical Tradition.* Edited by Philip A. Stadter. London: Routledge, 1992, 159-82.

Brenner, Sandy. "Coin of Herod the Great: Star or Crest." *The Celator* 14:10 (2000): 40-47.

———. "Herod the Great Remains True to Form." *Near Eastern Archaeology* 64 (2001): 212-14.

Brett, Agnes Baldwin. "A New Cleopatra Tetradrachm of Ascalon." *AJA* 41 (1937): 452-63.

Bringmann, Klaus. "The King as Benefactor: Some Remarks on Ideal Kingship in the Age of Hellenism." In *Images and Ideologies: Self-Definition in the Hellenistic World.* Edited by Anthony Bulloch, Erich S. Gruen, A. A. Long, and Andrew Stewart. Berkeley: University of California Press, 1993, 7-24.

Broshi, Magen. "Does 'State Necessity' Contradict 'Personal Need'?" *Jerusalem Cathedra* 1 (1981): 67.

———. "The Credibility of Josephus." *JJS* 33 (1982): 379-84.

Broughton, T. Robert S. *The Magistrates of the Roman Republic.* Vol. 2. New York: American Philological Association, 1952.

Brunt, P. A. "*Amicitia* in the Late Roman Republic." *PCPS* 191 (1965): 1-20.

———. "Stoicism and the Principate." *Papers of the British School at Rome* 43 (1975): 7-35.

Bryan, David J. "The Herodians: A Case of Disputed Identity: A Review Article of Nikos Kokkinos, 'The Herodian Dynasty.'" *Tyndale Bulletin* 53 (2002): 223-38.

Bull, Robert J. "Caesarea and King Herod's Magnificent City Plan." *AJA* 100 (1996): 370.

Burke, Peter. *The Fabrication of Louis XIV.* New Haven: Yale University Press, 1992.

Burkert, Walter. "Zur geistesgeschichtlichen Einordnung einiger Psudopythagorica." In *Pseudepigrapha,* I. Edited by Kurt von Fritz. Vandoeuvres-Geneve: Fondation Hardt, 1972, 25-55.

Burrell, Barbara, and Ehud Netzer. "Herod the Builder." *JRA* 12 (1999): 705-15.

Burrell, Barbara, and Kathryn Gleason. "The Promontory Palace at Caesarea, Israel: The 1993 and 1994 Seasons." *AJA* 99 (1995): 306-7.

Burrell, Barbara, Kathryn Gleason, and Ehud Netzer. "Uncovering Herod's Seaside Palace." *BAR* 19.3 (1993): 50-52, 76.

Busink, Th. A. *Der Tempel von Jerusalem, von Salomo bis Herodes. Eine Archäologisch-Historische Studie unter Berücksichtigung des Westsemitischen Tempelbaus.* 2 vols. Leiden: Brill, 1980.

Butler, H. C. *Publications of the American Expedition to Syria 1899-1900. Architecture and Other Arts.* Vol. 2. New York: Century, 1903.

Cairns, Francis. *Virgil's Augustan Epic.* Cambridge: Cambridge University Press, 1989.

Cavedoni, Celestino. *Biblische Numismatik.* 2 vols. Hanover: Hahn, 1855-56.

Chancey, Mark A. *The Myth of a Gentile Galilee.* Cambridge: Cambridge University Press, 2002.

———. *Greco-Roman Culture and the Galilee of Jesus.* Cambridge: Cambridge University Press, 2005.

Charlesworth, M. P. *The Virtues of a Roman Emperor: Propaganda and the Creation of Belief.* London: Humphrey Milford Amen House, 1937.

Bibliography

———. "Review of *Les Traités de la Royauté d'Ecphante, Diotogéne et Sthénidas,* by Louis Delatte." *Classical Review* 63 (1949): 22-23.

Chauveau, Michel. *Cleopatra: Beyond the Myth.* Translated by David Lorton. Ithaca: Cornell University Press, 2002.

Claridge, Amanda. *Rome: An Oxford Archaeological Guide.* Oxford: Oxford University Press, 1998.

Cohen, Eric W. "The Appendix of the Antonia Rock in Jerusalem." *PEQ* 111 (1979): 41-52.

Cohen, Getzel M. "The Hellenistic Military Colony: A Herodian Example." *TAPA* 103 (1972): 83-95.

Cohen, Shaye J. D. *Josephus in Galilee and Rome: His Vita and Development as a Historian.* Leiden: Brill, 1979.

———. "The Matrilineal Principle in Historical Perspective." *Judaism* 34 (1985): 5-13.

———. *The Beginnings of Jewishness.* Berkeley: University of California Press, 1999.

Collins, John J. "The Epic of Theodotus and the Hellenism of the Hasmoneans." *HTR* 73.1-2 (1980): 91-104.

———. "Cult and Culture: The Limits of Hellenization in Judaea." In *Hellenism in the Land of Israel.* Edited by John J. Collins and Gregory E. Sterling. Notre Dame, IN: University of Notre Dame Press, 2001. Reprinted in John J. Collins. *Jewish Cult and Hellenistic Culture.* Leiden: Brill, 2005, 38-61.

———. "The Jewish World and the Coming of Rome." In *Jewish Cult and Hellenistic Culture.* Leiden: Brill, 2005, 202-16.

———. "The King as Son of God in the Hebrew Bible." Paper presented at *Oxford Speaker's Lectures in Biblical Studies: Messiah and Son of God. Early Christology in Light of Biblical and Jewish Traditions,* Oxford University, May 2, 2006.

Cooke, Gerald. "The Israelite King as Son of God." *ZAW* 32 (1961): 202-25.

Corbishley, Thomas. "The Chronology of the Reign of Herod the Great." *JThS* 36 (1935): 22-32.

Corbo, Virgilio. "Macheronta. La Reggia-Fortezza Erodiana." *Liber Annuus* 29 (1979): 315-26.

Cotton, Hannah M., and Joseph Geiger. "The Economic Importance of Herod's Masada." In *Judaea and the Greco-Roman World in the Time of Herod in the Light of Archaeological Evidence.* Edited by Klaus Fittschen and Gideon Foerster. Göttingen: Vandenhoeck and Ruprecht, 1996, 163-70.

Cotton, Hannah M., Joseph Geiger, and Ehud Netzter. "A Greek Ostracon from Masada." *IEJ* 45 (1995): 274-77.

Cotton, Hannah, Omri Lernau, and Yuval Goren. "Fish Sauces from Herodian Masada." *JRA* 9 (1996): 223-38.

Cotton, Hannah, and Wolfram Weiser. "Neues zum 'Tyrischen Silbergeld' herodianischer und römischer Zeit." *ZPE* 139 (2002): 235-50.

Crawford, M. H. *Roman Republican Coinage.* 2 vols. London: Cambridge University Press, 2001.

———. "Roman Imperial Coin Types and the Formation of Public Opinion." In *Studies in Numismatic Method: Presented to Philip Gierson.* Edited by CN. L. Brooke,

B. H. I. H. Stewart, J. G. Pollard, and T. R. Volk. Cambridge: Cambridge University Press, 1983, 47-64.

Creighton, John. "Links between the Classical Imagery in Post-Caesarean Belgica and the Rest of the Roman world." In *Die Kelten und Rom: Neue Numismatische Forschungen, Studien zu Fundmünzen der Antike.* Edited by J. Metzler and D. Wigg-Wolf. Berlin: Mann, 2005, 87-107.

———. "Augustan Client Policy and Britain and the West." In *Herod and Augustus: Papers Presented at the IJS Conference, 21st-23rd June 2005.* Edited by D. M. Jacobson and N. Kokkinos. Leiden: Brill, 2009, 361-81.

Cross, Frank M. *Canaanite Myth and Hebrew Epic: Essays in the History of the Religion of Israel.* Cambridge: Harvard University Press, 1973.

Crowfoot, J. W., K. M. Kenyon, and E. L. Sukenik. *Samaria-Sebaste I: The Buildings of at Samaria.* London: Palestine Exploration Fund, 1942.

Crowfoot, J. W., G. M. Crowfoot, and K. M. Kenyon. *Samaria-Sebaste III: The Objects from Samaria.* London: Palestine Exploration Fund, 1957.

Curtis, Robert I. *Garum and Salsamenta: Production and Commerce in Materia Medica.* Leiden: Brill 1991.

Dar, Shimon. *Landscape and Pattern: An Archaeological Survey of Samaria, 800 B.C.E.-636 C.E.* 2 vols. Oxford: BAR, 1986.

Davies, John. "The Interpenetration of Hellenistic Sovereignties." In *The Hellenistic World: New Perspectives.* Edited by Daniel Ogden. London: Classical/Duckworth, 2002, 1-21.

Davis, Norman, and Colin M. Kraay. *The Hellenistic Kingdoms: Portrait Coins and History.* London: Thames and Hudson, 1973.

Day, John. "The Canaanite Inheritance of the Israelite Monarchy." In *King and Messiah in Israel and the Ancient Near East.* Edited by John Day. Sheffield: Sheffield Academic, 1998, 72-90.

Delatte, Louis. *Les Traités de la Royauté d'Ecphante, Diotogéne et Sthénidas.* Paris: Librairie E. Droz, 1942.

Delev, P. "Lysimachus, the Getae and Archaeology." *CQ* 50 (2000): 385-401.

Dentzer, J. "A Propos du Temple Dit de 'Dusares' à Si." *Syria* 56 (1979): 325-32.

Derfler, Steven L. *The Hasmonean Revolt: Rebellion or Revolution.* Lewiston: Mellen, 1989.

De Vaux, Roland. "The King of Israel, Vassal of Yahweh." In *The Bible and the Ancient Near East.* New York: Doubleday, 1971, 152-80.

———. "Mambre." *DBSuppl* 5 (1957): 753-58.

Dodge, Hazel. "The Architectural Impact of Rome in the East." In *Architecture and Architectural Sculpture in the Roman Empire.* Edited by Martin Henig. Oxford: Oxford University Committee for Archaeology, 1990, 108-20.

Donaldson, T. L. "Rural Bandits, City Mobs and the Zealots." *JSJ* 21 (1990): 19-40.

Doudna, Gregory L. *4Q Pesher Nahum: A Critical Edition.* London: Sheffield Academic, 2001.

Duncan-Jones, Richard. *Money and Government in the Roman Empire.* Cambridge: Cambridge University Press, 1994.

Bibliography

Eck, Werner. "Senatorial Self-Representation: Developments in the Augustan Period." In *Caesar Augustus: Seven Aspects*. Edited by Fergus Millar and Erich Segal. Oxford: Clarendon, 1984, 129-67.

Eckhardt, Benedikt. "'An Idumean, that is, a Half-Jew.' Hasmoneans and Herodians Between Ancestry and Merit." In *Jewish Identity and Politics between the Maccabees and Bar Kokhba*. Edited by Benedikt Eckhardt. Leiden: Brill, 2012, 91-115.

Edmondson, Jonathan, Steve Mason, and James Rives, eds. *Flavius Josephus and Flavian Rome*. Oxford: Oxford University Press, 2005.

Edwards, Ormond. "Herodian Chronology." *PEQ* 114 (1982): 29-42.

Efron, Joshua. *Studies on the Hasmonean Period*. Leiden: Brill, 1987.

Eitan, Abraham, Pirhiya Beck, and Moshe Kochavi. "Aphek." In *NEAEHL*. Edited by Ephraim Stern. Jerusalem: Israel Exploration Society, 1993, 62-72.

Elias, Norbert. *The Court Society*. Translated by Edmund Jephcott. New York: Pantheon, 1983.

Engnell, Ivan. *Studies in Divine Kingship in the Ancient Near East*. Uppsala: Almqvist and Wiksell, 1943.

Eshel, Hanan. "4QMMT and the History of the Hasmonean Period." In *Reading 4QMMT: New Perspectives on Qumran Law and History*. Edited by John Kampen and Moshe J. Bernstein. Atlanta: Scholars, 1996, 53-65.

———. *The Dead Sea Scrolls and the Hasmonaean State*. Grand Rapids: Eerdmans, 2008.

Farber, J. Joel. "The *Cyropaedia* and Hellenistic Kingship." *AJP* 100 (1979): 497-514.

Fatkin, Danielle Steen. "As the Romans Do? Bathing in Herodian Palestine." Paper presented at *The Society of Biblical Literature Annual Meeting*, San Diego, November 17-20, 2006.

———. "Royal Power and Bathing in Herod's Palestine." Chapter 3 of "Many Waters: Bathing *Ethe* of the Roman Empire." Ph.D. diss., Stanford University, 2007.

Feldman, Louis H. "Asinius Pollio and His Jewish Interests." *TAPA* 84 (1953): 73-80.

———. "Asinius Pollio and Herod's Sons." *CQ* 35 (1985): 240-43.

———. "Josephus' Portrayal of the Hasmoneans Compared with 1 Maccabees." In *Josephus and the History of the Greco-Roman World: Essays in Memory of Morton Smith*. Edited by Fausto Parente and Joseph Sievers. Leiden: Brill, 1994, 41-68.

———. *Josephus' Interpretation of the Bible*. Berkeley: University of California Press, 1998.

———. *Studies in Josephus' Rewritten Bible*. Leiden: Brill, 1998.

———. "On Professor Mark Roncace's Portraits of Deborah and Gideon in Josephus." *JSJ* 32 (2001): 193-220.

———. "How Much Hellenism in the Land of Israel?" Review of *Hellenism in the Land of Israel*, ed. John J. Collins and Gregory E. Sterling. *JSJ* 33 (2002): 290-313.

Fischer, Moshe L., and Alla Stein. "Josephus on the Use of Marble in Building Projects of Herod the Great." *JJS* 45 (1994): 79-85.

Fischer, Thomas. "Hasmoneans and Seleucids: Aspects of War and Policy in the Second and First Centuries B.C.E." In *Greece and Rome in Eretz-Israel*. Edited by Aryeh

Kasher, Uriel Rappaport, and Gideon Fuks. Jerusalem: Jerusalem Exploration Society, 1990, 3-19.

Fittschen, Klaus. "Juba II und Seine Residenz Jol/Caesarea." In *Die Numider: Reiter und Könige Nördlich der Sahara*. Edited by Heinz Günter Horn and Christoph B. Rüger. Cologne: Rheinland, 1979.

———. "Wall Decorations in Herod's Kingdom: Their Relationship with Wall Decorations in Greece and Italy." In *Judaea and the Greco-Roman World in the Time of Herod in the Light of Archaeological Evidence*. Edited by Klaus Fittschen and Gideon Foerster. Göttingen: Vandenhoeck and Ruprecht, 1996, 139-61.

Fleischer, Robert. *Studien zur Seleukidischen Kunst I: Herrscherbildnisse*. Mainz: von Zabern, 1991.

———. "Hellenistic Royal Iconography on Coins." In *Aspects of Hellenistic Kingship*. Edited by Per Bilde, et al. Oakville: Aarhus University Press, 1996, 28-40.

Flinder, Alexander. "A Piscina at Caesarea." *IEJ* 26 (1976): 77-80.

———. "The Piscinas at Caesarea and Lapithos." In *Harbour Archaeology: Proceedings of the First International Workshop on Ancient Mediterranean Harbours: Caesarea Maritima*. Edited by Avner Raban. Oxford: BAR, 1983.

Flusser, David. "The Great Goddess of Samaria." *IEJ* 25 (1975): 13-20.

Foerster, Gideon. "The Early History of Caesarea." In *Studies in the History of Caesarea Maritima*. Edited by Charles T. Fritsch. Missoula: Scholars Press, 1975, 9-22.

———. "Hellenistic and Roman Trends in the Herodian Architecture of Masada." In *Judaea and the Greco-Roman World in the Time of Herod in the Light of Archaeological Evidence*. Edited by Klaus Fittschen and Gideon Foerster. Göttingen: Vandenhoeck and Ruprecht, 1996, 55-72.

Foerster, Gideon, and Ehud Netzer. "Herodium." In *NEAEHL*. Edited by Ephraim Stern. Jerusalem: Israel Exploration Society, 1993, 618-26.

Fontanille, Jean-Philippe. "The Largest Herodian Coins: The Very First Dies." *The Celator* 19:2 (2005): 18-25.

Förtsch, Reinhard. "The Residences of King Herod and Their Relations to Roman Villa Architecture." In *Judaea and the Greco-Roman World in the Time of Herod in the Light of Archaeological Evidence*. Edited by Klaus Fittschen and Gideon Foerster. Göttingen: Vandenhoeck and Ruprecht, 1996, 73-119.

Freeman, Joanne. *Affairs of Honor: National Politics in the New Republic*. New Haven: Yale University Press, 2001.

Frova, Antonio, et al. *Scavi di Caesarea Maritima*. Roma: "L'Erma" di Bretschneider, 1966.

Frumkin, Amos. "The Hydrogeology of Israel and the Problem of Water Supply in Antiquity." In *The Aqueducts of Israel*. Edited by David Amit, Joseph Patrich, and Yizhar Hirschfeld. JRAS 46; Portsmouth: Journal of Roman Archaeology, 2002, 21-24.

Fuks, Gideon. "Josephus and the Hasmoneans." *JJS* 41 (1990): 166-76.

———. "Antagonistic Neighbors: Ashkelon, Judaea and the Jews." *JJS* 51 (2000): 42-62.

———. "Josephus on Herod's Attitude towards Jewish Religion: The Darker Side." *JJS* 53 (2002): 238-45.

Bibliography

Fulco, W. J., and F. Zayadine. "Coins from Samaria-Sebaste." *ADAJ* 25 (1981): 197-225.

Gabba, Emilio. "The Historians and Augustus." In *Caesar Augustus: Seven Aspects*. Edited by Fergus Millar and Erich Segal. Oxford: Clarendon, 1984, 61-88.

———. "The Finances of King Herod." In *Greece and Rome in Eretz-Israel*. Edited by Aryeh Kasher, Uriel Rappaport, and Gideon Fuks. Jerusalem: Jerusalem Exploration Society, 1990, 160-68.

Gafni, Isaiah M. "Josephus and *I Maccabees*." In *Josephus, the Bible, and History*. Edited by Louis H. Feldman and Gohei Hata. Detroit: Wayne State University Press, 1989, 116-31.

Galinsky, G. K. "The Anger of Aeneas." *AJP* 109 (1988): 321-48.

———. "Hercules in the *Aeneid*." In *Oxford Readings in Vergil's Aeneid*. Edited by S. J. Harrison. Oxford: Oxford University Press, 1990, 277-94.

Gagarin, Michael, David Mirhady, Terry L. Papillon, and Yun Lee Too, eds. *Isocrates*. 2 vols. Austin: University of Texas Press, 2000-04.

Garlan, Y. "A Propos des Nouvelles Inscriptions d'Iasos." *ZPE* 9 (1972): 223-24.

Geertz, Clifford. "The Politics of Meaning." In *The Interpretation of Cultures*. New York: Basic, 1973, 311-26.

———. "Centers, Kings and Charisma: Reflection on the Symbolics of Power." In *Local Knowledge: Further Essays in Interpretive Anthropology*. 3rd ed. New York: Basic, 2000, 121-46.

Geiger, Joseph. "Herodes *Philorhomaios*." *Ancient Society* 28 (1997): 75-88.

———. "The Hasmoneans and Hellenistic Succession." *JJS* 53 (2002): 1-18.

———. "Language, Culture and Identity in Ancient Palestine." In *Greek Romans and Roman Greeks: Studies in Cultural Interaction*. Edited by Erik Nis Ostenfeld. Aarhus: Aarhus University Press, 2002, 233-46.

Gera, Dov. *Judaea and Mediterranean Politics, 219 to 161 B.C.E.* Leiden: Brill, 1998.

Gerber, Douglas E. "Theocritus, *Idyll* 17.53-57." In *Corolla Londiniensis*. Edited by Giuseppe Giangrande. Vol. 8. Amsterdam: Gieben, 1981, 21-24.

Gersht, Rivka. "The Tyche of Caesarea Maritima." *PEQ* 116 (1984): 110-14.

Geva, Hillel. "The 'Tower of David' — Phasael or Hippicus?" *IEJ* 31 (1981): 57-65.

———. "Excavations in the Citadel of Jerusalem." *IEJ* 33 (1983): 55-71.

———. "The Temple Mount and Its Environs." In *NEAEHL*. Edited by Ephraim Stern. Jerusalem: Israel Exploration Society, 1993, 736-44.

Gibson, Shimon, and David M. Jacobson, *Below the Temple Mount in Jerusalem*. Oxford: British Archaeological Society, 1996.

Gigante, Marcello. *Philodemus in Italy: The Books of Herculaneum*. Translated by Dirk Obbink. Ann Arbor: University of Michigan Press, 1998.

Gihon, M. "Idumea and the Herodian Limes." *IEJ* 17 (1967): 27-42.

Gilbert, Michelle. "The Person of the King: Ritual and Power in a Ghanaian State." In *Rituals of Royalty: Power and Ceremonial in Traditional Societies*. Edited by David Cannadine and Simon Price. Cambridge: Cambridge University Press, 1987, 298-330.

Gilboa, A. "The Intervention of Sextus Julius Caesar, Governor of Syria, in the Affair of Herod's Trial." *Scripta Classica Israelica* 5 (1979-80): 185-94.

Gleason, Kathryn L. "Garden Excavations at the Herodian Winter Palace in Jericho: 1985-1987." *BAIAS* 7 (1987-88): 21-39.

———. "Ruler and Spectacle: The Promontory Palace." In *Caesarea Maritima: A Retrospective after Two Millennia*. Edited by Avner Raban and Kenneth G. Holum. Leiden: Brill, 1996, 208-27.

Goffman, Erving. *The Presentation of Self in Everyday Life*. Woodstock: Overlook, 1973.

Goldenberg, David M. "*Antiquities* IV, 277 and 288, Compared with Early Rabbinic Law." In *Josephus, Judaism and Christianity*. Edited by Louis H. Feldman and Gohei Hata. Detroit: Wayne State University Press, 1987, 198-211.

Goldschmidt-Lehmann, Ruth P. "The Second (Herodian) Temple, Selected Bibliography." *Jerusalem Cathedra* 1 (1981): 336-59.

Goodblatt, David. *The Monarchic Principle: Studies in Jewish Self-Government in Antiquity*. Tübingen: Mohr, 1994.

Goodenough, Edwin R. "The Political Philosophy of Hellenistic Kingship." *YCS* 1 (1928): 55-102.

———. Review of *Les Traités de la Royauté d'Ecphante, Diotogéne et Sthénidas*, by Louis Delatte. *CP* 44 (1949): 129-31.

Goodman, Martin. "The First Jewish Revolt: Social Conflict and the Problem of Debt." *JJS* 33 (1982): 417-27.

———. *The Ruling Class of Judaea: The Origins of the Jewish Revolt AD 66-70*. Cambridge: Cambridge University Press, 1987.

———. "Judaea." In *Cambridge Ancient History*. Edited by Alan K. Bowman, Edward Champlin, and Andrew Lintott. 2nd ed. Vol 10. Cambridge: Cambridge University Press, 1996, 737-81.

———. "Jews, Greeks and Romans." In *Jews in a Graeco-Roman World*. Edited by Martin Goodman. Oxford: Oxford University Press, 1998, 3-14.

———. *Rome and Jerusalem. The Clash of Ancient Civilizations*. New York: Vintage, 2008.

Goudchaux, Guy Weill. "Was Cleopatra Beautiful? The Conflicting Answers of Numismatics." In *Cleopatra of Egypt: From History to Myth*. Edited by Susan Walker and Peter Higgs. Princeton: Princeton University Press, 2001, 210-74.

Grabbe, Lester L. *Judaism from Cyrus to Hadrian*. Minneapolis: Fortress, 1991.

Gracey, M. H. "The Armies of the Judaean Client Kings." In *The Defense of the Roman and Byzantine East*. Edited by Philip Freeman and David Kennedy. Oxford: BAR, 1986. 311-23.

Grafman, R. "Herod's Foot and Robinson's Arch." *IEJ* 20 (1970): 60-66.

Grant, Michael. *Herod the Great*. New York: American Heritage, 1971.

———. *Cleopatra*. London: Weidenfeld and Nicolson, 1972.

Gressmann, Hugo. *Der Messias*. Göttingen: Vandenhoeck and Ruprecht, 1929.

Griffin, Jasper. "Augustus and the Poets: 'Caesar qui cogere posset.'" In *Caesar Augustus: Seven Aspects*. Edited by Fergus Millar and Erich Segal. Oxford: Clarendon, 1984, 189-218.

Gruen, Erich S. *The Hellenistic World and the Coming of Rome*. Berkeley: University of California Press, 1984, 745-52.

———. "Hellenistic Kingship: Puzzles, Problems and Possibilities." In *Aspects of Hellenistic Kingship*. Edited by Per Bilde, et al. Oakville: Aarhus University Press, 1996.

———. *Heritage and Hellenism: The Reinvention of Jewish Tradition*. Berkeley: University of California Press, 1998, 116-25.

———. *Diaspora: Jews amidst the Greeks and Romans*. Cambridge: Harvard University Press, 2002.

———. "Cleopatra in Rome: Facts and Fantasies." In *Myth, History and Culture in Republican Rome: Studies in Honor of T. P. Wiseman*. Edited by David Braund and Christopher Gill. Exeter: University of Exeter Press, 2003, 257-74.

Guidobaldi, Federico. "Pavimenti in Opus Sectile di Roma e dell'Ara Romana: Proposte per una Classificazione e Criteri di Datazione." In *Marmi Antichi: Problemi d'Impiego, di Restauro e d'Identificazione*. Edited by Patrizio Pensabene. Roma: "L'Erma" di Bretschneider, 1985, 171-233.

Gunkel, Hermann, and Joachim Begrich. *Introduction to the Psalms*. Macon: Mercer University Press, 1998.

Hadley, R. A. "Hellenistic Royal Iconography on Coins." *JHS* 94 (1974): 50-65.

Hahm, David E. "Kings and Constitutions: Hellenistic Theories." In *The Cambridge History of Greek and Roman Political Thought*. Edited by Christopher Rowe and Malcolm Schofield. Cambridge: Cambridge University Press, 2000, 457-76.

Hamilton, Mark W. *The Body Royal: The Social Poetics of Kingship in Ancient Israel*. Leiden: Brill, 2005.

Hansen, Esther V. *The Attalids of Pergamon*. 2nd ed. Ithaca: Cornell University Press, 1971.

Hanson, K. C. "The Herodians and Mediterranean Kinship. Part 1: Genealogy and Descent." *Biblical Theology Bulletin* 19 (1989): 75-84.

———. "The Herodians and Mediterranean Kinship. Part 2: Marriage and Divorce." *Biblical Theology Bulletin* 19 (1989): 142-51.

———. "The Herodians and Mediterranean Kinship. Part 3: Economics." *Biblical Theology Bulletin* 20 (1990): 10-21.

———. "When the King Crosses the Line: Royal Deviance and Restitution in Levantine Ideologies." *Biblical Theology Bulletin* 26 (1996): 11-25.

Harder, Günther. "Herodes-Burgen und Herodes-Städte im Jordanangraben." *ZDPV* 78 (1962): 49-63.

Hassall, Mark, Michael Crawford, and Joyce Reynolds. "Rome and the Eastern Provinces at the End of the Second Century BC." *JRS* 64 (1974): 195-220.

Hazzard, R. A. *Imagination of a Monarchy: Studies in Ptolemaic Propaganda*. Toronto: University of Toronto Press, 2000.

Healey, John. "The Immortality of the King: Ugarit and the Psalms." *Orientalia* 53 (1984): 245-54.

Heinen, H. "The Syrian-Egyptian Wars and the New Kingdoms of Asia Minor." In *Cambridge Ancient History*. Edited by A. E. Astin, M. W. Frederiksen, R. M. Ogilvie, and F. W. Walbank. 2nd ed. Vol. 7. Cambridge: Cambridge University Press, 1984, 412-45.

Hendin, David. "New Discovery on a Coin of Herod I." *INJ* 11 (1990-91): 32.

———. "Confirmation of Herod Coin Motif Now Possible." *The Celator* 6.3 (1992): 38.
———. "The Helmet on Herod's Large Coin." *The Celator* 12.7 (1998): 30.
———. *Guide to Biblical Coins*. 4th ed. New York: Amphora, 2001.
Hengel, Martin. *The Zealots: Investigations into the Jewish Freedom Movement in the Period from Herod I until 70 A.D.* Translated by David Smith. Edinburgh: Clark, 1989.
———. *The "Hellenization" of Judaea in the First Century after Christ*. Translated by John Bowden. London: SCM, 1989.
———. "Judaism and Hellenism Revisited." In *Hellenism in the Land of Israel*. Edited by John J. Collins and Gregory E. Sterling. Notre Dame: University of Notre Dame Press, 2001, 6-37.
Herzberg, Hans Wilhelm. *I & II Samuel: A Commentary*. Philadelphia: Westminster, 1964.
Hesberg, Henner von. "The Significance of the Cities in the Kingdom of Herod." In *Judaea and the Greco-Roman World in the Time of Herod in the Light of Archaeological Evidence*. Edited by Klaus Fittschen and Gideon Foerster. Göttingen: Vandenhoeck and Ruprecht, 1996, 9-25.
Heutger, Nicolaus. "New Light on Jewish Coins of the Second Temple Period." In *Actes du XIe Congrès International de Numismatique*. Edited by Marcel Hoc. Louvain la Neuve: Société Royale de Numismatique de Belgique, 1993.
Higgs, Peter. "Searching for Cleopatra's Image: Classical Portraits in Stone." In *Cleopatra of Egypt: From History to Myth*. Edited by Susan Walker and Peter Higgs. Princeton: Princeton University Press, 2001, 200-209.
Hoehner, Harold. *Herod Antipas*. Cambridge: Cambridge University Press, 1972.
Hohlfelder, Robert L. "Beyond Coincidence? Marcus Agrippa and King Herod's Harbor." *JNES* 59 (2000): 241-53.
Hölbl, Günther. *History of the Ptolemaic Empire*. London : Routledge, 2000.
Holloway, R. Ross. "The Tomb of Augustus and the Princes of Troy." *AJA* 70 (1966): 171-73.
Holum, Kenneth G. "The Temple Platform: Progress Report on the Excavations." In *Caesarea Papers 2*. Edited by Kenneth G. Holum, Avner Raban, and Joseph Patrich. Portsmouth: Journal of Roman Archaeology, 1999, 12-34.
Holum, Kenneth G., Robert Hohlfelder, Robert J. Bull, and Avner Raban. *King's Herod's Dream: Caesarea by the Sea*. New York and London: Norton, 1988.
Holum, Kenneth G., et al. "Caesarea." In *NEAEHL*. Edited by Ephraim Stern. Jerusalem: Israel Exploration Society, 1993, 270-91.
Hooke, S. H., ed. *Myth, Ritual, and Kingship: Essays on the Theory and Practice of Kingship in the Ancient Near East and in Israel*. Oxford: Oxford University Press, 1958.
Horbury, William. *Jewish Messianism and the Cult of Christ*. London: SCM, 1998.
Hornblower, Simon. *Mausolus*. Oxford: Oxford University Press, 1982.
Horsely, Richard A., and John S. Hanson. *Bandits, Prophets, and Messiahs: Popular Movements in the Time of Jesus*. Harrisburg: Trinity, 1999.
Humphrey, John H. "'Amphitheatrical' Hippo-Stadia." In *Caesarea Maritima: A Retrospective After Two Millennia*. Edited by Avner Raban and Kenneth G. Holum. Leiden: Brill, 1996, 121-29.

Bibliography

Hunt, Lynn. *Politics, Culture and Class in the French Revolution.* Berkeley: University of California Press, 1984.

Hurwit, Jeffrey M. *The Athenian Acropolis: History, Mythology, and Archaeology from the Neolithic Era to the Present.* Cambridge: Cambridge University Press, 2000.

Huzar, Eleanor G. "Mark Antony: Marriages vs. Careers." *CJ* 81 (1986): 97-111.

Ilan, Tal. "The Greek Names of the Hasmoneans." *JQR* 78 (1987): 1-20.

———. "King David, King Herod and Nicolaus of Damascus." *JSQ* 5 (1998): 195-240.

———. "'Things Unbecoming a Woman' (*Ant.* 13:431): Josephus and Nicolaus on Women." In Tal Ilan, *Integrating Women into Second Temple History.* Tübingen: Mohr, 1999, 85-125.

———. "Intermarriage in the Herodian Family as a Paradigm for Intermarriage in Second Temple Judaism." Paper presented at *The Society of Biblical Literature Annual Meeting,* Toronto, November 23-26, 2002.

———. *Silencing the Queen: The Literary Histories of Shelamzion and other Jewish Women.* Tübingen: Mohr, 2006.

Ingholt, Harald. "A Colossal Head from Memphis, Severan or Augustan?" *Journal of the American Research Center in Egypt* 2 (1963): 125-45.

Isaac, Benjamin. "A Donation for Herod's Temple in Jerusalem." *IEJ* 33 (1983): 86-92.

———. "Bandits in Judaea and Arabia." *Harvard Studies in Classical Philology* 88 (1984): 171-203.

Ita of Sion, Marie. "The Antonia Fortress." *PEQ* 100 (1968): 139-43.

Jacobson, David M. "Ideas Concerning the Plan of Herod's Temple." *PEQ* 112 (1980): 33-40.

———. "The Plan of the Ancient Haram el-Khalil at Hebron." *PEQ* 113 (1981): 73-80.

———. "The Design of the Fortress of Herodium." *ZDPV* 100 (1984): 127-36.

———. "A New Interpretation of the Reverse of Herod's Largest Coin." *ANSMN* 31 (1986): 145-65.

———. "King Herod's 'Heroic' Public Image." *RB* 95 (1988): 386-403.

———. "The Plan of Herod's Temple." *BAIAS* 10 (1990-1991): 36-66.

———. "King Herod, Roman Citizen and Benefactor of Kos." *BAIAS* 13 (1993-94): 31-35.

———. "Sacred Geometry: Unlocking the Secret of the Temple Mount, Part 1." *BAR* 25.4 (1999): 42-53, 62-64.

———. "Sacred Geometry: Unlocking the Secret of the Temple Mount, Part 2." *BAR* 25.5 (1999): 54-63, 74.

———. "Geometrical Planning in Monumental Herodian Architecture." *BAIAS* 17 (1999): 67-76.

———. "The Anchor on the Coins of Judaea." *BAIAS* 18 (2000): 73-81.

———. "Decorative Drafted-Margin Masonry in Jerusalem and Hebron and Its Relations." *Levant* 32 (2000): 135-54.

———. "Herod the Great Shows His True Colors." *Near Eastern Archaeology* 64 (2001): 100-104.

———. "Three Roman Client Kings: Herod of Judaea, Archelaus of Cappadocia and Juba of Mauretania." *PEQ* 133 (2001): 22-38.

———. "Placing Herod the Great and His Works in Context." *PEQ* 134 (2002): 84-91.
———. "Herod's Roman Temple." *BAR* 28.2 (2002): 18-27, 60.
———. "The Northern Palace at Masada — Herod's Ship of the Desert?" *PEQ* 138 (2006): 99-117.
———. "Has Herod's Place of Burial Been Found?" *PEQ* 139 (2007): 147-48.
———. "The Jerusalem Temple of Herod the Great." In *The World of the Herods: Volume 1 of the International Conference The World of the Herods and the Nabataeans Held at the British Museum, 17-19 April 2001*. Edited by Nikos Kokkinos. Stuttgart: Steiner, 2007, 145-76.
Jacobson, David M., and Shimon Gibson. "A Monumental Stairway on the Temple Mount." *IEJ* 45 (1995): 162-70.
Japp, Sarah. *Die Baupolitik Herodes des Grossen. Die Bedeutung der Architektur für die Herrschaftslegitimation eines Römischen Klientelkönigs*. Rahden: Leidorf, 2000.
———. "Public and Private Decorative Art in the Time of Herod the Great." In *The World of the Herods: Volume 1 of the International Conference The World of the Herods and the Nabataeans Held at the British Museum, 17-19 April 2001*. Edited by Nikos Kokkinos. Stuttgart: Steiner, 2007, 227-46.
Johnson, W. R. "A Quean, A Great Queen? Cleopatra and the Politics of Misrepresentation." *Arion* 6 (1967): 387-402.
Jones, A. H. M. *The Herods of Judaea*. Oxford: Clarendon, 1938.
———. *The Cities of the Eastern Roman Provinces*. 2nd ed. Oxford: Clarendon, 1971.
Kahn, Lisa C. "King Herod's Temple of Roma and Augustus at Caesarea Maritima." In *Caesarea Maritima: A Retrospective After Two Millennia*. Edited by Avner Raban and Kenneth G. Holum. Leiden: Brill, 1996, 130-45.
Kanael, Baruch. "The Coins of King Herod of the Third Year." *JQR* 42 (1951-52): 261-64.
———. "Ancient Jewish Coins and Their Historical Importance." *BiblArch* 26 (1963): 38-62.
Kasher, Aryeh, and Eliezer Witztum. *King Herod, A Persecuted Persecutor: A Case Study in Psychohistory and Psychobiography*. Berlin: de Gruyter, 2006.
Kashtan, Nadav. "Akko-Ptolemais: A Maritime Metropolis in Hellenistic and Early Roman Times, 332 BCE-70 CE." *MHR* 3 (1988): 37-53.
Kaufman, Asher. "Kaufman Responds to Jacobson." *BAR* 26.2 (2000): 60-61, 69.
Kemp, Barry. *Ancient Egypt: Anatomy of a Civilization*. London: Routledge, 1989.
Kershaw, Ian. *The Nazi Dictatorship: Problems and Perspectives of Interpretation*. London: Arnold, 1985.
Kindler, Arie. "Some Unpublished Coins of King Herod." *IEJ* 3 (1953): 239-41.
———. *Coins of the Land of Israel*. Jerusalem: Keter, 1974.
King, C. E. "Roman Portraiture: Images of Power?" In *Roman Coins and Public Life under the Empire: E. Togo Salmon Papers II*. Edited by George M. Paul and Michael Ierardi. Ann Arbor: University of Michigan Press, 1999, 123-36.
Kleiner, Diana E. E. *Cleopatra and Rome*. Cambridge: Harvard University Press, 2005.
Knudtzon, J. A. *Die El-Amarna-Tafeln*. Leipzig: Hinrichs, 1915.
Kochavi, Moshe. "Tel-Aphek." *IEJ* 23 (1973): 245-46.

Bibliography

———. "The History and Archeology of Aphek-Antipatris: A Biblical City in the Sharon Plain." *BiblArch* 44 (1981): 75-86.

Kockel, Valentin. "Archäologische Funde und Forschungen in den Vesuvstädten II." *AA* (1986): 443-569.

Kokkinos, Nikos. "A Coin of Herod the Great Commemorating the City of Sebaste." *Liber Annuus* 35 (1985): 303-6.

———. *The Herodian Dynasty: Origins, Roles in Society and Eclipse*. Rev. ed. London: Spink, 2010.

———. "Cleopatra and Herod: A Failed Seduction." *British Museum Magazine* 39 (2001): 17.

———. "The City of 'Mariamme': An Unknown Herodian Connection?" *MedAnt* 5 (2002): 715-46.

———. "Herod's Horrid Death." *BAR* 28.2 (2002): 28-35, 62.

———. "The Royal Court of the Herods." In *The World of the Herods: Volume 1 of the International Conference The World of the Herods and the Nabataeans Held at the British Museum, 17-19 April 2001*. Edited by Nikos Kokkinos. Stuttgart: Steiner, 2007, 279-303.

Krattenmaker, Kathleen. "Palace, Peak and Sceptre: The Iconography of Legitimacy." In *The Role of the Ruler in the Prehistoric Aegean*. Edited by Paul Rehak. Liege: Kliemo, 1995, 49-62.

Kreiger, Barbara. "Finding Herod's Tomb." *Smithsonian* 40.5 (2009): 36-43.

Krencker, Daniel. "Vergleichende Untersuchungen romischer Thermen." In *Die Trierer Kaiserthermen. Ausgrabungsbericht und grundsätzliche Untersuchungen römischer Thermen*. Augsburg: Filser, 1929, 1:174-305.

Krentz, Edgar. "The Honorary Decree for Simon the Maccabee." In *Hellenism in the Land of Israel*. Edited by John J. Collins and Gregory E. Sterling. Notre Dame: University of Notre Dame Press, 2001, 146-53.

Krupp, Michael, and Shraga Qedar. "The Cross on the Coins of King Herod." *INJ* 5 (1981): 17-18.

Kuhrt, Amélie. "Usurpation, Conquest and Ceremonial: From Babylon to Persia." In *Rituals of Royalty: Power and Ceremonial in Traditional Societies*. Edited by David Cannadine and Simon Price. Cambridge: Cambridge University Press, 1987, 20-55.

Kushnir-Stein, Alla. "An Inscribed Lead Weight from Ashdod: A Reconsideration." *ZPE* 105 (1995): 81-84.

———. "Another Look at Josephus' Evidence for the Date of Herod's Death." *Scripta Classica Israelica* 14 (1995): 73-86.

———. "Review: Nikos Kokkinos, *The Herodian Dynasty: Origins, Role in Society and Eclipse*." *Scripta Classica Israelica* 18 (1999): 194-98.

———. "Dates on Ancient Palestinian Coins." In *Measuring and Weighing in Ancient Times*. Edited by Ofra Rimon, et al. Haifa: Hecht Museum, 2001, 47-50.

———. "Some Observations on Palestinian Coins with a Bevelled Edge." *INJ* 14 (2001-02): 78-83.

———. "Coins of the Herodian Dynasty: The State of Research." In *The World of the Herods: Volume 1 of the International Conference The World of the Herods and the*

Nabataeans Held at the British Museum, 17-19 April 2001. Edited by Nikos Kokkinos. Stuttgart: Steiner, 2007, 55-60.

Laato, Antti. *A Star Is Rising: The Historical Development of the Old Testament Royal Ideology and the Rise of the Jewish Messianic Expectations*. Atlanta: Scholars, 1997.

Lalor, Brian. "The Temple Mount of Herod the Great at Jerusalem: Recent Excavations and Literary Sources." *Archaeology and Biblical Interpretation*. Edited by John R. Bartlett. London: Routledge, 1997, 95-116.

Lambert, W. G. "Kingship in Ancient Mesopotamia." In *King and Messiah in Israel and the Ancient Near East*. Edited by John Day. Sheffield: Sheffield Academic, 1998, 54-70.

Lämmer, M. "Eine Propaganda-Aktion des Königs Herodes in Olympia." In *Perspektiven der Sportwissenschaft*. Schorndorf: Hoffmann, 1973, 160-73.

Landau, Tamar. "The Image of Herod in Josephus' *Bellum Judaicum*." In *Josephus and Jewish History in Flavian Rome and Beyond*. Edited by Joseph Sievers and Gaia Lembi. Leiden: Brill, 2005, 159-81.

―――. *Out-Heroding Herod: Josephus, Rhetoric, and the Herod Narratives*. Leiden: Brill, 2006.

Laqueur, Richard. *Der Jüdische Historiker Flavius Josephus: ein Biographischer Versuch auf Neuer Quellenkritischer Grundlage*. Darmstadt: Wissenschaftliche Buchgesellschaft, 1970.

Lauffray, Jean. "Beyrouth Archéologie et Histoire, Époques Gréco-Romaines I: Periode Hellénistique et Haut-Empire Romain." *ANRW* 2.8 (1977): 135-63.

Launderville, Dale. *Piety and Politics: The Dynamics of Royal Authority in Homeric Greece, Biblical Israel and Old Babylonian Mesopotamia*. Grand Rapids: Eerdmans, 2003.

Lefkowitz, Mary R. "Influential Women." In *Images of Women in Antiquity*. Edited by Averil Cameron and Amélie Kuhrt. London: Routledge, 1993, 49-64.

Leschhorn, Wolfgang. *Gründer der Stadt: Studien zu einem Politisch-Religiösen Phänomen der Griechischen Geschichte*. Stuttgart: Steiner, 1984.

Lesko, Barbara S. *The Great Goddesses of Egypt*. Norman: University of Oklahoma Press, 1999.

Leveau, Philippe. "Caesarea de Maurétanie." *ANRW* 2.10.2 (1982): 683-738.

Levick, Barbara. "Propaganda and the Imperial Coinage." *Antichthon* 16 (1982): 104-16.

―――. "Messages on the Roman Coinage: Types and Inscriptions." In *Roman Coins and Public Life under the Empire: E. Togo Salmon Papers II*. Edited by George M. Paul and Michael Ierardi. Ann Arbor: University of Michigan Press, 1999, 41-60.

Levine, Lee L. "Towards an Appraisal of Herod as a Builder." *Jerusalem Cathedra* 1 (1981): 62-66.

Levy, Brooks. "Tyrian Shekels and the First Jewish War." In *Proceedings of the XIth International Numismatic Congress (1991)*. Edited by Tony Hackens and Ghislaine Moucharte. Louvain: Hoc Association, 1993, 267-74.

―――. "Tyrian Shekels: The Myth of the Jerusalem Mint." *SAN* 19 (1995): 33-35.

Lewis, Theodore J. *Cults of the Dead in Ancient Israel and Ugarit*. Atlanta: Scholars, 1989.

Bibliography

Lichtenberger, Achim. *Die Baupolitik Herodes des Grossen*. Wiesbaden: Harrassowitz, 1999.

———. "Jesus and the Theater in Jerusalem." In *Jesus and Archaeology*. Edited by J. H. Charlesworth. Grand Rapids: Eerdmans, 2006, 283-99.

Lieu, Judith. "Not Hellenes but Philistines? The Maccabees and Josephus Defining the 'Other.'" *JJS* 53 (2002): 246-63.

Liver, J. "The Half-Shekel Offering in Biblical and Post-Biblical Literature." *HTR* 56 (1963): 173-98.

Long, A. A., and D. N. Sedley. *The Hellenistic Philosophers*. 2 vols. Cambridge: Cambridge University Press, 1987.

Loomba, Ania. *Colonialism/Postcolonialism*. London: Routledge, 1998.

Lund, Helen S. *Lysimachus: A Study in Early Hellenistic Kingship*. London: Routledge, 1992.

Lyne, R. O. A. M. *Further Voices in Vergil's Aeneid*. Oxford: Clarendon, 1987.

———. "Vergil and the Politics of War." In *Oxford Readings in Vergil's Aeneid*. Edited by S. J. Harrison. Oxford: Oxford University Press, 1990, 316-38.

Ma, John. *Antiochos III and the Cities of Western Asia Minor*. Oxford: Oxford University Press, 1999.

MacConville, J. G. "King and Messiah in Deuteronomy and the Deuteronomistic History." In *King and Messiah in Israel and the Ancient Near East*. Edited by John Day. Sheffield: Sheffield Academic, 1998, 271-95.

Machinist, Peter. "Kingship and Divinity in Imperial Assyria." In *Text, Artifact, and Image: Revealing Ancient Israelite Religion*. Edited by Gary Beckman and Theodore J. Lewis. Providence: Brown Judaic Studies, 2006, 152-88.

Macurdy, Grace Harriet. *Hellenistic Queens: A Study of Woman Power in Macedonia, Seleucid Syria, and Ptolemaic Egypt*. Baltimore: Johns Hopkins University Press, 1932.

Mader, A. E. *Mambre: Die Ergebnisse der Ausgrabungen im Heiligen Bezirk Ramet El-Halil in Südpalästina 1926-1928*. 2 vols. Freiburg I. B.: Wewel, 1957.

Mader, Gottfried. *Josephus and the Politics of Historiography: Apologetic and Impression Management in the Bellum Judaicum*. Leiden: Brill, 2000.

Maehler, Herwig. "Egypt under the Last Ptolemies." *BICS* 30 (1983): 1-16, plates 1-3.

Magen, Itzhak. "Mamre." In *NEAEHL*. Edited by Ephraim Stern. Jerusalem: Israel Exploration Society, 1994, 939-42.

Magie, David. *Roman Rule in Asia Minor to the End of the Third Century After Christ*. Princeton: Princeton University Press, 1950.

Magness, Jodi. "The Mausolea of Augustus, Alexander and Herod the Great." In *Hesed Ve-Emet: Studies in Honor of Ernest S. Frerichs*. Edited by Jodi Magness and Seymour Gittin. Atlanta: Scholars, 1998, 313-39.

———. "The Cults of Isis and Kore at Samaria-Sebaste in the Hellenistic and Roman Periods." *HTR* 94:2 (2001): 159-75.

———. "Where Is Herod's Tomb at Herodium?" *BASOR* 322 (2001): 43-46.

Malthea-Förtsch, Marion. "Scroll Ornamentations from Judaea and Their Different Patterns." In *Judaea and the Greco-Roman World in the Time of Herod in the Light of Archaeological Evidence.* Edited by Klaus Fittschen and Gideon Foerster. Göttingen: Vandenhoeck and Ruprecht, 1996, 177-96.

Maov, Ze'ev. "Banias, Temple of Pan-1989." *Excavations and Surveys in Israel* 9 (1990).

Mantzoulinou-Richards, Ersie. "From Syros: A Dedicatory Inscription of Herodes the Great from an Unknown Building." *Ancient World* 18.3-4 (1988): 87-99.

Marcus, Ralph. "Review of *Les Traités de la Royauté d'Ecphante, Diotogéne et Sthénidas*, by Louis Delatte." *Classical Journal* 44 (1948-49): 500-502.

Marshak, Adam Kolman. "The Dated Coins of Herod the Great: Towards a New Chronology." *JSJ* 37 (2006): 212-40.

———. "Herod the Great and the Power of Image: Political Self-Presentation in the Herodian Dynasty." Ph.D. diss., Yale University, 2008.

———. "Rise of the Idumaeans: Ethnicity and Politics in Herod's Judaea." In *Jewish Identity and Politics between the Maccabees and Bar Kokhba*. Edited by Benedikt Eckhardt. Leiden: Brill, 2012, 117-29.

———. "Glorifying the Present Through the Past: Herod the Great and His Jewish Royal Predecessors." In *Christian Origins and Hellenistic Judaism: Social and Literary Contexts for the New Testament*. Edited by Stanley E. Porter and Andrew W. Pitts. Leiden: Brill, 2012, 51-81.

Mason, Steve. *Flavius Josephus on the Pharisees*. Leiden: Brill, 1991.

———. "Introduction to the *Judaean Antiquities*." In *Judaean Antiquities 1-4*. Translated by Louis H. Feldman. Leiden: Brill, 2000, xiii-xxxvi.

———. *Josephus and the New Testament*. 2nd ed. Peabody: Hendrickson, 2003.

Mason, Steve, et al., eds. and trans. *Flavius Josephus: Translation and Commentary*. Leiden: Brill, 1999-.

Mathieu, Bieke. "The Foundation Year of Samaria-Sebaste and Its Chronological Implications." *Ancient Society* 38 (2008): 183-96.

Mazar, Benjamin. *The Mountain of the Lord: Excavating in Jerusalem*. New York: Doubleday, 1975.

———. "Josephus Flavius and the Archaeological Excavations in Jerusalem." In *Josephus, the Bible, and History*. Edited by Louis H. Feldman and Gohei Hata. Detroit: Wayne State University Press, 1989, 325-29.

McCane, Byron R. "Simply Irresistible: Augustus, Herod, and the Empire." *JBL* 127 (2008): 725-35.

McCarter, Kyle P. *II Samuel: A New Translation with Introduction, Notes, and Commentary*. Garden City: Doubleday, 1984.

McKenzie, Judith S., Sheila Gibson, and A. T. Reyes. "Reconstructing the Serapeum in Alexandria from the Archaeological Evidence." *JRS* 94 (2004): 73-121.

McLaren, James S. *Power and Politics in Palestine: The Jews and the Governing of Their Land, 100 BC-AD 70*. Sheffield: Sheffield University Press, 1991.

———. *Turbulent Times? Josephus and Scholarship on Judaea in the First Century CE*. Sheffield: Sheffield Academic, 1998.

Meadows, Andrew. "Sins of the Fathers: The Inheritance of Cleopatra, Last Queen of Egypt." In *Cleopatra of Egypt: From History to Myth*. Edited by Susan Walker and Peter Higgs. Princeton: Princeton University Press, 2001, 14-31.

Bibliography

Meier, John P. "The Historical Jesus and the Historical Herodians." *JBL* 119 (2000): 740-46.

Mendels, Doron. *The Rise and Fall of Jewish Nationalism*. New York: Doubleday, 1992.

Meredith, David. "Berenice Troglodytica." *JEA* 43 (1957): 56-70.

Meshel, Ze'ev, and David Amit. "The Water Supply Systems of Cypros Fortress." In *The Aqueducts of Israel*. Edited by David Amit, Joseph Patrich, and Yizhar Hirschfeld. JRAS 46; Portsmouth: Journal of Roman Archaeology, 2002, 313-29.

Meshorer, Ya'akov. "Maritime Symbols on Ancient Jewish Coins." *INJ* 2 (1964): 8-10.

———. "New Denominations in Ancient Jewish Coinage." *INJ* 2 (1964): 56-59.

———. *Jewish Coins of the Second Temple Period*. Translated by I. H. Levine. Tel Aviv: Am Hassefer, 1967.

———. "A Stone Weight from the Reign of Herod." *IEJ* 20 (1970): 97-98.

———. "The Beginning of Hasmonean Coinage" *IEJ* 24 (1974): 59-78.

———. *Nabataean Coins*. QEDEM 3. Jerusalem: Institute of Archaeology, Hebrew University of Jerusalem, 1975.

———. "On the Nature of the Symbols on the Coins of Herod the Great." In *Festschrift for Reuben R. Hecht*. Jerusalem: Korén, 1979, 158-61.

———. "Again on the Beginning of the Hasmonean Coinage." *INJ* 5 (1981): 11-16.

———. *Ancient Jewish Coinage*. 2 vols. New York: Amphora, 1982.

———. "One Hundred Ninety Years of Tyrian Shekels." In *Studies in Honor of Leo Mildenberg: Numismatics, Art History and Archaeology*. Edited by A. Houghten et al. Wetteren: Editions NR, 1984, 171-79.

———. *City-Coins of Eretz-Israel and the Decapolis in the Roman Period*. Jerusalem: Israel Museum, 1985.

———. "Ancient Jewish Coinage Addendum I." *INJ* 11 (1990-91): 104-32.

———. *A Treasury of Jewish Coins: From the Persian Period to Bar Kokhba*. Nyack: Amphora, 2001.

Metcalf, William E. "Whose *Liberalitas?* Propaganda and Audience in the Early Roman Empire." *RIN* 95 (1993): 337-46.

———. "Coins as Primary Evidence." In *Roman Coins and Public Life under the Empire: E. Togo Salmon Papers II*. Edited by George M. Paul and Michael Ierardi. Ann Arbor: University of Michigan Press, 1999, 1-17.

Mettinger, Tryggve N. D. *King and Messiah: The Civil and Sacral Legitimation of the Israelite Kings*. Lund: Gleerup, 1976.

Meyshan, Josef. "Symbols of the Coinage of Herod the Great." *PEQ* 91 (1959): 109-121.

———. *Essays in Jewish Numismatics*. Jerusalem: Israel Numismatic Society, 1968.

Mielsch, Harald. *Die Römische Villa: Architektur und Lebensform*. Munich: Beck, 1987.

Millar, Fergus. "Triumvirate and Principate." *JRS* 63 (1973): 50-67.

———. "State and Subject: The Impact of Monarchy." In *Caesar Augustus: Seven Aspects*. Edited by Fergus Millar and Erich Segal. Oxford: Clarendon, 1984, 37-60.

———. *The Roman Near East: 31 BC–AD 357*. Cambridge: Harvard University Press, 1993.

Miller, Martin C. J. "Macedonian Royal Insignia on the Coinage of Alexander Jannaeus." In *Alpha to Omega. Studies in Honor of George John Szemler on His 65th Birthday*. Edited by W. J. Cherf. Chicago: Ares, 1993, 144-57.

Mowinckel, Sigmund. *He That Cometh: The Messiah Concept in the Old Testament and Later Judaism*. Translated by G. W. Anderson. Oxford: Blackwell, 1959.

Morrison, J. S. "Review of *Les Traités de la Royauté d'Ecphante, Diotogéne et Sthénidas*, by Louis Delatte." *JHS* 69 (1949): 91-92.

Moulton, Warren J. "An Inscribed Tomb at Beit Jibrin." *AJA* 19 (1915): 63-70.

Mowry, Lucetta. "Settlements in the Jericho Valley during the Roman Period (63 B.C.–A.D. 134)." *BiblArch* 15 (1952): 31-32.

Murray, G. W. "Troglodytica: The Red Sea Littoral in Ptolemaic Times." *GJ* 133 (1967): 24-33.

Murray, Oswyn. "Philodemus on the Good King According to Homer." *JRS* 55 (1965): 161-82.

Narkiss, Mordechai. "Notes on the Coins of the Herodian Dynasty." *Journal of the Jewish Palestine Exploration Society* 4 (1934): 8-14.

Negev, Avraham. "Caesarea." *IEJ* 11 (1961): 81-83.

———. "Caesarea." *IEJ* 13 (1963): 146-48.

Nesbit, R. G. M. "*Aeneas Imperator:* Roman Generalship in an Epic Context." In *Oxford Readings in Vergil's Aeneid*. Edited by S. J. Harrison. Oxford: Oxford University Press, 1990, 378-89.

Netzer, Ehud. "Herod's Building Projects: State Necessity or Personal Need?" *Jerusalem Cathedra* 1 (1981): 48-61.

———. "In Reply." *Jerusalem Cathedra* 1 (1981): 73-80.

———. *Greater Herodium*. Jerusalem: Hebrew University of Jerusalem, 1981.

———. "Searching for Herod's Tomb: Somewhere in the Desert Palace-Fortress at Herodium, Palestine's Master Builder Was Buried." *BAR* 9.3 (1983): 31-51.

———. "Herod's Family Tomb in Jerusalem." *BAR* 9.3 (1983): 52-59.

———. "Herod the Great's Contribution to Nikopolis in Light of His Building Activity in Judaea." In *Proceedings of the First International Symposium of Nicopolis (23-29 September, 1984)*. Edited by Evangelos Chrysos. Preveza: Demos Prevezas, 1987, 121-28.

———. "Cypros." In *NEAEHL*. Edited by Ephraim Stern. Jerusalem: Israel Exploration Society, 1993, 315-17.

———. "Jericho: Tulul Abu el-'Alayiq." In *NEAEHL*. Edited by Ephraim Stern. Jerusalem: Israel Exploration Society, 1993, 682-91.

———. "Masada." In *NEAEHL*. Edited by Ephraim Stern. Jerusalem: Israel Exploration Society, 1994, 973-85.

———. "The Palaces Built by Herod — A Research Update." In *Judaea and the Greco-Roman World in the Time of Herod in the Light of Archaeological Evidence*. Edited by Klaus Fittschen and Gideon Foerster. Göttingen: Vandenhoeck and Ruprecht, 1996, 27-54.

———. *The Palaces of the Hasmoneans and Herod the Great*. Jerusalem: Yad Ben-Zvi, 2001.

———. "Debate: Where Was Herod's Temple to Augustus? A Third Candidate: Another Building at Banias." *BAR* 29.5 (2003): 25.

———. *Hasmonean and Herodian Palaces at Jericho: Final Reports of the 1973-1987 Excavations*. 4 vols. Jerusalem: Israel Exploration Society, 2001-08.

———. *The Architecture of Herod, the Great Builder*. Tübingen: Mohr, 2006.

———. "In Search of Herod's Tomb." *BAR* 37.1 (2011): 36-70.

Netzer, Ehud, and Sarah Ben-Arieh. "Remains of an Opus Reticulatum Building in Jerusalem." *IEJ* 33 (1983): 163-75.

Netzer, Ehud, and Emmanuel Damati. "Cypros." In *Hasmonean and Herodian Palaces at Jericho: Final Reports of the 1973-1987 Excavations*. Vol. 2. Jerusalem: Israel Exploration Society, 2004, 233-80.

Nielsen, Inge. *Thermae et Balnea: The Architecture and Cultural History of Roman Public Baths*. Aarhus: Aarhus University Press, 1990.

Nongbri, Brent. "The Motivations of the Maccabees and the Judaean Rhetoric of Ancestral Traditions." In *Ancient Judaism in Its Hellenistic Context*. Edited by Carol Bakhos. Leiden: Brill, 2005, 85-111.

Noreña, Carlos F. "The Communication of the Emperor's Virtues." *JRS* 91 (2001): 146-68.

Noth, Martin. "God, King and Nation." In Martin Noth, *The Laws in the Pentateuch and Other Studies*. Philadelphia: Fortress, 1966, 145-78.

Obbink, Dirk. *Philodemus on Piety*. Oxford: Clarendon, 1996.

Oegema, Gerbern S. *The Anointed and His People: Messianic Expectations from the Maccabees to Bar Kochba*. Sheffield: Sheffield Academic, 1998.

Olami, Y., and Y. Peleg. "The Water Supply System of Caesarea Maritima." *IEJ* 27 (1977): 127-37.

Oleson, John P. "Herod and Vitruvius: Preliminary Thoughts on Harbour Engineering at Sebastos, the Harbour of Caesarea Maritima." In *Harbour Archaeology: Proceedings of the First International Workshop on Ancient Mediterranean Harbours: Caesarea Maritima*. Edited by Avner Raban. Oxford: BAR, 1983, 165-72.

Oleson, John P., Avner Raban, et al., eds. *The Harbours of Caesarea Maritima*. 2 Volumes. Oxford: British Archaeological Reports, 1989-94.

Osterhammel, Jürgen. *Colonialism*. Translated by Shelley L. Frisch. Princeton: Wiener, 1997.

Osterloh, Kevin. "The Judaean *Ethnos-Politeia:* Reinventing Jewish Collective Identity in a Hellenistic World Contending with Rome." Paper presented at Society of Biblical Literature Annual Meeting, Philadelphia, November 19-22, 2005.

Overman, J. Andrew, Jack Olive, and Michael Nelson. "Discovering Herod's Shrine to Augustus." *BAR* 29.2 (2003): 40-49, 67-68.

———. "Debate: Where Was Herod's Temple to Augustus? The Authors Respond." *BAR* 29.5 (2003): 24.

———. "A Newly Discovered Herodian Temple at Khirbet Omrit in Northern Israel." In *The World of the Herods: Volume 1 of the International Conference The World of the Herods and the Nabataeans Held at the British Museum, 17-19 April 2001.* Edited by Nikos Kokkinos. Stuttgart: Steiner, 2007, 177-95.

Paltiel, Eliezer. *Vassals and Rebels in the Roman Empire: Julio-Claudian Policies in Judaea and the Kingdoms of the East.* Brussells: Latomus, 1991.

Patrich, Joseph. "Hyrcania." In *NEAEHL.* Edited by Ephraim Stern. Jerusalem: Israel Exploration Society, 1994, 639-41.

———. "The Formation of the Nabataean Capital." In *Judaea and the Greco-Roman World in the Time of Herod in the Light of Archaeological Evidence.* Edited by Klaus Fittschen and Gideon Foerster. Göttingen: Vandenhoeck and Ruprecht, 1996, 197-218.

———. "The *Carceres* of the Herodian Hippodrome/Stadium at Caesarea Maritima and Connections with the Circus Maximus." *JRA* 14 (2001): 269-83.

———. "Herod's Theater in Jerusalem: A New Proposal." *IEJ* 52 (2002): 231-39.

———. "Herodian Caesarea — the Urban Space." In *The World of the Herods. Volume 1 of the International Conference The World of the Herods and the Nabataeans Held at the British Museum, 17-19 April 2001.* Edited by Nikos Kokkinos. Stuttgart: Steiner, 2007, 93-129.

Patrich, Joseph, and David Amit. "The Aqueducts of Israel: An Introduction." In *The Aqueducts of Israel.* Edited by David Amit, Joseph Patrich, and Yizhar Hirschfeld. JRAS 46; Portsmouth: Journal of Roman Archaeology, 2002, 9-20.

Patrich, Joseph, and Benjamin Arubas. "'Herod's Tomb' Reexamined: Guidelines for a Discussion and Conclusions." In *New Studies in the Archaeology of Jerusalem and Its Region.* Edited by Guy D. Stiebel, Orit Peleg-Barkat, Doron Ben-Ami, Shlomit Weksler-Bdolah, and Yuval Gadot. Vol. 7. Jerusalem: Israel Antiquities Authority, 2013, 287-300.

Paul, G. M. "The Presentation of Titus in the *Jewish War* of Josephus: Two Aspects." *The Phoenix* 47 (1993): 56-66.

Pelling, Christopher, "The Triumviral Period." In *Cambridge Ancient History.* Edited by Alan K. Bowman, Edward Champlin, and Andrew Lintott. 2nd ed. Vol. 10. Cambridge: Cambridge University Press, 1996, 1-69.

Perowne, Stewart. *The Life and Times of Herod the Great.* New York: Abingdon, 1959.

Pollitt, Jerome J. *The Ancient View of Greek Art: Criticism, History and Terminology.* New Haven: Yale University Press, 1974.

———. *Art in the Hellenistic Age.* Cambridge: Cambridge University Press, 1986.

Porat, Roi, Yakov Kalman, and Rachal Chachy. "Herod's Tomb and the Memorial Complex at Herodium." In *New Studies in the Archaeology of Jerusalem and Its Region.* Edited by Guy D. Stiebel, Orit Peleg-Barkat, Doron Ben-Ami, Shlomit Weksler-Bdolah, and Yuval Gadot. Vol. 7. Jerusalem: Israel Antiquities Authority, 2013, 257-86.

Price, Simon. "From Noble Funerals to Divine Cult: The Consecration of Roman Emperors." In *Rituals of Royalty: Power and Ceremonial in Traditional Societies.* Edited by David Cannadine and Simon Price. Cambridge: Cambridge University Press, 1987, 56-105.

Bibliography

Pritchard, James B. *The Excavation at Herodian Jericho 1951. Annual of the American Schools of Oriental Reseach* 32/33 (1958).

Putnam, Michael. *The Poetry of the Aeneid*. Cambridge: Harvard University Press, 1965.

———. "Anger, Blindness, and Insight in Virgil's *Aeneid*." *Apeiron* 23 (1990): 7-40.

———. *Virgil's Aeneid: Interpretation and Influence*. Chapel Hill: University of North Carolina Press, 1995.

———. "*Aeneid 12:* Unity in Closure." In *Reading Vergil's Aeneid: An Interpretive Guide*. Edited by Christine Perkell. Norman: University of Oklahoma Press, 1999, 210-29.

Qedar, Shraga. "The Coins of Marisa: A New Mint." *INJ* 12 (1992-93): 27-33.

Raban, Avner, et al. "The Underwater Excavations 1993-1994." In *Caesarea Papers 2*. Edited by Kenneth G. Holum, Avner Raban, and Joseph Patrich. Portsmouth: Journal of Roman Archaeology, 1999, 152-68.

———. "Land Excavations in the Inner Harbour (1993-1994)." In *Caesarea Papers 2*. Edited by Kenneth G. Holum, Avner Raban, and Joseph Patrich. Portsmouth: Journal of Roman Archaeology, 1999, 198-224.

Rajak, Tessa. "Roman Intervention in a Seleucid Siege of Jerusalem?" *GRBS* 22 (1981): 65-81.

———. "The Hasmoneans and the Use of Hellenism." In *A Tribute to Geza Vermes: Essays on Jewish and Christian Literature and History*. Edited by Philip R. Davis and Richard T. White. Sheffield: Sheffield Academic, 1990, 261-80.

———. "The Jews under Hasmonean Rule." In *Cambridge Ancient History*. Edited by J. A. Crook, Andrew Lintott, and Elizabeth Rawson. 2nd ed. Vol. 9. Cambridge: Cambridge University Press, 1994, 274-309.

———. "Hasmonean Kingship and the Invention of Tradition." In *Aspects of Hellenistic Kingship*. Edited by Per Bilde, et al. Oakville: Aarhus University Press, 1996, 99-115.

———. "Josephus." In *The Cambridge History of Greek and Roman Political Thought*. Edited by Christopher Rowe and Malcolm Schofield. Cambridge: Cambridge University Press, 2000, 585-96.

———. *Josephus: The Historian and His Society*. 2nd ed. London: Duckworth, 2002.

———. "Judaism and Hellenism Revisted." In Tessa Rajak, *The Jewish Dialogue with Greece and Rome*. Leiden: Brill, 2002, 3-10.

Rappaport, Uriel. "Notes sur la Chronologie des Monnaies Hérodiennes." *Revue Numismatique* 10 (1968): 64-75.

———. "Gaza and Ascalon in the Persian and Hellenistic Periods in Relation to Their Coins." *IEJ* 20 (1970): 75-80.

———. "The Emergence of Hasmonean Coinage." *AJS Review* 1 (1976): 171-86.

———. "Ascalon and the Coinage of Judaea." *La Parola del Passato* 201 (1981): 353-66.

———. "The First Judaean Coinage." *JJS* 32 (1981): 1-17.

Reinhardt, Eduard G., "Stratigraphic Excavations of Outer Harbour Deposits: Preliminary Report (1994)." In *Caesarea Papers 2*. Edited by Kenneth G. Holum, Avner Raban, and Joseph Patrich. Portsmouth: Journal of Roman Archaeology, 1999, 189-95.

Regev, Eyal. "Family Burial, Family Structure, and the Urbanization of Herodian Jerusalem." *PEQ* 136 (2004): 109-31.

———. "Herod's Jewish Ideology Facing Romanization: On Intermarriage, Ritual Baths, and Speeches." *JQR* 100 (2010): 197-222.

———. "Inside Herod's Courts: Social Relations and Royal Ideology in the Herodian Palaces." *JSJ* 43 (2012): 180-214.

Reifenberg, A. *Ancient Jewish Coins.* Jerusalem: Mass, 1965.

Reisner, George Andrew, Clarence Stanley Fisher, and David Gordon Lyon. *Harvard Excavations at Samaria, 1908-1910.* Cambridge: Harvard University Press, 1924.

Renov, I. "A View of Herod's Temple from Nicanor's Gate in a Mural Panel of the Dura-Europos Synagogue." *IEJ* 20 (1970): 67-74.

Rice, E. E. *The Grand Procession of Ptolemy Philadelphus.* Oxford: Oxford University Press, 1983.

———. *Cleopatra.* Stroud: Sutton, 1999.

Richardson, Peter. "Religion and Architecture: A Study in Herod's Piety, Power, Pomp and Pleasure." *Bulletin of the Canadian Society of Biblical Studies* 45 (1985): 3-29.

———. "Law and Piety in Herod's Architecture." *Studies in Religion* 15 (1986): 347-60.

———. "Religion, Architecture and Ethics: Some First Century Case Studies." *Horizons in Biblical Theology* 10 (1988): 19-49.

———. *Herod: King of the Jews and Friend of the Romans.* Columbia: University of South Carolina Press, 1996.

———. "Review: Nikos Kokkinos, *The Herodian Dynasty: Origins, Role in Society and Eclipse*." *JJS* 50 (1999): 156-58.

Ritmeyer, Katherine, and Leen Ritmeyer. "Reconstructing Herod's Temple Mount in Jerusalem." *BAR* 15.6 (1989): 23-53.

Ritmeyer, Leen. "Locating the Original Temple Mount." *BAR* 18.2 (1992): 24-45, 64-65.

———. "Where Was the Temple? The Debate Goes On: Ritmeyer Responds to Jacobson." *BAR* 26.2 (2000): 52-59, 72.

Rocca, Samuel. "Josephus and the *Psalms of Solomon*." In *Making History: Josephus and Historical Method.* Edited by Zuleika Rodgers. Leiden: Brill, 2007, 313-33.

———. *Herod's Judaea: A Mediterranean State in the Classical World.* Tübingen: Mohr, 2008.

Roller, Duane W. *The Building Program of Herod the Great.* Berkeley: University of California Press, 1998.

———. *The World of Juba II and Kleopatra Selene: Royal Scholarship on Rome's African Frontier.* London: Routledge, 2003.

Roller, Lynn E. *In Search of God the Mother: The Cult of Anatolian Cybele.* Berkeley: University of California Press, 1999.

Roncace, Mark. "Josephus' (Real) Portraits of Deborah and Gideon: A Reading of *Antiquities* 5.198-232." *JSJ* 31 (2000): 247-74.

———. "Another Portrait of Josephus' Portrait of Samson." *JSJ* 35 (2004): 185-207.

Ronen, Israel. "Formation of Jewish Nationalism Among the Idumaeans." In Aryeh Kasher, *Jews, Idumaeans and Ancient Arabs: Relations of the Jews in Eretz-Israel with Nations of the Frontier and the Desert during the Hellenistic and Roman Era (332 BCE–70 CE).* Tübingen: Mohr, 1988, 214-39.

Rooke, Deborah W. "Kingship as Priesthood: The Relationship Between the High

Bibliography

Priesthood and the Monarchy." In *King and Messiah in Israel and the Ancient Near East*. Edited by John Day. Sheffield: Sheffield Academic, 1998, 187-208.

Roth, Jonathan P. "Jews in the Roman Service during the Great Revolt." Paper presented at the Society of Biblical Literature Annual Meeting, San Antonio, November 20-23, 2004.

Roy, Jim. "The Masculinity of the Hellenistic King." In *When Men Were Men: Masculinity, Power and Identity in Classical Antiquity*. Edited by Lin Foxhall and John Salmon. London: Routledge, 1998, 111-35.

Rozenberg, Silvia. "The Wall Paintings of the Herodian Palace at Jericho." In *Judaea and the Greco-Roman World in the Time of Herod in the Light of Archaeological Evidence*. Edited by Klaus Fittschen and Gideon Foerster. Göttingen: Vandenhoeck and Ruprecht, 1996, 121-38.

———. "Wall Paintings of the Herodian Period in the Land of Israel." In Ehud Netzer, *The Architecture of Herod, the Great Builder*. Tübingen: Mohr, 2006, 350-76.

Rutgers, L. V. "Roman Policy towards the Jews." *Classical World* 13.1 (1994): 56-74.

Sachs, A., and J. Wiseman. "A Babylonian King List of the Hellenistic Period." *Iraq* 16 (1954): 202-12.

Safrai, Zev. "The Description of the Land of Israel in Josephus' Works." In *Josephus, the Bible, and History*. Edited by Louis H. Feldman and Gohei Hata. Detroit: Wayne State University Press, 1989, 295-324.

Saller, Richard. *Personal Patronage under the Early Empire*. Cambridge: Cambridge University Press, 2002.

Samuel, Alan E. *From Athens to Alexandria: Hellenism and Social Goals in Ptolemaic Egypt*. Louvain: Peeters, 1983.

———. *The Shifting Sands of History: Interpretations of Ptolemaic Egypt*. Lanham: University Press of America, 1989.

———. "The Ptolemies and the Ideology of Kingship." In *Hellenistic History and Culture*. Edited by Peter Green. Berkeley: University of California Press, 1993, 168-92.

Sandmel, Samuel. *Herod: Profile of a Tyrant*. Philadelphia: Lippincott, 1967.

Sarna, Nahum M. "Psalm 89: A Study in Inner-Biblical Exegesis." In *Biblical and Other Studies*. Edited by Alexander Altman. Cambridge: Harvard University Press, 1963, 29-46.

Schalit, Abraham. *König Herodes. Der Mann und Sein Werk*. Rev. ed. Berlin: de Gruyter, 2001.

Schmitt-Korte, K. "Nabataean Coinage — Part II. New Cont Types and Variants." *NC* 150 (1990): 105-33.

Schneider, Eugenia Equini, et al. *Elaiussa Sebaste I: Campagne di Scavo 1995-1997*. Rome: L'Erma Di Bretschneider, 1999.

Schick, Konrad. "Neue Funde im Norden von Jerusalem." *ZDPV* 2 (1879): 102-4.

Schniedewind, William. *Society and the Promise to David: The Reception History of 2 Samuel 7:1-17*. New York: Oxford University Press, 1999.

Schürer, Emil. *The History of the Jewish People in the Age of Jesus Christ (175 BC–AD 135)*. Edited, Translated, and Revised by Geza Vermes and Fergus Millar. Edinburgh: Clark, 1973-87.

Schutt, R. J. H. *Studies in Josephus.* London: SPCK, 1961.
Schwartz, Daniel R. *Agrippa I: The Last King of Judaea.* Tübingen: Mohr, 1990.
———. "Joseph Ben Illem and the Date of Herod's Death." In *Studies in the Jewish Background of Christianity.* Tübingen: Mohr, 1992, 157-66.
———. "Josephus on John Hyrcanus II." In *Josephus and the History of the Greco Roman World: Essays in Memory of Morton Smith.* Edited by Fausto Parente and Joseph Sievers. Leiden: Brill, 1994, 210-32.
Schwartz, Seth. "Israel and the Nations Roundabout: 1 Maccabees and the Hasmonean Expansion." *JJS* 42 (1991): 16-38.
———. "A Note on the Social Type and Political Ideology of the Hasmonean Family." *JBL* 112 (1993): 305-17.
———. "The Hellenization of Jerusalem and Shechem." In *Jews in a Graeco-Roman World.* Edited by Martin Goodman. Oxford: Oxford University Press, 1998, 37-46.
———. "Herod, Friend of the Jews." In *Jerusalem and Eretz Israel: The Arie Kindler Volume.* Edited by Joshua Schwartz, Zohar Amar, and Irit Ziffer. Tel Aviv: Eretz Israel Museum and The Ingeborg Center For Jerusalem Studies, 2001, 67-76.
Seager, Robin. "Some Imperial Virtues in the Latin Prose Panegyrics: The Demands of Propaganda and the Dynamics of Literary Composition." *PLLS* 4 (1984): 129-65.
Sear, David R. *Greek Coins and Their Values.* 2 vols. London: Seaby, 1982.
———. *Roman Coins and Their Values.* 4th rev. ed. London: Seaby/Spink, 1988.
Seeman, Chris, and Adam Kolman Marshak. "Jewish History from Alexander to Hadrian." In *Early Judaism: A Comprehensive Overview.* Edited by John J. Collins and Daniel Harlow. Grand Rapids: Eerdmans, 2012, 30-69.
Segal, Arthur. "Herodium." *IEJ* 23 (1973): 27-29.
———. *Theatres in Roman Palestine and Provincia Arabia.* Leiden: Brill, 1995.
Shachar, Ilan. "The Historical and Numismatic Significance of Alexander Jannaeus' Later Coinage as Found in Archaeological Excavations." *PEQ* 136 (2004): 5-33.
Shanks, Hershel. "Was Herod's Tomb Really Found?" *BAR* 40.3 (2014): 40-48.
Shatzman, Israel. *The Armies of the Hasmoneans and Herod.* Tübingen: Mohr, 1991.
Shaw, Brent D. "Tyrants, Bandits and Kings: Personal Power in Josephus." *JJS* 44 (1993): 176-204.
Sidebotham, Steven E., and Willemina Z. Wendrich. "Berenike: Roman Egypt's Maritime Gateway to Arabia and India." *Egyptian Archaeology* 8 (1996): 15-18.
Sievers, Joseph. "The Role of Women in the Hasmonean Dynasty." In *Josephus, the Bible, and History.* Edited by Louis H. Feldman and Gohei Hata. Detroit: Wayne State University Press, 1989, 132-46.
———. *The Hasmoneans and Their Supporters: From Mattathias to the Death of John Hyrcanus I.* Atlanta: Scholars, 1990.
———. "Review: Nikos Kokkinos, *The Herodian Dynasty: Origins, Role in Society and Eclipse.*" *JSJ* 32 (2001): 101-5.
Sievers, Joseph, and Gaia Lembi, eds. *Josephus and Jewish History in Flavian Rome and Beyond.* Leiden: Brill, 2005.
Silverman, David P. "The Nature of Egyptian Kingship." In *Ancient Egyptian Kingship.* Edited by David O'Conner and David P. Silverman. Leiden: Brill, 1995, 49-92.

Bibliography

Simonetta, Bono. *The Coins of the Cappadocian Kings*. Fribourg: Office du Livre, 1977.
Smallwood, E. Mary. *The Jews under Roman Rule: From Pompey to Diocletian*. Leiden: Brill, 1976.
Smith, R. R. R. "Kings and Philosophers." In *Images and Ideologies: Self-Definition in the Hellenistic World*. Edited by Anthony Bulloch, Erich S. Gruen, A. A. Long, and Andrew Stewart. Berkeley: University of California Press, 1993, 202-11.
Smith, William, ed. *Dictionary of Greek and Roman Antiquities*. 2nd ed. Boston: Little, Brown, 1870.
Spaer, Arnold. "Jaddua the High Priest?" *INJ* 9 (1986-87): 1-3.
Stager, Lawrence E. "Ashkelon." In *NEAEHL*. Edited by Ephraim Stern. Jerusalem: Israel Exploration Society, 1993, 103-12.
Stahl, Hans-Peter. "Aeneas — An 'Unheroic' Hero?" *Arethusa* 14 (1981): 157-77.
Stanley, Farland H., Jr. "The South Flank of the Temple Platform." In *Caesarea Papers 2*. Edited by Kenneth G. Holum, Avner Raban, and Joseph Patrich. Portsmouth: Journal of Roman Archaeology, 1999, 35-40.
Stanwick, Paul Edmund. *Portraits of the Ptolemies: Greek Kings as Egyptian Pharaohs*. Austin: University of Texas Press, 2002.
Sterling, Gregory E. *Historiography and Self-Definition: Josephos, Luke-Acts, and Apologetic Historiography*. Leiden: Brill, 1992.
Stern, Menahem. "The Reign of Herod." In *The World History of the Jewish People*. Edited by Michael Avi-Yonah. Vol. 1.7. New Brunswick: Rutgers University Press, 1975, 71-123.
———. "Judaea and Her Neighbors in the Days of Alexander Jannaeus." *Jerusalem Cathedra* 1 (1981): 22-46.
———. "Social and Political Realignments in Herodian Judaea." *Jerusalem Cathedra* 2 (1982): 40-62.
———. "Josephus and the Roman Empire as Reflected in the Jewish War." In *Josephus, Judaism and Christianity*. Edited by Louis H. Feldman and Gohei Hata. Detroit: Wayne State University Press, 1987, 71-80.
Stewart, Andrew. *Faces of Power: Alexander's Image and Hellenistic Politics*. Berkeley: University of California Press, 1993.
Stieglitz, R. R. "Stratonos Pyrgos — Migdal Sar — Sebastos: History and Archaeology." *Caesarea Maritima: A Retrospective After Two Millennia*. Edited by Avner Raban and Kenneth G. Holum. Leiden: Brill, 1996, 593-608.
Strange, John. "The Book of Joshua, A Hasmonean Manifesto?" In *History and Traditions of Early Israel: Studies Presented to Eduard Nielson*. Edited by André Lemaire and Benedikt Otzen. Leiden: Brill, 1993, 136-41.
———. "Herod and Jerusalem: The Hellenization of an Oriental City." In *Jerusalem in Ancient History and Tradition*. Edited by Thomas L. Thompson. London: Clark, 2003, 97-113.
Sullivan, Richard D. "The Dynasty of Judaea in the First Century." In *ANRW* 2.8. Berlin: de Gruyter, 1977, 296-354.
———. "The Dynasty of Cappadocia." In *ANRW* 2.7.2. Berlin: de Gruyter, 1980, 1125-68.

———. "Dynasts in Pontus." In *ANRW* 2.7.2. Berlin: de Gruyter, 1980, 913-30.

———. *Near Eastern Royalty and Rome: 100-30 BC.* Toronto: University of Toronto Press, 1990.

Sussman, Varda. "A Giant Cretan Oil-Lamp from Herod's Seaside Palace at Caesarea." *IEJ* 45 (1995): 278-82.

Sutherland, C. H. V. *Coinage in Roman Imperial Policy: 31 B.C.–A.D. 68.* London: Methuen, 1951.

———. "The Purpose of Roman Imperial Coin Types." *RN* 25 (1983): 73-82.

Svoronos, Jean N. *Ta Nomismata tou Kratous ton Ptolemaion.* 4 vols. Athens: Sakellariou, 1904-08.

Syme, Ronald. *The Augustan Aristocracy.* Oxford: Clarendon, 1989.

———. *The Roman Revolution.* Rev. ed. Oxford: Oxford University Press, 2002.

———. "Who Was Vedius Pollio?" *JRS* 51 (1961): 22-30.

Talgam, Rina, and Orit Peleg. "Mosaic Pavements in Herod's Day." In Ehud Netzer, *The Architecture of Herod, the Great Builder.* Tübingen: Mohr, 2006, 377-83.

Tarn, W. W. *Alexander the Great.* Cambridge: Cambridge University Press, 1948.

Tarrant, R. J. "Poetry and Power: Virgil's Poetry in Contemporary Context." In *The Cambridge Companion to Virgil.* Edited by C. A. Martindale. Cambridge: Cambridge University Press, 1997, 169-87.

Taylor, Jane. *Petra and the Lost Kingdom of the Nabataeans.* Cambridge: Harvard University Press, 2002.

Tcherikover, Victor. *Hellenistic Civilization and the Jews.* Peabody: Hendrickson, 1999.

Thackeray, Henry St. John. *Josephus: The Man and the Historian.* New York: Jewish Institute of Religion Press, 1929.

Thesleff, Holger. *An Introduction to the Pythagorean Writings of the Hellenistic Period.* Åbo: Åbo Akademi, 1961.

———. *The Pythagorean Texts of the Hellenistic Period.* Åbo: Åbo Akademi, 1965.

———. "On the Problem of the Doric Pseudo-Pythagorica. An Alternative Theory of Date and Purpose." In *Pseudepigrapha I.* Edited by Kurt von Fritz. Vandoeuvres-Geneve: Fondation Hardt, 1972, 59-87.

Thiering, Barbara. "The Copper Scroll: King Herod's Bank Account?" In *Copper Scroll Studies.* Edited by George J. Brooke and Philip R. Davies. Sheffield: Sheffield Academic, 2002, 276-87.

Thoma, Clemens. "John Hyrcanus I as Seen by Josephus and Other Early Jewish Sources." In *Josephus and the History of the Greco-Roman World: Essays in Memory of Morton Smith.* Edited by Fausto Parente and Joseph Sievers. Leiden: Brill, 1994, 127-40.

Thompson, Dorothy J. "Philadelphus' Procession: Dynastic Power in a Mediterranean Context." In *Politics, Administration and Society in the Hellenistic and Roman World.* Edited by Leon Mooren. Leuven: Peeters, 2001, 365-88.

Thompson, Peter, Georgia Papadopoulou, and Eleni Vassiliou. "The Origins of Entasis: Illusion, Aesthetics or Engineering?" *Spatial Vision* 20 (2007): 531-43.

Toher, Mark. "Herod, Augustus, and Nicolaus of Damascus." In *Herod and Augustus:*

Bibliography

Papers Presented at the IJS Conference, 21st-23rd June 2005. Edited by D. M. Jacobson and N. Kokkinos. Leiden: Brill, 2009, 65-81.

Trümper, Monika. "The Oldest Original Synagogue Building in the Diaspora: The Delos Synagogue Reconsidered." *Hesperia* 73 (2004): 513-98.

Tsafrir, Yoram. "Symmetry at Herodium, 'Megalomania' in Herodian Architecture, and the Place of Roman Technology." *Jerusalem Cathedra* 1 (1981): 68-72.

―――. "The Desert Fortresses of Judaea in the Second Temple Period." *Jerusalem Cathedra* 2 (1982): 120-45.

Tsafrir, Yoram, and Itzhak Magen. "Sartaba-Alexandrium." In *NEAEHL*. Edited by Ephraim Stern. Jerusalem: Israel Exploration Society, 1993, 1318-20.

Turcan, Robert. *The Cults of the Roman Empire*. Cambridge: Harvard University Press, 1996.

Turner, Eric. "Ptolemaic Egypt." In *Cambridge Ancient History*. Edited by A. E. Astin, M. W. Frederiksen, R. M. Ogilvie, and F. W. Walbank. 2nd ed. Vol. 7. Cambridge: Cambridge University Press, 1984, 118-74.

Van Henten, Jan Willem. "The Honorary Decree for Simon the Maccabee (1 Macc 14:25-49) in Its Hellenistic Context." In *Hellenism in the Land of Israel*. Edited by John J. Collins and Gregory E. Sterling. Notre Dame: University of Notre Dame Press, 2001, 116-45.

Vermes, Geza. "The So-Called King Jonathan Fragment (4Q448)." *JJS* 44 (1993): 294-300.

Villalba I. Varneda, Pere. *The Historical Method of Flavius Josephus*. Leiden: Brill, 1986.

Vincent, L. H., and E. J. H. Mackay. *Hébron, le Haram el-Khalil. Sépulture des Patriarches*. Paris: Leroux, 1923.

Wacholder, Ben Zion. *Nicolaus of Damascus*. Berkeley: University of California Press, 1962.

―――. "Josephus and Nicolaus of Damascus." In *Josephus, the Bible, and History*. Edited by Louis H. Feldman and Gohei Hata. Detroit: Wayne State University Press, 1989, 147-72.

Walbank, F. W. "Monarchies and Monarchic Ideals." In *Cambridge Ancient History*. Edited by A. E. Astin, M. W. Frederiksen, R. M. Ogilvie, and F. W. Walbank. 2nd ed. Vol. 7. Cambridge: Cambridge University Press, 1984, 62-100.

Walker, Susan. "Cleopatra's Image: Reflections of Reality." In *Cleopatra of Egypt: From History to Myth*. Edited by Susan Walker and Peter Higgs. Princeton: Princeton University Press, 2001, 142-47.

Wallace-Hadrill, Andrew. "The Emperor and His Virtues." *Historia* 30 (1981): 298-323.

―――. "Civilis Princeps: The Emperor between Citizen and King." *JRS* 72 (1982): 32-48.

―――. "Image and Authority in the Coinage of Augustus." *JRS* 76 (1986): 66-87.

Wargo, Eric. "Where Is Herod Buried? *BAR* 28.2 (2002): 32-33, 63.

Warren, Charles, and C. R. Conder. *Survey of Western Palestine*. London: Palestine Exploration Society, 1884.

Watzinger, Carl. *Denkmäler Palästinas. Eine Einfürung in die Archäologie des Heiligen Landes*. 2 vols. Leipzig: Hinrichs, 1933-35.

Weinfeld, Moshe. *Deuteronomy and the Deuteronomic School.* London: Clarendon, 1972.
Weingast, Barry R. "The Political Formations of Democracy and the Rule of Law." *American Political Science Review* 91 (1997): 245-63.
Welch, John W. "Herod's Wealth." In *Masada and the World of the New Testament.* Edited by John F. Hall and John W. Welch. Provo: Brigham Young University Studies, 1997, 74-83.
White, L. Michael. "Herod and the Jewish Experience of Augustan Rule." In *The Cambridge Companion to the Age of Augustus.* Edited by Karl Galinsky. Cambridge: Cambridge University Press, 2005, 361-88.
Whitelam, Keith W. *The Just King: Monarchical Judicial Authority in Ancient Israel.* Sheffield: JSOT, 1979.
Wightman, Gregory J. "Temple Fortresses in Jerusalem Part II: The Hasmonean *Baris* and Herodian Antonia." *BAIAS* 10 (1990-91): 7-35.
Williams, D. S. "Thackeray's Assistant Hypothesis: A Stylometric Evaluation." *JJS* 48 (1997): 262-75.
Williams, J. H. C. "'Spoiling the Egyptians': Octavian and Cleopatra." In *Cleopatra of Egypt: From History to Myth.* Edited by Susan Walker and Peter Higgs. Princeton: Princeton University Press, 2001, 190-99.
Wilson, John Francis. *Caesarea Philippi: Banias, the Lost City of Pan.* New York: Tauris, 2004.
Wilson, John Francis, and Vassilios Tzaferis. "Banias Dig Reveals King's Palace: But Which King?" *BAR* 24.1 (1998): 54-61, 85.
———. "An Herodian Capital in the North: Caesarea Philippi (Panias)." In *The World of the Herods. Volume 1 of the International Conference The World of the Herods and the Nabataeans Held at the British Museum, 17-19 April 2001.* Edited by Nikos Kokkinos. Stuttgart: Steiner, 2007, 131-43.
Witt, Reginald E. *Isis in the Ancient World.* Baltimore: Johns Hopkins University Press, 1997.
Wroth, Warwick. *A Catalogue of Greek Coins in the British Museum: Pontus, Paphlagonia, Bithynia and the Kingdom of Bosporus.* London: Longmans, 1889.
Yadin, Yigael. *Herod's Fortress and the Zealots' Last Stand.* New York: Random, 1966.
———. *The Temple Scroll.* 3 vols. Jerusalem: Israel Exploration Society, 1983.
Yavetz, Zvi. "The Res Gestae and Augustus' Public Image." In *Caesar Augustus: Seven Aspects.* Edited by Fergus Millar and Erich Segal. Oxford: Clarendon, 1984, 1-36.
Yule, Brian, and Anthony J. Barham. "Caesarea's Inner Harbour: The Potential of the Harbour Sediments." In *Caesarea Papers 2.* Edited by Kenneth G. Holum, Avner Raban, and Joseph Patrich. Portsmouth: Journal of Roman Archaeology, 1999, 262-84.
Zanker, Paul. *The Power of Images in the Age of Augustus.* Translated by Alan Shapiro. Ann Arbor: University of Michigan Press, 1990.

Index of Modern Authors

Allen, Frederic D., 234n2
Alon, Gedalyahu, 113n4
Amit, David, 256n24
Ariel, Donald T., 127, 127n13, 129n14, 132, 133n17, 157-58n24, 162nn28-29, 163n30, 164n30, 167, 167n32, 168-69, 168n32, 170n34, 171n35, 172n36, 231n1, 286nn7-8, 287, 323n9, 342-49, 344n1, 346n2, 348n4, 354n2
Arnold, Dieter, 40n22
Arubas, Benjamin, 261, 261n28
Atkinson, Kenneth, 71n33
Austin, M. M., 33n10
Avigad, Nahman, 63n21, 226n53
Aviram, Joseph, 122n9, 192n24
Avi-Yonah, Michael, 152n17, 332n13

Badian, Ernst, 5n2, 10n13, 303n18
Bahat, Dan, 305n19, 318n4, 319n5, 320n7, 330n12, 332n13, 333n14
Barag, Dan, 56n13, 150n15, 160n27, 212n41, 215n44, 217n45, 248n17
Barclay, John M. G., 103n25, 286n6
Barham, Anthony J., 219n46
Barkat, Amiram, 261n28
Ben-Arieh, Sarah, 223, 223n51
Ben-Dove, M., 318n4
Benoit, Pierre, 107n32
Berlin, Andrea M., 214n43, 215n43
Bernett, Monika, 58n15, 59n16, 103n24, 111n1, 112n2, 115n5, 150n15, 152n17, 153n17, 201n30, 203nn31-32, 211, 212, 212n41, 213, 214n42, 214-15n43, 216, 217n45, 236n4, 249n19, 250n19, 253n22, 283n3, 297-98n15, 299n16, 309n21
Berrin, Shani L., 58n15
Bickerman, Elias J., 46n3, 71n33, 162n28
Billows, Richard A., 26n1
Blake, Marian E., 225n52
Blau, Joseph L., 322n8
Boëthius, Axel, 204n33
Bowersock, G. W., 141n2, 243n11
Brandon, Christopher, 221n47
Braund, David, 5n2, 7n5, 9n10, 20n27, 22nn33-34, 104n26, 175n1
Brenner, Sandy, 157n23
Broughton, T. Robert S., 77n2, 83n8, 150n14, 347n3
Bryan, David J., 242n10
Bull, Robert J., 152n17, 207n37
Burke, Peter, 85, 86n9
Burrell, Barbara, 207n38, 217n45, 256n24, 261n28
Busink, Thomas A., 325n10
Butler, H. C., 215n44

Chacy, Rachel, 261n28
Chancey, Mark A., 273n35
Claridge, Amanda, 204n33, 223n51

Cohen, Eric W., 107n32
Cohen, Getzel M., 190n22
Cohen, Shaye J. D., 56n13, 80n5, 110-11n1, 293n12, 301n17
Conder, C. R., 320n7
Corbishley, Thomas, 316n3
Corbo, Virgilio, 225n52
Cotton, Hannah M., 178nn4-5, 179, 179n6, 180n7, 180n8, 181n9, 354n2
Coulter, Cornelia Catlin, 85n9
Crawford, Michael, 85-86n9, 133n17
Creighton, John, 20n28
Crowfoot, G. M., 209n40
Crowfoot, John W., 209n40, 215n44
Curtis, Robert I., 178n5

Davis, Norman, 32n9, 133n17
De Vaux, R., 295n14
Delatte, Louis, 28n5
Dentzer, J., 274n36
Dittenberger, Wilhelm, 155n20
Dodge, Hazel, 221n48
Donaldson, T. L., 77n2
Doudna, Gregory L., 58n15
Dowling, Melissa Barden, 85n9
Duncan-Jones, Richard, 164n30, 354n2

Eckhardt, Benedikt, 110n1
Edwards, Ormond, 343
Efron, Joshua, 60n17, 71n33, 80n5
Ehrenberg, Victor, 21n30
Eitan, Abraham, 252n21
Elias, Norbert, 85, 86n9
Eshel, Hanan, 58n15

Fatkin, Danielle Steen, 192n23, 193-94n25
Feldman, Louis H., 175n1
Fischer, Moshe L., 213n42, 215n43, 323n9
Fischer, Thomas, 49n7, 64n26
Fittschen, Klaus, 227n54
Fleischer, Robert, 31n8, 33, 33n10, 39n19
Foerster, Gideon, 122n9, 192n24, 196n26, 196-97n27, 197n27, 200n29, 201n29, 225n52, 226n53, 227n54, 290n10
Fontanille, Jean-Philippe, 127n13, 133n17, 157n23, 157-58n24, 231n1, 286n7, 287, 287nn7-8, 323n9, 342-49, 344n1, 346n2, 354n2
Förtsch, Reinhard, 196n26, 197n28, 200n29
Frova, Antonio, 152n17, 207n37
Fuks, Gideon, 103, 103n24, 285-86n6, 287-88n8, 289n9, 299n16

Gabba, Emilio, 146n10, 236n5
Gagarin, Michael, 28n4
Geertz, Clifford, 119n8
Geiger, Joseph, 178nn4-5, 180n8, 181n9
Geva, Hillel, 257n25, 284n5, 305n19, 317n4, 319n5, 322n8
Gibson, Sheila, 42n23
Gibson, Shimon, 318n4, 319n5, 320nn6-7
Gilboa, A., 82n6
Gleason, Kathryn Louise, 196n26, 207n37, 208n39
Goffman, Erving, xix, xixn3
Goldschmidt-Lehmann, Ruth P., 318n4
Goodblatt, David, 62nn19-20, 63n23, 79, 80n5
Goodenough, Erwin R., 27n3, 28n6
Goodman, Martin, 77nn2-3, 113n4, 116n6, 250n19, 300-301n17, 309n21
Goren, Yuval, 178n5, 179, 179n6, 180n7
Gracey, M. H., 182n13
Grant, Michael, 175n1
Grove, Martin, 221n47
Grueber, Herbert A., 86n9
Gruen, Erich, 65n26, 250n19
Guidobaldi, Federico, 225n52

Hadley, R. A., 32n9, 133n17
Hahn, David E., 28n6, 30n7
Hahn, Ulrike, 213
Hansen, Esther V., 251n20
Hanson, John S., 77n2
Harder, Günther, 253n22
Hasson, Nir, 261n28

Index of Modern Authors

Hazzard, R. A., 35n11, 130-31, 131n16, 162n28
Head, B. V., 162n28
Heinen, H., 37n15
Hendin, David, 61n18, 63n21, 129n14, 157n23, 270n34, 286n7
Hengel, Martin, 71n33
Hesberg, Henner von, 217n45
Höghammer, Kerstin, 235n3
Hohlfelder, Robert L., 152n17, 207n37, 221n47
Holum, Kenneth G., 152n17, 207n37, 214n42
Hornblower, Simon, 264n29
Horsely, Richard A., 77n2
Humphrey, John H., 201, 201n30, 207n37
Hurwit, Jeffrey M., 327n11
Huzar, Eleanor G., 105n27

Ilan, Tal, 108n33, 112n2, 293n12, 301n17
Isaac, Benjamin, 77n2, 265n30, 315n3, 316n3
Ita of Sion, Marie, 107n32

Jacobson, David M., 129n14, 192n24, 193n24, 196n26, 200-201n29, 221-22n48, 226n53, 235n3, 261n28, 280-81n1, 281, 281n2, 283n3, 285n6, 295n14, 305n19, 317-18n4, 318n4, 319n5, 320nn6-7, 325n10, 330, 330n12, 332n13
Japp, Sarah, 122n9, 123n10, 225n52, 226n53, 227n54, 252n21, 253n22, 256n24, 260n27, 261n28, 305n19, 314n2, 317n4, 319n5, 325n10, 333n14
Jones, A. H. M., 21n30, 264n29

Kahn, Lisa C., 213n42, 215n44
Kalman, Yakov, 261n28
Kanael, Baruch, 158, 160
Kasher, Aryeh, 56n13, 83n8, 98n12, 100n17, 150n15, 247n16, 252n21, 253n22, 273n35, 285n6, 296, 297n15
Kemp, Stephen, 221n47
Kenyon, K. M., 209n40

Kershaw, Ian, xxn5
Kindler, Arie, 155n20
Kleiner, Diana E. E., 40n22, 266n31
Kochavi, Moshe, 252n21
Kockel, Valentin, 200n29
Kokkinos, Nikos, 99n15, 100n16, 112n2, 124, 125n12, 134n18, 136n20, 158, 158n25, 231n1, 241, 241-42n10, 257-58n25, 267n32, 272n35, 285n6, 308n20, 315-16n3
Konstan, David, 85n9
Kraay, Colin M., 32n9, 133n17
Kreiger, Barbara, 261n28
Krencker, Daniel, 192n24
Krentz, Edgar, 66n30, 152n17
Krupp, Michael, 158
Kushnir-Stein, Alla, 155n21, 156n22, 231n1, 248n17, 343, 344, 344n1, 345-46n2

Lalor, Brian, 318n4, 319n5, 325n1
Lamden, Yitzhak, 120
Landau, Tamar, 80n5, 86n9, 281n1
Lauffray, Jean, 245n14
Lernau, Omri, 178n5, 179, 179n6, 180n8
Leschhorn, Wolfgang, 251n20, 264n29
Leveau, Philippe, 221n48
Levine, Lee I., 152n17
Levy, Brooks, 352, 354n2
Lichtenberger, Achim, 122n9, 123n10, 126n12, 149n13, 196n26, 200n29, 203-4, 204n33, 205n34, 206n36, 207n37, 247n16, 256n24, 258n25, 260n27, 261n28, 280n1, 281nn1-2, 296, 297n15, 305n19, 309n21, 314n2, 317n4, 319n5, 320n6, 323n9, 325n10, 333n14
Liver, J., 323n9
Lund, Helen S., 26n1, 32n9, 37n15, 133n17

Mackay, E. J., 295n14
Mader, A. E., 295n14
Magen, Itzhak, 295n14
Magness, Jodi, 160, 161, 261n28, 264n29
Mahieu, Bieke, 134n18, 143n4, 150n15
Malthea-Förtsch, Marion, 226n53

INDEX OF MODERN AUTHORS

Mantzoulinou-Richard, Ersie, 234n2
Maov, Ze'ev, 214n43
Marshak, Adam Kolman, 3n1, 5n2,
    45nn1-2, 79n4, 83n8, 111n1, 117n7,
    136n20, 157n23, 161n28, 227n54,
    241n9, 297n15
Mazar, Benjamin, 317n4, 319n5
McCane, Byron R., 152n17
McKenzie, Judith S., 42n23
McLaren, James S., 77n2, 80n5
Mendels, Doron, 285n6
Meredith, David, 251n20
Meshel, Ze'ev, 256n24
Meshorer, Ya'akov, 63n21, 113n3, 129n14,
    130, 131-32, 131n16, 132-33n17, 156n22,
    158, 158n26, 160-61, 169, 171n35,
    248n17, 342, 350-54, 354n2
Meyshan, Josef, 158, 160, 171n35, 172,
    172n36, 241n9
Mielsch, Harald, 196n27, 197n27
Millar, Fergus, 11, 21n30
Mirhady, David, 28n4
Moulton, Warren J., 136n20
Mowry, Lucetta, 253n22
Murray, G. W., 251n20

Negev, Avraham, 152n17, 213-14n42
Nelson, Michael, 214, 214n43
Netzer, Ehud, xxn4, 107, 107n32,
    120, 122n9, 123n10, 126n12, 149n13,
    151n16, 152n17, 192n24, 193n24,
    196n26, 197n28, 200n29, 204n33,
    205n35, 207n38, 211-12n41, 212n41,
    213n42, 214, 214n43, 215n43, 217n45,
    219n46, 221n47, 221-22nn49-50, 223,
    223n51, 225, 225n52, 226n53, 227n54,
    234n2, 252n21, 253n22, 256n24, 257,
    257-58n25, 260n27, 260-61, 261n28,
    264n29, 290n10, 295n14, 317n4,
    319n5, 320n6, 322n8, 323n9, 324-
    25n10, 330n12, 332n13
Nielson, Inge, 123n10, 192nn23-24,
    193n24
Nongbri, Brent, 49n7, 59n16, 60

Oleson, John P., 152n17

Olive, Jack, 214, 214n43
Overman, J. Andrew, 214, 214n43

Papadopolous, Georgia, 327n11
Papillon, Terry L., 28n4
Patrich, Joseph, 152n17, 201-2n30, 203-
    4, 204n33, 205, 205nn34-35, 207n37,
    214n42, 260n27, 261, 261n28
Peleg, Orit, 226n53
Pelling, Christopher, 93n2, 102n22,
    104n26, 105n27
Pollitt, Jerome J., 332n13
Porat, Roi, 261, 261n28
Pritchard, James B., 123n10

Qedar, Shraga, 158

Raban, Avner, 152n17, 207n37, 219n46
Rajak, Tessa, 59n16
Regev, Eyal, 123n10, 267n32, 267-68n32,
    286n6, 291, 291-92n11, 293n12, 293,
    293-94n13
Reinhardt, Eduard G., 219n46
Reisner, George Andrew, 209n40,
    212n41, 215n44
Reyes, A. T., 42n23
Rice, E. E., 266n31
Richardson, Peter, 56n13, 101n20,
    103n25, 113n4, 155n20, 169, 170n34,
    172, 172n36, 234n2, 235, 236n4,
    242n10, 244n12, 248n17, 249n18,
    274n36, 276n37, 283n3, 285n6, 288n8,
    289, 289n9, 290n10, 298n15, 307,
    308n20, 309n21, 319n5, 325n10,
    333n14, 354n2
Ritmeyer, Katherine, 318n4, 319n5,
    320nn6-7, 321n7, 325n10
Ritmeyer, Leen, 257n25, 318n4, 319n5,
    320nn6-7, 321n7, 325n10
Rocca, Samuel, 26n1, 61n18, 111n1, 113n4,
    117n7, 123n10, 143nn4-5, 152n17, 175n1,
    176n2, 181n9, 183n14, 184n15, 186n19,
    187n19, 189n21, 190n22, 203, 221n47,
    223n51, 231n1, 233, 233n2, 234n2,
    237n6, 244n12, 248n17, 253n22,
    255n23, 257n25, 260n27, 265n30,

Index of Modern Authors

266n32, 269n33, 280n1, 283n3, 284, 284n4, 294n13, 300, 301n17, 305n19, 306n19, 308, 309n21, 327n11, 329-30, 330, 330n12, 332n13
Roller, Duane W., 100n18, 101n20, 107n32, 150n15, 154n19, 175n1, 201n30, 208n39, 216n45, 217n45, 231n1, 234n2, 236n4, 237n6, 244n13, 252n21, 253n22, 258n25, 261n28, 267n32, 269n33, 314n2, 318n4, 325n10
Roller, Lynn E., 41-42n23
Ronen, Israel, 297n15
Roth, Jonathan P., 181nn10-11, 182n12
Roy, Jim, 31n8, 37n15
Rozenberg, Silvia, 227n54, 290n10
Rubenstein, Chaim T., 305n19, 330n12, 333n14

Sachs, A., 48n6
Saller, Richard, 5n2
Samuel, Alan E., 35n11, 37n15
Schalit, Abraham, 83, 83n8, 183-84n15, 183, 264n29, 313n1
Schick, Konrad, 223n51
Schneider, Eugenia Equini, 221n48
Schürer, Emil, 6n3, 22n34, 82n7, 101n20, 143n4, 175n1, 189n21, 203n32, 264n29, 285n6, 299n16, 305n19, 314, 314n2, 315, 348n4
Schwartz, Daniel R., 81n6
Schwartz, Seth, 49n7, 59n16, 64n25, 88n10, 305n19, 309, 309n21, 333n14
Sear, David, 131n16, 157n23
Seeman, Chris, 45nn1-2
Segal, Arthur, 193n24, 200n29, 207n37
Shacar, Ilan, 160n27
Shanks, Hershel, 261n28
Shatzman, Israel, 143n5, 145n7, 150n15, 173nn13-14, 181-82, 181nn10-11, 182n12, 183, 184, 184-85n16, 185nn17-18, 187-88, 188n21, 274n36
Shaw, Brent D., 77n2
Sidebotham, Steven E., 251n20
Sievers, Joseph, 242n10
Siliotti, Alberto, 264n29
Smallwood, E. Mary, 103, 103n24, 153n17, 175n1, 285n6, 305n19, 313n1, 314, 314n2, 315
Smith, R. R. R., 31n8, 37n15
Smith, William, 163n30
Stanley, Farland H., Jr., 214n42
Stein, Alla, 213n42, 215n43, 323n9
Stern, Menahem, 135-36n20, 308n20
Storvick, Olin J., 152n17
Strange, John, 305n19, 333n14
Sukenik, E. L., 209n40
Sullivan, R. D., 6n3
Sutherland, C. H. V., 343, 344n1, 347
Svoronos, J. N., 131n16
Syme, Ronald, 105n27, 175n1, 236n4, 347n3

Talgam, Rina, 226n53
Taylor, Jane, 274n36
Tcherikover, Victor, 46n3
Thompson, Dorothy J., 266n31
Thompson, Peter, 326, 327n11
Toher, Mark, 81n6, 283-84n4
Too, Yun Lee, 28n4
Trümper, Monika, 234n2, 246n15
Tsafir, Yoram, 264n29
Turner, Eric, 37n15, 269n33
Tzaferis, Vasilios, 273n35

Van Henten, Jan Willem, 66, 66-67nn30-32
Vann, Robert Lindley, 152n17
Vassiliou, Eleni, 327n11
Vincent, L. H., 295n14

Wacholder, Ben Zion, 26n2, 269n33
Waddington, W. H., 273-74
Walbank, F. W., 25n1, 27n3, 36n14, 39n19, 266n31, 269n33, 270n34
Ward-Perkins, John B., 329, 330, 330n12
Warren, Charles, 320n7
Watzinger, Carl, 226n53
Weingast, Barry, 85, 86n9
Weiser, Wolfram, 354n2
Welch, John W., 146n10
Wendrich, Willemina Z., 251n20
Wightman, Gregory J., 107n32

Wilson, John Francis, 273n35
Wiseman, J., 48n6
Witztum, Eliezer, 247n16, 285n6
Wroth, W., 39n19

Yule, Brian, 219n46

Zanker, Paul, 162n29, 212n41

Index of Ancient Literature

HEBREW BIBLE/OLD TESTAMENT

Genesis — 296
13:18	295n14
14:13	295n14
14:24	295n14
18:1-15	295n14
23:1-20	295n14
25:30	297n15
49:29-32	295n14

Exodus
15:11	45n2
20:4	289
21:2	299
22:1-2	299
22:2	299
23:14-17	333n14
30:11-16	323n9
34:23	333n14

Leviticus
11:9-11	180n7

Numbers
19:1-22	322n8

Deuteronomy
14:9-10	180n7
16:16-17	333n14

Joshua
12:18	252n21

1 Samuel
4:1	252n21
23:19	99n15
29:1	252n21

2 Samuel — 79

1 Kings — 84, 329
6-8	316n4

2 Chronicles — 29
2-4	316-17n4

Nehemiah
3:16	280n1

Ezekiel
40–43	317n4

Daniel
11:29-30	46n5

NEW TESTAMENT

Matthew
21:12-13	286n7
21:12-17	323n9
21:23-27	323n9

Mark
11:15-19	286n7, 323n9
11:27-33	323n9

Luke
19:45-48	286n7, 323n9
20:1-8	323n9

John
2:12-25	323n9
2:13-16	286n7

Acts
2:29	280n1
27:1	183n13

APOCRYPHA/DEUTEROCANONICAL WORKS

1 Maccabees   47, 50n8, 53, 58, 66-67

INDEX OF ANCIENT LITERATURE

1:16-19	46n5	14:41-49	67	*m. Bekhorot*	
1:16-20	21n29	14:42	270n34	8.7	353
1:36-40	47	15:15-24	65n27, 234n2	*m. Middot*	316
1:41-42	47	15:21	54	1.3	319n5, 321, 322,
1:41-55	42n23				322n8
2:1	60n17	**2 Maccabees**	45-47,	1.9	322n8
2:1–4:60	50n8		50n8, 58	2.1–5.4	316n4
2:48	59	1–2:18	114n4	2.2	320-21n7
2:50	59	2:19	136n20	2.3	333n14
3:1	45n2	2:24	136n20	*m. Parah*	322n8
3:1-9	59n16	2:35	136n20		
3:21	59n16	3	45n2	*m. Sheqalim*	
3:27-37	48n6	4:7-9	46n3	6.6	354n2
3:43	59n16	4:23-25	46n4		
4:26	65n28	4:27-34	46n4	**Tosefta**	353
4:33-34	65n28	6:1-6	42n23		
4:36-59	59n16	6:2	42n23	**Babylonian Talmud**	
4:59	49	6:18–7:42	47	*b. Avodah Zarah*	
5:1–6:63	50n9	8:1	45n2	39a	180n7
5:6-10	65n28	8:1-29	50n8		
5:55-62	59n16	9:1-19	48n6	*b. Bava Batra*	
6:1-17	48n6	10:1-9	50n8	3b-4a	79-80, 80n5
7:5-9	59n16	10:14-38	50n9	4a	116, 119n8,
7:13-14	59n16	11:1-34	50n8		284n4
7:19	322n8	12:2–13:26	50n9		
8:12-16	51n10	13:24	50n9	*b. Berakhot*	
8:17-32	64n27			48a	58n15
8:23-31	51n10				
10:1-21	270n34			*b. Keritot*	
10:20-21	270n34	**PSEUDEPIGRAPHA**		5b	169
10:62	270n34				
11:21	59n16	*Psalms of Solomon*		*b. Qiddushin*	
12:1-23	65n27, 243n11	17	71n33	66a	60n17
12:39–13:41	52n11			70	80n5
13:41	53	*Testament of Levi*	62n19		
13:42	53			*b. Sanhedrin*	
14:16-23	243n11			11	321n7
14:16-49	53n12	**RABBINIC WORKS**		19a-b	80n5
14:25-49	53n12, 66			107b	58n15
14:29	66	**Mishnah**			
14:31	67	*m. 'Avodah Zarah*		*b. Sukkah*	119n8
14:32	66n31	2.6	180n7		
14:33-34	67	3.1	289n9	**Jerusalem Talmud**	
14:36	67	3.4	289, 289n9	*y. Avodah Zarah*	
14:37	67	4.3	289n9	321	180n7
14:38-39	67				

Index of Ancient Literature

Midrash Halakhah
Sifre Deuteronomy
18   300n17

DEAD SEA SCROLLS
4Q169.3-4 i:6-9   58n15

GRECO-ROMAN AUTHORS

Alexander
Polyhistor   175, 268, 269n33

Appian
Civil Wars   82n7, 88n10, 93n1, 94n3, 102n22, 105n27, 164n30, 204n33
Mithridatic Wars   6n3
Punic Wars   13n18
Syrian Wars   46n5, 48n6, 250-51n20, 251n20

Aristotle   27n3
Politics   27-28, 28n4, 29, 30, 39, 39n20

Athenaeus
Deipnosophistae   266n31

Augustine
City of God   204n33

Caesar
African War   184n15
Civil War   183n13
De Bello Alexandrino   77n2
Gallic War   10nn11-12,

22n32

Cassius Dio   10n12, 12n17, 13n18, 20n27, 21n31, 22n34, 26n3, 62n19, 77n2, 82n6, 83n8, 93n1, 94nn3-4, 102n22, 105n27, 106n28, 134n18, 141n2, 143n4, 144n6, 145n7, 150n14, 151n16, 164nn30-31, 176n2, 208n39, 213, 244n13, 266n31, 287n8, 314n2, 346, 347n3, 351n1

Cato the Elder
De Agricultura   179n6

Cicero
Divinatio in Caecilium   13, 13n19
Epistulae ad Atticum   9n10, 14, 14n20, 20n27, 27n3, 93n1, 104n26, 184n15
Epistulae ad Familiares   6n3, 9n11
Epistulae ad Quintum fratrem   22n32
Pro Sulla   13n18

Dio Chrysostom   26n3, 31, 32, 33
Orationes   35, 35nn12-13, 40

Diodorus   11n14, 39n18,

128n14

Diogenes Laertius   27n3

Dionysius of
Halicarnassus   22n33
Roman Antiquities   27n3

Diotogenes   29
Peri Basileias   28, 30

Epiphanius of
Salamis   242n10

Eupolemos   269n33

Eusebius
Chronicon   272n35
Onomasticon   296, 297n15

Eutropius   145n7

Gaius Asinius
Pollio   175, 268

Homer   268
Iliad   153, 154n19

Horace
Epistles   252, 253n22
Satires   180n8

Isocrates   27n3, 31
Ad Nicoclem   27, 28n4, 29, 30n7, 33
Ad Philipp   30, 36
Cyprian Orations   28n4
Evagoras   37

Josephus   ix, xix, xx, 67, 68, 83, 87, 88, 108, 120,

INDEX OF ANCIENT LITERATURE

134, 231, 232, 236, 236n4, 242n10, 249, 250n19, 259, 261, 273, 282, 284-85, 307, 326, 339, 350

Jewish Antiquities   xxiin6, 6n4, 7n5, 8n9, 11n11, 10n13, 12n17, 21nn29-31, 43, 45n1, 48n6, 52n11, 56n13, 57n14, 58n15, 59n16, 60n17, 62-63nn20-23, 64n25, 65nn27-29, 75-76, 75-76n1, 77n2, 77-78n3, 78-81, 80n5, 81-82n6, 82n7, 83, 83n8, 84, 85n9, 87, 88n10, 90, 90n11, 94-95, 94nn3-5, 95, 95nn6-7, 96, 96nn8-10, 97, 97n11, 98, 98n12, 99, 99nn13-14, 100-102, 100nn16-18, 101nn19-21, 102nn22-23, 103n24, 105, 106, 106nn28-29, 108n33, 110n1, 111-12, 112n2, 113nn3-4, 114n4, 115n5, 116n6, 119n8, 124-25, 125n12, 130n15, 134n18, 135n19, 136n20, 140, 140n1, 141n2,

142-43, 142n3, 142-43n4, 143n5, 144, 144n6, 145nn7-8, 146n9, 148nn11-12, 149nn13-14, 150-51, 150n15, 151n16, 152, 152n17, 153n18, 154n19, 160, 160n27, 164, 164n31, 167n32, 168, 168n33, 170n34, 171n35, 172, 172n36, 175n1, 176n2, 177n3, 182, 182n12, 183n13, 184nn15-16, 184-87, 185n17, 186n18, 187nn19-20, 188, 188n21, 189n21, 190n22, 201n30, 203n31, 205, 205n35, 206n36, 208n39, 212, 213, 213n42, 214, 214n42, 215nn43-44, 218, 220, 233-34n2, 234n2, 235n3, 237, 237n6, 238n7, 240nn8-9, 241nn9-10, 243n11, 244n13, 245n14, 246, 246n15, 247-48, 247n16, 248n17, 249, 249nn18-19, 252, 252n21, 253n22, 255n23, 256-57, 257n25, 258n26, 260n27, 265, 265n30, 266n31, 267n32, 270n34,

272n35, 273n35, 274n36, 276n37, 279-81, 280n1, 281n1, 283n3, 284, 284nn4-5, 285n6, 287n8, 288, 289n9, 293n12, 297n15, 298-300, 298-99n16, 299n16, 300n17, 302, 303n18, 308n20, 313, 313n1, 314, 315, 315n2, 316, 316nn3-4, 318n4, 319n5, 322n8, 323n9, 324n10, 327n11, 333n14, 334n14, 350, 352n1, 353

Jewish War   xxiin6, 6n4, 7n5, 8nn8-9, 10n13, 12n17, 21nn30-31, 48n6, 56n13, 57n14, 58n15, 63nn21-22, 75-76, 76n1, 76-77n2, 77-78n3, 78-81, 80n5, 81-82n6, 82n7, 83n8, 84, 85n9, 87, 88n10, 90, 90n11, 94-95, 94nn3-5, 95, 95nn6-7, 96, 96nn8-10, 97, 97n11, 98, 98n12, 99, 99nn13-14, 100, 100nn16-18, 101-2, 101nn19-21, 102nn22-23, 103n24, 104, 104n26, 105, 106, 106nn28-29, 106-7, 107n31,

Index of Ancient Literature

108n33, 110n1, 111-12, 112n2, 113n3, 114n4, 115n5, 116, 116n6, 119n8, 122n9, 124-25, 125n12, 125-26n12, 135n19, 136n20, 140, 140n1, 141n2, 142-43, 142n3, 142-43n4, 144n6, 145n8, 148nn11-12, 149nn13-14, 150n15, 151n16, 152, 152n17, 153n18, 154n19, 160, 160n27, 168, 168n33, 171n35, 177n3, 182, 182n12, 183n13, 184nn15-16, 184-87, 185n17, 186nn18-19, 187nn19-20, 188, 188n21, 189n21, 190n22, 201n30, 208n39, 212, 213, 213n42, 214, 214n42, 215nn43-44, 218, 223n51, 233n2, 234, 235n2, 235n3, 236n5, 237n6, 240nn8-9, 241nn9-10, 243n11, 245n14, 252, 252n21, 253n22, 255n23, 256-57, 257n25, 258n26, 260n27, 264n29, 267n32, 270n34, 272n35, 274n36, 276n37, 281n1, 283n3, 284n5, 287n8, 288, 288n8, 289n9, 305-6n19, 308n20, 314, 314n2, 315n3, 316, 316nn3-4, 318n4, 322, 322n8, 323n9, 333n14, 350

Vita 60n17, 114n4, 185n17, 186n19, 187n19, 290n10

Justin Martyr 242n10

Kallixeinos of Rhodes 266n31

Livy 7n6, 8n7, 9nn10-11, 13n18, 16n23, 18, 18nn24-25, 22nn32-33, 36n14, 46n5, 104n26, 237n6

Periochae 82n7, 204n3

M. Junianus Justinus *Epitoma Historiarum Philippecarum Pompei Trogi* 6n3, 37n15, 62n19, 128n14

Macrobius *Saturnalia* 293

Marcus Antistius Labeo 300

Marcus Terentius Varro 175

Nicolaus of Damascus xx, 26, 26n2, 81n6, 87, 97, 108, 108n33, 112n2, 140n1, 177n3, 238, 238n7, 242n10, 258n26, 269n33, 276, 280, 284 *Universal History* 268, 283n3

Orosius 145n7

Pausanias 37n15, 151n16, 327n11

Persaeus of Citium 27n3

Philo 316 *Allegorical Interpretation* xxiin6, 333-34n14 *In Flaccum* 22n34 *Legatio ad Gaium* 134n18 *Special Laws* 300, 300n17

Philodemus 27n3, 28, 31, 35, 36, 40 *On Rhetoric* 29, 29-30

Plato 26n3, 27n3, 268 *Laws* 29, 30n7 *Minos* 39n20 *Philebus* 331 *Politics* 30n7, 35 *Republic* 30n7

Pliny the Elder 92 *Natural History* 37n15, 144n6, 179, 179n6, 180n7, 204n34, 252,

INDEX OF ANCIENT LITERATURE

253n22, 264n29, 269n33, 310-11

Plutarch
Agesilaus 27, 40, 40n21

Antony 10n12, 93, 93nn1-2, 94n4, 96n8, 96n10, 104, 104n26, 105n27, 106n28, 141n2, 164n30, 184, 185n16, 239, 240n8, 243n11, 266n31

Brutus 93n1

Cato the Younger 20n27

Crassus 10n12

Demetrius 37n15

Pompey 208n39

Tiberius Gracchus 13n18

Polybius 7n6, 10n13, 13n18, 18n25, 19n26, 20n27, 21n29, 36n14, 43, 46n5, 176n2, 183n13, 269n33, 270n34

Pompeius Tragus 62n19

Pseudo-Archytas 29

Pseudo-Aristotle
Rhetorica ad Alexandrum 28, 28n6

Ptolemy
Geography 154n19,

252-53, 253n22

Quintus Curtius Rufus
Historiarum Alexandri Magni Macedonis 37n15

Sallust
Bellum jugarthinum 19-20, 20n27, 176n2

Seneca 26n3
De clementia 37n15
De ira 37n15

Sextus Julius Africanus 242n10
Chronographiae 99n13, 252n21

Sozomen
Church History 296, 297n15

Statius
Silvae 196, 196n26

Sthenidas the Locrian 33

Stobaeus
Anthology 28n5, 30n8

Strabo of Amaseia 76n1, 81, 82n7, 114n4, 144n6, 145n7, 149-50n14, 268
Geography 13n18, 41n23, 62n19, 151n16, 234n2, 248n17, 281n2

Suetonius 213, 328, 346
Divus Augustus 16, 16n23,

150n14, 151n16, 163, 164nn30-31, 237, 237n6, 244n13, 330n12, 347n3

Tacitus
Annales 9n10, 22n34, 104n26, 204nn33-34

Historiae 8n8, 62n19

Theocritus
Idylls 37n15, 38, 38n16, 39, 39n19

Theophrastus
On Kingship 27n3, 28

Theopompus
Ad Alexandrum 27n3

Thucydides 140n1, 268, 283n3

Timagenes of Alexandria 175, 268

Velleius Paterculus
Roman History 204n33

Vitruvius
De Architectura 193n24, 204n33, 221n47, 224, 327n11, 330-31

Xenophon 27n3
Agesilaus 27, 37, 41
Cyropaedia 27, 29, 32, 32n9, 37, 40, 40n21

400

www.ingramcontent.com/pod-product-compliance
Lightning Source LLC
Chambersburg PA
CBHW020636300426
44112CB00007B/130